0058158

COLLIN COUNTY COMMUNITY

3 1702 00090 1300

D0984684

Learning Resources Center
Collin County Community College District
SPRING CREEK CAMPUS
Plano, Texas 75074
WITHDRAWN

RADWTRI 99
$15.95

The Winnebago Tribe

The Winnebago Tribe

Paul Radin

UNIVERSITY OF NEBRASKA PRESS ● LINCOLN AND LONDON

Manufactured in the United States of America

First Bison Book printing of this edition: 1990
Most recent printing indicated by the last digit below:
10   9   8   7   6   5   4   3   2   1

International Standard Book Number 0-8032-5710-4
Library of Congress Catalog Card Number 64-63594

The Winnebago Tribe originally was published as part of the Thirty-Seventh Annual Report of the Bureau of American Ethnology, Smithsonian Institution, Washington, 1923.

CONTENTS

	Page
Preface	xv

PART I

CHAPTER I.—History	1
General remarks	1
The Tale of Tcap'o'sgaga	10
How the Winnebago first came into contact with the French and the origin of the Decora family	17
What the Shawnee prophet told the Winnebago	21
Winnebago names of other tribes and peoples	27
CHAPTER II.—Winnebago archeology	28
General problems	28
Implements of stone and other materials	39
Copper implements	39
Earth works and mounds	40
Intaglio mounds	41
Conical mounds	41
Linear mounds	44
Effigy mounds	50
Description of Lake Koshkonong mounds	52
The conical mounds	52
Combinations of conical and linear forms	52
Linear mounds	53
Effigies	53
Bird effigies	53
Mammal effigies	53
Turtle and allied forms	53
The grouping	54
The man mound	54
Miscellaneous structures	55
CHAPTER III.—Material culture	56
Habitations	56
Clothing and adornment	61
Hunting	61
Fishing and agriculture	66
Games and amusements	72
Travel and transportation	75
Musical instruments	75
Divisions of time	76
CHAPTER IV.—General social customs	78
Male terms of address	80
Female terms of address	83
Joking relationship	85
Mother-in-law and father-in-law taboo	87

                                                                    Page
Puberty customs 87
Marriage 90
Adoption 91
CHAPTER V.—Burial and funeral customs 92
Description of funeral customs and wake 92
Generalized description of funeral customs and wake 96
Funeral customs of the Thunderbird clan (first version) 98
Death and funeral customs of the Thunderbird clan (second version) .. 98
Death and funeral customs of the Bear clan 100
Funeral customs of the Buffalo clan 106
Origin myth of the four-nights' wake 106
Grave-post marks 107
CHAPTER VI.—Warfare and the council lodge 108
Warfare 108
The council lodge 115
CHAPTER VII.—System of education 118
My father's teaching to his sons and daughters 118
System of instruction to son 118
System of instruction to daughter 129
System of instruction to children 132

                              PART II

CHAPTER VIII.—Social organization—General discussion 133
The twofold grouping 137
Functions of the twofold division 139
Clan organization 142
Reckoning of descent 144
Individual names 145
Attitude toward clan animals 147
Relationship to clan animals 148
The clan tie 150
Clan functions 151
The reciprocal relationship of the clans 152
The specific possessions of the clan 154
Immaterial possessions of the clan 155
The clan marks of identification 155
Influence of the clan upon ceremonial organization 156
CHAPTER IX.—Social organization—Specific clans 159
The Thunderbird clan 159
Introduction 159
Clan myths and names 164
The Warrior clan 170
Introduction 170
Origin myth 171
Clan songs 172
Eagle and Pigeon clans 172
Clan names 173
The Bear clan 177
Introduction 177
Origin myths 181

	Page
Clan songs	187
Clan names	188
The Wolf clan	190
Introduction	190
Origin myths	190
Clan songs	192
Clan names	192
The Water-spirit clan	193
Introduction	193
Origin myth	194
Clan names	194
The Buffalo clan	195
Introduction	195
Origin myth	195
Clan songs	197
Clan names	198
The Deer clan	198
Introduction	198
Origin myths	199
Clan song	201
Clan names	201
The Elk clan	201
Introduction	201
Origin myth	202
Clan names	202
Snake and Fish clans	202
Clan names	202
Clan names	203
CHAPTER X.—Shamanistic and medicinal practices	206
Introduction	206
Tales concerning Midjistega	207
Lincoln's grandfather	210
The uses of the stench-earth medicine	211
How an Indian shaman cures his patients	222
Thundercloud's fasting experience	227
CHAPTER XI.—Religion	229
Introduction	229
The concept of supernatural power	233
The concept and nature of the spirits	235
The power and localization of the spirits	240
The twofold intrepretation of the relation of the spirits to man	241
The guardian spirits	242
Personal religious experiences	243
How Wegi'ceka tried to see Earthmaker	243
Account of J.'s fasting	245
R.'s fasting	248
Aratcge'ka's fasting	248
Account of X.'s fasting	250
How Y. fasted and was blessed with a war bundle	251
What G. obtained in his fast	252
How a bear blessed a man	253

Page

How the daughter of Mank'erexka refused a blessing from Disease-giver   254
Fasting experience   256
J. B.'s fasting experience   260
How a man defied Disease-giver   261
Methods of bringing the spirits into relation with man   262
The folkloristic concepts   263
The cosmological ideas   268

PART III

CHAPTER XII.—Ceremonial organization   269
   Introduction   269
   Ceremonies associated with the clans   270
      The clan feasts   270
         The Thunderbird clan or chief feast   270
         The Bear clan feast (first version)   273
         The Bear clan feast (second version)   276
         The Snake clan feast   277
CHAPTER XIII.—Religious societies based on blessings from spirits   281
   Society of those who have received blessings from the Night Spirits   281
   Society of those who have been blessed by the Herok'a   295
   Society of those who have been blessed by the Buffalo spirits   296
   Society of those who have been blessed by the grizzly bear   299
CHAPTER XIV.—The Medicine dance   302
   Origin myth   302
   Organization of the bands   311
   Personal accounts of initiation   326
CHAPTER XV.—Miscellaneous dances   331
   The Hok'ixe're dance   331
   The Herucka dance   336
   Watconank'êwê feast   336
   The Captive's Death dance   336
   The Farewell dance   337
   The Soldier's dance   338
   Ceremony of Uangeru   339
   Feast to Buffalo Tail   339
   Kikre waci and Tcebokona^{n}k dances   339
CHAPTER XVI.—The Peyote cult   340
   General description   340
   John Rave's account of the Peyote cult and of his conversion   341
   O. L.'s description of the Peyote cult   346
   J. B.'s account of the leader of the Peyote   348
   Albert Hensley's account of the Peyote   349
   J. B.'s Peyote experiences   352
   J. B.'s account of his conversion   364
   Jesse Clay's account of the Arapaho manner of giving the Peyote cere-
      mony which he introduced among the Winnebago in 1912   367
   Development of the ritualistic complex   371
   Dissemination of the doctrine   374
   What the converts introduced   376
   The attitude of the conservatives   377

Page

CHAPTER XVII.—The clan war-bundle feasts 379

The war-bundle feast of the Thunderbird clan (first version) 379
Introductory remarks 379
Analytical presentation of the ceremony 380
Analysis of types of action and speeches 384
The development of the war-bundle feast and its place in the ceremonial organization of the Winnebago 384
Characterization of the spirits mentioned in the war-bundle feast 388
Description of the war-bundle feast 393
First division of the ceremony—in honor of the Thunderbirds 399
Sweat-lodge ritual 399
The Dog ritual 403
General placing of the tobacco 403
The tobacco offering to the spirits 405
The buckskin offerings to the spirits 417
Filling of the ceremonial pipe and smoking ritual 421
Basic ritual 423
The feast 433
The fast-eating contest 437
Continuation of the basic ritual 439
Second division of the ceremony—in honor of the Night Spirits 453
The tobacco offering 453
Basic ritual 457
The throwing out of the buckskins 465
Feast to the Night Spirits 471
Rite of those who have been crazed by the Night Spirits 471
Continuation of the basic ritual 473
Terminal address to the dog 479
Addenda 481
The war-bundle feast of the Thunderbird clan (second version) 482
The war-bundle feast of the Thunderbird clan (third version) 486
The war-bundle feast of the Bear clan 499
Index 503

ILLUSTRATIONS

PLATES

Page
1. Red Banks, Green Bay, Wis. 18
2. a, Black Wolf, chief of Winnebago. b, Four Legs, chief of Winnebago 18
3. Jasper Blowsnake 18
4. John Fisher 18
5. a, James Pine. b, John Rave and family 18
6. a, b, John Fireman. c, Whitebreast. d, John Raymond 18
7. a, Young Winnebago woman and daughter. b, Old Winnebago and daughter.... 18
8. a, Gray Hair. b, Red Wing. c, James Risehill. d, Albert Hensley (front view).... 18
9. a, John Baptiste. b, Hugh Hunter. c, Levi St. Cyr. d, Albert Hensley
    (profile view) 40
10. Winnebago bone implements 40
11. Four Legs' village on Doty Island, 1830 40
12. Aztalan 40
13. Wisconsin intaglios 42
14. a, Burial in a mound at Borchers Beach. b, Conical mound, Cutler Park,
    Waukesha, Wis. 42
15. A series of burial mounds 44
16. Stone chamber in burial mound, Buffalo Lake, Marquette County, Wis. 44
17. Zahn Mound, Calumet County, Wis. 44
18. a, Lodge made of reed matting. b, Lodge made of bark with covering of
    reed matting. c, Lodge made of bark 44
19. a, Lodge of bark. b, Modern lodge with canvas covering. c, Lodge of
    reed matting 56
20. a, Thomas Mallory. b, Winnebago in full dress 56
21. a, Winnebago women in modern dress. b, Winnebago women in old-style
    dress 56
22. a, Child in modern dress. b, Young boy in full warrior's costume 56
23. a, Group of Winnebago in old-style costumes. b, Winnebago family 60
24. Decorated moccasins 60
25. Decorated moccasins 60
26. a, Winnebago, showing modern headgear. b, Winnebago with deer-tail
    headdress 60
27. Beaded belts 60
28. Women's hair ornaments and small beaded bag 60
29. Beaded articles of modern type 60
30. Miscellaneous objects 60
31. Bow and bird arrow 70
32. Woven bags with old designs 70
33. Woven bags 70
34. Varieties of woven bags 70
35. Woven bags with old designs 70
36. Woven bags (Peabody Museum) 70
37. Openwork woven bags (Peabody Museum) 70
38. a, Wooden dishes. b, Wooden spoons. c, Wooden mortars and pestles 70
39. Moccasin game 74

xii   ILLUSTRATIONS

                                                                    Page
40. Snowshoes 74
41. *a*, Winnebago and daughter. *b*, Old Winnebago woman. *c*, Woman and
    child, showing cradle board. *d*, Woman and child, showing method of
    carrying infant 78
42. *a*, Infant with ornamented cradle board. *b*, Group of Winnebago 78
43. *a*, War clubs of the Upper Division. *b*, Whips 108
44. Drums 108
45. War clubs 108
46. Facial burial marks 200
47. Buckskin offerings 200
48. Buckskin offerings 200
49. *a*, Exterior of Medicine dance lodge. *b*, Interior of Medicine dance lodge 302
50. *a*, Exterior of Medicine dance lodge. *b*, Interior of Medicine dance lodge 302
51. Otter-skin medicine pouches used at Medicine dance 314
52. Pouches of animal skins used at Medicine dance 314
53. Skin pouches and feather fans used at Medicine dance 314
54. *a*, Peyote leaders. *b*, Burial huts 340
55. *a*, Oliver Lamere. *b*, John Rave 340
56. *a*, Thunderbird war bundle. *b*, Hawk war bundle 380
57. Contents of Thunderbird war bundle 380
58. Contents of Hawk war bundle 380

                              TEXT FIGURES

1. Sectional map of Wisconsin, giving the locations of some of the old villages 3
2. Map of Wisconsin, showing distribution of circular mounds 29
3. Map of Wisconsin, showing distribution of effigy mounds 30
4. Effigy mounds (panther or water-spirit type) 42
5. Bear effigy mound, Madison, Wis. 43
6. Burial mounds, upper Baraboo Valley, Wis. 43
7. Burial mounds in a group at Rice Lake, Rusk County, Wis. 44
8. Effigy and dumb-bell-shaped mounds 45
9. Linear mounds at Madison, Wis. 45
10. Linear mounds, Clyde Township, Iowa County, Wis. 45
11. Effigy and linear mounds, Pishtaka, Waukesha County, Wis. 46
12. Effigy mounds in the Wingra group, Madison, Wis. 46
13. Bird effigy mounds 47
14. Man mound, Greenfield Township, Sauk County, Wis. 47
15. Types of mammal effigy mounds 48
16. Types of so-called turtle effigy mounds 48
17. Effigy mound of unknown animal 48
18. La Valle man mound, Sauk County, Wis. 49
19. Group of mounds of different types, Lake Koshkonong, Wis. 49
20. Archeologic map of Lake Koshkonong 51
21. Wisconsin garden beds 55
22. *a*, Cross section of round lodge. *b*, Cross section of gable lodge 57
23. Pattern of men's buckskin leggings 58
24. Pattern of women's buckskin shirt 58
25. Pattern of men's moccasin 59
26. Pattern of women's moccasin 60
27. Men's lacrosse 72

Page

28. Grave-post marks 107
29. Seating arrangement in council lodge according to Thunderbird clan 116
30. Seating arrangement in council lodge according to Bear clan 116
31. Seating arrangement in council lodge according to Thunderbird clan 117
32. Seating arrangement in council lodge according to Wolf clan 117
33. Plan of village according to Thundercloud, of the Thunderbird clan 140
34. Plan of village according to John Rave, of Bear clan 141
35. Diagram of Bear lodge 181
36. Plan of Bear clan war-bundle feast as given by John Rave 273
37. Plan of Soldier's dance 338
38. Plan of Thunderbird clan war-bundle feast 482

PREFACE

The information included in this volume was obtained during the years 1908–1913 while employed by the Bureau of American Ethnology and on private expeditions. In all cases wherever it was possible the author tried to obtain his information in Winnebago, although the English version is printed here. Owing to the fact that the Winnebago have for some time been accustomed to the use of a syllabic alphabet borrowed from the Sauk and Fox, it was a comparatively easy task to induce them to write down their mythology and, at times, their ceremonies, and then have an interpreter translate them. As the author has a fair command of Winnebago grammar, he was able to control these translations and thus insure their approximate accuracy. On account of the importance of having as accurate a record of the ceremonies as possible, those few ceremonies that were obtained in syllabic text were subsequently taken down in phonetic text.

It has been the aim of the author to separate as definitely as possible his own comments from the actual data obtained, and for that reason every chapter, with the exception of those on history, archeology, and material culture, is divided into two parts, a discussion of the data and the data itself.

Certain subjects, such as mythology, art, and music, have been entirely omitted. In order to discuss the second a comparative study of woodland art and design would have been necessary, which would have entailed a prolonged study at different museums; and to discuss the latter, specific training and knowledge were demanded, which the author does not possess.

The following monograph does not claim to be a comparative study, but simply as intensive an investigation as the time spent allowed, of an unusually interesting tribe, made under exceptionally propitious conditions. It is principally the raw material that is presented here. Throughout the work, the Indian has been allowed to tell the facts in his own way. For that reason no attempt has been made to change the English, except when it was ungrammatical or unintelligible. This will explain the simple and at times poor English of the accounts.

The work ends rather abruptly because the section on mythology and the general conclusion have been reserved for special treatment.

In conclusion, the author wishes to thank all those Winnebago who helped him since he first came among them. In particular does he wish to thank his interpreter, Oliver Lamere, of Winnebago, Nebraska, without whom this work could hardly have been completed, and his three main informants, Jasper Blowsnake and Sam Carley, both of Black River Falls, Wisconsin, and John Rave, of Winnebago, Nebraska.

To Prof. Franz Boas he is under especial obligations for directing him to the Winnebago, for the methods of research inculcated in him at Columbia University, and particularly for impressing upon him the necessity of obtaining as much information as possible in text.

His thanks are also due to the following individual and institutions: To Mr. C. Brown, of Madison, Wis., for a number of illustrations previously published in the Wisconsin Archeologist, and to the American Museum of Natural History, the Peabody Museum, and the Milwaukee Public Museum for numerous photographs of objects in their collections.

His brother, Dr. Max Radin, he wishes to thank for financing his first visit to the Winnebago in 1908.

The manuscript was finished in 1913.

PAUL RADIN.

SANTA FE, NEW MEXICO, *May 11, 1916.*

THE WINNEBAGO TRIBE

Part I

CHAPTER I

HISTORY

General Remarks

At what time the Winnebago entered Wisconsin it is impossible to say. It seems quite reasonable to suppose that they came from the east. If we are right in assuming that they are the builders of the effigy mounds, then we are justified in assigning a certain significance to the distribution of the latter. One of the interesting points of this distribution is that many are found along the shore of Lake Michigan and northward to Two Rivers, that some are found in Rock County, and that they gradually decrease in number as one proceeds north. This would lead us to assume that the Winnebago entered Wisconsin from the south, probably from the southeast. We ought, then, to find effigy mounds in Illinois and, in general, on the route of their probable journey from the east. This is not the case, and it is very difficult to account for their absence unless we assume that all traces of them have disappeared; that the Winnebago first developed their mound-building habit after they had reached Wisconsin; or that the mounds in Illinois are their work (and that of kindred tribes), and finally that the type of mound developed along different lines after they had definitely settled in Wisconsin. It is also possible that since the effigy mounds are undoubtedly closely associated with the clan organization this type of social organization was adopted by the Winnebago only after they entered Wisconsin.

There can be no doubt but that the Winnebago and the closely related tribes like the Missouri, Oto, and Iowa represented the second of the Siouan migrations westward. There were probably four of these migrations, as G. F. Will and H. J. Spinden claim, succeeding each other as follows:

1. Mandan, Hidatsa, Crow.
2. Iowa, Oto, Missouri, Winnebago.

1

3. Omaha, Ponca, Osage, Kansa, Quapaw.

4. Dakota, Assiniboin.[1]

The linguistic grouping seems to bear out this theory with the exception of the Mandan, who are far more closely related to the Winnebago and their kindred than to the Hidatsa. It seems likewise strange that the Hidatsa and Crow, on the one hand, and the Dakota and Assiniboin, on the other, belonging to the first and fourth "migrations," should nevertheless speak dialects that are closely related. One might have expected that Dakota would be more like Omaha and its group.

The Winnebago themselves have no traditions telling of their migrations from the east. The majority of the people questioned asserted that the tribe had originated at Green Bay. This is, however, merely the origin myth of the Thunderbird clan, which apparently has displaced other origin accounts. While, in a few instances, other places were mentioned, the localities to which they referred were all in Wisconsin. There may be some significance in the origin legends of some of the clans which claim that they came from over the sea (the lake), but it is utterly impossible to determine whether we are here dealing with a myth pure and simple or with a vague memory of some historical happening.

The Winnebago have, however, some recollection of their separation from their kindred Siouan tribes. The accounts collected are short and fragmentary, but this may be due largely to the fact that no systematic attempt was made by the author to obtain detailed information on this point. The following fragmentary accounts will give some idea of the value of these recollections.

a. In the early days the Winnebago often went out hunting after they had finished hoeing their corn and other crops. During one of these travels they killed an elk and every lodge received a piece of the animal except one lodge in which a man, his wife, and six daughters with their husbands lived. Thinking that they were disliked by the rest of the tribe, these remained behind the next day when the others continued their journey. They have never been heard from since. It is said that the Quapaws do not know where they come from and we think that they may be descended from this family.

b. When the Winnebago lived on Lake Michigan the tribe was so large that each clan had its own chief and a general chief presided over the whole tribe. After a while it became so hard to obtain food that a band of Winnebago went south. They never returned. These are now in the Southwest. Some of them are the Missouri and some the Iowa. Band after band kept moving away until only one was left—the present Winnebago.

---

[1] The Mandans, Papers of the Peabody Museum. Vol. III, no. 4, pp. 97-98, Cambridge, 1906.

c. Four lodges once left the main tribe at Prairie du Chien or Mac-Gregor, Wisconsin, and never returned. This happened after all the other tribes had leagued together against the Winnebago. The reason these four lodges left the Winnebago was because they were afraid that war might break out again. Some people believe that the Oto

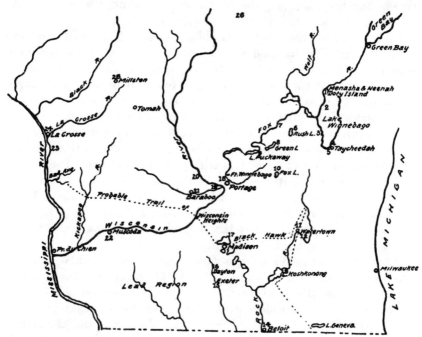

Fig. 1.—SECTIONAL MAP OF WISCONSIN, GIVING THE LOCATIONS OF SOME OF THE OLD VILLAGES.

EXPLANATION OF MAP.

[The numbers on the map indicate the locations of some of the Wisconson Winnebago villages.]

1. Doty Island village, 1634–1832.
2. Pesheu's village, 1797–1833.
3. Black Wolf s village, 1828.
4. Smoker's village, 1816.
5. Sarrochau's village, 1788.
6. Rush Lake village.
7. Yellow Thunder s village, 1828–32.
8. Sarcel's village, 1827.
9. Old Gray-headed Decorah's village, 1793.
10. Big Fox's village, 1832.
11. Watertown village.
12. Iron Walker's village.
13. Little Priest's village, 1832.
     Whirling Thunder s village, 1836.
14. Karraymaunee's village, 1832.
15. Spotted Arm's village.
16. Dayton village.
17. White Crow's village, 1832.
18. Choukeka's village, 1816.
     White Ox's village, 1832.
19. Old Gray-headed Decorah's village, 1793–1836.
20. Yellow Thunder's "forty."
21. Karraymaunee's village, 1832–42.
22. Sarcel's village, 1827.
23. Washington Decorah's village 1832.
24. Buzzard Decorah's village, 1787.
     One-eyed Decorah's village, 1832.
25. Little Decorah's village, 1857.
26. Big Hawk's village, Pike Lake.

are this lost branch, for they speak the same language with but few differences and use many old words that the Winnebago employed long ago but have now given up.

d. Some lodges left the tribe never to return. Some say there were four, others give different numbers (of long lodges). Some say only one lodge. My uncle used to say that there were four. "I think that it is believed that they went to the east," he said.

The other tribes of the second "migration" have semihistorical legends telling of their separation from the Winnebago. Major Bean told Maximilian that an Oto chief had informed him that originally the Winnebago inhabited the lakes and that they subsequently migrated to the Southwest, presumably in pursuit of buffalo. At Green Bay they divided, the Winnebago remaining there while the others continued their journey.

Dorsey was informed by Iowa chiefs [2] that "their people and the Oto, Missouri, Omaha, and Ponca 'once formed part of the Winnebago nation.' According to the traditions of these tribes, at an early period they came with the Winnebago from their priscan home north of the Great Lakes, but that the Winnebago stopped on the shore of a great lake (Lake Michigan), attracted by the abundant fish."

When the Winnebago were first discovered they were entirely surrounded by Central Algonquian tribes. To the north of them lay the Menominee on the shore of Green Bay, to the southeast the Miami, to the south and southwest the Sauk and Fox, and to the west the Ojibwa. The nearest of their kindred were in southern Iowa, western Wisconsin, and eastern Minnesota. Under these circumstances it is not strange that the Winnebago show marked evidence of Central Algonquian influence (fig. 1).

At what time the Winnebago were isolated from their Siouan kindred it is impossible to state. We doubt, however, whether this occurred before the sixteenth century. The Central Algonquian tribes in this region are clearly intruders. The Ojibwa came from the northeast and the Fox, Miami, etc., from the south and the southeast. It seems clear, to judge from the number of effigy mounds found in the territory occupied by the Fox and Miami, that the Winnebago had lived there for a considerable length of time before they were pushed westward and northwestward by these tribes. When the Menominee arrived, and from what direction, it is difficult to determine. On purely linguistic grounds, judging from the close relationship of Menominee to Fox, we might assume that they, like the Fox and the Miami, entered Wisconsin from the south. In that case they might either be interpreted as representing the northernmost extension of the same migration which carried the Miami northward along the shore of Lake Michigan or as representing a prior invasion along the same route. If the latter assumption is correct, they may have arrived in Wisconsin before the Winnebago. One point seems to confirm the thesis of their priority, namely, that they were never at war with the Winnebago, and it hardly seems possible that, had

[2] Handbook of Amer. Inds., Bur. Amer. Ethn., Bull. 30, part 1, p. 612, Washington, 1907.

they forced their way through the country occupied by the Winnebago, war would not have occurred.

The Winnebago call themselves *Hotcaŋgara*, which has been variously interpreted as "people of the parent speech" by James Owen Dorsey and as "big fish people" by other observers. Dorsey's explanation, which is the one most generally accepted, is most certainly wrong, and represents an interpretation read into the word to make it fit the legends which claimed that the dialect was the most archaic of all the Siouan languages. It is true that *ho* may mean "speech," but *tcuŋk* can only mean one thing, and that is "big, real." It is found with a number of animal names, such as *ketcuŋk*, "turtle," and *cvnktcuŋk*, "wolf." It corresponds strictly to the Dakotan *tank*, "large." *Ho* means "fish" in Winnebago. The name Winnebago, as is well known, is of Algonquian origin.

The Winnebago were first encountered by white men in 1634, when Jean Nicolet visited them as agent for Governor Champlain. Where he encountered them is not definitely known. The Winnebago as a rule claim that it was at Green Bay. Some discussion has arisen of late years on this question. No contemporary narrative of the event exists, nor have the Winnebago any clearly marked legend that might be interpreted as referring to it.

An excellent description of their history has been given by P. V. Lawson [3] and from this we will quote at some length, selecting those periods that are of greatest importance in the history of the tribe and which can be illustrated by semihistorical legends still known to the Winnebago.

Much of our knowledge of the early history of the Winnebago is derived from Baqueville de la Potherie's Histoire de l'Amérique Septentrionale. A good deal of his information was obtained from Nicholas Perrot. For the period covering the years 1640–1660 we have the following information: [4]

A few years ago, they numbered possibly 150 warriors. These savages have no mutual fellow-feeling; they have caused their own ruin, and have been obliged to divide their own forces. They are naturally very impatient of control, and very passionate; a little matter excites them; and they are great braggarts. They are, however, well-built, and are brave soldiers, who do not know what danger is; and they are subtle and crafty in war. Although they are convinced that their ancestors drew upon themselves the enmity of all the surrounding Nations, they cannot be humble. Their women are extremely laborious; they are neat in their houses, but very disgusting about their food.

---

[3] The Winnebago tribe, in Wisconsin Archeologist, vol. 6, no. 3, Milwaukee, 1907.
[4] Quoted in Lawson's paper, p. 90.

Perrot also gives an account of the relentless war waged against them:

This nation was a populous one, very redoubtable and spared no one; they violated all the laws of nature; they were Sodomites, and even had intercourse with beasts. If a stranger came among them, he was cooked in their kettles. The Malhominis (Menominees) were the only tribe who maintained relations with them; they did not dare even to complain of their tyranny.

Lawson goes on to say:

So aggressive were the Winnebago that although their only arms "were stone hatchets and knives," they declared war on all the other tribes. Envoys sent to them by the Ottawa were eaten, which cruel deed so incensed the surrounding tribes that they formed an alliance and sent frequent war expeditions against the common enemy, and greatly harassed them. As a result of disagreements among themselves and the continued troublesome activities of the allied tribes, civil wars broke out among the Winnebago. For better protection against the tribes they were finally forced "to unite all their forces in one village, where they numbered four or five thousand men," but an epidemic occurred which soon reduced their number to 1,500.

"Despite all these misfortunes, they sent a party of 500 warriors against the Outagamis (Fox), who dwelt on the other shore of the lake; but all those men perished, while making that journey, by a tempest that arose."

We suppose that this disaster occurred on Little Lake Butte des Morts, as it has been stated that the Winnebago resided on an island, which we suppose was Doty Island. The Winnebago being now greatly reduced by despair and famine, the other tribes were moved to pity by their condition and ceased to make war, and the Illinois sent 500 men, including "50 of the most prominent persons in their nation," to carry to them a supply of provisions. These the Winnebago received "with the utmost gratitude;" but at the same time meditated sacrificing the Illinois to the shades of their dead. A large cabin was erected to lodge their guests, and arrangements made for a dance in their honor. While the Illinois were dancing their bowstrings were cut, and the Winnebago "flung themselves upon the Illinois, massacred them, not sparing one man, and made a general feast of their flesh."

Reproaching themselves for this dastardly deed, and fearing the vengeance of the allied tribes when it should become known to them, the Winnebago "resolved to abandon the place which they were occupying," and "took refuge on an island, which has since been swept away by ice floes." There they considered themselves safe, as the Illinois did not use canoes. The Illinois, finding that their people did not return, investigated the place and found only their bones. In order to allow a proper period for mourning for the dead:

"They deferred hostilities until the second year, when they assembled a large body of men from all Nations who were interested in the undertaking; and they set out in the winter season, in order not to fail therein. Having reached the Island over the ice, they found only the cabins in which there still remained some fire, the Puans (Winnebago) had gone to their Hunt on the day before, and were traveling in a body, that they might not, in an emergency, be surprised by the Illinois."

They followed the hunters in the dead of winter, coming up to them on the sixth day and attacking their camp.

"So vigorous was their attack that they killed, wounded, or made prisoners all the Puans, except a few who escaped, and who reached the Malhouminis' village, but severely wounded by arrows."

He [Perrot] again refers to these traditional events as those of "the ancestors" of the tribe as he knew them, and which we judge to refer to ancestors of the Winnebago of possibly the year 1660. There is no record to say how many years before, though it was doubtless several score, for 50 years before La Potherie published his history Allouez had told the same story of the destruction of the Winnebago by the Illinois:

"About 30 years ago all the people of this nation were killed or taken captive by the Iliniouek with the exception of a single man, who escaped, shot through the body with an arrow."

This would place the event in about the year 1640.

He adds that when the captives were permitted to return to their homes this one was made a "Captain of his Nation," as having never been a slave. Shea commenting on this disastrous defeat of the Winnebago says, "If this strange event took place at all, we must ascribe it to an earlier date than 1639 (1634), when visited by Nicolet, who "found them prosperous, and we can hardly suppose a tribe almost annihilated and then restored to its former numbers in 30 years." . . . Nicolet, it will be remembered, was sent to this then unknown region for the purpose of "making peace" between the Winnebago and the Hurons. As the Winnebago were strong enough to command that attention from Governor Champlain, Doctor Shea is quite correct in supposing the Winnebago to have been "a prosperous tribe" in 1634. The events mentioned in the foregoing accounts are not historical, but traditional, for assuredly they did not take place after the coming of Nicolet, as he was followed by other white men in such short periods as to make it impossible for the occurrence of these stirring events to go unrecorded by others.

Charlevoix visited the tribe in 1720, and though a historian of note in old Canada, records the occurrence as history, though we have shown it to have taken place, if at all, more than a century before he went among them. He possibly got the story from the records of Allouez, made a half century before, though it may have been a riverside or cabin story heard by him at the time of his visit to this frontier of New France. He says:

"The Otchagras, who are commonly called Puans, formerly lived on the shores of the bay . . . but they were attacked by the Illinois, who slew great numbers of them; the rest took refuge on the river of the Outagamis (Fox River), which empties into the end of the bay. They settled upon the shores of a sort of lake (Lake Winnebago)."

Charlevoix . . . adds another disaster not mentioned by the other old writers. In this same narrative he records that "sometime after" the Winnebago had settled on Lake Winnebago:

"They undertook to revenge the defeat which they had suffered from the Illinois. Six hundred of their best men embarked to seek their enemy; but while they were crossing Lake Michigan they were surprised by a furious gale, which caused them all to perish." [6]

The Winnebago still tell of these events and practically in the same words as Perrot obtained them, as can be learned from the following versions obtained in 1910.

a. When the Winnebago first originated, they were holy and clever. They were equal to the spirits. In those days there lived a Winnebago who could fly like a bird, one who could fly as far as four days' journey from the village. There was another Winnebago who could scent anything as far away as four days' journey from the village. Then there was one man who could talk with the trees. They told him many things. Finally there was one who could transform himself into a buffalo. On account of these four men, it was quite impossible for an enemy to approach near the village without the knowledge of the Winnebago, for he who could scent well would scent them, he who could fly far would see them, and he who could converse with trees would be informed of their approach. The one who could transform himself into a buffalo always bore the brunt of the fighting. He would transform himself into a buffalo whenever he got angry. In consequence the Winnebago were feared by all. They could do what they pleased with the other tribes. If the other tribes did not make war on them, they would make war on the other tribes.

One day he who could transform himself into a buffalo had the sensation which generally preceded a battle. So he told the other three. Then the one who could fly went out to make a reconnoissance of the country around them, but returned without having seen anything; then the one who could scent well, scented all around, but likewise could find nothing; then the tree-converser asked the trees and they also told him that they knew of nothing. In spite of it all, however, the buffalo-man said that he still had the premonition of something happening. Then he who could fly again went out, this time going to a distance four days' journey from the village, but he saw nothing. Each time that he went out, however, he noticed a pile of rocks in a hollow near their village. When he returned he said to the people, "Over there, there is a pile of rocks which I never noticed before. I wonder what it can be?" Then the buffalo-man said again, "I really feel that I am going to fight. Look out for yourselves therefore." However, they told him that he was worrying himself unnecessarily, that he ought to go to sleep.

However, the buffalo-man stayed awake all that night, and just as he had anticipated, the whole village was surrounded by enemies in the morning. The other three men were at once awakened and the one who could fly made a rush at the enemy, but was killed. Then the one who could scent well made a rush at the enemy, but he, too, was killed. Up to this time the latter had been absolutely invulnerable. Then the one who could converse with trees made a rush, but he, too, was killed. Thus all three were killed. Then the people said to Buffalo-man, whose real name was Long-Wing, "O Long-Wing, your people are being destroyed! Do you try and accomplish something." Then Long-Wing answered, "*Ho!*" and, making a rush for the enemy, killed four of them, the holiest of their warriors. Then the enemy gave the signal for stopping the battle, which is "*Gu.*" This signal is held to be sacred both among the Winnebago and other tribes. There the battle ended.

The Winnebago felt terrible about the loss of their three warriors. The rocks that the one who could fly had seen in the hollow were the enemy. The name of the one who could fly well was Short-Wing;

that of the keen scenter was White-Dog; and that of the tree con-
verser was Buffalo.

Shortly after this battle a band of visitors from another tribe came
over to Long-Wing's lodge, which had been pointed out to them as
the lodge of the chief. The visitors entered it. In the meantime
the Winnebago held a hurried council and decided to kill these
visitors to avenge the death of their three warriors, whose loss they
were still lamenting. It was decided to scald the visitors to death
with hot water. The roofs of the lodges, which were gable-lodges,
could easily be opened.

When everything was in readiness they called their chief out and
closed the entrances firmly. The chief, however, begged them not
to kill the visitors in his lodge (for it was holy). The Winnebago,
however, paid no attention to him, and as they had already taken
the weapons from the strangers, they poured hot water through the
roof upon their heads. They killed all except two, who succeeded
in making their escape through the roof. One of these changed himself into a turkey and flew away and the other got to the roof and
kept jumping from one roof to the other until he came to the end of
the village, where he succeeded in making his escape. However, the
Winnebago noticed his shell neck ornament which had twisted
around to the back of his neck and one of them threw a stone hammer
at him and killed him. In reality, therefore, only one man escaped.

After they had brought the last body back to the village the chief
told them that they had not acted rightly, for they had killed people
in his (the chief's) lodge, and that from then on the lodge was to
remain as a warrior's lodge.

That same night an owl came to the top of the lodge and hooted,
saying, "The Winnebago will have bad luck." Then the Winnebago asked, "What can be the matter with us?" The chief interpreted the owl's meaning and told them that it meant that from
that time on the Winnebago would lose their power.

Shortly after all these things happened the Winnebago were
attacked by a disease that turned their bodies yellow and many died
of this sickness.

b. When the Winnebago were in trouble because all the other
tribes had leagued against them, they were living at a place near
Red Banks. The enemy had shut off all the water and the only
way they could get any was to tie their pack straps to their pails
and let down these pails in a deep canyon. However, this was also
discovered after a while and the enemy cut the pack straps.

So terrible were their straits that they finally spread their blankets
on the ground and offered tobacco to their medicine men and asked

them to make it rain. Then, after the rain had fallen, they wrung out their blankets and drank the water.

All this time the men of the tribe were being killed off. After a while they began to kill the male children too. Whenever they saw a child they raised up its dress and if it was a male child, they killed it. However, there was a young mother who had a boy, and fearing that if the enemy discovered him they would kill him, she tied a string to the end of the child's penis and pulled the string back under its legs so that the child was given the appearance of a girl. From this woman and her child all the pure blood Winnebago living to-day are descended.

The war against the Winnebago was ended by a young Winnebago chief painting himself blue and surrendering himself to the other tribes.

The most important events of Winnebago history during the eighteenth century were the various alliances into which they were drawn with and against the Fox Indians in the wars that the French waged against this brave tribe. The Winnebago at first allied themselves with the Fox, but afterwards joined the French. This alliance was destined to bring upon them a great disaster. Lawson describes this period in their history as follows.[7]

In pursuance of their policy to combine all the tribes against the Fox, the French in some manner won over the Winnebago, their former friends and allies. Thus we learn that in the autumn of 1729 word was brought to Quebec of an attack by the Winnebago, Ottawa, and Menominee on a Fox village, in which there were killed 100 Fox warriors and 70 women and children. Among the killed of the assaulting party were four Winnebago. . . . Another account gives this assault as on a party of Fox returning from a buffalo hunt, and as made by Ottawa, Chippewa, Menominee, and Winnebago. The Fox village contained 80 men, all of whom were killed or burned except three. The allied Indians burned the cabins and also killed 300 women and children. This probably occurred in the winter of 1729, as the reports are of the date of May 6, 1730.

The Winnebago having broken with their neighbors and friends, the Fox, by this treacherous and unprovoked slaughter, were now in terror for the consequences of their miserable acts. Further attempts against the Fox tribes having been projected from Quebec by the fall of 1729, Sieur Captain Marin appeared at the old French fort at La Baye (Green Bay), and repaired its fallen roofs. He had with him ten Frenchmen. On September 10th the Winnebago returned from their hunt and went to Marin to assure him that they still remained faithful to the French, at the same time presenting him with three slaves. They were rewarded with gifts of powder, bullets, hatchets, guns, and knives. Having ascertained that the Fox were not in their own country, the Winnebago took their families and camped on Dendo Island in the Fox River, adjoining their former location on Doty Island. Very soon thereafter the Fox and Sauk returned and surprised and killed some Winnebago fishermen. Then began a long siege of the Winnebago through the erection by the Fox on the Doty Island waterside of two forts to command the water in all directions.

In order to compensate the Fox for the loss of two of their number through treachery, and procure a cessation of hostilities, the Winnebago decapitated two Menominee who were with them, and delivered to them two others. But the Fox refused to be satisfied unless they also delivered to them four of their own number. This proposal the Winnebago considered an insult, and the siege was resumed. After the fighting had continued for about six weeks, Capt. Marin with five Frenchmen and thirty-four Menominee, came to the assistance of the besieged. When the treachery of the Winnebago in giving up several of their comrades to the Fox became known to the Menominee it required all Marin's powers of persuasion to prevent their deserting from his small command and leaving the besieged to their fate. After four days of fighting with the relief party under Marin it was discovered that the Fox had raised the siege by decamping in the night. Thus were the Winnebago, who had in the meantime been reduced by famine to the eating of boiled bear skins, delivered from the enemy. Marin's force thereupon retired, the Winnebago accompanying him to Green Bay, "where they established themselves in a fort."

For a more detailed account of the same events see Wisconsin Historical Collections, Vol. XVII, 88–100. The Winnebago have preserved a clear recollection of these stirring events in the semi-historical tale known as *Tcap'o'sgaga*.

THE TALE OF TCAP'O'SGAGA[8]

In the early days of their existence the Winnebago were a successful people. They all fasted and were blessed by the spirits. It is for that reason that they were powerful and were called *Hotaŋgara*.

At one time a Fox Indian, whose nation was about to be destroyed by its enemies, came to these much-feared Winnebago and said, "Brothers, I have come to you for aid."

The Winnebago lived on one side of the lake[9] and the Fox on the other and (because of the appeal) the former made friends of the latter, it is said, and the chiefs presented the pipe to one another. When chiefs exchange pipes with one another a very sacred bond is established. Thus many Winnebago and Foxes became friends, and Winnebago men married Fox women and Fox men married Winnebago women.

There was once a very famous warrior among the Winnebago whose crops were molested by the Foxes. *Tcap'o'sgaga's* wife[10] thereupon said to him, "Why don't you take them (the marauders) to task?" Then *Tcap'o'sgaga* went to the Foxes and said, "Boys, all the watermelons are yours when they are ripe, if you desire to eat them." "All right," they answered.

On the morning after the second night *Tcap'o'sgaga's* wife woke up very early and went out to inspect the crops. Again they had been disturbed, so she immediately went back exclaiming, "How terrible: The largest and best of *Tcap'o'sgaga's* crops have been

---

[8] This has also been published by me with the accompanying Winnebago text in the Proceedings of the Wisconsin Historical Society, 1914, pp. 192-207, Madison, 1915.

[9] Probably at the junction of the Fox River with Lake Winnebago.

[10] This name means White-throat.

damaged. Indeed, you (*Tcap'o'sgaga*) should have forbidden them." Then *Tcap'o'sgaga* went over and forbad them.

Early in the morning after the third night the old woman again woke up and went to inspect the crops. Again they had damaged almost everything. "The nicest of *Tcap'o'sgaga's* crops they have destroyed. He should have forbidden them. Why indeed did you not forbid it? They have utterly destroyed your crops." Then *Tcap'o'sgaga* got up and said, "I will go and forbid them." So he went over to the Foxes and said, "Leave my crops alone, I told you. Instead of that you have destroyed them. If again to-night you dare do this, as I am a man who thinks (of revenge), beware. Dare do it again (and take the consequences)," he said.

One of the wicked ones among the Foxes who was doing this said, "O pshaw: He acts as though he were the only man (i. e., great warrior) in creation."

The next morning *Tcap'o'sgaga* himself got up early and went to inspect his crops, and indeed they had been utterly destroyed. What had been left (from previous depredations) had now been utterly ruined, and even the vines had been torn up. *Tcap'o'sgaga* felt grieved and said, "Have my attendants go and call my war-bundle bearer."[11] They went and called him and when he (and others) had arrived (they asked), "What are we to do?" *Tcap'o'sgaga* said, "Put on the food." Then they prepared the food.[12] When the food had been cooked they went to invite as the feasters the most important (of the people). When the feasters finished, then he said, "I am going on the warpath. At the end of the path I see my enemy. I am going to have the pleasure of killing the ten men that my grandfathers (the spirits), who are in control of war, obtained for me. For ten chiefs I am going."

Near the door he indicated what would be the first stopping place. Then he placed the war-bundle across the entrance and jumped over it.[13] Then he put the war-bundle on his back and walked toward his boat, his attendants accompanying him. They had hardly pushed off when they were greeted by a "Here! here!" Then they saw a very long boat filled with chiefs, all of whom were dressed in their best finery; their faces painted blue and medals around their necks.[14] They (the Winnebago) permitted the boat to pass and then when it was exactly alongside of them, they shot the occupants and tipped the boat over. Soon after, a strong wind arose and all the people in the village started out to give chase (to the enemy).[15]

[11] The youths who carry the war-bundle on the warpath. They are generally the nephews of the war leaders.

[12] For the war-bundle or winter feast which is always given before a war party starts.

[13] It was always customary for the leader to do this.

[14] The boat contained the Fox chiefs who had come to make reparation for the damage inflicted upon *Tcap'o'sgaga's* crops.

[15] I. e., started on a tribal warpath.

The Foxes in their village said, "Say, I believe the chiefs have been killed. This is a time of war. *Tcap'o'sgaga* has been angered. When *Tcap'o'sgaga* gets very angry he generally does what he threatens." Then the bad Foxes said, "Perhaps they are eating the objects we donated".[16]

"The Foxes will not be coming back for some time" (the Winnebago said). (The Foxes) at the same time had gathered together and discussed the fate of the chiefs who had gone to give themselves up (to the Winnebago) and had never returned. "Very likely they are not alive any more," they said.

Tcap'o'sgaga returned to the Winnebago village after he killed (the chiefs) and then started for the smaller of the two villages in which the Foxes lived. It was at the smaller village that the lake was narrowest. Toward this one he was going, he said.

He had again planned a war-party. All those within the village who were likely to show any skill in killing men prepared themselves for (attacking) the smaller village. They started at dawn, and they reached the smaller village at night and ferried themselves across. By dawn all had crossed and the village was surrounded. As soon as it was broad daylight they gave the war-whoop in four different places. Then they rushed on to the small village and destroyed it completely. Then they burned up the houses and went home.

When they got home everyone was happy. They danced the victory dance and at night they had the *Hok'ixe're* dance. So happy were the Winnebago.

Although they thought they had killed all in the smaller village, one young girl who was lying on top of a small cliff, near where they crossed, fasting, had not been killed. Now the Foxes were living also in a large village right across the lake from the Winnebago. To this place the young woman who had not been killed went, and when she got to the big Fox village she told them the news, namely, "The Winnebago have completely destroyed us, I believe. Some of them (the enemy) I partially recognized. Go and see, however, whether they were Winnebago, for (if it was they) the lodges will be found burned to the ground, that being their custom when they go on a war-path."

Then the older Foxes went and when they returned, spies announced, "Yes, they were Winnebago, for the lodges have been burned down. It is true that the chiefs who had gone to make peace have been killed." Then the Foxes went into mourning for them. "There are many of the Winnebago and we will not be able to fight them," said the Foxes. Indeed the Foxes were afraid. Although a Fox disliked a Winnebago not one could he kill.

---

[16] I. e., the chiefs who went to make peace.

All the Foxes went into mourning.

Ten Winnebago youths proud of their tattoos had been out (in the woods) before these troubles began. As they were returning they said to the one who was their leader, "Let us go around the large village and court women." "Only if you go around the small village will you escape unharmed," said the leader. "We will go by the large village even if all of us are killed by the spirits," they said. "Well, let us go by way of the small village," the war leader said to them. "If you are afraid, as you say, you may go alone by way of the smaller village; we, however, will go by the way of the large village." The leader, however, refused and also went by way of the large village. That they would die, he knew very well, but nevertheless he accompanied them to the edge of the big village. When they got there (they said), "Let us paint ourselves."

Then they painted themselves, and as they were painting themselves an old man in deep mourning appeared and said, "Are you returning from your travels? Stay with us, for our men are giving a feast. I will tell them to come after you."

Then he went away and soon a young man came (and said), "You are invited. Come right along." "Men, you have seen that all are in mourning. Once more, let me tell you something. In the feast in which you are now to take part, do not lend your knives to anyone. Hold your knife ready," he told them. "All right," said they.

Then they entered the lodge and when all were in they (the Foxes) made room for them and they sat down. Then the host arose and spoke and pointed to a place that was nearest him, for the leader. Then toward another place he pointed for the second and thus each one (Winnebago) received a seat. With each Winnebago were placed several Foxes, making eight in all.

Then the host spoke, "As I rise, I will blow upon my flute and have a song started. I am anxious to have them start a song," he said. Then he rose and blew his flute and as soon as the song was started the Winnebago were seized. It was a long time before they could seize the war leader, but the others had lent their knives and were consequently seized easily. The war leader killed many, but finally his knife broke and he was seized. Then they bound him and prepared the torture. Ten posts they stuck in the ground. Then the war leader said, "I told you of this, but you doubted me. Here we are going to die."

Then the youths came after them and they began torturing them. They applied firebrands to them. They burnt them in those places where they would suffer most. Then the war leader said, "Well, my boys, we are now courting women."

Thus they burned them to death and destroyed them utterly.

The Foxes now offered tobacco to many different tribes, giving them beautifully decorated pipes. They desired to annihilate the Winnebago. All the different peoples liked this because they hated the Winnebago. They made their plans carefully, but even then they could not defeat (the Winnebago) in battle. They (the Winnebago) always kept on moving back as the others tried to overcome them. The Winnebago were driven into the water. They crossed to an island, taking with them the women and children. Here they lived in lodges and ate the crops as they stayed there. All summer they were besieged on this island, as the enemy hoped to destroy them.

One night a man wearing a black skin robe inside out, said, "This they are going to do to you, we heard. So far only the fleetest have come. Soon the slower ones will come, peeling basswood bark as they go along with which to bind the people. If some are still alive we can then take them home bound."

Tcap'o'sgaga felt sad and said, "He will die, the one who said that." Then he shot at him and tumbled him down. The one who had said this was sitting on top of a tree.

One day (the Foxes) said, "Turn over to us those Menominee who have married into your tribe. We are longing for some Menominee soup. If you give these (men) to us we will let up on you." The two Menominee among the Winnebago were great warriors and it was for them that (the Foxes) were asking. These Menominee talked to one another and the one who spoke first said, "It is a hard thing to be a son-in-law in a tribe not your own, my father used to say to me. Whenever the members of the tribe are in difficulties and they wish to save themselves, they turn (their attention to the strangers among them)." "Thus it is" (said the other), "but they may sacrifice me." "My friend, I feel the same way about it just as my father told me. I spoke to you because I thought that you might dread it."

Then the Winnebago gave the Menominee away, but the Foxes did not let up on them.

After a while the Menominee came to the aid of the Winnebago, but the Foxes said, "Wait a little; let us speak to you first." The Menominee listened and the Foxes told them, "The Winnebago are not to be pitied. There are two Menominee who had married among them and they handed them over to us. In this way we again drank Menominee soup. For this reason am I speaking to you. You may help them now, if you wish to, now that I have told you."

The Menominee had come to help the Winnebago, but now that the two Menominee had been handed over to the Foxes they turned back.

Tcap'o'sgaga had been offered tobacco. "Well," he said, "I will try it." At night he started out and jumped into the water. Across there were enemies, so he turned himself into a goose. In the middle of the lake, a lone goose suddenly squawked. Those across shouted, "*Tcap'o'sgaga* is over there." "Yes," was the answer. Then he went around the shallow water and crossed over, and as he sat there bathing some one went by. They said to him, "Are you cooling yourself off with water?" "Yes," he answered.

Then he got himself ready and went to the French and when he arrived among them he said, "Father, different tribes banded together are trying to destroy us." "My child, go home, for I will come to-morrow."

When *Tcap'o'sgaga* returned he went around the other tribes. He went across the island. When he was home he said to the Winnebago, "Our father is going to come." All therefore expected that their father would come. Soon after the French ship came in sight. The other tribes went toward the boat as it came in sight. The Winnebago saw them go toward it. The Winnebago were frightened as they saw the other people go toward the boat, thinking that the French might take part against them.

Then the other tribes spoke to the French. "Father, you know very well that the Winnebago are bad people. Just as a big dog jumps on to a small dog and would like to kill it, so the Winnebago used to do to us. Let us therefore reduce them to ashes." The Frenchman agreed with them and said, "You have spoken the truth and I will help you. I will let you go on (if you wish) but the result will be simply that you will reduce everything to ashes. This is what will happen if you continue. You know that the Winnebago gets very resourceful when he starves. That is his nature and therefore I will take him home with me and fatten him up for you. But you must do what I now tell you. From whatever different places you come, go back to them. If you don't do it, as long as I live, never will I sell any ammunition to you. If you do not let up on the Winnebago, I will give them ammunition and lend them my own men." "All right," said they.

Then they scattered and the women and children were taken into the boat. The men who could walk fast, walked. As soon as he had brought them back near the fort he gave them food with which to sustain themselves. When they were strong enough he bade them flee and gave them good guns and as much food as they could carry in their boats. Coffee, sugar, bread, and all kinds of food he provided for them and he said, "Children, as you're about to flee (remember this). Never hunt fish with a spear. You might thus let a fish escape and if it dies later on and (the enemy) hook a dead fish and inspect it, they will say, 'This fish was speared and got away and died and therefore they (the Winnebago) have passed here.' Likewise, if you build a fire, always cover up the embers, for if you should throw away any into the water (you would be detected)."

Then they went away in boats and returned to the lake. When they came to the narrow place where the main body of water lies there they went ahead along the left branch. Now this is all of this.

After a while the tribes came to see the Frenchman, for it was about the time fixed, and they said, "How have you been getting along?" Then he said, "Children, you know what kind of people the Winnebago are. We watched them very closely, but they got away, in what direction I do not even know. In the morning they were gone. I believe they went downstream, although I haven't even hunted for them upstream."

Well, all these different tribes looked for the Winnebago, for they wished to trail them and kill them. Now, although the Frenchman had expressly forbidden them, sure enough (the Foxes) found a fish that had been speared. "They've come past here," they said. However, when they came to the fork of the stream they didn't know which way (the Winnebago) had gone, but they noticed embers in the water. "They've gone by here." As it was impossible to go to the end of the stream in boats, all the half-breed Foxes got out (and walked). Soon they saw the oval lodges. "There they are," they said. For that reason the Foxes carefully looked them over and watched them. They inquired about them and found out that they had passed by.

The road (trail) was visible, so they chased them. Soon a cold autumn spell overtook them and they (the enemy) gave up the chase and returned home.

We will not follow the course of Winnebago history through all its vicissitudes from their defeat by the Foxes to the British and American occupancy, but only indicate important facts. An important local event was the coming of the Frenchman Decora among them and his marriage to the daughter of the chief of the tribe. An account of this has been preserved by the Decora family, although it is clearly mixed up with what we believe is an account of the first contact of the Winnebago with the French.

HOW THE WINNEBAGO FIRST CAME INTO CONTACT WITH THE FRENCH AND THE ORIGIN OF THE DECORA FAMILY

The Winnebago originated at a place called Red Banks (Green Bay, Wis.) (pl. 1). They had no tools to work with at that time. All they had were bows and arrows and a fire-starter. They had no iron, and if they saw a stone that was naturally sharpened in any way it was considered sacred and they offered tobacco for it. They had tobacco from the beginning. It was their most valued possession.

WITHDRAWN SPRING CREEK CAMPUS

They fasted and became holy. The greatest honor was to be a brave man, and for that reason they did nothing but go to war. They were prepared for war at all times. They tried to obtain war honors. They wished to go to war all the time and kill many enemies. If a person fasted and went without food for a long time, gave offerings of tobacco often, and was then blessed by the spirits, then it would be very hard to kill such a person in battle. The people knew that such powers could be obtained, and that is why they did these things all the time.

They gave many feasts. When a person gives a feast, then he offers the spirits tobacco and asks in return that their weapons be sharper than those of their enemies (i. e., that he kill an enemy and escape unharmed). That is why they used to give so many feasts, that they might be victorious in war. They make offerings to the war spirits, and if these then bless them they will become great warriors. They desired greatly to obtain these blessings.

Tobacco is the greatest possession they have. After Earthmaker created all things he created man. Man was the last of the created objects. Those created before were spirits, and he put them all in charge of something. Even the smallest insects are able to foresee things four days ahead. The human beings were the least of all Earthmaker's creations. They were put in charge of nothing, and they could not even foresee one day ahead. They were the last created and they were the poorest. Then Earthmaker created a weed with a pleasant odor and all the spirits wanted it. Some were almost certain that it would be given to them. They would each think to themselves, "I am going to be put in charge of that, for I am one of the greatest spirits in the world." Then the Creator said, "To all of you (spirits) I have given something valuable. Now you all like this weed and I myself like it. Now this is the way it is going to be used." Then he took one of the leaves and mashed it up. Then making a pipe he smoked it and the odor was pleasant to smell. All of the spirits longed for it. Then he gave each one of them a puff. "Now, whatever (the human beings) ask from me and for which they offer tobacco, I will not be able to refuse it. I myself will not be in control of this weed. If they give me a pipeful of this and make a request I will not be able to refuse it. This weed will be called tobacco. The human beings are the only ones of my creation who are poor. I did not give them anything, so therefore this will be their foremost possession and from them we will have to obtain it. If a human being gives a pipeful and makes a request we will always grant it." Thus spoke Earthmaker.

For that reason the human beings are in control of tobacco; it is their natural possession. This is the story that was handed down to us. The Winnebago made war and made many offerings of tobacco. It is said that the Winnebago were the bravest of all the Indians.

PLATE 1

a, RED BANKS, NEAR GREEN BAY, WIS., LEGENDARY ORIGIN
PLACE OF THE WINNEBAGO

b, RED BANKS, NEAR GREEN BAY, WIS.

PLATE 2

b, FOUR LEGS, CHIEF OF THE WINNEBAGO
VILLAGE ON DOTY ISLAND, 1827

(From Lewis's Aboriginal Portfolio)

a, BLACK WOLF, CHIEF OF THE WINNEBAGO
VILLAGE AT BLACK WOLF POINT, LAKE
WINNEBAGO, 1827

(From Lewis's Aboriginal Portfolio)

PLATE 3

JASPER   BLOWSNAKE

PLATE 4

JOHN FISHER

a. JAMES PINE

b. JOHN RAVE AND FAMILY

PLATE 6

a. JOHN FIREMAN
(Front view)

b. JOHN FIREMAN
(Profile view)

c. WHITEBREAST

d. JOHN RAYMOND

PLATE 7

a. YOUNG WINNEBAGO WOMAN AND DAUGHTER

b. OLD WINNEBAGO AND DAUGHTER

PLATE 8

a. GRAY HAIR

b. RED WING

c. JAMES RICEHILL

d. ALBERT HENSLEY (Front view)

WINNEBAGO TYPES

They say that the tobacco was given to them directly and that Earthmaker loves the Winnebago more than any other race. For that reason they were very clever. Now this is what the old men have said and handed down to us.

Once something appeared in the middle of the lake (Green Bay). They were the French; they were the first to come to the Winnebago. The ship came nearer and the Winnebago went to the edge of the lake with offerings of tobacco and white deerskins. There they stood. When the French were about to come ashore they fired their guns off in the air as a salute to the Indians. The Indians said, "They are thunderbirds." They had never heard the report of a gun before that time and that is why they thought they were thunderbirds.

Then the French landed their boats and came ashore and extended their hands to the Winnebago, and the Indians put tobacco in their hands. The French, of course, wanted to shake hands with the Indians. They did not know what tobacco was, and therefore did not know what to do with it. Some of the Winnebago poured tobacco on their heads, asking them for victory in war. The French tried to speak to them, but they could not, of course, make themselves understood. After a while they discovered that they were without tools, so they taught the Indians how to use an ax and chop a tree down. The Indians, however, were afraid of it, because they thought that the ax was holy. Then the French taught the Indians how to use guns, but they held aloof for a long time through fear, thinking that all these things were holy.

Suddenly a Frenchman saw an old man smoking and poured water on him. They knew nothing about smoking or tobacco. After a while they got more accustomed to one another. The Indians learned how to shoot the guns and began trading objects for axes. They would give furs and things of that nature for the guns, knives, and axes of the whites. They still considered them holy, however. Finally they learned how to handle guns quite well and they liked them very much. They would even build fires at night so that they might try their guns, for they could not wait for the day, they were so impatient. When they were out of ammunition they would go to the traders and tell their people that they would soon return. By this time they had learned to make themselves understood by various signs.

The second time they went to visit the French they took with them all the various articles that they possessed. There the French taught them how to sew, how to use an ax, and how to use a knife. Then the leader of the whites took a liking to a Winnebago girl, the daughter of the chief, and he asked her parents for permission to marry her. They told him that her two brothers had the right to give her away in marriage. So he asked them and they consented.

Then he married her.   He lived there and worked for the Indians and stayed with them for many years and he taught them the use of many tools.   He went home every once in a while and his wife went with him, but he always came back again.   After a while a son was born to him and then another.   When the boys were somewhat grown up he decided to take his oldest son with him to his country and bring him up in such a way that he would not be in danger, as was the case here in the woods.   The Indians consented to it and they agreed that the mother was to bring up the youngest child.

So he took his oldest boy home with him and when he got home he went to live with his parents, as he had not been married in his own country.   He was a leader of men.   The boy was with him all the time and everyone took a great liking to him.   People would come to see him and bring him presents.   They gave him many toys.   However, in spite of all, he got homesick and he would cry every night until he fell asleep.   He cried all the time and would not eat.   After a while the people thought it best to bring him back to his home, as they were afraid that he would get sick and die.   Before long they brought him back.   The father said: "My sons are men and they can remain here and grow up among you.   You are to bring them up in your own way and they are to live just as you do."

The Indians made them fast.   One morning the oldest one got up very early and did not go out fasting.   His older uncle, seeing him try to eat some corn, took it away from him and, taking a piece of charcoal, mashed it, rubbed it over his face, and threw him out of doors.   He went out into the wilderness and hid himself in a secret place.   Afterwards the people searched for him everywhere, but they could not find him.   Then the people told the uncle that he had done wrong in throwing the boy out.   The latter was sorry, but there was nothing to be done any more.   In reality the uncle was afraid of the boy's father.   They looked everywhere but could not find him.

After a full month the boy came home and brought with him a circle of wood (i. e., a drum).   He told the people that this is what he had received in a dream, and that it was not to be used in war; that it was something with which to obtain life.   He said that if a feast was made to it, this feast would be one to Earthmaker, as Earthmaker had blessed him and told him to put his life in the service of the Winnebago.

From this man they received many benefits.   He was called to take the foremost part in everything.   They called him the Frenchman, his younger brother being called *Tcap'o'sgaga*, White-throat.   And as they said, so it has always been.   A person with French blood has always been the chief.   Only they could accomplish anything among the whites.   At the present time there is no clan as numerous

as the descendants of that family and the object that he said was
sacred (the drum) is indeed sacred.   It is powerful to the present
day.   His descendants are the most intelligent of all the people and
they are becoming more intelligent all the time.   What they did
was the best that could be done.   The ways of the white man are the
best.   This is the way they were brought up.

This is the end of the history of the Decoras.

One of the interesting developments resulting from the Indian contact with the whites has been the appearance of prophets.   In almost
all cases these prophets were concerned with attempts to so adapt
the life of their fellow-Indians to the new conditions that they
would be better able to cope with the invaders who were sweeping
all before them.   Whether prophets sprang up only in response to the
peculiar conditions resulting from the presence of the whites it is impossible to say, but there seems no reason to believe that such had
always been the case.   It is quite possible that conditions similar to
those developing from the occupancy of America by Europeans had
occurred in pre-Columbian times when one tribe was hard pressed
by another.

The Winnebago seem to have had their share of prophets, and
seem likewise to have been influenced by some of the great prophets
of other tribes, like the Shawnee prophet.   An interesting account of
what he told the Winnebago has been preserved and we will give it at
length.

One of the suggestive things about the following account is the way
in which the informant, who is evidently a devout Peyote follower,
connects the teachings of the Shawnee prophet with the modern
Peyote movement, thus evincing a remarkable feeling for historical
continuity.

WHAT THE SHAWNEE PROPHET TOLD THE WINNEBAGO

Now this is what the Winnebago heard from the Shawnee prophet;
this is what he said, it is said, by those who heard him:

"Let the people give up the customs they are now observing and I
will give them new ones."   This is what he said.

Some of the Winnebago did this and threw away their war bundles.
But he had meant their bad customs.   Some also threw away their
good medicines.   At last they decided to go over to where he was.   A
man named Smoke-Walker led a number of young men over.   " We
will walk as the thunderbirds do," said the leader.   Then a great and
holy man called Dog-Head said that he also was going along.   He
was then an old man.   The leader said, "You had better not come
along for we are going to walk as the thunderbirds do, and for that
reason I wish only young men."   But Dog-Head said, "I am going

along nevertheless, and whenever you wish to walk like the thunder-birds and walk above the earth, then I can turn back. I will go along."

There were eleven who went along. When they got to the place where the Shawnee prophet was staying they found all the other tribes (represented) there except the Winnebago.

Then the prophet said, "It is good, my younger brothers." He called the Winnebago younger brothers. "There are many tribes here, but I wanted to see you here especially. It is good you have come. I want to talk to you, but it is impossible (because I can not speak your language)." Now the old man who had come along against the wishes of the chief could speak any Indian language, so the leader said to Dog-Head, "Older brother, you used to speak almost any language; can you still do it?" Then Dog-Head said, "My younger brother, I can understand what he is saying, but I don't know whether I could talk the language myself. I may or may not be able to speak it (enough to make myself understood). I don't know." Then the leader said, "It is good, older brother. Try to talk to him, and whatever you do will be better than nothing." Then Dog-Head said to the Shawnee prophet, "I can understand what you are saying, but I am afraid to talk to you because I don't know whether I could make myself clear to you." The prophet thanked him and said, "It is good. I want to talk to you Winnebago."

Then they had a long conversation and this is what he said, "Younger brothers, we are not doing the right thing and that is why we are not getting along very well in life."

At that time they (the other tribes) were having their night dances, so the Winnebago moved over to them. There they heard the prophet speak. He said that he had been sent by the Creator because the Indians were wandering away from their old customs. For that reason the Creator had sent him to tell them of it. He at first forgot all about it, for the devil misrepresented things to him and he believed him. The devil had told him that he would go to heaven and that he could not be killed. He had told him that he had given him a holy belt. He was a bad person. Whenever he got angry he would throw his belt down on the ground and it would change into a yellow rattlesnake and rattle. When he did this the rest of the people were afraid of him. He was very mean when drunk. They were afraid of him, not only on account of his belt, which he could turn into a yellow rattlesnake, but also because of the fact that he was very strong. If, when he was drunk, a number of people jumped on him, afterwards he would find out about it and hit them. If they would resist he would kill them.

It was utterly impossible for him to be killed. He was unkind to the women. They would go with him not because they liked him but because they were afraid of him. It was a dangerous thing to say anything about him. Whenever he wished to drink he would take some person's valuables and buy drink with it. These are the things he did. The Creator had sent him on a mission to the earth, but the devil had misled him.

On one occasion (when he was drunk) quite a number of people jumped on him and nearly killed him. When he awoke the next morning he asked his wife who had done it and she told him. "Well, they will hear of me soon. However, I want to go and take a bath first and cool off and then take my revenge, when I get back." When he was in bathing a man came to him and said, "They have told me to come after you, so let us go." Then he went back with him and he took him to the place from which he had originally started. Then the Creator said, "How are you getting on with the work which you were to do?" Then he remembered what he had been doing. Then the Creator said, "Is it for this that I created you?" Then he took his mouth and showed it to him and he saw that it was crooked and sticking out in all directions. Then he took his understanding (and showing it to him), he said, "Did I create you thus?" Then he looked into his ears and they were crooked and ragged. Thus he made him see all his bad characteristics and his evil mind. Then he took out his heart and showed it to him. It was all furrowed up and bad to look upon. "Did I create you thus?" said the Creator.

"Now, then, you will do better the next time," and he sent him back. This time, however, he (the prophet) did not come here to get revenge. He came to tell of the mysteries, but no one would believe him. "He is just getting crazier all the time," they said of him. Then he told all to gather in one place and he promised to say nothing but the truth. Then he made a small flat war club, cleared a piece of ground and laid it there. Then he said to those assembled, "If anyone can lift this, then I will not say it (i. e., talk about my mission)."

Now he (the prophet) was one of triplets. The third one was teased a good deal and one day he said, "I am getting tired of this teasing and am going home." Then he died. They had been teasing him about his head, which was very narrow. There were thus two left. The brother who was left was a powerful man. Bullets could not penetrate him, and indeed it was impossible to kill him in any way. It was this brother who had told him not to talk (about his mission). Then the prophet said to him, "Well, if you can lift this war club I will not speak about it any more." Then he tried to lift the little war club and failed. After that the brother made no more remarks about it.

Then he had them make a long lodge and they were told to go after a number of bears. As many as he told them to get, that many they would bring home with them. Thus they knew that he was telling the truth. All the people in the country listened to him and what he prophesied came true, so they believed him holy.

One day they told him that the whites were coming. After a short time they said, "They are still coming. There are very many of them." The lookouts were always watching and they saw them coming. Then the prophet said, "When they come, listen to them, and when they sleep we will attend to them." Now the whites had come; they had to cut through the roads to come. When they were near one of their number came over to ask where they could camp and they were told to camp right there. In the night, when they were asleep, they shot at them. They were half asleep and they ran away without their weapons. A tribe of Indians was just then going down the stream and these shot at the whites, too. Then they turned back and the commander had the bugle blow and called them to themselves. Then they took their guns and fought. Many Indians were killed. The one who had led the Winnebago over was killed in this battle.

Then his son started back home. His name was Small-Snake. As they were returning, unprepared for danger, a boat came down the stream and passed very close to them. The women (he was the only man among them) cried out. He was without any ammunition except two shots. Just as he got ready to shoot they were recognized. The people in the boat were not Americans but Frenchmen and they were very hungry. Thus they were saved, and the Frenchmen gave them plenty of ammunition. Then they passed safely on.

The Indians had scattered in every direction and no one knew who was alive. Then Dog-Head blessed them with a powerful medicine that he possessed. "My son (he was addressing Small-Snake), if I were to induce you to join the Medicine Dance, why that honor would perish with your death. Now they say that a man named Large-Walker had a vision in which he was blessed by a loon. The loon blessed him, saying, 'Large-Walker, I also bless you with this (medicine). When I work for the chief and when I sweep his lodge, I sweep all the bad things outside. It will be the same with this medicine. If a person partakes of something bad, he will not die, no matter how bad it is, but, on the contrary, he will live. Now when you wish to use this medicine, pour some tobacco for me and I will smoke it.' Then he looked at the loon and the loon had something growing out of his back. That is what he was referring to. Then the loon said again, 'When you want to dig it, don't dig it right away (i. e., without performing the proper rites). You must offer a white feather, a white deerskin, red feathers, and tobacco. Then you can dig it. If you make these offerings, you will never fail in anything. With this I bless you (this herb), and no one else in the world will know it.'"

This is what Dog-Head told Small-Snake: "As long as your posterity lasts, so long can you use this medicine. If I had given you clothes, when they were worn out, that would be the end of them. Your father spoke to me in your behalf and that is why I am giving you this medicine." Dog-Head told the truth, for even to the present day this medicine is being used. It is a purgative and a valuable medicine.

When the Winnebago returned the possessor of the medicine was careless and placed it in a hole in a cliff. When he came back for it it could not be found. He looked all over for it but it was apparently gone. Then they said, "We should not have done this. We should look before acting." Indeed, nowhere did they ever find it afterwards.

Now, it is four generations since the Shawnee prophet prophesied, and from that time there have been many prophets among us, as he is said to have told the people. Many have prophesied, but none have told anything that seemed reasonable. The Shawnee prophet was good, but those who have come after him have prophesied so that people might praise them, or just for the sake of talking.

It is said that the Shawnee prophet said that there would come a time when a woman would prophesy and that she should be immediately killed. The end of the world would be near then. Then he is said to have said that a little boy would prophesy and that one was to give ear to what he said.

The Peyote people claim that their ceremony is the fulfillment of this prophesy and that it is true. The Shawnee prophet had said that there would be springs of water in front of the people's lodges and it is so at the present time, for the water is at our very doors. His prophesy was correct and he told the truth. Then he said that trees would travel and this is happening to-day, for trees are loaded into trains and are carried all around the country. He told the truth and he knew what was going to happen. He said that one day we would be able to write our own language and we are doing that to-day, for we have a Bible in Winnebago and we are able to write to one another in our own language. All these things he was able to foretell four generations ago.

A Winnebago by the name of Noise-Thunder had also prophesied that we would be able to write our own language. One thing that he said, however, was not correct. He said that the bad thing that has come upon us will make us forget our own ways. He meant that we should not take up with the white man's ways. "Don't do it, for if you do, we will all die." Now, he was mistaken in that. "The Creator has given two plates and they are getting empty. He gave the men a plate for them to fill and the women a plate for them to fill. The women's plate is empty." He meant that the Creator had made men to hunt and the women to dig the soil and raise vegetables, and that the latter were not doing it. That is what he meant by saying that their plates were empty. Noise-Thunder insisted that this was the white man's fault; he thought that we were being weakened by the white man's food. Quite a number of people believed him. "The birds eat what was provided for them to eat, game and vegetables, and the whites eat what was provided for them. Why should we not eat what was provided for us?" He was right, but then the Creator also created the food that the whites are eating. We are now getting accustomed to it and are getting stronger on this food.

The Winnebago were decreasing in number, so the Creator gave them a medicine which would enable them to get accustomed to the white man's food; that, also, they might know the Creator and that he is the true bread and food. This they found out by using this medicine. They are going into it deeper and deeper all the time, they who had been lost, and this has all been accomplished by the medicine (the peyote).

The following notes were also obtained concerning other prophets:
"There was a prophet among the Winnebago recently named George Wilkinson. He claimed that he was the Trickster; that there were two worlds; that he had been to the first and that he was now on the second. After a while he was to return to *ma'una* (Earthmaker). He told all the Winnebago to plant their tobacco and cornfields again. (This is what he was ordered to say.) He said that the power of the war bundles was entirely exhausted, but that it could be restored if a person were to fast for four days. When the spirits addressed him by name they called him "He-Who-Stands-Blue." This happened fifteen years ago.

"Thundercloud claims to be the Hare."

Another man named Xuga prophesied the same, led them on a warpath, and lost a lot of people.

The most important religious revival of the last century among the Winnebago is the Peyote or Mescal religion. It is described in detail on page 388.

WINNEBAGO NAMES OF OTHER TRIBES AND PEOPLES

At the present time the Winnebago appears to have names only
for the following tribes and peoples:

Omaha, Oma^{n}ha^n.

Sioux, Ca^{n}ha^n.

Oto, Wadjokdjadja.

Iowa, Waxotc.

Pawnee, Pani.

Menominee, Kaγi.

Fox, Wacerekϵ.

Sauk, Zagi.

Potawatomi, Warax.

Ojibway, Regatci.

Kickapoo, JakdjΛnagi.

Osage, Worac.

French, Djimoxgemena.

Germans, Daγeri.

English, Zagana^{n}c.

Irish, Hit$^\epsilon$e waracicik.

Whites in general, Ma^{n}hi xedera.

CHAPTER II

WINNEBAGO ARCHEOLOGY

GENERAL PROBLEMS

One of the most interesting and important features of the area occupied by the Winnebago is the large number of earth mounds found. That these mounds were made by the Winnebago or the Sioux there seems to be little doubt. The participation of the Sioux in the construction of these earth mounds seems, however, to have been confined entirely to the so-called linear and conical types. The effigy mounds seem to have been the work of the Winnebago exclusively[1] (figs. 2, 3).

The first really serious study of the Wisconsin mounds was made by I. A. Lapham in 1850, and his work must be considered of considerable importance still, by reason of the admirable plats of mounds long since leveled. The next discussion is found in Cyrus Thomas's Report on the Mound Explorations, [2] but he makes no attempt to explain them. Our first accurate knowledge dates from the inception of the Wisconsin Archeologist in 1901. Any attempt to study the archeology of Wisconsin will necessarily have to be based on material there published. An extremely useful and suggestive summary of the data has been made by A. B. Stout. This little pamphlet and that on the Koshkonong region [3] by the same author are of prime importance in the study of Winnebago archeology.

In order to understand the archeology of this region clearly it will be best to say a few words about the regions which were the early habitations of the Winnebago and the tribes that were their immediate neighbors.

The Winnebago, when first found, were inhabiting the southern shore of Green Bay, Wis. Whether, at this time, they already extended farther south and west, it is impossible to say. The tradi-

---

[1] Cf. Radin, "Some Aspects of Winnebago Archæology," Amer. Anthropologist, n. s., vol. 13, no. 4, 1911.

Prof. Dixon in his article on "Some Aspects of North American Archæology," Amer. Anthropologist, n. s., vol. 15, no. 4, 1913, accepts this conclusion. "The association of the effigy mounds of Wisconsin and the adjacent area with the Winnebago or other Siouan tribes seems now reasonably certain, and one might therefore naturally regard the Serpent mound and the few others of this effigy type in the Ohio Valley as due also to tribes of the same stock," p. 561.

[2] Twelfth Annual Report of the Bureau of American Ethnology, pp. 47–49, Washington, 1894.

[3] "Prehistoric Earthworks in Wisconsin," Ohio Archæological and Historical Quarterly, vol XX, no. 1, Columbus, 1911; and "The Archæology of the Lake Koshkonong Region," Wisconsin Archeologist, vol. 7, no. 2, 1908.

tions speak only of Green Bay as their original habitat. On the other shore of Green Bay were the Menominee, who likewise have no recollection of having lived anywhere else. To the northeast, along Door Peninsula, were the Potawatomi, unquestionably intruders, who had come by way of Mackinaw. To the southwest lay the Sauk and Fox, the closely related Kickapoo, and the enigmatic Mascoutin. Finally,

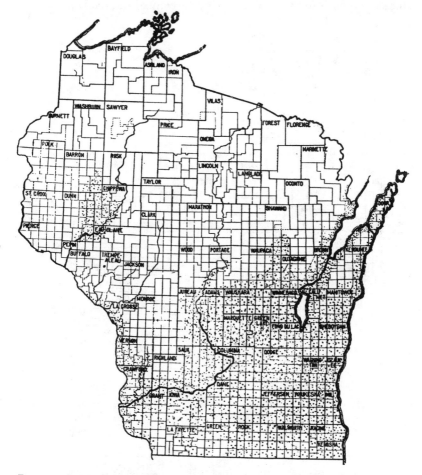

FIG. 2.—MAP OF WISCONSIN, SHOWING DISTRIBUTION OF CIRCULAR MOUNDS.

to the south lay the Miami. Such seems to have been the distribution of the tribes around Green Bay and Lake Michigan at the first advent of the whites. Within 50 years of the landing of Nicollet the places were entirely shifted. Winnebago villages are found scattered all along the Fox River and Lake Winnebago, the Sauk and Fox and Kickapoo are on their way farther south, and the Potawatomi are in possession of the southern shore of Green Bay and the western shore of Lake Michigan. Later still we find the Winnebago extending all

along the Wisconsin River and west of it to the Mississippi, and, at the
same time, occupying the territory south of Lake Winnebago through
the region of the Four Lakes, the shores of Lake Koshkonong and
farther down along the Rock River into Illinois. Their eastern
boundary was determined by the Potawatomi.

Let us return now to the distribution of the mounds. Of the three
kinds of mounds found in Wisconsin, the conical and oval ones are the

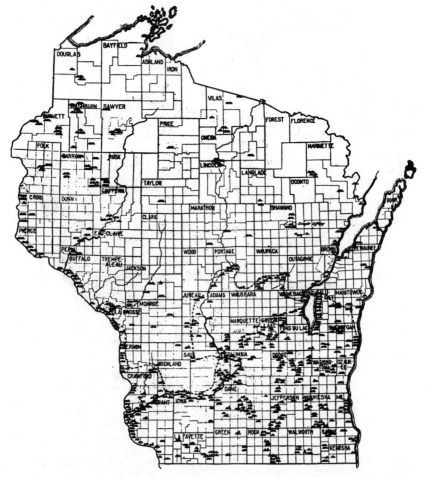

FIG 3.—MAP OF WISCONSIN, SHOWING DISTRIBUTION OF EFFIGY MOUNDS.

commonest, and they are met with in practically every county of the
State in which records have been made. They have also been found
in Minnesota. The so-called effigy mounds, on the other hand,
have never been found north of a line drawn through the southern
boundary of Lincoln County. They have, however, been found in
every area which the Winnebago occupied at one time or another,

with the exception of the eastern shore of Green Bay and the Fox River. At the same time they have been discovered in fairly large numbers in the counties of Sheboygan, Ozaukee, Washington, Waukesha, Racine, and Kenosha, which, as far as our historical information extends, had never been occupied by the Winnebago. Flint arrow points and pottery shards are found throughout the entire State. The distribution of copper implements has not yet been thoroughly investigated, but the present status of our knowledge has been ably discussed by Charles E. Brown.[4] To judge from the papers of Brown, implements of copper are found pretty generally distributed over the State, although certain objects seem to be found in greater abundance in some places than in others.

There are three types of mounds in Wisconsin and the territory immediately adjacent to it—the effigy, the linear, and the intaglio. All of these have been subjected to a variety of explanations at the hands of archeologists, from Lapham's time to our own. The cardinal error in all their attempts at explanation has perhaps been the assumption that the mounds were necessarily of great antiquity. For a long time it was not considered likely that the present inhabitants of the region, the Winnebago or their ancestors, had had anything to do with their erection. As soon, however, as systematic inquiries had been made among living Winnebago it was discovered that not only were they able to give more or less reasonable explanations of the uses of most of the mounds, but a number of the older people claimed to have distinct recollections of the erection of some of them. In obtaining notes on social organization the writer was told incidentally that it had been customary not very long ago to erect near the habitation of each clan an effigy of their clan animal. Subsequently, upon a more systematic inquiry, it was discovered that not only were such effigy mounds erected near clan habitations, but also on every plantation owned by a certain clan. In other words, these effigy mounds were, to all intents and purposes, property marks. Similar effigies are found in the porcupine quillwork, on the war bundles, and on the woven bags still used by the Winnebago in Wisconsin. This interpretation has been so fully corroborated that there can no longer be any possible doubt about it. The age of the mounds thus diminishes considerably. Of course some may have been erected long ago, but it is quite evident that the effigy mounds found near the Mississippi must have been erected during the eighteenth century, as the Winnebago did not reach this region before that time.

In connection with the effigy mounds two things need explanation— namely, why there are no mounds of this type near Red Banks, Green Bay, and why there are so many directly south of this region along

4 "The Native Copper Implements of Wisconsin," in Wisconsin Archeologist, vol. 3, no. 2; and "The Native Copper Ornaments of Wisconsin," ibid., vol. 3, no. 3, 1904.

the eastern shore of Lake Michigan, a territory in which the Winnebago have no recollection of ever having lived. The first question is very difficult to answer. There is always the possibility that some mounds may yet be discovered and again it is possible that all have been leveled considerably. The apparent persistency with which the Winnebago held to the custom of mound building during their forced migration since the eighteenth century, even when they lived in places for only a short time, and thè absence of any mounds in their legendary home, suggest the possibility that they never lived permanently near Green Bay.[5] This inference has not been drawn from a study of the archeological but from a study of the historical sources, by Mr. P. V. Lawson.[6] In this paper the writer tries to prove that all the old sources point to Doty Island situated in Fox River, at the foot of Lake Winnebago, as the place where Nicollet first met the Winnebago. Whatever the merits of the case may be, it is certain that, according to the Winnebago themselves, their original home was Green Bay. Into this tradition many legendary details have, of course, been woven, and it seems to us that the presumption of evidence favors Green Bay, although the complete absence of what seems to have been such a characteristic feature of Winnebago culture as effigy mounds suggests a possibility that the Green Bay settlement represented just the northernmost extension of the tribe. The large settlements found along Lake Winnebago so soon after Nicollet's landing make it reasonably certain that the Winnebago had been there before his arrival in Wisconsin.

We will also have to assume that the Winnebago erected the effigy mounds along the western shore of Lake Michigan, in an area that, since the coming of the whites, has been occupied successively by the Miami and Potawatomi. This would indicate that the Winnebago originally came in a compact mass from the south. They, however, have no recollection of this fact and it must indeed have taken place a long time ago. This is, of course, only an hypothesis.

The effigy mounds are unquestionably supposed to represent the eponymous clan animals of the Winnebago. It seems, however, as if three clan animals were never represented—namely, the wolf, the buffalo, and the fish. It is possible that the mound found near the asylum grounds at Madison, Wis., is intended to represent a wolf, but, even if this could be established, it would not explain the apparent absence of any more examples of one of the most important Winnebago clans.

[5] The absence of any mention of them in early records has no significance, for even in the nineteenth century, in regions where it seems incredible that they should have escaped notice, no mention is ever made of them by travelers.

[6] "The Habitat of the Winnebago," in the Proceedings of the State Historical Society of Wisconsin, 1906. Mr. A. C. Neville in a previous paper published in the Proceedings of 1905, sought to establish the thesis of a Green Bay home from the same data.

There are a large number of effigies that, for want of a better name. most Wisconsin archeologists have called "turtle" mounds. No explanations can be offered of these peculiar effigies unless they are attempts to picture fish or are altered water-spirit mounds. The Winnebago had no turtle clan, but the turtle plays an important part in their mythology.

Perhaps the most peculiar effigy mounds are the famous "Man" mounds, of which only two examples are in existence, and the so-called "intaglios." Good descriptions of both types have been given.[1]

The two "Man" mounds have generally been regarded as inexplicable or connected with some prehistoric rite, and it seemed useless to attempt any explanation. As there seemed to be no reason why these mounds might not fall into the same category as the clan mounds, the writer took the opportunity of inquiring about them among the older Winnebago. A number of the people asked knew nothing about them, but, fortunately, two very old members of the tribe interpreted them, as soon as they were described, as representations of the Warrior or Hawk clan. As this clan belonged to the Bird phratry, no one had ever looked for any but bird emblems.

No information has been obtained from living Winnebago that could throw any light on the "intaglio" mounds. We wish, however, to hazard a suggestion as to their possible meaning. "The intaglio effigies," to quote Mr. Brown, "may be described as being the reverse of the ordinary effigy mounds. They are excavated out of the soil instead of erected upon it, the earth removed from the shallow excavation being heaped up with care along the edges, giving form and prominence to the animal shapes depicted."[2] The Winnebago frequently placed symbols referring to water deities under water, and, as 10 of the 12 intaglios that have been described belong unquestionably to the Water-spirit clan, it may have been customary to keep these "intaglios" filled with water. The discovery of two supposedly Bear "intaglios" militates against this suggestion. However, according to the Bear clan legends, the ancestors of that clan came from the water, as did likewise those of the Wolf and Buffalo clans.

We now come to the most unsatisfactory problem of our area— namely, the nature and significance of the linear mounds. The various types have been best described by Mr. A. B. Stout and we will do best to quote him *in extenso:*

The principal classes of linear mounds are as follows:
The pure linear type is a straight wall-like mound of uniform width and height. They are usually about 2½ feet in height and from 10 to 20 feet in width. Some are so

---

[1] "The Preservation of the Man Mound," in vol. 7, no. 4, of the Wisconsin Archeologist, and " The Intaglio Mounds of Wisconsin," in vol 9, no. 1, of the same journal; both papers by C. Brown.

[2] Cf. Wisconsin Archeologist, vol. 9, no. 1, p. 6.

short that they approach the oval and platform mound types, while the longest are over 900 feet in length.

The straight pointed linear is usually of considerable length and differs from the pure linear as given above in having one end tapering to a long drawn out point. . . .

Club-shaped linears are frequently found . . . and kidney-shaped linears are not wanting. . . .

The various linear types described above are sometimes modified by an enlargement at one end. . . . This ranges from a low, flattened enlargement to a rounded, well built conical mound. Various projections or appendages to some of the linear forms . . . give figures that shade toward effigies proper. These types of linear mounds are mingled in the mound groups as shown in the various group plats. . . .

Besides the types already discussed there are peculiar combinations and composite mounds which do not admit of any rational explanation.[3]

Many explanations have been given by investigators and, for that matter, by Indians themselves, of the significance of these linear mounds. Not only is it necessary to account for the peculiar and manifold shapes, but for the equally strange combinations into which they have entered. With regard to the latter type, Mr. Stout refuses even to suggest an interpretation. He, however, takes a determined stand with regard to the linear mounds proper and interprets them as having been constructed for the purpose of symbolizing inanimate things, and consequently as really conventionalized effigies. This seems to him the only satisfactory explanation. "It is evident," he says, "that there are intermediate or transitional forms between the linears and the pure effigy types with which they are mingled."[4] He admits the existence of linear mounds extending westward into Minnesota and Manitoba, far beyond the limits of the effigy type, but he does not believe it necessary either to regard these latter as effigies or to change his interpretation of the significance of the former. Mr. Stout's interpretation is indeed a purely arbitrary one. Whereas his identification of the effigy mounds was based upon information obtained directly from some Winnebago Indians, that of the linear is based upon what he thought was the necessity of the case.

Inquiries made among the Winnebago of Wisconsin by the writer brought out the fact that the Indians were unanimous in claiming their forefathers as the authors of the mounds, but they were not at all unanimous as to their significance. By far the largest number of individuals, however, insisted that these linears were defensive works behind which they dodged during battle. These must not be confused with anything in the nature of breastworks or fortifications. The Indians claimed that these mounds ought to be found in great numbers along Lake Koshkonong, because it was there that a terrific struggle had once been waged by the Winnebago against one of

3 Ohio Archæological and Historical Quarterly, Vol. XX, no. 1, Jan., 1911, pp. 22–23.
4 Ibid., pp. 24–26.

their hereditary enemies. As a matter of fact, according to Mr. Stout, in the small area of 31 square miles around the lake, no less than 481 linear mounds have been found, and, if we take into consideration the fact that but 50 miles to the northwest, in the Sauk County area, 734 were found, we have within a radius of 231 square miles an enormous number of linear mounds. Whether, however, this has anything to do with the statements of the Indians mentioned above is very doubtful. When the writer called the Indians' attention to the fact that structures that were so low could hardly serve as an adequate protection against arrows they retorted by saying that the Indians did not stand up when attacked but lay stretched on the ground behind the mounds.

The same two areas that yielded such a large number of linear mounds were also rich in effigy and conical mounds, containing 225 of the former and 646 of the latter. The conclusion is thus forced upon us that we have here the seat of a large number of Winnebago settlements. The linear mounds may therefore be said to be characteristic features of certain villages. A similarly large number of linear mounds seems to exist in Crawford County, according to the investigations of Lapham. It is possible that a continuation of thorough and systematic studies like those made by Mr. Stout in Sauk County and Lake Koshkonong will bring to light many such linear mound areas closely associated with village sites.

With regard to the Winnebago interpretation given above it might be said that we know of numerous battles that occurred both along Lake Koshkonong and the Mississippi, and that it would require no manipulation of the facts to accept the Indians' explanation. It might, nevertheless, justifiably be asked why these peculiar shapes? They can hardly have had any importance in warfare.

As opposed to the view advanced above, various interpretations have been given at different times. Peet regarded the linear mounds as game drives, but this explanation seems to have been quite arbitrary. At least we know of no facts that were brought forth in its defense.

Although the interpretation that we were here dealing with defensive structures was by far the most common, two other explanations were obtained, one to the effect that the linear mounds were the bases of lodges and the other that some, at least, were snake effigies. It is impossible to say anything about the latter contention, although there may be more in it than is suspected. The other explanation, even though they had a special name for the projections that are often found at one end of the linears (natci, or wood houses), must be accepted with caution. The enormous length of some of the linears hardly seems to support such an assumption. The Winnebago themselves claimed that the reason lodges were built upon mounds was because they could thus shed water most easily.

The conical mounds were unquestionably used for purposes of burial. Whether, however, they were always constructed with that particular object in view may be seriously doubted, for in some cases the burials seem to represent clear evidences of being intrusive in character. A few Indians insisted that some of the conical mounds were used as platforms from which to address an audience; that some were "stations" in the game of lacrosse, and that some were bases of lodges.

The composite type of mound, characterized by the union of a conical and a linear or by the union of a number of each, was interpreted by the Winnebago questioned as lodge bases connected with one another, the conical mound being the base of the lodge and the "linear" acting as a sort of connecting passageway.

We mentioned before that Mr. Stout maintains the view that the linear are in reality conventionalized effigy mounds. Our main objection to such an interpretation would be that conventionalization is a method of artistic expression exceedingly rare among the Winnebago. Had it been common it would certainly have been found in use in their bead and quill work or in their woven bags. There is a possibility that some of the linears may be either very crudely constructed effigy mounds or that they may represent effigy mounds that have been changed through the influences of weather and general climatic conditions, as well as, to a smaller extent, by human hands, factors that have been neglected altogether too much in this connection, especially in the interpretation of what appear to be anomalies. From this point of view, it would be suggestive to compare some of the so-called "turtle" effigies with the water-spirit or "panther" type, on the one hand, and with the linears on the other. It is perhaps such "transitional" forms that have led Mr. Stout to postulate that all linears are effigies.

Summing up, we might say that the linears may be either effigies, in part representing a snake, or they may be, in part, altered or mutilated or crude effigies; or they may be the bases of lodges. We have the authority of a number of Indians that some are snake effigies. The interpretation that some are altered or mutilated has never been confirmed by the Indians themselves. Finally, that some of them are the bases of lodges is the statement of a large number of Indians, but it must await further evidence before it can be accepted.

That some of the mounds found in the Winnebago territory antedate, in part, the coming of the whites, and can consequently be regarded as constituting an archeological problem, there can hardly be any doubt. Nevertheless, many of them have been erected since

Nicollet's time, some even within the recollection of Winnebago still living. All were unquestionably erected by the Winnebago, and since there is no reason for believing that this tribe entered Wisconsin many centuries before the first appearance of Europeans in America, it is quite erroneous to state, as Mr. Stout does, that the evidence at hand justifies us in dividing the occupancy of Wisconsin into two principal periods, the effigy mound-building era and the time that has elapsed since that period.

The use of copper by the Winnebago prior to their contact with Europeans is another of the rather baffling questions connected with Winnebago archeology. There are references to its use in the myth of the Twins, but the sections of the myth where it is mentioned show marked evidences of European influence and can hardly be accepted as reflecting the original mode of life of the Winnebago. Copper is found in a number of mounds, but we have no way of determining whether these mounds are pre-Columbian or not.

In all likelihood, almost all the copper found in Wisconsin comes from the original copper workings at Isle Royale, Keweenaw, Ontonagon, and elsewhere, in the Lake Superior district. "A provisional description of the territory in which the greatest number of such artifacts have been recovered up to the present time may be given as extending from about the middle of Milwaukee County, northward along the west shore of Lake Michigan to Door County, thence westward to the Wisconsin River or slightly beyond, thence southward along this stream to Dane County and eastward to Milwaukee County, the starting point. Embraced within this territory are the extensive lake shore village sites, from which thousands of articles have already been recovered, and certain well-known sites in Green Lake and adjoining counties, the Rush Lake and similarly productive regions."[11]

The region thus described embraces the Winnebago territory and that subsequently occupied by the Central Algonquian tribes. It does not follow the line of Winnebago migrations farther than the Wisconsin River to the west or farther than the southern boundary of Dane County to the south or southwest. As far as the writer knows no one has ever been able to obtain any information from the Winnebago that would in any manner connect them with the authorship of the copper implements found associated with their old village sites. All Indians questioned denied that their ancestors had ever used copper before the arrival of the early French traders. For the Winnebago, it seems to the writer, the problem connected with the occurrence of copper implements is not whether the Winnebago made them, but how they came to obtain them. The solution of this problem would be immensely facilitated if we had accurate knowledge

---

[11] Brown, in the Wisconsin Archeologist, vol. 3, no. 2, p. 58.

of the distribution of copper among the Sauk, Fox, and Kickapoo, and if we were in a position to tell whether or not these tribes had copper before their arrival in Wisconsin. We might then be in a better position to decide whether the Winnebago obtained their copper from these tribes or from some northern tribe, presumably the Potawatomi or Menominee. It is generally supposed that they actually did obtain their copper implements through the intermediation of these two last-mentioned tribes, although there is no really conclusive evidence for it. That opportunities for their transmission through the Menominee or Potawatomi were plentiful is unquestioned, and the only problem is whether the systematic exchange was not conditioned by the appearance of the white traders.

The last problem connected with Winnebago archeology is the authorship of the numerous flint arrowheads. They are found all over Wisconsin, in every nook and corner of Winnebago territory, in every stage of manufacture, and yet the Winnebago of to-day regard them as having been made by some other tribe. The most common explanation of their origin is the legendary one that they were made by worms. In the few cases where the old men were of a different opinion, the writer was assured that they were the "bones" of the water-spirits, and consequently holy. Numerous myths speak of them in connection with the water-spirit. The Indians admit that they had at times used them as arrow points, but insist that in every case they were found in the earth; that in fact people were generally blessed with them. Mr. Skinner informs me that the Menominee, on the other hand, remember very well how they were made. Among the Winnebago, until recently, three kinds of arrow points were in use: one, properly not an arrow point at all but simply a sharpened arrow, the second consisting of sharpened portions of pieces of antlers, and the third consisting of a turtle claw that had been softened and straightened. It has generally been maintained that the presence of regular "quarries" absolutely clinched the hypothesis of a Winnebago origin for the flint arrow points, but it seems to us that we would first have to prove that in every case where such quarries are found no tribe but the Winnebago had ever occupied that territory, because had any Algonquian tribe been there they might be held as much responsible for these quarries as the Winnebago. That they were not used within the recollection of the oldest men among the Winnebago there can be no doubt, because this question was repeatedly put to them, with negative results.

It seems best, therefore, to attach some significance to current belief as to the origin of the flint arrow points and to assume for the present that they were either the work of the prehistoric ancestors of the Winnebago or that of some tribe that had occupied the territory before them; or—but this is extremely unlikely—that they were all of Algonquian origin.

IMPLEMENTS OF STONE AND OTHER MATERIALS

As pointed out before, we ought not to expect to find much strictly archeological data relating to the Winnebago in their Wisconsin habitat. As, however, they probably reached this habitat before the discovery of America, some of the archeological finds may easily go back that far. Unfortunately we have no way of determining, even approximately, the age of the artifacts.

We will now confine ourselves to a description of the more important types of artifacts and remains found on old Winnebago sites without going into the question of their respective age.

Implements and utensils were made of stone, clay, shell, bone, wood, antlers, and turtle claws (pl. 10). According to information obtained from the present Winnebago, which is supported by the testimony of the myths and tales, but few objects were made of stone. The most important of these was the stone hatchet. It may even be questioned whether the Winnebago originally made these, for they are given a supernatural origin by those few Winnebago who mentioned their existence, and it has been the author's experience that objects to which a supernatural origin is ascribed are generally either of recent origin or have been borrowed. None of the myths or tales even mention their existence. Nevertheless a large number of stone implements, most of them presumably stone hatchets, has been found at Doty Island, near Menasha, Wis. (pl. 11), which had at one time been one of their principal village sites. It is quite probable that the Winnebago obtained most of these from the neighboring Algonquian tribes who were well known for their skill in working stone.

COPPER IMPLEMENTS

The Winnebago are known to have used copper implements in fairly great abundance, the only question being whether they were the original makers of these objects. We do not think they were, and base our opinion on the answers given by present-day Indians and the total absence of their mention in the myths. Both iron and presumably copper are mentioned in certain myths, but these passages are clearly of European origin.

Practically all of our knowledge of the nature and distribution of copper objects in Wisconsin has been conveniently summarized in Mr. C. E. Brown's paper entitled "The native copper implements of Wisconsin,"[12] and all that we mention here is taken from this little monograph.

---

[12] The Wisconsin Archeologist, vol. 3, no. 2.

Following Brown's classification, we note the following copper objects in Wisconsin: Axes or hatchets (the most common), chisels, "spuds," gouges, spiles, spatulas, knives, spear and arrow points, harpoon points, pikes and punches, awls and drills, spikes, needles, and fishhooks.

The most important types of axes were the following: Those oblong in outline, with edges nearly parallel; those with straight edges and tapering, widest toward the cutting edge and becoming narrower toward the head. The head itself may be either flattened, rounded, or roundly pointed. This is the most common type found. The third type, according to Brown, resembles the second, "with the exception that the margin at the edges is slightly but distinctly elevated, thus giving a slightly depressed or concave surface in the center and from end to end on one or both broad faces of the ax. In some examples this margin is fully one-half inch in width at or near the middle."[13]

Three principal types of chisels were found: Those broadest at the cutting edge, with edges tapering gradually from this cutting edge to the head; those of nearly uniform width with straight parallel edges; and those with a more or less prominent median ridge.

According to Brown there can be no doubt as to their use. "It probably included the hollowing out of wooden canoes, troughs, and vessels . . ."[14]

Knives are quite common, there being two principal types—one with a straight back and oblique, curved, or straight cutting edge; and another distinguished from the latter by a greater breadth of its broad curved blade and terminating in a broadly rounded point.

Spear and arrow points are found in great profusion and fall into many types: The leaf-shaped, the stemmed and flat, the ridged, the beveled, the eyed, the notched, the toothed, the spatula-shaped, the short-stemmed, the barbed or pronged, the conical, the rolled socketed, and the ridged socketed.

EARTHWORKS AND MOUNDS

Aztalan.—Apart from the mounds there is one very famous earthwork in Wisconsin called Aztalan (pl. 12) which has for many decades puzzled archeologists. We will not enter into any of the numerous explanations given at different times by observers, but will confine ourselves exclusively to quoting the rather clear description given by Mr. G. A. West:[15]

The inclosure and associated earthworks at Aztalan, on the Crawfish River in Jefferson County, have long been considered among the most interesting and important

[13] The Wisconsin Archeologist, vol. 3, no. 2, p. 61.
[14] Ibid., p. 62.
[15] "The Indian authorship of Wisconsin antiquities," Wisconsin Archeologist, vol. 6, no. 4, pp. 219–222.

PLATE 9

a. JOHN BAPTISTE

b. HUGH HUNTER

c. LEVI ST. CYR

d. ALBERT HENSLEY (Profile view)

WINNEBAGO TYPES

PLATE 10

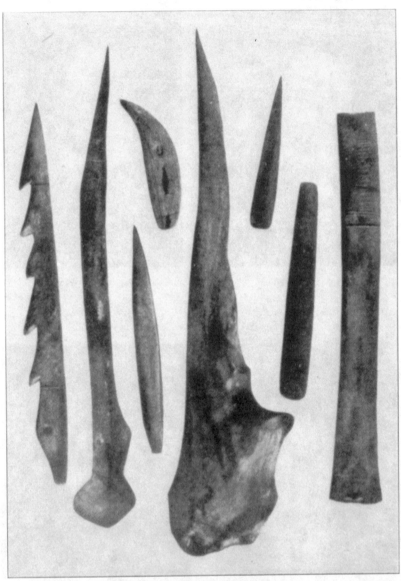

WINNEBAGO BONE IMPLEMENTS
(From Wisconsin Archeologist)

PLATE 11

FOUR LEGS' VILLAGE ON DOTY ISLAND, 1830

(From Waubun)

PLATE 12

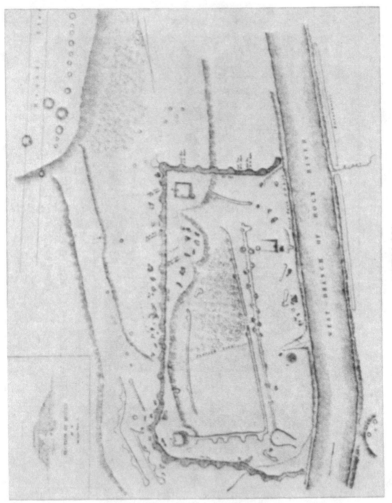

AZTALAN

(After Lapham)

of the aboriginal monuments of Wisconsin. The inclosure was first noticed by the government surveyor. In 1837 a hasty survey was made by N. F. Hyer, who afterwards published a brief description. . . . In 1850 Lapham made a careful survey of Aztalan. . . and in 1855 published a description illustrated with several fine plates and figures in his "Antiquities of Wisconsin." . . .

This interesting inclosure, now almost obliterated by many years of cultivation, may be briefly described as being in the shape of an irregular parallelogram, lacking one of the long sides which is supplied by the bank of the Crawfish which forms its eastern boundary. It is reported to contain 17¾ acres of land. The length of the north wall Lapham gives as 631, the west as 1,419, and the south as 700 feet. The width is given as about 22 feet and the height at from 1 to 5 feet. Along the outer edge of its entire length, at somewhat regular distances, were rounded projections which have been frequently referred to as "buttresses or bastions," but which Lapham determined "were never designed for either of the purposes indicated by these names."

"The distance from one to another varies from 61 to 95 feet, scarcely any two of them being exactly alike. Their mean distance apart is 82 feet. On the north wall and on most of the west wall they have the same height as the connecting ridge and at a little distance resemble a simple row of mounds.

"On the inner wall, opposite many of these mounds (projections), is a slight depression or sinus; possibly the remains of a sloping way by which the wall was ascended from within the inclosure."—Lapham, Antiquities, 43.

Within the wall at the northwest corner of the inclosure was a rectangular truncated pyramidal mound, its level top measuring 60 by 65 feet. At its southeast corner was a sloping ascent. At the southwest corner, also within the wall, was a square, truncated mound, the level area on its top being 53 feet wide on the west side, it being originally in all probability a square of this size. Lapham's figure shows the sides of the mound rising in two terraces to the top. There appeared to be a sloping way leading down from its top toward the east. It was the highest earthwork within the wall, which it overlooked. These two mounds he judged to have been the probable foundations of buildings or of other structures of perishable materials. From the eastern side of the last-mentioned mound a line of wall with a number of projections similar to those on the wall of the inclosure extended about two-thirds of the way to the river, where it angled and proceeded in a northwesterly direction, being broken near its middle to within about 250 feet of the north wall. Beginning near the angle and on the east side of and paralleling this wall for its entire length was a second line of wall with projections distributed at various distances along its sides.

Within the inclosure were also a number of excavations, conical mounds, embankments, and other earthworks, some of which our present knowledge enables us to identify as very probably effigy or emblematic mounds.

Opposite the southwestern angle of the wall of the inclosure were several embankments also with projections along their sides. Scattered at intervals along the entire front of the west wall were a considerable number of excavations irregular in outline and of different sizes from which some of the earth used in the construction of the wall was most probably taken.

A short distance west of these, and also extending along the front of the wall, is a long mound of the familiar tapering effigy type, an irregular line of conical mounds, and a single linear mound. Several hundred feet northwest of the inclosure on the higher ground was a double line of 60 or more conical mounds of different sizes, extending from west of the present Aztalan road across the road and in a general northerly direction into the present village of Aztalan. A small number of the more prominent of these can still be seen along the road.

On the east bank of the Crawfish opposite the inclosure were two long earthen embankments and a group of conical mounds. The larger of the two embankments

Lapham's plat shows to have been about 660 feet in length and probably 18 feet in width.

INTAGLIO MOUNDS

The intaglio mounds (pl. 13) are clearly the reverse of effigy mounds. They were discovered by Lapham 60 years or more ago and since that time no others have been found. Lapham himself located nine of them, all associated with earthworks, at Milwaukee, Pewaukee, Theresa, and Fort Atkinson. At about the same time

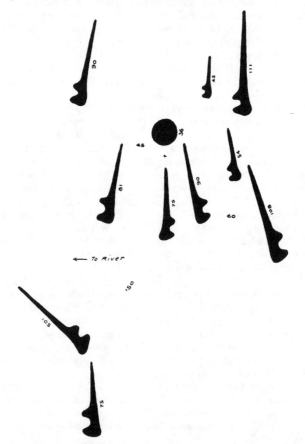

FIG. 4.—EFFIGY MOUNDS (PANTHER OR WATER-SPIRIT TYPE). FORKS OF THE MANITOWOC RIVER, CALUMET COUNTY, WIS.

Mr. W. H. Canfield located two near the earthworks at Baraboo. Those found by Lapham are undoubtedly intended to represent what most Wisconsin archeologists call the "panther," but which the Winnebago call the water-spirit (*wakdjexi*) (fig. 4), while those found by Canfield are probably intended to represent the bear (fig. 5).

PLATE 13

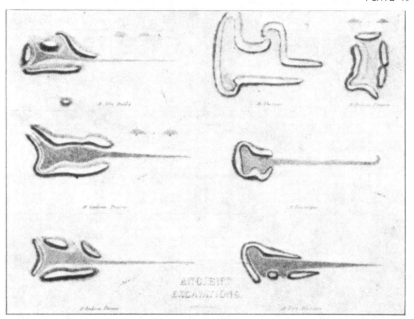

WISCONSIN INTAGLIOS

(After Lapham)

PLATE 14

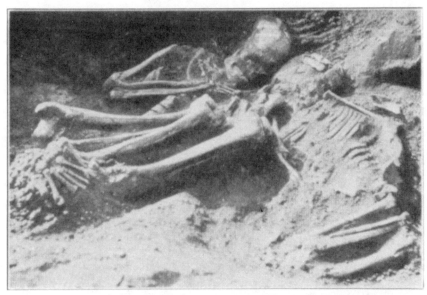

a. BURIAL IN A MOUND AT BORCHER'S BEACH
(From Wisconsin Archeologist)

b. CONICAL MOUND, CUTLER PARK, WAUKESHA, WIS.

The Fort Atkinson intaglio is the only one now in existence. "Its greatest depth (at the middle of the body) is slightly over 2 feet. The great tail of the animal reaches to within about 25 feet of a fine large conical burial mound." [16]

CONICAL MOUNDS

These are found all over the territory once occupied by the Winnebago, but we know definitely that the Central Algonquian tribes also erected them. In the following section we will describe but one group of these mounds found on territory formerly inhabited by the Winnebago and which was never, or only for a very short time, occupied by other tribes (pl. 14).

FIG. 5.—BEAR EFFIGY MOUND, MADISON, WIS.

This interesting group was located in Angelo Township, Juneau County, and is known as Mound Prairie, West Group (Fig. 6). Twelve mounds are preserved there with the following dimensions:

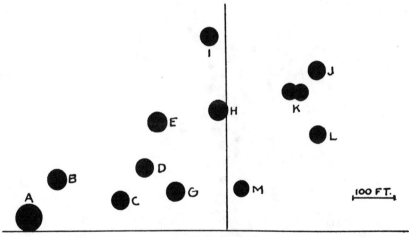

FIG. 6.—BURIAL MOUNDS, UPPER BARABOO VALLEY, WIS.

A 53 feet in diameter.
B 48 feet in diameter.
C 48 feet in diameter.
D 45 feet in diameter.
E 44 feet in diameter.
G 48 feet in diameter.

H 46 feet in diameter.
I 45 feet in diameter.
J 42 feet in diameter.
K 65 by 30 feet.
L 46 feet in diameter.
M 38 feet in diameter.

[16] C. E. Brown, "The Intaglio Mounds of Wisconsin," Wisconsin Archeologist, vol. 9, no. 1, p. 9.

As a rule, whenever the conical mounds represent the work of the Winnebago they are always found accompanied by linear and effigy mounds. At Lake Koshkonong, out of a total of 481 mounds 309 are conical. A similar proportion is found in other groups. Little has ever been found in them except burials and there seems little doubt that the vast majority of them were always used for this purpose. (Pls. 15–17; fig. 7.)

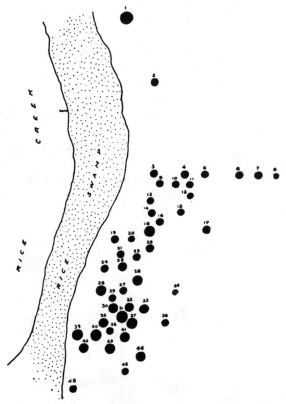

FIG. 7.—BURIAL MOUNDS IN A GROUP AT RICE LAKE, RUSK COUNTY, WIS.

In a number of places conical mounds are joined to linear mounds or to other structures, often producing irregular figures. Mr. A. B. Stout classifies them as belonging in general to three types. The commonest of these combinations are those called by Mr. Stout the dumb-bell and tadpole type (fig. 8).

LINEAR MOUNDS

Linear mounds, like conical mounds, are found all over the territory once occupied by the Winnebago. What purpose they could have served is not definitely known, although the modern Winnebago

PLATE 15

A SERIES OF BURIAL MOUNDS

(Aztalan, Jefferson County)

PLATE 16

STONE CHAMBER IN BURIAL MOUND, BUFFALO LAKE, MARQUETTE COUNTY, WIS.

(From Wisconsin Archeologist)

PLATE 17

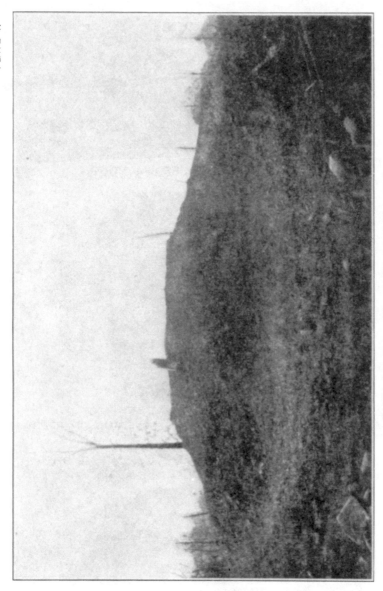

ZAHN MOUND, CALUMET COUNTY, WIS.

(From Wisconsin Archeologist)

PLATE 18

a. LODGE MADE OF REED MATTING

b. LODGE MADE OF BARK WITH COVERING OF REED MATTING

c. LODGE MADE OF BARK

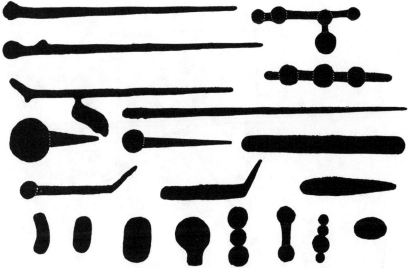

FIG. 8.—EFFIGY AND DUMB-BELL-SHAPED MOUNDS.

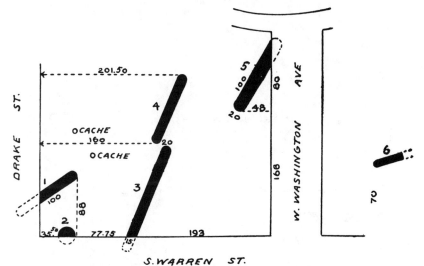

FIG. 9.—LINEAR MOUNDS AT MADISON, WIS.

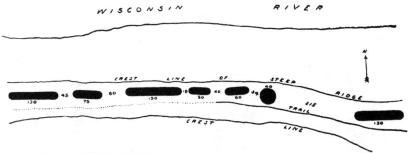

FIG. 10.—LINEAR MOUNDS, CLYDE TOWNSHIP, IOWA COUNTY, WIS.

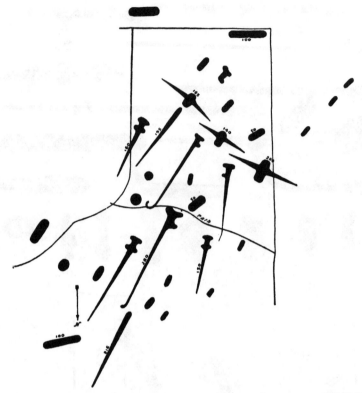

FIG. 11.—EFFIGY AND LINEAR MOUNDS, PISHTAKA, WAUKESHA COUNTY, WIS.

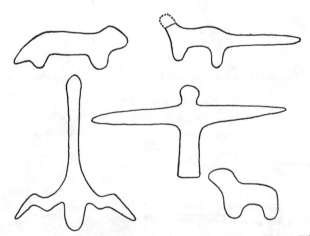

FIG. 12.—EFFIGY MOUNDS IN THE WINGRA GROUP, MADISON, WIS.

FIG. 13.—BIRD EFFIGY MOUNDS.

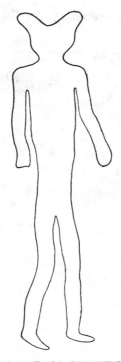

FIG. 14.—MAN MOUND, GREENFIELD TOWNSHIP, SAUK COUNTY, WIS.

FIG. 15.—TYPES OF MAMMAL EFFIGY MOUNDS.

FIG. 16.—TYPES OF SO-CALLED TURTLE EFFIGY MOUNDS.

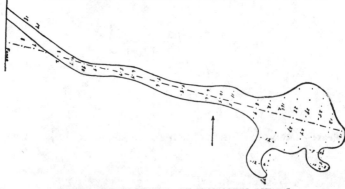

FIG. 17.—EFFIGY MOUND OF UNKNOWN ANIMAL.

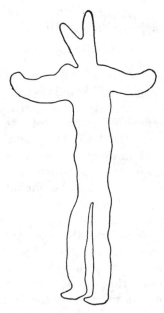

Fig. 18.—LA VALLE MAN MOUND, SAUK COUNTY, WIS.

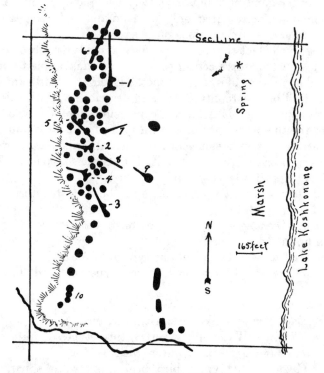

Fig. 19.—GROUP OF MOUNDS OF DIFFERENT TYPES, LAKE KOSHKONONG, WIS.

seem to be practically unanimous in explaining them as either the base of lodges or as defenses (figs. 9, 10, 11).

EFFIGY MOUNDS

Effigy mounds (figs. 4, 5, 11–18) are discussed at some length in the following pages. The following types are found: The bird, the bear, the panther or water-spirit, the deer (uncommon), the wolf (uncommon), the turtle, and the so-called man. The commonest by far are the bird, bear, and water-spirit, and this would seem to corroborate the statements of living Winnebago that these mounds represent the clan effigies, for these three clans were by far the most important and numerous in the tribe. Certain of the clans are apparently not represented, particularly the elk, the buffalo, the snake, and the fish, while but isolated examples of two fairly important clans, the wolf and the deer, are found. If the so-called turtle mounds (fig. 16) were really intended to represent that animal, we would have the only instance of a large number of mounds that can not possibly be connected with the Winnebago clans, for the tribe never had a Turtle clan. However, these mounds may not really have been intended to represent turtles. On the other hand, it is not absolutely necessary to believe that the effigy mounds represented only clan animals. It is possible that some were erected for religious purposes.

Owing to the fact that so many effigy mounds have been destroyed in the last two or three centuries, it is quite impossible to be certain of the distribution of specific types. Even those still in existence have not all been carefully noted and described. Until this is done, no even approximately definitive conclusions can be drawn as to the reasons for the prevalence of certain types in one area and others in other areas. To give some idea of their distribution, however, we will describe briefly their distribution in those sections of Wisconsin that have been fairly thoroughly studied:

Lake Mendota.—Two types of bird, bear, water-spirit, and the very rare effigy of a frog.

Lake Koshkonong.—Two types of bird, water-spirit, frog ? mink ? and an unknown mammal.

Fond du Lac.—Water-spirit, one type of bird, turtle.

Lake Waubesa.—Water-spirit, three types of bird, bear, turtle, and lynx.

Turtle Creek, Rock County. —Water-spirit, turtle.

Winnebago County.—Water-spirit, bear, bird.

Lake Wingra.—Water-spirit, turtle, three types of bird, and bear.

Manitowoc County.—Bird, water-spirit, turtle.

Sauk County.—One type of bird, bear, mink, water-spirit.

In general it may be said that effigies of the bird type are found over the entire region in which effigies are found, although certain types seem to have a restricted range—the bear type, westward from Lake Waubesa to Sauk County and probably beyond; the water-spirit, over the entire region from Milwaukee to Madison and as far north as Gills Landing in Waupaca County; the goose, at Lake

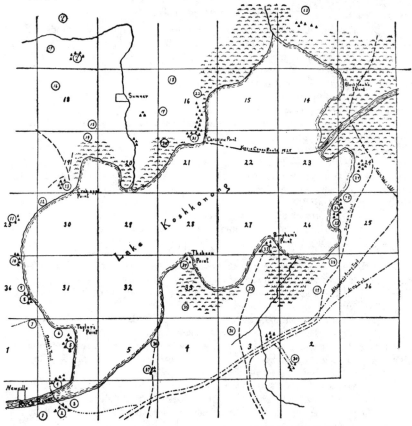

FIG. 20.—ARCHEOLOGIC MAP OF LAKE KOSHKONONG.

INDEX TO MAP.

1. Conch shell cache, 1842.
2. Black Hawk's camp, 1832.
3. Ogden group.
4. Rock River group and village site.
5. Tay-e-he-dah group and village site.
6. Taylor House group.
7. Fulton group.
8. Koshkonong group and village site.
9. John Son group.
10. Noe Springs group and village site.
11. North group.
12. Rufus Bingham group.
13. Le Sellier group and village site.
14. Goldthorpe burials.
15. Messmer Garden beds.
16. Kumlien group.
17. a-b-c. Koshkonong Creek mounds and village site.
18. Conch shell cache, 1867.

19. Draves group.
20. Skavlem group.
21. Carcajou mounds and White Crow's village.
22. Loge Bay mounds and garden beds.
23. Altpeter group and White Ox's village.
24. Man Eater's village.
24 and 25. Gen. Atkinson group.
26. Hoard group and Kewaskum's camp.
27. Fun Hunter's Point mound and cornfield.
28. Lookout group.
29. Haight's Creek group.
30. Atkinson's camp.
31. Indian cornfields.
32 and 33. Ira Bingham group and village site.
34 and 35. Thiebeau Point village site and cornfields.
36. French trader's cabin sites.
37. Camp site and cornfield.
38. Black Hawk Island camp site.

Waubesa and the upper Madison lakes; the lynx type, at Lake Waubesa, as far east as Lake Koshkonong, and as far west as Devils Lake in Sauk County.

DESCRIPTION OF LAKE KOSHKONONG MOUNDS

In order to give an idea of what a carefully planned survey of a particular region has yielded we will quote Mr. A. B. Stout's summary of his work at Lake Koshkonong (figs. 19, 20): [17]

A total of 481 mounds are here noted. This does not include the mounds entirely destroyed at Thiebeau Point, the Koshkonong Groups, and the Kumlien Group. There are 157 mounds on the east side and 324 on the west side of the lake. There are still well preserved 394 mounds. There is a total of 309 conical mounds of which 233 are on the west side, but of the 42 effigies 24 are on the east side of the lake.

In most cases the grouping as given is in no wise arbitrary. All the large and important groups are composed of mounds rather compactly arranged. Groups 3, 4, 6, 11, and 17 are more or less scattered and are considered as groups chiefly for convenience in description.

The largest group is the Koshkonong Group of 78 mounds. Next in rank are the General Atkinson Group of 73, the Noe Springs Group of 64, the Hoard Group of 36, the Le Sellier Group of 29, the Kumlien Group of 28, the Altpeter Group of 28, and the Rufus Bingham Group of 21. In these 8 well-defined groups are found 357 of the total of 481 mounds.

All of these mounds are found in an area of 42 square miles, of which 13 are covered with water and at least 5 more occupied by swamp and marsh lands.

THE CONICAL MOUNDS

As previously stated, this type is the most abundant. Most are low, many are no more than 2 feet in height. In fact, there are but 23 that are 4 or more feet in height. The largest of the conical mounds are as follows: . . . 60 by 12 feet in diameter; . . . 75 by 10; . . . 45 by 8; . . . 54 by 7; . . . 63 by 6.

. . . Some conical mounds are built with edges overlapping, forming a sort of chain of mounds. There is some evidence of superimposed mounds. . . .

Nearly all the conical mounds have been opened in a more or less desultory manner. The few clues at hand as to the results of such digging confirm the opinion that this type of mound was built for burial purposes.

It will be noted . . . that several mounds are oval in outline. Two others are pear-shaped . . . with the larger end built considerably higher. The oval type appears to grade into the short linear. This may be noted in the General Atkinson and Altpeter groups.

COMBINATIONS OF CONICAL AND LINEAR FORMS

The dumb-bell form.—Two mounds of the Altpeter Group are of this form . . . In these the ends are decidedly conical and may possibly be superimposed upon the ends of short linear mounds.

The tadpole type.—This type of mound consists of a more or less pronounced conical mound from which extends a straight pointed linear portion that varies in length . . . In No. 4 of the Koshkonong Group the conical part is 40 by 6 with the linear part comparatively low and short. In other cases . . . the conical part is wide and flattened. In still other cases the linear part is quite long . . .

Irregular forms.—Nos. 5 and 6 of the Noe Springs Group are unusual combinations of conical and linear mounds. The conical mounds are in some cases several feet

---

[17] "The Archæology of the Lake Koshkonong Region," by A. B. Stout and H. L. Skavlem, Wisconsin Archeologist, vol. 7, no. 2, 1908.

higher than the adjoining linear part. The surface examination made at the time of this survey gave the opinion that the conical mounds had been built upon the linear parts possibly at a later period.

LINEAR MOUNDS

The pure linear type.—This type is shown in . . . [fig. 8]. The mounds thus classed are straight and uniform in height and width. Some are so short as to almost approach the oval form.

The straight pointed linear type.—This form is shown in . . . [fig. 8] and is usually of great length, widest at one end and tapering to a point at the other . . . Twelve of this type are found. The longest measures 675 and the shortest 120 feet.

The angular linear type.—In group 9, No. 3 . . . [fig. 8] there is this peculiar type which is so abundant along the Wisconsin River in Sauk County.

The club-shaped linear type.—This form is shown in . . . [fig. 8] and is a slight variation of the pure linear type. There are three of this class.

The curved linear type.—This is a linear form having a slight kidney or crescent shape. There are but two mounds of this type at Lake Koshkonong.

In the Altpeter Group are three linear-like mounds that might be classed as effigies. No. 1 [fig. 8] is much like the "mink" type. No. 3 bears some resemblance to the same type, and No. 2 to the "tadpole" type. In the latter, however, the head end is but little higher than the adjoining linear part and bulges slightly more on one side.

EFFIGIES

The forms and sizes of the various effigies can be best understood by a study of the [various illustrations] . . . Not including the three mounds just mentioned or any of the "tadpole" type, there are 42 mounds that are plainly effigies. Three of these are nearly destroyed; the others are well preserved.

BIRD EFFIGIES

. . . All of these lie on the east side of the lake in two closely associated groups. There are six such effigies in the General Atkinson Group and four in the Hoard Group.

But two have the wings at right angles to the body and both of these are low and flattened with heavy broad bodies in marked contrast to splendid mounds of this class in other parts of the State.

Of the class having the wings extremely drooped . . . there are five. Nos. 28 and 29 in the Hoard Group have a conical-like breast, while those of the General Atkinson Group have the surface of the body nearly level. The two small bird effigies close to the Lake View Hotel . . . have a conical breast and wings half drooping.

MAMMAL EFFIGIES

All of the mounds shown in . . . [fig. 15] represent the animal as lying on one side with the fore limbs and the hind limbs united. It will be seen that there are several splendid examples of the "panther" type.

Nos. 4 and 31 are of similar form, but represent the animal with the tail raised. These two are on opposite sides of the lake and are the only effigies of this precise character.

Of the "mink" type there is an example in the Le Sellier Group.

Mound No. 1 of the Draves Group and the effigy in the Taylor House Group are the only ones of their class existing at the lake.

Of all the forms and types to be found in this region the mound shown in . . . [fig. 17] is perhaps the most . . . complicated, and it will be interesting to learn if there exists elsewhere in the State a mound of similar form.

TURTLE AND ALLIED FORMS

There are seven short . . . and two . . . long-tailed "turtle" effigies in this region.

Mound No. 60 of the Atkinson Group differs from the "turtle" effigy in profile as well as in outline. The head is considerably higher than the part midway between the hind limbs. No. 36 of the Hoard Group is similar, but has a truncated tail. Mound No. 61 shows still another departure in outline. . . . The four mounds just mentioned have no duplicates in the area. All the mounds shown in . . . [fig. 16] are similar in that the animal is represented from a dorsal view . . .

THE GROUPING

A study of the various groups shows that there was no uniform plan in their construction. In general they occupy prominent elevations near the lake. There is a rather promiscuous mingling of types and arrangement of mounds which suggests that a group is the result of several or many years of continuous building during which mounds were added as desired and simply grouped to suit the immediate topography.[18]

Stone

Arrow and spearpoints.	Knives.
Perforators and scrapers.	Grooved axes and hammers.
Hammerstones.	Celts, numerous, many broken.
Clubheads.	Pipes and fragments of pipes (of catlinite, steatite,
Grinding and polishing stones.	limestone, sandstone, etc.).
Gorgets.	Sawed pieces of catlinite.
Plummets.	Flint spalls, chips, flakes, fragments, nodules, and
Discoidals.	rejects.
Stone balls.	Burned stones from fireplaces.

Copper

Spearpoints.	Earring.
Awls.	Fishhook.
Blanks.	Chisel.
Rolled copper arrowpoints.	Knives.
Beads.	Rings.

Pottery

Pipe, broken, and fragments of others.	Potsherds, shell, sand and quartz tempered.
Pottery disks.	

Bone and shell

Bone beads, several styles.	"Jewel stones" from sheepshead perch.
Bone awl.	Jawbones of pickerel.
Columella of large sea shell.	Carapace of mud turtle.
Valves of fresh-water clamshells.	Shell beads, disk-shaped and cylindrical styles.
Bones of various birds and animals.	Shell gorget.

THE MAN MOUND

What probably constitutes the most interesting type of mound found in Wisconsin is the so-called Man mound, two examples of which are known, both from Sauk County, one from Greenfield Township and the other known as the La Valle Man mound. The second of these has long been obliterated, but is known to us from a plat made by Mr. Canfield in 1872 (figs. 14, 18.)

Lapham [19] described the Greenfield township Man mound as follows:

The figure is no less than 214 feet in length, the head 30 feet long, the body 100, and the legs 84. The head lies toward the south and the movement [of the body] is west-

---

[18] The following will give an idea of the material collected from one village site in this region. The village site is known as the White Crow site. The information is taken from the Wisconsin Archeologist, vol. 7, no. 2, p. 93.

[19] Quoted by Brown in Wisconsin Archeologist, vol. 7, no. 4, p. 140.

ward. All of the lines of this most singular effigy are curved gracefully, and much care has been bestowed upon its construction. The head is ornamented with two projections, or horns, giving a comical expression to the whole figure. [fig. 14.]

MISCELLANEOUS STRUCTURES

Stone chambers.—These are found in a number of places and were apparently always used for burial. According to the present Winnebago, chiefs were often buried in them (pl. 16).

Garden beds (fig. 21).—These were first described by Lapham. According to him[20] they were "low, broad, parallel ridges, as if corn had been planted in drills. They average 4 feet in width, 25 of them having been counted in the space of a hundred feet, and the depth of the walk between them is about 6 inches."

Mr. C. E. Brown also found some which he has described in[21] his paper on "Wisconsin Garden Beds:"

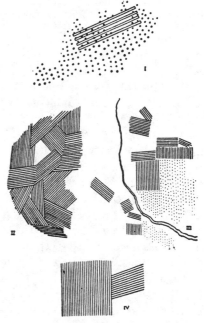

To the southwest . . . was a remnant of a fourth plot of beds with 11 rows. Their direction was northeast and southwest, and their length then about 52 feet, a portion having been obliterated by the plow. On another plot of ground, lying to the west of that upon which all of the above described are situated, occurred a fifth plot of beds, having a northeast and southwest direction. The rows numbered 12 and were about 48 feet long. A sixth plot of

FIG. 21.—WISCONSIN GARDEN BEDS.

beds, running north and south, numbered 28 rows, each about 84 feet long. Its dimensions were about the same as those of the first plot.

In summing up, Mr. Brown says:[22]

In concluding an examination of the evidence now available upon the subject of the age of the Wisconsin garden beds it may be stated that examples have now been located in 16 different localities in the State. The area in which these occur may be described as being bounded by Green Bay on the north and Racine County on the south, and extending from Lake Michigan westward to the Fox-Wisconsin waterway. In nearly every instance where garden beds are closely associated with mounds there is good reason to believe that their origin and age is identical. Like the mounds, most garden beds are prehistoric, but some were constructed in early historic times. Their association in some instances with plots of cornhills indicates that in these cases these two features of our archeology are also contemporaneous.

---

[20] Antiquities of Wisconsin. Smithsonian Cont. to Knowledge, vol. VII, p. 19, 1855.

[21] Wisconsin Archeologist, vol. 8, no. 3, p. 100.

[22] Ibid., pp. 104–105.

CHAPTER III

MATERIAL CULTURE

HABITATIONS

In former times the Winnebago seem to have had eight types of lodges: The round lodge (*tci p'ârap'â'ratc*), the long lodge (*tci se'rêtc*), the tipi, the grass lodge, the gable lodge (*nanhaitci p'â'rap'-aratc*), the platform lodge, the ceremonial lodge, and the sweat lodge. Of the round lodge and the long lodge there are three varieties—one made entirely of bark (pl. 18, *c*); another made entirely of reed mattings (pl. 18, *a*); and still another of bark with a roof covering of reed matting (pl. 18, *b*). The round and long lodges of all three types are occasionally seen even now, rarely as habitations, however, but as storehouses (pl. 19). Gable lodges are no longer found among the Winnebago, but the water has been informed that a few still exist among the Sauk and Fox living near Tama, Iowa.

The round and the long bark lodges are constructed in a very simple manner. These are built of poles of ironwood (*tcatcô'na*) driven into the ground, bent over and lashed to other poles which meet them from the opposite direction: The poles are tied together with basswood bark (*hincke'xuntc*). The same material is used in attaching to these poles the cedar bark that forms the walls of the lodge. The walls are supported on the inside by a varying number of poles (*tcicu' curuteanp*) attached to the corresponding poles of the other side. In many cases a series of transverse poles (*tcicu' nanjiŋk'ere*) are inserted beneath the exterior vertical poles. These can be seen in plate 18, *a*, *b*, *c*. The bark roofs are incased in frames made of irregularly distributed vertical poles with generally one transverse pole (pl. 18, *a*, *b*, *c*). If the roofs are of reed matting two or three of the external poles have poles attached to them which are arched across the matting (pl. 18 *a*, *b*, *c*). The reed matting lodges, as a rule, have no external vertical poles and only two transverse poles each, one on the outside and one on the inside (pl. 19, *c*).

Although considered of Winnebago origin by many Indians, these bark and reed matting lodges are in all probability of Central Algonquian origin. They are easily constructed and for that reason were generally used for temporary purposes in the olden times. Accord-

PLATE 19

a. LODGE MADE OF BARK

b. MODERN LODGE WITH CANVAS COVERING

c. LODGE MADE OF REED MATTING

PLATE 20

b. WINNEBAGO IN FULL DRESS

a. THOMAS MALLORY

PLATE 21

b. WINNEBAGO WOMEN IN OLD-STYLE SILK APPLIQUÉ DRESSES

a. WINNEBAGO WOMEN, SHOWING MODERN DRESS

PLATE 22

b. YOUNG BOY IN FULL WARRIOR'S COSTUME

a. YOUNG CHILD IN MODERN DRESS

ing to the oldest informants, the earliest type of lodge used by the Winnebago was the ten-fire gable lodge, of which there were two types, rectangular in form, one built on a platform and the other on the ground. Poles of cedar, forked at the top, formed the sides. Through the forks transverse poles were laid to which the gable roof was attached. Three poles ($na^nji'k'er\hat{e}$) were arranged in the center of the lodge for the better support of the roof. Beds were placed along both of the long sides on a platform raised 2 feet ($haza'tc$).

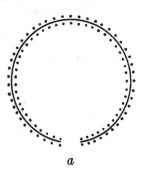

Frequently a platform 4 to 5 feet high was erected in the rear of the lodge and partitioned off. Here the favorite child of the family lived when he was fasting. In front of the lodge a spot was always kept carefully cleared ($nowaxi'nera$). There were two doorways to the lodge. Often the entrances were shaded with boughs. According to some informants, this was only done for the chief's lodge. According to another description of the gable lodge, there were only two centra poles, one at each entrance; these were always painted blue to symbolize the day (fig. 22, b).

a

As far as can be learned at the present time, the platform lodges were merely gable lodges on platforms. What purpose the platform served is now difficult to determine, but most Winnebago questioned said that it was provided as a protection against the dampness of the ground and insects.

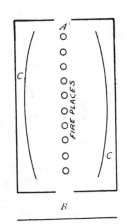

The ceremonial lodge was merely a large, long bark lodge. The grass lodge seems to have been a roughly constructed round lodge with a covering of grass instead of bark. The sweat lodge was a round bark lodge having a framework of four poles. The tipi was of a simple type provided with a three-pole framework.

FIG. 22.—*a*, CROSS-SECTION OF ROUND LODGE. *b*, CROSS-SECTION OF GABLE LODGE.

All the evidence obtained points to the fact that lodges of these types were used synchronously. According to the myths and the oldest informants, in ancient times a village occupied for a considerable period consisted entirely of gable lodges, but these seem to have given way to the round and long type, probably borrowed from the Central Algonquian. The gable type seems to have held its own, however, among the more western villages of the Winnebago. The round bark lodges were used in winter and the reed matting lodges in spring and summer. In the spring those who still lived in bark lodges covered the roofs with reed matting, as that material shed water more effectually than bark. The tipi was generally used on the hunt, the grass lodge merely for a shelter overnight.

All the duties connected with the construction of the lodge belonged to the woman. These duties do not seem to have been restricted to any special class of women except in the construction of ceremonial lodges, in which only women who had passed their climacteric could participate.

CLOTHING AND ADORNMENT

In discussing the personal adornment of men it must be remembered that in former times each costume generally had special significance and could be worn only on certain occasions. Moreover,

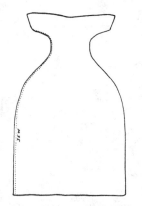
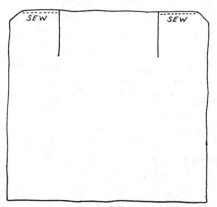

FIG. 23.—PATTERN OF MEN'S BUCKSKIN LEGGINGS.   FIG. 24.—PATTERN OF WOMEN'S BUCKSKIN SHIRT.

certain articles of dress, as arm bands and garters, could be worn only by certain people. The significance of most of the items comprising a man's costume, as well as the proper occasion for wearing them, has long been forgotten and today everything relating to dress and adornment is hopelessly confused. Illustrations of the various articles of apparel will be found in plates 20–23; figures 23–26.

The men's clothing is thus described by Skinner:[1]

The men's garments obtained in Wisconsin consisted of leggings of ribbon-worked cloth, or of plain buckskin. . . . Some of the latter are made skin-tight, with a broad flap fringed at the edge. The decorated flap of the cloth and the fringe of the buckskin are worn outside. Some are made by folding over a rectangular piece of leather and holding the sides together by means of thongs passing through from side to side, their ends serving in lieu of a fringe. Some little boys' leggings are skin-tight and fringed only at the top. The clout is of three pieces, a strip of plain, cheap material to cover the genitals, supported at each end by a belt, and two beaded broadcloth

[1] In "Notes Concerning New Collections," Anthr. Papers Amer. Mus. Nat. Hist., vol. IV, part II, pp. 292–293.

flaps falling over the front and rear, and sometimes merely two ornamented flaps tying on like aprons fore and aft and not passing between the legs at all. Shirts of cloth or buckskin are beaded about the collar, over the shoulders, and down the front over the chest, where the head opening is. Buckskin shirts are often fringed at the juncture of the sleeves with the trunk at the shoulders, as well as along the seams of the sleeves. Beaded garters are worn outside the leggings below the knees, and beaded, or German silver, arm bands may be seen.

The shirt worn by the women in former times seems to have been similar except as to length to that worn by the men, but the leg-

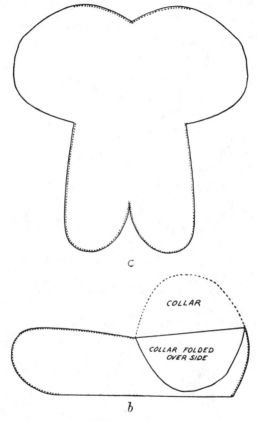

FIG. 25.—PATTERN OF MEN'S MOCCASIN.

gings were characteristically different. These consisted of a straight piece of buckskin folded around itself so as to leave no free flap. The upper part had a cuff. There was no flap at the bottom falling over the moccasin, as in the case of men's leggings (figs. 23, 24).

The skirt is a single piece of broadcloth, the ends of which are handsomely ribbon-worked in appliqué on the outer side. The garment is wrapped around the body, the ends meeting in front, bringing the ribbon-worked horizontal bands together, the opening being in front. The upper part of the garment is folded outward over the woven belt which confines it. A curious shirtwaist, short and beribboned, is worn outside the belt. A shawl or blanket of broadcloth, handsomely ribboned, completes the costume. This is worn not over the head, but the shoulders. . . . It may be observed that in the photographs which date back a number of years, the waists worn by the women are very much longer than those now in vogue, falling almost to the hips.

There is a marked difference between the moccasins worn by men and those worn by women (pls. 24, 25). The former are cut out as shown in figure 25, *a. b.* When folded, they have the shape

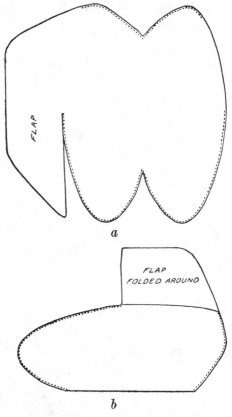

FIG. 26.—PATTERN OF WOMEN'S MOCCASIN.

shown in figure 25, *b.* There are two seams, one in front and one in the back. The women's moccasins are cut in much the same manner, but they have a large flap falling over the front (fig. 26, *a, b*). The string used in fastening the moccasins to the feet is always attached to the rear end (fig. 25, *a, b*).[2]

Hats.—As a rule no head coverings of any kind were worn, but in winter, according to the author's Wisconsin informants, the head was protected by a hoodlike covering.

---

[2] Excellent illustrations of Winnebago moccasins may be found also in Anthr. Papers Amer. Mus. Nat. Hist., vol. IV, pt. II, p. 291.

PLATE 23

a. GROUP OF WINNEBAGO IN OLD-STYLE COSTUMES

b. WINNEBAGO FAMILY

PLATE 24

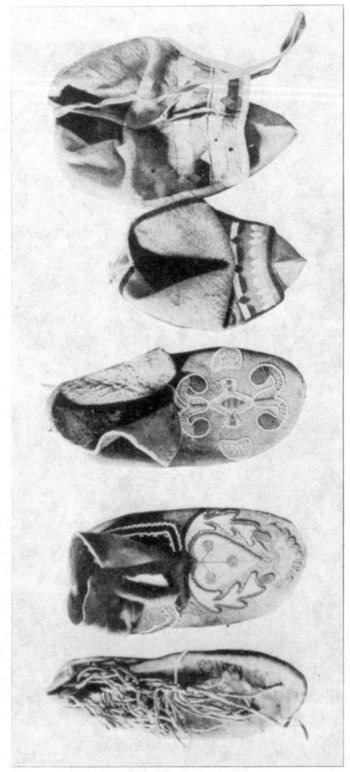

DECORATED MOCCASINS

a. Men's moccasin with partial quill decoration. *b, c.* Men's moccasin with beaded Algonquian decoration. *d.* Women's moccasin with beaded Winnebago decoration. *e.* Women's moccasin with silk appliqué work.

PLATE 25

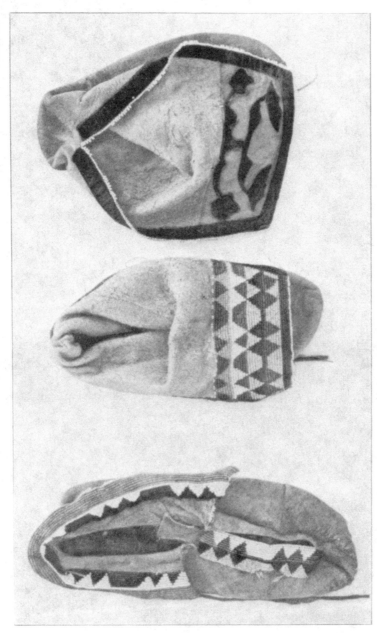

a *b* *c*

DECORATED MOCCASINS

a. Men's moccasin with beaded Winnebago decoration, *b.* Women's moccasin with beaded Winnebago decoration, *c.* Women's moccasin with silk appliqué work.

PLATE 26

b. WINNEBAGO WITH DEER-TAIL HEADDRESS

a. WINNEBAGO, SHOWING MODERN HEADGEAR

PLATE 27

BEADED BELTS

(c, d, e, f show old Winnebago patterns)

a   b   c   d   e   f   g   h   i

PLATE 28

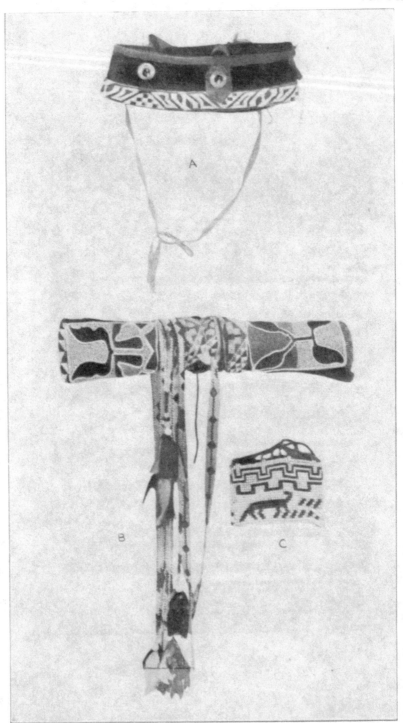

WOMAN'S HAIR ORNAMENTS AND SMALL BEADED BAG

PLATE 29

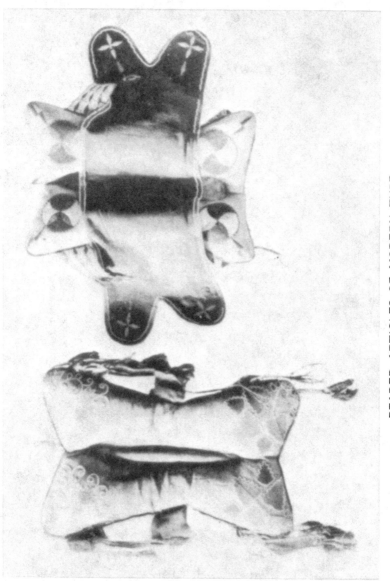

BEADED ARTICLES OF MODERN TYPE

PLATE 30

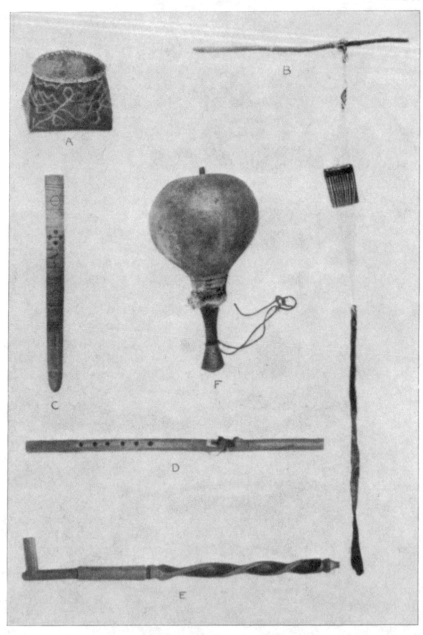

MISCELLANEOUS OBJECTS

a. Birch-bark receptacle.
b. Frame for stringing beads.
c. Staff with personal markings.

d. Wooden flute.
e. Catlinite pipe.
f. Gourd rattle.

Method of wearing the hair.—In former times the men wore their hair in two long braids, although some seem to have affected the Sauk and Fox roach. The scalp along the parting of the hair was always painted, the color varying with individuals. There is no indication of any distinctions in the method of wearing the hair among the various clans as found among the Osage.

A variety of coiffures exist among the Winnebago women at the present day and the assumption that these are all recent is unwarranted. It seems probable that in the old days the hair was usually worn in one braid, which on festive occasions was inclosed in a case. This consisted of two parts—a rectangular piece of broadcloth beaded, and long strips of beaded work (pl. 28).

Earrings and bracelets.—At the present time earrings are fashioned either of 10-cent pieces strung together or of various ornaments of German silver. Strings of beads also are worn occasionally. Bracelets now are made generally of German silver, while in former times beaded or quillwork buckskin was used.

Arm bands and necklaces.—Arm bands are made either of German silver or beaded work. The necklaces consist of long strings of various articles, as modern wampum, seeds, and elk teeth.

Belts, as well as cross belts, are now either beaded or woven, but formerly they were always woven from buffalo hair. Shell gorgets are generally of the type shown in plates 22, 24, 26, *b*. Tight collars are now made of beaded work. Bandoliers consist of long sashes with bags attached; both sash and bag are always gorgeously beaded. The bandoliers are worn in three ways, with the bag hanging on the right side, on the left side, or in front. Often the same individual wears two or three bandoliers. Garters are now made of beaded work; formerly these were generally made of the skins of various animals, preferably the polecat (pls. 27, 28, 29, 30, *b*).

Headdress and taildress.—The Winnebago headdress has been well described by Skinner (op. cit., p. 293), as follows:

The typical headdress is a roach or comb-like ornament woven from deer's hair and generally dyed red. A carved bone, somewhat like an elongate isosceles triangle in shape, spread out this roach and was attached near the front to another tubular bone in which an eagle feather was inserted. Often the latter was ornamented with dyed horse hair and rattlesnake rattles. . . . The whole was fastened on the crown of the head slightly back of the forehead. It was usually pinned to the hair, the scalplock serving to hold it on.

A taildress, consisting of the tail of some animal, was worn only at certain dances, particularly the Herucka.

HUNTING

In their original habitat hunting was the most important means of subsistence of the Winnebago. Practically all game available was hunted, very few animals being tabooed. So far as the author knows, the following animals only were not eaten: Skunk, mink, marten, otter, horse, the weasel, gophers of all kinds, crows (northern ravens?), and eagles.

Bow.—The bow and arrow and traps were used in hunting. The bow is of a very simple type, having ends more or less pointed by rubbing them on stones. In former times the bowstring was made of sinew.

Arrows.—There were five types of arrows, distinguished both by the nature of the arrowhead and by their use: *Ma^n p'axe'dera*, bird arrow; *ma'^nsantc p'a^ε'u^n*, rabbit, or small mammal, arrow; *ma^n k'etcûñk cako'k'ere*, deer and large mammal arrow; *mai^n su'ra*, or *mai^nso'k'ere*, used in battle; and the *ma^n p'a'^εuna*, also used in battle. The first two and the last were made entirely of wood, generally hickory, the last being merely a pointed stick. The third and the fourth were the only ones that had separate heads attached. The head of the third was, as the name implies, a turtle claw, and that of the fourth a fragment of flint. The Winnebago have no recollection of ever having made flint arrowheads and claim that those they used were found in the ground (pl. 31).

Traps.—One of the principal traps consisted of a heavy timber supported very slightly by an upright, to which a piece of wood was attached bearing bait at the end. No sooner does the animal—wolf, bear, fox, or raccoon—touch the bait than the heavy timber falls upon his head, killing him instantly. Another trap commonly used for rabbits may be described thus: The head of a post is hollowed out to receive the knob-shaped end of a long pliable piece of wood that fits into it very lightly. To the latter is attached a noose, so arranged that it draws away the knob-shaped head at the slightest touch. The rabbit must put his head into the noose in order to get at the bait; in so doing he invariably moves the lever, which springs back, jerking him into the air and strangling him.

For trapping deer a very ingenious method is used. Taking advantage of the animal's habit of following repeatedly the same trail, the hunter at some point of a deer trail piles across it a mass of brush to a height of about 4 feet. Behind this he plants a pointed stake so that it can not be seen by the animal. On encountering the obstruction the deer leaps over it and is impaled on the stake.

Knowledge of the habits of beavers and otters is utilized in the following way: Many of these animals live along winding creeks, and in proceeding from one place to another, instead of following all the meanderings of the streams, they cut across the land. The Winnebago hunter digs deep holes in these cut-offs and covers them with hay. Into these the animals fall and are unable to get out.

The bear hunt.—Bears were hunted by individuals or by the tribe. Before a man started on a bear hunt he went through the following ceremony, known as *wana{ʰ}tce're*, literally "concentration of the mind." He either built a special lodge or used his own for the ceremony. A kettle containing food was placed on the fireplace; this was intended for the particular bear the man wished to kill. The food generally consisted of corn or dried fruit; tobacco and red feathers also were offered, the former in small bark vessels. All these offerings were made not only as sacrifices to the bear but in order to make the feast as tempting as possible. When everything was in readiness, the host rubbed two sticks having rough surfaces against each other, called *nai'{ⁿ}carax* or *nai{ⁿ}waidjo'k'ere*. The host never ate. He continued his singing and rubbing until he attracted the attention of the bear, as indicated by the appearance of a little streak of flame passing from the fire toward the gifts he brought for him.

The same ceremony was performed before starting on a deer or a raccoon hunt. In addition to this ceremony, individuals always used the special hunting medicines that they obtained during their fasts. This was frequently chewed and then rubbed into the arrow (nowadays into the gun).[3]

There is a time of the year called *hiruci'c*, when bear break hickory or oak branches for the nuts or the acorns. It seems they are then very easy to approach. If a man killed a bear he would always refer to it in terms of respect.

The tribal bear hunt always took place in summer. As enemies were generally encountered on the way a winter or war feast was always given before the party started. This had nothing to do, however, with the hunt proper. Following is a fairly close translation of an account of a Winnebago bear hunt and buffalo hunt secured by the author:

Description of a bear hunt.—When the Winnebago went on the bear hunt they always traveled in large numbers. They would always be able to find bears in the groves of red timber-oak, and it would be very easy to kill them. Nevertheless the old people considered it a very dangerous affair, especially if the hunters came upon breeding bear. If anyone killed a breeding bear he would cause very much trouble. The male bear would get very angry and chase the man who had done the killing, and if it ever happened that he was out of ammunition, the man surely would be killed. The bear would jump upon him and tear him to pieces. It is said that when bears kill a human being they always eat him. Another way of getting at the bears was to clear away the ground for them. It is very easy to kill them then. This generally takes place at the time of the year when the acorns fall to the ground. The bears gather in the cleared spaces and lie down there. They lie in the timber under the trees. They look like black objects in the distance. It is customary to shoot at them from some distance, but care is always taken not to shoot all of them, nor to shoot when the wind was with them, for then they would scent the hunters

---

[3] Numerous descriptions of the *wana{ⁿ}tce're* are given in the Hare Trickster cycle.

or hear the noise and run away. For this reason the hunters are very careful about these two things—namely, the number of bears shot and the direction of the wind. The method of hunting bears when the acorns fall and they come to the open or cleared spaces is known as the *hiruci'c* method. When the bears eat acorns then only is it easy to find them and kill them without much effort.

Description of a buffalo hunt.—Whenever the Winnebago went buffalo hunting, they always went in large numbers, for the people used to say that on a buffalo hunt, they are likely to encounter their enemies and a fight might take place. It is even said that some people went purposely for the fighting. They generally went together with the *Homaⁿna* (Missouri ?), Waxotcera, Iowa, and *Wadjokdjadjera*, the Oto. Many women accompanied them. It is said that they could always tell where the buffalo were by the dust they encountered, for the dust raised by the trampling of the buffalo rose high in the air. They would always start out for the buffalo early in the morning on fast horses and try to ride up along the right side of the female buffalo, for they only killed the bulls afterward. They shot the buffalo with bow and arrows. When riding horseback, the bow is always drawn back with the right hand. The reason they try to kill the female buffalo first is because they always run away while the bulls do not.

While hunting the buffalo they were always bound to meet some of their enemies and a fight would ensue, so that when they returned, they would bring back not only buffalo but also scalps, and immediately after their return the Victory Dance would be celebrated.

A different account of a buffalo hunt was obtained from another informant (J. H.): [4]

Whenever we go on a buffalo hunt we camp in a circle, with the soldiers in front. They always carried long poles to be used in the construction of tipis. [This statement was made by a number of persons whose information was generally accurate. As they were bound for the open prairie where there was a scarcity of wood, buffalo manure was always carried for fuel.]

As soon as the chief decided to go on a hunt he gave a feast [war feast] to which he invited everyone. This was generally in June. As soon as the feast was over a hunting council was held. Then the chief appointed public criers who went around the village announcing the time for starting, etc. Then all went to the lodge of the chief of the Bear clan. There the ten best warriors were selected, who were to go ahead of the main body and reconnoiter for both buffalo and enemies. These started immediately and if they returned with the news that they had found many buffalo and enemy at the same time, fights frequently took place. Ten warriors always went ahead and the old warriors generally stayed in the rear behind the women in order to protect them better. As soon as they came to the place where the buffalo were seen they followed their trail and killed them. The flesh was cut up into large chunks, which were afterwards dried on the grass. Then when they had enough they all returned home, observing, of course, the same order of march as when they started. When they reached their home they gave another war feast at which all thanked the spirits for their successful return.

Pigeon hunt.—The pigeons are "chief"[5] birds and they would be hunted whenever the chief decided to give the chief feast. The entire tribe was always invited to participate in the meal served, so that many pigeons were needed. The pigeons generally make their nests near human habitations. Sometimes there would be 20

---

[4] As his grandfather was a Dakota, J. H. may have confused in his account Dakota customs with those of the Winnebago. Apart from this consideration, it should be said that J. H. was an exceedingly unreliable informant.

[5] They are called "chief" birds because the pigeon belongs to the same division as does the Thunderbird, or Chief, clan.

in one tree, but a really large tree would hold even more. The pigeons were hunted in the following manner: Long poles were taken and the pigeons poked out of their nests. In this manner many would be killed very easily in one day. They are then either broiled or steeped, when they have a delicious taste. Often it is unnecessary to hunt for them after a storm because large quantities die from exposure to inclement weather.

Method of slaughtering animals.—According to most of the author's informants, all larger animals were opened by making two long incisions, one on each side of the chest. This information may be accepted as correct with respect to the bear, but there is less certainty as to other large animals. There are two considerations, however, which seem to make the question of agreement among informants of secondary importance: First, the considerable differences in this and kindred matters among the settlements of the Winnebago, due to the large extent of territory they inhabited and the diverse influences potent at various places; and secondly, the fact that the distribution of food was entirely a matter of courtesy between individuals, so that considerable variation in custom was both possible and probable.

According to one informant the man who killed an animal had the least to say about its distribution and generally got the poorest share. This unquestionably does not give a very accurate impression of the custom, because subsequent questioning brought out clearly the fact that the manner of distribution depended entirely on the number of individuals present at the killing of the animal, and also on the age of these individuals and their social standing. Remembering that there is no "typical" division which an Indian thinks of in the abstract, but that he always has in mind particular instances of distribution, in order to ascertain definite rules it would obviously be necessary to obtain an adequate number of representative cases in which all the possibilities based on the factors of age, number, and social standing would be duly considered.

From another individual the following information was obtained: When two people went hunting the man who killed the animal received the head, breast, feet, lungs, and heart; his companion, the hide and the rest of the animal. A feast was given afterwards, however, at which the bravest warrior received all that was properly the share of the man who killed the animal. When four went out, the eldest always got the hide; he was granted also the right to apportion the animal. This last instance seems significant in view of the fact that at the tribal hunt the rights of the individual who killed the animal were subservient to many other rights, as those pertaining to seniority and social standing, and suggests that only when one or two individuals took the rather great risks of hunting by themselves was actual killing of the animal deemed of predominating importance in the apportionment.

Regulation of the tribal hunt.—It can not be said that there were many special regulations during the tribal hunt. The rules applying to the regulation of war parties held here too. (For a description of these, see p. 108.)

Individuals were strictly prohibited from taking the initiative except by permission. For instance, a man was not allowed to proceed beyond a certain point, or shoot before a certain time; in short, not to do anything by which he might endanger his own life, the safety of his companions, or the success of the hunt, such as scaring away the animals or causing them to stampede.

It is during the tribal hunts that the power of the Bear clan is at its height. For this reason it may perhaps be most appropriate to include here a description[6] of these powers, although this really belongs in the section on Social Organization:

Whenever the Winnebago are on their tribal hunt or whenever they move from one place to another, the soldiers (i. e., the Bear people) take the lead. Whenever they decide to stop at some place, the leader of the Bear people places his stick in the ground and the other soldiers do the same. The line of sticks is a slanting one. The main tribe follows behind at some distance and always camps a little behind them. None of the members of the tribe dare pass ahead of these sticks. If, for instance, during the fall move the tribe were passing through a country in which much game abounded, and if after the tribe had stopped at a certain place anyone should take it upon himself to go ahead and kill game on his own initiative, and he was discovered, the soldiers would go to his camp and burn it and everything it contained, destroy any supplies he had, and break his dishes. They would spare only his life and the lives of his family. If he resisted he would get a severe whipping. If even after that he resisted them and took his gun and attempted to shoot, the soldiers would not do anything but stand ready. But the moment he made an attempt to shoot, they would kill him and nothing would be said of the matter, for they would be putting into effect the law of the tribe. If, on the other hand, the man submitted to the action of the soldiers and apologized they would make him a better lodge and would give him more and better things than those they had taken away.

FISHING AND AGRICULTURE

Fishing.—In former times fishing seems to have been done exclusively by spearing or by shooting. The spear (*woca'*) consisted of a long stick provided with a bone or a horn point. Spearing was done preferably at night with the aid of torches made of pine pitch. In shooting fish a long arrowlike stick (*maⁿnuxinixini*) with a pointed end, whittled and frayed at the base like the ceremonial staff of the Bear clan, was discharged from an ordinary bow.

The most commonly used trap for fishing was a triangular weir loaded with a stone at its base and placed at the head of a waterfall caused by artificial damming of a stream.

Very few fish were taboo, the principal ones being the dogfish and the eel.

---

[6] By Thunder Cloud.

Names of the principal trees, etc.

raxgɛcok‘a′wa, resin-weed.
xaⁿdje, moss.
wax cutc, cedar (red cedar).
tcatcaⁿna, ironwood.
witci, flat cornered reed used for lodges.
sa, round reed used for mats.
hiⁿcgɛ′, basswood.
wazi, pine in general.
wazi paras, white cedar.
wacgɛ′, poplar.
tcaⁿ tca′wa, birch.
tcagu, walnut.

paⁿ dja′gu, hickory.
tcazu′kɛ, butternut.
naⁿ sa′ŋk‘, maple.
ruɣi, willow.
rak, ash.
tcacge′gu, oak.
maŋk‘a′rak, elm.
huksigu, hazel.
naⁿ p‘a′gu, cherry.
naⁿ ho′cgᵉ, box-elder.
heɣu′, cottonwood.

Names of the principal vegetables and fruits

tcera′bɛra, a water root.
woknɛⁿgɛra, root called "awl" root.
huⁿɛⁿkboi′dja, pea vine.
dora, a sort of artichoke.
paⁿkxi, root found in lowlands.
naⁿp‘ak, chokecherries.
k‘aⁿtc, plum.
kcë‘ crabapple.
tcosa′ⁿwaⁿ, fruit of a tree similar to crab-apple tree.
hazɛ′cutcgɛ, raspberry.
hasda′maŋkerɛ, blackberry.
hasdinɛŋk‘, blueberries.

hascdjek‘, strawberry.
hap‘u′nup‘unuxgɛ, gooseberry.
hotcʋŋkɛ′, cranberry.
k‘aⁿtc hiⁿcek, peaches (fuzzy plums).
kcë carotc, apple (long and round apple).
wak‘aⁿretcawa, wild currant (snake's navel).
dokɛ′wehi, prairie turnip.
huⁿn‘ŋk, bean.
huⁿnaŋk‘ naⁿdi, climbing bean.
huⁿn‘ŋk‘ mink, nonclimbing bean.
maⁿhiⁿtc, milkweed.

Animals and parts of animals whose flesh is not eaten

waŋkcʋŋk, dogfish.
djadja′ŋks‘k, mink.
doco′nAⁿk, otter.
ho wak‘aⁿ, eel (holy fish).
k‘aɣi, crow (really northern raven).
tcaxcɛ′p, eagle.

weasel.
marten.
no entrails (u′djwoju).
gopher.
horse.

Agriculture.—In the old days the Winnebago always raised in their permanent villages at least corn, squash, and beans. As the villages consisted practically of a group of families belonging to different clans, each clan apparently living by itself, the question of clan ownership of these fields was hardly considered. (This statement is made because some Winnebago spoke of clan ownership.) What actually occurred was, in the opinion of the author, as follows: Each group of families being segregated according to clan, it happened that certain family groups had fields in common. This must have happened rather frequently, for there seems to have been a tendency—although this can not be said with certainty owing to the meagerness of reliable information—for related families to hold together in these settlements. In general, however, each family owned and cultivated its own field.

In the middle of the field was usually placed an earthen representation of the clan animal. As to how squash and beans were planted, no reliable information is available. The corn was planted in small circular mounds which, to judge from those near Madison, Wis., were arranged in remarkably straight rows.

The author is unable to say what type of implements was used, as the Winnebago have been using those of European manufacture for many years and have no recollection of any other kind.

If anyone had more corn planted than he could take care of he gave a feast, to which he invited all who had hoes. At this feast dried corn was used. On this occasion the people sacrificed tobacco to their hoes, so that they might not cut themselves with these implements or have other accidents. Then they all joined in helping their host cultivate his corn.

In addition to the above-mentioned patches, most Winnebago had small fields of tobacco, which were regarded as very sacred. The tobacco grown on these was used only for sacrificial purposes. Sacred gourds also were planted in these fields.

Berry picking.—From the earliest times the Winnebago were known for their bountiful supply of berries. Every fall parties of men, women, and children went out to pick cranberries and whortleberries.

Customs when berries are ripening.—If a man has a son whom he loves very much, he has him fast as soon as the berries and other things begin to ripen. If this boy dreams of something good, then he (the father) gives a feast with the newly ripened food and the boy eats. If the boy does not dream of anything good after four days, the father makes him eat and has him try again.

Rice gathering.—In common with the Central Algonquian tribes, with whom they have come in contact, especially the Menominee, the Winnebago spent a number of weeks every year gathering wild rice. The following description of the manner in which this is done is taken from a newspaper article published by Prof. A. E. Jenks of the University of Minnesota:

Fox River from its source to Lake Winnebago was for hundreds of years a very productive field for this aquatic cereal, and along this river the Winnebago lived in plenty and peace with several wild rice eating tribes of the Algonkin stock. Probably a few families still gather their annual crop in that old domain; but most of the wild rice which the tribe now gathers is obtained in the sloughs of the Mississippi River near Lacrosse, Wis., and on the Iowa side of that river

The Winnebago gather the grain by running their canoes into the tall standing stalks before the grain is ripe. A stick is held in each hand of the harvester, one being used to draw the standing stalks over the edge of the canoe, while the other one is employed in tapping or striking the heads of the stalks, thus knocking the grain out of the fruit head into the canoe. After the canoe is full it is taken to the shore and emptied.

Preparation of foods.—Meats were prepared by broiling, in three ways—on stakes, over a rack, or under hot ashes. Only the ribs and the breast of most animals were considered good portions, but the head of the deer was included. Other portions were eaten, however. For infants the deer's tail was considered a delicacy. Now, when they eat meat provided by the white man, rib roast of beef is the favorite meat of the Winnebago.

The Winnebago were very fond of soups of all descriptions. Most of these were meat soups with the addition of vegetables or berries.

Most time was, however, spent in the preparation of vegetable foods, especially in the preparation of wild rice and corn. For the preparation of rice I will again quote Professor Jenks's article:

At this stage of the harvest when the Winnebago gather the wild rice, the kernel is very like a long oat and has a tenacious hull, which must be removed before the grain can be eaten. The necessity of removing this hull and the unripe condition of the grain make it necessary to dry it artificially. This is usually done by spreading the kernels yet inclosed in the hull upon a rack of lattice work, under which a slow fire is kept burning. The grain is cured and the hull made brittle by the heat and smoke. The next process is the thrashing. The Winnebago thrashes the grain by the use of a most primitive flail. He spreads a blanket, rush mat, or deerskin on the ground, upon which he puts the now cured grain. Along three sides of the blanket he erects a screen of similar material. At the open side of this screen the man squats on his knees, and beats the grain with a straight stick in each hand, thus releasing it from the hull. When it has been thrashed the woman gathers up the contents of the blanket and winnows the mass by letting it fall from a vessel held high in the air upon a blanket or mat laid on the earth; the wind blows away the chaff from the falling grain and leaves the clean kernels.

The Winnebago distinguished a number of different kinds of corn, the principal ones being *wahi'seretc*, yellow-stalked; *hiwarakona*, sweet corn; and *waruc'tcke*, red-colored corn. The cornstalk was called *wahu'*, the corn proper, $witca'^nwa^ns$, and the cob, *wosa'k'*. The corn is pounded on a rack ($waick^e$) and then shelled, the grain falling through the rack and the cobs remaining on top. After being shelled the corn is steamed. Then the stones necessary for cooking it are gathered and the corn is picked. When this is finished, a hole is dug in the ground and red-hot stones are put in. Over this the husks are put and upon these the corn; then another layer of husks, etc. The top always is covered with husks. Four holes are made through the husks, into which four pails of water are poured and the whole is covered with a thick layer of earth and the corn left there overnight. The next morning it will be entirely cooked. In shelling, the outer part of an oyster shell is used. When the shelling is over the corn is spread out and dried.

Squash is prepared as follows: After the skin has been removed the squash is cut into slices and the seeds taken out; the slices of squash are then put on poles to dry. The dried squash is called $hotca'^nwa^ndawus$. There are two varieties of this vegetable— $witca'^nwa^n$, Hubbard squash, and $witca'^nwansik$, small-kernel squash.

Fruit was dried, but by what process the author has not learned.

In addition to the vegetable foods above referred to, the following may be mentioned: *Tcera'pɛra*, a plant growing in the water, the root of which was eaten boiled with meat; *wokniŋkɛra* and *huⁿiŋk boi'dja*, awl plant and peavine, respectively, of which only the roots were eaten; and finally the *dora*, wild potato, a favorite dish. The skin was peeled off; then the potato was dried in the sun and afterwards boiled. *Naⁿpa'k'*, chokecherries, were eaten raw. *P'aŋkxi'* and *maⁿhi'ntc*, a lowland weed, and the milkweed, respectively, were also utilized. Of the former, the boiled root was eaten; of the latter, the boiled head. Small quantities of food which required grinding were put into a squirrel hide from which the hairs had been removed, and were pounded with a stone. A mill consisting of a dug-out trunk with handles attached was also used.

Preservation of food.—In former times meat was hung on long racks for preservation. Corn was cached (*woxe'*). Dried berries were kept in bags woven from vegetable fibers. These bags were always covered with designs, mostly of geometric patterns, although realistic designs, as elk, deer, thunderbirds, and water spirits, all unquestionably property marks, were frequently used. There were two types of bags, that closely woven (*p'aⁿ*) (pls. 32–36), just mentioned, and matting bags with fairly large openings in the meshwork (pl. 37). Food stored away at home was generally placed in a part of the lodge reserved for the purpose.

A Winnebago menu.—To give an idea of the favorite dishes of the Winnebago, the names of several mentioned in one of the myths are here appended: Small dried corn boiled with bear's ribs; jerked meat with bear's fat; deer's fat; deer's grease frozen in a hole in the ground; dried corn boiled with fruit; deer-loin soup.

Cooking and eating utensils (pl. 38).—With regard to the kind of cooking and eating utensils used in the old days there exists even among the Indians themselves considerable difference of opinion. According to some, their ancestors never used wooden utensils, mills, spoons, and plates, but utilized shells of various kinds or other natural objects suitable to their needs. Others state, on the contrary, that, in early times, in addition to such natural objects, wooden vessels of many kinds were fashioned from maple knots. These are said to have been burned out, a very tedious process, or even to have been cut out with adzes. It is quite impossible to decide this question now. Wooden implements and utensils in great variety are, of course, found among the Winnebago at the present time, but these are supposed by many to have been introduced by the neighboring Algonquian tribes and by early French traders. The main contention of the present-day Winnebago is, however, that their ancestors could never have made this woodenware without the aid of European implements, burning out being a tedious and unsatisfactory method.

PLATE 31

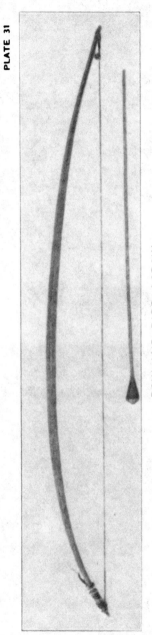

BOW AND BIRD ARROW

PLATE 32

WOVEN BAGS WITH OLD DESIGNS

PLATE 33

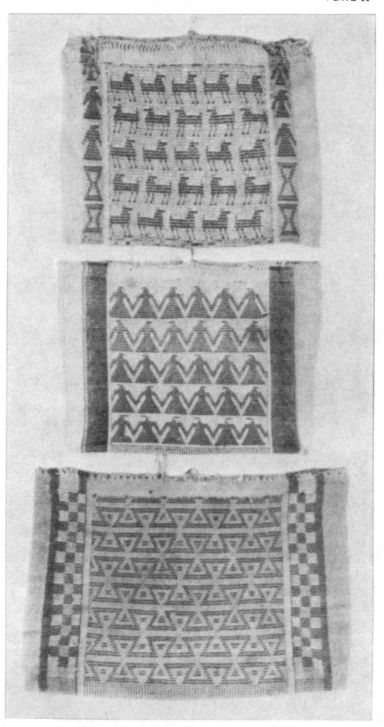

WOVEN BAGS

a. Deer and thunderbird designs   b. Thunderbird design

PLATE 34

VARIETIES OF WOVEN BAGS

PLATE 35

WOVEN BAGS WITH OLD DESIGNS

PLATE 36

a

b

WOVEN BAGS

(Peabody Museum)

PLATE 37

a

b

OPENWORK WOVEN BAGS
(Peabody Museum)

PLATE 38

a. WOODEN DISHES

b. WOODEN SPOONS

c. WOODEN MORTARS AND PESTLES

It might be said that all recollection of the making of wooden vessels could easily have been lost in the last century or two and that therefore too much weight should not be given to present ignorance of the subject. There are a number of reasons, however, why ignorance in this particular case might be significant. First, many indications point to workmanship of a low order among the Winnebago in the manufacture of artifacts; second, there are many suggestions of two cultural strata in this tribe; third, while the Winnebago in Wisconsin still use wooden vessels, many of them claim that these were introduced; and fourth, all the informants who gave this information were old people. If the author were to hazard an hypothesis, it would be the following: In very early times few objects were fashioned out of wood, but gradually contact with the Menominee led to the introduction of many wooden vessels, and finally the acquisition of European axes, knives, and other implements made it possible to manufacture such vessels in large numbers. A similar explanation was offered by an Indian with regard to the use of dugouts.

Besides wood as a material for dishes and spoons of various kinds and sizes, shells were utilized, while sticks served as knives.

All informants agree that neither bone nor stone were used in the manufacture of utensils.

For cooking, clay pots were used. These vessels, most of which were very large, with round bottoms, always hung over the fire. The material used in their manufacture was blue clay found at Green Bay, on or near the site of St. Paul, Minn., mixed with shell shards, glue from sturgeon vetrebræ, and the gelatinous substance in the horns of the deer. The addition of these ingredients greatly increased the cohesiveness of the clay. The material was either molded with the hands or in holes of the desired shape dug in the ground and lined with leaves. Finally, the vessels were dried over a slow fire in small kilns constructed for the purpose. None of the clay vessels were provided with handles. Some were ornamented with geometric patterns. The irregular incised designs on some Winnebago vessels are the impressions of grass blades with which the mold was lined.[7]

Fire making.—In former times fire was always made by means of a simple fire drill. This method is still used for ceremonial occasions.

Tanning.—The author never witnessed the process of tanning. The description obtained agrees exactly with that of Mr. A. Skinner here quoted:[8]

After the skin has been removed, the hair is scraped from it. During this process the skin is hung over an obliquely inclined log, one end of which has been smoothed

---

[7] One informant gave a description of pottery making in which a wheel was used, but as no other Winnebago corroborated this statement the author is convinced that it is inaccurate.
[8] Anthr. Papers Amer. Mus. Nat. Hist. pl, IV, pt. II, pp. 289-290.

off on the upper surface. The beaming tool is then grasped in both hands and pushed away from the user against the grain of the hair over the skin where it lies on the smoothed surface of the stick or log. This process is the same as that followed by the Northern Ojibway and Eastern Cree. The next step is to stretch the skin on a square, upright frame. A fleshing tool is then brought to bear, although the beamer is often made to answer this purpose. When the skin has been fleshed, it is soaked in a mixture of deer's brains and water. No grease is added. This preparation is kept in liquid form in a pail and lasts some time. After remaining in the brain fluid for a time, the skin is taken out and thoroughly washed. Then it is taken by the tanner—

who is always a woman—and dried. While the skin is drying, it is rubbed with a wooden spatula to make it flexible. It is now ready for the last step—smoking. For this process it is first sewed up into a cylindrical shape, and the upper end is tied together to form a bag. By this closed upper end it is then suspended over a shallow hole from a stick driven obliquely into the ground at an angle of about 45 degrees. In the hole a fire is built with dried wood. The open lower edge of the skin bag is pegged or fastened to the ground about the edge of the hole.

GAMES AND AMUSEMENTS

Lacrosse was the favorite game of the Winnebago. This was generally played on ceremonial occasions. Whenever played, the two divisions of the tribe, the Wañgᴇre'gi and the Maṇe'gi, were pitted against each other. There were two kinds of lacrosse, one played by men and the other played by women; these differed in a number of particulars.

Men's lacrosse.—The men's game was called *tcabonino'ṇugis hik'isik'*. There were either 12 or 22 men on each side, placed in the following manner: Two, one of each side, stood in front of the arched sapling which constituted one of the goals (*wak'a'rani*); these were called *woixᵉiŋgra*. There were, of course, two goals, each about 10 feet high, one at each end of the field. About midway between the goals a small mound was made from which the ball was thrown.

FIG. 27.—Men's lacrosse. *A*, Goal. *B, B'*, Goal guards of wañgeregi side. *C, C'*, Goal guards of maṇegi side. *D*, Mound from which ball is thrown.

Ten or twenty men, as the case may be, covered the ground between the mound and the two men stationed at each *wak'a'rani*. The lacrosse stick was called *tcabonadu'gis*, and the ball used either *tci-oko'nôñkra* or *waⁿiⁿi'ⁿṇa*. The object of the game was to put the ball through the goal four times. At the beginning of the game the ball was thrown straight into the air from the mound. (For plan of the game, see fig. 27.)

Ceremonial lacrosse.—The following description of a ceremonial lacrosse game was given by a member of the Bear clan:

The Wañgᴇre'gi and the Maṇe'gi people were to play lacrosse. So the Wañgᴇre'gi took an invitation stick and attached some tobacco to it and sent it to the Maṇe'gi people. Thus they fixed a day for the contest. The contest was to be in four days. In the meantime both sides were to get ready, for some might be without balls or sticks, etc. Then the Wañgᴇre'gi said, "We are the fleeter and will therefore go and look for food." When they returned the leader of the Wañgᴇrᴇ'gi said again, "We are the fleeter and will therefore win from our opponents. In addition to that we are holy and for that reason we will be strengthened in the coming contest." Then the leader of the Maṇe'gi said, "I will first pour tobacco and then I will arise with the blessing of life which was bestowed upon me and through which I know my men will be strengthened." Then they arranged the goals, i. e., the *wak'a'rani*, and arranged for the points. Then they took an emetic and went into a vapor-bath in order to strengthen themselves. The goals were now standing far apart from each other. Then the people who were to play gathered on the field and two men from each side began to tell their war exploits. First, one of the Wañgᴇrᴇ'gi men told how he had cut off an enemy's head; how proud his sisters had been at receiving the gifts and how they had danced in the Victory Dance. "With such a man you will have to play," he shouted to those on the other side. Then a man from the Maṇe'gi side said, "I also am a brave man. I did with the enemy as I pleased. Once when an enemy had been killed between the firing lines, I rushed for him and in the midst of bullets I cut off his head. With such a man you will have to fight," he shouted to those on the other side. Then he gave a whoop and the ball was thrown into the air and they began to play lacrosse. Those who first succeeded in putting the ball through the *wak'a'rani* four times would be declared the winners. All day they played and in the evening they stopped. Lacrosse was the favorite game among the Winnebago. This is all.

Women's lacrosse.—The women's game was called *naiyaca'radji uñk'isik'*. Ten women took part on each side; they all stood in front of the goal, which consisted merely of a line drawn on the surface of the ground, called *wak'a'rani* as in the men's game. The lacrosse stick (*tcabenoṇa*) was straight. The "ball" consisted of two balls tied together by a string (*naiyaca'radji$^\varepsilon u^n$ wa$^n i^n$ina*). This was put into play by being thrown from a point midway between the goals straight up into the air. The side that hit over the goal four times won.

Football.—Football was played by men. The *wak'a'rani* was merely a line drawn on the surface of the ground. The 16 or 20 men who took part on each side arranged themselves in front of either *wak'a'rani*. The ball used was a fairly large one made of deer's hair, covered with hide from the same animal. It was put in play in the middle of the field and the side that kicked the ball over the goal four times won the game.

Hit-the-tree game (*tcibonnoogis nai^{n}djá hap'a-na'^{n}-i*).—This consisted merely of a test of marksmanship. A tree (*na^n hadjina*) about 8 feet high and 8 inches in diameter was selected and the one who hit it from a certain distance received a prize. Any number of people could participate.

The kicking game.—This was a very rough sport in which men only took part. Two men took turns in kicking each other as hard as they could, the one who held out the longer being the winner.

The moccasin game.—One of the favorite games of the Winnebago. Five men took positions directly opposite their five opponents. Between the two rows of players, in front of each man was a receptacle, generally a moccasin, in which a small object was secreted. The sides in turn guessed in which moccasin it was secreted. The guesser pointed in turn with a long stick to each moccasin, all the time carefully scrutinizing the expression on the face of each man whose moccasin he touched. The bystanders and the other players on his side meanwhile sang songs and made all sorts of remarks and allusions in an attempt to catch off his guard the man in whose moccasin the object was secreted, so that he might disclose the fact by some gesture or expression. The person guessing had the right to touch each moccasin without forfeiting his chance. As soon as he wished to guess he overturned with his stick the moccasin in which he thought the object was hidden. The seriousness with which a player scrutinized his opponents is well shown in plate 39.

Women's dice game.—The women's dice game (*kᵉ'ansu*) was played with either bone or wooden dice. Eight of these are used. After being shaken, they are allowed to fall into a wooden bowl. The dice are white on one side and black or blue on the other. One of the dice has a mark on each side. The count is as follows: 1 dark, 7 white, count 2; 2 dark, 6 white, 1; all dark, 0 white, 4; 3 dark, 5 white, 0; 4 dark, 4 white, 0; marked dice dark, 7 white, 10; marked dice white, 7 dark, 10; marked dice white, 1 other white, the rest dark, 2; all dice white, 4; 2 white, 6 dark, 1; 1 white, 7 dark, 2.

The side gaining all the counters, which consist of small sticks, wins.

Cup-and-ball game.—"A cup-and-ball game is composed of eight worked phalangeal bones of the Virginia deer (*Odocoileus virginiana*). It differs from those seen by the writer among the Cree and Ojibway in that the topmost phalangeal unit of the game as played among those people does not have the joint removed, whereas in the Winnebago specimens all the bones are cut into conical form. The top is generally surmounted by a bunch of leather thongs with many perforations. The striking pin is of bone. The count is one for each unit, five for catching the tails or thongs at the top, and the same if all the units are caught together, which occasionally happens. The bottom unit nearest the striking pin has four small perforations set at equal distances about the lower edge. Above these holes are two, three, four, and six dots, respectively, cut in the bone. The count gained by catching this bone through any one of the holes varies according to the number of these dots. The striking pin may be of bone or wood. Sometimes these games are stained with dye or paint. The string and pins are short, so that the game is much more difficult and clumsy than in the Cree and Ojibway forms." [9]

⁹ A. Skinner, op. cit., pp. 295–296.

PLATE 39

MOCCASIN GAME

PLATE 40

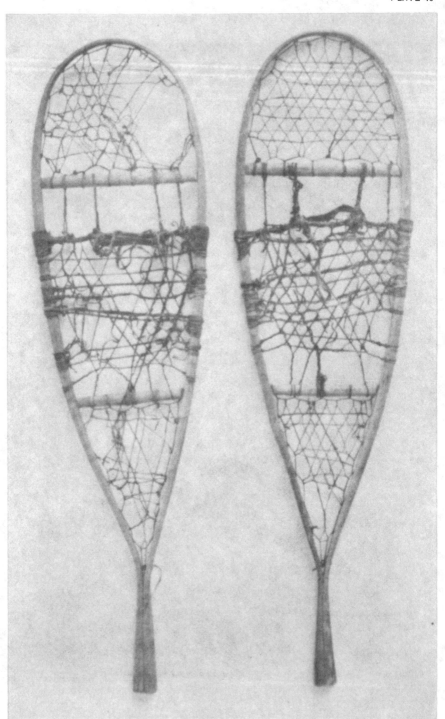

SNOWSHOES

Tree game.—Two trees are selected about 20 feet apart, one having a branch about 15 feet from the ground. A number of people stand ready at the side of this tree and the one whose turn it is to play tries to hit the branch. When he succeeds in doing so all run toward the other tree. As soon as the player gets the ball he tries to hit the runners. If successful in this before the others have reached the tree he wins; otherwise they are "safe" and he must try again. The Winnebago called this game *hahi'bidjike$^\varepsilon$u^n*.

TRAVEL AND TRANSPORTATION

Canoes and dugouts.—All the boats found in the early days in the territory originally inhabited by the Winnebago were dugouts, yet a number of the tribe questioned denied positively that boats of this kind were in common use before the coming of the whites. According to these informants, in former times the Winnebago always had their home in a birch country, and had at hand, therefore, the requisite material for making canoes; moreover, birchbark canoes were much easier to construct than dugouts, for which logs had to be hollowed by burning—a process that might consume weeks. Only when the whites introduced the ax and the knife did it become practicable to make dugouts. These implements became available at the time of the southern migration of the tribe into a region where birch bark was scarce, and one result of the change was the substitution of the dugout for the canoe. The validity of this explanation is supported by the same line of argument as in the case of the wooden vessels.

Snowshoes.—The snowshoes of the Winnebago were similar to those used by the Menominee, with this difference, that the two pieces of wood forming the "handle," instead of being tied together for their whole length, as among the latter, were left unfastened for about 5 inches at the end. This difference is immediately detected (pl. 40) by the present-day Winnebago, who can easily identify, by the feature mentioned, snowshoes belonging to the tribe.

MUSICAL INSTRUMENTS

The musical instruments of the Winnebago seem to have been restricted to the flute, drum, and gourd. The flute was made of red cedar and usually had a range of five or six notes; it was used at many ceremonies, and especially by young men when courting. The drum consisted of a framework (in later days a wooden pail or a barrel served the purpose), over which a skin was drawn very tight. A small quantity of water was always kept in the drum so that the skin could be wet as often as necessary. Rattles consisted of dried gourds filled, in olden times, with seeds, in more modern times with buckshot (pl. 30, *d, f*).

Divisions of Time

The Winnebago reckoned time from the beginning of each new month (*wira*). There are slight differences in the names of the months between the Nebraska and the Wisconsin branch of the tribe, as appear below:

Nebraska—

1. Hundjwi′ra, month when the bears are born.
2. Húndjwiro-a′gᴇnina, last bear month.
3. Wák‘ek‘ iru′xᵉ, raccoon-breeding month.
4. Hoi′doginâ‛na, fish become visible (because of the ice clearing away).
5. Maiⁿ da′wus, month that dries the earth.
6. Mank‘era, dig-the-earth month (when the crops are sowed).
7. Wixo′tcera, the month that makes them gray (the month when the tassels of corn appear and the fields look gray).
8. Wida′djox, when the roasted ears of corn burst.
9. Wiza′zek‘e, name of a bird that appears this month.
10. Pca′maiⁿna‛xora, when the deer paws the earth; or Huⁿwaiⁿjukᴇra, when the elks shout, or whistle.
11. Tcaik‘i′ruxe, deer-breeding month.
12. Tca′hewakcu‛, when the deer shed their horns.

Wisconsin—

1. Hu′ndjwi tconína, first bear month.
2. Hu′ndjwiro-a‛gᴇnina, last bear month.
3. Wâk‘e′k‘iruxewi′ra, raccoon-breeding month.
4. Hoi′doginâna, fish becoming visible.
5. Maiⁿda′wus, drying-of-the-earth month.
6. Mank‘e′ra, digging month.
7. Maiⁿṇa? ᵉuⁿṇa, cultivating month.
8. Wixo′tcerera, tasseling month.
9. Huⁿ waiju′kᴇra, elk-whistling month.
10. Tco′maiⁿna‛xora, when the deer paw the earth.
11. Tcaik‘iru′xira, deer-breeding month.
12. Tcahe′yakcu‛na, when the deer shed their horns.

According to a member of the Bear clan, the following were the activities throughout the year. The accounts given of these activities differed in certain details, depending upon the clan connection of the informant, because he naturally associated some months with specific activities of his clan, such as clan feasts.

1. Members of the Bear clan give their feast.
2. Month in which the various Winter Feasts are given.
3. Month in which people hunt.
4. Month in which people begin to fish.

5. Month in which people hunt deer. At this time deer are very tame and frequent the streams.

6. Month in which people plant corn, squash, and beans.

7. Month in which people hunt deer. At this season deer are very fat. The hunters return to their homes at the beginning of the eighth month.

8. Month in which people dry corn and store it away.

9. Month in which people tie the rice stems into bundles and go through them with their canoes.

10. Month in which the people go on their fall move and hunt the larger animals.

11. Month in which the people go on their fall move and dry their meat.

12. Month in which the people return to their winter quarters.

From this calendar of activities it is apparent that the longest period the Winnebago remained at home continuously was three months, the twelfth, first, and second. They were at home also throughout the sixth and eighth months. Whether they were in their villages at intervals during the fourth and fifth months is hard to determine. It is probable that the fishing or hunting trips consumed a considerable portion of, if not the entire, month. During the ninth, tenth, and eleventh months the Winnebago were undoubtedly away from their villages all the time.

CHAPTER IV

GENERAL SOCIAL CUSTOMS

Birth.—During pregnancy a woman had to observe carefully certain restrictions. She was not allowed to roam the woods alone for fear of meeting snakes or other animals, the sight of which was believed to forebode ill luck to a pregnant woman. She was not permitted to have dogs or cats around her nor to sleep during the day. Every morning during her pregnancy she had to take a cold bath. Among the restrictions may have been food taboos, but no information on this phase of the subject was obtained.

When the time for delivery came, it was the custom for the woman to occupy a small lodge erected especially for her use. None of her male relatives were permitted to be present and her husband was not even permitted to stay at home. He was supposed to travel continually until the child was born, in the belief that by his movements he would help his wife in her delivery. According to one informant the husband had to hunt game, the supposition being that this procedure on his part would cause his wife to have enough milk for the child. This traveling of the husband was called, therefore, "Looking-for-milk." It was considered improper for a woman to cry out during labor pains, and by doing so she subjected herself to the jests of her elder female relatives. The cradle-board was always made before the child was born (pls. 41, *c*, 42, *a*).

The positions commonly assumed by women in delivery may be described thus: Supported by the arms, which were passed over a pole held in the crotches of two forked sticks driven into the ground; suspended between two stakes; or flat on the back.

The infant's navel string was cut off and sewed into a small bag, which was attached to the head of the cradle-board.

On the birth of a child the sisters of the husband were supposed to show his wife especial marks of courtesy. They always gave her valuable gifts, such as goods or a pony. They were glad that he had offspring, the people said, and even permitted their brother's wife to give the presents received from them to her own relatives. The presentation of these gifts was called "Cradling-the-infant." Gifts were presented also to the wife's brothers.

Some time after the birth of a child, if a boy, the father always gave a feast to Earthmaker and thanked him.

126

PLATE 41

a. WINNEBAGO AND DAUGHTER

b. OLD WINNEBAGO WOMAN

c. WOMAN AND CHILD, SHOWING
CRADLE-BOARD

d. WOMAN AND CHILD, SHOWING
METHOD OF CARRYING INFANT

PLATE 42

a. INFANT WITH ORNAMENTED CRADLE-BOARD

b. GROUP OF WINNEBAGO

Names.—A newborn child received a birth name immediately. There were six such names for male children and six for female children, which were given according to the order of birth:

Male	Female
1. K'u'nu.	1. Hi'nu.
2. He'nu.	2. Wi'ha.
3. Ha'ga.	3. Aksi'-a (generally pronounced Aksi).
4. Na'ŋxi.	4. Hi'nuŋk'.
5. Naŋxixô'nu.	5. A'ksigaxô'nu.
6. Naŋxixonu'niñk'a.	6. A'ksigaxônu'niŋk'a.

The meanings of these names are unknown to the present Winnebago, who reject the idea that they ever had any meaning apart from indicating the order of birth. Originally, of course, these names had meanings, but at the present time they resemble no other Winnebago names and baffle all attempts at interpretation. This is not surprising, because they represent in all probability archaic names which undoubtedly have been considerably modified through long-continued use. The Dakota have a similar set of names but only four in number. The two additional names among the Winnebago indicate by their form that they have been derived from one of the other four. In this connection it is interesting to note that the fifth of the male names is, as one might expect, merely the fourth name of the series with the addition of a diminutive suffix, whereas the fifth of the female names is the third of that series with a like addition. The sixth name of each series is formed by adding another diminutive suffix to the fifth name.

A few words may not be out of place here with regard to the relation of the male to the female series, and to the possible interpretation of two of the female names. He'nu [1] of the male and Hi'nu of the female series, it will be noted, differ only in the first vowel. A similar phenomenon is found in such relationship terms as *hi'niŋk*, male child of elder brother, and *hi'ûnuŋk'*, female child of elder brother. Remembering that in those Siouan languages which distinguish between female and male oral stops the difference often consists merely in the change of a vowel, this difference between He'nu and Hi'nu may be suggestive. The name K'u'nu may be connected with *k'u'niŋk*, "a grandmother," in which *k'u* is unquestionably the stem, meaning probably "old." In the female series there is a possible relationship between Hi'nu and Hi'nuŋk', as *k'* seems to be a very common ending in relationship terms. Hi'nuŋk' itself is identical with the word for "woman" and it seems hard to imagine that it is not the same, especially since it is also found as the relationship term for female child of younger brother.

---

[1] Hi'nu is also the name for a man's elder sister.

On first thought it might be imagined that the application of the same name to so many people would cause great confusion. As a matter of fact, however, in a village of, say, 20 families, there could have been a maximum of only 40 having the same name. Taking into account deaths and departures, the number was greatly diminished. Moreover, as in general only relations or close friends were addressed in this way, strangers commonly being addressed by their nicknames, the seeming danger of confusion is almost entirely obviated. In those cases, however, in which confusion might result a nickname, or sometimes a clan name, was added to the birth name when speaking of an individual.

Naming feast.—The clan name was generally bestowed on a child at a special feast held for the purpose or at any feast that happened to be given within a reasonable time after its birth. The bestowal of the clan name was not infrequently delayed by a father's inability to gather the requisite amount of food to be presented to the old man who was to select the name. Occasionally it even happened that a father under such conditions permitted the relatives of his wife to bestow a name on a child, which of course was a name from its mother's clan. The author has personal knowledge of a case in which the first child of a man had a name belonging to his mother's clan while the other children had names belonging to their father's clan. When questioned, the man said that at the time of the birth of his eldest child he was too poor to pay for the honor of having his child receive a name and that he had allowed his wife's relatives to give it a name. When his other children were born, however, as he was in better condition financially he had been able to name them in the usual way. Although a child, irrespective of his individual name, always belonged to his father's clan, there seemed to exist a feeling that a person having a name not taken from his own clan was more or less incomplete. A person possessing no clan name was regarded as having low social standing.

When a child was adopted it retained its former birth name and clan name.

Relationship terms.—The system of relationship terms used by the Winnebago is as follows:[2]

MALE TERMS OF ADDRESS

Tcok'a', p. and m. grandfather (direct address).
Hi'tcok'ê, p. and m. grandfather and father-in-law.
K'u'nǐŋk'a, p. and m. grandmother (direct address).
Hik'ârok'e, p. and m. grandmother and mother-in-law.
Dja'dji, father (direct address).

---

[2] Abbreviations: p., paternal; m., maternal; br., brother; sr., sister.

Hi-a′ntc, father.
Na′ni, mother (direct address).
Hi-u′ni, mother.
Hi′ni, elder brother (direct address?).
Ni′ni, elder br. (?).
Hi′suŋk‘, or Hisûŋkêdji^n, younger br.
Hi′nu, elder sr.
Wai′tcke, younger sr.; or (Tcûñgŭa′k‘ (obsolete) (direct address?).
Hiwaŋgê′, wife of elder br.
Hiwaŋgê′, wife of younger br.
Hitca′^{n}, husband of elder sr.
Hitca′^{n}, husband of younger sr.
Hi′nîŋk‘, son of elder br.
Hi′nîŋk‘, son of younger br.
Hi′nûŋk‘, daughter of elder br.
Hi′nûŋk‘, daughter of younger br.
Hi′nûŋktce′k‘, wife of son of elder br.
Hi′nûŋktce′k‘, wife of son of younger br.
Hitcû^{n}ckê′, son of elder sr.
Hitcû^{n}ckê′, son of younger sr.
Hitcû^{n}jôŋk‘, daughter of elder sr.
Hitcû^{n}jôŋk‘, daughter of younger sr.
Hinûnktce′k‘, wife of son of elder sr.
Hinûnktce′k‘, wife of son of younger sr.
Wadoho′tci, husband of daughter of elder br.
Wadoho′tci, husband of daughter of younger br.
Wadoho′tci, husband of daughter of elder sr.
Wadoho′tci, husband of daughter of younger sr.
Nîngïa′k‘, son (no longer in common use) (direct address).
Hinîŋk‘, son.
Hirakewa^n, stepson.
Hitca′xa^n, stepdaughter.
Nûngŭăk‘, daughter (no longer in common use) (direct address).
Hinûŋk‘, daughter.
Himûŋktce′k‘, wife of son.
Watoho′tci, husband of daughter.
Hitcû^{n}ckê′, son of son.
Hitcû^{n}ckê, son of daughter.
Hitcû^{n}jô′ŋk‘, daughter of daughter.
Hitcû^{n}jôŋk‘, daughter of son.
Hinûŋktce′k‘, wife of grandson
Wadohto′ci, husband of grand-daughter.
Hinûŋga′s, p. br.
Hi-uni′nîŋk‘, wife of p. br.

Hi'ni, Hisû'ŋk', older and younger sons of p. br., respectively.
Hi'nu, waitckê', older and younger daughters of p. br., respectively.
Hinûŋktce'k', wives of sons of p. br.
Watoho'tci, husbands of daughters of p. br.
Hiniŋk', sons of sons of p. br.
Hinûŋk', daughters of sons of p. br.
Hitcû'ⁿwiⁿ, p. sr.
Hitca'ⁿ, husband of p. sr.
Hitcûⁿcke', sons of p. sr.
Hitcûⁿjo'ŋk', daughters of p. sr.
Hinûŋktce'k', wives of sons of p. sr.
Wadoho'tci, husbands of daughters of p. sr.
Hitcûⁿckê, sons of sons of p. sr.
Hitcû'ⁿjô'ŋk', daughters of sons of p. sr.
Hide'k', m. br.
Hitcû'ⁿwiⁿ, wife of m. br.
Hide'keniŋk', sons of m. br.
Hidcû'ⁿwiⁿ, daughters of m. br.
Hitcûⁿckê', sons of sons of m. br.
Hitcûⁿjô'ŋk', daughters of sons of m. br.
Hitcû'ⁿwiⁿ, wives of sons of m. br.
Hitca'ⁿ, husbands of daughters of m. br.
Hi-uni'nîŋk', m. sr.
Hinûŋga's, husband of m. sr.
Hi'ni, Hisû'nk, older and younger sons of m. sr., respectively.
Hi'niŋk, male children of male children of m. sr.
Hi'nûŋk, female children of male children of m. sr.
Hinu, waitckê, daughters of m. sr., respectively.
Hinûŋktce'k', wives of sons of m. sr.
Wadoho'tci, husbands of daughters of m. sr.
Tcido', elder br.
Hitcûⁿckê', children of br.
Hitcûⁿjôŋk', daughters of br.
Hiciga'ⁿ, wife of br.
Hisû'ŋk', younger br.
Hitcôŋk', younger sr.
Hi'nu, elder sr.
Hicikᵉe', husband of sr.
Hinî'ŋk', sons of sr.
Hinûŋk', daughters of sr.
Hiciga'ⁿ, wives of sons of br.
Hicikeᵉ', husbands of daughters of br.
Hinûŋktce'k', wives of children of sr.
Wadoho'tci, husbands of daughters of sr.
Hicikᵉe', husband of father's sr.

Hiko′nô, husband.
Hitca′ⁿ, brother of wife.
Hitca′ⁿwiⁿ, wife.
Hiwaŋge′, sister of wife.

After one's grandchild's generation the children of a man whom one called either Hi′niŋk‘ or Hitcûⁿckê′, or of a woman whom one called either Hi′nûŋk‘ or Hitcûⁿjô′ŋk‘, were all called Hitcûⁿckê′ or Hitcûⁿjô′ŋk‘.

A special term, Wotcû′ⁿwoŋk‘, was used by parents-in-law when addressing each other.

It will be noticed that, taking self as the starting point, the distinction between forms—one series to be used in speaking of a person and the other in directly addressing one's own blood relative—has been developed for only grandfather, grandmother, father, mother, son, and daughter. It is probable that in former times brother and sister also were included in this double series.

FEMALE TERMS OF ADDRESS

As compared with the distinction between male and female terms of address found among other Siouan tribes, that existing among the Winnebago is very weak and there seems to be no indication that it ever was much stronger, although caution must be observed in drawing inferences as to past relationship terms, since it is a well-known fact that they have a tendency to disappear. At the present time there are only four terms used among the Winnebago by women specifically; *tcito*, elder brother; *hitcô′ŋk‘*, younger sister; *hiciga′ⁿ*, wife of brother; and *hicikᵉe′*, husband of sister.

A cursory examination shows that the following forms are linguistically related:

hini.
hinîŋk‘.
hicikê′.
hitcûⁿckê′.
hitcáⁿ.
hitcû′ŋk‘.
hitcak‘â′ro (friend).

hinu.
hinuŋk.
hiciga′ⁿ.
hitcûⁿjô′ŋk‘ (tcuⁿ—gŭ′ak, obsolete) hitcû′ⁿwiⁿ.
hitcaⁿwiⁿ.

It is clear that we are dealing here with a change of terminal vowel (from *i* to *u*; from *e* to *a*; from *a* to *u*), indicative of sex. In the form *hitcuⁿwiⁿ*, *wiⁿ* is undoubtedly identical with *-wiⁿ*, meaning "female," found with all animal female names. Terminal *k‘*, *k‘e*, *ga*, is a suffix that may be related to the termination *k‘e* found with so many animal names. We may perhaps say, then, that we have here only three stems, *hini*, *hicik‘*, and *hitcû′ⁿ*. For a complete list of stems used in relationship terms there must now be added to these the following: *Hik‘â′ro—k‘ê hitcok—k‘ê′, hi-a′ntc hi-u′ni, hisû′ŋ—k‘, waitc—k‘ê′, hinûñgás, hide—k‘ hiwañ—gê′, tcidó,* *wadohótci*, and *hinû'ñk—tcek'*. Hınûnga's might be said to be divided into *hinug* and *gas*, but there is no reason to assume that such a division of the word is justifiable, and for that reason it has not been included in the enumeration of *hinû'n—k'* stems. The form *tcido*, elder brother, spoken by females, is baffling, all the more so if we assume that there never was a form for "younger brother" used by women.

Let us now separate the terms applied to relatives through marriage from those applied to blood relatives.

Blood relatives	Relatives through marriage	Blood relatives	Relatives through marriage
Hini	Hicikᵉé	Waitc—k'ê'	Hitca'ⁿ
Hitcûⁿckê'	Hiciga'ⁿ	Hinûñga's	Hi-uni'nîŋk'
Hik'âro—k'ê'	Hitcû'ⁿwiⁿ	Hide'—k', hídekɛnî'ŋk'	Hinûŋga's
Hitco—k'ê'		Tcido'	
Hi-a'ntc	Wadoho'tci	Hitcû'ⁿwiⁿ	
Hi-u'ni; hi-unini'ŋk	Hiwaŋgê'	Hiníŋk'	
Hisû'ŋ—k'	Hinuŋk'tce'k'		

Three terms are applied sometimes to blood relatives and sometimes to relatives through marriage: *Hitcû'ⁿwi*, *hi-uni'nîŋk'*, and *hinûŋga's*. It is the author's belief that in all these cases the terms have been applied to relatives through marriage on account of the extremely close relationship the husbands of *hitcu'ⁿwi* and *hi-uni'nîŋk'* and the wives of *hinûŋga's* bear to one's parents; that it is really an act of courtesy toward people whose children are in one case (*hitcû'ⁿwiⁿ* and *hi-uni'nîŋk'*) regarded as one's brothers and sisters and in the other case as the same as one's sister's children. There never was the slightest confusion as to the position held by the wife of one's father's brother (*hi-uni'nîŋk'*), or one's mother's brother's wife, or the husband of one's mother's sister; nor is there the slightest indication that they ever were considered as identical with any blood relatives who bore the same name.

The foregoing list contains twenty-two terms of relationship applied by the Winnebago to all relatives, blood or otherwise, for five generations—one's own father's, grandfather's, son's, and grandson's. The two tables following show first, how these terms were distributed over the five generations, and second, to how many people of these five generations the same name was applied.

Generation	Male	Female
1. Grandfather's	Hitcok'ê'	Hi'k'ârok'ê'
2. Father's	Hi-a'ntc, hide'k'	Hi-u'ni, hi-uninŋk'
	Hinuŋga's, hitca'ⁿ	Hitcû'ⁿwiⁿ
3. One's own	Hini, hisû'ŋk'	Hinu, waitckê', hinûŋk' tce'k'
	Hitcûⁿckê', hideke-	Hitcûⁿjô'ŋk', hitcû'ⁿwiⁿ,
	Nîŋk', hitca'ⁿ,	Hiwaŋgê', hiciga'ⁿ
	Wadoho'tci, hicikᵉe	
4. Son's	Hiniŋk', hitcûⁿckê',	Hinû'ŋk', hinûŋk' tce'k',
	Hini, hisû'ŋk',	Hitcuⁿ jô'ŋk', hínu,
	Wadohótci	Waitckê'

Generation	Male	Female
5. Grandson's	Hitcûⁿckê', hínîŋk',	Hitcûⁿjô'ŋk', hínûŋk',
6. Great-grandson's	Hitcûⁿckê', hínîŋk',	Hitcûⁿjô'ŋk', hínûŋk',
	(Hitcûⁿjô'ŋk')	(Hitcûⁿckê')
7. Great-great-grandson's	(Hitcûⁿjô'ŋk')	(Hitcûⁿckê')

For the first three generations no term is repeated except *hitcû'ⁿwiⁿ*; for the fourth generation eight terms are repeated and two terms are added, *hinîŋk'* and *hi'nûŋk'*. After that all the terms are repeated and no new terms are added. Only three sets of terms are repeated for more than two generations—*hitcûⁿckê'*, *hitcûⁿjô'ŋk hinuŋk'tce'k, wadoho'tci*, and *hi'nîŋk', hi'nûŋk'*. After the fifth generation only one set of terms is used.

Distribution of all relationship terms [3] *occurring more than once.*—
Hi-uni'niŋk', wife of p. br.; m. sr.
Hi'ni, elder br.; son of p. br.; son of m. sr.
Hisûŋk', younger br.; son of p. br.; son of m. sr.
Hi'nu, elder sr.; daughter of p. br.; daughter of m. sr.
Waitckê', younger sr.; daughter of p. br.; daughter of m. sr.
Hi'nîŋk', son of elder br.; son of sr. (sister speaking).
Hi'nûŋk', daughter of elder br.; daughter of sr.
Hitcûⁿckê', son of elder br.; son of daughter and son; son of br.; son of p. sr.
Hitcûⁿjô'ŋk', daughter of elder br.; daughter of daughter and son; daughter of p. sr.; daughter of br.
Hitcû'ⁿwiⁿ, p. sr.; daughter of m. br.; wife of son of m. sr.
Hitca'ⁿ, husbands of sisters; husband of p. sr.; husband of daughter of m. sr.
Hiciga'ⁿ, wife of br.; wife of son of br.
Hicikᶜe', husband of p. sr.; husband of daughter of br.

JOKING RELATIONSHIP [4]

A man was not permitted to take even the slightest liberties with any of his near relatives or with his mother-in-law or his father-in-law, but a curious exception to this rule was permitted for his father's sister's children (*hitcûⁿckê'* and *hitcûⁿjô'ŋk'*); his mother's brother's children (*hitcûⁿckê'* and *hitcûⁿjô'ŋk'*); his mother's brothers (*hide'k'*); and his sisters-in-law and brothers-in-law. In the two cases last named not only was a man permitted to joke with those relatives but he was supposed to do so whenever he had an opportunity. Under no circumstances were any of these individuals supposed to take offense. This relationship was of course reciprocal. If a person

---
[3] A more specific study of these relationship terms is reserved for a special article on Siouan Relationship Terms.
[4] The joking relationship was discovered among the Winnebago by the author. Since then it has been found to exist among the Crows and the Creeks, etc.

attempted liberties with people who did not belong in the category of the "joking relationship" they would stop him immediately, saying, "What joking relation am I to you" (*Djagu' niŋk' idajütcgad-ja*^{n})?

It is impossible to determine the significance of the "joking relationship." Two points of interest may be referred to, however: First, that it existed between a person and such close relatives as the children of his father's sister and his mother's brothers and their children, on the one hand, and his relatives by marriage only, as his brothers-in-law and sisters-in-law, on the other; and second, that his mother's brother was at the same time a person with whom he was on particularly intimate terms. With regard to the first point, the author suggests the following explanation: Both groups just mentioned had this in common—they did not belong to the man's clan and with the exception of their mother's brother they did not belong to any individuals but those of their own generation. Now we know that the prohibition of marriage into a man's mother's clan extended only to members of her generation and that theoretically, at least, he could marry her brother's children. In the same way the children of a man's father's sister, belonging as they did to the side into which he had to marry and not belonging to the generation of his father, belonged also to the group into which he theoretically might marry. The author has never heard any Winnebago state that a man may not marry any of the individuals included in the "joking relationship," with the exception of his sister-in-law, but he feels certain that such marriage would be considered improper, although equally certain that it would not be regarded as incest, as would be the case if a person were to marry the son of his mother's sister or of his father's brother. The suggestion is offered, therefore, that the "joking relationship" implies, first, close relationship of individuals who have different clan membership, and, second, perhaps, the possibility of marriage. If there is any explanation for the existence of the relationship between a man and his mother's brother I feel that it is probably to be sought in the first of these suggestions. The second is really advanced merely to suggest some reason for the grouping together of blood relations with relations by marriage.

The "joking relationship" is very peculiar from the point of view of a European, and for that reason it is perhaps likely that we exaggerate its importance. In actual practice joking was probably indulged in only during the first moments after meeting, except by the habitual punster. An important psychological factor may have been the opportunity for relaxation it afforded an individual who was constantly surrounded by close relatives in intercourse with whom he had to observe at all times strict rules of propriety.

Mother-in-law and Father-in-law Taboo

In former times the mother-in-law and father-in-law taboo was in full force. No man was allowed to talk directly to his mother-in-law or to look at her, and the same rule held with regard to the attitude of a woman toward her father-in-law. Even accidental meetings of these relatives, as on the road, were attended with great embarrassment. The author never learned of any way in which either the mother-in-law or the father-in-law taboo could be relaxed even temporarily, much less done away with entirely.

Puberty Customs

From the age of five, children, male and female, were taught the customs of their ancestors in a series of talks always delivered by an elderly male relative, perhaps the father. The specific training differed, of course, for boys and girls and for individuals. Personal training ceased at the age of puberty, when all, both boys and girls, were sent out to fast. For boys this fasting constituted the only puberty rite. After their faces had been blackened with charcoal they were sent to some neighboring hill with the injunction not to return till dawn. Gradually they would be sent out for two, then three, nights; if after that trial they were not blessed they would be advised either to desist entirely or exhorted to fast until they were blessed, no matter how long the time required to secure the desired result. While fasting the boys and girls used the following formula:

Waxop' inixjiwina hina'djire na^{n}dje'je wahadjex.
Spirits am I likely to be blessed? that is why I am praying.

One old Indian informed the author that in former times the young boys and girls were offered either bread or charcoal for their fast. If they took the charcoal, well and good; but if they took the bread, they were unceremoniously kicked out of the house and the charcoal was thrown after them. From the other statements of this informant one might gather that the young boys and girls generally took the bread, because, he said, after they had been kicked out, they would always resolve to go to the wilderness (in that way running the risk of being captured or killed by an enemy), in order to spite their parents. My informant was of the opinion that the parents purposely treated their children roughly, so that they might feel all the more miserable while fasting and thus pray all the more intensely.

A faster is always told to be careful as to what kind of spirits bless him, as he might be blessed by a bad spirit. Therefore a faster's blessings are always reviewed by the elders. J.'s old grandmother used to call the children in at dusk, as the evil spirits are around then.

All boys do not seem to have approached the ordeal of fasting with the proper religious feeling.   One instance in particular showed anything but a reverent attitude; this is so amusing that it is here given in the exact words of the Indian:

When I was a young boy, my folks made me fast together with a boy named Modudjeka. We were supposed to go to the hills and cry until the spirits blessed us. However, whenever we looked at each other and at our charcoal-blackened faces we could not refrain from bursting out laughing. Whenever we made up our minds to cry, something or other would induce us to look at each other and the laughing would begin all over again. When the time for our return to the house came, we didn't present the slightest indication of having cried, so we took some saliva and made long streaks on our faces.

Young girls and women are also encouraged to fast to obtain the war honors.

Menstrual lodges.—Fasting at puberty by girls was inseparably connected with their retirement to menstrual lodges.   Sometimes there was only one girl in each menstrual lodge, sometimes there were as many as three.   From the time of her first menstrual flow to her climacteric a woman retired to a menstrual lodge every month for a few days.   An excellent account of Winnebago customs in this respect was obtained in a text from a male informant, and, although somewhat discursive, it is given in full here:

As soon as a woman begins to have her menstrual flow she has to retire to a menstrual lodge and to be careful never to come in contact with any sacred objects. If she did, these objects would all lose their power. Everything that is holy would immediately lose its power if a menstruating woman came near it. A holy woman or a holy man or even a holy child would be affected by the proximity of a menstruating woman. Their holy condition would immediately disappear. In a similar way, if food were served to a sick person from the same dish used for a menstruating woman the sick person would become far more sick.

The food for a menstruating person is always cooked separately. Special dishes are used and special fireplaces are made.

If a person possessed any medicines, they would lose all their power if a menstruating woman came in contact with them. If any person should enter a menstrual lodge, in after life, whenever he fasted, he would not be blessed by any spirit. However, there is one thing that a menstruating woman is afraid of, and that is the war bundle. These war bundles are kept in cedar [leaves?] mixed with medicine to prevent danger from just such a source. If a menstruating woman comes near a war bundle, her flow would increase and never cease, and after a while she would die,[5] and only if the owner of the war bundle personally attends to her can she be cured. For that reason whenever a war-bundle feast is being given a woman is very careful, and even if it is a few days before her menstrual flow she will not go.

---

[5] This explains what puzzled the author for some time—namely, the fact that although contact with a menstruating woman destroyed the efficacy of everything holy, in the case of the war bundle the reverse was true and the woman was destroyed. Many of the Indians who spoke of this matter also seemed to believe it was the war bundle that killed the woman. From this account, however, it is perfectly clear that it is not the war bundle at all that killed the woman, but the poison in which the war bundle was wrapped. The war bundle is therefore no exception to the general rule, and it is only on account of the serious consequences that would accrue to so many people from any impairment of its powers, and the care taken to prevent this by surrounding it with special medicines, that it offers externally an exception to the fatal effects of contact with a menstruating woman.

The menstrual lodge is never far from the lodge in which she lives. Indeed, it is within speaking distance, so that the occupants of her parents' lodge can hear her. All the utensils she uses are very small. The women stay from 4 to 10 days in the menstrual lodges. The older women stay out the shorter time because they are over it sooner.

It is said that if the young girls have any lovers they always come to the menstrual lodges at night. This is therefore the time for wooing. It is said that the girls cohabit with their lovers in these menstrual lodges. Those girls who have parents are attended by watchers, so that no unworthy men may visit them. They are especially guarded against ugly men, who are very likely to have love medicines. However, generally it is of no avail to struggle against such men, for they are invincible.

The women always take their blankets with them when they go to a menstrual lodge, for they never lie down but remain in a sitting-posture, wrapped in their blankets. The women are always watched, so that when their menstrual flow comes everything is in readiness and lodge poles are placed around them and a lodge erected above their heads just about large enough to fit their body. They are not permitted to look upon the daylight nor upon any individual. If they were to look out during the day the weather would become very bad, and if they were to look at the blue sky it would become cloudy and rain. If they looked at anyone that person would become unfortunate. For four days they do not eat or drink anything; not even water do they drink. They fast all the time. Not even their own body do they touch with their hands. If they ever have any need of touching their bodies they use a stick. If they were to use their hands in touching their own body their bones would be attacked with fever. If they were to scratch their hands their heads would ache. After the fourth day they bathe in sight of their home. Then they return to their homes and eat. (This, of course, holds only for those whose menstrual flow ceases in four days.) If any women have to stay longer than four days they have to fast for that entire period. They always fast during this period and often some spirits bless them. When a woman who has stayed in the menstrual lodge for 10 days is ready to return to her lodge, she bathes herself and puts on an entirely new suit of clothes. Then her home is purified with red-cedar leaves and all the sacred bundles and medicines removed. Only then can she enter her parents' lodge. As soon as she returns to her parents' lodge after her first menstrual flow she is regarded as ready to be wooed and married.

Thus the teacher of our customs, the Hare, has willed it. At a feast all the young girls nearing the age of puberty will be absent, but the old women, who have passed their climacteric, sit right next to the men, because they are considered the same as men as they have no menstrual flow any more.

If the Winnebago can be said to be afraid of any one thing it may be said it is this—the menstrual flow of women—for even the spirits die of its effects.

If the above account may be taken as a fairly accurate description of the customs connected with the menstrual lodge as they existed in former times, then one point must be regarded as of great interest, namely, that the women permitted their lovers to meet them there. So far as is known to the author, among other tribes having menstrual lodges it would have been considered a crime for any man to come near them. According to our informant the women were indeed guarded while they were in the menstrual lodges, but not so much to protect them against the intrusion of all men, as against the intrusion of unworthy men. From other information obtained, however, it appears that women were married to these same lovers after the former left the menstrual lodge, so that the presence of men in these lodges may be taken either as a part of the wooing or as one of the methods of marriage. Some theorists may be inclined to look on this feature of the practices connected with the menstrual lodge as a survival of a "women's house." To those the fact may be emphasized that it is only a few times in the life of a woman that such a feature exists, because she is married shortly after leaving the lodge. [6]

MARRIAGE

Girls were usually married as soon as they reached marriageable age, and the same was probably true of men. In most cases marriage was arranged by the parents of the young people, and it rarely happened that the latter refused to abide by the decision—a fact that seems to have been due not so much to implicit obedience as to the wise precautions taken by the parents in mating their children. If, however, the young people absolutely refused to abide by their parents' choice, the latter always yielded. In former times children were betrothed to each other at an early age. At the betrothal presents were exchanged between the parents of the prospective bride and groom. The girl was said to be *dohore'na*.

Generally a man took but one wife, although he was permitted to marry more than one if he wished. In polygamous marriages the second wife was usually a niece or a sister of the first wife. According to a very reliable informant it was the wife herself who often induced her husband to marry her own niece. This she did if she noticed that he was getting tired of her or losing his interest in her.[7]

There was no ceremony connected with marriage. As soon as the customary presents were exchanged, the man came to the woman's lodge and the marriage was consummated.

A man generally lived with his parents-in-law during the first two years after his marriage. During these two years he was practically the servant of his father-in-law, hunting, fishing, and performing minor services for him. Many Winnebago interpreted these enforced services of a son-in-law as part of his marriage obligations toward his father-in-law. After the first two years he returned to

---

[6] Were it not for the fact that his informant in this case was exceedingly reliable the writer would be inclined to regard with suspicion the statement as to the use of the menstrual lodge as a rendezvous for lovers. It seems, however, that the very fact that the informant shows so great abhorrence of the menses would have prevented him from attributing to men intimacy with women at this time had there been any doubt in his mind on the subject. Nevertheless his statement on the point under discussion seems peculiar and the author would not be surprised if he had exaggerated greatly the number of men willing to brave the bad luck and weakness incident on contact with women during the menstrual period.

[7] As one of my informants said, "A man can marry a woman and her niece. If the man is not steady and goes around with other women, it is customary for the wife to call her niece, and she would marry her aunt's husband. This is done to steady the man. In this way one or the other will always be with him. The same is true of sisters."

his father's lodge, where his seat had always been kept for him. With his own folks he stayed as long as he wished, leaving it generally as soon as he decided to live alone—a decision that was usually reached as soon as he had one child or a number of children. However, he did not always build his own lodge, especially in the olden times, when it was customary for those Winnebago who lived in permanent villages to occupy the long gable-roofed lodges, that frequently were large enough to house as many as 40 people. In such cases a man and his family generally alternated between his parents-in-law and his own parents.

ADOPTION

Adoption of individuals was quite frequent in former times. As far as the writer knows, however, it always took the form of replacing of a deceased child by some other child physically resembling the one lost. I do not know whether there were any additional considerations if the child adopted happened to be a prisoner. As the name for adoption (*wanaŋxe'rek'inaŋk*) indicates, it is closely connected with the common belief in reincarnation, meaning either the exchange of one spirit for another or the replacing of the spirit. A special feast could be given for adoption or it could be done at one of the regular feasts. As the child adopted was often the "friend" (*hitcak'â'ro*) of the deceased and in any case had parents living, presents were always given to his parents.

Perhaps a better idea of the nature of adoption can be obtained from the following few words of an informant:

When a child dies, then the father mourns for many years, and if during that time he happens to meet a child that resembles his dead child he asks to be allowed to adopt him. The parents of the child can hardly object to such a request.[8]

---

[8] There is no doubt in my mind that quite a number of parents believe that such a person is really their reincarnated child.

CHAPTER V

BURIAL AND FUNERAL CUSTOMS

There appear to have been two distinct methods of burial among the Winnebago—simple inhumation and platform burial. Within recent times, owing to the influence of their Algonquian neighbors, platform burial has entirely disappeared and inhumation alone is practiced. It has even become customary to erect a typical Algonquian burial-hut over the grave (see pl. 54, *b*).

When the old culture was still intact inhumation was definitely associated with the lower phratry and platform burial with the upper phratry. Whether this marked difference in burial customs was merely another example of that specialization in function so characteristic of these two divisions of the tribe, or whether it was due to distinct historical origins, it is difficult to determine. I am, however, inclined to regard the latter interpretation as by far the most probable.

All the customs are described in full detail in the various accounts that follow and in Chapters VII and VIII. Each clan seems to have had a few details peculiar to itself, but, in the main, the rights were identical. They may briefly be divided into the following sections: 1. Preparation of the body for burial. 2. Rites in the house of the deceased, consisting mainly of speeches of consolation to the bereaved. 3. Speeches addressed to the deceased and the narration of the myth of the journey to spirit land. 4. Rites at the grave. 5. The recounting of war exploits by specially invited warriors, at the grave. 6. The elaborate four nights wake at the home of the deceased.

DESCRIPTION OF FUNERAL CUSTOMS AND WAKE

Informant, member of the Thunderbird clan:[1] When an individual dies his relatives get some one to bury him and the chief mourner will also invite some person to talk to the corpse before it is buried. The person addressing the dead man or woman tells the deceased how he is to go (to spirit land) and what he is to do on the way there. The body is then dressed by the person who is going to bury it. All the relatives come to the lodge and the deceased is dressed in his best clothes; beads are put around his neck, bracelets on his wrist, rings

---

[1] This description is a generalized one.

140

on his fingers, and earrings in his ears. The body is then put in the casket.

By the time this is all finished the gravediggers have about completed their work. Then the mourners blacken their faces with charcoal and the corpse is taken up by the man to whom this duty is delegated. The mourners follow behind, weeping. Thus they proceed to the grave. When they get there the corpse is laid in the grave. Then the chief mourner steps across the center of the grave and the others do the same. When they start back, they are told under no circumstance to turn around and look in the direction of the grave.

The grave is then filled in.

Then the overseer goes around to the various people in the village and invites them all to come to (the wake). The brave men and warriors are especially welcomed.

The mourners prepare food and when the sun goes down the chief mourner takes a stick made of hard wood and lights it and carries it to the grave, placing it at the east end. It is supposed to be still burning when placed there. After this is done (the man returns) and the overseer gets everything in readiness for the feast. When all is ready the chief mourner speaks as follows:

All my relatives who are sitting here, I greet you. I have done nothing of any consequence which could justify you to come here and honor me, yet being relatives of mine, you have (in the kindness of your hearts) come to comfort me. I have prepared cooked food and boiled water for my child (the dead person), and tobacco is also handy, all of which the attendant when he is ready will pass around to all and give to whomsoever he pleases. That is why I am greeting you.

Then the attendant takes the water and tobacco and gives it to the one who is to speak to the soul of the departed person. This one then rises and greets all those present and speaks as follows:

To-night we are greeting you not for the sake of jollification, but because we are afflicted (with grief). Now, it is the custom to speak to the soul of the departed. It is a sacred action, yet even I, they tell me, can do it, provided no worthier person can be found. They [2] even tell me that my words will not cause the spirit of the departed to lose his way in his journey (to spirit land).[3] For that reason I will speak to the departed and say the best I can. I greet you all.

Then he takes some tobacco in one hand and passing it behind him through the lodge says:

Here it is, the tobacco. I am certain that you, O ghost, are not very far away, that in fact you are standing right in back of me, waiting for me to reach you the pipe and tobacco, that you might take it along with you, that likewise, you are waiting for your food to take on your journey. However, four nights you will have to remain here.

---

[2] This and what follows is the customary ceremonial modesty.

[3] It is believed that if the chief speaker makes a mistake or exaggerates while thus addressing the spirit of the deceased, the latter will lose his way in his journey to spirit land.

Now here are these things, and in return we ask you to act as mediator (between the spirits and us). You have made us long for you, and therefore do you see to it that all those things that belonged to you and that you would have enjoyed had you lived longer—such as victories on the warpath, earthly possessions, and life—that all these you leave behind for us to enjoy. This do you ask for as you travel along. This also I ask of you, do not cause us to follow you soon; do not cause your brothers any fear. I have now lit the pipe for you.

Then the pipe is passed on to all those present. After that he drinks a little water and passes it around again. It is only after the pipe and water have passed all the way around that the people begin to eat. When the meal is over, the attendant takes the pipe and some tobacco and places it before a warrior and tells him to talk to the spirit and tell him the route to take.

Then the warrior rises and speaks as follows:

Ho, I greet you all. We are not greeting one another because we are happy (as in the case of an ordinary feast), but because it is the custom to do it. Now I will tell the soul of the departed one the route to take and the care he must observe in his journey. I shall tell them (the ghosts) over whom I have control to guide him safely to his destination. I will not exaggerate when I relate my war exploits, but tell only those things that really happened to me. It has been said that if, in talking, I tell falsehoods the spirit of the departed would stumble on the road.[4] So, therefore, I will tell only the truth, and I will tell the chief of the spirits to guide our dead one safely over all the obstacles. Now I am not going to speak of anybody else's exploits, but only of my own. Only those over whom I have control will I put at the disposal of our dead one to guide him. The spirit-tobacco, the spirit-food and fire, they will carry for him, and they will lead him by the hand until he reaches his destination. I greet you all.

Then he begins an account of his war exploits. He tells all that he did in detail. Sometimes the account of a war exploit would last two to three hours. When he is through, the people retire for the night.

For three nights they do this and every evening they place a burning ember at the grave. This is supposed to be taken by the spirit of the dead man on his journey.

The fourth night they invite all the brave men in the neighborhood and everybody else. They prepare plenty of food, and the relatives of the mourners bring objects for the mourning games and try to comfort the mourners as best they can. The fourth night, likewise, they place a burning ember at the grave of the dead man.

As soon as the attendant prepares the food the chief mourner gets up and speaks as follows:

I greet you all. I know that I am not performing any great action in greeting you,[5] but I was in trouble, and all my relatives have come to comfort me. I feel strengthened by their actions. You all have asked me to live (not to succumb to my sorrows),

---

[4] It is believed that a warrior is in control of the spirits of all the people he has killed. His function at the wake is to put these spirits at the disposal of the dead man, to guide him, and to take care of him.

[5] I. e., if I were a great man and this were a ceremony of rejoicing, then a greeting would mean something. This is another example of ceremonial modesty.

and I shall try to overcome my grief and sorrow. I will not forget all the good you have done for me. You have been a comfort to me and you have helped me in many things. Now this is the last night, and I am glad that it is a good night for the warriors to relate their experiences. If they should say anything funny, I hope that you will not hold back your laughter. I, too, will laugh with you. You are free to make all the noise you care to, for I will feel all the better if you do it. This is what I want you to remember. I greet you all who are present here.

Then the one who is to address the spirit speaks:

I greet you all. We have come to this (wake) for a purpose, much as we would wish that the occasion for it had never happened. Now I will tell the spirit of the departed the route he is to take, nor will I, by my words, cause him to go astray. On an occasion like this not everyone can talk to spirits (spirits of departed people); not everyone can do it. My grandfather obtained the right to speak to them and handed it down to my father, and he in turn gave it to me. Now I will tell the spirit of the departed the right road to take and I will not cause him to stumble. I shall breathe upon the spirit of the departed, and I wish all those present to do the same. It is said that for those who do not make this sound it is a sign that they will die soon. Now all of you say it.

Then he says "ha-a" and "ha-a," and all join with him in repeating it.

Then he speaks again (addressing the spirit of the departed):

I suppose you are not far away, that indeed you are right behind me. Here is the tobacco and here is the pipe which you must keep in front of you as you go along. Here also is the fire and the food which your relatives have prepared for your journey. In the morning when the sun rises you are to start. You will not have gone very far before you come to a wide road. That is the road you must take. As you go along you will notice something on your road. Take your war club and strike it and throw it behind you. Then go on without looking back. As you go farther you will again come across (some obstacle). Strike it and throw it behind you and do not look back. Farther on you will come across some animals, and these also you must strike and throw behind you. Then go on and do not look back. The objects you throw behind you will come to those relatives whom you have left behind you on earth. They will represent victory in war, riches, and animals for food. When you have gone but a short distance from the last place where you threw objects behind, you will come to a round lodge and there you will find an old woman. She is the one who is to give you further information. She will ask you, "Grandson, what is your name?" This you must tell her. Then (you must say), "Grandmother, when I was about to start from the earth I was given the following objects with which I was to act as mediator between you and the human beings (i. e., the pipe, tobacco, and food)." Then you must put the stem of the pipe in the old woman's mouth and say, "Grandmother, I have made all my relatives lonesome, my parents, my brothers, and all the others. I would therefore like to have them obtain victory in war and honors. That was my desire as I left them downhearted upon the earth. I would that they could have all that life which I left behind me on earth.[6] This is what they asked. This likewise they asked me, that they should not have to travel on this road for some time to come. They also asked to be blessed with those things that people are accustomed to have on earth. All this they wanted me to ask of you when I started from the earth.

---

[6] The deceased had apparently died young, and what he desires is that the difference between his years and the normal length of life be distributed among his relatives. He means not only the actual years but also whatever he would have accomplished in those years.

"They told me to follow the four steps that would be imprinted with blue marks, grandmother." "Well, grandson, you are young but you are wise. It is good. I will now boil some food for you."

Thus she will speak to you and then put a kettle on the fire and boil some rice for you. If you eat it you will have a headache. Then she will say, "Grandson, you have a headache, let me cup it for you." Then she will break open your skull and take out your brains and you will forget all about your people on earth and where you came from. You will not worry about your relatives. You will become like a holy spirit. Your thoughts will not go as far as the earth, as there will be nothing carnal about you.

Now the rice that the old woman will boil will really be lice. For that reason you will be finished with everything evil. Then you will go on stepping in the four footsteps mentioned before and that were imprinted with blue earth. You are to take the four steps because the road will fork there. All your relatives (who died before you) will be there. As you journey on you will come to a fire running across the earth from one end to the other. There will be a bridge across it but it will be difficult to cross because it is continually swinging. However, you will be able to cross it safely, for you have all the guides about whom the warriors spoke to you. They will take you over and take care of you.

Well, we have told you a good road (to take). If anyone tells a falsehood in speaking of the spirit road, you will fall off the bridge and be burned. However (you need not worry) for you will pass over safely. As you proceed from that place the spirits will come to meet you and take you to the village where the chief lives. There you will give him the tobacco and ask for those objects of which we spoke to you, the same you asked of the old woman. There you will meet all the relatives that died before you. They will be living in a large lodge. This you must enter. Ho-o-o, ha-a-a.

GENERALIZED DESCRIPTION OF FUNERAL CUSTOMS AND WAKE

Informant, member of Bear clan. When a person died a member of his friend (*hitcakâro*) clan was immediately sent for, who took charge of the body and of all the funeral arrangements. The overseer dressed the deceased in his best clothes and all his finery, for it was said that he was going on a long journey. Then some clansman painted the dead man's face with the clan markings and delivered a speech to the corpse. When he concluded the clan songs were sung and the body was carried to the grave. All the mourners marched in single file. After the body had been buried or placed on a scaffold, as the case might be, a post was placed at the head of the grave, and the warriors among the mourners counted their coups and drew representations of their victories on the posts. The purpose of the warriors in counting coups at the grave was to put at the disposal of the deceased the spirits of all the enemies they had killed, and also to give him additional strength for overcoming the obstacles on the road to the spirit land. Food was placed on the little shelf in front of the window of the grave-house, to be used by the spirit during the four days that he hovered around this earth before departing on his journey. Then a light was lighted and finally, toward evening, all departed for their homes, returning as they had come, in single file, and being very careful not to look back toward the grave after they had first started.

The same evening the four nights' wake began. The overseer, who was in full charge, had everything prepared. Before the wake formally commenced the chief mourner made a short speech. Then the overseer lighted a pipe and passed it around to all, who took a puff each and returned it to him. Then sweetened water was passed around, of which all partook. The feast followed. Taking on a plate a small portion of all the food to be eaten, the overseer threw it outside for the spirit of the deceased. In the case of a nursling the mother added a small quantity of milk from her breast to the other food on the plate. After the feast the chief mourner made another speech, explaining why the rites were performed and how they had been handed down for many generations. He concluded by thanking the people for all they had done for him.

There was always an abundance of tobacco at a wake. Most of it was given to the warriors, a number of whom were invited, for they played a very important rôle on such an occasion. It was believed that every warrior was in control of the spirit of an enemy he had slain and he was supposed always to be willing to put the spirit at the service of any member of his tribe who had just died, if the proper offerings were made. At the proper time tobacco was given to the warrior, who, rising, narrated his war exploits, at the conclusion of which he ordered the spirit of the enemy he had slain to take charge of the deceased. Then tobacco was given to another warrior, who followed the same procedure, which was continued until midnight. Then most of the people departed to their homes, but some stayed overnight in the lodge in which the wake was held.

The proceedings of the second and third nights of the wake were exactly the same as those of the first, but somewhat longer. The beginning of the ceremony on the fourth night was the same as on the three preceding nights; after a while, however, it deviated in the following manner.

J. F., rising, tells the spirit of the departed the road he is to take in his journey to spirit land, the obstacles he is to meet, and how he is to overcome them. After he has finished the warriors begin to tell some more war exploits, and this continues generally until 3 o'clock in the morning, depending entirely upon the amount of gifts given to the warriors. The gifts generally consist either of 12 pieces of calico each 3 yards, or of beads, or of 12 quarter dollars. The warriors always gamble for these gifts and play the favorite game of the deceased. If a man had died they generally play moccasins; if a woman, ka^nsu. When all the presents have been exhausted, then the relatives of the deceased comb the mourner's hair, give him presents, and tell him that he is now free to cease mourning and to marry if he wishes.

In former times the period of mourning is supposed to have lasted four years.

When a person is in mourning he always cuts his hair short and does not comb his hair. In former times people often mutilated themselves by cutting off either entire fingers or finger joints.

The overseer always takes all the belongings of the deceased, but he must give the latter's relatives an equal amount of new material.

FUNERAL CUSTOMS OF THE THUNDERBIRD CLAN

(FIRST VERSION)

Informant, member of the clan When a member of the clan dies they send after a man of the Thunderbird clan who is to speak to the corpse, paint it, and give him a war club to take along with him (to the land of the spirits). Then they go after a man from the lower phratry to bury him, for these clans (of the lower phratry) belong on earth and they have the right to dig into the ground and bury people.

When the one who is to be the general overseer arrives and arranges everything, he prepares the corpse, putting a sack of tobacco in one hand and a war club in the other. Then he paints him. He paints the forehead with a red and a black mark and paints the lower part of the face to the end of the nose with scattered dots. He paints the jaw red and he makes a red mark across the mouth and the throat. Then he speaks as follows:

You have departed at this (young) age. You have taken your relatives by surprise and have left them a long part of your life (i. e., you have lived but a small part of your apportioned share of years). As you go to spirit land, you will find on the road many feathers, many good plants, and many good kinds of clay, scattered around, the blue clay, the red clay, and the white clay. You will also find the sweet-smelling plants and good life. For all these things do you ask. If anything comes across your path, throw it behind you without looking around. In four days you will depart and objects with which to mediate between us and the spirits will soon be furnished you. For four nights your people will tell you what to do and when they hear you singing on the road they will know that it is you. There (in spirit land) you will go to live and the songs that I will sing you will sing as you travel on your road.

Then he sings (the four clan songs).

When the gravediggers are finished they take the body and carry it to the grave, the mourners following. They take the body to the grave and there lower it.

DEATH AND FUNERAL CUSTOMS OF THE THUNDERBIRD CLAN

(SECOND VERSION)

Informant, member of the clan. When a member of the Thunderbird clan dies, the clansmen discuss what is to be done for the spirit of the deceased. Then they go and call the leader of their band and he comes and addresses the body as follows:

You are about to leave all your relatives. They will remain on earth, objects of pity to all. You will proceed on your road, turning to your left after you start until you come to him who is in charge of the spirits. Whenever you see him, the following request do we wish you to make of him, namely, that he bestow upon us all that you fell short of in your life on this earth. The means of offering, the tobacco, which Earthmaker gave us, we have given you some to take along. As you go along the road you will come to a place where the road branches off. Do not turn to the right, for that road leads to the bad spirits. Turn to the left and soon you will come to a guard. Point your pipe at him and he will be thankful. This man will have a complete suit of clothes and he will look terror-inspiring. He will smoke with you and then you may speak to him as follows: "Grandfather, before I left the earth, the people told me to ask you to point out to me which road I should travel in." Then he will tell you and you will pass ahead and after a while you will come to a fire-girdle. The man who is in charge of it will have a complete suit of clothes just like the first man. Point the stem of your pipe toward him and he will be very thankful and smoke with you. Then make your request, namely, to be permitted to pass, and he will grant it. As you go along after that you will come to a round lodge in which you will find an old woman. Point your pipe at her and she will be thankful and smoke it, and then ask her to let you pass and she will permit you to go ahead. Your hair will now be white but you will not be unconscious. On the contrary, you will have complete possession of all your senses. Then you will come to where he who is in control of spirits sits.· Go to him and point your pipe toward him. Then when he is smoking it, ask him to show you the road to Earthmaker, our father, and he will point it out to you. Then you must proceed until you come to Earthmaker. When you get to him, point the stem of your pipe toward him and, if he takes it and smokes it, then you must say, "Earthmaker, my father, you know very well what kind of a life I have led." And he will answer, "You have done well, my son."

The informant then skips to the opening night of the four nights' wake. The address to the spirit that follows is probably delivered by the chief mourner before the formal opening of the wake.

Address to the spirit.[7]—Ha ho-o-o-o, I want you to listen, you who have become like a spirit. You have made those of your relatives who remained behind on earth miserable and lonely. They have given you much food to take along with you and they have given you a pipe and some tobacco so that you may offer them to the spirits you meet on your road and make some requests of them. The first request that they wish you to make is to ask the spirits to distribute to your clan all the successful warpaths which would have fallen to your share had you lived your normal quota of years; and that all the food, etc., that you have not used be bestowed upon those whom you left behind on earth. The last request you should make of those on the road is to pray that a long time may elapse before any of your relatives traverse this road.

Now follows a description of the obstacles to be met on the road.

When you reach Earthmaker, offer him your pipe, and if he accepts it speak to him as follows: "Grandfather, as I was leaving the earth my relatives asked me to request of you humbly that you bestow upon the clansmen that I left behind me all that I would have accomplished had I lived longer. Now this is what I wished to ask of you, grandfather." Thus you should speak: "Ha ho-o-o-o."

[7] Spirit here is *waxop'ini*, spirit, deity, not *naɣɣidak'*, ghost, noncorporeal embodiment. What is meant is that the deceased has become like one of the spirits, in that he lives, enjoys consciousness, etc., without at the same time having any corporeal existence.

Then all the other people answer *ha-ho-o-o-o*. Now someone lights a pipe and passes it around so that everyone can take a puff. All take a puff, children and women as well as men. After that water is passed around. Then all eat. A little portion of everything served is put aside and thrown out for the spirit to eat. Then a warrior, the person who has charge of the wake, speaks:

> I greet you all. I first wish to pour some of the tobacco that you have offered me for our grandfather who is in control of war-giving powers. (Probably the Thunderbirds are meant.) I will tell the spirit as carefully as I can all that I know about the road he must travel. My father impressed upon me very earnestly the need of being very truthful in speaking to the spirit of one recently deceased, for if I were a bad man I would cause the spirit to stumble. For that reason I always feel that I ought not to speak very much whenever I am called upon to talk.

Then a warrior was called upon to tell of his war exploits. He told as accurately as it was possible how he had killed a man, broken his collar bone, and then flayed him; how he had then chopped and cut up his body and mutilated him in such a way that he could not be identified; and how finally he had stolen his dogs. All night he spoke in this strain. He went on to tell how he had killed and utterly destroyed an entire village so that no one was left to tell of the massacre. All night he told of his war exploits. Thus they lighted the road for the spirit (i. e., held the Four Nights' Wake).

The second and third nights were just the same as the first, only that different warriors spoke and different war exploits were told. They are very proud of their war exploits and they would try to tell of their bravest deeds, those that had been most dangerous and which had required the greatest heroism. When the mourners listen to the narrative of such an exploit they become strengthened. All those people on whom the warrior had counted first coup and all those whom he had killed would carry the light for the spirit of the deceased. Those on whom he had counted second coup were commanded to clear the road, and a woman whom the warrior had captured was ordered to carry along the food. The ceremonies of the fourth night are the same as those of the first three nights.

DEATH AND FUNERAL CUSTOMS OF THE BEAR CLAN [8]

Informant, member of the clan. Mr. J. M. died in June, 1911. In accordance with the old Winnebago customs, the first individual to be notified of the death was Mr. J. F., a member of the Wolf clan. To Mr. F. fell the lot of taking charge of all the funeral rites—dressing the deceased, laying his body in the casket, burying him, and, finally, conducting the elaborate funeral wake.

---

[8] This is practically a reprint of "Description of a Winnebago Funeral," by Lamere and Radin, Amer. Anthrop., n. s. vol. 13, no. 3, 1911.

One of Mr. F.'s most important duties was to invite the warriors to extend invitations to all those who wish to participate in the feast. After the body has been buried the overseer goes to the home of the deceased and takes away all those things with which the deceased had been in daily contact.

In addition to F., another man was sent for, Mr. A. W., also a member of the Bear clan. He went through the Bear clan ceremony, which was as follows: When the deceased was fully dressed, just before he was to be laid in the casket, A. W. walked up to him and, taking some paint from a little bundle he carried, he painted a red mark across his forehead, then a black one immediately below this one, and finally daubed the whole chin red. When he was through with this preliminary work he addressed those present as follows:

You relatives, all that are seated here, I greet you. This ceremony is not anything that we have originated ourselves, but it was known to be the proper thing to do by our ancestors. It is for that reason that I have made the markings upon the face of my son in order that he may be recognized by his relatives in spirit land; and I have also given him the material with which he may talk, i. e., tobacco, that with it he may entreat the spirits to bestow all those years that he fell short of upon his relatives still living.

Now, it is said that the members of the Bear clan hold death as a blessing and not as anything to mourn about. I do not mean that I do not feel sorry for the children of the deceased and that I rejoice in his death, but it is the belief of the members of the Bear clan that the same happiness comes to them at death that comes to us during life when a bear is killed and brought to the village for food.

For now, indeed, my son will walk in a road that has been cleared of all obstacles and his claws will be sharp, and his teeth will be sharp, and nothing, indeed, will cross his path. And in this, his walk to the spirit land, may he tread down upon us the life that he has fallen short of on this earth. And he will walk just as the original Bear clansmen walked when they originated and when they approached the earth. And now I will sing him the songs that they sang as they came on earth, so that he may take them along with him on his journey to the spirit land. It is said that there is no other place besides this prepared for us in the hereafter.

Then he sang the four clan songs.

When the songs had been sung, it was just about noon and, as dinner was ready, we all sat down and A. W. filled a pipe and when he was ready to smoke it began to speak again to the following effect:

Relatives, all that are present, I greet you. It is good that this many of you have come here, and it is said that the soul of the deceased remains hovering around about this place four days and that we should partake of food with him for that period. It is for that reason that we act in this way. And it is good that this many of you have come here and have helped us out with food and dress.

He then mentioned the things that had been given by different individuals. Then he lit a pipe and took a few puffs and sent it around to all the others in the lodge. Then a pitcher of water was passed around from which we all took a sip.

During the morning Mrs. R. came in and combed the hair of the deceased's wife and gave her some presents, telling her at the same time that she hoped that she would dry her tears as a sign of appreciation of the gifts. Another person came in in the morning bringing a pair of leggings and a blanket for the deceased. He also brought the casket. While the body of the deceased was being prepared this same person spoke as follows:

Relatives, all that are present, I greet you. If my nephews will come here and sit near me, I will talk to them.

Then the sons of the deceased came and sat near their mother and sisters and the man continued:

My sister, it is said that it is best for a person not to weep; and that a widow should not mourn too much, for then the people would make fun of her; as well as for the fact that having children she must for their sake look forward to life and live for them. And it is also said that we should keep up this mourning for at least four years. Now there is nothing amusing about what I am going to say (although it may sound so)— namely, that we should not cry on such an occasion as to-day, but, on the contrary, keep up a good spirit. I do not mean that I am glad that my brother-in-law is dead. But if you were to weep some one might come in and say that it behooves you more to show him your teeth than your tears. They mean that you should smile.

And again it is said that one should not cry, for when a body is laid in the ground there is no more hope of its ever returning to this earth again. My nephew, the one that had been advising you in your daily affairs, is gone and you are left alone to look after yourself, your little brothers, and your mother; and therefore I want you all to love ane another and remember your mother.

While we were eating C. P. came in and spoke as follows:

Relatives, all that are present, I greet you. It is good that you all have come here and are comforting this house of mourning. It is good that J. H. has brought a casket and clothing for the deceased and food for the wake. And indeed he has also promised a hog for the feast. I know that he did not do this in order to have some one speak of it in public, but how can I refrain from expressing my thanks? My brother also came with the intention of furnishing some of these things, but inasmuch as J. H. has furnished them beforehand he placed ten dollars in the hands of the wife of the deceased. He did not, however, tell her for what purpose he gave her the money and I therefore take the liberty of telling her that the gift is meant for anything that she may desire to buy. Now, my relatives, this is no time for happiness, but I am glad, nevertheless, that so many have come and I am thankful for what you have done. I greet you all.

Then the casket was put in the spring wagon and taken to the Winnebago Cemetery. When we got there the casket was lowered into the grave. When this was over, A. W. spoke as follows:

Relatives, all that are present, I greet you. This many of you have followed my son to his last resting place. Further than this place he will not walk in this life. Truly this many of you have felt sorry for him. All the rites that were taught me in this connection I have already performed. I have given the deceased the emblem (i. e., the whittled stick known as *namanxinixini*) and the material to talk with (the tobacco), so that he may plead for us, his relatives, when he gets to the end of the journey, that we may live the life he fell short of upon this earth, and that he may tread firmly upon us as he walks to the spirit land. All that I know I have said before. I was taught nothing that I was to do or say at this place except that we should step over the grave just as our forefathers did when they originated. They were holy and they entered this life on a perfect day just as this day to-day, and, inasmuch as they were holy, all the ground that they touched was holy. It is for that reason that we should step over the grave.

Then we stepped over the grave. After that we went to our homes.

The same evening the wake began. When all the invited guests had arrived and were seated, the feast was spread before them. Then A. W. spoke as follows:

Relatives, all that are seated here, I greet you. It is good that this many of you have come to-night. You know that we are not creating any new ceremony, but are simply following up what our forefathers have learned to be true and good. And, as it is said that we should not weep aloud, therefore you will not hear any of us making any utterings of sorrow. And even though we weep silently should anyone come to us we will look upon them smiling. We therefore beg of you, should you find us happy in mood, not to think the worse of us. And now I am ready to turn over the tobacco and water to J. F. Thus I express my thanks to you all that are present.

Then J. F. took the tobacco and water and spoke as follows:

Relatives, all that are seated here, I greet you. It is good that so many of you have come to our humble affair and, as our ancestors said that this was the proper way to do, so I am glad that it was given to me to handle the corpse, as I am certain that I will be strengthened by it. I will now pass the tobacco to Mr. X. He is a brave man and he will light the pipe and pass the water before we eat and after supper he will tell the deceased a route to the spirit land. Now I thank you and I greet you.

Then the brave man took the tobacco and filled the pipe and after taking a few puffs from it, passed it to the left and it thus went round, each person taking a puff from the pipe and a sip from the pitcher of water. Then the feast began. When it was over and all the dishes were cleared away, and everyone was properly seated, then the brave man greeted them again:

Relatives, I greet you. As we are not creating anything new, and as our ancestors knew it to be good, and as it is said that if anyone exaggerates a story in a case like this it will cause the soul to stumble, therefore I will tell my war exploits to my relative (the deceased) exactly as I remember them. I greet you all.

He then proceeded to tell his war exploits. When he had finished he again spoke as follows:

Relatives that are present, I greet you. As I said before, I do not wish to cause the soul of my recently deceased relative to stumble and I have tried to tell my story as accurately as I could. It is said that the souls of the ones killed in a battle are at the mercy of the victor, and I therefore command the souls of the ones I have killed to lead and guide my relative safely through the spirit land. I greet you all.

He then passed the tobacco to another brave man present who in his turn greeted those present and related his war exploits. After two warriors had told their war exploits they stopped for the night, to continue on the second night. The second and third nights were the same as the first. About the evening of the fourth night, when all the people invited were present, A. W. spoke in the same strain as on the first night, and when he had finished he passed the management of the feast to J. F. The latter then passed it to F. F. now lit the pipe and passed it around, together with the water. Then all partook of the feast. After supper A. W. reported all the donations that were made to them, naming each giver and the amount of the gift and thanking them and praising them for their generous gifts. Then F. told the following story:

THE JOURNEY OF THE SOUL TO SPIRIT LAND [9]

Ho! Ha! Are you all ready? I am going to speak about the four nights during which you listened to your relatives and to the words they had to say. I am placing the sacrificial tobacco in the rear part of the lodge for you. As you go home do not look back. Before you are far away you will come to a lodge. You may enter this lodge. A door faces the rising sun and a door faces the setting sun. As you enter you will find a woman on your right. Go and sit down opposite her. Then your great-grandmother will say to you, "My great-grandchild, what did they say to you when you were leaving, when your life was over?" "My great-grandmother, as I listened to my beloved relatives they said very little indeed. They said that I was breaking their hearts (in leaving them), and that they hoped that none would follow me soon. Then they asked me to make four requests:

"First. I was to ask for life, that the flames from the lodge fires might go straight upward. Yet they were satisfied if at my departure the flames swayed to and fro.

"Second. Whatever fruit had been predestined for me and that I did not taste, my relatives should hereafter not be deprived of.

"Third. They also mentioned nuts, all manner of herbs, all serviceable hides and skins, all medicinal roots and grasses. They commanded me to make a request for all things that exist in the earth.

"Fourth. That if anyone has a friend his weapon might have a keen edge on one side. Now, my great-grandmother, this is the number of requests they commanded me to make."

"My great-grandchild, although you are young, you are wise. My great-grandchild, my lodge is a place where all who enter must pass an examination. Earthmaker looks upon it as a keen-edged instrument. No clouds of ill omen ever pass over it. Now, my grandchild, as to those four requests you put to me, it shall be as you say. The nuts and herbs you have requested shall be given you. There will be nothing of that food predestined for you that your relatives will not taste. The hides and skins, the grasses they will possess in plenty. And if they have friends their weapons will be keen on one side. All that they have requested through you shall be given them. Here is the food set before you in this wooden bowl."

Then you are to answer to her, "My grandmother, this was what my relatives longed for. These are the things I was to leave behind me for those on earth."

Now, be sure that you only take a taste and push the dish away from you. For then the old woman will say, "My great-grandchild, all that you have left behind you in that dish represents the vegetable kingdom on this earth. Many who are older than you have eaten all that I gave them, my great-grandchild. You have a wise head on young shoulders. All that you have left in the dish shall grow on the face of the earth. Earthmaker is waiting for you in great expectation. There is the door to

---

[9] Obtained from Henry Clowd.

the setting sun. On your way stands the lodge of Herecgu'nina, and his fire. Those who have come (the souls of brave men) from the land of the souls to take you back will touch you. There the road will branch off toward your right and you will see the footprints of the day on the blue sky before you. These footprints represent the footprints of those who have passed into life again. Step into the places where they have stepped and plant your feet into their footprints, but be careful you do not miss any. Before you have gone very far, you will come into a forest of wacke'ja^n broken by open prairies here and there. Here, in this beautiful country, these souls whose duty it is to gather other souls will come to meet you. Walking on each side of you they will take you safely home. As you enter the lodge of the Earthmaker you must hand to him the sacrificial offerings. Here the inquiry that took place in the first lodge will be repeated and answered in the same manner. Then he will say to you, "All that your grandmother has told you is true. Your relatives are waiting for you in great expectation. Your home is waiting for you. Its door will be facing the mid-day sun. Here you will find your relatives gathered. Inasmuch, then, as our ruler will nod assent and express his approval by word of mouth, so shall we now do the same."

At this word all those assembled at the wake shout, *Ho-ha!*

Then a warrior told his war experiences and after thanking the people passed the tobacco to the next warrior, who in turn related his war experiences.

The amount of gifts was then figured out and they tried to arrange matters so that the warriors were through with their stories about midnight. At midnight games were played with the donations as prizes. The gifts generally consisted of twelve 3-yard pieces of calico or money equal to that amount of calico; twelve strings of beads, etc. These were the gifts used as prizes. Other donations of food were made for the four nights' feast. A. W. was in charge of the games and he likewise designated what games were to be played. As they generally play the games the deceased was fond of so in this case they played the moccasin game and cards. After the donations were exhausted and the games finished a brave man was called upon to give a war whoop in thankfulness for the sun, and also to all the spirits above and below. Then A. W. greeted and thanked the guests again for coming, and the wake was over.

In olden times the widow was supposed to continue single for four years. She is strongly admonished, nevertheless, not to continue in low spirits, and to consider herself free to act in any way that will make her happy. She is told to play games or dance, or in fact do anything that will make her forget her sorrow, and she is told that no one will hold her conduct against her as disrespectful to the deceased. As this admonition is given to her by the sister or aunt of the deceased's husband, the only people who could properly reproach her—namely, the members of her husband's clan—it has all the more weight. The prohibition of weeping is further strengthened by the fact that it is customary to say that any woman who weeps too profusely at the death of her husband is in reality thinking, in the midst of her tears, of the one she is going to marry next. The people will then tell one another not to put themselves out too much as the widow will soon forget her mourning and show no respect to the memory of the dead, but instead look after her own pleasures.

FUNERAL CUSTOMS OF THE BUFFALO CLAN

Told by a member of the clan.[10]   If a Buffalo clan man dies some members of his clan who are called upon would speak as follows:

To-day when you ceased to breathe we were aware of it.   Therefore relatives who are present, I greet you.   Here my brother's life has ended, and for the last time I will talk to him about the road he is to take.

Hanho, my brother, the place at which we originated was called Bad Lake.   There were four buffaloes there and from the youngest one are we descended.   They lived holy lives, and we hope you will walk in their path.   That you may strike everything (you meet on your journey) you must take along with you a war club.   You shall walk armed with sharp teeth; and it will be impossible for bad spirits to walk back and forth across your path.   And your sight shall be holy as you walk.

Then the speaker painted the face of the deceased.   On the right side of his forehead he painted a rainbow with blue and red paint. After that he sang the clan songs.   When he was through singing, a member of the Water-spirit clan spoke as follows:

Relatives, I greet you.   When one of you passes away and you ask me to work, I am always willing to be of service.   And I shall do it all the more willingly now because I am certain that I shall obtain some of the years that the deceased left "unlived."   I do it with that belief, and furthermore I pray that no bad animals abuse the deceased on his journey.   It is said that one cheers the soul of the dead in thinking thus.   Therefore I do it and also that I myself may be strengthened thereby. I came back willingly when I was asked to work and I am doing this so that no bad animals should abuse the soul of the deceased.

Then one of the callers would talk to the mourners, saying as follows:

Relatives, I greet you.   To-day one of your relatives has disappeared.   You must, however, keep up your courage and not cry, for Earthmaker above has ordained that we should disappear.   If a piece of earth caves in, it disappears, and when a rock crumbles it is disappearing.   Thus, it is said, it must be.

ORIGIN MYTH OF THE FOUR NIGHTS' WAKE

Two friends went out to cut arrow-sticks, and were surprised by a war party and killed.   When they were shot they thought they had stumbled and went right on (in the spirit).   After the enemy had killed the first one they chased the second one and killed him, and so their bodies lay apart.   Then the war party left and the two spirits started to follow them.   Soon they came to where their bodies were lying.   Then they said, "Let us follow the enemy a little."   Soon they caught up to the war party and one of the spirits pushed one of the

___
[10] This account is quite fragmentary and was obtained in connection with the clan myth.   It is given here on account of the speeches.

men on the back of his head. He immediately became paralyzed from the touch. Then they pushed another man and he could not walk. So they laughed and turned back in order to return to their home.

They had not yet learned that they were dead. One went to his camp and told his wife that he was hungry but she paid no attention to him. The other had the same experience. Then each man started to go to the other man's lodge and they met midway. The first man said, "I came back hungry and asked for food, but they would not give me any, so I thought that I would go to your place." The second one said the same thing. Then they said, "Let us lie down a while." Just then the people began to cry, for they had brought back the bodies of the two dead men. Then one of the men said, "My friend, we have been killed." The other one began to cry.

So the people gathered together and had a meal. One of the ghosts said, "We must try and get something from the meal that they are having, for the people said, 'We are giving this meal in honor of the departed.'" Then the other friend said, "Now we are going to eat, for they are cooking for us."

These two were born again and told about this, and that is how we know it. This is the origin of the Four Nights' Wake. It is claimed that the spirits of the spirit land have a four nights' feast before they start.

Grave-post Marks

(DRAWINGS BY INDIANS)

(Fig. 28)

Warrior has been on the warpath (homani'na).

Warrior was a leader of a warpath (sak$^{\varepsilon}$ĭ').

Warrior was a helper on a warpath (wagixô'na) (rek$^{\varepsilon}$ĭ^{n}').

Warrior counted one of the three coup (wa'ŋgonʌŋk).

Warrior had made a captive (waŋgîni).

Warrior had killed a horse on the warpath or stolen one from the enemy.

If a person had killed a man and cut off his head, he is allowed to paint the top (upper part?) of the grave-post red.

Fig. 28.—Grave-post marks: 1, Has been on the warpath; 2, has been leader on warpath; 3, has been helper on warpath; 4, has counted one of the coup; 5, has made a captive; 6, has killed horse on warpath or stolen one from enemy; 7, has killed a man and cut off his head.

CHAPTER VI

WARFARE AND THE COUNCIL LODGE

WARFARE

War was one of the most important elements in the life of the Winnebago. The life of the warrior was the ideal toward which all men strove. It not only satisfied certain emotional needs but it was so inextricably interwoven with social standing in the community and with individual prestige that Winnebago life is unthinkable without it. It is not surprising, then, that the prayer for success on the warpath was the most important prayer that men offered up to the spirits and that it was reechoed in almost all the ceremonies. (Pls. 43, 44, 45.)

An element of culture fraught with so much significance to the individual and the social group was bound to be surrounded by innumerable customs, regulations, and restrictions. It was a life that was at stake every time an individual went on the warpath, and remembering the value of each life to a small community, it is not to be wondered at if there is a definite attempt on the part of the social group to restrict individual activity in this particular regard. An individual might go on the warpath either alone or in company with a few people, but the community, in the person of the chief, insisted that he show some warrant for his action. If no warrant of any kind could be given, he subjected himself to the only restrictive measures the chief and the community could adopt, disapproval, jeers, and temporary loss of social standing and prestige. So much, as far as his own person was concerned. If his action jeopardized the life or lives of other members of the tribe he had then to face the relatives of these people, just as any individual who had committed some wrong. It is hardly likely that many men would willingly run any risks of unnecessarily antagonizing their fellow tribesmen when the proper means of preparing for the warpath was open to all. A careful perusal of the system of education given on page 118 makes it clear that a sufficiently large number of methods for obtaining consent to lead a party were given, and that it was possible for every male individual to go on the warpath frequently if he so desired. Certain requirements were, however, necessary. It was not left to each individual to decide for himself whether he possessed these, but the final decision always lay in the hands of the chief.

PLATE 43

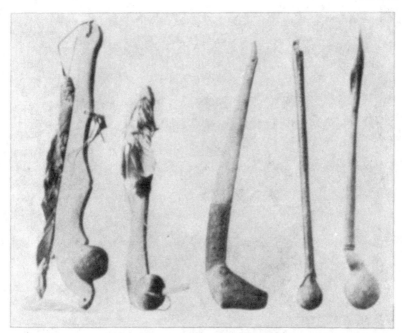

a. WAR CLUBS OF THE UPPER DIVISION

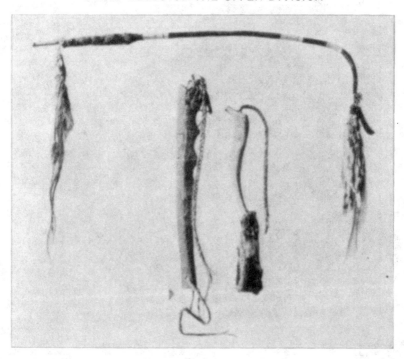

b. WHIPS

PLATE 44

DRUMS

PLATE 45

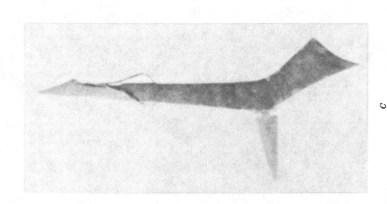

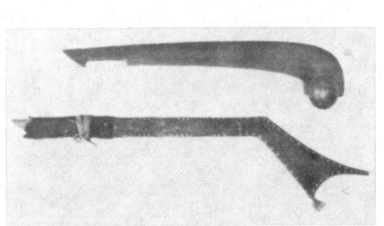

c

WAR CLUBS

a, c. Of lower division. *b.* Of upper division.

Any man who has been specially blessed with war powers may go on the warpath. Such a man must not merely be blessed with those general war powers that individuals obtain during their puberty fast, but must likewise be blessed with a definite enemy to kill or capture, as the case may be, immediately before he starts out. In practice this meant that whenever a person wished to go on the warpath he fasted in order to obtain the necessary guarantees of success. An account of the powers granted by the spirit or spirits was then placed before the chief and if, in his opinion, they justified the undertaking, the man was permitted to go. If they were insufficient the chief expressed his disapproval and the contemplated undertaking had either to be given up or the man would be compelled to fast again for increased powers. There were a number of men who were unable to obtain the requisite powers. To them one of two alternatives was left open: they might either purchase sufficient powers to go on a warpath or they might volunteer to join a large warpath. A volunteer needed no special blessing. If he had one, it would certainly benefit him, but it was not necessary except as an additional precaution, for the leader of the war party (*dotca*ⁿ*huŋka*) was supposed to be blessed specifically with every element necessary for a successful undertaking. As the Winnebago express it, he was blessed "with a complete road." In a war leader's blessing, everything must be provided—sufficient food, a definite number of enemies to kill, the exact place where they are to be killed, the exact time when they are to be killed, the exact manner in which they are to be killed, the exact manner in which the participants are to return to their homes, the safe return of all participants, and an infinite number of other minor points. As a volunteer went at the request of another man, the latter, and not he, took upon himself entire responsibility and the chief dealt directly with him. The chief would, in such a case, be particularly careful to see that every life that was risked was amply safeguarded. Otherwise the war party would not be permitted to start.

A man may go on the warpath for two reasons: either to revenge a slain relative or in a general way because he thinks he has received sufficient power and wishes to obtain glory. If the incentive was revenge, he might pursue one of two methods. He might go to the shaman with offerings of tobacco and presents and tell him about the death of his relative and his desire for revenge; or he might take the matter in his own hand, fast, and after having stealthily prepared for the necessities of the warpath inform a friend and steal out with him in the middle of the night. Were he to take the first method, it would be the shaman who would fast and who would afterwards lead the party, taking along with him as many men as would follow him.

When a man went on a warpath for the sake of glory he generally led a large party and all sorts of special arrangements were made, because then a war leader was necessary and volunteers were always needed. It is believed that the same holds true for larger war parties.

In discussing the essential requisite for a successful war party we have stated that a special blessing was necessary for this purpose. There is, however, one noteworthy exception to this rule, if we are to accept the statements of members of the upper phratry—all members of the Warrior clan may go on a warpath without fasting and without receiving a blessing. This statement was vigorously denied by members of the lower phratry.

When a war party returns, a very interesting ceremony takes place. At some distance from the village a victorious war party sends a messenger ahead to tell all those at home that the war party has been unsuccessful and that all have been killed, and that those at home should put on mourning. Secretly, however, the leader tells someone to look for a pole for the Victory dance, and shortly after all the preparations for mourning have been made the victorious warriors rush into the village. Before entering the village that warrior who has counted first coup is offered a pipe, from which he always takes a few puffs. The same pipe is then handed to the one who counted coup second, and so on, until the fourth man is reached. Then the prizes (*waixewe*) are given to the victors, who afterwards give them to their sisters. The scalps are not taken into the village, but are left outside, and warriors who have remained at home rush out to count coup upon them. Then the scalps are carried around the village four times.

The widely-known Plains custom of "counting coup" is also practiced among the Winnebago. The individual who strikes the dead body of the enemy first obtains the first honor, the one striking it second the second honor, the one striking it third the third honor, and the one who actually killed the enemy obtaining the fourth and least important honor.

The following are descriptions given in the words of the informants:
Description of war customs and the manner of conducting a war party.—Informant, member of the Thunderbird clan.

When a man is ready to go on the warpath, he looks around for as many men as he wishes to take along and then gives a feast. At the feast he fixes the time at which the war party is to start. The man giving the feast (i. e., the leader of the war party) would get up and tell those present that he intended going on a warpath and give his reason; then he would say that whosoever so desired could come along.

Many went along. Indeed, there was quite a crowd. The first stopping place (*higiɣara*) was always near the outskirts of the village. There the leader appointed four men to go after food and wood for the fire. During their absence two camping places would be arranged, one on each side of the war leader. As soon as the four men returned with the food the attendants skinned and prepared the animals for eating. Then the war leader asked for food, and it was brought to him. Now the female relatives of the men came to the camp, bringing with them moccasins for the journey. After that the chief asked some man to tell stories and some to take care of the fireplace, while two brave warriors were put in charge of the camp. Toward morning a number of warriors who had not been asked to join this particular war party might stray in (*hotcu'ŋgit^ee*).

Before the war leader enters the *higiɣara* he places his war bundle crosswise in front of the entrance of the *higiɣara* and sings some songs. When he is finished, his attendants place the war bundle on his back, and only then does he really enter the *higiɣara*, followed by all the other members of the war party.[1]

When they approached the place where they expected to find the enemy, two distinguished warriors were appointed to reconnoiter, and they proceeded ahead of the war party until they saw the enemy. Then they returned to the camp and reported to the war leader. From that time on they would practice their various individual powers (*waruxʌ'p naŋkgigire'jê*).[2]

When the two warriors sent out to reconnoiter return, the attendant offers them the pipe that he had prepared for the war leader. They smoke it and say, "Those whom we are after are entirely unaware of our presence." Then the members of the war party would thank them for their information. All would now start out against the enemy. When near the enemy, they practice their powers again and paint themselves with their war paints. To those spirits who have bestowed blessings upon the various members of the war party offerings are now made. Especially to the spirits who are in control of war powers are offerings made. To them they also pray for life and for war honors in the coming encounter. They even offer tobacco to those spirits from whom they have not received blessings, asking them for aid because of their careful observance of all the customs and precepts they were taught. Some offered tobacco to a medicine they possessed and asked the medicine to remember them in the coming encounter. Others boiled water (for a spirit) and asked him to assist them in obtaining a war honor, while others again offered tobacco to their war bundles and prayed that the powers contained therein might be strong and that they might kill some of the enemy and obtain war honors. All prayed that the enemy might not kill them and that they might finally return home safe. Those who had no supernatural powers to fall back upon would get frightened at such a time and they would say, "Alas! how will I fare! I should have fasted. I should have given feasts. I should have offered good medicines to the spirits and fasted until I was blessed, so that I, too, might now have some powerful medicine to use. Had I fasted and obtained a blessing from the spirits who are in control of war powers, had I given feasts, this all would have been a source of strength to me now and I would know positively whether or not I am going to be killed in the coming encounter."

When everything is in readiness the war leader rises and appoints four warriors to give the war whoop. Then, as soon as the war whoop has been given, they would rush upon the enemy, imitating as they ran the sounds of the spirits who had blessed them. The first four to kill and count coup obtained the corresponding four war honors. Those who captured a man also obtained war honors. Beside these principal ones there were minor war honors. Those who obtained no honors at all would return home crying. After they had killed all those in the village of the enemy they would burn it to the ground and then start for their homes in the best of spirits.

When they were near their home they sent a messenger ahead to inform their relatives to put on mourning, for all those who had started out on the warpath had been killed; that he who had in reality obtained the first war honor had been killed first,

---

[1] *Higiɣara* is the special arrangement of the camp used on individual warpaths.

[2] When a war party has located the enemy, they prepare for the attack and run about, practicing their individual magical powers. "The war-club running" (*waruxa'p naŋkgigire'jê*) referred to is the practice of running about in preparation for the attack upon the enemy so that they may not get tired out too easily.

etc. Then the war leader would secretly tell some one to select a stake (for the Victory Dance) and after a short time all the members of the war party would rush in and march around the entire village striking the scalps that they had tied to sticks. Then they would all go to the place where the stake had been put up and there they would distribute the war prizes to the sisters of the men who had won them and the women would walk around proudly with the prizes around their necks. Then, in the daytime they would dance the Victory Dance and in the evening they would dance the Hok'ixere Dance for four nights.

Description of a war party.—Informant, member of the Thunderbird clan.

If a man wishes to go on the warpath he must fast and be blessed by the spirits in a specific manner. If a man is thus blessed, he gives a feast and announces his intention of leading a war party. The chief always has a representative at such a feast (a member of the Buffalo clan), and as soon as it is over this man goes to the former and reports to him. If the chief thinks that the blessing is insufficient and might cause the death of many men he takes the war leader's pipe and lays it across his path and the war leader is then compelled to abandon his undertaking. This action on the part of the chief is sacred and must be accepted as final. The war leader dare not step across the pipe. Should the chief, however, not do this, then the war leader knew that there was no objection. Usually some members of every clan go along, but especially members of the Thunderbird, Warrior, and Bear clans.

The action of the war leader is controlled by many rules. He must be the one who has fasted and been blessed with all that is essential for conducting a war party. He must have his food provided for him by the spirits, know the exact location of the enemy, their numbers, and their sex.

After the war party has traveled for about four days, the men offer tobacco to the leader and he tells them where he is going, the number of the enemy, etc. If, after that, any of the members of the war party do not approve of the undertaking then they place a pipe across his path and the war leader is compelled to return. If nothing is said, then all is well. The war leader always goes ahead of his party and his attendants behind him, followed by the other members of the party. Whenever the chief stops his attendants run to his side, take his war bundle and place it in front of him. Then the leader sits down, neither turning to the right nor to the left but looking straight ahead. The attendants get two poles and place them on each side of him, bend the ends over to form an arch, on each side of which are placed small oak sticks arranged in a row. Under this structure the war leader stays. Here he sleeps and is fed by his attendants. No one is permitted to go ahead of this improvised structure. On each side of him two fireplaces are placed, two for the Upper clans and two for the Lower clans. If the war party is traveling westward the two fireplaces on the north side belong to the Lower clans and the two on the south side to the Upper clans. If a man is going on a warpath for the first time, he stays in the rear of the party and has a little fire of his own. He remains in the rear in this way until the battle begins. Then he joins the others.

A member of the Warrior clan is selected by the war leader to act as guard and he goes back and forth behind him encouraging the men and telling them not to steal away alone or go too far ahead of the party, since that always results in the loss of life. It is for this reason that it is not considered correct for a man to try and steal away and perhaps obtain a war honor in this selfish manner. Whenever the war leader stops he tells his companions what they must do in order to obtain food, all this information having been provided for in his blessing. If he tells some one to go to a certain place and kill a deer, he is certain to find a deer at the place specified. Whenever the war leader gets up and steps over his war bundle the attendants come and place his war bundle on his back and he then proceeds on his march, followed by the other members of the party. Whenever he comes to a river he takes some of the tobacco which is always kept on hand and offers it to the spirit who controls this particular war party. The others do the same. Then he would cross the river. Whenever he drank any water the others would also do so, and if he refrained so would the others. If at any time during the night when they are camping the war leader should wake up and sing some songs, be they grizzly bear, black root paint, or night songs, all those others who knew similar songs would likewise begin to sing.

Miscellaneous war customs.—There were, in former times, many miscellaneous customs connected with warfare, most of which have now been forgotten. However, in myths and accounts of war parties a number of them are still mentioned.

When a war party surprised a lodge, all the occupants were killed or captured and the poles that were spliced together to form the arches were released so that they sprang back to either side and assumed a vertical position.

When a war party surprised a lodge in which there were children they generally killed them, cut off their heads, pried open their mouths so as to give them the appearance of laughing, and then placed the heads on their bodies again and arranged them against the door, so that when their father came home he would find them greeting him as usual. A brave warrior would never flinch at such a sight, but would prepare a meal as usual and speak to the children as if they were alive and offer them something to eat. Only then would he bury them. Immediately after they had been buried he would go on the warpath to revenge them.

Frequently the skulls of slain enemies are used as lodge weights and their skin is taken off and used as mats, door-flaps, etc.

War honors.—"It is the ideal of every Winnebago youth," says an informant, "to kill an enemy in full sight of his friends and thus to gain for himself a headdress and an eagle feather." Most deeds considered valorous, according to Winnebago ideas, have associated with them certain insignia which are always worn in public, giving evidence to all that so-and-so has performed such and such a valorous deed.

These insignia consist of the following:

Headdress and feather.—Denote that an individual has scalped and killed a man and torn off his scalp still bleeding. He is entitled to a red headdress and eagle feather. This also includes the man who has counted first coup (*sarinîgwahi'na*).

Red headdress.—If he has killed the enemy and not scalped him (*tcasî'ntc wak'e'rê.*)

Eagle feather.—Worn by one who has counted second coup.

Hanging eagle feather.—Worn by one who has counted third coup.

Eagle feather stuck crosswise in hair.—Worn by one who has counted fourth coup.

Waŋgirusgitc.—Consists of a rope worn around the neck. It is worn by the leader of that warpath who has captured an enemy.

Uâ'ŋkerê.—Arm band worn by the person who did the actual capturing. If two enemies are captured he can wear an arm band on each arm.

Red-dyed eagle feather.—A red-dyed eagle feather worn by a war leader who has brought a captured enemy to camp and tortured him with embers.

Ankle-band of skunk or polecat.—An ankle-band of the skin of a skunk or polecat worn by one who has seen an enemy dead on the battle field and kicked him. If he does it for the second time, he may wear skunk skins on both legs below the knee. If the leader does it he is allowed to use an otter skin.

Rope tied to belt.—A rope of any desirable length tied to a belt may be worn by an individual who has succeeded in either capturing or killing an enemy's horse. At a dance no one would dare step on it. If an individual does not want to wear this, he may in its place wear a rope around his body.

Legs painted white.—An individual who has been on the warpath in winter may paint his legs white, from the knee down.

Gun painted red.—An individual who has killed an enemy with a gun may carry this gun at a dance and paint it red.

Spear.—If a person kills an enemy with a spear, he may carry this and tie to it any symbol (eagle feather, etc.) that he has gained.

Kokê'reʳûⁿ.—An individual who was a well-known warrior and had fought in front of his comrades, and one whom the enemy respected, was entitled to a long stick with eagle feathers. At a dance he had the privilege of dancing with the stick in front of his comrades.

Hand on face.—Any warrior making all four coups, who did not care to wear a dress, might paint a man's hand in black upon his face.

Raven's skin around neck.—If an individual captured more than one woman in war, he was entitled to wear a raven skin around his neck.

Body painted yellow and wounded spot red.—If a man had been wounded on the warpath, he had the right at a dance to paint his body yellow and the wounded spots red, with red streaks running from the wounds.

Otter skin around knee and naŋgisʳo.—A great warrior, one who has gained all the war honors, can, if he does not wish to wear his separate insignia, wear instead an otter skin attached below the knee, whose ends are not quite united. He may also wear a naŋgisʳo consisting of a stick, whittled and painted red, in his hair.

Valorous deeds are also perpetuated on the grave posts when the warriors who have accompanied the corpse to the grave count coup and draw a picture symbolizing their particular deed on the post. It should therefore be remembered that the markings on these posts do not refer at all to the valorous deeds of the deceased but to those of warriors who happened to count coup at the grave.

THE COUNCIL LODGE

The clan in the council lodge.—There is one place where the clan finds representation as a political unit, and that is the council lodge. No unanimity seems to exist with regard to the positions of the various clans in the council lodge, but here again the position of those clans with specific governmental functions seems to be far more stable than that of the others. The clans are generally so seated as always to be opposite their "friend" clan, from which fact a clan frequently calls its friend "my opposite." It is, however, interesting to note that this seating does not hold for two friend groups, the Water-spirit-Buffalo and Elk-Deer. The Water-spirit clan occupies a high position in the council lodge, apparently quite out of proportion to its present importance in the social organization of the tribe, but in consonance with its former importance.

Councils.—No important undertaking was ever attempted without the holding of a council. On such occasions the principal members of each clan would assemble in a long lodge and discuss in great detail. Nothing comparable to a vote that might express the desire of those assembled was taken, but the opinions of those present were always presented in their speeches. As a rule the chief, or some person especially interested in definite matter, led the discussion. Owing to the complete absence of specific examples of councils it is very difficult to obtain a very clear idea of their working. The numerous councils relating to treaties with the whites are of very little interest or significance in this connection.

There was unquestionably a regular order of entering and seating in the council lodge. What this order was it is impossible to determine now, for the statements made by different informants were contradictory. Since, however, the contradictions in the seating arrangements seemed to be correlated with different clan membership the discrepancies may be due, not to lack of knowledge but to actual differences. A few examples of the seating arrangements follow (figs. 29–32):

Description of order of entering the council lodge.—Informant, member of Bear clan. The Buffalo clan would always be the last to enter the council lodge because the members remained outside making announcements until all the others had entered. The members of the Thunderbird clan enter first, making a circuit of the lodge before taking their seats. The members of the Warrior clan followed and took their seats just opposite those of the Thunderbird clan. Then the Water-spirit clan follows, and then come the rest as indicated in the diagram. This is the only place where the Bear clan is not in control of the arrangements.

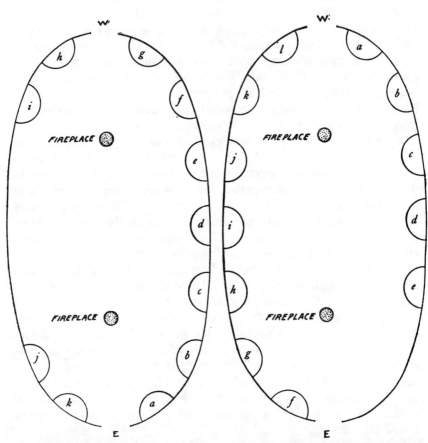

FIG. 29.—Seating arrangement in council lodge according to Thunderbird clan: *a*, Warrior clan; *b*, Water-spirit clan; *c*, Deer clan; *d*, Elk clan; *e*, Pigeon clan; *f*, Wolf clan; *g*, Bear clan; *h*, Snake clan; *i*, Buffalo clan; *j*, Eagle clan; *k*, Thunderbird clan. (The order of importance is from *k-a*.)

FIG. 30.—Seating arrangement in council lodge according to Bear clan: *a*, Thunderbird clan; *b*, Bear clan; *c*, Wolf clan; *d*, Pigeon clan; *e*, Eagle clan; *f*, Snake clan; *g*, Fish clan; *h*, Elk clan; *i*, Buffalo clan; *j*, Deer clan; *k*, Water-spirit clan; *l*, Warrior clan.

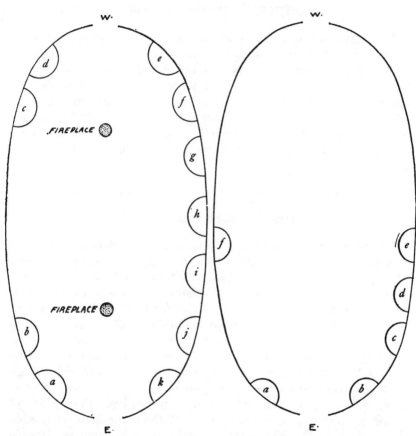

FIG. 31.—Seating arrangement in council lodge according to Thunderbird clan: *k*, Thunderbird clan; *j*, Eagle clan; *i*, Buffalo clan; *h*, Snake clan; *g*, Bear clan; *f*, Wolf clan; *e*, Pigeon clan; *d*, Elk clan; *c*, Deer clan; *b*, Water-spirit clan; *a*, Warrior clan.

FIG. 32.—Seating arrangement in council lodge according to Wolf clan: *a*, Thunderbird clan; *b*, Eagle clan; *c*, Buffalo clan; *d*, Water-spirit clan; *e*, Bear clan; *f*, Wolf clan.

CHAPTER VII

SYSTEM OF EDUCATION [1]

The Winnebago seem to have had a more or less formal system of instruction. This consisted of a series of precepts on different aspects of life, such as the duty of fasting, of being a warrior, of behavior to one's parents and relatives, how to treat one's wife and women in general, how to bring up children, how to behave to strangers, etc. These formal teachings were called $hok'i'ku^n$, which means "precepts" or "teachings." Doubtless those obtained do not constitute all the different types existing, but they seem fairly representative.

My Father's Teaching to His Sons and Daughters

SYSTEM OF INSTRUCTION TO SON

My son, when you grow up you should see to it that you are of some benefit to your fellowmen. There is only one way in which you can begin to be of any aid to them, and that is to fast. So, my son, see to it that you fast. Our grandfather, the fire, who stands at all times in the center of our dwelling, sends forth all kinds of blessings.[2] Be sure that you make an attempt to obtain his blessings.

My son, do you remember to have our grandfathers, the war chiefs, bless you. See to it that they pity you.[3] Some day when you go on the warpath their blessings will enable you to have specific foreknowledge of all that will happen to you on that occasion. This will likewise enable you to accomplish what you desire without the danger of anything interfering with your plans. Without the slightest trouble you will then be able to obtain the prizes of war. Without any trouble

---

[1] This chapter was originally intended for special publication and the notes prepared for it then have been retained.

[2] The fire ($p'etc$) is regarded as a spirit by the Winnebago. As a spirit he possesses many gifts that are of use to human beings in their sojourn on earth, and in order to obtain them, mortals must make offerings of tobacco to him. He may also appear to them during their fastings and bless them with a number of powers. In addition to his other powers, it is believed that he is the messenger of Earthmaker and the other spirits and that he transmits both the messages, as well as the offerings that mortals make to them, by means of the smoke that rises upward. The old man speaks of the fire first, because being always around them it is a comparatively easy task to make offerings to it.

[3] This is the regular expression used for blessing. The idea seems to be that through fasting and crying you are to put yourself in a "pitiable" condition and that then the spirits, seeing your state, will pity you and grant you what you have asked. The word "grandfathers" is used in the sense of ancestral spirits, the thunderbirds, who are regarded as the dispensers of war power, not only by members of this clan but by all Winnebago.

you will be able to obtain these and in addition glory and the war honors.[4] If, in truth, you thirst yourself to death,[5] our grandfathers who are in control of wars—to whom all the war powers that exist in this world belong—they will assuredly bless you.

My son, if you do not wear out your feet through ceaseless activity (in fasting), if you do not blacken your face for fasting, it will be all in vain that you inflict sufferings upon yourself. Blessings are not obtained through mere desire alone; they are not obtained without making the proper sacrifices or without putting yourself time and again in proper mental condition. Indeed, my son, they are not to be obtained without effort on your part. So see to it that, of all those spirits whom Earthmaker created, one at least has pity upon you and blesses you. Whatever such a spirit says to you that will unquestionably happen.

Now, my son, if you do not obtain a spirit to srengthen you, you will not amount to anything in the estimation of your fellowmen. They will show you little respect. Perhaps they will make fun of you.

Do not die in the village. It is not good to die there. Whenever a person is grown up that is what is told him. Nor is it good, my son, to let women journey ahead of you from amidst the village. It is not good thus to let women die before you.[6] Therefore, in order to prevent this, our ancestors encouraged one another to fast. Some day you will travel in a difficult road; there will be some crisis in your life, and then when it is too late you will begin to reproach yourself for not having fasted at the proper time. So that you may not have occasion to blame yourself at such a time I counsel you to fast. If you do not obtain a blessing when the other women are dividing the war prizes brought home from the warpath by their brothers, your sisters will stand aside envying them. If, however, you are blessed by the spirits in control of war power, and if you then return victorious, how proud your sisters will be to receive the war honors and to wear them around their necks and participate with them in the victory dance! And in this way your sisters likewise will be strengthened by your war deeds. You will keep well, in health.

My son, it will indeed be good if you obtain war powers, but our ancestors say it.is difficult. Especially difficult is it to be leader on

---

[4] There are four war honors, the highest going to the Indian who first touches a dead enemy, the second belonging to the one who kills him, and the last two to those who touch him second and third. The war prizes generally consisted of necklaces of wampum which were given to those who had obtained the first war honors. The victor also would be given the privilege of first smoking the pipe on his return to his home. The prize of the wampum necklace was always given by the victor to his elder sisters.

[5] That is, fast.

[6] That is, obtain war power so that you can go on the warpath and prevent yourself from dying in the village or have women die before you.

the warpath.[7] So they say. If you do not become an individual warranted to lead a war party, yet mistaking yourself for one although really an ordinary warrior, you "throw away a man," your act will be considered most disgraceful. A mourner might harm you in revenge for the fact that you have caused him to mourn, and burn you with embers. Your people will all be sad, both on account of your disgrace and on account of the pain inflicted upon you.

My son, not with the blessing of one of the spirits merely, nor with the blessing of twenty, for that matter, can you go on the warpath. You must have the blessing of all the spirits above the earth, and of all those on the earth, and of all those who are pierced through the earth;[8] of all those under the earth; of all those who are under the water; of all those that are on the sides of the earth, i. e., all the four winds; of the Disease-giver;[9] of the Sun; of the Daylight;[10] of the Moon; of the Earth; and of all those who are in control of war powers—with the blessings of all these deities must you be provided before you can lead a successful war party.

My son, if you cast off dress[11] men will be benefited by your deeds. You will be an aid to all your people. If your people honor you, it will be good. And they will like you even the more if you obtain a

---

[7] Among the Winnebago any individual who has been blessed with the necessary powers to lead a warpath may do so, but it is absolutely essential that his blessing directing him be of such a nature that every possible contingency is included therein. Such complete blessings are, of course, not common nor can they be obtained except through unusual exertions. If you are blessed with just the ordinary or incomplete war powers and you nevertheless undertake to lead a war party, you may either be defeated or perhaps only partially successful, and, what is worse, you may lose some of the warriors who started with you. Your recklessness has thus caused the death of some of your fellow tribesmen. It is understood that every warrior before starting on the warpath turn his "blessing" over to the chief of the tribe for examination, and if the chief considers it complete the warrior is not held responsible for the lack of success or loss of life. If the chief does not consider an individual's blessing sufficient to justify the object he has in view and forbids the warrior to go, and if the latter nevertheless goes; or granted the case he does not even submit his "blessing" to the chief for scrutiny, and sneaks out, then he is held directly responsible for any mishap on the warpath. The relatives of any individual thus killed may hold the war leader responsible and demand compensation; or, as is indicated by B. a few lines later, a mourner (i. e., one who has been placed in mourning by the criminal foolhardiness of the war leader) might attack, perhaps kill him, without being held guilty of any crime. It must of course be understood that such occurrences would seldom take place. We must, however, remember throughout these "teachings" that one of the objects of the old men was to draw the most alluring pictures of the rewards that would fall to the lot of those who followed in the footsteps of their ancestors, and, on the other hand, to draw the most lurid pictures of the wretchedness that befell those who deviated, no matter in what details, from the customs sanctioned by age.

[8] According to the Winnebago creation myth, when Earthmaker, the creator of the earth, first came to consciousness and began creating life the earth on which we were to live was in continual motion, and nothing that the former could do seemed to be able to stop it. From above he threw down grass, trees, etc., but all was of no avail. Finally he hit upon the happy expedient of pinning the earth down at the four corners by means of four enormous snakes, or, as some say, by means of four mythical animals known as water spirits. It is to these that the old man is referring here. According to the story, even these were of no avail, and it was only when he finally placed four mythical beings known as "Island Weights" at the four corners that our planet stopped spinning. These "Island Weights" seem to be identical with the spirits of the four cardinal points, but they are not to be confused with the four winds mentioned later.

[9] A deity conceived of as dealing out life-giving powers from one half of his body and death-giving powers from the other half. He is also supposed to disseminate disease. Disease-giver is a literal translation of the Winnebago word, but this probably does not convey the exact meaning. There seems to be no parallel to this peculiar deity among the other Siouan tribes or among the Algonquian.

[10] Daylight or light is conceived of as something different and distinct from the sun.

[11] That is, if you give away things frequently, especially to poor people.

limb.[12] They will indeed like you very much if you obtain a limb, or, even better, two or three. If you do thus, wherever people boil an animal with a head [13] you will always be able to eat.

If on account of your bravery you are permitted to tell of your war exploits during the Four Nights' Wake for the benefit of the soul of the deceased, do not try to add to your glory by exaggerating any exploit, for by so doing you will cause the soul to stumble on its journey to the spirit land.[14] If you do this and add an untruth to the account of your war exploit, you will die soon after. The war spirits always hear you. Tell a little less. The old men say it is wise.

My son, it is good to die in war. If you die in war, your soul will not be unconscious. You will have complete disposal of your soul and it will always be happy.[15] If you should ever desire to return to this earth and live here again, you will be able to do so. A second life as a human being you may live, or, if you prefer, as an inhabitant of the air (a bird) you may live, or you may roam the earth as an animal. Thus it is to him who dies in battle.

My son, fast for an honorable place among your fellowmen. Fast, so that when you are married you may have plenty of food; that you may be happy and that you may not have to worry about your children. If in your fastings you have a vision of your future home, the members of your family will be lacking in nothing during their life. Fast for the food that you may need. If you fast a sufficiently large number of times, when in after life you have children and they cry for food you will be able to offer a piece of deer or moose meat without any difficulty. Your children will never be hungry.

---

[12] That is, a war honor, but more specifically if you "count coup" first. The honor of killing an enemy and the three honors associated with first touching his dead body are always spoken of as "the four limbs of the body."

[13] That is, wherever people give a Winter Feast. At this feast a deer, head and all, is served to the invited guests. The head may only be eaten by brave warriors.

[14] At the death of a clansman an elaborate wake takes place. To this wake, as the principal participants, three or four warriors who have counted "coup" are always invited. It is believed that the souls of all the enemies one has killed become the slaves of the victor and he may command them to do his bidding at any time. If the victor tells his exploit and then commands the enslaved soul to take care of the recently departed person in whose honor the wake is being given, the soul of the conquered enemy will be of considerable aid in overcoming the obstacles that are supposed to infest the path between this earth and the land of the spirits. These can not be overcome by the merits of the individual alone. If, however, a warrior becomes vainglorious, the soul of the recently departed individual will fall into the abysm of fire which surrounds one of the heavenly earths through which he must pass. That is what is meant by "stumbling."

[15] It must be remembered that the Winnebago believe that all that constitutes "life," "consciousness," continues to exist after death, the only difference being that in the former case an envelope, the body, is present and, in the latter case, it is not. Winnebago philosophy does not concern itself with what happens when a soul becomes "unconscious" at death, which would, of course, be the case with all those who do not die in battle; but it does insist that to him who dies on the warpath the moment of death does not even deprive of consciousness. He goes right on living, as if he were still an inhabitant of this earth, the only difference being that the corporeal envelope has fallen off his soul and that, although he sees and hears human beings, he himself is not visible nor his voice audible.

My son, never abuse your wife. The women are sacred. If you abuse your wife and make her life miserable, you will die early. Our grandmother, the earth, is a woman, and in mistreating your wife you will be mistreating her. Most assuredly will you be abusing our grandmother if you act thus. And as it is she that is taking care of us you will really be killing yourself by such behavior.

My son, when you keep house, should anyone enter your house, no matter who it is, be sure to offer him whatever you have in the house. Any food that you withhold at such a time will most assuredly become a source of death to you. If you are stingy about giving food the people will kill you on this account. They will poison you. If you hear of a traveler who is visiting your people and you wish to see him, prepare your table for him and have him sent for. In this manner you will be acting correctly. It is always good to act correctly and do good, the old people used to say.

If you see an old, helpless person, help him with whatever you possess. Should you happen to possess a home and you take him there, he might suddenly say abusive things about you during the middle of the meal. You will be strengthened by such words. This same traveler may, on the contrary, give you something that he carries under his arms and which he treasures very highly. If it is an object without a stem,[16] keep it to protect your house. If you thus keep it within your house, your home will never be molested by any bad spirits. Nothing will be able to enter your house unexpectedly. Thus you will live. Witches, instead of entering your house, will pass around it. If, in addition to possessing this medicine, you also fast, your people will be benefited by it greatly. Earthmaker made spirits up above and some he made to live on this earth; and again some he made to live under the water and some to live in the water; and all these he put in charge of something. Even the small animals that move about this earth the creator put in charge of some power. Thus he created them. Afterwards he created us human beings and as he had exhausted all the powers to be disposed of we were not in control of anything. Then he made a weed and placed it in our charge. And he said that no matter how powerful are the spirits that exist they would not be able to take this weed from us without giving something in return. He himself, Earthmaker, would not be able to demand it for nothing. So he spoke. This weed was the tobacco plant. Earthmaker said that if we would offer a pipeful of tobacco to him, whatever we should ask of him he would immediately grant. Not only he, but all the spirits created, longed to have some of this tobacco. It is for this reason that when we fast and cry piteously for some spirit to take pity on us, if we give them tobacco they will bless us with those

16 A plant without a stem, presumably some root, used for warding off danger.

powers that the creator gave them. So it will be. Earthmaker made it thus.

My son, you must fast. If you breathe upon sick people,[17] I mean if you are blessed with that kind of power, you will be able to restore people to health. You will be of help to your people. If you can, in addition, draw out the pain from within the body of an individual, you will indeed be a help to your people. They will respect you. You will not even have to work for all your necessities, for those whom you treat will cheerfully support you as long as you live. If you should die, your name will be held in great respect and people will frequently talk about you. Ah, that man he had indeed great power!

My son, if you are not able to fast,[18] try at least to obtain some plants that are powerful. There are people who know the qualities of the different plants, who have been blessed by the spirits with this knowledge. It is pitiable enough that you could obtain nothing through fasting, so ask those that are in possession of these plants at least to have pity upon you. If they have pity upon you, they will bless you with one of the plants they possess, and you will thus have something to help you in life and to encourage you. One plant will not be enough. Of all the plants that cover the earth and lie like a fringe of hair upon the body of our grandmother, try and obtain knowledge of these, that you may be strengthened in life. Then you will have reason to feel encouraged. A real medicine man has even more justification for feeling encouraged than an ordinary one, because such a one has been blessed with life by the Water-spirits. If, therefore, you wish to obtain the real powers of curing people, so that you will have the power of making them arise from their sick beds, you must long and patiently wait and labor. If, however, you obtain the true powers—that is, if you obtain blessings from the Water-spirits—then some day, when your children are in need of medicine, you will not have to go and look for a medicine man, but you will only have to look into your medicine bundle. Whatever trouble your children have you will be able to cure it. Should anything be the matter with the people of your tribe they will call upon you. You can then open your medicine bundle and the individual who is wanting in life will be benefited from the stock of medicines

---

[17] Sickness is due to the presence of some object within the body. Illness can therefore only be cured if this object is extracted. This is generally accomplished by the shaman sucking it out through a bone tube. Among the Winnebago the shaman before applying the tube squirts some water upon the afflicted person and breathes upon him. This is what the "breathing" refers to.

[18] Not everyone who fasts is blessed with power. For those who are thus unable to obtain blessings directly from the spirits there is only one method of protection against evils left—the purchase of plants with magical properties from those who have been blessed with them. These can be obtained by any individual no matter how unsuccessful he has been in obtaining blessings through personal fasting. All that is needed is sufficient riches for purchasing them. Of course it goes without saying that those who have been blessed with power may and do also provide themselves with these medicines.

that are in your possession. You will indeed never be embarrassed. You will know just wherein his ailment lies. As you have obtained your power with great effort, therefore what you say will be so. If you say he will live, he will live. If the relatives of the patient make you good payments, you may perform what you are accustomed to in your treatment of people. Then you can ask your medicine to put forth its strength for you and it will do so. If you make good offerings of tobacco to the plants and if you make feasts in their honor, if, indeed, you make much of your medicine, if you talk to it as though it were a human being, then when you ask it to put forth its strength it will do so. The payments that you receive you can take with a good conscience and your children will wear them and will be strengthened thereby. So be very diligent in the care you bestow upon them. The medicines were placed here by Earthmaker for a good purpose. We are to use them to heal ourselves. For that purpose Earthmaker gave them to us. If anyone tries to obtain the life sustainers—that is, the medicines—and inflicts suffering upon himself in order to obtain them, our grandmother will know about it. So whatever you spend upon it, be it in labor or in goods, she will know about it. All that you gave in obtaining your medicines she will know. They will be returned to you. The people will thus be providing themselves with something for the future. The people always look forward to the future and for all possible happenings they will have some medicine provided. You must try to obtain some of the medicines that most people possess. If you want paint-medicine, make yourself pitiable. If your paint-medicine overcomes your enemy and you keep it in your home, you will never be wanting in wealth. The most valued possessions of the people will be given to you. The people will love you and the paint-medicine will be the cause of it. Whatever you receive will be in consequence of the possession of the paint-medicine. The paint-medicine is made of the blood of the Water-spirits, and therefore it is holy. People used to fast and thirst themselves to death and a Water-spirit would appear to them and bestow his blessings upon them. Whatever he told them would come true. The Earthmaker put the Water-spirit in charge of these things so that he would bless the people with them. That was his purpose.

Some people who wished to find good medicines obtained the race medicine. Try and learn of it. Others had gambling medicine, and still others again had hunting medicine. There are medicines for very purpose.

There is a courting medicine and a medicine to prevent married people from wishing to separate, and there is a medicine for making one rich.

If one wishes to make a person crazy, there is a medicine for that purpose.

If some one had made another one sad at heart and he wished to revenge himself, he would use a medicine that would make that person crazy. Thus he would poison him.

If a person wished to marry a certain girl and she did not want him, he would poison her with a medicine that would make her become a harlot. All the men would fall in love with her by reason of the medicine he gave her.

If they wished a man to be continually running after a woman, they had a medicine for that purpose. All these medicines they possessed. You can obtain any of them you like if you ask for them in the proper way.

Some people have knowledge of plants that will cause a person to sleep all the time. Others again have medicines that will cause them to stay awake all the time. Some know how to overcome the viciousness of dogs that watch over women by means of medicines; some again have medicines that will make people single them out even in crowds. If this person uses his medicine in a crowd of people, the one on whom it is used will consider him a great man no matter how many there should be in the crowd. Some have a medicine to be used for preventing an individual from getting tired. Others have a medicine to be used when they have dog contests.

Whatever they did, for that they would have medicines.

Whenever they plant a field they protect it with medicine tied on to a stick. No one will then go through that field without suffering for it. If you did not have that protection, people could go through your field whenever they wished. In short, try to obtain as many medicines as you possibly can, for you will need them all. People should always look out for themselves so that they may learn what is necessary to make life comfortable and happy. If you try to obtain the knowledge of these things you will get along in life well. You will need nothing; and whenever you need a certain medicine, instead of being compelled to buy it, you will have it in your own possession. If you act in this manner and keep on fasting you will never be caught offguard during your life. If you have a home, it will always look nice and you will be lacking in nothing. So, do what I tell you and you will never regret it in after life. Try and learn the way in which your ancestors lived and follow in their footsteps.

If you thus travel in the road of the good people, it will be good and other people will not consider your life a source of amusement.[19]

If you can not obtain a blessing from the spirits try also to have some good plant take pity on you. This I am telling you and if you do not do it, you will suffer for it. All that I am saying will be of great benefit to you if you pay heed to me, for (you will need medicines for) whatever you do in life, if you are not fortunate enough to obtain blessings from the spirits. If you are ever on the warpath, you will need medicine in order to escape being hit or in order to prevent yourself from getting exhausted or from feeling famished. If you manage to be fortunate in all these things you may be certain that the medicines have caused it.

My son, help yourself as you go along life's path, for this earth has many narrow passages and you can never tell when you will come to one. If, however, you have something with which to strengthen yourself you will come safely through the passages you meet.

Let every one think you a desirable person to know. Associate with people. If you act in this manner, every one will like you. (You will live) a contented life. Never do anything wrong to your children. Whatever your children ask you to do, do not hesitate to do it for them. If you act thus people will say you are good-natured. If you ever lose a friend by death and if you have riches cover[20] the expenses of the funeral of the deceased. Help the mourners to feed the people at the wake. If you act thus you will be acting well. Then you will be truly a helper of the people and they will know you as such. Indeed, all of them will know you. For the good you do, all will love you.

My son, do not become a gambler. You might, it is true, become rich, but in spite of your wealth all your children will die. No gambler ever had children. It is an affair of the bad spirits entirely. Now if you do all that I have told you, you will unquestionably lead a happy and contented life.

Thus would the old people speak to a child whom they loved very much, that he might obtain the means of warding off what is not good. Anyone who acted contrary to these teachings would have himself to blame for the consequences.

---

[19] This dislike of being made fun of, or of being the laughing stock, plays an important rôle among the Winnebago. It is not at all comparable to the same feeling as found at the present day among civilized people of Western Europe, for it is infinitely deeper and closely associated with social ostracism. The despondency caused by being made fun of, would frequently drive a person away from home or lead him to embark on any undertaking that would bring death. Owing to the social consequences coming in its train, a man would consequently do most anything in his power to ward it off. Correlated with this negative aspect of the use of "fun-poking," there is a positive one. There are certain relatives who have the privilege of making fun of or playing practical jokes on you. This "joking-relationship" exists among many tribes in America, but the relatives between whom it is permitted differ in every case. Among the Winnebago it exists between uncles and nieces and nephews and between brothers-in-law and sisters-in-law.

[20] That is, buy the funeral apparel for the deceased.

If you ever get married, my son, do not make an idol of your wife. The more you worship her, the more will she want to be worshipped. Thus the old people said. They warned the young men against the example of those men who always hearken to what the women say, who are the slaves of women. Often they would speak in the following manner: "You have had many warnings, but it may happen that some day you will not pay any attention to them. Then, when they call upon you to take part in the Winter Feast you may perhaps refuse to go. When a war party is leaving you may listen to the voice of your wife and not join them. Thus you will be as one who has been brought up as a woman.[21] Men of every description do what is demanded of them, you alone do not act as a man should. You never perform a man's deed. If you were to go to a Winter Feast, you would be handed a lean piece of meat.[22] Why should you subject yourself to the danger of being made fun of? A real brave man, when he goes to a Winter Feast, will receive a deer's head, while you will only receive a lean piece of meat. That is all they will give you to eat. It will stick in your throat."[23]

My son, if you keep on listening to your wife, after a while she will never let you go to any feast at all. All your relatives will scold you and your own sisters will think little of you. They will say to one another, "Let us not ever go over to see him. He is of no help to anyone." Finally, when you have become a real slave to your wife, she might tell you to hit your own relatives, and you would do it. For these reasons, my son, I warn you against the words of women. Steel yourself against them. For if you do not do so you will find yourself different from other men. It is not good to be enslaved by a woman.

My son, this also I will tell you. Women can never be watched. If you try to watch them you will merely show your jealousy and your female relatives will also be jealous. After a while you will become so jealous of your wife that she will leave you and run away. First, you worshipped her above everything else, then you became jealous and watched her all the time, and the result will be that she will run away from you. You yourself will be to blame for this. You thought too much of a woman and in worshipping her you humbled yourself, and as a consequence she has been taken away from you. You are making the woman suffer and making her feel unhappy. All the other women will know of this, and no one will want to marry you again. Everyone will consider you a very bad man.

---

[21] He may mean a berdash, but it is far more probable that he merely means to call him a woman, an insult sufficiently great.

[22] A man who has distinguished himself as a warrior is always invited to eat the head of the animal, offered at the Winter Feast. Those next in distinction are given the fat pieces of meat, and the lean pieces—to the Winnebago, the poorest—are given to those who are of no importance.

[23] I. e., the meat will stick in your throat, because you will feel so much ashamed of yourself.

My son, whenever people go on the warpath go along with them. It is good to die on the warpath. You may perhaps say so, because you are unhappy that your wife has left you. My son, not for such reasons, however, must you go on the warpath. You will be merely throwing away a human life. If you want to go on the warpath, do so because you feel that you are courageous enough, not because you are unhappy at the loss of your wife. If you go on the warpath you will enjoy yourself. Do not go, however, unless you have fasted, and unless you have fasted for that particular warpath. If you have not fasted and attempt nevertheless to go on the warpath, a bullet will surely seek you out and kill you. This is what will happen to you if you do not fast.

If you exert yourself in fasting you will assuredly perform some brave war exploit. You must tell your sisters and sister's children and your mother's sisters all about your exploit. Remember, also, that the keepers of the war-bundles can give you good advice in all that pertains to war. For their deeds they will be given a good dish of meat.[24] This they will give you to eat.

Of such things did my ancestors speak, and I would wish you to do as they did. That is why I am telling you all these things. I myself never asked for any of this instruction, but my father did. All human beings ought to ask for it. Never let anybody be in a position to puzzle you in regard to what is right. Ask for this instruction, my son, for it is not an ordinary thing. In the olden times if a person loved his child very much, he would only give him instruction after he had begun fasting all day for the first time. When a young boy has just matured, those who have been preaching to him always ask him one question, namely, whether he had begun to fast. And this the young boy must always answer truthfully, for if he has begun his fast the instruction would stop. The old men do not preach to men, but only to boys.

(What follows is apparently an illustration of how a young man asks his instructor for information of how to conduct himself in life.)
The young man will go to an old man and say, "Grandfather, I would like to know how I am to conduct myself in life. Bless me and if you can really give me any information, do so." Then the old man was very thankful and said, "It is good; you speak correctly." Now the one who was asking something of the old man had taken very good care of the old man's body and had led a good life. He had no scars of any kind; that is, he had never done anything shameful. The young man brought all sorts of food and placed it in the lodge of the old man. Then he also brought him a fine horse. Only then did he ask him again about the life that his ancestors had led, and what kind of a life he ought to live. He asked

---

[24] I. e., you will be given a position at the Winter Feast and offered some of the choice pieces of meat.

him what the old people do when they give a child a name, and what they say. All these things the old man told him. "It is good," he said, "for you to know these things so that if anyone comes to you and asks you for information you will be able to tell them something and will not have to behave like a fool. If you are asked to give a little child a name, this little child will really be a means of increasing your power. That is why you ought to give a feast for it and smoke the child's tobacco. You must also give the child a name for his dog. Give him the name Yellow-Tree for a male dog. The name Yellow-Tree is given for the following reason. When the Thunderbirds strike at a tree it looks yellow. Just as leaves wither so do trees wither when the Thunderbirds strike them. They then begin to rot and become very much discolored. That is why they give a dog this name. If you ever have to give a dog-name for a female child call it She-Who-Stays-In-Her-Own-Place. This is all that I wish to tell you."

SYSTEM OF INSTRUCTION TO DAUGHTER

This is the way the old men used to speak to the little girls:

My daughter, as you go along the path of life, always listen to your parents. Do not permit your mother to work. Attend to your father's wants. All the work in the house belongs to you. Never be idle. Chop the wood, carry it home, look after the vegetables and gather them, and cook the food. When in the spring of the year you move back to your permanent settlements, plant your fields immediately. Never get lazy. Earthmaker created you for these tasks.

When you have your menses, do not ask those in your lodge to give you any food, but leave the lodge and fast and do not begin eating again until you return to your own lodge. Thus will you help yourself. If you always fast, when you marry, even if your husband had amounted to nothing before, he will become an excellent hunter. It will be on account of your fasting that he will have changed so much. You will never fail in anything and you will always be well and happy. If, on the contrary, you do not do as I tell you—that is, if you do not fast—when you marry he will become very weak, and this will be due to you. Finally he will get very sick.

My daughter, do not use medicine. If you marry a man and place medicine on his head he will become very weak and will not amount to anything. It may be that you do not want to have your husband leave you and this may induce you to use medicine to keep him. Do not do that, however, for it is not good. You will be ruining a man. It is the same as killing him. Do not do it, for it is forbidden. If you marry a man and you want to be certain of always retaining him, work for him. With work you will always be able to retain your hold on men. If you do your work to the satisfaction of your husband, he will never leave you. I say again, it is not proper to use medicine. Above all, do not use medicine until you have passed your youth. You will otherwise merely make yourself weak. You will lead a weak life. It may even happen that you will cause yourself to become foolish.

Do not use a medicine in order to marry. If you marry remain faithful to your husband. Do not act as though you are married to a number of men at the same time. Lead a chaste life. If you do not listen to what I am telling you and you are unfaithful to your husband, all the men will jeer at you. They will say whatever they wish to (and no one will interfere). Every man will treat you as though he were on the "joking relationship" with you. If you do not listen to me, therefore, you will injure yourself.

Thus the old people used to talk to one another. Thus they would warn one another against certain actions. They used to instruct the young girls as they grew up (just as I am doing to you now). That is why I am telling of these things now.

My daughter, as you grow older and grow up to be a young woman, the young men will begin to court you. Never strike a man, my daughter. It is forbidden. If you dislike a man very much, tell him gently to go away. If you do not do this and instead strike him, remember that it frequently happens that men know of medicines; or if they themselves have none they may know from whom to get them. If you make a man feel bad by striking him, he may use this medicine and cause you to run away with him and become a bad woman. It is for this reason that the old men used to warn the young girls not to strike the men who are courting them, but whom they dislike. Pray with all your heart that you do not become such a woman.

Do not act haughtily to your husband. Whatever he tells you to do, do it. Kindness will be returned to you if you obey your husband, for he will treat you in the same manner.

If you ever have a child, do not strike it. In the olden times when a child misbehaved the parents did not strike it, but they made it fast. When a child gets hungry, he will soon see the error of his ways. If you hit a child, you will be merely knocking the wickedness into him. Women should likewise never scold the children because children are merely made wicked by scoldings. If your husband scolds the children, do not take their part, for that will merely make them bad. In the same way, if a stranger makes your children cry, do not say anything to the stranger in the presence of the children, nor take their part in his presence. If you wish to prevent a stranger from scolding your children, keep them home and teach them how to behave by setting them a good example. Do not imagine that you do the best for your children by taking their part, or that you love them if you talk merely about loving them. Show them that you love them by your actions. Let them see that you are generous with donations. In such actions they will see your good work and then they will be able to judge for themselves whether your actions equal your words.

My daughter, do not show your love for other children so that strangers notice it. You may, of course, love other children, but love them with a different love from that which you bestow on your own children. The children of other people are different from your own children, and if you were to take them to some other place after you had been lavishing so much love upon them they would not act as your children would under the same circumstances. You can always depend upon your own children. They are of your own body. Love them, therefore. This is what our ancestors taught us to do.

If a wife has no real interest in her husband's welfare and possessions she will be to him no more than any other woman, and the world will ridicule her. If, on the other hand, you pay more attention to your husband than to your parents, your parents will leave you. Let your husband likewise take care of your parents, for they depend on him. Your parents were instrumental in getting you your husband, so remember that they expect some recompense for it, as likewise for the fact that they raised you.

My daughter, the old people used to teach us never to hurt the feelings of our relatives. If you hurt their feelings, you will cause your brothers-in-law to feel ashamed of themselves. Do not ever wish for any other man but your husband. It is enough to have one husband. Do not let anyone have the right to call you a prostitute.

Do not hit your relatives at any time. For if you did that or if you were on bad terms with one of them, it may chance that he will die, and then the people will say that you are glad that he is dead. Then, indeed, you will feel sad at heart and you will think to yourself, "What can I best do" (to make up for my conduct). Even if you were to give a Medicine Dance in his honor or donate gifts for the Four Nights' Wake, many people will still say, "She used to be partial and jealous when he was alive. Now that he is dead she loves him. Why does she act this way? She is wasting her wealth. (She really does not love him and therefore), and she ought not to spend so much money upon him now." Then, indeed, my daughter, will your heart ache; then, indeed, will you get angry. That is why the old people would tell their children to love one another. If you love a person and that person dies, then you will have a right to mourn for him, and everyone will think that your mourning is sincere. Not only will your own relatives love you, but everyone else will love you likewise. If, then, in the course of your life you come to a crisis of some kind, all these people will turn their hearts toward you.

My daughter, all that I am trying to tell you relates to your behavior (when you grow up). In your own home the women all understand the work belonging to the household and that relating to camping and hunting. If you understand these and afterwards visit your husband's relatives, you will know what to do and not find yourself in a dilemma from which you can not extricate yourself. When you visit your husband's people do not go around with a haughty air or act as if you considered yourself far above them. Try to get them to like you. If they like you, they will place you in charge of the camp you happen to be visiting. If you are good-natured, you will be placed in charge of the home at which you happen to be visiting. Then your parents-in-law will tell your husband that their daughter-in-law is acting nicely to them.

SYSTEM OF INSTRUCTION TO CHILDREN

Informant, member of the Thunderbird clan: I still keep up the old system of teaching my children at the camp fire. In the morning I wake them up early and start to teach them as follows:

My children, as you travel along life's road never harm anyone, nor cause anyone to feel sad. On the contrary, if at any time you can make a person happy, do so. If at any time you meet a woman in the wilderness (i. e., away from your village), and if you are alone and no one can see you, do not scare her or harm her, but turn off to the right and let her pass. Then you will be less tempted to molest her.

My children, if you meet anyone on the road, even though it is only a child, speak a cheering word before you pass on. Fast as much as you can, so that when you grow up you can benefit your fellowmen. If you ever get married you must not sit around your lodge near your wife, but try and get game for your wife's people. So fast that you may be prepared for your life.

My daughters, if at any time you get married, never let your husband ask for a thing twice. Do it as soon as he asks you. If your husband's folks ever ask their children for something when you are present, assume that they had asked it of you. If there is anything to be done, do not wait till you are asked to do it, but do it immediately. If you act in this way, then they will say that your parents taught you well.

My son, if you find nothing else to do, take an ax and chop down a tree. It will become useful some day. Then take a gun and go out hunting and try to get game for your family.

As soon as I see that the children are showing signs of restlessness then I stop immediately.

Part II

CHAPTER VIII

SOCIAL ORGANIZATION—GENERAL DISCUSSION

We are justified in assuming that the twofold division of the Winnebago and the southern Siouan tribes, Dhegiha and Tciwere, had a common historical origin. Our identification is based upon the existence in these three tribal units of specific similarities apart from those of social organization. Positive proof that the type of social organization is historically identical among these tribes is not, however, forthcoming. This will become even more apparent when we consider the twofold division from the point of view of the names they bear, the subdivisions within them, and their specific functions.

According to our informants, the twofold organization among the Dhegiha and Tciwere only existed upon specific occasions, when the tribe was on the tribal hunt. We are in complete ignorance as to whether in olden times this arrangement was reflected in the village, but we know that whether it was or not, the twofold division was present in a very definite manner in the consciousness of the people themselves; that is, every individual definitely knew to which one of the two divisions he belonged and that certain names and functions were associated with them. The moment, however, that we stop to analyze these names, functions, etc., we realize at once that to-day they connote different ideas in the different tribes under discussion. The names of the divisions seem particularly significant in this connection. Among the Omaha they are known as Ictacunda and Hanga, probably connoting Sky people and Leaders; among the Ponca, as Wajaje and Tciju, Earth and Thunder; among the Kansa, as Yata and Ictunga, Right side and Left side; among the Osage as Tciju and Hanga, Peace and War side. The names for the Kwapa, Oto, Missouri, and Iowa are not known. It will be seen at a glance that the terms Tciju and Ictacunda are identical, and it will also be noticed by reference to the monographs of J. O. Dorsey and Miss Alice C. Fletcher and Francis La Flesche, that these names as well as the name Hanga are names of subdivisions within these divisions. Were these names first used to designate the two divisions or the subdivisions? There seems to be no reason for believing that the names were first applied to the larger divisions, whereas a number of facts speak strongly in favor of the reverse. In no case, for instance, can it be shown that the two divisions, per se, have any functions except that of regulating marriage. The various political and ceremonial functions displayed pertain to the subdivisions composing them. Owing to the massing together of a number of such functions on each side, we often obtain the impression that these belong to the larger unit, as such. And indeed this may be said to be true at the present time, in so far as the functions of one subdivision have become identified with the larger unit. All that we wish to point out here is that the names of the two divisions may be different, and that they may connote different ideas in the different divisions of an historically related culture, due to specific historical development within each. Among the Dhegiha there seem to be a number of reasons for assuming that the present names of the two divisions are not the historically primary ones.

It is far more difficult to discuss the names of the subdivisions or "gentes" within the two larger divisions. From a comparative point of view it must be regarded as significant that the names of the subdivisions within the Tciwere tribes tally almost exactly with those of the Winnebago and that those of the Dhegiha tribes tally with the names of many of the two latter, although they possess, in addition, a large number not found among them. The Tciwere and Winnebago have animal appellations for their clans, the Dhegiha have animal appellations plus a type of designation descriptive of animal taboo. Which of the two types is the older it is difficult to say. This fact might be noted, however, that the animal names have, to a large extent, been forgotten and that the descriptive taboo appellations have not; that in a number of cases there is some reason for believing that these animal appellations have been reinterpreted and in other cases replaced by nonanimal designations; that the origin myths of these divisions always explain why a certain animal is associated with a subdivision, and rarely the origin of the taboo name; and lastly, that the majority of personal names are strictly comparable to the clan names of the Winnebago and the Tciwere. On the other hand, the descriptive taboo type of name is found frequently among the band appellations of the Plains Indians, with whom the Omaha had come into intimate contact and by whom they had been influenced along definite lines of ceremonial and social development. For these reasons we would like to suggest that the animal appellations are historically primary and that the taboo type became subsequently popular and spread over the whole tribe. Examples of changes in the names of subdivisions are by no means isolated. The Winnebago exhibit a tendency to substitute names indicative of the function of a clan for the old animal names—and this has gone so far that a large number of individuals would probably deny to-day that the Hawk and the Warrior clan are one and the same. Again, among the Osage, Kansa, and Quapaw we find Sun and Star clans, and, if we were to imagine that for some reason or another the latter type of name became popular, it might here become dominant within a comparatively short time.

Like a twofold division, the clan may connote a number of different things to the minds of the Indians. The Omaha apparently used the term *tonwoqgtho^n*, which means literally "place-of-habitation-of-those-related," *gtho^n* being the possessive-reflexive pronoun. It would thus seem to coincide with a geographical unit. The Quapaw use the term *enikaciga*, evidently meaning "people"; the Kansa, the term *wayumida*, "those-who-sing-together"; the Osage, the term *peda*, "fireplace"; and the Winnebago, the term *hokik'a'radjera*, "those-related-to-one-another." The remarks made about the specific names of the twofold divisions apply here. There is no reason for assuming that these are historically primary. A possible historical hint that they are not will be mentioned later.

The twofold division apparently regulates nothing but marriage. It has at the present time no other function, per se. Nevertheless, a number of ethnologists, and for that matter Indians themselves, speak of the functions of the two sides. If we consider the Omaha "circle," we notice that practically all the ceremonial functions are on one side; that among the Osage "war" and "peace" functions are found on both sides; and that, as a matter of fact, the functions of war and peace apparently relate to a certain reciprocal relation existing between the two divisions. Indeed, there is no reason to justify the use of these terms. Among the Iowa, J. O. Dorsey quotes Hamilton to the effect that the regulation of the hunt and other tribal affairs was in the hands of one "phratry" during the autumn and winter, and in that of the other in spring and summer. It is, however, doubtful whether this was the case. Among the Winnebago, as we shall see, the functions of war and peace were grouped together on one side, the functions of the other side being confined to those relating to the policing and regulation of the hunt. But the only fact of importance to us here is not whether there appears a balancing of functions connected with the social organization, but whether the Indian thinks there is; and here the consensus of opinion favors the view that no Omaha would, for example, suppose that the Hangacenu division, as such, was the custodian of the real pipes of peace. This belonged to the Inkesabe gens, and there is not a shred of evidence to support the view that it was delegated to that clan by the larger unit. The same reasoning applies to the Hanga clan. That the importance of the possessions of the latter clan played an important part in the associations of the Omaha, even to the extent of impressing its name upon the whole division, we do not doubt for a moment. Other reasons may have led to the designation of the other half by the name of one of its component clans.

Similarly, among the Ponca, the Wajaje half corresponds to the Wajaje clan, the keepers of the sacred pipe; and among the Osage, the Tciju and the Hanga divisions of one side, and the Wajaje divisions of the other, correspond to the clans with the same name that are associated with important ceremonial-political functions. On the other hand, we have the fact that among the Kansa the names of the two large divisions are distinct from any of the clans in those divisions, and the same is true for the Tciju division of the Ponca. If we correlate this last fact with the apparent absence of any association of important ceremonial or political functions with specific clans, the suggestion might be permitted that no incentive existed in the minds of these people for the clan becoming identified with the larger divisions. Among the Winnebago the names for the divisions are quite different from those of the clans composing them, but at the present time the fact that the clan in each division has definite functions and powers has reacted on the interpretation of the social organization, and it is quite customary to refer to one half as *huŋk* or "chiefs," and to the other as *manap'e* or "soldiers," although the latter is not common.

In short, we have a right to see, in all the facts mentioned, indications of a possible historical development whose characteristics seem to lie in the identification of the name and function of an important clan with that of a much larger division.

The Winnebago social organization has long since broken down, but its details are still so well preserved in the minds of the older men, and particularly in the literature of the tribe, that no difficulty was experienced in reconstructing it. This reconstruction, however, does not enable us to determine the relation of the clan and dichotomous division to the distribution of the tribe over the large area once occupied in Wisconsin. That the 4,000-odd individuals composing the tribe at the advent of the whites lived together is extermely doubtful. The nature of the woodlands of Wisconsin and the fairly extensive territory over which the Winnebago were found scattered not long after Nicolet's first visit are facts that practically exclude such a hypothesis. The myth that speaks of a village that at one time was so long that those living at one end did not know what was transpiring at the other contains too many literary touches to justify its use as an historical document.

The question, therefore, of village groups is of considerable importance, because there may have been, cutting across the general organization, another smaller, perhaps looser social unit, that of "band" or village, setting off one group against another. Systematic questioning has elicited from various individuals the information, also corroborated by historical records, that the villages were generally known according to geographical location or according to names descriptive of the haunts of certain animals. Even to-day the group scattered over the Nebraska Winnebago reservation are commonly known by similar designations. There we find, for instance, the following names: *kozo-atcira*, "those living on the peninsula"; or *k'uha^ntcira*, "those living below", i. e., in the timber; *niwa'hatcira*, "those living near the dirty water"; *hṳtc x^ᵉdgominangera*, "where big bear settles," etc. If we may then suppose this to have been a customary association, we may quite properly ask whether the name of the village had any influence on the social organization; whether there is even a hint at a genetic relation between these two types of group names. All that can be said is the fact that formerly *honi*, "band," seems to have been used instead of *hokik'aradjera* for clan; that an archaic name of the Wolf clan, *regoni* or *degoni*, may mean Lake band; and that the villages all had geographical names. All of which, however, is, I realize, hardly sufficient evidence.

No satisfactory demonstration has as yet been made indicating that the clan organization was ever associated with an historically simple social structure, whereas quite a number of reasons lead us to suspect that it was in all cases preceded by other types of organization. In North America there is quite considerable evidence tending to show that the village group organization often preceded in many places the clan, and for that reason the facts brought out above may be of more than casual significance. That a system of clan names different from that now in use existed is borne out by the archaic names for the Bear and Wolf clans. That another system was making headway against the animal-name type of change, namely, the substitution for animal designation, with correlated associations of descent or connection with an animal ancestor, of designations indicative of the functions of the clan. If the association of the social unit with a common animal ancestor was preceded by an association of a social unit with geographical location, we would then be able to demonstrate what is so rare in ethnology—the historical succession of types of naming.

THE TWOFOLD GROUPING

The Winnebago are divided into divisions, one known as the *waŋgeregi herera*, "those who are above," the other as the *manegi herera*, "those who are on earth." Descent was reckoned in the paternal line. But these appellations refer to the animals after whom the clans are named, the term *waŋgeregi* covering the birds, the term *manegi*, land and water animals. So firmly has the idea of division of animal forms become associated with the two divisions that, as mentioned before, were a new clan introduced now among the Winnebago its position would depend exclusively upon the nature of the animal associated with it. As similar reasons dictate clan groupings among some of the Central Algonquian tribes, a few words concerning this type of association will not be amiss. The groupings of the fauna into a distinct number of categories is extremely common in North America. Among the Winnebago, a number of other Siouan, and Central Algonquian tribes, there was a fivefold classification; earth animals, sky animals, empyrean animals, aquatic animals, and subaquatic animals. Among the Winnebago the thunderbird belongs to the empyrean; the eagle, hawk, and pigeon, to the sky; the bear and wolf, to the earth; the fish, to the water; and the water-spirit, below the water. This religio-mythological conception has unquestionably received a certain amount of sympathetic elaboration at the hands of shamans, and particularly at the hands of the leaders of such ceremonies as the Winter Feast, the Clan Feast, and the Clan Wake, as well as at the hands of those who had in their keeping the clan origin myths.

The characteristics of the thunderbird, eagle, bear, and water-spirit as clan animals, and as animals connected with a division of fauna, are also related to the general conception of these animals per se. The eagle and hawk are birds of prey; the thunderbird is generally a deity granting long life, and associated with peace, although his connection with war is also common. Similarly, the bear is supposed to have a "soldier" nature, and the water-spirit is intimately associated with rites pertaining to crossing streams, calming the sea, and ownership of water property. This correlation unquestionably indicates an influence of the religio-mythological conception of the animal upon the social group with which it is associated. How far this can go is abundantly attested by the names and behavior of the *waŋgeregi* and *manegi* divisions.

On the other hand, we may legitimately ask what influence the two divisions had in molding the attributes of these animals, or upon the behavior of the groups with which their name was associated. The functions of a warrior may have determined, as they certainly have accentuated, the "warrior" characteristics of the eagle and hawk, nor is there any easily intelligible reason why the thunderbird should be associated with peace. From our knowledge of the social organization of other Siouan tribes, the political functions of the clan seem to be the characteristic feature of the organization, and this being the case, the possibility of associations of warlike and peaceful attributes with animals may as much be ascribed to the influence of the social unit as vice versa. With regard to such functions as the exogamy of the two divisions or that of the clans, or of the reciprocal burial relationship of the *waŋgeregi* and *manegi* divisions, we, of course, know that the characteristics of the animal in question have nothing to do with the matter. We must then realize that we are dealing with reciprocal influences—of the religio-mythical conception of animals on the one hand, and of political functions of social units on the other. In some cases, such as the specific associations with the water-spirit, it is probable that the religio-mythological conception of the animal is dominant. The association of the thunderbird with fire has likewise not been due to any activity of the social unit; and thus examples might be multiplied. In this connection, the fact that animals with whom a multitude of associations have already been established are subsequently associated with social units is fundamental. From this point of view, the animal names of social organization are intrusive features, and we will consequently expect to find historical adjustments. This, we think, is what has taken place here. The animal name with its religio-mythological conceptions was a remarkably strong unit, and as a result reciprocal influences took place. Although the religio-mythological influence must thus have been marked, it appears to have changed none of the marital and other functions of the two divisions nor the political functions of the clans. What it did change, and change fundamentally, was the interpretation of the social organization.

Functions of the Twofold Division

The only function that the *waŋgeregi* and *manegi* divisions seem to have had was the regulation of marriage. A *waŋgeregi* man had to marry a *manegi* woman, and vice versa. The only other function was, according to some informants, reciprocal burial. Here the religio-mythological interpretations seem in part to have determined this relation, for a *manegi* man buried a *waŋgeregi* man because, as a "land division," it pertained to him to place a corpse in the earth. This, however, seems to be a doubtful function, for earth burial seems in olden times to have been characteristic only of the *manegi* division, the *waŋgeregi* clans employing scaffold burial. In addition, the burial relation was one of the many reciprocal duties of the "friend-clan," and if it was ever postulated of the *waŋgeregi* and *manegi*, this was likely due to the fact that the "friendship" relation seems also to have existed between two clans belonging to the two different divisions. According to one myth, however, the four clans of the *waŋgeregi* paired off as "friends" with four clans of the *manegi*. This would then be practically equivalent to saying that the *manegi* buried the *waŋgeregi*.

Thus far we have spoken only of the socio-political functions. The two divisions, however, play a part in a number of social and ceremonial connections: first, in the organization of the village; second, in the arrangement of the clans while on the warpath; third, as the basis of organization at the "chief" feast; and lastly, as the basis of organization of the ceremonial lacrosse game.

According to the majority of the older people, when the old social organization was still intact, each village was divided into two halves by an imaginary line running due northwest and southeast, the *waŋgeregi* clans dwelling in one half, with the chief's lodge in the south, and the *manegi* clans dwelling in the other half, with the bear or soldier lodge in the north (fig. 33). Although this arrangement has now become almost legendary, it was corroborated by many of the older people. To what extent every village was organized on this basis it is impossible to state. When this question was

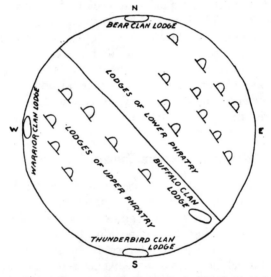

Fig. 33.—Plan of village according to Thundercloud, of the Thunderbird clan.

directly put to individuals, the answer was always in the affirmative. Quite a number of old individuals, however, denied vigorously that such had ever been the organization of the village, and claimed instead that the lodges of the Chief and the Soldier (Bear) clan were in the center of the village (fig. 34).

In looking over the clan affiliations of the informants, we noticed, however, that the first arrangement was always given by members of the bird clans, and the second arrangement by members of the Bear clan and generally also by others on the *manegi* side. This fact, of course, makes the decision as to the relationship of these two types of village organization quite difficult. There can be no question as to the existence of a twofold division of the tribe as far as marital relations were concerned, nor as to the segregation of specific clans in different villages. When on the warpath the twofold division manifested itself in the arrangement of fireplaces, so that the question to be resolved here is whether we can credit the statements that this twofold division expressed itself in the arrangement of the village, and, if it did, whether this was characteristic of the whole tribe or only of parts of the tribe. That this was true for part of the tribe can be accepted. Whether it was true for the whole tribe, however, can not be definitely answered until we know more of the Dhegiha and Tciwere. In the subsequent discussion of the clan we will touch on this subject again.

The twofold organization is reflected in the arrangement of the fireplaces when on the warpath, each division having two fireplaces,

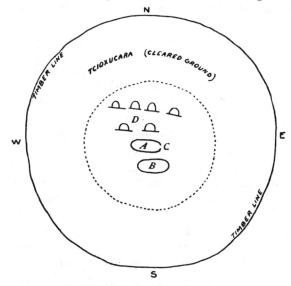

Fig. 34.—Plan of village according to John Rave, of Bear clan. *A*, Lodge of chief of tribe (Thunderbird clan). *B*, Lodge of chief of Bear clan. *C*, Lodge of Warrior clan. *D*, Lodge of Buffalo clan.

whose location is determined by the direction in which the party is going. When going west, for instance, the two fireplaces for the *waŋgeregi* are on the south, and the two for the *manegi* on the north side. However, when on the tribal move or hunting, no indication of the division exists.

As the basis of ceremonial organization, we find the twofold division present only once—at the chief feast (*huŋk woḣa*), but as this feast is to all intents and purposes a feast given by the bird clans in general, there is really nothing surprising about its use. The name *huŋk woḣa* would seem to indicate that we are dealing simply with a feast of the Thunderbird clan, and this indeed may have been the case historically. *Huŋk* to-day, however, is frequently used to indicate the *waŋgeregi* division.

As the basis of organization in a game, the twofold division finds expression in ceremonial lacrosse. There the *waŋgeregi* are always pitted against the *manegi*. A well-known myth is associated with this arrangement, according to which the animal ancestors of the *waŋgeregi* and *manegi* decided their respective rank by playing a game in which they were organized on this basis. The *waŋgeregi* won and for that reason the chiefs of the tribe have been selected from this division. A division into two halves when playing ceremonial lacrosse is characteristic not only of the Winnebago but of the Omaha, Menominee, Sauk, Fox, and other tribes. Among the former two, these sides are identical with the two aforementioned political divisions of the tribe, but among the latter two, where no such division exists, the tribe seems to divide itself into two halves merely on this occasion.

Up to the present we have treated the two divisions as social units per se, but now, before entering on the discussion of the clans, it may be well to point out the fact that the *waŋgeregi* people are sometimes spoken of as the Bird clan (*waniŋk hokik'aradjera*), and that the four clans composing this side are so intimately related, and their clan origin myths so similar, that the assumption of the four clans representing one clan that subsequently split up into a number of divisions is not outside the realm of historical possibility. This is, however, quite immaterial, for whether we have one bird clan opposed to eight other animal clans is of little consequence, for historically it is not the bird clan that is opposing the other clans, but one social unit, the division, set off against another. The numerical equality that exists between these two sides, in spite of the disparity in the number of clans, is perhaps another confirmation of the fundamental character of the twofold structure.

CLAN ORGANIZATION

There are 12 clans among the Winnebago with the following names:

A. *Waŋgeregi herera* (those who are above):[1]
    1. *wakandja*, thunderbird.
    2. *wonaγire uaŋkcik*, war-people.
    3. *tcaxcεp*, eagle.
    4. *rutcgε*, pigeon (extinct).

B. *manegi herera* (those who are on earth):
    5. *huntc*, bear.
    6. *cuŋktcuŋk'*, wolf.
    7. *waktcexi*, water spirit.
    8. *tca*, deer.
    9. *huⁿwaⁿ*, elk.

---

[1] All the clans of the upper phratry are also called *ahuirasara*, "Those-with-wings." This name is found in ceremonies.

10. *tce*, buffalo.

11. *ho*, fish.

12. *wak'a^n*, snake.

Another list was obtained in which only 10 clans were mentioned, the Fish and the Snake being omitted. The clans omitted are, however, regarded by all as of recent origin.

There are two older lists of Winnebago clans obtained by Morgan [2] and Dorsey.[3] Morgan gives the following clans:

Wolf.	Eagle.	Snake.
Bear.	Elk.	Thunder.
Buffalo.	Deer.	

Dorsey's list is more complete, although owing to the fact that he did not know of the existence of the twofold division, he classes the four Bird clans as subclans of one larger Bird clan. His list differs from the author's only in the absence of the Fish clan and in the fact that he was still able to obtain two archaic names for the Wolf and Bear clans. Dorsey's list follows:

Wolf.	Bird.	Buffalo.
Bear.	*a.* Eagle.	Deer.
Elk.	*b.* Pigeon.	Water-monster.
Snake.	*c.* Hawk.	
	d. Thunderbird.	

Foster gives a grouping of the clans according to the fauna.[4] His list hardly was intended as an enumeration of the clans. According to Foster, we have the following grouping:

I. Thunderbird family or invisible Thunderbird people.

II. The air family, the visible Thunderbird people.

III. The land or quadruped family.

IV. The water family.

An interesting variant of the names of the Thunderbird and Warrior clans was given by one informant. He called the Thunderbird the good thunders, and the Warrior the bad thunders. This is strikingly reminiscent of the Menominee and was perhaps borrowed from them.

The main differences in the above lists are the order of the clans, the position of the Wolf clan, the presence of a general Bird clan called *wanink* by Dorsey, the double names for the Wolf and Bear clans, and the absence of a Fish and Warrior clan in Dorsey's and of a Hawk clan in the list obtained by the author.

The position of the Wolf clan, in spite of Morgan's and Dorsey's agreement, does not belong in the place assigned to it by them. In all probability their main informant was a member of this clan who wished to give his clan a greater importance than properly belonged

[2] Ancient Society, p. 157.

[3] Siouan Sociology. Fifteenth Ann. Rept. Bur. Amer. Ethn, pp. 240–241.

[4] Quoted in J. O. Dorsey's MSS. of Winnebago clan names (B. A. E.).

to it.   There is no doubt but that in older times the Wolf clan played a far greater part in the affairs of the tribe than it does to-day, but that it ever was the principal clan of the tribe is out of the question.

With regard to Dorsey's postulation of a Bird (*wanink*) clan, all that can be said is that the author obtained nothing confirmatory of it.   It is just possible that Dorsey, who apparently did not know of the existence of the two phratries, misinterpreted a popular grouping of the four clans of the upper phratry, as representing a fundamental division.   Historically it may, indeed, be true that the four clans of the upper phratry represent the subdivision of one clan.

The archaic names for the Wolf and Bear clans can not be translated with any degree of certainty any longer.   It is barely possible that *degoni* means "lake band" and *tconank* means "blue back." Whether these are simply a second set of names, or whether they represent an historically older set, it is impossible to say to-day.   The probabilities are that they are terms of respect.

The absence of the Warrior clan in Dorsey's list and the presence of a Hawk clan is rather interesting, for it shows that only 25 years ago the bird name for this clan was still in use.   The Warrior and Hawk clans are identical, the latter being, however, the appellation that is preferred to-day.

In addition to the names given above, some of the clans have names indicative of respect, such as *hung*ᵉ for the Water-spirit, *haga* for the male members of the Bear clan, and *warowina* for the female members.   It is also possible that the names *degoni* and *tconank*, mentioned by Dorsey for the Wolf and Bear clans, were terms of respect.

RECKONING OF DESCENT

Descent is patrilineal and a man's name generally belongs to his father's clan.   Formerly there never was an exception to the rule that the name must belong to the father's clan, but of recent years the Winnebago have become very lax in this particlular.   The irregularities in the giving of names were due to two causes—first, the intermarriage of Winnebago women with white men or with Indians of other tribes where the clan organization was either unknown or where descent was matrilineal, and, secondly, to the fact that the wife's parents were often in a better position to pay for the naming feast than the parents of the father.   When a Winnebago woman marries a man who either has no clan or who reckons descent in the mother's line, the children are always considered as belonging to the mother's clan.   This, however, lasts for only one generation.   As a result the male children of such a marriage perpetuate the clan of the mother, although they transmit it thereafter in the male line.

Another irregularity that has grown up within recent times is the occasional transmission of the clan war-bundle in the female line. In olden times it could only be transmitted in the male line, so as to prevent its passing out of the clan. It was, however, not always passed to the eldest son, but to that one who, by his actions and the interest he manifested in learning the legends and songs pertaining to the ceremony, showed himself capable of properly providing for the bundle. Now it happened occasionally that a man either possessed no son or that his son did not show sufficient interest in all that pertained to the bundle. In such a case the father had the alternative of giving it to some near relative in the male line, and if there were none of either giving it to some distant relative in the male line or the son of his sister or daughter. This, of course, happened very rarely, and in all probability the female line would eventually have to return it to the clan to which it originally belonged.

We have described these two instances of transmission in the female line in some detail in order to show how simply they can be explained without the intervention of any theory that the Winnebago reckoned descent in the female line originally. Such a claim has been made by Morgan and reiterated by Frazer. It seems to be based on the fact that Carver found the daughter of a Winnebago chief, known to the whites as Glory-of-the-Morning, and her children occupying an exceptional position among the tribe, or at least among the division of the Winnebago living at the upper end of Lake Winnebago, Wis. Her position and that of her children, one of whom has become well known in Winnabago legends, *Tcap'osgaga*, was, however, due to the fact that she married a Frenchman named Decora. She was not the chieftainess of the tribe nor were any of her children, strictly speaking, chiefs of the tribe. In any case her position had nothing to do with female descent and at best but illustrates what we have said before about the clan to which children of such a union belong.

INDIVIDUAL NAMES

Before turning to the specific study of each clan a few words must be said about the individual names. From a purely descriptive point of view the names can be arranged in nine classes:

I. Color.
II. Physiological characteristics.
III. Social functions.
IV. Animal and plant forms.
V. Animal characteristics.
VI. Natural phenomena.
VII. Quality.
VIII. Episodes of a legendary character.
IX. Personal achievement.

According to the majority of our informants only one of these classifications seems to be generally present in the minds of the Winnebago to-day—that commemorating incidents relating to the origin of each clan. Thus, for instance, because the first thunderbird alit on a tree the name *He-who-alights-on-a-tree* is given; because a wave swept over the shore as the wolf arrived at Green Bay the name *Wave* is given, etc. However, the most representative names of this type are *Gives-forth-fruit-as-he-walks, Makes-the-day-tremble, He-who-comes-singing, Judge-of-the-contest*, etc. The vast majority of the names, although many of them can doubtless be interpreted as referring to incidents that occurred during the various origins of the clan, clearly belong to the first seven divisions mentioned above. Yet the Winnebago interpret them all in terms of category VIII.

As an example of the Winnebago viewpoint let me give the following: [5]

Four men [the clan eponymous ancestors] Earth-Maker sent here from above; and when they came, all their various characteristics were used for making proper names. Thus at the present day, the characteristics of the thunder-birds, all of their actions, are used as proper names. (At the beginning), four men came from above. And from that fact there is a name, He-who-comes-from-Above. . . From above, four men Earth-Maker sent down. And since they came like spirits, there is a name, *Spirit-Man*. . . And as there was a drizzling fog when the four men came from above, so there are names, *Walking-in-Mist, Comes-in-Mist*, and a woman they would call, *Drizzling-Rain-Woman*. It is said that when they first came to Dérôk, they alit upon some brushes, and bent them down; and from this fact there is a name, *She-who-bends-the-Brushes*. On the limb of an oak-tree that stood there, they alit; and they bent it down as they alit on its branches. From this there is a name, *She-who-bends-the-Branches-down*. And since they alit on the tree, there is a name, *He-who-alights-on a-Tree;* . . . and from the tree itself there is the name, *Oak-Woman*. . . And because they stepped from the oak-tree to the ground, . . . there is a name, *He-who-alights-on-the-Ground*. . . And since they came with the thunder-birds, there is a name, *Thunder-bird* . . . and *White-Thunder-bird* . . . and *Black-Thunder-bird* . . . And since the thunder-birds thunder, there is a name, *He-who-thunders* . . . And since they make the noise *tcinwin*, people are called *He-who-makes-Tcinwin* . . . When the thunder-birds walk, rain accompanies them; and from this fact we have a name, *He-who-walks-with-Rain* . . . And since the thunder-birds come walking, we have a name, *Walking-Thunder;* and since the thunder-birds walk with a mighty tread when they start out, there is a name, *He-who-comes walking-with-a-Mighty-Tread;* . . . and since the earth shakes when they commence walking, there is a name, *He-who-shakes-the-earth-with-force* . . . And since there is always wind and hail when the thunder-birds come, we have a name, *He-who-comes-with-Wind-and-Hail*. Now, since one of the thunder-birds came first, there is a name, *He-who-walks-First;* and since one of them was the leader, therefore, there is the name *Thunder-bird-Leader* . . . Now since the thunder-birds flash (their eyes) in every direction, so we have the name *Flashes-in-every-Direction* . . . Now, we don't see the thunder-birds, but we see their flashes only; and thus there is a female name, *Only-a-flash-of-Lightning-Woman;* and since the thunder-birds (flash) streaks of lightning, there is a name, *Streak-of-Lightning;* and since cloudiness is caused by the thunder-birds walking in the clouds, there is a name, *He-who-walks-in-the-Clouds*. Now since the thunder-birds have long wings, there is a name, *He-who-has-Long-Wings* . . . Now when the thunder-birds come, they come with terrible thunder-crashes, it is said; and as many people as there are on this earth, . . . and as many plants as there are on the earth, indeed, everything, the earth itself, they deluge with rain, and thunder-crashes (are heard); for all this they have a name; they call him *Warudjáxega*.

The point at issue in this interpretation of names is, can we accept it as historically primary? We do not think so, for the following reasons: A large number of the names are clearly descriptive of animal habits, others express the influence of social organization, and others refer to personal achievements, etc. Secondly, the interpretation is of too specific a nature to be regarded as one that could possibly have dictated an original system of naming; and, thirdly, in spite of its prevalence, other systems of interpretation are present. As a matter of fact in the above quotation, our informant distinctly mentions the fact that the characteristics of thunderbirds were used for names, although he insists that the names referred specifically to the ancestors of the Thunderbird clan. According to J. O. Dorsey the interpretations obtained by him were largely symbolical. He makes no mention of the interpretation obtained by the author, although this may be due to the fact that he was but imperfectly acquainted with Winnebago ethnology. It seems best, therefore, to regard the ancestor-episode type of name as but one, perhaps the last, that developed among the Winnebago.[6]

ATTITUDE TOWARD CLAN ANIMALS

When the animal names became associated with the social groups they were accompanied by the specific associations clustering around these animals. These associations were probably of the same type, if not indeed identical with those grouped around the animals as guardian spirits. The clan animals are among the principal guardian spirits to-day, and we must expect to find an explanation of the attitude toward them as clan animals in the attitude exhibited toward the guardian spirit. To a certain extent it would be quite correct to say that the guardian became the clan animal. This does not, however, mean, in the slightest degree, that the guardian spirit of the individual became the clan animal, but merely that the concept of the guardian spirit became associated with a local group.

The guardian spirit is at the present time conceived of as an immaterial being in control of an animal species. The attitude toward this spirit is a purely religious one, and exhibits a marked absence of taboo of any kind. It is an open question whether a vision must be attested by obtaining some part of the animal "embodiment" of

---

[6] For fuller discussion cf. P. Radin, The Social Organization of the Winnebago Indians, Museum Bulletin 10, Anthropological Series 5, Geological Survey of Canada, 1915.

the spirit, but there is no doubt that every vision is symbolized by a special gift from the "spirit." The guardian spirit unit may thus be said to consist of a special religious attitude plus a symbol.

The attitude toward the clan animal differs from that toward the guardian spirit in this characteristic respect, that more emphasis is laid upon identification with the animal itself than with the "spirit." As far as could be determined, the clan animal is the thunderbird with his characteristics of lightning and thunder, of the bear who likes honey and raisins, etc. The animal is engraved as clan symbol and used as a property mark, and he is brought into intimate contact with the group by the postulation of descent. Naturally, descent is not from the "spirit" animal but from the living animal species. Nevertheless the clan animal has, at the same time, retained its place as a guardian spirit, and in a most suggestive way, for the blessing of a clan animal is more easily obtained by a member of the clan than by an outsider. The clan animal is, in short, a clan protector.

In this change of attitude two considerations seem pertinent: first, the possibility of the "spirit" of the guardian spirit being a product of the esoteric elaboration connected with religious societies, and that its apparent absence in the clan animal represents an exoteric conception; secondly, under the influence of the social functions of the clan, an originally strong religious conception of the clan animal gave place to an identification with the animal species itself. It might be objected that there is no inherent correlation between social organization and animal species as contrasted with spirit animals. It seems certain, however, that descent could only be reckoned from the animal, and as long as descent is postulated it must be from the animal. With regard to the historical priority of the "spirit" conception, little can be definitely said except that the systematization it has undergone suggests the influence of esoteric societies, and that the visions obtained during fasting appear to speak of the guardian "spirit" as an animal. On general psychological considerations we are inclined to believe in the contrast of the material and spiritual conception of the animal as a real fact, although it would be hazardous to say whether one or the other lies at the basis of the attitude of the individual toward his clan animal.

RELATIONSHIP TO CLAN ANIMALS

The question of descent from the animal brings us to the consideration of the whole intricate relationship of the individual to the clan animal, a subject that has played so prominent a part in discussions of totemism. There are two distinct sources for the determination of this relationship—data obtained in reply to direct questioning, and that contained in some miscellaneous myths and in the origin myths. Part of the oral data is merely a reflex of the origin myths, but part is not. The value of this "unwritten" material lies in the fact that it represents the popular, exoteric attitude, the attitude that, on the whole, is not the result of conscious rationalization, and that this exoteric view may very likely have been the basis for the priestly esoteric interpretation.

The prevalent conception of the relationship of the individual to his clan animal is that of descent from an animal transformed at the origin of the present human race into human beings. This view is expressed in some of the origin myths and the general statements of individuals. Direct descent from an animal was never postulated. The definition of the term "animal" is, however, very difficult. The Indians themselves seem to make a distinction between the animal of to-day and the animal of the heroic age. The main characteristics of the animal of the latter was his power of transformation into human form and vice versa. Although the animals have lost this to-day, they are nevertheless descended from this animal. The human beings are, however, descended from precisely the same "animals," so that it might be well to bear in mind that descent from the transformed animal does not mean descent from the animal of to-day. This view is more systematically expressed in some places. According to one miscellaneous myth, the existing human beings and animals were descended from the same being, who once possessed infinite powers of transformation now into human and now into animal shape. At one time, presumably the beginning of our present creation, these "beings" either consciously or unconsciously exhausted all their "transforming" power, and the form into which they changed themselves, human or animal, remained fixed for all time. The existing animals have never succeeded in regaining their power of transformation. Among human beings this power has only been vouchsafed to those few who have obtained it as a special gift from some spirit. Even then, however, it is ludicrously incomplete as compared with the same powers of primordial "beings." This conception of the animal-human archetype must not be regarded as at all flavoring of a philosophy developed after contact with Europeans. The error that has always been committed in discussions upon the nature of descent from the animal lies in confusing our concept of animal species with the term "animal" as used by primitive people, and in the lack of discrimination between the possible connotations of that same term, as applied to animals of to-day and as applied to those animals that were brought into intimate contact with the clan ancestor.

There is no reason for regarding the specific descent from the totem as a development of this older Winnebago idea of the origin

of human and animal forms.   The latter conception is entirely a
religious one, the former merely an extension of the genealogical
tendency prevalent in many types of social organization.   Instead
of being simply descended from an individual in a given social unit,
the bond of membership within this unit has been strengthened by
the postulation of blood relationship to the clan animal.   The idea
of descent may thus be looked upon as one of the elements necessary
for the stability of a political unit and may be far older than its
specific extension to those clan animals.   A very illuminating example of a case in point can be selected from the history of the war
bundle in the Thunderbird clan.   This bundle, like the others, was
obtained as a gift from the thunderbird in his capacity as a guardian
spirit.   The ceremony connected with it has, however, been markedly
influenced by the clan organization and as a result we find descent
from the thunderbird and night-spirit, the two most important
spirits in the ceremony, postulated of the original owner of the war
bundle.   The same tendency is exhibited in the numerous stories of
the relation of an individual of the heroic age to a village.   Here
the individual, generally a transformed guardian spirit or animal,
comes to the aid of the people in their struggle against cannibals,
defeats the latter and marries into the village, becoming thus the
eponymous ancestor of the subsequent village group.

At the same time no strong correlation apparently exists between
a totemic organization and the extension of descent to include the
clan animal, this seemingly being a peculiarity of certain cultures
only.   Bonds other than descent from the animal are frequently
found and must unquestionably be considered as older than the
latter in a number of cases.   On the Northwest coast, among the
Creek, Iroquois, and other tribes, descent from the totem is not
found.   Among the Winnebago themselves, in addition to the above,
we find the idea that the Thunderbird clan takes its name from the
fact of its members imitating the actions of that animal.   Some
versions of the origin myth give no reasons at all for the name, while
in others an animal is killed, becomes reincarnated as a human
being in a certain village, and the group takes its name from the
fact.   The descent from the totem, however, where it has not been
primary, owing to its being a reflex expression of the social organization, quite generally supplants the other interpretation.

In intimate relation with the attitude toward the clan animal is the
conception of the tie binding one member of the clan to another.
In no case did an individual regard the tie between him and another
member of the same clan as based upon descent from the same animal.
Blood relationship was always given as the reason for exogamy, as is

shown by the very word for clan (*hokik'aradjera*). This concept of blood relationship was extended to the mother's clan generation. As we have pointed out, there is no reason for assuming that blood relationship is the primary explanation. The number of explanations for exogamy existing between one clan and another, and between the clans of one side as opposed to those of another, indicate clearly how readily interpretations of this phenomenon change. The Bear does not marry into the Wolf clan because they are friends (*hitcak'oro*), and does not marry into the Buffalo clan because it belongs to the same side, or no reason at all is assigned. Before the question of the clan tie can be thoroughly understood, the kind of blood relationship that is here meant must be more carefully defined. This is not a very general but a very definite notion, and may be said to extend not beyond four generations, in fact not beyond the direct knowledge of some living individual. This will be brought out more clearly by the following tables, based on actual genealogies:

(F) Thunderbird—Bear (M) 1.	or:
(F) Bear—Eagle (M) 2.	(F) Thunderbird—Bear (M) 1.
(F) Eagle—Wolf (M) 3.	(M) Bear—Eagle (F) 2.
(F) Wolf—Thunderbird (M) 4.	(M) Bear—Thunderbird (F) 3.
(M) Thunderbird—Bear (F) 5.	

All these marriages are permitted. In the first case a man marries into his maternal grandmother's maternal grandfather's clan; and in the second, a man marries into his paternal grandmother's clan. We will consequently have to consider blood relationship as extending only to four, sometimes three, generations, and have to regard the statement of blood relationship as the tie binding the members of the clan together as purely fictitious and secondary. That, nevertheless, this fictitious tie called forth the same feeling as that of real relationship, there is abundant evidence to show, and that it was of considerable importance in the development of the Winnebago clan-unit is borne out by the fact that the clan was called "those-who-are-relatives-to-one-another."

CLAN FUNCTIONS

The association of political functions with definite social units is a common phenomenon in most cultures where a tendency toward socialization exists. It is strictly comparable to the association of ceremonial and religious functions with ceremonial units. In this connection, the difference between an association with a group unit and an association with an individual is of fundamental importance. Is the former, for instance, merely an extension of the latter? This only individual history can demonstrate. Such a genetic relationship between the two depends probably as much upon the nature of the political function as upon anything else. The exact time when this socialization took place is of no great import here. Among the Winnebago, for instance, some individuals claim that the functions of the public crier were inherent in the Buffalo clan, while others insist that any person who had counted coup four times was eligible for the office. Now, in this case not only is it possible but it is extremely probable that the office of public crier was originally connected with an individual, and that subsequently it became associated with the Buffalo clan, probably by reason of a certain relationship existing between this clan and the Chief clan. It must, of course, be remembered that a grouping had already taken place, because the requirement of having counted coup four times made a large number of warriors potentially public criers. Its association with membership in the Buffalo clan represented, on the one hand, a restriction of the number of individuals, and on the other hand, the addition of another qualification. Historically, then, the qualification of membership in the clan supplanted the other qualifications, at least in the eyes of a number of individuals. What has been said of the development of the functions of the Buffalo may also be generally applied to the Warrior or Hawk clan.

Political functions may, however, become connected with a group unit without the individual playing any rôle either in directing or in developing it. The functions of preserving peace and of acting as intermediary, that among the Winnebago are connected with the Thunderbird clan, and the police and disciplinary functions connected with the Bear clan, may represent such types of association. In the absence of historical data, no demonstration can be made. It will, however, be shown later that association of ceremonial-religious functions with a social unit has actually occurred. That the police and disciplinary functions of the Bear clan developed from functions of individuals, on the basis of requirements similar to those of the public crier, is quite improbable, and no indication of that exists. Similarly the functions of the Thunderbird clan do not lend themselves readily to such an interpretation. But even should we accept the necessity for the priority of the one over the other types of association, we must still insist that psychologically the functions are in each case associated with a group unit.

Four of the Winnebago clans have specific political functions the details of which are discussed elsewhere. The Thunderbird, the chief clan, and in addition to the fact that the chief of the tribe is selected from it, has important functions connected with the preservation of peace; the Warrior clan has functions connected with war; the Bear clan, those relating to policing and discipline, both within the village and while on the hunt, etc.; and the Buffalo clan, those relating to the office of public crier and intermediary between the

chief and his people.   The Wolf, Water-spirit, and Elk clans seem
also to have possessed minor political-social functions.   Thus the
Wolf people are regarded as "minor" soldiers; the Water-spirit
people are connected with the passage of streams, etc.; and the Elk
are connected with the care of the fireplaces while on the hunt and
warpath.   This accounts for seven of the twelve clans, and it thus
seems as if the association of political functions with clans was a type
that had found great favor among the Winnebago, and was perhaps
being extended to every clan.   Among the Dhegiha, associations of
ceremonial functions with social units seem to have found corresponding favor, while among the Central Algonquian neither type
prevailed.

Marked political and ceremonial functions of the clan are thus the
distinguishing characteristics of the Siouan social organization and
have given an entirely different color to clan structure there.

THE RECIPROCAL RELATIONSHIP OF THE CLANS

We have seen that one of the bonds between the clans was the
fact of belonging to the same side.   But there is a special bond between certain clans known as "friendship" relation (hitcak'oro).
This always subsists between two, although it seems occasionally to
have been extended to three or four clans.   Most informants gave
these groups in such a manner that the "friendship" relation was not
postulated between clans belonging to different divisions.   One individual postulated them just on this basis, i. e., Thunderbird-Bear,
Warrior-Wolf, etc.   There can, however, be no doubt that the prevalent arrangement is: Thunderbird-Warrior; Eagle-Pigeon; Bear-Wolf;
Buffalo-Water-spirit; Elk-Deer; Snake-Fish.   Most informants did not
claim any pairing for the Snake, while some associated it in a three-
fold grouping with the Buffalo and Water-spirit.   The four clans of
the Waŋgeregi are generally united in a fourfold group of "friend
clan," although some divide them into Thunderbird-Warrior and
Eagle-Pigeon.

Under the term "friend clan" is included the idea of mutual service.
This becomes especially marked on two occasions: first, when a member of one clan visits his "friend clan," and second, when an injustice
has been done a member of the "friend clan."   On the former occasion every possible privilege is extended to him, even to his occupying the seat and bed of the host.   There is no indication of "wife-
borrowing," however.   On the latter occasion, the "friend clan" will
seek to revenge the injustice just as if the wrong had been done one of
its own members.   The respect shown by one clan to its "friend clan"
is again apparent at the naming-feast.   There he may be called upon
to give the dog names for an individual of the clan with which he is
associated, and, at times, to lend one of his clan names to the latter.

The relation of *hitcak'oro* or "friend clan" is thus strictly analogous to that which exists between two individuals who are *hitcak'oro* to each other. It is one of the characteristic traits of Siouan culture that two individuals often form a strong, inextricable friendship. Not only are they always together but the death of one on the warpath involves that of the other. The same intimate relationship seems to exist between an uncle (*hidek'*) and his nephew (*hitcųcge*). There is, however, one fundamental difference between such relation as that existing between *hidek'* and *hitcųcge*, the members of the family group, and the members of the same clan, on the one hand, and clan *hitcak'oro*, on the other. In the former there is the bond of blood, real or fictitious; in the latter, only that of mutual service. On the other hand, while the *hidek'-hitcųcge* relation, the individual *hitcak'oro* and the clan *hitcak'oro* all may be of different historical origin, they are psychologically the same. The postulation of even a fictitious blood bond between the different individual *hitcak'oro* and the clan *hitcak'oro* is not unheard of. For the *hitcak'oro* relation of individuals this is always possible, for if one individual dies, his *hitcak'oro* is generally adopted to fill his place. On the other hand, the myths seem to indicate that no blood bond was regarded as existing between them, for they generally married each other's sisters.

What historical relation the clan *hitcak'oro* bears to the individual *hitcak'oro* relation, it is impossible to state, but the remarks made before are pertinent here, and no genetic relationship need be postulated.

THE SPECIFIC POSSESSIONS OF THE CLAN

Among the Omaha a number of clans have in their possession certain objects around which not merely the clan but also the tribal reverence is centered. Historically, we believe that these were originally possessions of an individual clan, which subsequently became identified with the entire tribe. Among the Winnebago nothing remotely comparable to these clan possessions exists, and the few specific objects possessed by the clan have never become of real tribal significance.

The specific material possessions of the clan consist of certain war bundles, one in each clan; and two crooks in the possession of the Bear clan. There also exist war clubs, of which there are two types, one found among the *waŋgeregi*, the other among the *manegi* divisions. In connection with the clan bundles there are certain ceremonials known as clan-bundle or war-bundle feasts, popularly as Winter Feasts. The distribution of the clan bundle differentiates these from the specific possessions of the Omaha clans, and suggests a hint as to their historical associations. To all intents and purposes, as their individual history shows, these bundles are merely gifts from one spirit, the thunderbird, and a secondarily associated night-spirit (*hąhe*). The Winter Feast might thus be interpreted as a society of those who have obtained blessings from the thunderbird. The bundle remains in the possession of a certain family, however, and cannot pass out of the clan. The war bundle may therefore be said to be primarily the personal possession of a family which has become associated with all the members of the clan to such an extent that it is almost regarded as a clan possession.

In the possession of the two crooks by the Bear clan we have an example of specific clan property. The crooks are in the nature of emblems and are used on the warpath to indicate the extreme line of advance. They are thus of tribal significance. When not in use they are kept in the lodge of the Bear clan.

IMMATERIAL POSSESSIONS OF THE CLAN

Although there are no specific material possessions, each clan has certain "immaterial" possessions. They all have the added connotation of sacredness. For the Bird clans, it is the possession of fire; for the Bear, the doorway of his lodge; for the Wolf and Water-spirit, water. They were not obtained for all the clans. We indicated before that these "possessions" may have been primarily connected with the animals associated with the clan, upon which an additional socio-religious interpretation has been superimposed. The whole subject is, however, closely related to that of clan etiquette, for which, of course, no explanations can be given now.

THE CLAN MARKS OF IDENTIFICATION

As if more fully to set off the social unit of the clan, there have come to be associated with it definite marks of identification, such as symbols, property marks, facial decorations, and songs.

The symbols of only two clans were obtained, although a number of other clans seem to have possessed them. These were the war club (*namątce*) of the Thunderbird clan and the peculiarly whittled stick (*namaxinixini*) of the Bear clan. When a member of the Thunderbird clan died a miniature war club was buried with him. Whether the *namaxinixini* was buried with a member of a Bear clan we do not know.

The property mark consisted of the effigy of the clan animal, and was woven on such objects as bags, tobacco pouches, etc. It was also frequently engraved on wooden objects. Its most peculiar uses, however, were the emblematic earthen effigy mounds, in the shape of the clan animal, which were erected near the habitation of each clan in the village and in the center of clan squash fields, cornfields, etc.

Associated with every clan was also four clan songs. These were supposed to be the four songs sung by the ancestors of each clan when they came to this earth. They were always sung on the death of an individual, and were supposed to serve as a mark of identification in the journey of the soul to the land of the spirits. The use of these songs was so intimately associated with death that when some hardened offender, let us say, some individual who had killed a member of the tribe and who refused to make atonement of any kind, was pursued, he defiantly sang his clan songs.

As a last element in the clan complex may be mentioned the specific facial decorations existing in each clan.

We have now completed the discussion of clan organization. As we saw, it consisted of a large number of cultural elements of the most heterogeneous historical origin. So many indications are there, indeed, of interpretations, reinterpretations, and secondary association that it is impossible to form any correct idea of what is historically primary, except the self-evident fact that it had grown around a strong social-political unit.

INFLUENCE OF THE CLAN UPON CEREMONIAL ORGANIZATION

Perhaps the most characteristic trait of Winnebago culture is the existence of two strong socialized units, that of the clan and that of the secret society. Historically both are old, and even if we are of the opinion that the clan is historically younger, the political unit upon which it is superimposed is probably an ultimate historical fact. From the earliest times one would have supposed reciprocal influences to have occurred repeatedly. The nature of these influences, in so far as they are not conditioned by chance, would depend upon the respective center of gravity in either unit. It is evident that for the clan the organization was of paramount importance, and that the addition of cultural associations probably tended to strengthen its stability in this respect. On the other hand, the absence of political or governmental functions in the religious societies, and the clustering of the most multitudinous religious and shamanistic ideas within them, rendered the emotional unit of the latter the center from which influences would radiate. At the same time, the ceremonial unit of organization seems to have been so firmly fixed that any influence of the clan unit of organization upon it does not seem likely. As a matter of fact, in the typical schematic, religious society like the Medicine Dance, the Grizzly-Bear Dance, and Night-Spirit Dance, no influence is perceptible. However, these religious societies may be regarded as presenting no possible points of contact. Where, however, the bond of union is supernatural communication with a guardian spirit who subsequently became the clan animal, an obvious point of contact is given, and this brings to mind a very suggestive fact of Winnebago culture, namely, that there are, strictly speaking, no religious societies based on communication from a clan animal. There are, however, clan and clan-bundle (Winter) feasts which, in many respects, are absolutely identical with the religious societies, and which furnish, it seems to us, an example of just those two kinds of influence that we wished to point out, one radiating from the clan as an organization, the other from the entire clan unit.

In the Winter Feasts the unit of organization is the clan. Generally all the clans were represented in the person of the owner of each specific clan war bundle. The order of invitation was traditionally fixed, but it seems that in a number of cases the "friend" clan always had the position of honor. The war-bundle owner was not, however, supposed to represent the clan at all, but the spirits to whom offerings were being made. In every case, although the participants were supposed to represent a fairly large number of animals, the main blessings that were contained in the war bundle were from the thunderbird and night-spirit and the main offerings were indeed made to them. There seem thus to have been two separate ceremonies involved, one to the thunderbird and the other to the night-spirits.

The question arising with regard to the clan basis of these ceremonial organizations is whether we are to imagine that the ceremonial unit of organization was displaced by the clan unit, or whether we are to suppose that the ceremony is of comparatively recent origin, let us say at least long after the clan organization had been perfected, and that a number of things combined to determine the acceptance of the clan as a unit of organization, as opposed to the traditional ceremonial one. To the foregoing we must also add the fact that the Winter Feast seems to be related to similar ceremonies of the Central Algonquian, whose influence on the Winnebago must first be determined. If, then, we are not in a position at present to suggest the course of development, there can be no doubt that the content of the ceremony is strictly comparable to that of the religious societies, and that there are hints that the ceremonial unit of organization had begun to assert itself. If this could be definitely established, it would indicate that the clan basis of organization is historically primary.

The clan unit of organization is found in no other Winnebago ceremony, although the specific clan feasts show marked influences radiating from the clan unit. The clan feast is a typical ceremonial complex, both in type of organization and in content. The difference between it and a society like that of the night-spirit lies in the fact that although the five principal participants must have specific blessings (bundles), they must at the same time belong to the clan. To what extent a member of one clan who has obtained a bundle from some other clan spirit can take part in the specific clan feast of the latter it is difficult to determine, but in the buffalo feast, assuming that this is unquestionably the real Buffalo clan feast, any person who has obtained a bundle from the buffalo can participate, although the leader must always belong to the Buffalo clan. This example may be taken as an indication of the historical origin of these feasts, namely, that they are really religious societies in which the influence of the clan has restricted the number of individuals who are ordinarily supposed to occupy the five places of honor. That this restrictive influence of the clan was caused by the identity of the clan animal with the guardian spirit there can be little doubt.

CHAPTER IX

SOCIAL ORGANIZATION—SPECIFIC CLANS

The Thunderbird Clan

INTRODUCTION

The Thunderbird clan was unquestionably the most important of all the Winnebago clans. In numbers it seems to have equaled the three other clans of its phratry, and, since the upper phratry had about as many individuals as the lower phratry, the Thunderbird clan must have comprised about one-fourth of the entire tribe. How are we to explain this? Historical data are, of course, missing, so that any explanation reached is entirely hypothetical, but still it seems justifiable to hazard some interpretation. The most plausible hypothesis is to assume that the Winnebago were originally organized on a village basis and that the largest of these villages and the earliest to adopt the clan organization were those that took the thunderbird as their totem.

In the origin myths, the origin of the Thunderbird clan is always given as Green Bay, and in contradistinction to the accounts of other clans, the ancestors of the clan are supposed to have originated at Green Bay and not to have traveled there from some other place. How much credence is to be given to such a localization it is hard to say, but assuredly it should not be dismissed as entirely worthless.

The origin myths of the Thunderbird clan possess some interesting features which deserve a few words of comment. In the first version we have an account of the creation of the world which is almost identical with that given in the origin myth of the Medicine Dance (p. 302). None of the other clan origin myths contain it. How are we to explain this? As a secondary accretion or as an original and archaic feature? On internal evidence we suspect that it is a secondary accretion and that the original version began with the second paragraph. There seems to be no intelligible reason for having Earthmaker create two sets of individuals. If we suppose that the original version began with the second paragraph and that the general account of the creation was subsequently added, we would have a satisfactory explanation of this feature. Only one of the three versions obtained contains this general account of creation, and thus we have another reason for doubting its age.

There are other indications of an assimilation with the general origin myth in our versions, such as the absence of animals on the earth and the ascription of certain geographical features to the activity of the thunderbirds. Throughout, however, we are always confronted with the possibility that we may be dealing with an old village origin myth. There seems to be no doubt but that the episode of the origin of death, so distinct from that given in the general origin myth, is archaic. Other features, on the other hand, like the description of the origin of fire, are clearly reflections of certain possessions always associated with the Thunderbird clan.

A perusal of the following versions and the versions of the other clan origin myths indicates clearly how personal the accounts are. The members of the Thunderbird clan, as we shall subsequently show for the members of the other clans too, make claims of power and importance for their clans that are hardly justified by what we know of their actual power. As sources of information, therefore, we must be extremely cautious in our use of these origin myths.

Before leaving this subject it might be well to point out the number of different explanations given in these myths of the relations of the members of the clan to their eponymous clan ancestor. If a Winnebago were asked what this relation was he would answer offhand that the members of the different clans were descended from certain spirit-thunderbirds who were transformed into human beings at Green Bay.

In the first version the ancestors of the Thunderbird clan are created by Earthmaker and brought down to earth by the four spirit-thunderbirds the first Earthmaker had created. They are apparently human beings and not heroic birds, as most of the members of the clan assure you. To complicate the situation we have even the mention of the fact that the second set of people who came to visit them were members of the Thunderbird clan.

In the second version we have the customary identification of the ancestors of this clan with birds. At the end of this version we have the distinct statement, which is, however, clearly not part of the myth but an explanation by the informant, that the members of the clan call themselves thunderbirds because they, like the true thunderbirds, caused a drizzling rain and fog when they went about.

It is only in the myth of the origin of the Warrior clan that we have what can be interpreted as an account identical with that given offhand by the Winnebago. Here we are told that the warriors or hawks when they entered the lodge at Green Bay began to look different and that their feathers were worn off.

From these facts it is quite clear that, as far as the Thunderbird clan is concerned, the prevailing belief as to the relation of the members of the clan to the clan ancestor is but feebly substantiated by the origin myths.

As mentioned before, the chief of the tribe was selected from the Thunderbird clan, although the selection was apparently restricted to certain families. The functions of the chief of the tribe were connected with peace. He could not lead a war party, although, according to some, he could accompany one. His lodge stood either in the center of the village or at the south end, according to which of the two descriptions one cares to accept, and contained a sacred fireplace, around which only members of the Thunderbird clan could sit. This lodge was an asylum for all wrongdoers. No one could be killed there, and a prisoner who succeeded in making his escape to it was spared. Even a dog destined for a sacrifice at the war-bundle feast was freed if he took refuge in it. The Thunderbird chief always acted as intercessor between wrongdoers and their avengers. Even in so extreme a case as the murder of a clansman, he would always attempt a reconciliation by which the life of the murderer might be spared. If necessary, the chief would mortify himself, and with skewers inserted in his back have himself led through the village to the home of the nearest kinspeople of the murdered person.

The chief seems to have had some other miscellaneous functions, the most important of which was, perhaps, his right to prevent an unauthorized war party to depart from the village. If he, as an older man and guardian of peace and the best interests of the tribe, felt that a war party was taking too many risks, he would take his pipe and place it across the path of the one contemplating an unwarranted expedition and thus signify his disapproval. If then the war party chose to go, any mishap was directly chargeable to the leader who disobeyed. Should anyone be killed, the leader was regarded almost in the same light as a willful murderer, and the kinsmen of the deceased warrior could demand redress.

Our main informant for the Thunderbird clan summarized the functions as follows:

The chief is chosen from one of the "greater" Thunderbird clans [1] and must be a man of well-balanced temper, not easily provoked, and of good habits. The one sacred object he possesses is his pipe. He must be a peacemaker and love all the people in the tribe, the little children included.

If he saw a man, woman, or child passing by, he was to call them in and give them food to eat, for they were his brothers and sisters. All the relatives he has are to look after his possessions and keep him well supplied, for he was supposed to give away things constantly. If any person came to borrow some object from him, he would tell

---

[1] He divided the Thunderbird clans into two groups, the real Thunderbird and the Warrior clans. This latter he insisted was identical with the thunderbirds who caused the rain and who were quite different from the other thunderbirds.

the man that, since he was without this particular thing, to keep it and use it for all time.

The public crier, a member of the Buffalo clan, was supposed to report to the chief early every morning and receive instructions. The crier would then go all around the village making the chief's desires known.

The chief had a representative at every council, generally his brother.

The chief of the village is a peacemaker, and if two members of the tribe ever get into difficulties (i. e., quarrel) he is supposed to intercede. If in a quarrel a person should be killed, the chief would go to the murderer and tell the latter to permit himself to be tied up—i. e., to give himself up to the relatives of the murdered man. If the murderer consents to do so, then his arms are tied behind him and the chief walks in front of him carrying his sacred pipe. Thus they would go to the lodge of the murdered man's relatives. When they got there the chief would extend the stem of the pipe toward them. They might refuse to accept the pipe thus extended, but if any member of the family, even if it be a small child, were to take a puff from it, then the murderer would be forgiven and turned free.

This is the capacity of a Winnebago chief.

Another description of the chief's rôle as intercessor for a murderer is as follows:

When the Thunderbird chief wishes to save a murderer they take one of their own chiefs, one who is well beloved, paint his back blue, and put skewers in his back, to which they tie cords. Thus he is taken to the lodge of the murdered person's relatives. The chief, when he gets there, holds his pipe of tobacco in both hands. Should the relations not wish to accept the peace offering they close the door in his face. Then he returns.

The Thunderbird clan possessed a type of war club called a bald-headed war club, which was sacred to this clan alone, and a miniature of which was always buried with a dead body. The only other possessions were the clan war bundles. The Winnebago often speak as though each clan had but one of these palladiums, but there seems to be little doubt but that there were at least two and probably more in each clan. These war bundles must be regarded as the common possession of the clan at the present time, for they can not be alienated from the clan.[2] For all practical purposes, however, they are the private property of certain individuals or families.

Fire was considered a sacred possession of the Thunderbird clan. As mentioned before, an individual was supposed never to ask for a firebrand from the fire of any member of the clan and was never permitted to sit near such a fireplace. If, nevertheless, anyone should be immodest enough to ask for one of these objects, he would be refused, but he would be permitted to ask for any conceivable thing else. The following incident will serve as an example of the definite way in which this peculiar custom works. An old Winne-

[2] This point was very forcibly impressed upon the author when he tried to obtain the war bundle of a man who had become a member of the Peyote cult. The man was perfectly willing to part with it, but after repeated requests to those who happened to possess it at that particular time, he admitted that it belonged to the clan, although they could not have taken it away from him had he remained a believer in the old faith.

bago told the author that long ago a young man wanted to marry a girl belonging to his phratry and refused to listen to the entreaties of his father and mother. Finally the father, in desperation, went over to the lodge of a man belonging to one of the clans into which the young man could marry and asked for one of the sacred possessions. It was, of course, refused, and when the man was asked what other requests he wished to make, he asked that the host's daughter be allowed to marry his son. This was, of course, granted, and thus the boy was compelled to marry into the proper phratry.

One Winnebago interpreted the custom in an entirely different way. Exactly how much importance is to be attached to this explanation it is hard to say. According to this informant, the insult lay not in going to the fireplace or taking a firebrand, but in asking for it. The insult apparently consists in not taking it for granted that anyone entering the lodge was permitted to do what he wished. In other words, his asking was a breach of etiquette.

The typical method of burial in the Thunderbird clan was scaffold burial. It has long since been discontinued.

The burial customs seem to have been the same for all the clans. It may, however, be that in former times there were slight differences. For instance, in the first version of the Thunderbird clan origin myth the statement is made that the branch of a tree was placed at the grave and a small stick, painted red, attached to it. The author has no recollection of ever hearing the same statement made in connection with any other of the clans.

There are four songs associated with the Thunderbird clan. These are supposed to have been sung by the clan ancestors when they came to this earth, and are now always sung when a member of the clan dies, and on a few other occasions.

According to one informant, members of the Elk, Warrior, Deer, and Buffalo clans acted as servants to the Thunderbird clan on various occasions. The same informant also claimed that the Warrior clansmen took specific orders from the Thunderbird clansmen when on the warpath.

According to another informant, Thunderbird marks at death are a half circle on the forehead, made with charcoal. The proper marking is, however, that shown in plate 46.

Two dog names used in the Thunderbird clan are obtained— pinzakirutcga; ka-iwakitcanga.

The only feast specifically connected with the Thunderbird clan was the so-called chief feast, of which a description will be found on page 270. One of the divisions of the war-bundle feast is often considered as sacred to the thunderbird, but this is always the deity thunderbird, not the ancestor of the clan.

CLAN MYTHS AND NAMES

ORIGIN MYTH (TOLD BY A MEMBER OF THE CLAN)[3]

In the beginning, Earthmaker was sitting in space when he came to consciousness, and there was nothing else anywhere.[4] He began to think of what he should do, and finally he began to cry and tears began to flow from his eyes and fall down below him. After a while he looked down below him and saw something bright. The bright objects were hidden tears that had flowed below and formed the present waters. When the tears flowed below they became the seas as they are now. Earthmaker began to think again. He thought, "It is thus, if I wish anything; it will become as I wish, just as my tears have become seas." Thus he thought. So he wished for light and it became light. Then he thought, "It is as I have supposed; the things that I wished for have come into existence as I desired." Then he again thought and wished for the earth, and this earth came into existence. Earthmaker looked on the earth and he liked it, but it was not quiet. It moved about as do the waves of the sea. Then he made the trees and he saw that they were good, but they did not make the earth quiet. Then he made the grass to grow, but still the earth was not yet quiet. Then he made the rocks and stones, but still the earth was not quiet. However, it was nearly quiet. Then he made the four directions (cardinal points) and the four winds. On the four corners of the earth he placed them as great and powerful people, to act as island weights. Yet the earth was not quiet. Then he made four large beings and threw them down toward the earth, and they pierced through the earth with their heads eastward. They were snakes. Then the earth became very still and quiet. Then he looked upon the earth and he saw that it was good. Then he thought again of how things came into existence just as he desired. Then he first began to talk. He said, "As things are just as I wish them, I shall make one being in my own likeness." So he took a piece of clay (earth) and made it like himself. Then he talked to what he had created, but it did not answer. He looked upon it and saw that it had no mind or thought. So he made a mind for it. Again he talked to it, but it did not answer. So he looked upon it again and saw that it had no tongue. Then he made it a tongue. Then he talked to it again, but it did not answer. So he looked upon it again and saw that it had no soul. So he made it a soul. He talked to it again, and it very nearly said something. But it did not make itself intelligible. So Earthmaker breathed into its mouth and talked to it, and it answered.

---

[3] Told in connection with the origin of the Thunderbird wake.

[4] This myth is reprinted from Radin, Winnebago tales, Journal of American Folk-Lore, vol. XXII, no LXXXV, 1909. It has apparently been somewhat influenced by the Bible.

As the newly created being was in his own likeness, Earthmaker felt quite proud of him, so he made three more just like him. He made them powerful so that they might watch over the earth. These first four he made chiefs of the Thunderbirds. And he thought, "Some will I make to live upon the earth of those I have created." So he made four more beings in his own likeness. Just like the others he made them. They were brothers—Kunuga, Henaŋga, Hagaga, and Naŋγiga. He talked to them and said, "Look down upon the earth." So saying, he opened the heavens in front of where they sat and there they saw the earth (spread out below them). He told them that they were to go down there to live. "And this I shall send with you," he added, and he gave them a plant. "I myself shall not have any power to take this from you, as I have given it to you; but when of your own free will you make me an offering of some of it, I shall gladly accept it and give you what you ask. This shall you hold foremost in your lives." It was a tobacco plant that he had given them. He said, also, "All the spirits that I create will not be able to take this from you unless you desire to give it, by calling upon them during fasts and offering it to them. Thus only can the spirits get any of it. And this also I send with you that you may use it in life. When you offer anything it shall be your mediator. It shall take care of you through life. It shall stand in the center of your dwellings and it shall be your grandfather." Thus he spoke to them. What he meant was the fire. And then he gave them the earth to live upon.

So the four Thunder spirits brought the four brothers down to the earth. The oldest one, Kunuga, said, while on their way down, "Brother, when we get to the earth and the first child is born to me I shall call him *Chief-of-the-Thunders*, if it be a boy." On they came down toward the earth. When they got near the earth it began to get very dark. Then the second brother said, "Brother, when we get to the earth and a child is born to me, if it is a girl it shall be called *Dark*." They came to a place called Within Lake [5] at Red Banks, a lake near Green Bay. On an oak tree south of the lake is the place where they alighted. The branch they alighted on bent down from their weight. Then said the third brother to his brothers, "The first daughter born to me shall be called *She-who-weighs-the-tree-down-woman*." Then they alighted on the earth, but the Thunder spirits did not touch the earth. Then said the fourth and last brother to his brothers, "Brothers, the first son that is born to me shall be called *He-who-alights-on-the-earth*." The first thing they did on earth was to start their fire.

Then Earthmaker looked down upon them and saw that he had not prepared any food for them, so he made the animals that they

---

[5] This lake is probably Green Bay itself.

might have something to eat. The oldest brother said, "What are we going to eat?" Then the youngest two took the bow and arrows that Earthmaker had given them and started toward the east. Not long after the third brother came into view with a young deer on his back and the youngest brother also came with a young deer about 2 years old on his back. The deer that were killed, and those that killed them, were also brothers. They were very much delighted that they had obtained food. Then said they, "Let us give our grandfather the first taste." Saying thus, they cut off the ends of the tongues and the heart and threw them into the fire with some fat. The first people to call on them were the War clan people. They came from the west. Then came four others. They were the thunders. Thus they were called the youngest brothers. Then came those of the earth. Then came those of the Deer clan. Then those of the Snake clan. Then came those of the Elk clan. Then came those of the Bear clan. Then came those of the Fish clan. Then came those of the Water-spirit clan and all the other clans that exist. Then there appeared on the lake a very white bird—swan they called it. And after that, all the other water birds that exist came. And they named them in the order of their coming until the lake was quite full. Then the people began to dress the deer meat. Suddenly something came and alighted on the deer meat. "What is that?" they said. Then said Kunuga, the eldest brother, "It is a wasp, and the first dog that I possess, if it is black, *Wasp* I shall call it." Thus he spoke. "And as the wasp scented and knew of the deer dressing so shall the dog be toward other animals, and wherever the dog is, and animals are in the windward, he shall scent them." They made a feast with the deer for Earthmaker and threw tobacco into the fire and offered it to him. And to the other clans they showed how fire was to be made and gave them some, "For," they said, "each of you must now make fire for yourselves, as we shall not always lend you some." There the people made their home. It was just the time of the year when the grass comes as far as the knee.

One day they reported that something very strange was near the camp; but they said to themselves, "We will leave it alone." In a little while it moved nearer. Thus it moved toward the camp and soon it began to eat deer bones. They allowed it to become one of their clans and took it into their house. It was the dog or wolf. They killed one and made a feast to Earthmaker, telling him all about what they had done.

In the beginning the Thunder clansmen were as powerful as the Thunder spirits themselves. It was the Thunder people who made the ravines and the valleys. While wandering around the earth the Thunder people struck the earth with their clubs and made dents in the hills. That is the reason that the upper clans are chiefs of all the others and that the least of all are the dog people. So it was.

One day the oldest of the brothers lay down and did not rise again, and he did not breathe and he became cold. "What is the matter with our oldest brother?" the three others said. Four days they waited for him, but still he did not arise. So the second brother was asked by his youngest brother what the trouble was; but he did not know anything about it and told him to ask his third brother; but this one did not know either. Then the two older brothers asked the youngest one, but he did not know either. Then they began to mourn for him, not knowing what to do or think. They fasted and blackened their faces, as we do now when we are in mourning. They made a platform and laid him on it. When the snow fell knee-deep the three brothers filled their pipe and went toward the place of the coming of daylight—the east. There they came to the first being that Earthmaker had placed in the east, the *Island-weight*, as he was called. They came to him weeping and went into his tent, turning the stem of the pipe in his mouth. They said, "Grandfather, our brother Kunuga has fallen and is not able to rise again. Earthmaker made you great and endowed you with all knowledge, and thus you know all things." He answered and said, "My dear grandsons, I am sorry, but I do not know anything about it; but as you have started to find out I would refer you to the one ahead of me (the north). Perhaps he can tell you."

So, weeping, they started for the next one. When they got there and told him their troubles, he told them he could not help them; "but," he said, "perhaps the one ahead of me knows." So they started for the third one (the west), but from him likewise they could learn nothing. He also referred them to the one ahead (the south). When they reached the fourth and last one, they entered the lodge, and behold there sat the three to whom they had gone before. Here they asked the last one for help, and not only he but the other three also answered them: "Grandsons, thus Earthmaker has willed it. Your brother will not rise again. He will be with you no more in this world, and as long as this world lasts so will it be with human beings. Whenever one reaches the age of death one shall die, and those that wish to live long will have to attain that age by good actions. Thus they will live long. Into your bodies Earthmaker has placed part of himself. That will return to him if you do the proper things. This world will come to an end sometime. Your brother shall keep a village in the west for all the souls of your clan, and there he shall be in full charge of all of you, and when this world is ended your brother shall take all the souls back to Earthmaker—at least all those who have acted properly. Thus it is. Now you may go home and bury your brother in the proper manner." The Thunder people thanked the four spirits and left the tent. When they got home they took their brother's body, dressed him in his best clothes, and painted his face. Then they told him where he was to go and buried him with his head toward the west and with his war club. They placed the branch of a tree at his grave, and painted a little stick red and tied it to the tree, so that nothing should cross his path on his journey to the spirit abode. If any object or animal should cross his path on that journey, he must strike it with his club and throw it behind him, so that those relatives he had left behind on earth might derive blessings in war and attain long life. He must have his pipe and food along with him on his journey, and thus the things that he throws behind him will be a blessing for those still remaining on earth. Also the life he leaves behind him (i. e., the years that, had he lived to a normal age, are still due him) and the victories that he might have gained, all these he is to give to his relatives. The riches he might have had or, in fact, anything that he could possibly have had, he is asked to give to these relatives. Then they will not feel so unhappy and lonesome.

SECOND VERSION (TOLD BY A MEMBER OF THE CLAN)

In the beginning four brothers started from above and came toward this world. They came to a country called (*ni jahe*, cliff place?), and there they alighted on a tree. From there they started around the world, going from left to right.[6] The first time they went around they went through space, but the second time they went along this earth, at a place called *derok* (Within Lake). There they built lodges for themselves. While doing this the oldest suddenly became quiet, as if stricken. Finally, he asked the second brother what he should do, and the second brother said to him, "You are the oldest and ought to know what to do. How can I, who am younger, know anything? Perhaps the third-born brother might know." So he asked the third-born, but he said, "You are the older and ought to know. How can I, being the younger, know? Perhaps the youngest brother will know." So they asked that one and he said, "Yes, I know something." The thing about which they did not know anything was the making of the fire. The younger one, saying he knew something, took a piece of an oak tree and began twisting it until it began to smoke, and then the fire started. Then he placed it on the ground. After the fire began to blaze and seemed well started they finished building their lodge. From that time on whenever they saw anything new the brothers would give it a name. Animals and all the things that exist were thus named. And then they were to prepare a meal, and the second brother reached out his hand and produced the food that they wanted (i. e., he seemingly reached out from where he was seated and brought in deer's meat, etc.). Not having

---

[6] The ceremonial manner of passing around a lodge. Supposed to be comparable to the path of the sun.

any cooking utensils they broiled their meat on sharp sticks. Then the oldest one began making utensils for cooking. He took clay and slippery elm bark, mixed them together, and made a pot out of it, which was then heated over a fire.

Within Lake was their main stopping place during their wanderings. Now the members of the other clans began gathering at this place and all the other clans got to this place and obtained their fire from the Thunderers. From that time on they also began intermarrying. The rule was that the upper clansmen married the women of the lower clans and vice versa. The oldest one of the brothers made friends with the Water-spirit clan and the second brother made friends with the Bear clan. The reason why the upper clans and the lower clans intermarried was to prevent their marrying their own relatives. The second brother is the ancestor of the War clan people.

The Thunderers do not say that they were descended from the Thunderbirds, but they claim that in wandering about there was always a drizzling rain and fog which they caused and on account of the similarity of this to the actions of the Thunderbirds they called themselves the Thunderers.[7]

From the gathering at Green Bay the clan names originated. The names were taken from incidents of their journey to this place. The older brother kept on naming everything; the different parts of our body; the different parts of animals, etc. When he finished, he suddenly stopped breathing and died. His death occurred at dawn. The brothers did not know that he had died. For a long time they waited for him to come to life again, but he never came to life again. Thus death originated. His body died, but his spirit traveled west toward the setting of the sun, making a road for all who were to come after him. He was the chief of the village of the spirits.

THIRD VERSION (TOLD BY A MEMBER OF THE CLAN—FRAGMENTARY)[8]

"Well, my younger brother, what shall we speak of? Let us speak of the Winnebagoes. You are right. Of them we will speak. What shall we eat? If we see an animal let us eat him. I will go and look. See I have brought a deer. We will eat him." So they built a fire and broiled that deer. They cooked it and then ate it. Then they heard something. They listened and two persons came into the tent. They took a seat opposite. "Ha, ha, you that sit opposite, what relation will you be to me?" "What relation should I be to you?" "You shall be my chief." "Listen, some are saying

---

[7] The word Thunderers is the same as Thunderbirds. One and the same being is meant.

[8] This account seems to begin after the Thunderbirds have reached Green Bay and are sitting in the lodge waiting for the other clans to arrive.

something. Ha ha, our friends have come. Sit opposite (those opposite said). As long as we live we will attend to the fire for you." "Listen, our friends, they are speaking." "Ha, ha, sit opposite me" (a new clan has entered). They sat down. "You Water-spirit clan, what relation, my friend, will you be to me?" "What relation shall I be to you? You will be my chief." "Good. Now listen, a dog is howling. Let us wait for him." So the Thunderbirds waited for him. "Let us call him." "Ha, ha, my friend, we wish to teach the two-legged walkers something. As we say so will the Winnebagoes ever be." Again the Thunderbirds spoke, "Listen, some one has said something. Two people have come. We will call them the Buffalo clan."

The Warrior Clan

INTRODUCTION

There are not many members of this clan left, although it seems to have been quite important in the old days, to judge from the number of effigy mounds all over Wisconsin. There seems little doubt but that those bird effigies with unsplit tail are supposed to represent this clan.

Only one version of the origin myth was obtained. There is little to be said about it except that it mentions the fact that it was customary to have names for dogs. One statement seems to point toward cannibalism. As was pointed out in the preceding discussion, there is a boastful claim that they were chiefs.

Although, at the present time, this clan is known only as the *wonaɣirɛ ŭa'ŋkcɪk* (fear-inspiring men), its older name was hawk, and as such it was still known to J. O. Dorsey. When the present name began to be popular, it is impossible to say, but we feel confident that it has been in partial use for a considerable length of time. The change is quite in line with the rather common habit of referring to the Thunderbird clan as the chief clan and the Bear clan as the soldier clan. In other words, we have a name indicative of the functions of a clan superseding the older animal name. It is only in the case of the Warrior clan, however, that this substitution has been complete.

There is no indication in the myth that the Warrior clan was ever localized. A number of informants stated that the clan was but a division of a general bird phratry. In version 2 of the Thunderbird clan origin myth it is stated that the second of the two brothers was the ancestor of the Warrior clan. Dorsey, as we have seen, obtained the same information.

The Warrior clan seems to have had a lodge in the northwest corner of the village. In this lodge they claimed that prisoners were confined and certain tribal regalia deposited. The informants were not, however, at all clear about these facts, some even denying that there was a Warrior lodge and insisting that prisoners were confined in the Bear or Soldier lodge.

According to one informant the Warrior and Bear clans could give each other orders that had to be obeyed.

The members of the Warrior clan claimed that all the members of the clan were warriors and did not have to fast in order to obtain the right of starting out on a war party. This was vigorously denied by the members of the other clans, who referred to this claim with derision. There seems, however, to be no reason for questioning the fact that the clan had a special lodge and that it was intimately connected with war functions. Exactly what these were it is quite impossible to state, as they have not been exercised for a very long time.

The first two clan songs are given on page 172. The clan facial decoration, used only at burial, and which were supposed to be marks of recognition in the spirit land, are as follows: A red line alternating with a black and another red line across the forehead, and a red line around the mouth. One informant claimed that only the three marks on the forehead were necessary, and that in times of war blood was used for the red marks (pl. 46).

According to an informant of the Thunderbird clan, the Warrior clan functions were as follows:

The Warrior clan's position in the tribe is that of general warrior. He can kill an enemy at any time without breaking any of the rules of the tribe. Every other clansman who wishes to go on the warpath must fast and be blessed by the spirits with specific blessings before he can do this.

There may have been a special feast associated with the Warrior clan, but the author never heard of it. The clan possessed a number of war bundles.

ORIGIN MYTH

(TOLD BY A MEMBER OF THE CLAN)

In the beginning, Earthmaker made four men. Then he sent them to the earth. Within Lake, there, they landed and they alit on the branch of a tree. There were four branches and each one alit on one branch. And then on the earth they jumped and started walking toward the east. There they erected a camping place. There they started the fire. It was the principal fire. Then they started to look for food, but they were unable to find any. So the second brother was sent, but he was not able to get any animal, but he brought a man. Because he brought it, for that reason, the first male child we have shall be called *He-who-eats-humans*. Then the second one, him whom they called the warrior, was sent. Thus it was. And then all of them went toward the chief's lodge. They walked as chiefs, all four of them. The four of them went there. The chief's lodge was an oval lodge, and there they entered.

The Snake clansman was the one appointed to get the food. He went after the food. It was an Eagle-people feast. Two fish the Snake clansman brought, and with these the Eagle chief gave a feast. The Deer clan acted as attendants. Thus they ate the fish. And when they were finished with the eating, on either side, they left the head and the tail of the fish. This they left of their meal. "And if we have a dog we will call him *Leaves-fish-on-both-ends*," they said. Then they sat down. As they were sitting some one peeped in. It was the dog. Only his nose he stuck in. Then they said, "Whose nose does it look like?" So the chief spoke. "If we ever have a dog and if we wish to keep it permanently, *Whose-nose-does-it-look-like*, we will call it.

Then all of a sudden their bodies began to be different and their feathers began to look as if they were worn off. They were about to enter the chief's lodge. Then the chief passed the fire to the Deer clan and when they were through the lodge was purified with the incense of smoking cedar leaves. Then again into the very long lodge they entered. This was at Red Banks. Then the upper people taught the lower people the things to make them good. Thus Earthmaker ordained everything, and as he ordered, so it was. That is the way they were. Holy they were. And all (of my clan?) lived as chiefs. This is all that I was taught.

CLAN SONGS

First song

The blue flame they caused to start.
The blue flame they caused to start.
The blue flame they caused to start.
The blue flame they caused to start.

Second song

The fire they started.
The fire they started.
The fire they started.
The fire they started.

EAGLE AND PIGEON CLANS

No information was obtained about either of these clans. The Pigeon clan has been extinct for some time and only a few survivors of the Eagle clan are left. Neither of these clans seems ever to have been of great importance. They had war bundles and an Eagle feast is mentioned.

Facial paintings of these two clans, it is claimed, were the same as those for the Thunderbird clan (pl. 46). This was denied by others. According to one informant the Pigeon clan was borrowed from another tribe.

CLAN NAMES

WANINK' HIK'IK'A'RADJERA (THE BIRD CLAN)[9]

Ahugidjinewiŋga	Young bird that sheds its first feathers as it flaps its wings.
Ahugip'arawiŋga	Spreads her wings (said of a young bird just learning to fly).
Ahumanip'aga	He who hits the ground with his wings (refers to a cloud).
Ahup'ahiga	Sharp wing (said of a thundercloud).
Ahuperewiŋga	Transparently clear wings.[10]
Ahuru-aŋga	He who raises his wings (i. e., the edges of a cloud).
Ahusak'a	Strikes his wings.[11]
Ahuseretcga	Long wings (as a far-extended cloud, clouds being the plumage of the thunderbirds).
Ahusgawiŋga	White wing.
Ahutcowiŋga	Green wing.
Ahusururewiŋga	Slow wing.
Adedjirehiga	He who sets the prairie grass on fire suddenly (i. e., the lightning).
Codjega	He who kindles the (fire?).[12]
Hadjare	She who has been seen.
Hadjatcexiwiŋga	Difficult to be seen.
Hanp' hik'inohiga	He who misses the day.
Hanp'ok' guwiŋga	Owl returning hither.
Hanptcek'a	New day.
Hicdja Kereredjaŋga	Hawk-face.
Hitcaxcepewiŋga	Eagle woman.
Hitcaxcepsepga	Black eagle.
Hitcaxceptcoga	Green hawk.
Hiwetcoga	Green tail.
Hiwitcajaŋkega	Forked-tailed hawk.
Hohanp'guga	Returning light.
Hohanbmaniwiŋga	Walks in the light.
Hohanpdjik'ega	Light that comes hither regularly.
Hohanpdjikerega	Light flashes suddenly.

[9] The following list of names is based partly upon the manuscripts of Winnebago personal names prepared by the late Mr. J. O. Dorsey, and now in the possession of the Bureau of American Ethnology. This list has been revised and the phonetics of the Winnebago names corrected and transcribed by the author, but the English renderings of the names have been left as Mr. Dorsey obtained them, as the author obtained practically the same translations. Many of the names were obtained independently by the author. Dorsey's list is itself the amalgamation of two lists, that obtained by Dr. Foster and his own. He subsequently revised Foster's list, but to those names of the latter's list for which he could not obtain any translation he appended Foster's initials.

[10] Dorsey has "thin" wings, adding "as is a transparent fleecy cloud." However, the word *peres*, which is the full form for *pere*, means "clear," and is generally used in describing water in a brook. The interpretation of this and many other names as referring to clouds necessarily and not to the simple characteristics of the wings of the thunderbirds, is not obtained frequently to-day, but there seems to be no reason for believing that it was not customary a generation or two ago. For a discussion of the meaning of the names in general see the introduction to the section on social organization.

[11] Dorsey's rendering "stiff wings" is most certainly incorrect.

[12] Foster translates "misty" and Dorsey "smoke," but *cotc* means to kindle a fire, literally to cause the blue flame that appears just as the flames start up.

Hokorohiga.................He who makes a noise by dragging something.
Hopiŋga...................Good voice.
Horutcerega...............He who has eaten fish.
Hotca^{n}t^{c}i^{n}wiŋga...........Audible voice.
Hotcu^{n}tcu^{n}wiŋga.........Fishes in several places.
Huŋk' naŋk'awairega.......Chief whom they are afraid of.
Idjanikwahiga.............He who makes them shriek with fright.
Jibinik'a..................Short person (common to all clans).
K'aɣihitcaŋk'a............Changing crow.
K'aɣijiŋk'aga.............Yellowish crow.
K'aɣinu^{n}p'aga............Two crows.
Ki'zahuŋgewiŋga..........Fighting chief.
Ma^{n}cdja^{n}ixga^{n}wiŋga........Makes an effort in moving.
Ma^{n}cu^{n}p'i^{n}wiŋga...........Beautiful quill feather.
Ma^{n}cu^{n}sepga...............Black quill feathers.
Ma^{n}cu^{n}sgawiŋga...........White quill feather.
Ma^{n}cu^{n}tcowiŋga............Green quill feather.
Ma^{n}hinu^{n}p'aga...............Two knives.
Manihidadjega.............Strong walker.
Ma^{n}emanik'a...............Walking storm.
Maŋk'iksuntcga.............He who shakes the earth by striking.
Na^{n}ma^{n}tce K'urusga.......He who has taken his war-club.
Ma^{n}ma^{n}tce naŋk'ik'awairega.He of whose war-club they are afraid.
Ma^{n}a^{n}cotcga.................He who raises a dust on the earth.
Ma^{n}naŋksuntcga...........He who makes the earth shake by walking.
Maŋxek'iga.................He who drys the ground.
Ma^{n}suziwiñga..............Yellow arrow point.
Ma^{n}dadjehimaniga.........He who walks on the wind.
Mantcguna^{n}cicga...........Breaks a bow with his feet.
Maŋxicutcga................Red cloud.
Maŋxik'ok'iwaharetcga.....Overlapping clouds.
Maŋxik'ucina^{n}jiŋk'a........He who stands beyond the sky.
Maŋxik'ucena^{n}jiŋk'a.......Sky reached standing.
Maŋxip'asewiŋga..........Cloud-point.
Maŋxipi^{n}wiŋga............Beautiful cloud.
Maŋxirukanaga^n...........Master of the clouds.
Maŋxisepga................Black cloud.
Maŋxitcopga...............Four clouds.
Maŋxiwiwak'andjaŋk'a....Sacred cloud.
Maindjatcinaŋk'a...........He who sits having come hither to the earth.
Ma^{n}odjaŋguwiŋga...........Coming back near the ground.
Naŋxiksewahiga...........He who scares some one.
Na^{n}isawagicicga...........He who breaks a treetop by hitting it.
Na^{n}isawarutcga............He who eats a treetop.
Na^{n}najojopk'ega............Swallow.
Na^{n}odji^{n}wiŋga.............He who strikes a tree.
Naŋxekiga.................Withered tree (blasted by lightning).
Na^{n}wa^{n}huga..............He who comes singing.
Naŋk'awairega............He whom they fear to see.
Nijuga....................Rain man.
Nijumaniwiŋga............Walking rain.
Nijuxotcga................Gray rain.
Ninoha^{n}phiga..............He who makes the water shine.
Nizihutcgewiŋga...........Drizzling woman.

Notcaⁿpga................Lightning in the tree.
Nuwaŋk k'íriga............He who comes back running.
P'etcaⁿruhiga..............Crane rib.
P'etcawiŋga...............Crane woman.
P'etcga...................Fire person.
Xora cutcewiŋga..........Red bald eagle.
Xora huŋga...............Bald eagle chief.
Xorap'aga................Bald eagle head.
Rac tcaⁿtᶜiⁿwiŋga.........Audible name.
Rek'uhuhiga..............South wind.
Rutcgeniŋk'a.............Little pigeon.
Sakewarutcga............He who eats raw flesh.
Saⁿdjamaniŋga...........Grizzled walking person.
Si-ok'uruspiŋga..........Leaves good footprints.
Sincawatcoga.............Tail.
Tcatcga..................Wind person.
Tconirajireka.............He who is the first one named.
Tcaⁿphak'irutcewiŋga.....Lightning crossing itself.
Tcaⁿpjigewiŋga. ....Lightens again.
Djaⁿperacanaⁿtcaⁿtᶜiⁿwiŋga .Lightning visible only once.
Djaⁿphak'iwaresga........Forked lightning.
Djaⁿpherega..............He who is? lightning.
Djaⁿphaniwiŋga...........He who makes? or accompanies? lightning.
Djaⁿphik'icgaŋga.........He who makes? moving lightning.
Djaⁿpguhiga..............Lightning that returns.
Djaⁿberewiŋga............Lightning that goes.
Djaⁿpdjega...............Standing lightning.
Djaⁿpdjikerewiŋga.........Lightning that flashes suddenly.
Djaⁿpkcaⁿkcaŋga.........Zigzag lightning or lightning circling and recoiling.
Tcaⁿtᶜiⁿminaŋk'a..........Sitting in sight.
Tcexohaⁿphiga...........Lightens the highland marsh.
Tci-ohaⁿphiga.............He who lightens up the lodge.
Tciwaijega................He who makes one abandon lodge and flee.
Tᶜa-aninaŋk'a.............Kept aflying?
Tᶜaⁿguhiwiŋga............He who returns flying.
Wahok'ega................The marksman.
Wak'andja hadjagip'iwiŋga.Thunderbird that likes to be seen.
Wak'andja ciciga.........Bad Thunderbird.
Wak'andja yŭŋgiwiŋga....Thunder queen.
Wak'andjagipeniga........Young Thunderbird waiting.
Wak'andjaga..............Thunderbird.
Wak'andja giw'iŋxga.....Thunderbird whirling.
Wak'andjaguw'iŋga.......Thunderbird returning.
Wak'andjan'iŋgen'iŋk'a ....Very small Thunderbird.
Wak'andjap'iŋga..........Good Thunderbird.
Wak'andjaxega...........Yellowish Thunderbird.
Wak'andjaxiguhiga.......Thunderbird returning smoke.
Wak'andjaxunuga.........Thunderbird small.
Wak'andjasepga..........Black Thunderbird.
Wak'andjatconiw'iŋga......First Thunderbird.
Wak'andja tcoga..........Green Thunderbird.
Waktc'emaniw'iŋga.......He who walks killing.
Wani-ak'axiga.............Crow hankering for flesh.
Wan'ñk'tcaⁿw'iŋga........Changing bird.

Wap'akonaŋk'maniga.......The great dreadful one that walks.
Warutcexiga..............He who makes (the grass) rusty-yellow by eating.
Wasuhimaniga.............Walking hail.
Watcirukonaŋga...........Judge of the contest.
Wazika...................Pine.
Waŋgerutcga..............Man eater.
Wip'amaŋkerew'iŋga......Rainbow.
Wiragocgew'iŋga..........Star woman.
W'iŋɤanasega.............He who pens up ducks.
Wonaŋɤirebuŋga..........Warrior chief.
Wodjiⁿguhiga............He who returns and strikes.
Wodiⁿw'iŋga.............She who strikes.[13]
Koxmaniŋga..............Walking and making the sound of *kox'*.
Ahu-awiŋga..............Raise her wing.
Ahutco..................Blue wing.
Naⁿsgedjawiŋga.........Real tree woman.
Maŋxisepga.............Black cloud.
Maŋxisgaxedega.........Big white cloud.
Ahu-ijipga.............Short winged.
K'eratcosepga..........Black sky (means properly the firmament).
Keredjüⁿsepga.........Black hawk.
Maŋxiruzuga............He who makes the clouds have rays before them.
P'etcda-ehiga.........Fire starter.
P'etckerega...........Has fireplace.
Hok'awas..............Darkness.
Nûŋik'isumaniga.......Hails as he walked.
Tcoraminaŋk'a.........Sits blue.
Huŋgit'ega............Speaks as a chief.
Noroxoga..............Scratches tree.
Naⁿnawahiguga.........He who brings up a stick in his mouth.
Maⁿhodjaⁿpga.........He who flashes on the earth.
Hanaⁿdjadjairewiŋga...Seen by all.
Waŋgedjarega..........Belongs to the upper regions.
Maŋxixoruxutcga.......Looks at the clouds.
Maⁿcuŋginoga.........Flapping and shaking his feathers.
Ahugiciniwiŋga........Shining wings.
Heɤeniŋga.............Young swan.
Maŋk'uhodjaⁿpga......Flashes under the earth.
Warudjaxega...........Comes making a noise.
Waŋgedjahuga..........He who comes from above.
Naⁿiⁿnek'iga.........Lone tree.
Waŋgwaxopniga.........Holy man.
Ximaniga..............Walking in mist.
Xiguga................Comes in mist.
Xawiⁿanaⁿzogiga......Bends the brush.
Tcacgoguga............Oak tree.
Naⁿnazogega..........Bends the tree down.
Naⁿdjidjega..........Comes on the tree.
Maⁿdjidjega..........Comes on the ground.
K'onihega.............He who thunders.
Tciwiⁿdjikerehiga....Makes *tciwiⁿ* in coming.
Wak'andjamaniga.......Thunder walker.
Maⁿcdjaⁿmaniga......Mightily walking.

---

[13] This ends Dorsey's list of Bird clan names. Those following were collected by the author.

Maŋgiksuntcga............Shakes the earth.
Tconimaniga..............Walks first.
Djaⁿpdjirehiga.............Streak of lightning.
Maŋxiwimaniga...........He who walks in the cloud.
Ahu-iseretcga..............Long wings.

THE BEAR CLAN

INTRODUCTION

Seven versions of the Bear clan origin myth were obtained, so that for this clan, at least, a fairly intensive study of the variations and their significance can be made. Perhaps the most interesting fact to point out is the apparent existence of two recognized versions, one called the minor or false and the other the true. The complete version was only told when the interrogator had paid enough.[14] The minor version is not at all concerned with the origin of the Bear clan but appears to be largely an account of the origin of the reciprocal relations of the Bear and Wolf clans. The second is the real origin myth. The version obtained does not, however, seem complete.

The typical origin myths (excluding the fifth version) are of two types, those that speak of Earthmaker creating the ancestors of the clan and those that do not mention his name. Undoubtedly those versions that do not mention Earthmaker's name are the older. Those that speak of Earthmaker show clearly the influence of the general origin myth and of shamanistic systematization. This is particularly apparent in the sixth version, which was told in connection with the bear feast.

The subject matter of the myths relates to the manner in which the bears came to the great gathering at Green Bay, the older versions having them originate from the water and the later versions having them created by Earthmaker and sent to the earth. In the former they are distinctly heroic animals and in the latter vague spirit animals. The nature of the relation of these animals to the present clansmen is not clearly stated in the myths, and there is not the slightest mention of the present current belief on the subject. The myths seem almost entirely concerned with the question of the origin of the disciplinary functions of the clan and of its relationship to the Wolf and a few of the other clans.

It is difficult to explain the remarkable differences in the various versions. Comparing them with versions of the clan origin myths of the other clans, it seems likely that the short accounts represent the more archaic versions and the longer accounts those versions that

[14] My informant said, "If a person asked me about the origin of life (i. e., of my clan) and did not give me enough gifts or make enough offerings, I would tell him the minor version. Not until he gave me all that was necessary would I tell him the true account."

have been subjected to literary and shamanistic remodeling. Only the shorter accounts show in their subject matter and presentation certain affinities to the origin myths of the other clans, the longer ones being entirely different. Another cause for these marked differences may lie in the circumstance that since the longer accounts were associated with semi-esoteric ceremonies, the war-bundle feasts, they were known to but few individuals in the clan, whereas the shorter legends could be learned by anyone who chose to pay for them. To this must also be added the fact that presumably some of the accounts current were based on hearsay knowledge.

The Bear clan was, next to the Thunderbird clan, the most important in the tribe. Its lodge was either in the center of the village, opposite that of the Thunderbird clan, or at the extreme end, depending upon the scheme of village organization accepted as correct. In it were confined the prisoners of war and the insignia of office possessed by the clan, such as the so-called standards, really crooks, and the so-called *namaxinixini*. Some individuals also claimed that unmarried men were allowed to sleep in the lodge, although they were not clear as to whether they did this in order to guard the prisoners confined there or simply used it as a club house.

The clan songs are given on page 187. The same songs are used when gathering the clansmen together to select soldiers.

Apart from the war bundle or war bundles, the Bear clan possessed three insignia—a war club of a definite shape, the curiously whittled baton of authority called *namaxinixini*, and the crooks used in battle called *hoke're*u^n. Whenever the clan was exercising any of its functions the leader would always hold in his hands the *namaxinixini*.

The functions of the clan were probably the most important in the tribe and were entirely disciplinary. The author obtained the following description from an old Winnebago:

The Bear clansmen are the soldiers or sergeants-at-arms of the tribe. They have complete control of everything concerning discipline. Whenever the Winnebago are traveling or moving (i. e., on their various seasonal moves), the Bear clansmen lead, and wherever they decide to stop, there the leader would put his stick in the ground and the other Bear clansmen would do the same, arranging them all in a row pointing toward the direction in which they were going. The main body of the tribe would follow at a certain distance. No member of the tribe would dare pass ahead of the row of sticks. If, for instance, the tribe was on the fall move and traveling toward a country in which there was plenty of game, should any individual go back and around the sticks in order to kill game on his own account, the soldiers (Bear clansmen) would, as soon as he was detected, go over to his lodge and burn it up with all its contents and break all his dishes. The only thing they would spare would be his life and that of the other members of his family. If the one who had transgressed the rules made any attempt at resistance he would be severely whipped. If he refused to submit to this and took up his fire arms to fight, the soldiers would stand there calmly, but the moment he made an attempt to shoot they would kill him. In such a case nothing would be said either by the rest of the tribe or his relatives about the matter. If, on the other hand, he submitted to whatever punishment the Bear clansmen inflicted on him without resistance and apologized to them, then they would build him a new lodge and supply it with better goods than those which they had been compelled to destroy.

This is the way in which the soldiers act when they are on duty. They never jest and their word is a command. If it is not immediately obeyed, their next move is to punish. For that reason one generally listens to them and their commands. When they are not on duty they are the same as other people. Different members of the tribe are on duty at different times, for the leader changes them about frequently.

If a field of rice is found in some swamp or lake the Bear clan people are informed and they go over and keep watch over it and give every person an equal chance at picking it. If a person sneaks away and takes advantage of the others, the Bear clan people punish him.

The Bear clansmen guard the village almost all the time. When a council is held they guard the council lodge, and when a person is tried for some crime, particularly that of murder, a trial which generally takes place in the Thunderbird clan lodge, then they carefully guard this lodge, lest the prisoner try to escape or his relatives or confederates try to rescue him.

Certain actions and remarks are not permitted in the Bear clan lodge. They are the following:

To peep into the lodge.

To make the remark that they live in a nice lodge.

To sit in the doorway.

To give a deep sigh or snort inside the lodge.

Should any person do one of these forbidden things, the Bear clansmen would be compelled to give the most valued thing in the lodge to the offender.

If a man seduced a woman, he was brought to the lodge of the Bear clan and severely whipped. If the soldier whipped him too severely, he in turn was whipped.

If a murderer was brought to the Bear clan lodge and the chief of the tribe asked that the man be freed, the rest of the tribe would beg the relatives of the murdered man to relent; but if the murderer was turned over to the soldiers, they would take him to the lodge of the murdered man's relatives and let one of them kill him.

According to one informant, the Deer clansmen acted as servants to the Bear clan.

The Bear and the Wolf clans are friends, and although, as we indicated on page 153, each clan is paired off with another, the relationship of the Bear and Wolf clans is particularly intimate. It was even claimed that a Bear clansman would revenge the death of a Wolf clansman. For no other clans did the author hear this statement made. The women are addressed by the men and by each other as "my opposite," referring unquestionably to the positions in

the council lodge.   According to another informant, the Bear clan is
the Deer's friend, and therefore they bury one another.

Burial, as was the case for all members of the lower phratry, was
in the ground.   Opinions varied as to what clan was supposed to
bury a Bear man, some people claiming that it would have to belong
to the upper phratry, others that it was incumbent upon the Wolf
clan.   It seems that the latter custom is the one followed at the
present time and one which is considered old, to judge from the
account of an actual funeral (cf. p. 100).   The body was always
buried with a miniature Bear clan war bundle.   According to one
informant, a bow and arrows were occasionally placed in the hands
of the corpse, in addition to some tobacco.   According to another
informant, the facial marks were charcoal across the forehead and
red marks under the lips in direct imitation of the bear.

The facial decoration for the corpse consisted of two parallel marks
across the forehead, the upper one red and the lower one black, and
the painting of the entire chin red (pl. 46).   The red paint on the
chin was interpreted as a smile, for the Bear clansmen were supposed
to greet death with a smile, as they were returning to their clan
ancestors.   The statement was also made that Bear clansmen should
not mourn the death of any of their comrades.

There is a specific Bear clan feast at which no one is permitted to
laugh or talk, nor is anyone allowed to make any noise while drinking
soup.   The feasters must eat with their left hand.

One of the most interesting of the ceremonies associated with the
Bear clan is the so-called bear or soldier dance (*manu^npe waci*).   It
was described to the author as follows:

When sickness comes upon a Winnebago village the people go to the chief and say
"Sickness has come upon us, O chief! See that your soldiers arise!" And the chief
goes to the lodge of the leading Bear clansman and, offering him tobacco, speaks as
follows: "My soldier, I am offering you tobacco, for my people have been smitten
with disease." Then the latter rises and thanks him. He then informs all his clansmen and they give a feast. Then, of those participating, a number of males and
females are selected, who on the next day, accompanied by the leader, go around
the village four times. If a dog crosses their path, they kill it. After they have
made the fourth circuit they enter the village from the east end. They thereupon
visit the sick individuals one after another, dance in their presence, and lay their
hands upon them. After they have visited all the sick they go to the chief's lodge,
where a feast is spread for them by the chief's people. The next day all those who
had been ill become well.

It is quite clear that this "healing" function of the clan is intimately associated with the powers supposed to be bestowed upon
individuals by Bear spirits.   In fact, we are really dealing with a
society possessing the power of healing disease in which membership,
however, is restricted to members of the Bear clan.

The following dog names were obtained:

A black dog with yellow eyebrows and breast is called *hesiga'ruɣega*, Opens-beehives; black female dog, *hotckihiga*, Picks-acorns; black dog with white around the neck, *hotc hagawanuga*, Runs-for-acorns. The chief also had the privilege of calling a dog *noruxuga*, to show his superiority over the other members of the Bear clan. From another informant the following were obtained: *Tcapiracotcga*, Eats-everything-except-hide; *tcahoraweka*, Pulls-out-deer-liver.

ORIGIN MYTHS

FIRST VERSION [15]

Informant, member of the clan: In the beginning a bear came walking on the ocean. When he got to the shore he flew off as a raven and alit on the shore. The first being he saw was a Dog clansman. Then he entered the lodge and sat opposite him. That is

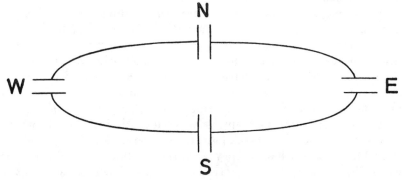

FIG. 35.—Diagram of Bear lodge.

why they call one another friends, or ''he who sits opposite me.'' From the fact that he flew off as a raven we have a name (*kaxijigaga*). The lodge had four doors, one on each end and one on each side (fig. 35). They landed at Green Bay, where a great gathering was held of all the clans. The other Bear clansmen claim that it was water foam that flew from the water, and it is from that fact that they obtained so much life. The fact that he (the bear) changed himself twice is the reason for his greatness among his fellow clansmen. Originally it was the fourth born who was sent from across the ocean.

SECOND VERSION

Informant, father of above: In the beginning 10 brothers started from across the ocean to the great clan meeting. When they got near, four waves came ashore and a raven flew from the waves, but when it alit (on land) it was a bear that walked. They were the greatest

---

[15] There are so many versions of the origin of the Bear clan that I think it best to give all I obtained. They are all discussed on p.177.

in power, as they had changed themselves twice. There they crossed the tracks of the Wolf clan, and they said, "Our friends have gone by." Then they went and sat opposite the Wolf people. The Wolf and Bear clans must bury one another.

The 10 men left their father and mother across the ocean.

The Bears should paint their faces with charcoal from burnt basswood and red paint. The face should be painted red and black alternately crosswise in stripes, or black on the upper half and red on the mouth and chin. Women are painted with red markings on each cheek and with charcoal markings in the center of the cheek.

THIRD VERSION

Informant, member of the Bear clan: It is supposed that Earthmaker ordered a meeting of all the animals to take place at Green Bay, and that the Soldiers (another name for the Bear clan) were also to attend.

In the beginning Earthmaker created all things in the form of animals, but at this gathering they (the originators of the various clans?) were to become human. When all was in readiness to start, it was decided that the families of those animals who were to become the ancestors of the Winnebago clans were each to send one representative, and that the one who was thus chosen, accompanied by his wife, was to become transformed on that occasion. Of the soldiers (i. e., the bears) the youngest was sent. He had three brothers, of whom the eldest had black hair, the second dark red hair, and the third blue or green hair. They were the chiefs of the villages from which they had started.[16] Only the youngest, however, was sent to the earth to attend the meeting. When he emerged at a place to the north of Green Bay he came from out the earth. When they emerged (the bear and his wife) it was a very fine day. As they were coming they heard voices in the distance saying, "The soldiers are coming." As they started to walk their footprints seemed imprinted with the blue of the sky—i. e., with daylight. A name has originated from this fact (haⁿbamanina, "He-who-walks-with-the-day"). As his wife was with him, he immediately started to hunt. (It seems that by this time the bear had some followers, for some would from time to time ask whether they were going to eat, and he would answer yes and tell them to hunt for food.)

When the youngest of the brothers started, the brothers who remained behind told him "to remember them" with regard to tobacco, red feathers, and food, and therefore after he had started he told some of his followers to go ahead and bring food of such and such a kind, so that when he arrived at certain camping places those sent

---

[16] It must be remembered that all this is taking place in the heavens, in the spirit abode of the bears. The color translations are only approximate.

ahead would be there before him ready with the food. After the first meal they started out again, and soon they came across the track of a member of some other clan, and they said, "Our friend has gone by." The latter clan had also said in coming, "Our friend must have come by." Then they came to the place where a large lodge had been constructed. When all were inside, the animal-beings wished to start a camp fire, and they called upon all those present to start it; but no one except the Thunderbirds could do it, so they made the Thunderbirds chiefs of the tribe. As, however, they were to have a number of chiefs, they called upon the Water-spirits to be chiefs of the lower division. Of the third division, the soldiers were to be the chiefs. The latter were to be in charge of discipline. That is the origin of the Bear or Soldier clan.

FOURTH VERSION

Informant, member of the clan [so-called "true" version]: Earthmaker made all things, and then he created man and woman, and he placed them in the south. He gave them charge of some of the day or life. All the creatures on the earth and all the birds of the air he was in charge of. He was going to start up from below and walk toward the north. All the creatures went with him. He walked forth with all the creatures. When he arrived on earth all the other clans had already gathered at one place. When he arrived they said, "Our soldiers have come. Make room for them." So it was said. And he said to them, "The things Earthmaker created me for, those I will do. Therefore, wherever you live or wherever you gather together I will look after your village; even to the edge of the clearing, that far I will make it sacred for you; and if you are ever overcome by sickness and you ask me to arise and help you, your sickness will leave you. And while he spoke of his power for four days the weather had been good, and no wind blew from any direction. The soldier was thus in charge of affairs. And as he spoke thus all birds with sharp claws flew above him in a circle.

On the fourth day all the clans left for their respective homes. Now even to this day he, the bear, is still in charge of the people.

FIFTH VERSION

Informant, same as of fourth version [so-called "minor" version]: In the south, where he emerged and came upon our earth, there was a spring which gave forth white water. When he was about to come out, the hill in which he was confined shook and the spring shook also. He was not the first to come out, for his attendants preceded him. Then he came out. There were 11 men. The oldest one told him to go and look around at the fields. He sent out four to look at the fields (the raspberries and all other fruits). The acorns and nuts they called beans. The four that emerged soon came upon the footprints of human beings.

And then they returned from the fields where they had been searching for food. "Oh, my; oh, my," they said, "over there we came across the foorprints of human beings." So they spoke. "Go again," he said, "go around a larger circle." So they went farther than before, and there they saw the people who had made the footprints. "Our friends are going about here," said the ones who had made the footprints and who were wolves. "Never shall we disobey one another's word, my friends," said the bear. And the wolf answered, "It shall be so."

If one of the Bear clansmen had been killed and it was reported to the Wolf clan, the latter would revenge him. The Bear clan would act similarly. Then the bear said to the wolf, "My friend, whenever you die I shall put you away so that your soul may not be bothered by bad insects." And the wolf answered, "My friend, it shall be so, and when you die I will likewise put you away so that the bad spirits may not abuse your soul." Then they parted, after shaking each other's hands. The bears returned to their home in the south. The next time they came, it was to stay. They scattered themselves all over the earth, seeking newly ripened fruit of all kinds. In this manner they are still living on earth.

SIXTH VERSION [17]

Informant, member of the clan: Earthmaker made us and as he created us thus the story has come down. The story of our creation is told as follows:

"Get ready. We will converse together over this affair." So spoke the one in the south. He was but one of those whom Earthmaker had created. There were four brothers. The name of the oldest one was Black Person, that of the second Red Person. (Indeed he was very red.) The third one was called Blue Person, and the fourth one White Person.

"Younger brother, how is it going to be? I (the oldest), who am speaking, not fitted do I feel myself for the task. My temperament is indeed not fitted for the task. Perhaps you might have something to tell them. Try, therefore, to say something to them. They are about to have a gathering and it is time to start. Try to say something to them." "Older brother, the truth do you speak. I also feel even as you have said; I am not fitted for it. I really don't consider myself equal to the task. My younger brother only is the one fitted for it. He is clever. Our younger brother, he only must be the one." "The truth you have spoken, my brother. Our youngest brother only is fitted for the task. The announcement of the gathering has already been made, so let us council over it imme-

---

[17] Told as the origin myth of the Bear feast.

diately. Let us get ready. Our younger brother, he is patient and strong-minded. On the earth he must go and we will remain here. To take care of the home we will remain here. Whatever he says it shall be so. In that wise will we think. Earthmaker has ordained that the gathering shall take place and that we are to live our lives there (on earth). Our younger brother he will go and live on the earth. As he is about to go to the earth, we will ask him to remember us.

"Younger brother, when you arrive on earth, whatever offerings you obtain, send them back to us as you walk along. When you start out you will appear with life. This you will take with you. This will be your task. Be careful that you perform everything correctly. When you arrive there, it will be necessary to give names to the human beings and to their dogs.

"Younger brother, when you start out toward the earth you will be holy. And when you are on earth and your first boy is born, call him He-who-is-very-black, and call the second one (*wajiga*) Brown-bear, the third one Blue-bear, and the fourth one White-bear. And if girls are born to you, call the first one Night-walking-woman, the second one Daylight-as-she-walks, the third one She-who-thrusts-herself-within-a-lodge, and the fourth one Visible-footprint-woman. And if your daughters have dogs which they wish to keep let them give them the following names (*wadogega*, untranslatable): Dog-pair, Third-born-girl, and Red-female-dog. Thus let it be."

When they (the bears) started, those at the gathering place listened: "Our soldiers have started; their whoops are audible." When the bear came on earth, he came across some tracks. "Our friends have gone by," he said. Finally the bears (man and woman) arrived at the gathering place; there they found all the clans assembled. The Water-spirit was the first one to come; then came the birds and then the bears. When all were assembled, they began to construct a large lodge. When it was finished, the one who had arrived first, the Water-spirit, was addressed by some of the other people. "Our chief, how are we going to make fire? Had you not better start?" "True you speak, but I do not know how. I am unable. Let some one else try it." But they all regretted and declined, saying they did not know how. So it was decided that he who made a fire would be chief. All thereupon tried, but only the Thunderbird succeeded. So he became the chief and the others all thanked him. Then the fire was distributed and all the clan fireplaces were made. Thus it was at the creation council. Now all things were finished and arranged. The Thunderbirds were the rulers of the village. The other people measured their acts by him. When the chief said do so and so, they would obey. Then the chief went out to look for food for himself and for his people, and they began to bring back food in the form of their relatives—i. e., in the form of the animals after whom they were named. Then the Bear people made a rule that they were to have a feast at which offerings would be made to their clan animal. And it was for him that they placed a shallow kettle at the feast. This is all.

Informant, member of the Thunderbird clan.

At a large spring sat a male bear. He looked upon his body and it was very blue. It was even bluer than the blue of the sky. As the blue from the sky illuminated, so he was. He sat as though he was part of the day. He was a chief and his name was Blue-chief. Toward one side he looked and there stood twelve men. Then the earth began to quake and something came out from the spring. Because something had come out from under the earth that is why the earth quaked. Blue-bear named him Earth-shaker. Then the earth began to quake again and now it was worse than before and Blue-chief named the one who emerged Earth-quaker. And then for the third time the earth began to tremble, even much more than before. So much did it tremble that the day itself trembled; and those that were not solidly attached to the earth came to the top and all manner of fruit was scattered over the earth. When he came out Blue-chief named him Gives-forth-fruit-as-he-walks. And again for the fourth time the earth began to roar and tremble and even the day trembled. Then one came out. So he was named, Makes-the-day-tremble. Thus they were all named as they came out. Then Blue-bear was told by Earthmaker, "This is all that remains to be done; your friends are waiting for you." There Blue-bear talked with Earthmaker, the latter telling him what he was to do. Then they started to the place where all the other clans were gathering, at Red Banks. As they came, all the leaves that had rough edges became human and all the trees that had prickers became human, and all the birds that had sharp claws and were able to claw anything, they all became human, and the snakes that had sharp fangs became human. Thus they went. Those of the air went in the air and those of the earth went on the earth, and nothing could cross their path. Even the earth trembled as they walked.

When they got to the gathering place they were told that seats were reserved for their friends (meaning them). But, said Blue-bear, "We did not come for that purpose, so we will not sit down. We were intended for something else by Earthmaker. As long as this world exists we will take care of you within the confines of your villages. We will not permit any evil spirits to enter these confines. The seats you offered us will remain as they are, so that if at any time the clans are gathered again our place will be reserved. Then the crowd dispersed and went home.   Blue-bear said that he would go home but that the rest were to live on this earth and that they would be the soldiers of this earth.   That is the origin of the Bear clan.

When a bear is killed on earth, the Bear clansmen do not mind it, but they laugh and feel good.   When one of the Bear clan dies, they say, "Don't cry, for he has gone home."   Then they paint his jaws red to give him the appearance of laughing.

When a bear is killed on earth the spirit returns to Blue-bear, and so it is with the Bear clansmen.   This is the story of the Bear clan.

All the birds, trees, snakes, and everything of its kind have soldiers. The sharp-clawed birds are soldiers of the birds and all the snakes that have fangs and all the trees that have prickers are soldiers of their kind.   All the animals and living things of the earth have soldiers among them.   The ugliest tempered ones of their kind are soldiers of whatever class they belong to.   Oftentimes when a person gets angry on earth they would say, "The soldier; it is because he has a soldier nature.''   (Whoever has the power of hurting one of his fellow-beings and does it has a soldier nature.)   This is the story of the Soldier clan.

If they had said in the beginning, "This or that clan will never do anything wrong," then the rest of the clans would never have done so. The Soldier clan opens the way for anyone, of any clan, at any time, to take up his soldier nature.

CLAN SONGS

Song 1

Winnebagoes, on the road they are coming.
Winnebagoes, on the road they are coming.
Winnebagoes, on the road they are coming.
Winnebagoes, on the road they are coming.

Song 2

Speaking Winnebago, they are coming.
Speaking Winnebago, they are coming.
Speaking Winnebago, they are coming.
Speaking Winnebago, they are coming.

Song 3

Who can be behind?
Who can be behind?
Who can be behind?
Who can be behind?

Song 4

Who can be above?
Who can be above?
Who can be above?
Who can be above?

CLAN NAMES

HUNDJ HIK'IK'ARADJERA (BEAR CLAN)[18]

Hagɛdja minaŋk'a	Sitting opposite.
Awasarega	He who is shut in.
Cagep'ahiga	The one with black claws.
Ciⁿsasak'a	Coarse-grained fat.
Roguⁿiⁿnega	He who is coveted.
Hahi-atciwiŋga	Dwelling on a hillside.
Hak'iridjewiŋga	Comes back.
Hak'irutcewiŋga	Crosses each other.
Hazhoniwiŋga	Hunts for berries.
Haⁿheoratcewiŋga	Travels by night.
Haⁿhewiŋga	Night.
Haⁿbeniŋk'a	Small day.
Haⁿpmaniga	He who walks by day.
Himaniwarutcga	He who eats as he walks.
Hiniguhega	His little one who is returning.
Hinuŋk'hadjariga	He who saw a woman.
Hinuŋk' inek'iminaŋk'a	Woman sitting alone.
Hinuŋk' djopga	Four women.
Hodihuga	He who comes climbing a tree.
Hundjhurega	Black bear who is coming.
Hundjga	The bear.
Hundjxedega	The big bear.
Hundjxunuga	Small bear.
Huŋgatcak'iriga	He who has come back to see the children.
Huŋgitᶠega	Prophet.
Huŋkorohiga	He who is the chief's flesh.
Huŋk'uniga	He who is made chief.
Inek'inaⁿjiŋga	He who stands alone.
Inek'iminaŋk'a	He who sits alone.
Gisɛweminaŋk'a	He who sits quiet.
Maŋk'axga	Dirt.
Maniwarutcga	He who eats as he walks.
Maⁿok'ipiwiŋga	She for whom the land is large enough.
Maⁿzitciga	Iron lodge.
Maⁿzanaⁿpiŋga	Iron necklace.
Maⁿzasaⁿwiŋga	Whitish metal.
Maⁿzawiŋga	Metal woman.
Maⁿcgodaniga	Three notches.
Maⁿnaⁿhaⁿpewiŋga	She who throws out the dirt with her paws.
Manaⁿpega	Soldier.
Maⁿp'ezirehiga	Earth thrown up yellow.
Maⁿrotcaⁿwiŋga	Straight earth woman.
Maⁿsorekega	Land cut in strips.
Maⁿtco-icdjajiripga	Grizzly bear with striped eyes.
Maⁿtcoga	Grizzly bear.
Maⁿwaksuntcga	Shakes the ground by his weight.
Motciwiŋga	She who dwells in the ground.
Naⁿcgadjewiŋga	She who plays on a tree.
Naⁿnetcûⁿsepwiŋga	Black root.

---

[18] The following names are from the Dorsey manuscript.

Naᵃnuzokˈiwiŋga.........Bends a tree by pulling.
Naⁿsaᵃnehiga............He who makes a tree whitish by scratching off the bark.
Naⁿtcgepiŋga............Good heart.
Naⁿtcgetcexiwiŋga.......She whose heart is difficult.
Naⁿtcujiwiŋga...........Yellowish red hair.
Noxtcuxiga..............Breaks up a tree into small pieces.
Noruxoga................Scrapes a tree.
Hokˈawasmaniwiŋga......Who walks in darkness.
Hokˈawasminaŋkˈa.......He who sits in darkness.
Reziwakˈantcaŋkˈa.......Holy tongue.
Rohaⁿminaŋkˈa..........Many sitting.
Si-asga.................Foot good to the taste.
Tciwojuga...............Fills the lodge.
Tcuga...................Ladle.
Tcugiga.................Spoon.
Wajiga..................Yellowish-red bear.
Wakˈizanaⁿpˈiŋga.......He who has a white spot under his throat.
Wamaniga...............Walks on the snow.
Wamanukˈega...........He who steals habitually.
Wamaŋksgaga...........With a white breast.
Wasaⁿhimaniga..........He who walks on melting snow.
Wasemqmakˈaŋga.......Vermillion.
Waŋkˈanaⁿsewiŋga......Pens up a male.
Waŋkˈhokˈisakˈa........Half a man.
Woixdjahiriga...........Laughing at his antics.
Wohiŋkcahirega.........He at whom they laugh.[19]
Maiⁿnukonuga...........In charge of land.
Tconaŋke huŋkˈa........First chief.
Septcoga................Real black.
Naⁿdjudjewiŋga.........Red hair.
Manaⁿpˈe huŋkˈa........Soldier chief.
Hokˈiwaiguⁿwiŋga.......She who retraces her steps.
Moradjawiŋga...........Earth wanderer.
Maⁿnusaŋkˈⁿ himinaŋkˈa ..Sits as the earth alone.
Moniŋga.................Hunts about the earth.
Anaⁿtcuⁿxedga..........Big armful.
Watcoginiwiŋga.........Goes ahead of them (common to all clans).
Maⁿmanˈwiŋga..........Walks on the earth.
Maŋguwiŋga............Earth coming woman.
Hotcaŋgitˈega...........Speaks Winnebago.
Haⁿpˈ emaniga..........Walks with the strength of day.
Haⁿbominaŋga..........Sits in the day.
Tcoraminaŋkˈa.........Sits blue.
Hundjxonuga...........Small bear.
Haⁿbirukonuga..........In charge of day.
Morutcaⁿwiŋga.........Goes around the earth.
Motciwiŋga.............Lives in the earth.
Tci-omaⁿtciga..........Lives in the earth permanently.
Ni-anaⁿjiŋga ....Stands on the water.

[19] The following names were obtained by the author.

The Wolf Clan

INTRODUCTION

Three versions of the origin myth of this clan were obtained. The second is the most interesting, for it gives the popular account of descent from the clan animal-ancestor, although it claims that he, in turn, was created by Earthmaker. One other important characteristic is the statement that the original clan ancestor married a human being and that from them the present members of the clan trace their descent. A similar type of descent is mentioned in a number of myths that can best be interpreted as village origin myths. The ownership of war bundles has also at times been linked up with descent from some spirit.

Very little is known at the present time about the functions of the Wolf clan. It is quite clear, however, that the clan once possessed powers of considerable importance. From the fact that the Wolf people are still occasionally called "minor soldiers" and that they are so closely linked with the Bear clansmen it is likely that their functions were similar in nature to those of the Bear people. They probably assisted the latter.

Water was sacred to the Wolf clan as it also was to the Water-spirit clan. A person was not allowed to tell a Wolf clansman that he looked like a wolf nor allowed to sit on a log in a Wolf clan lodge. If a man kills a Wolf clansman accidentally and then sits on the log in a Wolf lodge, he has to be freed.

According to one informant, the Wolf clan at one time possessed four sticks, which they would use and with which they kept time while the drum was beaten.

According to one informant, the Wolf clansmen were the only people who were allowed to intermarry.

The Wolf clansmen give a feast when a Bear child is born, to show respect for their friend. They give the child a name of their own clan.

The Wolf feast is held in the spring of the year, when the ice melts from the creeks and everything begins to grow. At the feast the clan origin myth is told and the members of the other clans are allowed to hear it. The food used is boiled rice.

ORIGIN MYTHS

FIRST VERSION (TOLD BY A MEMBER OF THE CLAN)

In the beginning the Wolf clan people came from the water. Therefore their bodies are of water—i. e., their sacred possession is water. There were four male wolves and four female wolves, and as they came up from the sea and swam toward the shore, one after the other, they caused waves to go before them. Therefore one of their clan names is *Wave*. They first appeared as wolves and later on they became humans. After swimming to the shore they lay on their backs to dry themselves; and that also is a name, a female name, *She-who-spreads-herself-out-to-dry*, and another name is *He-who-comes-up-first*. When they became human they built themselves a lodge and lived in it, but they had no fire. Then the Thunders came down and alit on a big oak tree that stood near their lodge. At first the Thunders were afraid of the Wolf people and they would not enter their lodge. That is why we have a name *He-who-is-afraid*. They asked the Thunders to come into their lodge and they had great difficulty in persuading them. After they entered the Wolf lodge they wanted to go home again immediately, but the Wolf clan people asked them to stay over for four days. From that fact a name has originated, *One-who-is-waited-for-by-the-Thunders*. The Thunders stayed, but not in the lodge of the Wolf people. They built themselves one just outside their door. Then they built a fire in it. After the four days were over the Thunders went home.

When a Wolf clansman dies the relatives paint his forehead blue (pl. 46) and the soul of the deceased is supposed to go west, and it never looks back as it goes on its journey, as this would be an indication of its longing for something in this world, and it should not do that. When the soul gets to the spirit home the relatives already there would ask the newcomer, "What did our relatives say when you were about to come?" And the deceased would answer, "They said that they would not come for some time."

The food that is prepared at the four nights' wake is supposed to last them forever.

This is the end of the story of the creation.

SECOND VERSION (TOLD BY A MEMBER OF THE CLAN)

All people claim to have come from some animal, and all are supposed to come from Earthmaker.

Four married wolves had a lodge in the middle of the ocean. They had four colors. The wolves all had children. One of them had 10, and the youngest one of these 10 is the one that came to this earth. When they came to this island, the first thing they saw was the footprint of the bear, and they said, "Our friend has gone by." There (at the place of gathering) they saw human beings and they liked their ways. Therefore they went home again and asked to come to earth and live with the human beings, and they were given permission to do so. Wherefore the two (man and wife) came here again the second time. When they were about to come everything was calm, and there were no waves on the ocean. They started out swimming, and they caused two waves to go before them. When they came to the humans they both got married. When they came to this land

they sang songs, but I do not know them. I was not taught them.
Finally children were born to both of them, and they gave them
names. They called one of them *Wave* on account of the wave
coming before them on their starting out. Because the four original
wolves in the middle of the ocean had four different colors, therefore
they have names *White Wolf, Green Hair, Gray Wolf,* and *Black
Wolf.* When the clan began to get larger they taught their children
these names.

When a large number of different clansmen are traveling and they
have to cross some large stream and the wind is high, they call upon
some Wolf clansman to calm the wind. This clan holds the water
very sacred. They do not even die in the water.

It was at this first meeting that they made friends with the Bear
clan. Therefore these two clans love one another.

THIRD VERSION—TOLD BY A MEMBER OF THE CLAN (FRAGMENTARY)

The original wolf brothers appeared from the bottom of the ocean.
When they got to the top of the water they started for the shore
singing. When they got to the shore they saw footprints of bears
who had just gone by. They said, "Our friends have just gone by."
That is why they are the friends of the Bear clan. They were going
to the meeting place. There a black hawk was gathering together
all the different clans. Finally he finished and he said, "It is done."
When he said this a wolf howled. They had forgotten him. They
said, "We have forgotten him. Let some one go after him." So
some one went after him . . .

CLAN SONGS

First song

This body of mine that I am walking.
This body of mine that I am walking.
This body of mine that I am walking.
On the earth I am speaking.

Second song

This body of mine that I am walking.
This body of mine that I am walking.
This body of mine that I am walking.
In the waters am I speaking.

CLAN NAMES

CÛŋKTCÛŋK' HIK'IK'ARADJERA (WOLF CLAN)[20]

Cûŋgewaksiga............Hunting dog.
Cûŋktcaŋk'a.............Wolf.
Regoniwiŋga.............Wolf (archaic name).

[20] The following names are from the Dorsey Mss.

Hicdjasgaga................White-faced.
Hicdjadjopga..............Four-eyed.
Hiⁿp'iwiŋga...............Good-haired.
Hiⁿtcoga..................Blue-furred.
Hominaŋk'a...............She who sits howling.
Manidjopga................Four walking.
Manaŋkᵉoga...............Throws up the earth (with his hind legs).
Maⁿok'acutcaminaŋk'a.....He who sits on the tree banks.
Niedjahuga................Coming from the water.
Niedjawanik'iriga.........He who brings them back from the water.
P'etcoga..................Green forehead.
P'e-osgaga................He who has a white forehead
P'ûⁿzakega...............Big sand person.
Xe-acaraminaŋk'a.........He who sits on a bare hill.
Xe-omik'a................He who dwells in a hill.
Xe-oratcega..............He who travels to the hill.
Sintcega..................Bushy tail.
Tcarawiga.................He who holds a deer in his mouth.
Tcasirawiga...............He who carries deer-feet in his mouth.
Tconaŋkehûŋga............Chief wolf.
Tconaŋketcòwiŋga.........First wolf.
Tconiminaŋk'a............Sits as a leader.
Wanuniniga...............He from whom nothing is hidden.
Warawaieinega............He who carries something in his mouth.
Warawaiguga..............Comes back with something in his mouth.
Waruxewiŋga..............She who chases.
Wirap'ega................He who lies in wait for them.

THE WATER-SPIRIT CLAN

INTRODUCTION

A rather poor version of the Water-spirit clan was obtained. It is, however, one of the few clan origin myths that contains the definite statement that the clan ancestors changed into human beings when they gathered at Green Bay.

The functions of the Water-spirit clan were, in former times, exceedingly important. Almost all the informants were agreed that a chief was selected from that clan, but the exact nature of this chieftain-ship is not clear. One informant, himself a member of the Bear clan, said that the Water-spirit clan was the chief of the lower phratry; that the clans were arranged in three groups, one over which the Thunderbird clan ruled; another over which the Water-spirit clan ruled; and a third over which the Bear clan ruled. He insisted, however, that just as the Thunderbird clan rules over the whole tribe in a general way, so the Water-spirit clan ruled over the clans of the lower phratry. Other informants claimed that the Water-spirit clan originally ruled over the entire tribe and that its place was subsequently usurped by the Thunderbird clan. It might be best to regard the function of the Water-spirit clan as akin but subsidiary to that of the Thunderbird clan.

Members of the clan were buried by members of the Thunderbird clan.

Water was sacred to the Water-spirits. It was considered an insult for a stranger to peep into a pail standing in one of their lodges.

One informant explained the custom as follows:

"If one enters a Water-spirit clan lodge and looks into a pail and there should be no water in it, the person will turn away and this action of his will be construed as begging. It would be proper to take a drink of water if some were there."

A round spot is painted with blue clay on the forehead of a Water-spirit man (pl. 46).

The Water-spirit feast is held in the fall and spring. Cracked or ground corn is used. Water-spirit people partake before anyone else at this feast.

ORIGIN MYTH

(TOLD BY A MEMBER OF THE CLAN)

In the beginning, when the clans began to form, the Bird clans came upon the earth first and alit upon an oak tree at Red Banks; and when they alit upon the oak tree they became human as we are now. Then the Water-spirit clan was to appear at Within Lake; and the waters began to whirl around in the lake and all the bad things that inhabited the waters began to appear. Just before the Water-spirits appeared some burned embers came up from the waters and the whirling became faster and deeper. As all the great things began to appear it always seemed as if the Water-spirits were the next to appear, but not until the last did they come up. Thereupon the waters began to quiet down. Then a white Water-spirit appeared with its horns curved toward each other, and when it came upon the earth it became human and walked. Then the other clans said, "Now, then, this is the chief. This is all that we have been waiting for. Now we shall divide ourselves" (into groups). Then they started for the lodge of the Thunderbird clan and entered it. There they named one another and divided one another into clans and there they counciled with one another.

CLAN NAMES

WAKTCEXI HIK'IK'ARADJERA (WATER-SPIRIT CLAN)

He-adaja^{n}jaŋk'a	Shining horns.
Hena^{n}pga	Two horns.
Heṛ'i^{n}wiŋga	Handsome horn.
Hesatcaŋk'a	Five-horned.
Hedjopga	Four-horned.
Maŋk'a^{n}ojuga	He who plants medicines.
Maŋk'a^{n}hodja^{n}pga	He who looks at medicines.
Ma^{n}i^{n}sinip'i^{n}wiŋga	Good cold spring.

Maⁿjiwiŋga	Yellowish-red earth (refers to deposits from iron springs).
Maⁿnuŋp'aga	Second earth person.
Ni-acgadjewiŋga	She who plays on the water.
Ni amaniwiŋga	She who walks on the water.
Ni-aⁿp'ᵐwiŋga	She who makes water good.
Ni-aⁿdagewiŋga	Still water.
Nicanaga	Stream person.
Nihuga	He who discharges water.
Ni-otᶜaⁿpwiŋga	She who jumps into the water.
Nidjobega	Four streams.
Niwak'itcaŋga	Selects (?) water.
Wakdjexicicik'a	Bad Water-spirit.
Wakdjexihuŋga	Chief of the Water-spirits.
Wakdjeximaniga	Walking Water-spirit.
Wakdjexip'iŋga	Good Water-spirit.
Wakdjexisaⁿwiŋga	White Water-spirit.
Hep'iŋga	Good horn.
Wadjxedega	Big boat.
Hip'ahiga	Sharp tooth.
Rabawiŋga	Beaverskin woman.
Rabewiŋga	Beaver.
Hejipga	Short horn.

THE BUFFALO CLAN

INTRODUCTION

The first version of the origin myth of the Buffalo clan is of considerable interest because it gives us an idea of the manner in which a myth had to be bought. It is one of the few origin myths that gives a precise location for the origin of a particular clan. What lake is meant by *de cicik* it is impossible to say. Considerable importance should be attached, however, to the fact that their place of origin differed from that of most of the other clans, because it may indicate that the people who came to be known under the name Buffalo joined the tribe after the other clans.

The Buffalo clansmen seem to have had the function of acting as the public criers and in general of being an intermediary between the chief and the tribe. This, however, has been denied by some informants, one of them a member of the clan. Their lodge was at the southeast corner of the village. Some informants deny that they had a special lodge, however.

The Buffalo and Water-spirit clans are friends and are supposed to bury each other's members.

ORIGIN MYTH [21]

Informant, member of the clan: "Listen, my grandson. Those who originated from the buffaloes and the way in which they origi-

---

[21] The following myth is given in the precise manner in which the individual who told it to me obtained the information from one of the old men who was privileged to narrate it. Unfortunately it was impossible to obtain any other clan origin myth in the same way.

nated, they have heretofore told one another thus. This it is. Whenever one asked about it, they would tell him, but they would never tell him unless he brought some present. Even when they had a child whom they loved very much (and for whom they were accustomed to do everything), even to such a one they would not tell it unless he brought them gifts. Thus they would not even say the least thing about the story of their origin merely because they loved some one. It is really essential to make a gift. And if some one came, carrying a gift, the old man would ask him what he wanted and what he would like to know, as this was not the only thing gifts were made for. Then he would announce his desire. However, he would not be told in public but when he was alone. Then the old man who had the right to tell the origin myth would announce subsequently at some feast that he had told so-and-so the story of the origin of their clan and that if anyone wished to be told of the same he should in the future, when he himself had died, go to this young man and ask him in the proper way. Remember, he would add, that before everything else it is the duty of an individual to try and learn of the origin of his clan.

"Father,[22] this I give you, a full suit of clothes. This I am giving you." "Thanks, my son. What do you wish? What do you wish to hear?" "Father, what did we originate from?" "My son, you have done well. My son, he who makes the most gifts obtains life therewith." "Well, then, father, you need not tell me now, but later, when I have made a sufficient number of gifts, then you may tell me." "My son, you have spoken well and if you do as you say, you will travel unharmed along the road of life." "Father, these also I give you, some beads and a blanket." "Thanks, my son, it is good. Now, my son, what I told you was true. I did not tell it to you because I coveted anything of yours, but truly because it is true—this, that we must make a sufficient number of presents. Whoever does as you have done will obtain the possibility of a good life for himself." "Now again, father, I give you these gifts. There is enough food for you in it." "My son, you have done well, very well indeed, for the life that I am to give you is holy; and as you know, even if one was loved very much they would not tell him this merely because they loved him, as it is holy." "Father, this I give you as a gift, a horse, as I desire to know what we originated from." "Now, then, my son, you have done well. This is what I meant when I said it is holy. Therefore, my son, you have done well. Come and sit down here. Listen very carefully so that if afterwards anyone should ask you for this story you will be able to tell it well."

---

[22] He is now proceeding to give the dialogue that ensued between the old man and himself when he brought the presents.

"My son, we first originated in human form at Bad Lake (*de cicik*).[23] From four buffalo spirits who are there, did we originate. The youngest one was clever and from him did we originate. The buffaloes asked one another what they were to do, and they then began to exert their powers, and the youngest one obtained the knowledge that there was to be a gathering of all the animals. So they all landed at a place called Red Banks. So it is said. And to the elk was given the charge of the seating arrangements.

"Thus did we originate. And then they counciled with one another as to how they should travel along the road of life. And as they arrived at Red Banks, each one would ask the other to do some work. And there they made a sacred (covenant)—that they would never fail to grant one another's requests. Likewise they agreed that when they died they would bury one another. The Buffalo clan and the Water-spirit clan were to bury one another, and they were to ask one another to work."

CLAN SONGS

Song 1

Finally you have cried.   I heard you.
Finally you have cried.   I heard you.
Finally you have cried.   I heard you.
Finally you have cried.   I heard you.

Song 2

This earth you have made me hear.
Finally you have cried.
You have made me hear.
You have made me hear.

Song 3

This day you have made me hear.
Finally you have cried.
You have made me hear.
You have made me hear.

"My son, here is some more information that one in your position should seek. This should be the second thing to ask for: 'What should one say when one gives a feast?' This you should ask for, and you should boil food for the informant and then you will be taught the proper speeches. Afterwards, when anyone boils food (i. e., gives a winter feast) a kettle should first be put on for Earthmaker and one should ask him for life; that the people may live to be strong and good. Include tobacco in your offering, for although Earthmaker made the tobacco he will not take any of it of his own accord. Not until it is offered to him by humans will he take it.

---

[23] The name *de cicik* is applied to-day to Lake Michigan. However, our informant in this case applied it to Devils Lake in Sauk County, Wis.

Thus he made the tobacco so that humans may ask life with it, and he will grant them their desires.   This is all."

TCE HIK'IK'ARADJERA (BUFFALO CLAN)

Moratcega	He who travels the land.
Tcanimaniwiŋga	Sho who walks ahead.
Tceniŋ ksiga	Suckling buffalo calf.
Tcega	Buffalo.
Tcep'anuⁿpga	Two buffalo heads.
Tcetcaⁿiwiŋga	First buffalo.
Tcedojeniŋk'a	Buffalo yearling.
Tcedoniŋk'a	Young buffalo bull.
Tcewiŋxedega	Big female buffalo.
Wirukanaŋga	He who is in control.
Hehekmaniga?	Shaggy walker.
Tcehatcowiŋga	Buffalo hide blue.
Maŋgiksuntcga	Shakes the earth by striking.
Tcep'aga	Buffalo head.
Manok'azuhiga	Kicking up the earth.

THE DEER CLAN

INTRODUCTION

The first version of the origin myth of the Deer clan is in part like that of version 6 of the Bear clan origin myth and in part like that of version 1 of the Thunderbird origin myth.   It is the only myth that shares with version 1 of the Thunderbird origin myth the account of the origin of death.

The Deer clan does not seem to have had any important functions, although in myth 1, it is stated that they claimed a "partial" chieftainship, whatever that may mean.

It was considered an insult to tell a member of this clan that he resembled a deer.

The facial painting is the same as that used for the Elk clan. (Pl. 46.)

The Deer clan people tell one another not to sing their clan song very loudly, and also not to make any sudden movement of their limbs, for each movement might cause the death of a human being. For the same reason they are told not to weep too loudly, as each deer's limb is a symbol of one of the four directions.   When, therefore, a Deer clansman moves a limb too hard when he is weeping over the decease of a member of his clan, he might be "putting some human being in the earth," and the wind would blow hard.

The dog names obtained were *uankcigohoniga* and *naⁿnatcgisga*.

ORIGIN MYTHS

FIRST VERSION (TOLD BY A MEMBER OF THE CLAN)

This is the origin story of the Deer people. In the beginning a black deer accompanied by an elk appeared in the center of the earth, and they went in the direction of the east. There they were going. Then the black deer said, "My dear younger brother, I am heavy on account of my excessive fatness, go you alone and I will remain here." So he remained there and did not go; and then to the center of the earth, to the place from which they started, he returned. Then he came back to the earth, and again they asked him. Four times they asked. There the necklace of money ornaments he recognized, the black deer did.[24] Thus the Deer clan beat them, and therefore they have the name *Black-Deer-chief*. As they went so they returned again. Again the necklace made of money he (the black deer)[25] recognized. The earth they went around. Then again the black deer went to the east. It was a large one who went ahead, and as he was going along, to his astonishment, they reached the place from which they had started.

"My younger brother," said Black-deer, "you try to do it." [26] And the second-born went ahead and the others followed, and again they were drawn back to the place from which they started. Then the third-born went first and the others followed and the same thing happened. Then they told the fourth-born to go first, and he went in front and suddenly he struck his horn, the one on the right, upon the earth, and, behold, grass suddenly appeared. It was a very white bud that he had caused to appear. Then he struck his left horn on the earth, and he made a tree appear and the fruit of this tree was meant to be eaten. Then they ate the fruit of the tree. The top of the tree there they ate. Thus they said. And they call a woman even to-day *She-who-eats-the-top-of-the-tree*. And then they began to walk and the earth trembled from their walking. Toward the east side they went. From this fact they have a name, *He-who-shakes-the-earth*. And again as some of the brothers were small they have the name *Small-deer*. They also have the name *Walking-leader*. And they also have names *She-who-comes-back* and *He-who-comes-back*, because in the beginning they always came back to the place from which they started. Whatever actions they went through, from these they derived their names.

---

[24] The thought is not quite clear here, due to the fact that something has probably been omitted by the narrator.

[25] There seems to be a contest between the deer and the elk as to who would be able to see the "money-necklace" first. Under the term "money-necklace" they evidently mean the medallions distributed by the American Government to those whom they recognized as chiefs. The recognition of the "money-necklace" is evidently going to decide the chieftainship between the deer and the elk.

[26] Some power is evidently drawing them back to the place from which they started.

The four cardinal points and the winds that are there, they are in control of. If on a very nice day a deer's voice is heard, that day will become bad, and if on a very bad day a deer's voice is heard, that day will become nice. The deer people are those who are in control of the weather. And they also have a name, *He-who-plays-with-the-winds*, and a woman is called *She-who-goes-with-the-wind*. The deer would always sit with the wind back of them. Thus they roamed all over the earth. Not one place on this earth did they miss.

Once, when they had come home, their eldest brother suddenly fell down (dead). "What is the matter?" they said. And the second-born said, "Our oldest brother is not saying anything; I don't know what the matter is." And then they asked their youngest brother and he said, "Our oldest brother is dead. That is the way Earthmaker arranged things." And then he talked to the dead brother and he said, "Earthmaker has made a place for you to go to now that you are dead. You have not attained a large share of life and you have left us who remain on the earth in a pitiable condition. But now that you are going home I want to ask you something. Those years that are still coming to you, distribute among your relatives. This I beg of you. And this is the second request: May the warpaths that you did not go on (by reason of your death), may the war honors that you did not obtain, may all these things be distributed among us. This I ask of you, my dear brother. And this is the third request: May the food that you did not eat, the nuts, the sweet fruits, etc., all that you liked on earth, may it all be distributed among us. This is what I ask of you. And this is the fourth request, my dear older brother: May all the wearing apparel that belonged to you as well as all the materials that you stored in back of your tent, never to be touched by you, but may we who are left behind use it all. This I ask of you. Wherever you are going, may these requests of those whom you left here behind on earth be before you."

Then the younger brother took some red paint and he said, "Brother, I am going to paint you. Thus they will recognize you at home. That is the way we will always do it hereafter. Those who are to live after us will paint us in the same way. Now this is the manner of painting. The forehead and the corners of the eye are to be painted in black and red streaks, respectively, and the chin and the front part of the throat are to be painted red." Then he dug a grave. Then they buried him. Then they sang the songs and when they were finished with this, they traveled around the earth and came to the gathering place of the clans. When they came to that place they were people—i. e., human beings. They lived their own life just as they had as deers. All the incidents of their traveling as well as all the characteristics of deers were used in the names

PLATE 46

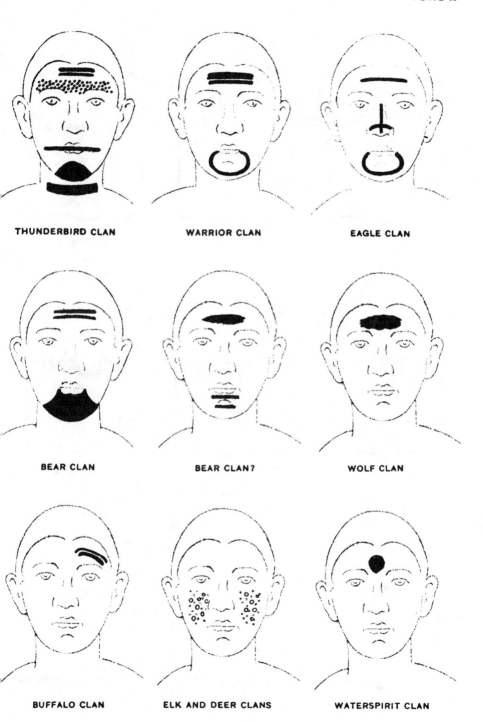

THUNDERBIRD CLAN   WARRIOR CLAN   EAGLE CLAN

BEAR CLAN   BEAR CLAN?   WOLF CLAN

BUFFALO CLAN   ELK AND DEER CLANS   WATERSPIRIT CLAN

FACIAL BURIAL MARKS

PLATE 47

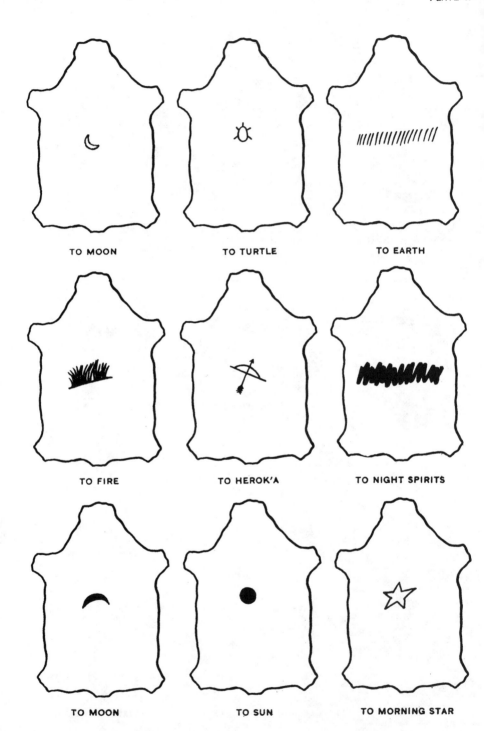

BUCKSKIN OFFERINGS

PLATE 48

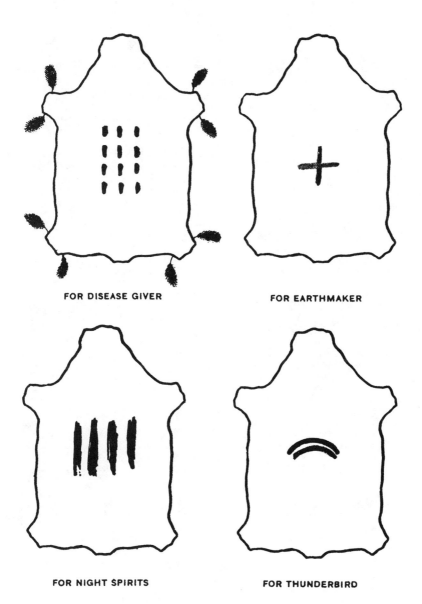

FOR DISEASE GIVER

FOR EARTHMAKER

FOR NIGHT SPIRITS

FOR THUNDERBIRD

BUCKSKIN OFFERINGS.

they gave one another.   Thus they have the names *White-hair, Fast-one, Little-white-teeth, Diffident-one, Horn, Pronged-horn*, etc.; and for dogs they have names also.   That is the way the deer people lived in the beginning at Red Banks, Within Lake.   Bands of people gathered together there, and all the clans that exist now originated there.

SECOND VERSION (TOLD BY A MEMBER OF THE CLAN)

The Deer clan people came up at the beginning of the earth. Only one is spoken of as appearing at the beginning.   He started forth but returned again that he might look for a companion.   For that reason a name exists in the tribe, *He-who-comes-back*, and another is *He-who-appears-first*.   After they had appeared on earth the deer blew on the original fire, which was only smoldering, and made it blaze up.   For that reason they claim a partial chieftainship.   The first one that appeared had a chief's medal around his neck.

CLAN SONG.

I use the cries of the four directions.
I use the cries of the four directions.
I use the cries of the four directions.
I use the cries of the four directions.

CLAN NAMES

TCA HIK'IK'ARADJERA (DEER CLAN)

Tcasephûŋk'a............Black deer chief.
Wagizenaⁿpᶜiⁿga..........Wears shells around neck.
Tcanûŋkcaⁿpᶜiⁿwîŋga......Deer vagina.
Maŋk'isagaγepga...........Appears in the middle of earth
Tcatconiwîŋga............First deer woman.

THE ELK CLAN

INTRODUCTION

In the Elk clan origin myth we find the clear statement that Earth-maker created the ancestors of the clan, and that they were human beings.   The myth resembles a village origin myth more than it does a clan origin myth.

The Elk clan seems to have had certain functions relative to the distribution of fire through the village and in camp.   It was never a very large clan.

The Elk people claim half of the fire, and thus half of the chieftain-ship.   They never hold fire toward any one.

Elks are buried by the Snake, Water-spirit, and Eagle clans, although the first has the preference.

White clay is used in painting the dead.

According to another informant, the facial painting consisted of white and blue dots on the face (pl. 46).

ORIGIN MYTH

(TOLD BY A MEMBER OF THE CLAN)

Earthmaker created all human beings. When he was about to create them, then he thought it would be good to see something moving. So he made a man and he was very good. But Earthmaker thought he ought to have company, so he made a woman. Then he thought to himself, "How should they know one another." So some one came to life through the water and this one was an animal. He made a village in the west for the human beings, and he thought about it and then he thought he would ask the humans what they would like to live through (i. e., become reincarnated), and they said the elk, because the elk never committed any crime. The humans were not to commit any crime. So the four elks started for the meeting place at Green Bay, Red Banks. They had up to that time supposed that they were the only living things, but Earthmaker let the oldest of the elks know of the existence of the other clans. So there they came and lived as Winnebagos. Thus it is said. This is all that they ever tell.

CLAN NAMES

HU^{N}WA^N HIK'IK'ARADJERA (ELK CLAN)

Roha^{n}maniwiŋga............Many walking.
Rek'uhumaniwiŋga........She who walks with the wind.
Tcatchiruxewiŋga..........She who pursues the wind.

SNAKE AND FISH CLANS

No information of any consequence was obtained about these two clans. Almost all the informants claimed that they were recent additions to the tribe. Only a very few survivors of either clan are still living.

CLAN NAMES

WAK'A^N HIK'IK'ARADJERA (SNAKE CLAN)

Haŋkcimiŋk'a.............Lying snake.
Hip'ahiga.................He who has sharp teeth.
Hirodiŋga.................She who has attained her full growth.
K'ik'urudiwiŋga...........She who crawls.
K'irixminaŋk'a............Sits coiled up.
Gisewek'inaŋk'a..........Sits quiet in her (home).
Hokciga..................High snake.

HO HIK'IK'ARADJERA (FISH CLAN)

Ho-apcudjewiŋga..........Red fish scale woman.

CLAN AFFILIATIONS NOT OBTAINED

Ha^{n}boguwiŋga.............East woman.
Huŋkminaŋk'a............Sitting chief.

K'ik'arasintcga............Licks herself.
Maŋk'uhoradjega..........Roams under the earth.
Maŋkerewiŋga.............
Ksismainga...............Sits solidly attached.
Mañk'urudjewiŋga........Her earth she spreads out.
Tcisgamaniga.............Walks as a white house.
Sinihimaniwiŋga..........Cold walking woman.
Sannaguga................Coming white.
Waŋk'inek'iga.............Lone man.
Warutcanxonuniga.........Small attendant.
Hominaŋkpiŋga...........Sits good as she comes.
Nannawahiguga............He who brings something in his mouth.
K'izahiyuŋgiwiŋga........Fighting princess.
Mogisagominaŋk'a.........Lies in the middle of the earth.
Waxurutcmanewiŋga.......Moves along as she walks.
Waŋktcoga................Green man.
Hihinanpga...............Comes out.
P'iŋk'ik'uŋga.............Fixes himself.

CLAN NAMES

FIRST FOUR GIVEN IN EACH CLAN

Although it has been discontinued for some time, the Winnebago claim that in former times it was customary to assign definite names to the first four children born in each clan. In all probability this custom extended not only to the fourth but even to the sixth child, as lists were obtained that gave six names. This would correspond to the fixed number of birth names. No significance need be attached to the exact number, as it was intended beyond any doubt to cover the number of children generally born within one family. Within these limits, then, the names were fixed, at least theoretically.

First four names of Thunderbird clan; informant, member of clan:

First. Nanozok'a......................Bending bough of tree.
Second. Nodjanpga.....................Lighting the tree.
Nainsawagicicga......................Broken tree top.
Hanantcnaŋxguŋga....................All heard it.

First four names of Thunderbird clan; informant, member of Warrior clan:

First. Hop'iŋga........................Good one.
Second. Warudjaxiriga.................Makes noise as he comes?
Third. Wak'andjamaniga ....Thunder walker.
Wak'andjahuŋga......................Thunder chief.

Informant, member of Thunderbird clan:

First. Wak'andjahuŋga................Thunder chief (male).
Second. Mandjidjega...................He who alights on the earth (male).
First. Hok'awas wiŋga.................Darkness (female).
Second. Nannazogewiŋga...............Bends (weighs) the tree down (female).

Informant, member of Elk clan:

First. Wak'andja sepga...............Black thunderbird.
Second. Wak'andja-teoga..............Green thunderbird.
Third. Wak'andja sgaga................White thunderbird.
Fourth. Wak'andja cutcga.............Red thunderbird.

Names of Warrior clan; informant, member of the clan:

First. Wonaɣire waŋkcik'a............Warrior man (male).
   or Naŋxedega....................Big tree (male).
Second. Nani^{n}nek'iga..................Lone tree (male).
Third. Ma^{n}cdja^{n}maniga.................Walks mightily (male).
Fourth. Wonaɣirega....................War (male).
Fifth. P'etcda-ehiga....................Fire-starter (male).
Sixth. Hûngmaniga.....................Chief walker (male).
First. Ahugiciniwiŋga................Shining wings (female).
Second. Ahutcowiŋga...................Blue wing (female).
Third. K'izahiyuŋgiwiŋga..............Fighting princess (female).
Fourth. Ahup'i^{n}wiŋga..................Good wing (female).
Fifth. Nijumaniwiŋga ....Rain walker (female).

First four names of Eagle clan; informant, member of Warrior clan:

First. Naŋk'iridjega....................Returns to the tree.
Second. Ahusak'a.......................Strikes his wings.
Third. Tcaxcephuŋk'a..................Eagle chief.
Fourth. Tcaxcepx'nunik'a..............Small eagle.

Bear clan; informant, member of the clan:

First. Tconaŋkhuŋk'a..................Bear chief (male).
Second. ?.............................? (male).
Third. Wak'izna^{n}p'iŋga................He who has white spot under his throat (male).
Fourth. Hundjxedega...................Big bear (male).
Fifth. Hirocicga.........................(Male).
Sixth. Noroxuga......................Scrapes a tree (male).
First. Hok'iwaigu^{n}wiŋga...............Retraces her footsteps (female).
Second. Tconaŋketcowiŋga.............Blue bear (female).
Third. Na^{n}cgadjewiŋga................Plays on wood (female).
Fourth. Asgawawiŋga..................Delicious bear (female).
Fifth. Hundj hinuŋk'a.................Female bear (female).
Sixth. Sitca^{n}t$^{ci n}$wiŋga..............Visible footprints (female).

Bear clan; informant, member of the Thunderbird clan:

Maiŋxga^{n}higa...........................Shakes the earth.
Waksuŋksuntcga......................Makes (it) quake.
Hashiwenimaniga......................Gives forth fruit as he walks.
Ha^{n}bixga^{n}higa..........................Makes the day tremble.

Bear clan; informant, member of the clan:

First. Maŋk'isakhominaŋk'a............He who sits in the middle of the earth.
Second. Hokere'u^{n}animaniŋga..........He who carries the ensign.
Third. Ha^{n}bidja^{n}dja^{n}higa...............Makes the day tremble(?)
Fourth. Nai^{n}sawahicicga.................Breaks the tree tops.

Wolf clan; informant, member of Bear clan:

First. Hi^{n}tcoga..........................Blue hair.
Second. Keratcoga......................Blue sky.
Third. Cuñktcuŋk' xotcga................Gray wolf.
Fourth. Cuñktcuŋk' sgaga...............White wolf.

Wolf clan; informant, member of Thunderbird clan:

First. Cuŋktcuŋk' xotcga................Gray wolf.
Second. Cuŋktcuŋk' sepga...............Black wolf.
Third. Cuŋktcuŋk' sgaga.................White wolf.
Fourth. Cuŋktcuŋk' cutcga?............Red wolf(?)

Wolf clan; informant, member of the clan:

First. Cuŋktcuŋk' sgaga.................White wolf.
Second. Cuŋktcuŋk' xotcga..............Gray wolf.
Third. Hi^{n}tcoga.........................Green hair.
Fourth. Cuñktcuŋk' sepga...............Black wolf.

Water-spirit clan; informant, member of Eagle clan:

First. Wakdjexi sgaga....................White water-spirit.
Second. Wakdjexi piŋga.................Good water-spirit.
Third. Wakdjexi tcoga..................Green water-spirit.
Fourth. Wakdjexi sepga.................Black water-spirit.

Elk clan; informant, member of the clan:

First. Hu^{n}wuŋga.......................The elk.
Second. Hezaztcga.....................Prong-horned.
Third. Hu^{n}wuŋgapga..................Black elk.
Fourth. Hi^{n}sgaga......................White hair.

Deer clan; informant, member of Elk clan.

First. Tcaga.............................The deer.
Second. Tca'i^{n}nek'iga..................Lone deer.
Third. Tcasgaga........................White deer.
Fourth. Tcasepga.......................Black deer.

CHAPTER X

SHAMANISTIC AND MEDICINAL PRACTICES

INTRODUCTION

The shamanistic and medicinal practices of the Winnebago differ in no respect from those found all over the woodland area and there is consequently no need for discussing them at length. The stories told about *Midjistega* and old Lincoln are the famous tricks and sleight-of-hand performances known all over America. There does not seem to be as much said about the conjuring lodge as is the case among the Ojibwa. This apparently is identical with the Winnebago *warukʌ'na*, "exerting one's powers." The lack of specific information relating to this subject obtained by the author may, however, be due to accident.

The Winnebago make a fourfold classification of their medicines: Those that affect a person by direct administration; those that affect him by their odor, like love and racing medicines; those that affect him at a distance; and those that are shot at an individual. Most of the medicines are obtained by fasting, although they can also be bought. The most important of these medicines are those called the stench-earth medicine (see p. 211) and the black-earth medicine.

Medicine may be used in a number of ways, but principally as offerings or as means of killing animals or men. It is often chewed. In order to make arrows or guns unerring, medicine is frequently rubbed upon them.

Sympathetic magic is of course well known. The procedure is the common one. A picture of the man to be harmed is drawn on the ground and shot at, stabbed, etc. The man is then certain to die a short time after, in the same manner as the figure has been mutilated.

There are two general magical ceremonies. *Warukʌ'na*, to know something by exerting one's powers; *wanaⁿtcere*, to hypnotize in the distance. (For description of latter, see p. 63.)

Example of warukʌ'na.—J.'s older brother and a friend had failed to return home and so J.'s grandfather went to a man called C. English and, offering him some tobacco, asked him to find out something about his son—i. e., to exert his powers. English did so and told the old man that they were camping and making sugar and that if

206

the old man went to a certain place he would find them. He went and found it was so.

Tales Concerning Midjistega

Recently the Potawatomi were going on the warpath and a number of other tribes were going along with them. As they were making their preparations they spent the evenings exhibiting the various powers they possessed and which they had obtained during their fasts.

One day Robert Lincoln's father heard that a Winnebago was going to come and give a grizzly bear dance. Old Lincoln and a few other Potawatomi decided to go over and watch him. When they arrived at the lodge they were told that the name of the Winnebago was *Midjistega*. They were also told that this *Midjistega* was going to make some gunpowder (in a magical manner). When they heard this, the Potawatomi said that if he could make his teeth protrude from his mouth he might be able to make gunpowder, but that otherwise he could not.

In the middle of the lodge where this performance was to be held there was a wooden dish filled with charcoal near which *Midjistega* was sitting. He had beautiful hair and he had marks made by white clay in the corners of his eyes and mouth. When the singers in the lodge began to sing for him he ran around the lodge on all fours, four times. Then he took up the dish of charcoal and shook it. While doing this he made a noise like a grizzly bear. Then his teeth began to protrude. When he had gone around the lodge four times the charcoal turned into gunpowder. Then he took a handful of it and threw it into the fire and it exploded. The members of the different tribes present took some of it and put it in their war-bundles. It is only a short time ago that a Winnebago war-bundle that was supposed to have some of this gunpowder was stolen. It belonged to a man named Buchanan.

Old man Lincoln had never seen any Winnebago before this, but he could understand their language and he interpreted all that *Midjistega* said. The Potawatomi around him asked whether he had learned the language from some of his Winnebago relatives but he said he had not.

After showing that he could make gunpowder in this way, *Midjistega* made some plug tobacco. He cut the bark of some walnut trees into the shape of plug chewing tobacco and put it in a white deerskin on top of which was placed a piece of real plug tobacco. Then *Midjistega* said, "Now since I have made gunpowder I will also make some plug tobacco." Then he took the bundle and danced around the lodge with it and by the time he had danced around the lodge the third time the odor of tobacco became very strong. After he had danced around for the fourth time he opened up his package and there was the tobacco. Then he spoke to the people, "You people of different tribes, the one that is dancing with me will obtain the first war-honor on the warpath that you are planning now, for I am giving him that honor and that power."

After this he told them that he would make them some paint, as they seemed to be short of it then. He took a wooden dish and filled it full of ashes and covered it up with a white deerskin. Then he danced around the lodge. As he was dancing around for the third time, old Lincoln thought he noticed yellow-colored paint. The fourth time he danced around, the paint turned into a red color. When, finally, *Midjistega* took the cover off, there was red paint of a very fine quality. Then the members of the different tribes distributed it among one another.

After this he made some axes. He molded some clay into the shape of axes and put them into a deerskin. On top of this bundle he put a real metal ax. Then taking this bundle he started to dance around the lodge. As he went around the lodge the third time, old Lincoln thought he noticed something shining. After he had gone around the fourth time he took the cover off and there were some real axes. They were all new and bright.

Then he decided to make some hoes, and then some awls. All of these he made of clay. Then he made some needles of deer hair. Then, noticing some boys playing with some basswood bark, he asked them to give him some, and out of it he made ribbons of four different colors, blue, white, red, and black.

Then he said, "As I have made almost everything, I will now try and make some whisky. If I fail there will be no harm done anyhow." Old Lincoln told his people what *Midjistega* was saying. Then they placed a new pail full of water before him. He took a flute and began to dance around the lodge. After he had made the first circuit of the lodge he held the flute near the pail, almost sticking it into the water. The second time he approached the pail he stuck the flute into the water just a little bit. The third time he came near it he stuck the flute into the water and stirred it around. By that time Old Lincoln could smell the odor of whisky pretty strongly. Then *Midjistega* went around the lodge for the fourth time and finally stirred the water with his flute for a long time, and taking a drink from the pail said, "It is whisky." Then he passed it around and everyone present took a drink. Old Lincoln, however, did not touch it. Then his father told him to drink it, as it was holy and had been made by a spirit. Then Old Lincoln drank some, and, sure enough, it was whisky, although it was colorless.

After that, all the people went on a warpath. However, the person to whom *Midjistega* had promised the first war honor only obtained the second one, Old Lincoln himself obtaining the first. The first war honor was a quantity of wampum beads and the second a wampum belt. Both the one who got the second prize and Old Lincoln brought back with them an enemy's head.

From that time on *Midjistega* stayed with the Winnebago and he and Old Lincoln became great friends, living together, one of the reasons being that Old Lincoln could understand Winnebago.

One day they ran short of corn meal, so they decided to go and trade some furs for corn meal. They had plenty of furs because they spent most of their time hunting. When they got to the trader's store *Midjistega* said, "Say, trader, the boys have been out of paint for some time and you ought to give them some." "No, *Midjistega*, I can't do that." Then *Midjistega* again said, "Well, the paint boxes are small and aren't of much value anyhow, and you ought to make them a present of some. However, I always knew you were very stingy." Then the trader said, "My business is to trade you my wares for your furs and I will not give you any paint for nothing." Then *Midjistega* said, "If I had some flour I could make some paint myself. However, I am short of flour, too." Then the trader said, "*Midjistega*, you can not do it, for even the whites do not know how to make paint (in that way), so how could you, who are only an Indian, do it?" Thus they spoke to and fro and finally the trader said, "*Midjistega*, I will bet you my store against your furs that if I give you some flour you can not make paint out of it. If I win you are to give me your furs, and if you win I will give you my store." Then the bet was agreed upon.

Then a lodge was prepared and *Midjistega's* drum and flute were carried into it. Then the trader had some flour carried over to the lodge and it was poured into a dish. The trader, suspecting that there might be some trick, stirred up the flour thoroughly. He satisfied himself that there was nothing at the bottom of the dish. *Midjistega*, in the meantime, painted the corners of his mouth and eyes with ashes and then the singers sang for him. Then he handed the flute over to Old Lincoln and told him to blow it for him every now and then. The trader sat near the entrance of the lodge with his employees. Then *Midjistega* jumped up and ran all around the lodge on all fours. Then he took the dish with the flour and shaking it, began to dance around the lodge with it. After he had danced around for the third time it suddenly turned into a yellow color, and Old Lincoln noticed the change in the expression on the trader's face. As he went around for the fourth time it suddenly changed to a red color. When he got back to his starting place it was quite red and was an excellent quality of paint. Then he said, "Well, trader, I have won your store," and the trader answered, "You have won my store. I did not think that an Indian could do it." Then *Mid-*

jistega said, "I can also make some sugar. If you don't believe it, give me some more flour." However, the trader said, "There is no need of your proving it; I believe you now." However, he sent one of his employees after some more flour and out of this *Midjistega* made some maple sugar. He made it in the following way. He sprinkled some water on the flour and said, "This shall be the size of pheasants' dung." Then it formed into little round lumps. Then the trader said, "*Midjistega*, my store is worth several times the value of your furs, and you have made me a poor man. However, I wish to ask you for one thing—this sugar—so that I can eat some of it once in a while." Then *Midjistega* gave it to him. *Midjistega* and his friend carried the contents of the store home. They had to make several trips. All the people at home got a blanket.

Then the trader said, "*Midjistega*, there is not a white man living who would believe that you can do this and if, therefore, I ever call on you to do it again, I hope that you will come with your friends (and do it). This is the only way I can ever win any of my money back again." However, no one ever heard of the trader after that.

Midjistega also made all the different varieties of corn at the Potawatomi meeting.

Old Lincoln had always heard of the remarkable power the Winnebago were supposed to possess in these matters but he had never actually witnessed any exhibition of it until he saw *Midjistega* perform (these tricks).

A man named Young Rogue, a brother of Robert Lincoln, could roll up a piece of clay about the size of a marble and then roll it on the ground and it would change into a toad and jump away. He was also able to shoot a blade of grass right into a log.

Lincoln's Grandfather

Lincoln's grandfather was the leader of the medicine dance and every time any relation of his died he would tell the daughters of his relative to stop their crying and that he would avenge the death of their father and kill four people. Shortly after he said this the four whom he had picked out died.

If there was a man with great wealth in the tribe he would make a wooden snake and send it toward the man. Immediately after this it always happened that the rich man would be bitten by a snake. The latter would then send for the medicine man and give him all that he possessed. Then the former would ask him, "When do you want to get well?" If the sick man said "In three to four days," the medicine man would say, "You must like to suffer."

For this reason the children of Lincoln's grandfather always had plenty of wealth.

The Crow (i. e., Menominee) Indians knew what a wonderful man he was and whenever he went to visit them they gave him many presents. He would be invited to a feast as soon as he arrived.

On one occasion when they had a feast in a lodge (in his honor) one of the Menominee marked the ground in front of him and dared Lincoln's grandfather to come over, saying that if he did he would injure him. When the Winnebago crossed the mark he was pushed in all directions and finally shoved into a pit, bruising himself a great deal. When he came out, the old man said, "You have probably never heard of me. To-morrow noon, soldiers will hit you." Then the Menominee asked, "If soldiers hit me, what will be the result?" "You will die." Then the Menominee said, "You have nothing to do with my life," and made a jump at him.

The Menominee who had been told that he was going to die said the next morning to his nephew, "Nephew, let us go to the lake and look around. I can't forget what the old man told me yesterday." So they took their spears for fishing and went out. While they were on the lake they saw a deer drinking at the edge of the water. The man took a shot at the deer, and the deer ran back into the timber. The man and his nephew pursued it. After a while the man gave a yell and then all was quiet. The nephew went over to the place and there the man was found dead. At his side a very large snake, with hair on its back, was standing.

The next morning one could hear the mourning songs all over the woods. Then they went to look for the Winnebago, for they believed that it was his fault. They told him not to worry about it, and gave him a horse to appease him. The day after they all had left the camp, the Winnebago pointed to some hawks that were circling around and told the Menominee to watch the foremost one. Then he pointed his finger at that one and made a sound with his mouth and the bird fell down dead. This Winnebago had the power to do this to all birds. He always told the Winnebago not to eat these birds because they were not good.

The Uses of the Stench-Earth Medicine[1]

There once was a man who had consumption and who knew that he was going to die soon. His relatives were about to move him to some other place and so he told them just to build him a separate lodge and leave him alone—that he wanted to die there. He asked them likewise not to come back to see him. They obeyed him and left him to die alone.

One day he decided to go out into the wilderness and die there. He went to the top of a hill and lay down. He noticed many birds

---

[1] This is the literal translation. What plant is meant the writer was not able to determine.

of prey hovering around the hill and he felt certain that they were there so that they could devour him as soon as he was dead. However, the birds told him they had come to cure not to devour him. Many carnivorous birds and many wolves were there. The turtle also came because he was the owner of some medicines.

Then the animals who had gathered on the hill began to doctor him. The raven began first. He ejaculated *e-he-a! e-he-a!* gave him some medicine and began to exert his powers until he felt better. Then the wolf began. He walked around ejaculating certain sounds and spitting medicine on him. The man became much better. He was almost completely restored to health. Then the turtle began to exert his powers, ejaculating at the same time *ahi! ahi! ahi! ahi!* and walking around the man and giving him some boiled medicine to drink. Now he was almost entirely cured. Finally a black hawk began to doctor the man. He put some medicine on the place where the man's pains seemed to be situated and he was immediately cured. Then all those who had cured him said, "Human! In a similar way you shall cure your fellowmen." They then gave him as much medicine as he would need. The raven gave him his "medicine chest," consisting of a flute and a gourd. With these things he blessed him. He also gave him a song which he was to sing. Then the wolf gave him his medicine chest, consisting of a gourd and a flute, and told him that he would not fail to cure any sick person he treated and that if the sick people offered the proper amount of tobacco, red eagle feathers, and food, no matter how serious their disease was he would be able to cure it. Then he told the man that Earthmaker had placed him in charge of these things and that he in turn would bless him with them for all eternity. As long as any of his posterity was left they would enjoy the benefit of these blessings.

And this is true, for even to the present day his descendants use this medicine.

Then Black Hawk said, "I, also, bless you. Earthmaker placed me in charge of some medicines and with these I bless you. If you are careful in offering tobacco and food to these medicines they will always help you to the utmost of their power. Whatever you ask they will accomplish for you. They will be able to understand you. So, if anyone is sick, you will be able to help him. In this way I bless you. If you are ever in any difficulty, think of me and I will help you." (What he meant is that if he ever was in any difficulty, he should think of the medicines with which Black Hawk had blessed him, and that that would be the same as if he thought of him.)

Then the Buffalo said, "My grandson, Earthmaker placed me in charge of certain medicines. Why should you then wish to die? Your condition is 'pitiable,' and therefore I want to bless you.

All those spirits whom Earthmaker made with his own hands were placed in charge of certain things. All these spirits have had compassion upon you. All those whom Earthmaker created as holy have blessed you. Earthmaker has placed me in charge of certain medicines and I am so completely in control of these that I can do what I please with them. There exist no beings either on the earth or under the earth whom I can not cure. With all these do I bless you. All your previous blessings were from spirits who live either on earth or in the heavens. The medicinal plants I bless you with are called Buffalo medicines. The other medicines are called 'stench-earth medicines.' As long as you and your descendants live these medicines will be efficacious. The owners of the stench-earth medicines they will be called. In this manner I bless you."

Then the hitcara said, "I bless you with those things that Earthmaker placed me in charge of. I was created by Earthmaker. Medicines, grass, trees, and bushes (for use in the making of medicines), with these I bless you. I bless you with my utterance. With my mouth, I bless you. If a human is suffering and places tobacco in your hands, then you may mention my name and pour a pipeful of tobacco into the fire. I will grant whatever you request. All the medicinal plants with which I bless you shall belong to you and your descendants as long as the earth endures. Your children can use them, and they will protect them. If any part of their body is weak from disease they can heal themselves with them. Many things will you gain through these medicines. You may also eat them. Human! you have dreamed, not only for yourself but for all your descendants. As long as this earth endures, so long will your descendants use these medicines with which I have blessed you. In this way I bless you."

Then the wildcat said, "Grandson, Earthmaker placed me in control of medicines also. I bless you. The other spirits have blessed you with certain medicines, and to these I now add my own. I can not tell you anything about the heavenly blessings. The spirits above have already bestowed these upon you. I will, however, tell you this: There is nothing either upon this earth or under it that I can not accomplish. I bless you with the power to do the same. With the blessings I give you, you will be able to accomplish anything you wish whenever you put these medicines to use. If a person were dying, and his relatives offered tobacco and food to you, you would be able to cure him. When you use my name, concentrate your mind upon me, and offer me tobacco. If I smoke the tobacco you will then know that your request has been granted. All the medical plants that I am giving to you, all the herbs that I am blessing you with, to all these, make an offering of tobacco. Whatever you ask they will grant you. All the animals that tread upon the air, all those

on the earth, have medicines that you are to use on earth.
Whatever you say on earth it will be so. You have been blessed with
all the things that are on and under the earth."

All the fowls and insects of the air, all the beings that have wings,
blessed him and gave him medicines, which he was to mix with other
medicines. He was told to make use of all the insects of the earth
and air, some of which we never see. All those who live on earth, all
the fishes in the water, and all the different kinds of water-spirits
blessed him with medicines. He was blessed with, and told to use
as medicines, all those plants that live in the water. He was blessed
with the leech, one of the animals that lives in the water, and he
was to use it in medicine mixing. They say that it is good to mix the
leech with other medicines to relieve pain. He was blessed with all
the trees, that we see to-day, which he was to use as medicines.
Their bark, leaves, and roots are considered very good for such purposes. He was blessed also with all the small undergrowth, whose
leaves, bark, inner bark, blossoms, and roots he was to use for
medicine. He was blessed with all the weeds, and he was to use
their heads and leaves for medicine, but their roots were to be used
for other purposes.

Thus all the different kinds of plants that grow on this earth
blessed him. The earth also blessed him and said to him,
"Grandson, as the other spirits are blessing you, I, also, will bless
you. Earthmaker has placed me here, and I therefore bless you
with all plants that grow upon me, and all the trees and weeds and
animals that exist on this earth, and lastly, with life and myself
(i. e., earth). You may use me, and especially the blue clay that you
derive from me, for medicines. Should you use as medicine all these
things with which I have blessed you, especially if you use me, as
medicine, you will be able to accomplish all that you attempt.

"If a person who is sick offers you tobacco (i. e., asks you to cure
him), remember that I also would like to smoke and that it is for
that reason that I have blessed you."[2]

Birds, especially eagles, are used in the making of medicines.
The entire body of a raven, including the heart and brains, are used,
and also the following snakes: The gray snake, the black snake, the
blue snake, the yellow snake, the bull snake, and the snake that
breaks itself in two. The rattlesnake is used in a mixture given to
women when in labor. If a woman hurts herself during pregnancy
and kills the child within her womb, she can be made to deliver the
embryo if she uses the medicine mentioned above.

---

[2] According to general belief the spirits are supposed to have entered into a sort of "bargain" with the
human beings by which they were to bestow their blessings upon them in exchange for tobacco, buckskin, and feathers. Of course, it must be understood that individuals must have the necessary requirements, such as a certain attitule of mind, fasting, etc., before their offering of tobacco has any meaning
to the spirits.

Toads are used, but only for poison medicines. The quail's heart is used for the same purpose. If a person is killed outright, his heart is used as a medicine, as the human heart is regarded as having great efficacy in such medicines. It is used in war, for compelling people to give you presents, and for courting women. The bear likewise is used for a variety of purposes. Its liver is especially powerful. It is rubbed over the body whenever in pain. It is often used by women who have injured themselves in childbirth, or in the form of tonics, poultices, and emetic; or for toothaches, bathing sore eyes, earaches, headaches; as snuff, as a physic, for burns, strictures, boils, hemorrhages, injections in the rectum, consumption, measles, dysentery, chills, nosebleed, pains in the stomach, and headaches caused by poisoning.

Sometimes a woman would take a hair of her husband and stick it into some bad medicine. In such a case he would never leave her for he would become very much enamored of her. If ever she went away, he would miss her very much. However, he always had a headache. Finally he would get sick and lose his appetite and then his eyesight. That is why it is forbidden to use this medicine, although some still do it.

Many Winnebago are blind, because there is a medicine that causes blindness. If one person offends another who possesses such a medicine, the latter would cause the offender to become blind.

The Winnebago have medicines for every purpose; for courting, for becoming rich, for obtaining good looks, etc. Even if a person is very holy, these poisoners can poison him. If a man was a good hunter or if he was wise and good, these bad shamans would poison him. If an individual was a great medicine man and these bad shamans got jealous, they would poison him. Indeed, only if a person was poor and lowly would they like him. Such a man they would never poison for they had no reason for being jealous of him. A bad shaman is always treated with the greatest respect and honor, because he kills many people.

A warrior is also greatly respected and flattered. It is the Indian's greatest desire to become a warrior. All desire that, and they also wish to become great medicine men and bad shamans.

This is the way they prepare and use their courting medicines. The courting medicine known to me is a plant of apparently two varieties, one of which has a blue blossom and the other no blossom at all. Otherwise they are alike. The one with the blue blossom is the male and the one without the blossom is the female. When I go out to dig this plant, I do not dig for these two specimens unless I can find them growing together closely. Even then I do not dig any two specimens unless the male is found growing on the east side. For that reason it is very hard to find them. As soon as I find two that fulfill all the conditions I dig them out and mix them together with their own roots. Then I take the blossom of the male and mix it together with the center leaf of the female flower. After that both are ground together thoroughly. Then I go to the woman I wish to court and, at night, when she is asleep, I touch first any part of her body, then a place not far from her heart, and finally the top of her head with this mixture. Finally I make her smell it. I then wake her up and go home. The girl will wonder who had touched her and she will think a good deal about the incident and never forget it. The next time I see her she will like me and she will do whatever I ask of her. The medicine would be working. If I did not see her for a long time, she would get lonesome, and the only thing that would cure her would be to marry me.

There is another medicine which I am now going to describe. When it first sprouts, which is in the spring, it is quite white. This must be taken and dried. Then one must chew it and go near the woman with whom one desires to talk. Approach her on the side from which the wind is blowing so that she can smell the medicine. As soon as she smells it, even although the man chewing it is one whom she has hitherto disliked, she will get to like him. This is the way in which the medicine works.

A man who was blessed was told of all these things. He cured all diseases. If a person had been shot and one blessed with the stench-earth medicine was called, he could be cured. In the same manner, if one is stabbed in what would generally be considered a fatal way and if a man blessed with stench-earth was called in time he would save him. The same cure is effected in cases of broken arms and of patients who are on the point of death. It is for this reason that those blessed with the stench-earth medicines are always praised, and that the people say "They surely are in charge of life; for their blessings really come from the spirits, just as they claim." [3]

[The "stench-earth" medicine men could undoubtedly cure the sick, but they also used it to poison people. The courting medicine was a poison medicine, and therefore it was not good. These people cured the body, but they killed the soul. It would have been much better had they saved their souls. They were really working for the devil. It is from him that they got all the bad medicines. Whenever they were offended, they would go and get poisons to kill the offender. Thus the devil [4] was really causing them to kill their own souls and the souls of those they poisoned. It is the same with all

---

[3] The following portion in brackets is the comment of our informant, who is a member of the Peyote sect.

[4] Although he really means the Christian devil many of the traits of the old Winnebago deity Herec-gu'nina, the chief of the bad spirits, are clearly discernible.

the other medicines, like the courting medicine, etc. The Indians were destroying their own souls. So Earthmaker decided to give them a new medicine. We have now all broken away from the old things. We have broken away from the devil and are earning our salvation through Earthmaker. For this reason I am thankful both for my sake and that of my people.]

This is a medicine that is good for consumption, for stomach trouble, for a cold, for a sore throat, and. for general illnesses. It consists of the following ingredients:

1. Waraxa'dax hoske'rera, English unknown.
2. Waraxa'dax ma^{n}nap'a'rara, English unknown.
3. Enai'^{n}tcox mank'a'^{n}na, English unknown.
4. Nicu'tcera, red water.
5. Mank'a'^{n}skaka, white medicine.
6. Mank'a'^{n} niyetco'tcera, medicine of the water.
7. Gi'xuk'unina, English unknown.
8. Mank'a^{n}ne'xeda, English unknown.

If a woman has any trouble with her womb this medicine will cure her immediately. She must not, however, drink it, but inject it. It makes no difference how severe her illness is, this medicine will always effect a cure. This man was blessed with the knowledge of its efficacy.

This is another medicine:

1. Mank'a'^{n} manup'ara'ra, medicine that spreads over the ground.
2. Xa^{n}wiwingi'ckera, medicine to tie with.
3. Mank'a'^{n} p'orop'orora, round medicine.
4. Hap'o'skra, English unknown.
5. Mank'a'^{n} kere'xera, sweet flag.
6. Na^{n}p'aca'k'onank' hura, English unknown.
7. Huntc p'istara, bear liver.

This is all ground together and mixed with water. When thoroughly mixed it is put into a bladder and injected by means of a wing bone.

This is a medicine for diarrhea:

1. K'etcû'nk'sire tco'ra, English unknown.
2. Aseni ho-ap hodô'p'iricera, curled sumac leaves.
3. Mank'a'ni tetco'tcera, medicine of the water.
4. Waraxadax skaka', English unknown.
5. Na^{n}da'nicura, maple sugar.

These are all ground together into a fine powder and sweetened with maple sugar. Otherwise no one would take it, for it does not taste good. It is called hasawañ'kemank'.

This is medicine used by women when their menstrual flow is not very good:

1. Tcemanaŋk'e, English unknown.
2. Wazi p'ara'ske abera, pine with flat leaves (?).
3. Wacutci abera, red cedar leaves.
4. Maŋk'a p'orop'oro abera, round medicine leaves.

All four of these ingredients are ground, mixed together, and then mixed with water. They are then drunk by any woman having trouble with her menstrual flow. After she has taken it she makes knots in the belt and ties it around her waist. As many knots as she makes that many days will it take her to get well. She also smokes herself with cedar leaves.

The next medicine that I wish to speak of is compounded as follows:

1. K'ewaxgu'ᵉuⁿsera, scent of a toad.
2. Waniŋkcu'tc na'ntckera, heart of a red bird.
3. Hactce'kera, strawberries.
4. Waŋkcik na'ntckera, human heart.
5. Xawiⁿjaⁿ, a plant.

If this medicine were mixed with whisky and given to any person, the latter would surely die within a year. The frog that is used in this medicine becomes alive in the stomach of the person who drinks it and kills him. If he took the same medicine and mixed it with paint and then rubbed it over his face, all who looked at him would take a liking to him and give him presents, and the women would fall in love with him and want to marry him. The reason that the women become smitten is because they can not resist the sight of a ripe strawberry. The human heart in the mixture is the object that makes the medicine so powerful, and the red bird heart strengthens it. Whenever these two, the human heart and the heart of the red bird, are used in medicines, the medicine is always remarkably efficacious.

If a woman makes fun of you and you feel hurt about it and want to revenge yourself, get one of her hairs and dip the root into this medicine and then tie it up. Hang the medicine bag in the woods and whenever the wind blows the woman will get lonesome for you and her head will ache. Finally she will get crazy. She will never cease talking about you. This is one of the medicines this man was blessed with. Some of them die from the effects of it. It is not a good thing, but the Winnebago thought that it was a very great thing. (Now that they know the Creator, they know that it is bad.)

Here is another medicine that we have, and it is prepared in the following way: Four trees of a certain species are peeled near the roots lying on the east side. Then the second bark is also peeled. Then these are taken and boiled together with a square-stemmed weed. The whole mixture is used to induce vomiting. This vomiting would rid a person of a spell cast upon him which was preventing him from killing game. In the particular case mentioned above the spell was the following: A man killed a deer, and a pregnant woman ate a piece of the intestine. From that time on the man was unable to kill any more deer.

The above medicine is used to break the spell of ill luck in hunting caused by the following actions: If a man cohabits with a widow, or if one who is a widower eats together with another person, or if he smokes out of the same pipe as another person. Not only would the medicine free him from his ill luck in hunting, but it would give him good luck in cards and speed in running.

Here is an astringent medicine. It is compounded of a mixture of the "clear" medicine and the "plant that spreads itself on the ground." It is used for the following purposes: As an application for swellings, for illness after childbirth, and for general sores and eruptions of the skin. In case of illness after childbirth it is injected. For sores, etc., it is taken internally.

Here is another medicine, called bladder medicine. It is made of the roots of a certain weed. These roots are boiled and then drunk. If one is troubled with stricture, the drinking of this medicine will enable him to pass water immediately. The same medicine is used to alleviate a toothache and to stop too profuse a menstrual flow.

Now this is another medicine. It is made of the leaves of a certain plant. These leaves are rolled up and then drunk down with water. The medicine is used for all stomach complaints.

Here is another medicine used for diarrhea and dysentery. It is made from the roots of a plant that has many thorns and beautiful white blossoms. The roots are scraped and the scrapings boiled and gulped down. At least a pint of this concoction must be taken. It can also be used as a mouth wash for those troubled with sore mouths.

We have another medicine used to rid a person of superfluous bile. This acts as a strong physic and not only cures a person of his indisposition but also gives him a great appetite.

Here is another medicine. It is called the medicine for burns. It consists of the leaves of a certain weed that is dried. If anyone has a burn, he chews some of this dried weed and then applies it to the burn.

Here is also a medicine for private diseases, compounded of the following:

1. Doxıcu'tckera hara, red willow bark.
2. Maⁿsixu'tckeda hara, English unknown.
3. Nap'a'hira hara, sharp tree.

These barks are pulverized and mixed together with skunk oil.

The next medicine I am going to describe is used in poisoning. It is called small-part-of-a-black-root-tree. It is used for many purposes. If, for instance, I wish a person to become blind or if I dislike him or were jealous of him because he was better off than myself, I would do the following: I would get a small part of a black root and pulverize it. Then I would mix it with ghost snuff and put it into my medicine bag. When I am ready to shoot the person I shake my bag and make the medicine fly out, and it would enter his eyes and make them sore. Soon he would become blind. I also use this medicine when I go on the warpath. I wrap it in a piece of buckskin and wear it around my neck. As long as I wear it in this manner I will never be shot.

This medicine is also used as a poultice. If a man has a pain anywhere, he makes four incisions in his body at that place, with the point of a knife, and applies the medicine.

Here is another medicine. It is kept in a large bundle. It is used in the following way: At a medicine dance a person may put an eagle feather on the nose of an otter-skin bag and then open the bundle containing his medicine and bring the medicine in contact with the nose of the otter-skin bag. The individual then enters the medicine-dance lodge. He makes note of the place where the person whom he dislikes is sitting. After a while he gets up and makes a circuit of the lodge four times and shoots at this person. He sees to it that one of the feathers attached to the otter-skin bag lodges just where he wishes it. Either he wishes to kill the man outright or to make him suffer for a long time. Should the victim die, the man who does the shooting must be very careful for he might easily injure himself. He must know, for instance, exactly when his victim is going to die and then as soon as he is dead he must open his medicine bundle and let the feather return, which it does as soon as the person at whom it was shot is dead. A black hawk is then heard in the distance. As soon as it approaches the man utters curious sounds and the feather alights right in the medicine bundle. When the feather returns, however, it is always black, though when it started it was red. One might imagine that there had been two distinct feathers.

If the man who shot the feather does not know when his victim dies and consequently does not make the necessary preparations for opening his medicine bundle, such as imitating the cry of a black hawk, or if, worse still, he is asleep, the feather will land upon him and he would likewise die.

This same medicine is also used for the following purpose: If a person offends you and you wish to take revenge by killing him, take your medicine bundle and whenever you come across the footprints of your prospective victim then open your medicine bundle and take out a striped feather from it and sing a song. When you are finished, make certain sounds and stab the footprints. You can arrange to have your victim die immediately, or, if you wish, to have him suffer for a long time, by becoming paralyzed.

This same medicine is used in a similar way in times of scarcity of food. The people offer a shaman tobacco and he would do the following: He would take his medicine bundle and walk till he came to the footprints of a bear. Then he would follow the tracks of the bear till he came to his lair. Here he would open his medicine bag, dip the striped feather in the medicine, and sing for some time. When he has finished he makes certain sounds and stabs the bear's footprints. Wherever the bear happened to be at that time, he would not be able to walk, and the people would soon overtake him. For that reason this medicine is valued very highly.

This medicine is also used when one desires something belonging to another. All that is necessary to do in such a case is to use the songs accompanying the medicine. Then all the things one has coveted would immediately be brought. For this reason they thought a good deal of this medicine.

If ever anyone uses it in gambling, he will win.

If again he casts his thoughts upon women, then the power of this medicine would go in their direction, and he will lose while gambling. All the women will, however, like him. He can marry whomsoever he wishes. The same thing will occur when a woman uses this medicine. If she casts her thoughts upon men, she will become foolishly enamored of them. For that reason the old people used to forbid women to use it.

This medicine bundle is also used on the warpath. If a man uses it upon himself and rushes upon the enemy, all those who are in front of him will suddenly find themselves unable to move. A person who goes on a warpath, after he has carefully applied the medicine to himself, is invulnerable. It is impossible to kill him, for no bullets can penetrate his body.

This medicine was likewise used in hunting for bear, and deer could easily be killed with it. Even those who are not accustomed to hunting could kill game easily if they used it.

Many of the medicines mentioned above were obtained from the man who was blessed with the stench-earth medicine. Everyone believed that the cures effected by him with this medicine were real. They believed that this medicine could cure them, and, indeed, it did cure them. It was this man, too, who originated the stench-earth medicine feast. It is a very sacred feast, considered more sacred than any other feast among the Winnebago. When the feast is given, an entire deer is boiled and cut into pieces much larger than any one person could eat. Nevertheless the host orders those whom he has invited to leave nothing upon the plate. Should any guest leave anything upon his plate, the host would give him a small piece of a root and tell him to chew and eat it. This the guest would have to do, and from that time on he would never know when he had had enough to eat. He would never get satiated. Whenever the man who had been blessed gave the feast personally, no one was ever known to leave anything upon his plate. While eating the guests kept time. They never shook their plates, for if anyone did so the others would immediately give him whatever remained on their plates. They would assume that anyone who shook his plate was the possessor of the stench-earth himself and that he intended to eat up these extra portions with the aid of this medicine. If, however, the shaking was done unintentionally and he failed to eat up the extra portions placed on his plate, then he would make a noise like a raven, and those who wished to help him consume this food would also cry like the raven, approach him, and flap their arms as the birds do their wings. Then all would eat.

When the man who obtained these blessings died, he left all these medicines that he had been the first one to use to another person. With the medicines he of course left all the songs. All that he used to do when he doctored a sick person he bequeathed to his successor. The last man who had these medicines was not a holy man but he knew all their uses and for that reason he was considered a powerful and holy man. To-day only the poison medicines are remembered; the good medicines are all gone.

This is the end.

How an Indian Shaman Cures His Patients[5]

"I came from above and I am holy. This is my second life on earth. Many years before my present existence, I lived on this earth. At that time everyone seemed to be on the warpath. I also was a warrior, a brave man. Once when I was on the warpath I was killed. It seemed to me, however, as if I had merely stumbled. I rose and went right ahead until I reached my home. At home I found my wife and children, but they would not look at me. Then I spoke to my wife but she seemed to be quite unaware of my presence. 'What can be the matter,' I thought to myself, 'that they pay no attention to me and that they do not even answer when I speak to them.' All at once it occurred to me that I might, in reality, be dead. So I immediately started out for the place where I had presumably been killed and surely enough, there I saw my body. Then I knew positively that I had been killed. I tried to return to the place where I had lived as a human being but for four years I was unsuccessful.

"At one time I became transformed into a fish. However, the life of the fish is much worse than ours. They are very frequently

___
[5] The shaman is represented as in the lodge of the patient and as speaking to him and his relatives

in lack of food.   They are nevertheless very happy beings and have many dances.[6]

"At another time I became transformed into a little bird.   When the weather is good the life of the birds is very pleasant.   But when it is cold they are compelled to undergo many hardships on account of the weather as well as on account of lack of food.   When it was very cold I used to go to the camp of some people who were living in the neighborhood and try to steal some meat from their racks. A little boy used to stand near these racks and we were very much afraid of him because he carried something in his hands with which he shot and which made a dreadful noise.   Whenever he shot it we would all fly away.   What the boy was using was a bow and arrow. At night we slept in a hollow tree.   If I entered the tree first and the others came in behind me I would be almost squeezed to death. If, on the other hand, I waited until the last I would sometimes have to stay outside and when the weather was cold I might have frozen to death.

"At another time I became a buffalo.   The cold weather and the food did not worry me much then, but as buffaloes, we would always have to be on the alert for hunters.

"From my buffalo existence I was permitted to go to my higher spirit-home, from which I originally came.   The one in charge of that spirit-home is my grandfather.   I asked him for permission to return to this earth again.   At first he refused, but then after I had asked him for the fourth time, he consented.   He said to me, 'Grandson, you had better fast before you go and if any of the spirits take pity upon you (i. e., bless you), you may go and live in peace upon earth.'   So I fasted for four years and all the spirits above, even to the fourth heaven,[7] approved of my coming.   They blessed me. Then I fasted 10 days more and then 20 and then 30.   Finally all the spirits blessed me, even those under the earth.   When I was ready to come to this earth, the spirits gathered together in a council-lodge and 'counciled' about me.   All the spirits were present. They told me that I would never fail in anything that I wished to do.   Then they decided to make a trial of my powers.   They placed an invulnerable spirit-grizzly bear at one end of the lodge and sang the songs that I was to use when I returned to earth.   Then I walked around the lodge holding a live coal in the palm of my hand and danced around the fireplace saying *wahi-!* and striking the hand containing the coal with my other hand.   The invulnerable bear fell forward prone upon the ground and a black substance flowed

---

[6] This is commonly postulated of both the life of the fishes and that of the snakes.

[7] He is probably referring to the four earths, although it is, of course, possible that there were four heavens. However, I never obtained the slightest indication of such a belief.

from his mouth. Then they said to me, 'You have killed him. Even so great a spirit as this you have been able to kill. Indeed, nothing will ever be able to cross your path.' Then they took the 'bear' I had killed and cut him into small pieces with a knife, piled these in the center of the lodge, and covered them with some dark material. 'Now,' they said, 'you must again try your powers.' I asked them for the articles that I would have to use and they gave me a flute and a gourd. Then I made myself holy. All those who had blessed me were present. I walked around the object that lay piled up in the center of the lodge and breathed upon it. This I did for the second time and all those within the lodge breathed together with me. Four times I did this and then the spirit-grizzly bear got up and walked away in the shape of a human being. 'It is good,' they said. 'He has restored him to life again. Surely he is holy.' After a while they said to me again, 'Just as you have done here, will you always do below. Whenever you wish to, you will be able to kill a person or restore him to life. Most assuredly you have been blessed.'

"Then they placed a black stone in the shamans' lodge that stood above. There again they made a trial of my powers. There I blew four times on the stone and I blew a hole through it. For that reason, if any person has a pain and he lets me blow upon it, I can blow it away. It makes no difference what kind of a pain it is. My breath was made holy by the spirits.

"The spirits on the earth and those under the earth also gave me a trial of my powers. They placed an old rotten log before me. I breathed upon it four times, and spat water upon it and it got up in the shape of a human being and walked away.

"My ability to spit water upon the people whom I am treating I received from an eel, from the chief among the eels, one who lives in the center and in the deepest part of the ocean. He is absolutely white and he is the one who blessed me. Whenever I spit water it is inexhaustible, because it comes from him, the eel.

"Then I came to this earth again. They, the spirits, all gave me advice before I left them. When I came upon this earth I entered a lodge and there I was born again. As I said, I thought that I was entering a lodge, but in reality I was entering my mother's womb. Even in my prenatal existence, I never lost consciousness. Then I grew up and fasted again and again, and all those spirits who had blessed me before sent me their blessings again. I can dictate to all the spirits that exist. Whatever I say will come to pass. The tobacco you (the patients) offer me is not to be used by myself. It is really intended for the spirits.

"Spirits, a person is sick and he offers me tobacco. I am on earth to accept it and to try to cure him.

"'You will live (this is addressed to the patient), so help yourself as much as you can and try to make yourself strong. Now as I offer this tobacco to the spirits you must listen and if you know that I am telling the truth, you will be strengthened by it.'"

(What follows is the shaman's offering of tobacco to the spirits.)

"*Haⁿ ho!* Here is the tobacco, Fire. You promised me that if I offered you tobacco you would grant me whatever request I made. Now I am placing tobacco on your head as you told me to, when I fasted for four days and you blessed me. I am sending you the plea of a human being who is ill. He wishes to live. This tobacco is for you and I pray that the one who is ill be restored to health within four days.

"To you too, Buffalo, I offer tobacco. A person who is ill is offering tobacco to you and asking you to restore him to health. So add that power which I obtained from you at the time I fasted for six days and you sent your spirits after me who took me to your lodge which lies in the center of this earth and which is absolutely white. There you blessed me, you Buffaloes, of four different colors. Those blessings that you bestowed upon me then, I ask of you now. The power of breathing with which you blessed me, I am in need of now. Add your power to mine, as you promised. The people have given me plenty of tobacco for you.

"To you, Grizzly-bear, I also offered tobacco. At a place called Pointed Hill lives a spirit who is in charge of a ceremonial lodge and to this all the other grizzly-bears belong. You all blessed me and you said that I would be able to kill whomsoever I wished, and that at the same time I would be able to restore any person to life. Now, I have a chance to enable a person to live and I wish to aid him. So here is some tobacco for you. You took my spirit to your home after I had fasted for ten days and you blessed me there. The powers with which you blessed me there I ask of you now. Here is some tobacco, grandfathers, that the people are offering to you.

"To you, the Chief of the Eels, you who live in the center of the ocean, I offer tobacco. You blessed me after I had fasted for eight days. With your power of breathing and with your inexhaustible supply of water, you blessed me. You told me that I could use my blessing whenever I tried to cure a patient. You told me that I could use all the water in the ocean, and you blessed me with all the things that are in the water. A person has come to me and asked me for life; and as I wish him to live, I am addressing you. When I spit upon the patient may the power of my saliva be the same as yours. Therefore I offer you tobacco; here it is.

"To you, the Turtle, you who are in charge of a shaman lodge, you who blessed me after I had fasted seven days and carried my spirit to your home, where I found many birds of prey (literally, birds with sharp claws). There you blessed me and you told me that should, at any time, any human being have a pain I would be able to drive it out of him. For that reason you called me One-who-drives-out-pains. Now before me is a person with a bad pain and I wish to take it out of him. That is what the spirits told me when they blessed me, before I came down to earth. Therefore I am going to heal him. Here is the tobacco.

"To you, who are in charge of the snake lodge, you who are perfectly white, Rattlesnake, I pray. You blessed me with your rattles to wrap around my gourd and you told me after I had fasted for four days that you could help me. You said that I would never fail in anything that I attempted. So now, when I offer you tobacco and shake my gourd, may my patient live and may life (an additional number of years) be opened to him. That is what you promised me, grandfather.

"I greet you, too, Night Spirits. You blessed me after I had fasted for nine days, and you took my spirit to your village which lies in the east, where you gave me your flutes which you told me were holy. You made my flute holy likewise. For these I ask you now, for you know that I am speaking the truth. A sick person has come to me and has asked me to cure him; and because I want him to live I am speaking to you. You promised to accept my tobacco at all times; here it is.

"To you, Disease-giver, I offer tobacco. After I had fasted two days you let me know that you were the one who gives diseases and that if I desired to heal anyone it would be easy for me to do so were I blessed by you. So, Disease-giver, I am offering you tobacco, and I ask that this sick person who has come to me be restored to health again as you promised when you bestowed your blessing upon me.

"To you, Thunderbirds, I offer tobacco too. When you blessed me you said that you would help me whenever I needed you. A person has come to me and asked me to cure him, and as I want him to live, I wish to remind you of your promise. Grandfathers, here is some tobacco.

"To you, the Sun, I offer tobacco too; here it is. You blessed me after I had fasted for five days and you told me that you would come to my aid whenever I had something difficult to do. Now, someone has come to me and pleaded for life, and he has brought good offerings of tobacco to me because he knows that you have blessed me.

"To you, grandmother, the Moon, I also offer tobacco. You blessed me and said that whenever I needed your power you would aid me. A person has come to me and asked for life, and I therefore call upon you to help me with your power as you promised. Grandmother, here is some tobacco.

"To you, grandmother, the Earth, I too offer tobàcco. You blessed me and promised to help me whenever I needed you. You said that I could use all the best herbs that grow upon you, and that I would always be able to effect cures with them. Those herbs I ask of you now, and I ask you to help me cure this sick person. Make my medicine powerful, grandmother.

"To you, Chief of the Spirits, I offer tobacco. You who blessed me and said that you would help me. I offer you tobacco and ask you to let this sick person live, and if his spirit is about to depart, I ask you to prevent it.

"I offer tobacco to all of you who have blessed me."

Then the shaman blew upon his flute, breathed upon the sick man and sang four times. Then he walked around the lodge and spat water upon the patient. After this he sang four times and stopped. The spirits would now let him know whether the patient was to live or die.

In this manner a shaman treats his patients for four days, and after that takes his offerings and goes away. If the sick person happens to recover, the shaman would tell him that he would never be sick again.

THUNDERCLOUD'S FASTING EXPERIENCE

Then he (Thundercloud) told of his fasting experience. "At the very beginning, those above taught me (the following). A doctor's village existed there; and all the various spirits that lived up in the clouds came after me, and instructed me in what I was to do. In the beginning they taught me, and did the following for me. 'Human, let us try it,' they said to me. There, in the middle of the lodge, lay a dead, rottening log, almost completely covered with weeds. There they tried to make me treat (the sick person). Then once he breathed, and all those that were in the lodge also breathed; then the second time he breathed, and all breathed with him; then for the third time he breathed; and then for the fourth time he breathed. As a young man he, the dead log, arose and walked away. After the fourth breathing, he arose and walked away. 'Human, very holy he is,' they said to me.

"There, from the middle of the ocean, they (the spirits) came after me, for there, in the middle of the ocean, is a shamans' village. There they blessed me—as many (spirits) as there are in the middle of the ocean—they all blessed me. There they made me try my power. As many waves as there are, all of them as large as the ocean, they asked me to blow upon; and as I blew upon them, everything became (as quiet) as (water) in a small saucer. So it became. Then I blew for the third time, and again it was that way. The fourth time they made the ocean choppy, and had (the waves) piled one upon the other; and they told me to blow again and show my power. And I blew, and the ocean, mighty as it was, became quiet again.

" 'This, human, is the way you will have to do,' they said to me. 'Not anything will there be that you can't accomplish. Whatever illness all (the people) may have, you will be able to cure it,' they told me. All those who are on earth (the spirits) blessed me. 'If any human being who has suffered, pours tobacco for you, then, whatever you demand, that we will do for you,' they said to me. At Blue-Clay-Bank (St. Paul) there is one who is a dancing grizzly-bear (spirit), and there they came and blessed me. If ever I should meet with some great trouble, they would help me, they said. I should pour as much tobacco as I think (necessary) for them, and they will smoke it, they told me. Songs they gave to me; and the power of beholding them, a holy thing, they permitted me, they told me; and their claws, which are holy, they gave to me, they told me. Then the grizzly-bears danced, performing while they danced. Their abdomen they would tear open, and making themselves holy, they would then heal themselves. Then they did it again, and shot bear-claws at each other, and they were badly choking with blood. Then they made themselves holy, and cured themselves. Now, again, they did the following: they made a front paw disappear in the dirt, and after a while they pulled out a prairie-turnip. Then, again, they grabbed a hold of a small plum tree that stood there, and breathed upon it, and shook it, and many plums began to fall.

"Then all sorts of 'shells' they gave. 'All of this, human, we bless you with; and if you do (what we desire), you will obtain (what you desire),' they said. Then he sang, and breathed (upon me), and squirted some water on my chest. 'Very true this is; very holy it is, I believe,' he said. 'You will get well,' he said to me."

CHAPTER XI

RELIGION

INTRODUCTION

We know that in all religions there are two factors to be considered—a specific feeling and certain beliefs, conceptions, customs, and acts associated with that feeling; that the belief most inextricably connected with that religious feeling is the one in spirits more powerful than man and controlling everything in life which he values.

The beliefs themselves play an important part with all people, but the importance of the specific feeling varies with each individual. A perusal of the fasting experiences (see pp. 245–260) will make this quite clear. It is because we do not separate the actions and testimony of the religious man from that of the intermittently religious and the nonreligious man that most presentations of the subject are so confused and vague. It is, of course, extremely difficult to obtain the real attitude of the intermittently religious and the nonreligious man, because it is the religious individual and leader who gives form to the expressions which religion assumes in ceremony and prayer. Yet we must recognize that there is a difference and that it is often this difference that accounts for certain contradictions in the information obtained. The one place where it is possible, at least among the Winnebago, to obtain some idea of the emotional make-up and attitude of the intermittently religious man, is the fasting ordeal, and from a comparison of those experiences it is quite clear that a sufficiently large number of people were not able to obtain that thrill which they had been taught to expect. It is also clear that the shamans and religious leaders recognized this fact and provided for it by advising such people to buy the requisite protection against the trials and misfortunes of life, or as they put it, "the crises or narrow places of life." Such a person would certainly not be regarded as one of the leaders of the tribe.

The ideal that the parent held before the eyes of his children is quite eloquently put in the system of instructions (see p. 118).

My son, when you grow up, you should try to be of some benefit to your fellowmen. There is only one way in which this can be done, and that is to fast . . . If you thirst to death, the spirits who are in control of wars will bless you . . . But, my son, if you do not fast repeatedly it will be all in vain that you inflict sufferings upon yourself. Blessings are not obtained except by making the proper offerings to the spirits and by putting yourself, time and again, in the proper mental condition . . . If you do not obtain a spirit to strengthen you, you will amount to nothing in the estimation of your fellowmen, and they will show you little respect . . . My son, as you travel along life's path, you will find many narrow passages (i. e., crises), and you can never tell when you will come to them. Try to anticipate them, so that you will be endowed with sufficient strength (by obtaining powers from the spirits) to pass safely through these narrow passages.

Among the Winnebago religion is definitely connected with the preservation of life values. It is not a phenomenon distinct from mundane life, but one of the most important means of maintaining social ideals. What these are can be gleaned from practically every prayer; they are success, happiness, and long life. The vast majority of investigators are often surprised at the intense religious life which, among the North American Indians, exists side by side with an intense realism and with a clear understanding and appreciation of the materialistic basis of life. The explanation, to judge from the Winnebago data, is simple enough. The Indian does not interpret life in terms of religion, but religion in terms of life. In other words, he exalts the world around him and the multifarious desires and necessities of the day, so that they appear to him bathed in a religious thrill. At least that is what the devoutly religious man does and most of the religious data presented in this volume emanates from him. Still we are convinced that for the vast majority of Winnebago, in other words, for the intermittently religious, there are many moments in life and many actions which are seen through this pleasurable religious thrill.

Every Winnebago will admit that to perform the wana^ntce're ceremony (p. 63) and, on the following day, to agree to start at a certain hour, would not necessarily result in killing a bear. The bear tracks are to be followed and a person is to persevere until the bear is captured, in spite of the fact that the wana^ntce're ceremony is supposed to insure the capture of the animal.

Or again let us take the following example. No man can hope to go on a warpath and kill an enemy unless he is authorized to do so by a definite blessing received during fasting. If we were to accept this statement as such, we might be led to believe that the Winnebago were willing to risk their young men on so dangerous an undertaking as a warpath, on the sole strength of a fasting experience. It does not stand to reason that they would, and a careful inquiry into the subject has shown that they never did. What actually happened was that the prospective war leader translated into religious terms the exact conditions and requirements of every particular war party. That is why the chief of the tribe and the shamans insisted that only such a person who had been blessed with the most specific kind of knowledge, such as the number of men he must take

along, the amount of food required, the number of moccasins necessary, the number and strength of the enemy, where he was to meet
them, etc.—that only such a man might start on a warpath. If an
individual failed to give the proper assurances and guarantees to the
chief, his expedition was not countenanced. If, nevertheless, he
went, any mishap was directly chargeable to him.

In other words, we are dealing here with a more or less fixed way of
describing the mundane happenings of life. The terminology is
religious, but does that mean that there is always a religious feeling
attached to it? That is the crucial question to determine. We
believe that the religious element in such a happening depends upon
the religious susceptibility of the individual concerned. It is quite
possible that a devoutly religious man may think of the religious aspect of a rite or action more than one who is but indifferently religious,
but he will never for one moment forget that the questions involved
here are of a purely human nature. The most that can be said of
the religious element of the two particular cases mentioned above
is that they will spur the person on. Perhaps it is the realization
that such is the case that often prompts the more matter-of-fact
individuals to lay such stress on fasting preparatory to starting on
a warpath. There, indeed, seems to have been a matter-of-fact
movement in the tribe, for the members of the Warrior clan claimed
that they could dispense with the fasting, and that mere membership
in that particular clan gave them the right to go on a warpath whenever they wished to. This we know was vigorously denied by other
individuals.

The Winnebago has no disinterested, unselfish love for the spirit
or deity to whom he prays, except in so far as every man is likely to
develop such an attitude at some crisis or when his mind is fixed
intently on the attainment of some personal advantage. Then,
naturally enough, the spirits who are to bestow these blessings are
addressed in the most laudatory terms. To show how intimately
these spirits are bound up with the worldly affairs of man and how
little they mean to him apart from this we have but to point out
that, for the vast majority of Winnebago, the spirits' freedom of
action is conceived of as definitely restricted. There seems to be a
purely mechanical relation of cause and effect between the offerings
of men and their acceptance by the spirits. The latter are not free to
reject them except in theory. Was it not ordained by Earthmaker,
when the earth was created, that in return for tobacco the spirits were
to bestow blessings on man? So every Winnebago believes. The
religious leaders insisted that only when the proper offerings were
made in the proper way would the spirits bestow their blessings.
But after all is said and done, the chances that the proper conditions
would not be fulfilled were negligible. And we doubt whether this

rather high conception was shared by all the Winnebago. Our impression is that many Winnebago believed the offering would be mechanically followed by the blessing. Take, for instance, the following example: A middle-aged Winnebago while hunting was suddenly surprised by the enemy. He succeeded in making his escape into a cave. All hope of final delivery seemed to be gone, for the enemy stationed themselves before the entrance. Now this man had never been blessed in his youth and knew little about the proper procedure to observe when making offerings to the spirits. In this terrible crisis he turned instinctively to the spirits. He took some tobacco and put some in the different nooks of the cave, and said: "Spirits, whoever you are, and wherever you are, it is said that you love tobacco and that in return for it you bless people. Here is some tobacco, and I ask that I may return to my people." There was, as far as we know, no promise made that in return he would make further offerings to them or that he would thereafter love them and honor them. He escaped and unquestionably believed that it was due to the intervention of the spirits, but the spirits were, quite clearly, constrained to act because they had received tobacco.

There can be little doubt that many Winnebago felt as this man did. We find an expression of the same attitude in a myth. The Winnebago are represented as making offerings to the buffalo spirits, and the smoke is ascending to the home of these spirits through a hole in the sky. The younger buffalos can not resist the temptation of approaching the opening to catch a few whiffs of their favorite tobacco. They are thereupon warned by the older buffalos not to go too close, for the tobacco fumes might tempt them too strongly; and should they succumb to the temptation and accept the offerings, they would then have to appear on earth and be killed by man. As might have been expected, there is in the relation of the spirits to man something similar to the securing of the food animal by some such ceremony as the $wana^nkere$. The spirits are dazzled, hypnotized by the offerings, and accept.

In the second of the examples given above we were dealing with a food animal—the buffalo. If there is any plausibility in the explanation we advanced before that the Winnebago interprets religion in terms of life, the relation of the spirits to the food supply ought to show it. Now, it is characteristic of the Winnebago religion that the great generalized spirit deities, like Earthmaker, Sun, Moon, etc., have little to do with the securing of specific kinds of food. As a rule, some generalized spirit-animal presides over the various species of animals, and he gladly permits the animals to appear on earth to be killed by man when the proper offerings are made. This seems to have been a secondary interpretation, however, developed probably under the influence of the shamans as a substitute for the purely mechanical attitude mentioned above. To picture the food animals as desirous of being killed and eaten by man is, however, but another way of saying that the food animals were killed and eaten, and were secondarily and weakly brought into the general religious life, because everything was seen through a religious vista. It is by no means certain that this was always the case, and there seem to be innumerable indications in the myths that there was a time when the securing of the food animals was not connected with religion as such.

Just as the securing of food animals is to-day connected with certain spirits, so are the various activities of man during his life. But characteristically it is not a generalized conception of life, but life as consisting of a prescribed number of years, with so many war honors, so much wealth, so much food consumed, so many children, etc. The spirits are exhorted to give to every man his allotted number of years, food, etc. These are apparently his by right, and if he dies before his time the ghost of the deceased is asked to beg the spirits to distribute among his relatives the "unused" years, food, etc. So here, too, we have a clear example of the explanation of purely materialistic conception of life in terms of religion.

It will be best to discuss the main features of Winnebago religion under the following heads:

I. The religious concepts:
    1. The concept of supernatural power.
    2. The concept and nature of the spirits.
    3. The power and localization of the spirits.
II: 1. The twofold interpretation of the relation of the spirits to man.
    2. The guardian spirits.
    3. Personal religious experiences.
III. Methods of bringing the spirits into relation with man:
    1. Fasting.
    2. Mental concentration.
    4. Offerings and sacrifices.
    5. Prayers.
IV. The folkloristic concepts:
    1. The concept of evil.
    2. The concept of disease.
    3. The concepts of death, after-life, and reincarnation.
    4. The concept of the soul.
V. The cosmological ideas.

THE CONCEPT OF SUPERNATURAL POWER [1]

The Winnebago have no such belief in a "magic power" as Mr. J. N. B. Hewitt and Mr. W. Jones would have us believe exists among

[1] For a general discussion of this concept in North America cf. my paper on the "Religion of the North American Indians," Journal of American Folklore, vol. 27, no. 106, pp. 344–351.

the Iroquois and Fox.[2] In the article mentioned above we have given our reasons for believing that these ethnologists were mistaken in their interpretation.

In the Winnebago language the four words most commonly used in speaking of the spirits are *wak'a^n*, *wak'a'ndja*, *xop*, and *waxop'i'ni*. *Wak'a^n* seems exactly equivalent to our word "sacred," while *wak'a'ndja*, which is identical with the Omaha word *wakonda*, means thunderbird. In all likelihood it originally meant "he who is sacred" or something like that. It has nothing to do with the word "thunder," which is *k^{c}oire* in Winnebago. The word *wak'a^n* also means snake, for the snake is a holy animal among the Winnebago, the messenger of the spirits. The word *xop*, identical with the Omaha *xube*, is more difficult to define. It means sacred and awe-inspiring and seems to be associated, in the eyes of the Winnebago, with the intensely emotional aspects of religion, where self is completely forgotten. Those ceremonies, in which the performers work themselves into a frenzy of excitement and dance naked, are always referred to as *xcp*. The word *waxop'i'ni* is clearly a noun compounded of the indefinite prefix *wa-* and the suffix *-ni*, which possibly is an old agentive nominalizer, or, more probably, an old stem meaning "man." It occurs also in the word *manka'ni*, medicine-man. In other words it means "he who" or "that which is holy." *Waxop'i'ni* is the only Winnebago word for spirit. Both the words *wak'andja* and *waxop'i'ni* are very definite terms referring to individualized spirits.

As to the use of the adjectives *wak'a^n* and *xop*, there seems to be little mystery about them. They are used much as our words "holy" and "sacred." Anything in any way connected with the spirits is either *wak'a^n* or *xop*. If a Winnebago were to come across some unusually shaped object he might offer tobacco to it, and upon being questioned he would undoubtedly say that the object is *wak'a^n*. What is it that he means by *wak'a^n*? From my experience in the field he simply means that it is "sacred," and if pressed for a more definite answer he would probably say that it has the power of

---

[2] According to Mr. Hewitt, *orenda* is a "magic power which was assumed . . . to be inherent in every body . . . and in every personified attribute, property, or activity . . . This hypothetic principle was conceived to be immaterial, occult, impersonal, mysterious in mode of action . . . The possession of *orenda* . . . is the distinctive characteristic of all the gods, and these gods in earlier time were all the bodies and beings of nature in any manner affecting the weal or woe of man." (Article "Orenda" in the Handbook of American Indians, Bureau of American Ethnology, Bulletin 30, pt. 2.) According to W. Jones, the *manito* "is an unsystematic belief in a cosmic, mysterious property, which is believed to be existing everywhere in nature . . . The conception of this something wavers between that of a communicable property, that of a mobile, invisible substance, and that of a latent transferable energy; . . . this substance, property, or energy is conceived as being widely diffused amongst natural objects and human beings . . . the presence of it is promptly assigned as the explanation of any unusual power or efficacy which any object or person is found to possess: . . . It is a distinct and rather abstract conception of a diffused, all-pervasive, invisible, manipulable, and transferable life-energy, or universal force . . . (Finally) all success, strength, or prosperity is conceived to depend upon the possession of (this force)."—"The Algonkin Manitou" (Journal of American Folklore, vol. 18, no. LXX, pp. 183–190, 1905).

bestowing blessings upon him—in other words, of acting like a spirit, a *waxop'i'ni*. That is why he offers tobacco to it. We would be inclined to say that the individual finding such an object has created a new spirit. Such a new spirit may be forever confined to the particular family to which the individual belongs. It might die with him, or, on the other hand, it might acquire great importance and popularity and become a tribal spirit. What seems to have happened, in the vast majority of cases, however, among the Winnebago, is that owing to the marked development of the spirit-deities and cosmogonic myths, such "sacred" objects were interpreted as being either some manifestation of a spirit, some transformation which he had assumed, or as inhabited by a spirit.

The reason why, in our opinion, so many ethnologists have apparently misinterpreted the nature of *wak'a^n* is due to the fact that when something that, from the European viewpoint, is immaterial and inanimate, like vapor, light, movement, etc., is called *wak'a^n*, then it seems difficult for them to imagine that it can be so except by virtue of some intimate connection with a definite spirit, and if that can not be demonstrated, then the only solution left is to fall back upon the "magic power" idea. By doing this they clearly show that for them the test of individualization is corporeality of a fairly definite kind, dependent mainly upon visual sensations. This brings us to a fundamental problem, not only for Winnebago religion, but for North American religion in general.

The Concept and Nature of the Spirits

Those Indians who have never spent any time thinking upon the nature of spirits can not truly be said to have any concept of their nature, whether vague or definite. They simply repeat what they have heard from the more religiously inclined. An answer prompted by a moment's consideration, as is often the case when an ethnologist interrogates them, does not necessarily reflect the current view of the subject, nor, for that matter, even the same Indian's belief after he has given the matter some thought. Many Winnebago, with whom the author was fairly well acquainted, refused to answer certain questions offhand and asked for time to reflect about them. It seems justified, when we are studying a subject like religion to ask for information from those who have, in all probability, formulated the beliefs—the shamans. It is from them that we must strive to learn whether the spirits are conceived of as anthropomorphic, theromorphic, dream-phantasms, or indefinite entities in general.

In trying to discover this the author found, not only that he was asking a leading question, but that he was asking an unnecessary question. It was soon quite clear that the Winnebago did not base their test of the existence of a spirit on the presence or absence of corporeality; in other words, upon such sense perceptions as sight and hearing. It is because we Europeans do insist that the presence or absence of corporeality is the test of reality or unreality that we have been led to make the classification into personal and impersonal. But the Winnebago apparently does not insist that existence depends upon sense perceptions alone. He claims that what is thought of, what is felt, and what is spoken, in fact, anything that is brought before his consciousness, is a sufficient indication of its existence and it is the question of the existence and reality of these spirits in which he is interested. The question of their corporeality is of comparative unimportance and most of the questions connected with the personal or impersonal nature of the spirits do not exist.

It is clear that if comparatively little stress has been laid by the Winnebago on the personality of the spirits, it will be difficult to define them precisely except by their names, by their attributes, and by the nature of the blessings which they bestow on man. What seems to stand out most prominently in the attitude of the Winnebago toward their spirits is the intense belief in the reality of their existence, which is due first to what might be called the "emotional authority" for their existence, and secondly, to the fact that the life values of man are intensely real and the spirits are theoretically in control of these life values.

To the average Winnebago the world is peopled by an indefinite number of spirits who manifest their existence in many ways, being either visible, audible, felt emotionally, or manifesting themselves by some sign or result. From a certain point of view, all the spirits demonstrate their existence by the result, by the fact that the blessings they bestow upon man enable him to be successful, and this holds just as much for the spirit who manifests himself in the most intangible, emotional manner as for that one who is visible to man.

In all those areas where a well-developed ritualistic organization exists a fairly large number of theromorphic and anthropomorphic spirits is found. In many cases these are real deities. This is true for the Winnebago. Exactly how definite and distinct this theromorphic and anthropomorphic nature of the spirits is will depend largely on the individual history that the spirit has undergone. Where tricksters and animal heroes have become spirits or deities their theromorphic nature is marked. Other deities, like Earthmaker, Disease-giver, the Thunderbirds, etc., have become markedly anthropomorphic, owing to the reinterpretations and remodeling of the shamans. Often enough the reinterpretations are not thorough and we find deities of an apparently mixed type.

Those who care to get a detailed description of the various deities of the Winnebago should read the various prayers found in such ceremonies as the war-bundle feasts, buffalo dance, sore-eye dance, etc. We will enumerate but a few of them here.

The principal deities of the Winnebago are: Earthmaker, Sun, Moon, Earth, Morning Star, Disease-giver, Thunderbird, Water-spirit, etc.

Earthmaker.—He is known to the Winnebago under three names: *Ma^n'una*, earthmaker; *waja^{n}gv^{n}zera*, he-who-makes-something; and *waxopi'ni xedera*, the great spirit. Of these the last is the most archaic, which might imply that originally Earthmaker was merely the great spirit. In the hands of the shamans, to whom the development and elaboration of the great Winnebago ceremonies like the medicine dance and the war-bundle feasts were due, he became almost a true monotheistic deity, benevolent but unapproachable. In the older myths, like the trickster and hero cycles (cf. for instance, the *wak'djvŋk'aga* and hare cycle), he is hardly mentioned except as a clear afterthought. In another cycle, like that of the twins, where he is definitely mentioned, he is treated like a spirit similar to the other spirits, although superior to them, but in no way re-sembling the benevolent deity that we find in the origin myth of the medicine dance (p. 302). How and when this development took place, and whether the introduction of Christianity had anything to do with it, it is difficult to say. All indications seem to be over-whelmingly against the latter assumption, although it can not be entirely dismissed. As we have indicated in a previous paper,[3] there appears to have been a well-developed pre-Columbian belief in a good and bad spirit among the woodland Indians. The Winne-bago shared in this belief and Earthmaker developed his present position through the displacement of the chief bad spirit called *Herecgunina.*

The older conception of Earthmaker seems to crop out also in the occasional attempts of individuals to obtain blessings from him. (Cf. the tale of Wegi'ceka, p. 243.)

Little can be learned as to the actual appearance of Earthmaker In the origin myth of the medicine dance he is described as though he were clearly anthropomorphic. The symbol associated with him in the war-bundle feasts, the cross, is unquestionably supposed to represent the four cardinal points.

Earthmaker is not supposed to bestow any definite blessings on man. He is, in a general way, expected to give them life. There is but little real worship of him because he is far removed from man and is supposed to come into relation with them only through his intermediaries, the spirits. According to the cosmological myths he

---

[3] The Religion of the North American Indians, Journ. Am. Folklore, vol. 27, no. 106.

created everything with the definite purpose of benefiting mankind in contrast to the creative acts of the old Trickster. It is very instructive to notice how he gradually usurped the place formerly held by the older spirit-deities and clan ancestors. In the clan origin myths there are a number of versions where he directs certain spirit animals, the ancestors of the clan, to go down to earth, while in other apparently older versions nothing is said of him.

Sun.—The sun is known to the Winnebago generally as *hanbwira*, orb of day, and ceremonially as *hanboradjera*, day-wanderer. He does not occupy to-day the position he formerly held. There are a number of indications that seem to point to the fact that his worship diminished when that of Earthmaker began to assert itself. Many of his functions and powers were likewise taken over by the Thunderbirds, who, although they distinctly belong to the older strata of Winnebago beliefs, have yet assumed their present importance apparently in connection with the development of the Earthmaker belief.

The sun is occasionally spoken of in myths, but rarely as a culture hero. In only one myth collected was he the hero of the myth. There he appears as the husband of the moon and as an anthropomorphic being who possesses an all-powerful disk (the sun).

Offerings are frequently made to him, but he rarely blesses an individual. In other words, he is not a true guardian spirit. He only blesses men and upon them he always confers success in war.

Moon.—The moon, like the sun, probably formerly occupied a more important place in the Winnebago pantheon. She is a female deity and blesses women, although, like the sun, she is not a true guardian spirit.

Earth.—Earth, like the moon, is a female deity. She is one of the oldest deities of the Winnebago and appears as the grandmother in some of the oldest myth cycles, like that of the hare. Offerings are made to her at the various ceremonies, particularly at the medicine dance and the war-bundle feasts. She never appears as a guardian spirit.

The earth is one of the deities who has received considerable reinterpretation at the hands of the shamans. In the myths she is a purely folk-mythological figure in no way interested in furthering she welfare of mankind. On the contrary, she is spoken of as the tister of those bad spirits who are bent on destroying the human race. Her rôle as a beneficent deity probably developed in connection with that of the hare, her grandchild, according to the old folklore notions, transformed when he became associated with the founding of the medicine dance or its older Winnebago predecessor from a typical trickster to an heroic animal deity.

Morning Star.—This is one of the spirits belonging to the older strata of Winnebago beliefs, who apparently was not displaced by the newer deities. He is both a great deity and a guardian spirit. That he developed out of the indefinite "folklore-spirits" is abundantly attested by the rôle he plays in the myths.

Morning Star is preeminently associated with war.

Disease-giver.—This is but an approximate translation of his name in Winnebago, which is *hocere$^{\varepsilon}u^n$ wahira*. He is a very peculiar figure, being described as an anthropomorphic figure, dealing out death from one side of his body and life from the other. He is preeminently a guardian spirit who only appears to the bravest and holiest fasters. His specific blessings seem to be connected with war and the curing of disease.

He appears in none of the myths and in but few of the ceremonies. He plays a very important rôle in the war-bundle feasts.

It is rather difficult to explain his origin. He seems hardly to be a deity of the people and can best be understood, it seems, if we regard him as largely a construction of the shaman. Certain of his characteristics may have been borrowed from some neighboring tribe.

Thunderbird.—Thunderbird is another of the older folkloristic conceptions that has been remodeled and reinterpreted by the shamans. He might be said to be the most popular of Winnebago deities. He is found everywhere—in the oldest myths, the clan origin myths, and the newest myths; he is a clan ancestor, a popular guardian spirit, and a popular deity. In contradistinction to practically all of the other deities, he is regarded as easily approachable by man.

To the popular mind he is distinctly theromorphic in form, causing lightning by the flashes of his eyes and thunder by the flapping of his wings. In some of the versions of the clan origin myth we still find this conception. In the hands of the shamans he became an anthropomorphic deity, characterized by baldness and the wearing of bay wreathes. Something of the older conception still clings to him, however, for he frequently acts as a bird and the flashing of his eyes still causes lightning. His baldness itself is an archaic feature, because the Thunderbird originally was supposed to be a kind of eagle.

Many representations of the Thunderbird can be found on various articles and in the effigy mounds.

He blesses men with practically everything, but particularly with victory on the warpath.

Water-spirit.—The meaning of the Winnebago word for this deity, *wak'tcexi*, is unknown. The translation "Water-spirit" does not claim to have anything to do with the real meaning of the word, but it was preferred by the Winnebago because this deity is always pictured as a water monster.

He is one of the older folkloristic conceptions and has not been very greatly reinterpreted by the shamans. The Thunderbird is supposed to be at eternal enmity with him, and for that reason he is regarded by most of the Winnebago as a sort of a mixed deity, partly evil and partly good, but always to be feared and capable of bestowing great blessings on man. Owing to the fact that he has become identified as the clan ancestor of one of the most important Winnebago clans, he has undergone a partial rehabilitation.

The Water-spirit is an important figure in the older myths, and in them seems to be identified with the bad spirits. The attitude of the Winnebago toward him is full of inconsistencies. He is evil, yet his "bones" are the most prized possessions of man on account of the remarkable power with which they are endowed. He is an evil spirit, yet according to an apparently old myth (the Traveler) one of the Water-spirits is the spirit deity in control of the earth.

In addition to these marked anthropomorphic and theromorphic spirit deities, the Winnebago, as mentioned before, have a large number of vague spirits, like fire, light, etc., and a legion of animal spirits. The latter show some interesting transitions extending all the way from purely nonspirit heroic animals to distinct spirits, conceived of as animal in shape but noncorporeal. In many cases it is, of course, quite impossible to say how marked the "spirit" nature of the animal is, because it often depends on who is looking at it. To the ordinary nonreligious Winnebago the hare is mainly an heroic animal; to the religious Winnebago or a member of the medicine dance he is a spirit-animal or even a spirit-deity. In the same way different conceptions are held about the nature of the animal clan ancestors, some thinking of them as heroic animals and others as generalized noncorporeal spirit-animals and spirit-deities. Wherever guardian spirits are animals they also become noncorporeal spirit-animals. One of the reasons given by the Winnebago for the fact that the different guardian spirit-animals do not object to the killing of animals of their own species is because, in killing a bear a Winnebago is not killing his guardian spirit, the bear, for the latter is a generalized spirit-bear in control of all the bears who appear on earth.

In a number of cases it is not at all difficult to trace the development of a trickster hero, an anthropomorphic hero, or an heroic animal, into a spirit to whom offerings are made. Thus, for instance, kettles and often buckskins are offered to *wak'djvŋk'a'ga*, hare, and the twins, at the war-bundle feasts.

The Power and Localization of the Spirits

According to the Winnebago, spirits possess the power of bestowing upon man all those things that are of socio-economic value to him. These may vary from such very important economic things as rain or success on the warpath to the most insignificant trifles. Practically any spirit, no matter how indefinitely conceived, can bestow generalized blessings. On the whole, however, these powers are conceived of as being in the hands of a comparatively small number, and the same powers are frequently possessed by different spirits. This will become clear after a careful perusal of the fasting experiences.

As to the prevalence of the belief in the localization of spirits, not only among the Winnebago but over all North America, there can no longer be any doubt. Among the Winnebago there are as many spirits as there are lakes, hills, rivers, etc., and all these are looked upon from two points of view, first as the bestowers of certain blessings and, secondly, as the protectors of their own precincts. In the first case they are generally identical with the guardian spirits. In the second case they are simply vague, indistinct spirits to whom offerings are made for temporary protection. So when a Winnebago crossed a river or lake he poured tobacco into the water as a recompense for trespassing, and uttered the prayer that no storms should arise or that he should not come to grief.

As to whether the spirits here are the lakes, rivers, hills, etc., or some being inhabiting them, the answer is, unquestionably the latter.

THE TWOFOLD INTERPRETATION OF THE RELATION OF THE SPIRITS TO MAN

We mentioned before (p. 231) that the interpretation of the relationship between the spirits and man was largely mechanical, blessings being secured apparently independent of any volition on the part of the spirits, for if the Winnebago make the requisite offerings to the Thunderbirds they must accept them and bestow on the suppliant the powers they possess. While this interpretation was undoubtedly the popular one, the shamans tried to develop another explanation—what might be called a "contract" theory. The spirits possessed the various powers without which man could achieve only a modicum of success; and man possessed tobacco, corn, eagle feathers, buckskin, etc. His principal possession, however, was tobacco, and this had been given him directly by Earthmaker. The contract was definite and distinct: man was to give the spirits tobacco, etc.; and the spirits were to give man the powers they controlled. Accompanying this change of interpretation, there was a difference of attitude, the principal characteristic of which was a heightened religious feeling. This change of interpretation is clearly shown in the concept of the guardian spirit.

THE GUARDIAN SPIRITS

In the concept of the guardian spirits we have a mixture of both the "mechanical" and the "contract" theories. The guardian spirits themselves are, to our mind, but the transformed localized spirits; in other words, the *genii loci*. They are supposed to protect the individual to whom they appear in the same way as the *genii loci* protected their precinct. While theoretically every Winnebago could have his own guardian spirit, there seems to have been a marked tendency for certain guardian spirits to be inherited. This was so, not because there was any distinct development of the idea of inheritance, but because certain definite powers were associated with the spirits, like success in hunting, fishing, etc. In terms of everyday life this simply meant that a good hunter would try to make his sons and near relatives good hunters; in religious terminology it meant that a son was blessed by the same guardian spirit as the father. (Cf. the fasting experience on p. 245.)

The following fasting experiences will show clearly what powers are supposed to be possessed by the various guardian spirits. The attitude with which the faster approaches the ordeal clearly varies from that of childish playfulness to one of considerable religious intensity, always remembering that we are dealing with boys and girls before the adolescent stage. Perhaps the best way of putting it would be to say that we are dealing with a stereotyped expression of life, reading as follows: "I am a successful hunter; I am a prominent warrior, etc.; and I am told that I have become such because I have done what my elders told me, have practiced these professions diligently, and made offerings to the spirits." Such a formula might be put in the mouth of the youthful faster, but it meant nothing until it was interpreted much later in terms of each man's experience in life.

The youth's fasting experience is carefully tested by the elders, and if found wanting in any respect the youth has either to try again or give up.

The guardian spirit is not supposed to be in permanent attendance upon man. It is only when he is needed, in the crises of life, that he is brought into relation with man; and it is quite characteristic of the markedly materialistic basis of the belief that the spirit is only called into aid for the particular needs of the case.

Personal Religious Experiences [4]

HOW WEGI'CEKA TRIED TO SEE EARTHMAKER [5]

Once there was a Winnebago whose name was Wegi'ceka. As soon as he was grown up his father begged him to fast. The old man told his son that Earthmaker, when he created this earth, made many good spirits and that he put each one of them in control of powers with which they could bless human beings. Some he placed in control of war powers. If these spirits bless an individual, he will always be victorious on the warpath. Earthmaker told the human beings to fast for these powers and then they would be rich and powerful. Now, my son, if Earthmaker has put all these spirits in charge of something, he himself must be in charge of much more power. Thus the old man reasoned and the son thought the same. So he tried to "dream" of Earthmaker. "I wonder what sort of blessings Earthmaker bestows on people," he thought to himself.

None of the spirits blessed Wegi'ceka during his fastings. He was always thinking of Earthmaker and asking him to bless him. Wegi'ceka made himself extremely "pitiable" and wept. He could not stop. "Perhaps I will be able to see Earthmaker if I weep," he thought to himself. "Indeed, if Earthmaker does not bless me I will die during my fast."

He fasted continuously without stopping. Verily, he fasted for Earthmaker. First he fasted for 4 nights, and then for 6 nights, and then for 8 nights, for 10, and finally for 12 nights. Yet he received no blessing of any kind. After fasting 12 nights he stopped and ate something. He kept fasting on until he had grown to be a fully developed man. Then he stopped and married and, accompanied by his wife, he moved away from his village to some uninhabited place. There he lived alone with his wife. There again he fasted and his wife helped him. As before, he tried to have Earthmaker bestow a blessing upon him. This time he made up

---

[4] Some religious experiences belonging to Winnebagoes well known to the tribe have been cast in a literary form and handed down from one generation to another. The literary mold in which they have been cast does not in the least interfere with their value as excellent examples of personal experiences, and for that reason I will include one of them here.

[5] Earthmaker is supposed never to bless any human being, but there are a number of accounts of individuals who tried without success, nevertheless, to have him bless them. What the people, however, meant by lack of success was not so much a total lack of success as an incomplete blessing. So, for instance, Wegi'ceka does really receive a cane as a blessing from Earthmaker, and he has the right to call upon him afterwards in the same way as he calls upon other "guardian spirits." Earthmaker does not, however, appear to him in the way an ordinary spirit would—that is, he neither appears to him as a man nor in the form of a voice conferring some blessing, but as a flash of light.

his mind once and for all that if Earthmaker did not bless him he would die during his fast. "It is true," he said to himself, "that no one has ever heard of anyone being blessed by Earthmaker, but nevertheless I will either obtain a blessing from him or die in the attempt."

As time passed on his wife gave birth to a male child. Then the man said, "We will offer up our son to Earthmaker," and the woman consented. So they sacrificed their son to Earthmaker. Then they placed the body of the child on a scaffold and wept bitterly. "Surely," he said to himself, "Earthmaker will bless us to-night." And indeed during the night he came to him. Wegi'ceka felt positive that it was he. He wore a soldier's uniform and a cocked hat and he was pleasing to the sight. Wegi'ceka looked and wondered whether it was really Earthmaker. Then this person took a step forward toward Wegi'ceka. "Indeed it must be," he thought. Then he took another step in his direction and uttered something. Wegi'ceka looked and saw that it was not Earthmaker but a pigeon. The spirits had fooled him. His heart ached, but, undaunted, he again fasted, and after a while Earthmaker seemed to come to him and say, "Man, I bless you. For a long time you have wept and made yourself pitiable. I am indeed Earthmaker." When Wegi'-ceka looked again he beheld something pleasing to the sight and he liked it. The clothing the man wore was pleasing and Wegi'ceka now felt certain that this person was Earthmaker. He looked at him again and it seemed to him as if Earthmaker was getting smaller and smaller, and as he looked for the fourth time he saw that he had been looking at a little bird all the time. Then his heart ached all the more, and he cried even more bitterly than before. Then for the third time Earthmaker blessed him and spoke to him. "You have tried to 'dream' of Earthmaker and you have worried yourself to death. Behold, I am Earthmaker and I will bless you and you will never be in want of anything. You will be able to understand the language spoken by strange tribes and you will never be wanting in the goods of life." Then he looked up for the first time, but when he saw the individual who had spoken to him he thought that there was something wrong. Soon he saw that the one who had spoken to him was a bird.

Then for the last time he tried to "dream" of Earthmaker. He did not eat anything and positively resolved to die if Earthmaker did not appear to him. He felt bad, for he thought that all the bad birds (spirits) were laughing at him.

He fasted, and soon Earthmaker, far above, heard his voice and said, "Wegi'ceka, you are weeping bitterly. For your sake, I will come to the earth." Then Earthmaker told Wegi'ceka that when he (Wegi'ceka) looked at him he would see a ray of light extending from above far down to his camp. That far it would reach. "Only thus, Wegi'ceka, can you see me. What you ask of me (to see me face to face) I can not grant you. But, nevertheless, you may tell (your fellowmen) that you saw me." Thus he spoke to him. He did not bless him with war powers. Only with life did he bless him.

Then Wegi'ceka tried to draw a picture of the flash of light extending from the heavens to his camp, just as he had seen it, upon a cane. To that cane he sacrificed. The descendants of Wegi'ceka are using cane even to the present day.

ACCOUNT OF J.'S FASTING

When I reached the age of puberty my father called me aside and told me to fast. He told me that it was his fervent wish that I should begin to fast, so that I might become holy and invincible and invulnerable in war. I would become like one of those Winnebagoes of whom stories are told. In future generations the people would speak of me often. For these reasons he wished me to fast. He assured me that if I fasted I would really be holy and that nothing on this earth would be able to harm me. I would also live a very long life, he told me. I would be able to treat the sick and cure them. That holy I would be, he told me. If I acted in this way, my father told me, no person would dare to make fun of me and they would always be careful of the manner in which they addressed me, both because they respected me and because they were afraid of incurring my enmity. For these reasons my father counseled me to fast and to continue fasting from the late fall until spring. During that time I should fast without stopping. In the spring, however, I was to stop, because many bad spirits are about at that time and they might deceive me. If he thought that I was not doing enough fasting he would urge me on with words, saying, "My son, fast, because if you receive knowledge of anything (i. e., if you have been blessed repeatedly), nothing will be able to harm you. You will live long; and I want you to live long." In this way my father used to speak to me and in this way he used to plead with me in a piteous manner. "Remember," he used to say to me repeatedly, "that if you do not fast none of the spirits will bless you."

There was a hill near our place called the Place-where-they-keep-weapons. This hill was very high and it looked steep and rocky. It must have been a very holy place. There my father had lived (when he was blessed by the spirits). Within this hill lived the spirits that we call Those-who-cry-like-babies.⁶ These spirits were supposed to have arrows and bows. There were supposed to be twenty of them in this hill. My father had control of these spirits.

---

⁶ These spirits are the same as those generally known as the Herok‘a, or Those-without-horns.

If he (my father) blessed a man he would do as follows: He would take his bow and arrows and, holding them in both of his hands, take the man around the hill and then into the lodge (i. e., into the hill). There he and the man he wished to bless let their breath pass into the middle of the lodge (i. e., into the hill). There stood a stone pillar and upon this stone pillar, at about arm's length, he drew the pictures of different animals. My father had only one arrow, but that arrow was a holy one. Then my father danced around the stone pillar and sang some songs, and when he was finished he began to breathe upon the stone pillar; and, walking around it, he shot it. When he looked at it, he saw that the stone had turned into a deer with large horns. This deer fell dead at his feet. He repeated this a number of times and the little spirits who were following him breathed with him and said, "Winnebago, whenever you wish to kill a deer with one horn, do as you have done here. Then offer tobacco to us and you will be able to obtain whatever you wish."

"Now, my son, I want you to be able to do as I do. I want you to be able to kill deer whenever you wish, and at any particular time." My father was a very good hunter and I wanted to be very much like him. I knew that what he was saying was true and that it would be good to follow his advice. I was also told that if I traveled around the hill where these spirits lived, then all earthly things would agree with me and that I would be the gainer thereby. If I did this, they told me, then I would never suffer any pains in my body and I would never be troubled in any way.

And this they told me about the ghost village—that when I go there I will be able to steal a costly shawl from the spirits and be able to escape with it; that then all the inhabitants of the ghost village would chase me, but that they would not be able to overtake me and would be compelled to turn back as soon as I reached the earth. In this ghost village there are no grown-up children.[7]

Now, all that I have spoken of, I dreamed. I really dreamed that I was stealing a costly shawl and that I would have plenty of them all the time. I dreamed that I would obtain ten or even more shawls in one year and that I would not have to pay anything for them. What the spirits meant by shawls was supplies. However, all this took place before I ate the peyote. Since then I know that these things were not true, and that what I must depend upon is not supernatural power, but myself, and my own endeavors. Supernatural powers do not come from anywhere. They do not exist at all. The blessings I had received were not holy and I am not holy.

[7] He is evidently referring to the spirit home of the Herok'a, or Those-who-cry-like-babies.

This I know now. The whole thing is untrue. Therefore I stopped using these supernatural powers some time ago.[8]

The old people made me fast so that I might obtain blessings, and that I might lead a life similar to that led by my ancestors. My father asked me to fast so that I might be of some help to my fellow-men as I grew up. It is through fasting that individuals obtain the power of curing disease and restoring a person to health again.

Spirits from above also came to me. They took me to the spirit-shaman village. As the shamans gathered around me they said that the blessing would be very difficult to give me. Then the shaman sitting far in front made himself holy and breathed upon me (i. e., performed the actions of a shaman when treating a patient). When he was finished, then he began to sing and all those in the lodge began to breathe, helping him. Then the second shaman made himself holy and began to breathe and sing. In this way four of them made themselves holy. They were showing me what to do when I came back to earth. If a person on earth is sick (this is what they meant), and is in an almost hopeless condition where no one else could cure him, then they would call for me and offer me tobacco with which I was to sacrifice to the spirits who had taught me.

Indeed I am holy. If a man is sick I can restore him to health. That is what I used to think. I really (had it been true) should have felt it, for I labored earnestly and honestly to be a holy person. Yet in spite of all my exertions I was very unfortunate. I had married twice and both of my wives and all my children died. Indeed, how could I ever consider myself a holy man (i. e., if I couldn't even cure my own wife and children of what value were my "supernatural powers")? For a long time I knew that, at least I should have known it.[9] (I was not holy.) Then I ate the peyote and now I really see myself as I am. Indeed I am not holy. My body is without a soul. I thought myself holy. So I have stopped the practice of the shaman.

---

[8] The informant had become a convert to the Peyote belief only a short time before he wrote down this account of his fasting, and it is interesting to see that, although he no longer believes in the efficacy of the supernatural powers, he still believes that they exist. Two years after this, however, the same informant explained them, as all the older members of the Peyote cult explain them, namely, as delusions, either caused by the abnormal condition of the youth while fasting or as snares of the devil.

[9] In the words "I should have known it" are summed up the essential change of attitude between the Peyote Winnebago and the older Winnebagoes. The latter, too, had observed the apparent failure of the supernatural powers on many occasions, but instead of attributing them to any diminution of efficacy in the "powers," attributed them, on the contrary, to a lack of something in the individual trying to use the "power," in so far as they thought about it at all. But the essential difference between the two cults, the older one and the Peyote, lies not so much in the logical conclusions their adherents have drawn from the failure of the "supernatural powers" to behave as they were expected to, as in the fact that the Peyote people make the failure of the "power" the subject of discussion and the old Winnebagoes accept the whole concept of "supernatural power" as such, and do not permit it to rise into their consciousness.

R.'S FASTING.

(R. WAS A MEMBER OF THE BEAR CLAN)

There was a village near Big Lake (Lake Winnebago), and at this village the upper people and the earth people played lacrosse.[10] The Bear was the chief clan of the lower people, and those representing that side in the game defeated the representatives of the other side by sheer strength. Then one of the upper people said, "What effeminate fellows those Bear people are. They are very strong, but it would be much better if instead of being so strong in playing lacrosse they were strong when on the warpath." Thus he spoke. Then one of the Bear people (the one whose fasting is about to be described) felt very much grieved and went out into the wilderness to fast. His desire was to be blessed by those spirits who are in control of war, and in his longing to be blessed by them he cried bitterly. Soon he heard some one saying, "Do not cry any more, we have come after you from above. The spirits have blessed you. You are going to be taken to the lodge of your friends." When the young man got there he saw four men. They were called cannibals, and they were brothers. "Our friends have blessed you and we also bless you," said the four spirits. These four spirits were catfish. Then some white crane spirits said, "Our friends have blessed you. With spears they have blessed you. Indeed, for good reason was your heart sad (i. e., did you make yourself suffer while fasting). With victory on the warpath do we bless you. Here is your bundle. Here also are your spears and your bow and arrows. This bundle you must use when you go on the warpath. Here also are some songs to use when you start out and when you return. With these songs I bless you. Here they are:

SONGS

Ho'sto k'ⁿine'djaⁿe'dja rahi'jê?
Where they gathered, there did you go?
K'âro' hitcak'âro' ha'gixewi're.
Well, my friend, shout at it for him.

"When the enemy is close upon you and aim their guns at you, if you sing these songs they will not be able to hit you. If you sing these songs then, those who gave you a name will honor you.[11] Thus we bless you. With life also we bless you."

ARATCGE'KA'S FASTING [12]

Aratcge'ka, Left-handed-one, went out to fast. "A spirit I wish to bless me. I am fasting because I was told to do so. A shaman

---

[10] In playing lacrosse the upper and lower divisions were always pitted against one another.

[11] The sense is not quite clear here, but it is believed that he means that by singing one of these songs he will be victorious and be able to count coup or distinguish himself in some such way, and thus be worthy of being honored by his elders.

[12] This account of a fasting has been cast in a literary mold. It evidently relates to the fasting experience of a well-known man.

I would like to be. I would like to be able to treat people the way
he does, and I have for that reason blackened my face and fasted for
eight days." Then I was blessed and they (the messengers of the
spirits) came after me. Up above, to a shaman spirit-lodge they
took me. There I saw the chief, and he said to me, "What you
desire, what you are thirsting yourself to death for, that you are to
be blessed with. For that reason these people have brought you
here. Here you are to give an exhibition of your powers. I am the
one who has caused you to be brought here (i. e., blessed you), I am
the ruler of this village and I sent for you to give you the following
powers:

"If ever an Indian is sick, even if he is so sick that he is practically
dead, I give you the power of restoring him to life. Now you are to
show your powers. Here is a log so rotten and decayed that it is
practically falling apart.[13] Upon this you are to exert your power
and show that you have been blessed. This is what the spirits
meant when they blessed you." Then he walked around the log,
breathed upon it, and spat water upon it, and it became human.
Then he walked around it again and again spat water upon it,
and it began to move. Then for the third time he spat water
upon it and walked around it and it began to groan. Then he
walked around it for the fourth time, and again spat water upon
the log, and it got up and walked away. He had restored the log to
life. Then the spirit said to him, "Man, with this power you are
blessed. That for which you longed, that for which you fasted, you
are blessed with. Giving-humans-life, thus the people will call you."

Then all the spirits who are above said as follows: "Brother-in-law,[14]
that you may live I am telling you this story."

In the wilderness I went, and there near an oval hill I sat down
and wept. Below the hill lay a round lake and there I saw the rising
dew coming in a fog. This first spread itself out over us, and then,
in turn, shrank and became small. All this time I sat there weeping.
There was something moving in the lake, but although I was looking
in that direction I did not see anything. They (evidently the
spirits) were sneaking up on me. Two (flames of) fire suddenly
burst forth extending from above to the lake. Then a report like

---

[13] This log is supposed to represent a human being in a similar condition—that is, practically on the verge of dissolution.

[14] The account is suddenly interrupted here to tell the listener why Aratcge′ka is telling the story of his fasting. The personal religious experiences were very sacred and rarely told even to near relatives. As far as I know, they were only told before death or when a person was very ill, as in the present case. The purpose seems to have been to transfer the benefits of the blessing to the sick person and cure him in much the same way as is done when an accredited shaman goes through his entire performance. Of course, Aratcge′ka's blessing related directly to the curing of disease. But evidently it was believed that blessings connected with other powers were equally efficacious.

that of a gun sounded. The two (spirits) were causing it. Suddenly a great noise was heard. I kept right on crying, for I was trying to be blessed. I sat there with staring eyes looking at the spirits. "I must be receiving a blessing," I thought. I continued crying and after a short time it began to rain very much. "How is this," I thought to myself, "only a little time before it was so nice and now it is raining." Yet in spite of the rain no water seemed to fall upon me. "How is it," I thought, "here it is raining and yet no rain is falling upon me." Then I looked above and I saw that it was very cloudy, yet straight above me in a direct line the sky was blue. This blue spot was like a round object covering me as though it were an umbrella. The Thunderbirds were blessing me. With the blue sky, they were blessing me. Soon the noise stopped, and when I looked above I saw four (men) standing with packs upon their backs. These (the spirits) killed. Then they blessed me with the power of killing. They spoke to me and said, "Stop your crying. What you have longed for and fasted for, with that we have blessed you. Just as these four men have been killed, so you will be able to kill people. But you will also be able to restore them to life again. Upon your body now we will make a mark and those whom you wish to bless will be given an opportunity of. selecting life for themselves,[15] so that, even when a person be practically dead he will be restored to health. What is above you, the blue sky, that we place on one of your fingers,[16] and with that we bless you. If the patient picks the finger with the mark upon it, he will live."

The Thunderbirds were the spirits speaking to me. They had spears and little war-clubs in their hands and (wreathes) made of flat cedar leaves upon their heads. Thus did four Thunderbirds bless me.

"Well, brother-in-law, I want you to live and I want you to pick life for yourself—i. e., pick the finger with the blue mark upon it. Do it carefully and do not attempt it when you are tired. Here are my four fingers and one of them has the blue sky upon it (i. e., the blue mark that betokens life). If you choose that, you will certainly live. You are the second person (to whom I have offered my fingers). Now do not miss it, for if you miss it you will surely die. Be careful, then, in picking it."

Then the brother-in-law picked the little finger and Aratcge'ka said, "Brother-in-law, it is good. You will live." Then he turned his little finger around and there a circular blue mark was visible.

ACCOUNT OF X.'S FASTING

The spirits can bless you with everything. My father used to tell me how much he loved me and how much he wished me to fast.

---

[15] That is, a sick person will have to guess at the part of the body that has been blessed by the Thunderbirds, and if he guesses correctly he will become well.

[16] That is, we will place a mark made with blue clay upon your finger.

He wanted me to fast all the time. I would therefore, to please him, fast off and on through the winter. The longest I ever fasted at any one time was six days. I was blessed by a yellow snake who lived near Medway, Wis. It was at that place that I fasted one winter. The spirit-snake that lives there blessed me with life and the right to draw bad blood from sick people (i. e., "cup blood"). These blessings are truly efficacious, but after they have been handed down to the next generation they lose their power (unless renewed). That same winter, not long before the beginning of spring, I fasted again for four days and early on the morning of the fourth day as I was walking along a ravine, crying and putting myself in a "pitiable condition," so that the spirits might take pity upon me, some one came to meet me. Up to this time, in spite of all my exertions and fastings, I had not been blessed by any of the spirits. The one who was coming toward me was walking very fast and when I stopped to look at him I saw that he was a man. His entire body was painted red and he wore an eagle feather on his head and garters around his legs. When he came near to me he said: "Human, I bless you. You may now go home and eat (i. e., break your fast). Every day I will bring the blessing of life to you. This also (I wish to tell you), if you think of me when you are in any difficulty, you will pass through it safely. The sick you will be able to heal through the blessing I give you. I am the Sun. Even if a day is cloudy, then know that I am keeping life for you beyond the clouds."

HOW Y. FASTED AND WAS BLESSED WITH A WAR-BUNDLE [17]

Our war-bundle is eight generations old. In the beginning my clansmen had no war-bundles. Whenever they had war, they had nothing from which to receive strength. The only powerful possession they had was fire. That was the only thing they carried when on the warpath. Soon they discovered that other clans had war-bundles and that they received them by fasting for them. So K'erex un'sak'a started to fast for one. He fasted from early autumn until summer and he received a blessing. Then he went to his father and told him, "Father, you told me to fast. Let us now go and see with what I have been blessed." So the old man accompanied his son.[18] When the old man got there he found a snake dried and dressed up and standing in an upright position. The snake had long hairs on its back, scattered here and there. The father on seeing it said, "My son, this is really too great. If you accept this and carry it with you on the warpath, you will not leave any human beings alive (i. e., you will always want to go on the

---

[17] This is the account of the origin of a war-bundle claimed to be eight generations old.

[18] Evidently the spirit had told him to go to a certain place and that there he would find certain objects, namely, the material objects with which he had been blessed.

warpath).'' The son therefore refused it, and went out to fast again. Then the spirits blessed him again and again he went to his father and asked to accompany him to the wilderness and see what blessings he had obtained. When they came to the wilderness [19] they found two wild cats (already stuffed) standing there and facing in opposite directions. Then the old man told his son again not to accept this blessing because it would be too powerful,[20] but the young man said, ''This is the last blessing that I am going to get,'' and accepted it.

(What follows was obtained at a later time from the same informant and relating to the same blessing.)

The first blessing K'erex'un'sak'a received was from the Thunderbirds. They dropped a flute and two feathers from heaven. But these he refused. The second blessing was also from the Thunderbirds. This time they told him to go to a certain place where he could see them himself. He went there and found four men sitting there broiling meat. They gave him a piece of meat. It was only when he fasted for the fourth time that he was blessed with a warbundle.

WHAT G. OBTAINED IN HIS FAST

I never fasted much. I only fasted three times and I don't believe that I ever fasted for more than two days at a time. However, I never was blessed with anything (i. e., any object). I knew, however, that I came from the home of the Thunderbirds (i. e., that I was a reincarnated Thunderbird). My spirit father and mother [21] were Thunderbirds. The Thunderbirds are beings whose glance can penetrate any object. For that reason I also can do it. For instance, I have seen a man through a tree. This I did once during a thunderstorm when a man had sought shelter behind a tree.

---

[19] Whenever the word ''wilderness'' is used all that is meant is an uninhabited place far away from the village.

[20] By ''too powerful'' the old man means that the feasts, offerings, etc., that would be necessary for so great a blessing would be quite beyond the means or the ability of the young man. It is to be remembered that the bestowal of a blessing does not in itself insure its efficacy, but that this can only be assured if the proper offerings and the proper emotional attitude accompany its subsequent use. Evidently the old man did not feel that the young fellow would be equal to the task. I have been told by many of the older Winnebagoes that when the old system was still intact the older people always made it a point to warn impetuous youths against taking upon themselves responsibilities that they might possibly not be able to fulfill, a very excellent device, it seems to me, for not multiplying the chance of failures and consequently the necessity of explaining them. However, one need not believe that this was the reason for their caution.

[21] He says ''spirit father and mother'' because when he lived with the Thunderbirds he was, of course, a spirit. It is quite impossible to determine whether he means that he was a human being who was living among the spirits as a spirit or whether he was a spirit who had desired to become reincarnated as a human being. Originally, of course, there were no human beings, but only spirits, of whom a portion became permanently transformed into human beings. However, even very powerful shamans never claim more than three reincarnations, so that he can obviously not be referring to this primitive condition and is either referring to the fact that he is a Thunderbird residing temporarily on this earth, or—and this would be the more common form—a human being who lived for some time as a Thunderbird and then returned to earth. In the latter case one would expect him to obtain great blessings in his fast, and the fact that he did not and had nevertheless such great powers suggests that he is really a reincarnated Thunderbird.

When I was ready to go down among the human beings (i. e., when I became reincarnated) I was given the power to overcome my enemies in battle. And this I have actually done. All the Thunderbirds have small war-clubs. I also had one when I came. Whenever I went on the warpath I made myself a war-club and used that only in battle. I believe that I was invulnerable. Whenever I got tired of living among human beings I knew I could return to the Thunderbirds. I thought I knew all this and that I had these powers. For that reason when I ate peyote I still held on to these beliefs for a long time, thinking that when I returned to the Thunderbirds inasmuch as they are above it would be the same as going to everlasting life, as the Peyote people said. Finally, one night, at a peyote meeting, in thinking over these things, I resolved to give them up. I could, nevertheless, not bring myself to do it. Then the peyote began to strangle me; [22] at least I thought so.

I also had the power of causing or stopping rain. All that I had to do was to offer tobacco to the Thunderbirds and make my request.

HOW A BEAR BLESSED A MAN [23]

Once a band of Winnebagoes used to give a feast to the bears. A bear had blessed one of their number with life and victory on the warpath.

It was a spirit-bear that had blessed him. The man was fasting and the spirit blessed him and said, "Human, I bless you. In war you will be able to do as you wish (i. e., you will be able to kill an enemy whenever you desire). The first time you go on the warpath you will come back with the fourth war honor; the second time you go on a warpath you will return with the third war honor; the third time you will return with the second war honor; and the fourth time you will return with the first war honor and receive the first prize, which you are to give to your sister." This is what the man "dreamed." He believed it and was happy. Then the spirit-bear said again, "Human, I said that I blessed you and I really mean it. Earthmaker created me and gave me control of many things. Human, I bless you. As many years as Earthmaker bestowed upon you, that number I also bless you with. You will reach the limit of the years that were granted you. With my body I also bless you. Whenever you are hungry and wish to kill a bear, pour a pipeful of tobacco for me. If then you go out hunting, you will be successful. Don't abuse the bears. I am the chief of the bears. I bless you. Never before have I blessed a human being, as long as I have lived here. As long as your descendants live on this earth, so long will this

---

[22] According to the Peyote people, if a member does not wish to do or tell something that he ought to, the peyote begins to strangle him and he finds no relief until he tells what is on his mind.

[23] This is really the "origin myth" of a bear feast.

blessing last. Should your descendants perform the feasts in my honor well, I will bless them with life and victory on the warpath. Whenever you offer me tobacco I will smoke it. If you put on a kettle of food for me I will be thankful to you. When you put this kettle of food on the fire and offer me tobacco see to it that you keep away menstruating women . . . [24]

HOW THE DAUGHTER OF MANK'EREXKA REFUSED A BLESSING FROM DISEASE-GIVER [25]

The daughter of Mank'erexka was fasting. She was his third daughter. She decided to fast during the summer. In her fast she was told that she was blessed and that on the following day a big deer would come across the waters for her to eat. Then she went to her father and said, "Father, I have been told to eat a big deer, and that to-morrow very early in the morning it will come out of the water." "It is good, my daughter. That deer has been given to you by the spirits and you may eat it."

Early the next morning a big deer came across the waters. "Let it be," the people said (to her). "As soon as it comes near we will chase it." So they got into a boat and chased it. Then they killed it and gave it to some other person instead of the young woman. "My daughter, what are you going to do? Are you going to eat the deer?" "No, father, if I were to eat the deer I would have killed it myself. But you people have killed it, so I will not eat any of it."

Then she rubbed some charcoal on her face and went to the place of fasting and said, "What you (the spirits) gave me others have taken away and eaten." Early in the morning she looked around toward the water. She was very weak, for she had not eaten for a long time. Nine days she fasted. She was saying to herself, "As soon as I see a deer I will tell the others and call my father." In the morning she went out in search of the deer. She was so weak that she could hardly crawl along. But she managed to reach the edge of the waters and, as she looked across, she saw a deer coming. So she immediately went to her father and told him. He got up immediately and, taking a spear, jumped into a boat, pursued, and speared it. Then the girl said, "Now I will eat." So they called her uncles, Wolf and Elk.[26] When they came she put tobacco in their hands and said, "My uncles, I have offered tobacco to the different spirits and asked them to bless me. Now I am about to eat and I would

[24] The rest of the story is a description of a bear feast and how, in spite of the warning of the spirit-bear two menstruating women took part in the feast; how, thereupon, two bears suddenly appeared and killed them, and how for that reason the bear feast was given up.
[25] This account has been cast in a literary mold, but there is no doubt that it represents a real fasting experience. It is included here principally because it contains a number of extremely interesting features.
[26] These are the names of individuals.

like to have you put some food in your mouths."[27] "My niece, it is good. You have indeed made yourself 'pitiable.' You have thirsted yourself to death and I, too, pity you. If any spirit has blessed you, he has done so with good reason. I, too, once thirsted myself to death and the spirits blessed me with life. With this life, my niece, I also bless you. I will gladly partake of your feast." Thus spoke Wolf. Then Elk said, "My niece, I, too, was told to fast; and in my fast the spirits blessed me with the power of having complete control over all my actions. This dream (i. e., the blessings I obtained) I now give to you.[28] With these blessings you will be able to live as you desire. I will now gladly partake of your food."

When they were through eating, she also ate, and then they all went home. After a while her father said to her, "My daughter, I am going to ask you a question. It is said that those who have been blessed might tell their dreams if they were asked." "All right," said the daughter, "I will tell you. Eight days I fasted and then the spirits blessed me. They told me that if at the end of four days I should place offerings south of the place known as the Big Eddy and situated down the stream the powers with which I had been blessed would be shown to me. The one who blessed me was the chief of the Wakᶠaiⁿtcûⁿ, the spirits who live in the earth. He said that Earthmaker had created him and given him great power; that he had placed him in charge of 'life.' In four days he told me, 'I will appear to you. The day on which I appear to you will be a perfect day. Whatever you wish to make for yourself, you may do. You will never be in want of anything, for you can make implements for yourself out of my body. With these I bless you, for you

---

[27] The feast referred to here is the feast called Haⁿdaginantc Wadu-itcanenaⁿ or faster's feast. It is given whenever a man or woman who has been blessed is about to break his fast. At this feast it is customary, according to some informants, for the faster to narrate his blessing. However, these feasts have now been discontinued for so long a time that it is extremely difficult to obtain any accurate information.

[28] The transference of certain blessings is very common, but, to my knowledge, it is rarely done in this manner. As a rule if a person was unable to obtain blessings, he sought to offset this handicap in life by purchasing supernatural powers from some of his more successful fellow-men. However, these powers seem to be connected almost exclusively with medicines. That blessings such as those bestowed upon individuals during their fast, such as long life, invincibility, hunting powers, etc., were transferred, does not seem probable, although it is, of course, possible. The writer was told of a number of cases where this seemed to have been the case, but on closer study it was conclusively shown that no real transference had taken place, but that in those instances where a person had said, "I transfer this and that dream to you," the transference had no validity unless the individual to whom the dream had been bequeathed actually fasted and obtained the same dream. An individual would in such a case always be careful to select as his "dream-heir" one who would in all likelihood obtain the same dream. It is only in this sense that one might actually speak of a transference. In those instances where a man is blessed with supernatural powers that are to extend to all his posterity this is what is really meant, namely, an infinite repetition of the same blessing, one that has, however, become so certain within definite families that it might be considered automatic.

have made yourself suffer very much [29] and my heart has been rent with pity for you. I bless you, therefore, with life, and this you may transmit to your descendants.' All this, father, the spirit said to me." "My daughter, it is not good. These spirits are trying to deceive you. Do not accept it. They will never bestow upon you what they have promised." "All right, father, but let me at least give them the offerings of deerskin, red feathers, and tobacco. I will not accept these blessings, for you forbid it."

Then after four days she took her offerings to the place where she was to meet the spirit and told him that her father had forbidden her to accept the blessing. "'You are not a good spirit,' he said." "He is right, for one side of my body is not good but the other is," answered the spirit. "That is the way in which Earthmaker created me." Thus the wak'ai^{n}tcu^n spoke.[30] Then the woman looked toward the lake and she saw a tree standing in the water. The spirit climbed upon this tree and wrapped himself around it. Then he took a tooth and shot the tree and knocked it down.[31] "This is what you would have been able to do," said the spirit. "The people would have respected you very much. You would have been able to cure weak or nervous people. But you did not listen to what I told you. You refused it."

FASTING EXPERIENCE

(INFORMANT, CLAN UNKNOWN)

A man fasted and was finally blessed. When he was to be blessed a spirit came after him. He came from the south. "Human," he said, "I was told to come after you." Then the man looked at him and he saw that it was a man speaking to him. So he went along with him. He did not go far before he came to a village and in the middle of this village he saw a long lodge. There he was taken and there he was blessed. The one that was in charge of the village blessed him first.

"I bless you with victory in wars. Whenever you go on the war-path and when you are about to make the rush, do not forget me. If you pour some tobacco for me and then fight, the enemy will not be able to kill you. I am in charge of wars."

---

[29] When people are blessed by the Water-spirits they make medicines from the bones of the spirits. They are also supposed to make what the Winnebagoes call "implements." What is actually meant by this term it is very difficult to state precisely. But it seems that they meant sharpened bones, etc., used in connection with the administration of magical medicines in painting the body, and in connection with shamanistic practices of all sorts. It is not common for other spirits beside the Water-spirits to bless an individual with the use of "his bones," but this is occasionally met with. In the trickster cycle the trickster, in one of his escapades. is squeezed into the skull of an elk, and he persuades the people that he is an elk-spirit and blesses them and permit them to use his bones.

[30] This characteristic would seem to identify the wak'ai^{n}tcu^n with the disease-giver, although it is possible that a number of Winnebago deities had such characteristics.

[31] This is a symbolistic representation of the powers she was given.

So he spoke to him. "Thus will your life be. Look at yourself."
So he looked at himself and his hair was very white. As one who
had attained a full life he saw himself. "All that are within this
lodge bless you," the spirit continued. "You have come to the
Buffalo village." This he was told, so he looked at the lodge full
of people. And those whom he had seen up to that time as human
beings now were buffaloes.

"Human, they bless you is why they went after you. Human,
if anyone is weighted with life and a reasonable amount of tobacco
is given, such a one would be able to do the following":

A dead man was placed in the middle of the lodge, and all of
those in the lodge tried their power, but none succeeded in restoring
him to life. At last the spirits let the man try it. So he tried.
When he arose, all those in the lodge began to make sounds and
when he began to exert his powers he sang buffalo songs. When
he was through with these songs, he walked toward the dead man,
in the middle of the lodge. He blew on him once, then again and
again. Now the man began to open his eyes. Then he blew on
him for the fourth time and he caused him to rise.

"Human, you have overcome all of us," said the buffalo chief.
"Human, thus shall you ever do to people. If anyone is sick and
the proper offerings are made to you, send some tobacco to our
council lodge and I will remember you. You must send all the
tobacco that is offered to you. I will remember it. This council
lodge is given to you and to your posterity as long as it lasts. As
long as the earth lasts that long your posterity will have occasions
on which to pour tobacco. Whatever blessing they ask, we will
bestow upon them while we smoke their tobacco. As many as are
the kettles that they offer to us, we will never accept one without
giving them a blessing. We are in control of wars; the Earthmaker
has given us control of them, and if you ask for it we will give it to
you. And if you ask for life we will bestow that blessing upon you
and accept your offerings."

They also blessed him with plants for medicine. This is the way
they did it. Each of the spirits caused him to see a plant and to
know the purposes to which it could be put. They told him to make
offerings to the plants whenever he gave a feast, so that the plants
would become more powerful. They also blessed him with a drum.
"This you must beat when you give a feast and it will tell us your
wants. We will understand the drum. We will make your drum
holy for you, and you must treat it as such," they told him. "You
must keep it holy. Whenever you are on the warpath you must
take it with you and it will help you. Human, your enemies you will
overcome; your weapons only will be sharp if your posterity will
never give up this ceremony." So they spoke to him. "Whenever

you give this ceremony, no matter what blessing you ask, we will bestow it upon you, when you offer tobacco. A flute you must also keep holy. You must make it yourself, so that it remains sacred." They also told him to make a war bundle. The Buffalo chief told him this. So he made one out of a buffalo head and a buffalo tail. These he made sacred so that people might offer tobacco to them. This was done long ago and yet they still do it.

Then they told him that four differently colored buffaloes would bless him—a white one, a black one, a red one, and a yellow one.

After a while he was blessed the second time. This time the spirits came after him from above and took him to the home of a spirit buffalo. This is the one that blessed him.

"Earthmaker has placed me here," said the spirit, "and he has given me control of many things. Grandson, I bless you. I am in control of war power, and if you ever go on the warpath don't forget me. If you pour a pipeful of tobacco for me before you go into battle, the enemy will only be able to shoot your shadow." Thus he spoke to him. "I will take your body, and in that way it will only be your shadow that the enemy will try to shoot with all their strength. You will be without a body, and how then can they hit you, being without a body?" This is what the spirit told him. So, therefore, whenever he went on the warpath it was impossible to kill him. For the spirit had said, "I am also in control of life and I will give you your life back, that you may control it. The spirits have given you a tobacco-pouring feast and whenever you give it, remember that I wish to smoke also. When you pour tobacco for me I will grant you whatever you ask. If you ask for war, or if you ask for life, I will accept your tobacco. As long as this earth lasts I will smoke your tobacco and accept the kettle of food that you place on the fire for me."

Thus he spoke to him. The man, however, still kept on fasting, and finally the spirits came for him again. There in the middle of the earth lived a buffalo-ghost. There he went and the buffalo-ghost said to him: "I also bless you. You were given counsel and I who am a buffalo also counsel you. I am in control of many things. Earthmaker placed me here to live and he put me in control of many things. Human, look at me," he said. The man looked at him. Then he saw that his body was covered with flattened bullets. "Thus you will be," said the ghost to him. "It will be impossible to kill you, and you will attain to old age, and when you get tired of living you may do as you please. I give you the privilege of controlling yourself." Then he gave him a song and he caused him to see a war prize, a wampum. After a while he spoke to him as follows:

"I also will always smoke at your feast, and if a kettle is ever put on the fire for me, I will be thankful to you. Whatever the people ask of me I will always take it into consideration. If they ask for war or if they ask for life, remember that I have been given control of these things." Thus spoke the buffalo-ghost. There he received all the things with which he was blessed.

In the course of his life he made use of all his blessings. His first victory occurred when he went on the warpath for the first time. He had joined a war party and a fight occurred toward the evening of the same day. As he was walking along he suddenly saw a gun directed against him at close range. He jumped right and left and in that way escaped being shot. Then the enemy tried to capture the one who had been blessed by the buffalo, holding him tightly by the arm. But he struck the enemy twice against an object and tore his stomach open. Then he walked away. As he was going he thought to himself, "Why did I not kill him outright?" So he went back with the intention of doing this, but as he approached the man the latter directed a gun against him. Thinking, however, that it was not loaded, he did not dodge, and he was shot. His breast was filled with shot and he was killed. But he did not remain dead long. He soon came to consciousness and sat up, uttering sounds like a buffalo.

Then he remembered that a buffalo ghost had blessed him. He had indeed said to him, "When you are about to fight do not forget me." He remembered this, so he exerted his power. All the blood that was in his stomach he vomited forth and felt better. Just then one of his relatives came along and asked him, "How have you been getting along?" and he answered, "I have killed one. There lies his body. Take his scalp for me." "All right," said his relative, and did what he had been told, and brought it to him, saying, "Here it is." A horse was there also, and this the relative likewise led away and started back to (the camp). When he met the war leader, the latter asked him, "How have you been making out?" He answered, "I give you these trophies," and handed the leader the scalp and the horse. "Ah, it is good," he said, and put a wampum belt on him. Then the war leader sang a song and started to run, and the buffalo-blessed one reminded himself of his blessing and went back also. He was all shot to pieces. But he did not die, for he had been blessed with power, so how could he die? The buffalo ghost he had seen with flattened bullets in his belt had fulfilled his promise, and the wampum belt that he had seen in his fasting had now become true.

He went to many wars after this, but he was never harmed. He doctored many people and caused them to have more life. After a while he made a war bundle consisting of a flute that he had constructed himself, a buffalo tail, and a buffalo head. Then he made offerings to them. These many things he made sacred. Since then buffalo feasts have been given.

J. B.'S FASTING EXPERIENCE

I fasted all the time. We moved back to a place where all the leaders used to give their feasts. Near the place where we lived there were three lakes and a black hawk's nest. Right near the tree where the nest was located they built a lodge and the war-bundle that we possessed was placed in the lodge. We were to pass the night there, my older brother and myself. It was said that if anyone fasted at such a place for four nights he would always be blessed with victory and the power to cure the sick. All the spirits would bless him.

"The first night spent there one imagined himself surrounded by spirits whose whisperings were heard outside of the lodge," they said. The spirits would even whistle. I would be frightened and nervous, and if I remained there I would be molested by large monsters, fearful to look upon. Even (the bravest) might be frightened, I was told. Should I, however, get through that night, I would on the following night be molested by ghosts whom I would hear speaking outside. They would saȳ things that might cause me to run away. Toward morning they would even take my blanket away from me. They would grab hold of me and drive me out of the lodge, and they would not stop until the sun rose. If I was able to endure the third night, on the fourth night I would really be addressed by spirits, it was said, who would bless me, saying, "I bless you. We had turned you over to the (monsters, etc.) and that is why they approached you, but you overcame them and now they will not be able to take you away. Now you may go home, for with victory and long life we bless you and also with the power of healing the sick. Nor shall you lack wealth (literally, 'people's possessions'). So go home and eat, for a large war-party is soon to fall upon you and as soon as the sun rises in the morning they will give the war whoop, and if you do not go home now they will kill you."

Thus the spirits would speak to me. However, if I did not do the bidding of this particular spirit, then another one would address me and say very much the same thing. So the spirits would speak until the break of day, and just before sunrise a man in warrior's regalia would come and peep in. He would be a scout. Then I would surely think a war party had come upon me, I was told.

Then another spirit would come and say, "Well, grandson, I have taken pity upon you and I bless you with all the good things that the earth holds. Go home now, for the war-party is about to rush upon you." And if I then went home, as soon as the sun rose the war-whoop would be given. The members of the war-party would give the war-whoop all at the same time. They would rush upon me and capture me and after the fourth one had counted coup, then they would say, "Now then, grandson, this we did to teach you. Thus you shall act. You have completed your fasting." Thus they would talk to me, I was told. This war-party was composed entirely of spirits, I was told, spirits from the heavens and from the earth; indeed, all the spirits that exist would be there. These would all bless me. They also told me that it would be a very difficult thing to accomplish this particular fasting.

So there I fasted, at the black hawk's nest where a lodge had been built for me. The first night I stayed there I wondered when things would happen; but nothing took place. The second night, rather late in the night, my father came and opened the war-bundle and taking a gourd out, began to sing. I stood beside him without any clothing on me except the breech-clout, and holding tobacco in each hand I uttered my cry to the spirits as my father sang. He sang war-bundle songs and he wept as he sang. I also wept as I uttered my cry to the spirits. When he was finished he told me some sacred stories, and then went home.

When I found myself alone I began to think that something ought to happen to me soon, yet nothing occurred, so I had to pass another day there. On the third night I was still there. My father visited me again and we repeated what we had done the night before. In the morning, just before sunrise, I uttered my cry to the spirits. The fourth night found me still there. Again my father came and we did the same things, but in spite of it all, I experienced nothing unusual. Soon another day dawned upon us. That morning I told my elder brother that I had been blessed by spirits and that I was going home to eat. However, I was not telling the truth. I was hungry and I also knew that on the following night we were going to have a feast and that I would have to utter my cry to the spirits again. I dreaded that. So I went home. When I got there I told my people the story I had told my brother; that I had been blessed and that the spirits had told me to eat. I was not speaking the truth, yet they gave me the food that is carefully prepared for those who have been blessed. Just then my older brother came home and they objected to his return, for he had not been blessed. However, he took some food and ate it.

That night we gave our feast. There, however, our pride received a fall, for although it was supposedly given in our honor, we were placed on one side (of the main participants). After the kettles of food had been put on twice, it became daylight.

HOW A MAN DEFIED DISEASE-GIVER

Once a man said, "Why do you always make offerings and feasts to the Disease-giver? What benefit has he ever been to you that you do it? If I were ever to see him, I would kick him off the earth. The only thing he can give you is disease."

In the fall of the year in which the man said this the people, as usual, went out hunting and the man got lost and was forced to camp out in the wilderness overnight. So he built a fire and sat alongside of it. Suddenly he saw a man coming toward him. As soon as the stranger came up to him he took a seat on the opposite side of the fireplace. Then the stranger said, "I am the one whom you threatened to kick off this earth whenever you met him. You, furthermore, boasted that I could not kill you." Then he pointed his finger in a line with the man's heart. But the man remained seated near the fireplace without moving. Then he did this again, yet the man still remained in his former position. Then the third time he did it and said, "In the center of the heart." The man, however, remained seated just as before. Then the stranger exclaimed, "Who are you anyhow?" and pointed his finger at him. But the man did not move. Then the stranger (Disease-giver) pleaded with the man to die so that it might not be said that he had failed in the "mission" for which he had been created. He promised the man that if he would oblige him and die he could come back to earth again within four days. Finally the man consented. He went home and told his folks that he was going to a certain place to die for the space of four days and that they should, under no conditions, go to see him there, for in that case he would surely die. Then he dressed himself in his best clothes and went to the place where he was to meet Disease-giver. (He rested his head against a tree and died.) However, on the third day his wife could not resist the desire to see him, so she went to the place where her husband was leaning against the tree. Then he really died. After his death a red spot was visible upon his forehead.[32]

METHODS OF BRINGING THE SPIRITS INTO RELATION WITH MAN

Fasting.—Fasting has been discussed before. There are two things to be remembered in connection with it—first, that it is a method of superinducing a religious feeling; and, secondly, that this religious feeling in turn is bound up with the desire for preserving and perpetuating socio-economic life values. Among the Winnebago the desirability of the conditions superinduced by fasting lay not so much in the emotional pleasure it gave, although this is not to be underestimated, as in the belief which the shamans had developed, that such a state was essential for placing people in a position enabling them to overcome certain crises in life, which it was reasonable to believe might take place.

Mental concentration.—To the religiously inclined Winnebago the efficacy of a blessing, of a ceremony, etc., depended upon what they

---

[32] This is not supposed to be a myth but the real experience of a man named James Smith.

called "concentrating one's mind" upon the spirits, upon the details of the ritual, or upon the precise purpose to be accomplished. All other thoughts were to be rigidly excluded, they believed. This was the insistent admonition of the Winnebago elders to the youth who was fasting. He was to center his mind completely on the spirits, for his blessing would be in direct proportion to the power of concentration he was capable of. The Winnebago believed that the relation between man and the spirits was established by this concentration and that no manner of care in ritualistic detail could take its place. Very frequently failure on a warpath or lack of efficacy of a ritual was attributed to the fact that the Indian or Indians had been lacking in the intensity of their "concentration."

Offerings and sacrifices.—The theory of offering and sacrifice held by the Winnebago has been discussed before. To the important deities offerings were made at the great ceremonies. These offerings consisted of tobacco preeminently, buckskins, and whatever the particular spirit was supposed to like. The animal spirits were given their favorite foods—honey to the bear, for instance. Dogs were offered to Disease-giver at the war-bundle feasts. Whether human sacrifices ever existed it is difficult to say. In the tale of *Wegi'ceka* a child is offered to Earthmaker, and there is reason to believe that this may represent a survival of human sacrifice.

Tobacco could be offered at any time and was so offered to the various *genii loci* whenever an individual passed their precincts.

Prayers.—For examples of prayers reference must be made to the descriptions of the ceremonies. Among the Winnebago, and doubtless everywhere else, the objects of the prayer are always the socioeconomic life values. What in these values is stressed depends upon the ambitions of the individual, and consequently it happens that individuals may pray for abstract blessings or ideal objects, although this is rare. Prayers are undoubtedly always accompanied by a religious feeling when made by the religious man, but frequently become mere formulas in the hands of the lay Indian.

THE FOLKLORISTIC CONCEPTS

The concept of evil.—It is extremely difficult to understand exactly what the Winnebago concept of evil is. They undoubtedly postulate the existence of evil and they have theoretically a host of evil spirits, the *waxop'i'ni cicik*. Youths will be warned not to fast at certain times and children will carefully be kept at home after dark for fear of the evil spirits. Yet in spite of all this, no even fairly definite idea of what these evil spirits are and what they look like can be obtained. One almost gets the impression that the notion of evil spirits belongs to an older strata of Winnebago beliefs and that what we find to-day

is but a faint survival of former times.   The older myths are full of
references to the evil spirits, and the cosmological myths represent
the world as infested with evil spirits who are on the point of exter-
minating the human race until the culture heroes come to the rescue.
It would almost seem as if, from a purely matter-of-fact point of
view, these early culture heroes had destroyed all the evil spirits.
Certainly they are not regarded as of great consequence, for if they
were we ought to find a certain number of prayers addressed to them
asking them not to harm anyone.   They seem to be mere bogies,
personifications of fear, and that is perhaps why they are so intimately
connected with darkness.

At the present time the vast majority of Winnebago ascribe evil,
in so far as they explain it at all, to three causes—either to some
failure on their part to perform a rite in the prescribed way, to
the fact that they have not invoked the spirits for protection (i. e.,
attempted to pass through life without the aid of the spirits), or to the
evil machinations of other men.   Often one derives the impression
that they accept evil and do not try to explain it.   It seems to be a
trait characteristic of the Winnebago, and perhaps characteristic of
other North American tribes, that explanations are developed for
the positive aspects of things.   Certainly it would require some
thought on the part of a Winnebago to explain why a war party
that had, in the opinion of the chief, all the necessary requirements
for victory, should nevertheless be defeated.   He would doubtless
find some reason, after a while, but it would be an afterthought and
would probably vary from individual to individual.   In some cases
lack of success would be ascribed to the fact that an individual had
been misled by an evil spirit, but this is clearly a secondary explanation because the individual, when questioned, would admit that he had
no way of telling whether this was so until he had failed in something.   We base this statement on an actual instance.

There is some evidence to show that there may have originally
existed among the Winnebago a belief that the spirits were neither
good nor bad; that they could be either at different times.   In two
notable instances, that of Disease-giver and Water-spirit, this is true
at the present time.   The former deity is the only one to whom
prayers are addressed beseeching him not to present to man his
death-dealing side.

In the myths we find a definite incarnation of evil in the case of
a spirit called *Herecgu'nina*.   The meaning of this word as given by
a Winnebago, and which seems to be justified, is "he whose existence
is doubtful."   If this is an old Winnebago word it would confirm
the view advanced above, that the Winnebago were not very much
concerned about the evil spirits.   There is, however, a possibility
that *Herecgu'nina* is, in part, a post-Columbian development due

to Christian influence. The one place where he plays an important rôle, the myth of the twins, shows definite indications of European influence. The only thing that militates against such an assumption is the fact that there does not seem to be any particular reason why the existence of a chief evil spirit should have been doubted, even if we were to grant that Christian influence extended the belief. The French of the seventeenth and eighteenth centuries had a very definite idea of the devil and made it a point to tell the Indians that all their former habits were due to deceptions the devil had practiced upon them. To-day such an answer is the first that a Christianized Winnebago or a member of the new Peyote cult will give an ethnologist. Perhaps, after all, it is a very old Winnebago conception, a confirmation of the view promulgated before, that in former times the Winnebago had a very definite conception of evil spirits taking an active part in the affairs of man to his detriment. The figure of *Herecgu'nina* is well defined and it would be ridiculous, in our opinion, to believe that the shamans would have done anything to develop it. We have clear indications of what the shamans were trying to do with this conception. They were attempting to bring it into some relation with the concept of Earthmaker, a beneficent All-Father, and to do so they were even willing to claim that *Herecgu'nina* was the first attempt of Earthmaker to create a spirit; that Earthmaker was dissatisfied with his work and threw it away; that then *Herecgu'nina* watched Earthmaker create spirits and imitated him, the evil spirits representing these imitations. The shamans, we should expect, would have done all in their power to lessen the importance of *Herecgu'nina*, even to deny his existence, and, in this connection, it may be of significance that one Winnebago interpreted his name to mean, "He-who-seems-to-exist-but-who-does-not."

Whatever the case may be, this much is clear, that in the twin myth he is represented as a deity as powerful as Earthmaker, whom Earthmaker can not destroy; upon whom the twins play jokes but whom they cannot really harm.

The concept of disease.—Disease is rarely ascribed to the spirits. Like lack of success, it is regarded as a fact of existence, and when it is explained it is believed to be due either to the carelessness of man in trying to pass through life without the aid of the spirits or to the evil machinations of other men.

The deity known as Disease-giver is the one exception to the rule that the Winnebago spirits do not directly cause disease, for he is sometimes described as scattering death broadcast over the earth.

The concepts of death, after-life, and reincarnation.—Death is rarely, if ever, ascribed to the spirits. It likewise is a fact of existence and,

when explained, is laid at the door of some evil man.   Death at old
age is clearly taken for granted.   Where explanations are advanced,
they are always for the deaths of individuals before their time, or
at least before what the Winnebago consider their time.

The Winnebago look at death in two ways—as being, first, a different kind of consciousness from that possessed in life, and, secondly,
as being a cessation of certain kinds of intercourse between individuals.
Death is regarded as a "stumbling," after which the individual goes
right on as if nothing had happened.   He does not know he is dead
until he sees his body.   The individual is divested of all his corporeal
investment and desires.   In the myth of the journey of the soul to
spirit land the ghost is not entirely a spirit until the old woman
whom he meets brains him, thus, by destroying the seat of consciousness, depriving him of all corporeality and carnal desires.
The ghost then becomes a spirit, in some cases of the same type as
the true spirits.

Although the Winnebago know that after death they will never see
people again, they do not feel that all kinds of intercou se have
ceased.   The deceased may appear to a living individual in dreams
or visions; he may talk to him or make his presence felt in a multitude of ways; and since, as we pointed out before, the test of existence is the consciousness of some kind of contact, such intercourse
may be of a very intense type.

This lack of a feeling of discontinuity between the living and the
dead is emphasized by the Winnebago concept of after-life and
reincarnation.

After-life is but life on earth, only idealized.   Everything is provided.   All carnal desires have been done away with and men and
women spend their time in one long round of enjoyment and bliss.
Something of the fear of ghosts lingers here, however, for when living
individuals try to reach spirit land—and a number of such instances
are mentioned in the myths, particularly in the origin myth of the
Ghost dance—these spirits are likely to be harmful.

By the belief in reincarnation the Winnebago entirely bridge the
gulf between life and death.   In other words, we seem to have a
cycle consisting of life (consciousness), after-life (unconsciousness
from a corporeal viewpoint), and life (reincarnation).   To live again
is the greatest desire of the Winnebago, and practically every secret
society holds this out as the lure to the outsider.   If you join the
Medicine Lodge you will become reincarnated, they say, and the other
ritualistic organizations make the same claim.   But not only by
joining an organization is it possible to be reincarnated; if you live
an upright life, if you die on the battlefield, reincarnation also awaits
you.

The author was fortunate enough to obtain an account by a well-known Winnebago shaman of his various reincarnations.

T. C.'s account of his two reincarnations.—I once lived in a party that numbered about 20 camps. When I had grown up to be a lad, although one not large enough to handle a gun, a war party attacked us and killed us all. I did not know, however, that I had been killed. I thought that I was running about as usual until I saw a heap of bodies on the ground and mine among them. No one was there to bury us, so there we lay and rotted.

I (i. e., my ghost) was taken to the place where the sun sets (the west). There I lived with an old couple. This place (spirit land) is an excellent place and the people have the best of times. If you desire to go anywhere, all that you have to do is to wish yourself there and you reach it. While at that place I thought I would come back to earth again, and the old man with whom I was staying said to me, "My son, did you not speak about wanting to go to the earth again?" I had, as a matter of fact, only thought of it, yet he knew what I wanted. Then he said to me, "You can go, but you must ask the chief first."

Then I went and told the chief of the village of my desire, and he said to me, "You may go and obtain your revenge (upon the people who killed your relatives and you)."

Then I was brought down to earth. I did not enter a woman's womb, but I was taken into a room. There I remained, conscious at all times. One day I heard the noise of little children outside and some other sounds, so I thought I would go outside. Then it seemed to me that I went through a door, but I was really being born again from a woman's womb. As I walked out I was struck with the sudden rush of cold air and I began to cry.

At that place I was brought up and I was taught to fast a great deal. Afterwards I did nothing but go to war, and I certainly took revenge for the death of myself and my relatives, that being the purpose for which I had come to earth.

There I lived until I died of old age. All at once my bones became unjointed, my ribs fell in, and I died the second time. I felt no more pain at death, then, than I had felt the first time.

This time I was buried in the manner used at that time. I was wrapped in a blanket and then laid in the grave. Sticks were placed in the grave first. There in the grave I rotted. I watched the people as they buried me.

As I was lying there, some one said to me, "Come, let us go away." So then we went toward the setting of the sun. There we came to a village where we met all the dead. I was told that I would have to stop there for four nights, but in reality I stayed there four years. The people enjoy themselves there. They have all sorts of dances of a lively kind all the time. From that place we went up to the place where Earthmaker lived and there I saw him and talked to him, face to face, even as I am talking to you now. I saw the spirits too, and, indeed, I was like one of them.

From that place I came to this earth again for the third time, and here I am. I am going through the same that I knew before.

The concept of the soul.—This concept is not clearly developed as a separate entity among the Winnebago on account of their strong belief in reincarnation. Their notion of the soul is merged in that of the noncorporeal ghost who eventully comes to earth again.

THE COSMOLOGICAL IDEAS

The cosmological ideas are of two types—those that are clearly of a folkloristic origin and those that have been developed by shamanistic reinterpretations. To the former class belong all the creative acts of the tricksters and culture heroes, like *Wak'djuŋk'aga* and Hare, and to the latter the systematic creation of the world by Earthmaker.

What is probably the oldest form of the Winnebago cosmological notions is that concerned with the general destruction of the bad spirits by Hare and by such spirits as the Thunderbirds, Morning Star, etc., and the removal of obstacles. Often the present characteristics of the earth are formed accidentally, as, for instance, the origin of the valleys, mountains, and lakes, as given in the myth of "Holy One." Even in the thoroughly remodeled general origin myth, Earthmaker is not conceived of as having purposely created the world.

The Winnebago believed that there were four worlds, one beneath the other, presided over, respectively, by Earthmaker, Trickster (*Wak'djuŋk'aga*), Turtle, and Hare. Hare rules over the world on which man lives. There seems to be some confusion as to who rules over the last earth, because it is also definitely stated that Traveler (a Water-spirit) is in control of it.

PART III

CHAPTER XII

CEREMONIAL ORGANIZATION

INTRODUCTION

The Winnebago had four types of ceremonies: clan ceremonies, in which only members of the clan could participate; religious societies, for which only people who had obtained blessings from the same spirits were eligible; the Medicine Dance, in which only initiated individuals could take part; and a semipermanent organization like the *hok'ixe're* dance, in which only individuals who were returning from a war party and had counted coup could participate. In this grouping we do not include ordinary feasts, such as the feasts connected with different medicines and the pleasure dances.

Every clan seems to have had a clan war-bundle feast (often called winter feast) and also a specific clan feast. We have reason to suspect that the war-bundle feasts were originally private feasts given by the owner of a war bundle. Then as the war bundles became of great importance to the clan to which the owners belonged, they were after a while regarded as clan possessions. But even at the present time, while many would contend that the war bundle belonged to the clan as such and could not be alienated, everyone realizes that it is the property, whether held in trust or not, of a certain individual, and that he can, up to a certain point, do what he wishes with it. For a detailed analysis of a winter or war-bundle feast see page 379.

The clan feasts were specific feasts at which offerings were made to the clan animal. A good description of one is that of the Snake clan on page 377.

Perhaps the most characteristic ceremonies of the Winnebago were those of secret societies in which membership was dependent upon blessings from one and the same spirit. There were at least four of these—the society of those who have been blessed by the night spirits, the society of those who have been blessed by the buffaloes, the society of those who have been blessed by ghosts, and the society of those who have been blessed by grizzly bears.

In order to prevent any misunderstanding with regard to the buffalo societies, it might be well to point out that there were three of them—

269

the Buffalo clan feast, the society of those who have been blessed by the buffaloes, and the society of those who wear buffalo headdresses; the last apparently of Sioux origin.

The medicine dance has been described by the author in some detail,[1] and a general description will be found on page 302.

Of the semipermanent societies, the *hok'ixe're* dance is given after every successful war party by those four individuals who have counted coup. It has only a temporary existence, for it ceases to be an organization as soon as each individual performance is over. Its main purpose seems to be the desire to transfer to the victor, from the skulls or the scalps of the slain enemies obtained on that particular warpath, the valor and prowess for which the slain person was noted.

In addition to the above ceremonies there were a number of pleasure and miscellaneous dances that are described on page 331.

There were apparently a number of very important feasts connected with certain medicines, the principal one of which was the Black Earth Medicine feast; but unfortunately no account of this was obtained, owing to lack of time.

CEREMONIES ASSOCIATED WITH THE CLANS

THE CLAN FEASTS

THE THUNDERBIRD CLAN OR CHIEF FEAST

Introduction.—The chief feast, or, as it may more properly be called, the feast of the bird clans, is generally given once a year, sometimes in late spring. It was also given on certain other occasions for specific purposes. At the present time it is given by the members of the Thunderbird clan and the prevalence of the appellation "chief feast" would seem to indicate that it was at all times the feast of the Thunderbird clan. We ought then to expect to find clan feasts of the other members of the *waŋgeregi* division, namely, of the Warrior, Eagle, and Pigeon clans. No such feasts are given to-day, however, and the members of these latter three clans always speak of the chief or bird feast as their specific clan feast. As such it is also regarded by the members of the *maⁿnegi* division.

In the total absence of historical data it is quite useless to speculate about the significance of one feast sufficing for four clans, where in strict analogy to the feasts of the other clans we would expect to find one for each clan; yet the idea that naturally presents itself is that we are in reality dealing with one clan that has become split up into four subclans. Such a view has been expressed by J. O. Dorsey,[2] but the data upon which he based his opinion seem to us highly

[1] The Ritual and Significance of the Winnebago Medicine Dance, Journal of American Folklore, vol. XXIV, No. XCII, 1911.

[2] Siouan Sociology, 15th Ann. Rept. Bur. Amer. Ethn., p. 241.

unsatisfactory. Apparently his statement is based upon the occurrence of four mythical ancestors. The similarity of the Winnebago social organization with that of the Dhegiha and Tciwere branches of the Siouan family, in which subclans seem to be found, appears to have influenced Dorsey considerably in making this assumption.

It is true that in their account of origins the Warrior clan speak of themselves as having sprung from the second of the birds mentioned in the origin myth of the Thunderbird clan and this statement permits us to infer that the other two clans bear a similar relationship to those four ancestral birds who, according to legend, alit on a tree near Red Banks. But this is, of course, merely a mythical account, and the data imbedded in the clan myths must be used with the greatest caution in so far as they can be expected to throw any light on early conditions of social organization.

All that we can say now is that the chief feast will have to be considered as belonging to all the four bird clans. But this is not to be interpreted to mean that an amalgamation of four historically distinct feasts has taken place, nor that, on the other hand, the four clans were originally subdivisions of one unit.

The Chief feast.—Informant, member of the Thunderbird clan:[4] The chief of the tribe is at the head of all the different bands and groups of people that exist among the Winnebago. As chief he has full charge of them. All the others are, so to say, his attendants and servants. When his people wish anything they go to him and ask him to obtain a blessing for them. Thus all the members of the tribe, the children as well as the mature men, go to him, and to help them the chief gives the feast known as the chief feast. He sacrifices to Earthmaker, and all who are present offer up some little gift in thankfulness, as this is a thing of supreme sacredness. All those who are present—the children, the women, the middle-aged, and the old men—in fact, whosoever attends the feast, see to it that they eat some of the food distributed.

As this feast is given in honor of their chief, all the members of the tribe, but most particularly the members of the Bird clan, prepare large offerings, so that there should be abundant food to eat. They bring all kinds of food—different kinds of meat, different kinds of vegetables, all manner of berries—in short, all sorts of edibles. These are to be offered to the spirits, and by means of these offerings they expect that their life will be filled with all that is good. It is to obtain these blessings that the feast is given.

When his people get sick, when it appears that an epidemic is likely, then the chief also gives the chief feast. It is for the purpose

---

[4] Unfortunately, it was not possible to obtain a full and detailed account of this feast. As in type, however, all the clan feasts are identical, this deficiency can be made up in part by comparing it with those feasts like the snake, bear, and buffalo that have been obtained in considerable detail.

of stopping the spread of the sickness, whatever it may be, and for repairing the ravages caused thereby. For this the feasters pray "May our people recover and thrive," they say. "May they never. get sick." Then they make all those present offer up tobacco. As each one offers tobacco Earthmaker is aware of it and accepts. Thereby do we live and become strengthened. If Earthmaker smokes the tobacco offered him he will give life in return. The people offer tobacco that they may obtain life.

They call the Thunderbird people chiefs, and it is from among their ranks that they select the chief of the tribe.[5]

It is the duty of the chief to ward off all evils. This is one of their missions in life. They preach only what is good.

"Chief," they used to say to him, "try to do something for your people. Try to accomplish something difficult for them. Try to accomplish something difficult for your village. If you accomplish such a thing for the benefit of your people they will look up to you and respect you. Have pity on your people and love them. If a man is very poor, help him. Give him and his family food. Whatever they ask, give it to them. If your people get into trouble with one another, take your pipe and, walking in front, die for them, if necessary. From actions like these they will know that you are really their chief. There, in front of them, with your pipe in your hands, you will be lying on the ground, dead.

"If your people are about to sacrifice a dog and he gets loose and runs into your tent, you must let them have something in place of this dog for their feast. Do not let them kill the dog in your lodge. This would be sacrilegious. Grant the dog his life. Similarly, if an individual who has murdered a person escapes and takes refuge in your lodge, give him his life. Use all the wealth you have and give it to him, that he may employ it to make peace with the relatives of the person he has killed. Help these people who are in need. Do not think of your wealth. When that is gone you will get some more. Do your duty. Do not pass anyone unnoticed, not even a child. If people have come and asked you for something, do not let them go away without attempting to do something for them. You are a chief. Do some good for your people. In that way you will show that you are a chief. 'Our chief,' they will all call you. The children that see you will call you chief. Whoever talks to you will call you chief. If you are good to your people, they will show their respect by being bashful in your presence. If you are not good to them they will not think you a chief and they will not be bashful in your presence. So, at all times, do as a chief ought to do. Be good-natured to all the people and in this way you will show that

[5] What follows is a typical speech delivered by a member of the Thunderbird clan.

you are indeed a chief. And then even the people of other tribes will say that such and such people have a good chief."

Informant, member of the Bear clan: The Indians always celebrated in summer. It was a season of rejoicing because the chief fed the tribe. It somewhat symbolized a mother bird feeding her young ones. The Thunderbird clan is in charge of the tribe, and when the chief feeds the tribe all rejoice and the standard is raised.

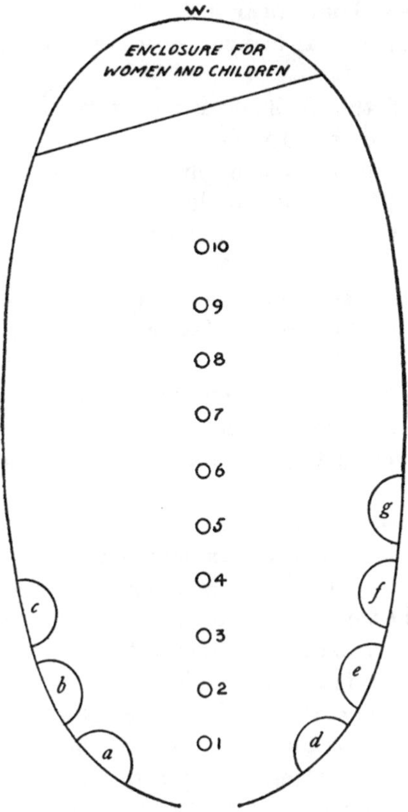

THE BEAR CLAN FEAST (FIRST VERSION)

Two versions of the Bear clan feast (fig. 36) were obtained, fortunately both from a man and a woman. The feast was generally given during the month called *Hundjwi'ra* (i. e., bear month), corresponding roughly to our January.

Informant, member of the clan (female): The host tells his sister's son, or, if he should not happen to have any, a member of the Wolf clan, to build a long lodge. This attendant then fills kettles either with blueberries or raspberries or any other fruit that the bears are fond of, and places them on the fireplace. Sometimes dried corn is also brought.

FIG. 36.—Plan of Bear clan war-bundle feast as given by John Rave. *a*, Host. *b*, Relatives of host. *c*, Warrior clan. *d*, Wolf clan. *e*, Thunderbird clan. *f*, Eagle clan. *g*, Buffalo clan. 1, Buckskin for earthmaker. 2, Buckskin for turtle. 3, Buckskin for thunderbird. 4, Buckskin for sun. 5, Buckskin for moon. 6, Buckskin for morning star. 7, Buckskin for earth. 8, Buckskin for fire. 9, Buckskin for heroka. 10, Buckskin for night spirits.

The participants enter the lodge at dusk. The host precedes the invited guests. In entering they proceed in a direction contrary to the hands of the clock. The host always sits at the southeast end of the lodge and the guests occupy seats next to him, proceeding from the southeast to the northwest.

When all are seated the host rises and addresses his guests as follows:

"Members of my clan who are seated here, I greet you all. To those from whom I have sprung I make these offerings of tobacco and this headdress (i. e., red feathers). I was told by my ancestors that if I did this I would obtain for myself, for my relatives, and for the members of my clan, sufficient blessings to guide us all safely through life, and to make our lives pleasant. I will not tell the origin myth (of our clan) because it is sacred and it must not be told without the proper ceremony, for the telling would then injure an individual. Besides there are many clans beside our own represented here and it is not proper that these should hear it."

He then speaks of the four ancestral bear-beings who were created in the beginning.

When the feast is ready one of the Wolf clansmen gives four soldier whoops. Then the fire is allowed to die out, and as soon as the lodge is in complete darkness the feasters begin to eat. Before eating, the host sings four songs. These are the clan songs and are only sung at these feasts or on the occasion of the death of a clans-man.

Those who partake of food at the feast may be members of any clan except the Bear clan. The members of the latter clan do not eat at their own feast.

Everyone attending must bring his own wooden spoon and must use it with his left hand. There are four wooden dishes in which the food is served. These are arranged in the lodge in a certain manner.

The guests sit around these dishes and eat with their own spoons.

The feast is given in the first bear month. Some one generally watches the moon and as soon as the new moon is visible the feast begins. The feathers and the tobacco to be offered are placed in four little troughs made of basswood bark, each about 1 foot long. These are then placed on the south side of the fireplace.

When the meal is over the attendant or Wolf clansman generally says a few words of thanks to the host and then the host in turn thanks those who have participated and tells them that the feast is now over. All now pass out, the one next to the host leaving first and the rest in succession, the host himself remaining until the end.

When the feast is over the tobacco and the feathers are taken away from the lodge and carried in a southern direction to a place (under a tree) that has been especially cleared and sanctified. Any person may therafter go there, offer tobacco, and ask for long life.

Informant, member of the clan (male): "Well, soldiers, your moon is about to appear. It is good. So come forth, for it is at this time that the spirits asked to be remembered. Let us send, on this occasion, to the place at which we all originated, whatever we possess of wealth. This is what the spirits asked of old. Let us therefore put the kettle on and prepare the feast.

"This is the way in which we prepare the feast. I offer only one small kettle. Here is my offering. I pray that what I offer may suffice and bring enough blessings from the spirits to include all the

Indians who exist and especially those who are present at this feast. For that reason do we deliver these speeches. We were told that at the place where we originated our ancestors now remain, regarding it as their home. There they expectantly await us. So our ancestors spoke. Our offering at this feast is intended for that purpose. Let us pour tobacco for them. Let us place at the edge of the fire the four bark receptacles. Now listen to me for I am going to pour tobacco.

(He now addresses the four original clan beings.)

"On the north side, Earthmaker created you. Four brothers he placed there (you being one of them). And when one of them started for the earth those remaining asked to be remembered at this feast. These are the objects they asked to be given as offerings— tobacco, feathers, and boiled food. Earthmaker gave you that kind of life-giving material. We, in turn, ask you for this, so that when you take our offerings you will grant us what we ask. Here they are, the offerings with which you wished to be remembered. The spirits promised to give them. We are praying now not only for our own, but for all the clans. Our life will be strengthened, it was said. These words that I am telling you now, they used. We must act very cautiously in this, they said.

"If you place a portion of boiled food away as an offering, you must use it only in that particular place. Do not do otherwise. This way only is the correct way to do it."

Then he spoke to the attendant and said, "Are you ready? Go and get all these people who are to eat. They must bring their spoons with them."

Then the attendant brought the people into the lodge and put some food in their plates.

"Place the people around the plate and let them be seated," the host said. "Now turn the fire down and get ready. Hold your spoons in your left hand, for with that only are you allowed to eat. None of you must talk nor laugh. You must do what I tell you. Before the meal begins let us sing. Let us do it now." (They then sing the four clan songs.)

"Thus they have told us. That way it was at the place where we began life.

"Now the meal is over. We have had a minor council. We have acted correctly. It is good that you who are present have come at our request. You have eaten very well, and we thank you for it. This is what those from whom we originated told us to do. This council-feast they pleaded for. 'We should act very cautiously, they said. That you have done. It is good that you have eaten for our benefit. Now is about time for us to finish. I greet you all."

THE BEAR CLAN FEAST (SECOND VERSION)

Informant, member of Bear clan: As soon as the first bear month is visible they have their feast. They do not use meat but products of the earth. The feast is held at night, never in the daytime. The people always save up food some time before giving the feast. The favorite dishes of the bear are sugar and blueberries. When they can not obtain these they use other vegetables. Indeed, any product of the earth is all right.

When they prepare to give the feast they get the food ready and have some tobacco on hand. On the first day of the first bear month they put on the fire some kettles with dried corn mixed with fruit and others containing green corn. The latter is boiled. They also have ground sugar. When these are ready the feast attendant goes around the village to invite the people. When all have entered the lodge and taken their proper seats, then the host rises and addresses them:

"All my relatives who are seated here, I greet you. It is not through blessings of our own that we can always make offerings of tobacco. My grandfather was blessed by a spirit called Black Fur, a spirit who is in command of all the other spirits. This spirit told us that we could perform the ceremony in this way. It is for that reason we have made an effort to heat water for him.[6] The first request we make is that if we ever go on the warpath, we may conquer. Our grandfather was also blessed with life by the bear spirit [7] and he told him that he would grant him and his posterity whatever they asked. We shall therefore send to this spirit a pipeful of tobacco, two kettles full of food, and some tree sap.[8] So much will we send him, accompanied by an offering of tobacco.

"As soon as the attendant gets everything ready the feasting will begin."

Then the attendant puts food in every plate, and when he has finished the host speaks again.

"Relatives, it is said that when the plates are supplied to you filled with food, then you should begin to eat. Do not, however, use your right hands in eating."

The host tells the feasters to use their left hands in eating, and they obey him. Before starting to eat all the fires are put out and the people eat in the dark.

In the spring of the year this feast is given again. Twice a year it is given.

The feast [9] was always given with some choice dried corn that had been put away for this event. Once when it was time to give the feast in the first bear month, the two daughters of the man who was

[6] Boil soup and prepare food in general.
[7] Black Fur is apparently a ceremonial expression for bear.
[8] Ceremonial name for maple sugar.
[9] What follows is an account of why this particular feast was discontinued.

to give it had their menses and were fasting. When the feast was about to be held there was no food and their mother gave the girls some of the sacred food and the unclean girls boiled it and ate it.

The following spring when the girls were out helping their mother tan some hide a bear approached them and tried to kill the girls. The old woman fought the bear off as best she could, but he paid no attention to her and tried to get at the girls. Finally he killed the girls. Then the old woman attacked the bear and finally threw him down and killed him, using her tanning stick as a weapon.

Now this bear was not an ordinary bear such as live on this earth, but his body was covered with blue clay. He had come out of a spring of water shortly before he came to this place. The girls had eaten sacred food when they were unclean, and that is why this bear came and killed them.

Since then that particular band has stopped giving this bear feast.

THE SNAKE CLAN FEAST

When a person wishes to give a snake feast, four chickens must be obtained. The nephew of the feast giver is then told to prepare these chickens and make the general preparations.

The feast is given in the fall, just as the snakes are supposed to go into their winter quarters and close their doors. The winter is their night, and then they go to sleep.

Shortly before the feast begins the host takes out a bundle containing four snake skins—a yellow-snake skin, a rattlesnake skin, a blow-snake skin, and a bull-snake skin. In honor of these he gives his feast and makes his offerings.

As the fall of the year is to the snakes the same as our evening, the Winnebago give this feast in their honor then, in much the same way as we have our supper before retiring for the night. The snake skins are representatives of the first four snakes Earthmaker made and which he pierced through the earth in the direction of the east. The snake skins are kept to represent the four original snake-beings and to keep evil away from homes. That is why offerings are made to them. Four men only are invited to this feast (as main participants), and they must each eat a chicken.

The host himself opens the door for the snakes. In front of him, next to the fireplace, he makes four holes in the ground, thus opening the door for them. There he likewise places tobacco for them. First he pours tobacco in the fire, for the fire is the mediator between the people and the spirit. The fire tells the spirit the wishes of the people and is, in general, in charge of the members of the tribe. For that reason they always pour tobacco upon it.

Now the host rises and speaks. "Grandfather (fire), you who stand in the center of the lodge, I offer you tobacco, for you are the interpreter (between the spirits and human beings), and I know that you will deliver the requests I address to our grandfather-who-crawls (the snake), just as I have said them. I offer you tobacco.

"To you likewise, grandfathers, you whom Earthmaker created first and placed within the earth; you whom Earthmaker placed in control of abundance of life and whose war clubs were made heavy, so that nothing could miss them; to you we offer these things. Whatever you can give us, we ask of you in return. Here are our offerings of food, tobacco, and eagle feathers. We place them here at your door. We ask that you bless us with victory in war. We know that the weapons you carry make you invulnerable, and we wish likewise to be invulnerable. You never fail to obtain what you desire with your clubs, and we ask that the same power be bestowed upon us. As the years pass may the blessing we obtain increase in power. When you look out upon the world life emanates from your eyes. May this life be given to our posterity. As we strut about in the short number of days allotted to us may you keep out of our path, so that we may not be frightened. Yet should we cross any of your paths may we be strengthened thereby. It is said that you are the grass, and that is why we ask you to bless us. Bless us because you are in possession of the life which we desire. For these reasons do we offer you tobacco, feathers, and food."

Then the host poured tobacco into the four holes that he had made in the ground and placed feathers there. Then he took a little food from each of the kettles and poured it into the four holes. After that he greased the heads of the snake skins which were lying before him with kettle grease and poured tobacco on the heads of the snakes. He asked all his relatives to offer tobacco likewise and he put tobacco into the holes again and poured some upon the heads of the snakes.

When those invited have arrived, someone who is a good speaker sits near the entrance, while another good speaker sits near the farthest end. After all have entered, the leader of the four participants makes the circuit of the fireplace four times. He then sits down, and the host greets each one in turn, as follows:

"I greet you all. It is good. How could I say aught but that it is good? I am a poor worthless fellow, yet you have remembered me. It is good. You did not look upon my unworthiness and think within your hearts he is a worthless fellow, but you thought of the spirits, and therefore you came to sit with me so that I might see your face. It is good. I have obtained four chickens, and the attendant is now cooking them. I suppose he has cooked them by this time, and we will soon be able to eat them.

"I am attempting to cook water for the beings first created, so that we might be blessed with victory in war, and with life. That is what we are asking and what we would like to obtain from them before they (the spirits) retire for the night. It is our desire to be blessed year in, year out.

"Your plates will be filled soon, so let me greet you again, you (humans) who are taking the place of the spirits. All you who are present I greet."

The attendant now takes the kettles from the fire and takes the plate of the first of those sitting in the row. Then he takes the sharp stick that he holds in his hand, sticks it through one of the four chickens, and puts it in the plate of the first man. He passes the plate around the kettle four times, going from right to left, and finally he places it before the feaster. The feaster then says, "I thank you all," and the attendant passes on to the next one, and so in succession until he comes to the last person. Then the one first invited rises and says, "All those present, the host and the three other guests, do I greet." Then the speaker addresses the one sitting next to him, who greets him in return. In the same way he greets the third and the fourth one. Then he speaks as follows:

"It is good. Who would not be thankful for this? The host and his relatives present here are praying for life and victory, to the four greatest spirits Earthmaker ever made, to those spirits whom he pierced through the earth so that it might hold together. All the snakes whom we see on the earth are ruled by these four. From them have they asked blessings. The first human beings on earth saw these spirits face to face and, we are told, they used them for protection. These we see before us as the host has laid them out. We are told that blessings can be obtained by the use of these snakes.

"I am indeed not a fit person to be invited to such a gathering as this, but the host has kindly overlooked my faults. My grandfather fasted and thirsted himself to death and he was blessed and his spirit taken to a spirit-home. That is what happened to my grandfather, for he told me this himself. The place where he was blessed was at Red Banks at a place where a creek flows into the sea (Green Bay). At the fork of this creek there was a hill lying east and west. It is there that the yellow snake-chief lives. To the home of this snake-chief my grandfather was taken. This snake was at this place gathering tobacco for all the spirits. There my grandfather was even blessed with their bodies. For this reason I always pour tobacco for them. And I have been given to understand that the spirits do not overlook the least fault (in the performance of the feast). They are always in our midst just as even the grass and the dust represent snakes. They know everything, they say. It is not safe to cross their path. As, however, the host is now making an offering to them, should we cross their path now it would even strengthen us. It is good. These clubs are heavy and they will not fail to strike everything within their reach. The host has asked for that power so that he might have victory (in war). They, the spirits, also have life to dispose of and that we ask of them also, giving them these offerings of tobacco, feathers, and food. They will bless us I am certain, for I am told that they even know our thoughts and wishes (before we express them), and are willing to grant them if we pour tobacco while making them. However, to-day we have done more. We have openly made a great offering to them. How could any spirit fail to see such an offering? For that reason (I know) they will surely bless us. And the blessings asked for the posterity will surely be granted. I feel that when I go home and talk to my children afterwards, they will be strengthened by the fact that I have taken part in the feast. All who are present, I greet. You, the host, I also greet. I greet you all."

Then the second one invited rises and speaks. He thanks the host for the privilege of having been invited and encourages him and assures every one that they will surely be blessed, telling them why they should be blessed.

Then the third one rises and says approximately the same as his predecessor. He also tells how his grandfather was blessed by the snakes, etc.

Then the fourth one speaks, telling what the snakes do and that he himself was a member of the Snake clan and was consequently descended from the snakes. Inasmuch as he had partaken of the feast, all who were present would surely be blessed by the snakes. He assured them that what they asked would surely be granted. Then he greeted them and concluded.

After that, all the four participants greet each other in turn again and when this is over they sit down and begin the feast. Each person must eat a chicken apiece. They must not leave anything on the plate, for it is a sacred feast. After they have eaten the chicken they are given soup to drink.

When the feast is over the host throws cedar branches into the fire and the plates and the spoons are held over the smoke in order to purify them. The host then rises and says:

"You, the first invited, and you, the second invited, etc., I greet you all. It is good that you have come and occupied seats at my request and I am grateful to you for it. Even were that all the blessing I was to receive, it would (be enough). But you have assured me that I would receive the blessings I longed for. You truly encouraged me. You told me of your grandfathers' blessings, so that I feel positive that I am blessed, for your grandfathers' blessings were surely great and I am sure everything could be obtained with them. Surely your grandfathers' blessings were equal to those of the spirits. It is good that you have indeed partaken of my feast. This must be what the older people said: 'Your life is (naturally) weak and you can only be strengthened by the counsel and advice of brave men.' Truly you have counciled with me and given me enough to live on. I thank you for the speeches you have delivered, for it is life to me. It is good. I greet you all."

CHAPTER XIII

RELIGIOUS SOCIETIES BASED ON BLESSINGS FROM SPIRITS

SOCIETY OF THOSE WHO HAVE RECEIVED BLESSINGS FROM THE NIGHT SPIRITS

Informant, member of Thunderbird clan: Once a man went hunting so that he might be able to get the game with which to give a feast. All of those who were to participate in the feast went along with him. After they had killed some deer they built a lodge. Then all the other feast-givers came into the lodge, bringing something toward the feast, as well as the tobacco which they were to offer. Some brought other things, even dogs, as their contribution to the feast. The dogs would be killed, singed, then boiled, and prepared in the same way as the deer. The meat would then be mixed with dry corn. The attendants, who were generally the nephews of the feast-givers, would look after the boiling of the food. Every time they gave a feast they selected these nephews to do the cooking and the general work connected with this ceremony.

The nephew who acts as attendant accompanies a feast-giver on the warpath, where likewise he has to endure a great deal. Should his uncle be killed, it is his duty to be killed likewise and not to return home.

He acted in this way because of his love for his uncle. The attendants do all the work whenever their uncles give a feast. They also arrange for the place where the feast is to be held; make the four invitation sticks; blacken them with charcoal and decorate them at the ends with fine and fluffy white eagle feathers. Then they prepare a bundle of tobacco containing about a pipeful. After these preparations have been made one of the nephews goes around the village and presents the invitation sticks to every individual who had been blessed by the Night Spirits. These are called the night-blessed children. The night-blessed children thanked the messengers and assured them that they now felt they were obtaining life. Then those to whom the invitation stick had been presented go around asking their relatives to accompany them to the feast. There the guest and his relatives would meet at the appointed time. All those who received invitation sticks do the same.

281

The host at the same time puts himself in readiness to receive the guests.

The two drums to be used are placed in the proper position with tobacco on top as an offering. The two gourds to be used are arranged in the same way, with offerings of tobacco on top. These four articles are placed in a row in front of the host, who pours tobacco upon them again and asks them for life.

The host now rises and speaks as follows (first, however, offering tobacco to the fire, and telling the people of his own band how he had obtained his blessing, and from what source it had come):

"Grandfathers, when you blessed my grandfather with life you promised that as often as we would boil food for you and offer you a pipeful of tobacco, you would smoke it. So it has been said. Boiled water from an animal whom you considered the same as our own body, and spirit food he extended to you, as well as a pipeful of tobacco. This we also are sending you. And what could we ask of you in return but war? That it may be directed toward us, we pray you. Grandfathers, you who are called Happy Nights, when you blessed our grandfather you blessed him with endless war. So it has been said. That is what we ask for, that as you blessed our grandfather, so you bless us. We ask for the same things. You, likewise, grandfather, you who are called The-one-with-rounded-wood, when you blessed my grandfather you blessed him with life. That is what he said, and you asked him in return to make offerings of tobacco. Here is the tobacco. This night we are going to ask life of you. We desire that you give us and all who will be here to-night, life. As many people as will be seated here, we ask life for all of them."

Then all who are present rise and, holding tobacco in each hand, walk around the lodge, pouring tobacco on the drums and the gourds, and some of it into the fire. They pour tobacco into the fire for the Night Spirits. For the Beings-with-rounded-wood they offer tobacco by pouring it upon the drums. The offering is made both to the drums and to the gourds directly. The tobacco bundles tied to the invitation sticks are offered to the four cardinal points and the four specially invited guests smoke this tobacco, because they are supposed to represent the four cardinal points. Behind the respective invited guests are placed two women, next to the wall, so that they might lead in the dance. When the invited guests come to the feast these women remain outside until the starting songs have been begun.

The host sings these songs first and when he has finished the first invited guest enters the lodge, ejaculating peculiar sounds (that are probably meant as greetings). Continuing these sounds, he walks around the lodge until he comes to the place from which he has started. There he stops and speaks. "You who obtain life, you that council, relatives, all who are seated here, I greet you. It is good that you have taken pity upon me. All those that I have along with me, my relatives, you have caused them to think that they were to obtain life; that a great life was to come to us through you. And all this you have done when we were leading worthless lives. It is good. If such an invitation were to be extended to people when they are sick and weakly, it would heal them; it would overcome their illness, it is said. It is good. When I think that our sick people will get well by reason of this feast, I am thankful. Up to the present our children have all been sickly, but from now on we will have no cause to worry. I am thankful. The principal tree of the night-soldiers, standing in front of their doorway and which is in full bloom, has not a dead leaf upon it, not one that has dried. It is beautiful to look upon. They obtained it for us and caused it to come down to us, and we feel grateful. It will strengthen our families. This lodge that we have entered is like the first lodge (the night-soldiers' lodge), and just as we were strengthened by it, so will we surely be strengthened by entering this lodge to-day. In the night-soldiers' lodge fine white feathers are scattered all over the ground, ankle deep, it is said. As we are about to go over the past, we certainly will be strengthened thereby. The lodge of the night-soldiers was fair to behold from the inside, we are told. We will consider ourselves blest with life to-day, even although we are not children of the night-blessed ones, and even although we will not be able to conduct ourselves as it is meet. We will, however, do what we can in order to obtain life. You children of the night-blessed ones, who are seated around here, I greet you."

Then he sings the entrance songs and walks around the lodge. His singing is generally finished at about the time that he has made the complete circuit of the lodge. Then he starts around the lodge again uttering the peculiar sounds mentioned before, until he comes to the seat of the host. There he stops and makes a circle in the air (with his hand) and addresses him as follows:

"I greet you. A great day has come to me and all my relatives have tasted thereof in the hope that they might thereby be strengthened. I have also brought along with me a pipeful of tobacco to be given to you, that we may all be strengthened. So it is said. It is for that reason that I am acting thus and am greeting you."

With these words he concluded and walked to the place that had been assigned him in the lodge, opposite the host and, still standing, he said the following: "Children of the night-blessed spirits who are seated here around me, I greet you all. The councilor, I mean the host, has seen fit to give me and my relatives a seat. We will sit in it so that we may be strengthened thereby. We will now take our seats, but before that let me send forth my greetings to all."

Then the second invited guest enters. He utters the same sounds as his predecessors and makes the circuit of the lodge. When he reaches the place from which he started he stops and addresses the host as follows:

"Councilor, you who obtain life, relatives who are seated here, I greet you all, and your seats do I greet likewise. You that are seated in the first place, I greet you, too. All you children of the night-blest spirits who are in this lodge, I greet you. It is good that you wish me to live; that I am here. I am not a child of a night-blest one, that this invitation should have been extended to me, but you probably knew the nature of my life and that is why, I suppose, you extended this honor to me. My relatives are even greater weaklings in the properties and goods of life than I am. That happens to be our manner of life. It is good. Henceforth we shall be stronger as we journey through life. Our men, women, and children shall all live in peace. As many of us as are living to-day, that many shall continue to live (on account of my participation in this ceremony). I am thankful.

"Of all the spirits that exist, these truly are in control of most life. So it is said of the Night Spirits. This is a great thing. These spirits have given us the occasion for a great counciling. Many of us are not able to take part in it, especially the one now speaking. The songs that have been used by our fathers we will not be able to sing, but whatever we say I know will be acceptable to you, children of the night-blest spirits. I send forth greetings to you all."

Then he sang an entrance song, and after he had made the circuit of the lodge, he sang another one. Then he went around the lodge again making his strange utterances, until he came in front of the host. Here he made a circle (with his hand) and stopped. Then he greeted the host as follows:

"A great day has come upon us, both upon me and upon all of my relatives. We all have tasted thereof so that we might live thereby. We have all brought you a pipeful of tobacco, just as we were told. It is said that we would thus strengthen one another, and that is why we have done it. I greet you all."

Then he went to his seat, the second one in the lodge, and sat down. Then all the members of his band sat down, each sending forth a greeting as they took their seats. When they were all seated the third man invited prepared to enter.

The third one invited now entered, uttering strange sounds, and made the circuit of the lodge, when he paused and addressed the host as follows:

"Councilors, life-obtainers, relatives who are seated in your respective seats, I greet you all. Here I have been blessed, although I am not worthy of it. My grandfather, and my father, too, once said to me, ' Some day when there is a dearth of people, some night-blest one will take pity on you. Submit to it.' Thus he spoke to me and what he referred to was this feast. These feasts are all sacred, but this is the most sacred one. That is what he used to tell me. It is not to be trifled with, even in respect to the rituals within the lodge. Never should one cross the lodge directly. If you trifle with this rule you will bring sorrow upon yourselves. The so-called night-soldiers are not to be trifled with. So he told me. The so-called night-soldiers, like soldiers on this earth, are stern. Truly they are stern, said my father. If we were to slight one of them we would most assuredly be punished for it, and punishment by them means death. So he spoke to me. But, said he, ' if, on the other hand, any one attends to all that pertains to this ceremony it will be a means of obtaining life. It will be a good thing to do, and one would thereby obtain a good life. Therefore, I have always looked upon the Night dance with awe, for it is a very holy thing.' So spoke my father. For that reason, consequently, whenever my father gave a Night feast he would encourage us to pay careful attention to it, and that is why I have always tried to do so. Remember, however, that I am not a child of the night-blest ones, and that, therefore, I have very little to say. However, I will start a song, which will be a greeting to this lodge, and I will sing it as I am passing around the lodge. Children of the night-blest ones, who are seated here, I greet you."

Then he sang an entrance song, first at the west end of the lodge and then near the position occupied by the host. When he had finished the circuit of the lodge he went around again, making the accustomed peculiar utterances, until he came in front of the host. There he stopped and addressed the host as follows:

"I greet you. You have caused this day to come upon me and all my relatives. We have all tasted thereof and we have all felt ourselves in connection with life. We are thankful. We have thought of this blessing of life in connection with ourselves. I greet you."

Then he walks to the place assigned to him in the west end of the tent and sits down. The other members of his band do the same, one after the other, greeting the people in the lodge at the same time.

When they are all seated the fourth one comes in. He repeats the utterances of the former guests and then starts around the lodge until he reaches the entrance. There he stops and addresses the host:

"Councilors and life-obtainers, I greet your seats. I likewise greet you, host. You who are seated in the north and you who are seated in the west, your seats I greet. Children of the night-blessed spirits who are within this lodge, all of you I greet. It is good. As far as I understand this Night ceremony is considered a life-giving one. The so-called happy Night Spirits alone are in control of most of life. So I was told, and that is why this ceremony is called a life-giving one. If I participated in this ceremony, I would be able to call it life, I was told. But I did not pay any attention to it. They told me it was good and that I would at the same time be making offerings to Those-with-the-rounded-wood, and that thus I would be able to make use of all the plants that these spirits control, so that I would never be embarrassed when I wished to use them. I have caused people who were ill to become well by means of this ceremony. All of the plants that these spirits control are good ones, and it is easy to obtain life with them. In this ceremony we may also obtain life by dancing. But we must dance earnestly. The leaders of this ceremony have held council over everything, and yet they have selected us for a seat of honor, so that we might greet them in this lodge and that we might be able to use this song while greeting them. You children of the night-blessed ones, I greet you all."

Then he sang an entrance song, and when he finished he repeated the utterances used in entering and gradually made the circuit of the lodge singing. When he was through singing, he again continued the utterances until he came to the place of the host, where he made the circle (with his hands) and stopped. Then he addressed the host as follows:

"I greet you. You wish me to live, and therefore caused a great day to come upon me and upon all my relatives. We have all received a taste of it, and we have all thought of ourselves in connection with life. We are also bringing you a pipeful of tobacco, so that we may strengthen one another. That is what we thought and that is why we are doing it. I greet you."

Then he walked around the lodge until he came to his seat. There he stopped and addressed his seat as follows:

"Seat that is reserved for me and for my relatives, we are about to sit in you; we will do it, and we will think that our lives have been helped thereby. I greet you." Thus he spoke and sat down. Then all the other members of his band sat down one by one.

When they were all seated the lodge was full. Then the host rose and spoke as follows:

"You who are seated in the first position, I greet you; you who are seated in the north position, I greet you; you who are seated in the west position, I greet you; and you who are seated at the end of the road, I greet you. Children of the night-blessed ones who are here, I greet you. My father and my grandfather spoke to me of this ceremony, and they told me it was good. They told me that the one who first obtained it was named 'Little Red Turtle.' He fasted and was blessed by those whom he called the Beings-with-round-wood. By these was he blessed at the noon hour, and he was taught what to do. There they taught him all. At a place where the stars touched land they caused it to become night, and there they blessed him and taught him how to make four circles and also certain songs. Since then this ceremony has been performed. He was really blessed, and he was told exactly how everything should be performed. So it is said. As he was very fond of the Night feast, he spoke in its behalf, and told of all the medicines that were associated with it and of the use to which they could be put. I myself know that these medicines are good to live on. If anyone uses them he will receive benefits therefrom and his children will receive life. I know that they are good. I would not have you think that I am one of those blessed by the Night Spirits because I say this. But I know that all the medicines of which I have personal charge and to which I make offerings of tobacco, for whom I boiled food, always make the individual to whom I offer them the better for it, provided that I do everything correctly. I was told to do this, and that is why I do it. I am now going to sing some songs audibly, and all these songs will be songs about medicines. I know that we will cause you to fan your faces (from perspiration brought on by making you work too hard), but forgive us for it. Children of the night-blessed ones who are seated here, I greet you, and to take the place of their sister whom they always place ahead of them so we also will have our sisters lead the dance for us."

Two women now rise and stand side by side in front of the men and hold, one in each hand, the invitation sticks that had been returned. These two women lead in the dance. The men who shake the gourds stand with their backs to the women, facing the drummers. All sing together and all the dancers have partners at their sides. It is a very interesting dance. Then all get up and start around the lodge, making strange utterances. When they have made the complete circuit of the lodge they stop and sing. When they finish this song they start around the lodge again, repeating the utterances. They stop at the west end of the tent, where they sing again. They thus sing at both ends of the lodge. They use all the songs they intend to. When the last song is over the individual who has sung it makes four circles and then takes the drum, gourd, tobacco, etc., and places them in front of the guest who occupies the first seat of honor. Then all sit down. Then the east leader rises and speaks as follows: [16]

"Councilors and life-obtainers, relatives who are seated here, I send you all greetings; and to you who are on the north side, and you who are on the west side, and you who are at the end of the road, your seats I greet. Our host has passed over to me the means of our meditation, the instruments through which we ask life. This instrument for asking life is the foremost thing we possess, so the old people said. We are thankful for it. We know that Earthmaker

---

[16] From now on we will use the terms East Leader, North Leader, West Leader, and South Leader to designate, respectively, the first, second, third, and fourth guests in the order of their invitation.

did not put us in charge of anything, and that for that reason the tobacco we received is our greatest and foremost thing. So the old people said. We were told that we should use it to ask for life. This must have been what they meant. This, the instrument with which to ask life, is, I feel sure, sufficient to attract them and they will surely take notice of it. We may also follow him who is taking the place of the spirits, and we will consider all those who are in the lodge blest. Those whom we call Nights have been offered tobacco, and the same has been offered to the four cardinal points, and to all the life-giving plants. To this many tobacco has been offered. It will strengthen us. This is what we call imitating the spirits, and that is why we are doing it. Children of the night-blessed ones who are seated here, I greet you all. The song we will now start is a pipe-lighting song."

When he finished singing he greeted all those in the lodge and then he lit his pipe. Then he took a number of puffs. First he inhaled some smoke and blew it toward the east, then toward the north, then toward the west, then toward the south. Then he passed it around and all smoked, except the host, who is not permitted to do so. Then the east leader spoke again as follows:

"Night-blessed ones who are seated here, I greet you. The instrument with which to ask life I will now place here, and if any of you want to fill your pipes you may do so."

Then the leader of the north band rose and spoke as follows:

"Councilors and life-obtainers, you who sit in the direction where the day comes from, you who sit on the other side, in the west, and you who sit at the end of the road, your seats I all greet. We, too, have been anxious to obtain the instrument whereby we ask life, and therefore we fill a pipe for ourselves. I greet you."

Then the leader of the south band rose and said as follows:

"If the leader of the north band has finished his greeting, I also would very much like to have the instrument with which we ask life brought to me. We will immediately go and fill a pipe. I am speaking now because I wish to tell you what I intend to do. I greet you."

The leader of the north band did not pass the pipe that he had filled all around the lodge, but merely passed it to the members of his band. Only they smoked from it. In the same way the leaders of the other bands, with the exception of the host's band, passed the pipe only to members of their individual band. Only the host passed his pipe all around the lodge. When the smoking was over the leader of the east band rose and greeted everyone. Then he spoke as follows:

"Our grandfathers used to carry on this ceremony, I have been told. They told me that if at any time the giver of this ceremony can not find enough people to invite he would take pity on me. This is what I should say, my father told me. In the direction from which the day comes, there where the Nights are, live the night-soldiers, who blessed my grandfather and who made him try his powers in the middle of the ocean—there where it is deepest. They placed a round object of wood before him, and the night-soldiers said that they would not take it away, and that every time my grandfather tried to seize it he would not miss. 'You have done well, human, you have won,' they said to him. For this reason it was considered an instrument of war, he told me. If you do your utmost in offering tobacco, it will be an instrument of war, he said.

And he also said the following: "All the plants with which I have been blessed are useful and a person can receive life through them if he takes good care of them. These plants can be very powerful and some of them can even be used in playing jokes, we are told. But we have never used any of them in such a manner, for if we did our plants would surely lose their strength. I have been told that should I frequently use any of my plants for the purpose of playing jokes and then for the purpose of curing a sick person, they would have no power at all. If, however, I never used them in jokes my medicine would always be powerful. Therefore I have never used them in that manner. Nor have I ever poisoned anyone with them. I never considered myself great or used a Night's trick-medicine or used fire, although I was told I could do so. This I never did. When I use one of the plants I like to have it do its work. I am saying this, although I am not a child of the night-blest ones. It is now about time to permit our sisters to get hold of the 'chief sticks' and to permit them to sit here and sing together with us."

The women are then permitted to take two sticks apiece and sing wherever they are sitting. As soon as the men sing the women join in.

"This is the way to do, I was told, and that is why I am doing it. Children of the night-blessed ones, who are seated here in this lodge, I send you all greeting."

When he is through with his starting song he stands up and speaks to them again, as follows:

"Night-blest ones who are within this lodge, I greet you. I was not invited to take this seat because I was a wise man. I do not for a moment imagine that, but it was done in order to help me obtain life. We will now rise and go forth and we will brush against your faces, but you must take pity on us. Children of the night-blessed ones, I greet you. We will not remain seated here but we will rise and go forth in order to obtain the round stick. That is why I am making this announcement to you. I greet you."

They then rise and make four circuits of the lodge, first stopping at the first seat, then at the second, then at the third, and lastly at the fourth. When they get back to their starting place they sing dancing songs, first stopping at the west end of the lodge and then at the entrance. This they repeat. By this time all the songs they had intended using have been sung, so they make four circuits of the lodge and then, taking the drum, gourd, etc., place it in front of the north band. When the dancers are all seated the leader of the north band rises, and greeting everyone speaks as follows:

"I was not pitied because I was a child of the night-blest ones, my father told me. Yet if I performed my duties aright I would be able to make the proper speeches when called upon, I was told. That I have been pitied now is due to the fact that these people here wished to have me obtain life. Certainly my invitation to this ceremony has made me think of life, as my father used to tell me. I do not for a moment imagine that they invited me because I was a great man. Nevertheless my father told me to say that it was good; and that if I really meant all that I said, my life would certainly be strengthened thereby. My father knew how to perform this ceremony correctly, but I am not able to do so. Although I was told it was a good thing, nevertheless I was not able to pour tobacco. Those whom we call the Ones-with-the-rounded-wood are in charge of very much life and they are holy. This affair is not a thing to be trifled with, my father told me. Yet in spite of this we will sing some songs, even though we know that we will not be able to sing them as they have been sung heretofore. Perhaps, however, you will be kind enough to be satisfied with whatever we do. Children of the night-blessed ones, I greet you."

Then he sang the starting song, and when he was finished he rose again and, greeting all, spoke as follows:

"When Those-with-the-rounded-wood start to walk their sisters are placed in front of them. Our sisters we will now place in front of us, so that thereby they may be blest with life and hold the principal sticks and staffs. We will use the toys so that we may be strengthened thereby, we think, and that is why I greet you."

Then they permit the women to lead the procession. These women walk in front, side by side, and are followed by the ones carrying the gourds, who dance with their backs toward them. Then come the drummers and the feast-givers, and after these, all those who desire to join in. They walk around the lodge making strange utterances. Four times do they make the circuit of the lodge and then they come and stop at the east end, where they sing. When they are through here they start around the lodge again and stop at the west end and sing. Then they start again, making the same strange utterances as before, until they come to the east end of the lodge, where they sing once more. When they have in this manner sung all the songs that they wish to use the leader of the north band makes the four circles as before and brings the tobacco, gourds, etc., to the west band. Then they all take their seats. Now the leader of the west band rises and speaks as follows:

"Councilors, life-obtainers, relatives, to you all who are seated here, I send forth my greetings. You who occupy the first seat, you who occupy the north seat, and you who occupy the seat at the end of the road, I greet. I do not mean to say anything of consequence. I was taught this ceremony, but I do not know anything about it. However, I always honored it, for I was told that it was a good thing. Indeed, I knew it, but I could never perform it well. I was told that if I performed it well I would obtain life thereby, just as others have done. Well, some of you are able to do it. It is a very great council feast. How, indeed, can the spirits ignore what you have done for them to-day? If they acknowledge it, we who are representing the directions will receive blessings through the host who is giving the feast. That is what I mean. When we hold our mediators (that is, the drums, tobacco, etc.) we will be strengthened thereby. So with this in our minds, let us take and hold them. Children of the night-blessed ones, I greet you."

Then he sang the starting song, and when he had finished he rose and spoke again.

"Councilors, I send you greetings, as well as to you who sit in the first seat, to you who sit in the north, and to you who sit at the end of the road. It is said that when the night-soldiers come they walk over the entire extent of the earth. When they blessed my grandfather they blessed him with life. So he used to say of himself. We will now plead for these powers in our songs. We will place our sisters in front and follow them. That is what I wanted to announce to you. Children of the night-blessed ones who are seated here, I greet you."

Then they made the complete circuit of the lodge until they came to the place where they had been sitting. There they made a circle. Then they made another circuit of the lodge and stopped in front of the south position and made a circle. Here they made another circuit of the lodge and stopped at the east end and made a circle. Then they made the last circuit of the lodge and stopped in front of the north band and made a circle. By this time all the songs that they were to use had been sung. The leader now made four circuits and brought the gourds, drum, tobacco, etc., in front of the south band. All now took their seats and when they were seated the leader of the south band arose and spoke as follows:

"Councilors, life-obtainers, I greet you. You who sit in the first seat, you who sit in the north, and you who sit in the west, I greet. Children of the night-blessed ones who are seated within this lodge, I greet you all. It is good that to-night you have tried to imitate your grandfathers, that you have tried to take the place of the spirits. You have said enough with which to obtain life. But I am more unfortunate. I can never do what my ancestors did or say what they said, and for that reason I suppose my talk will be quite worthless. I was told that if at any time I should be pitied, not to talk foolishly about this ceremony. If I am a bad man I will act foolishly in this affair, I was told.

"My grandfather was blessed by those whom we call the night-soldiers, who blessed him with certain utterances. As many black-birds as there are, that many appeared to him as Night Spirits. Our utterances will be an imitation of those he received when he was blessed. We can only guess at these.

"We were told that when we hold the mediators we will be strengthened by them. Night-blessed spirits who are seated here, I greet you."

Then he began the starting songs, and when these were finished he rose and spoke again.

"Councilors, life-obtainers, I greet your seats. You who sit in the east, you who sit in the north, and you who sit in the west, I greet you all. Children of the night-blessed ones, I greet you. Those whom we call night-soldiers treated their sisters as holy and placed them in front. In imitation of these soldiers we will now put our sisters in front, so that we may be strengthened thereby. I wish to announce that we now place the women at the head of our procession. Let us all come together, so that we may be strengthened. That is our desire and that is what we are pleading for. I greet you."

When they are ready to begin the dancing songs all rise and form in line, having the women lead them. Then the men with the gourds, their backs turned to the women, follow, then the drummers. Then all those join who feel so inclined. When they have finished all the songs they intend to use they bring back the drum, gourd, etc., to the middle of the lodge and stop dancing. Then they return to their seats and then the leader rises and says:

"Councilors, relatives who are seated here, I greet you. You who are seated in the first seat, you who sit in the north, and you who sit in the west, night-blest ones who are within this lodge, I greet you all. Whenever a night-blessed child holds council, when he is invited to a feast and is given the position at the end of the road, the intention of the feast-giver is to enable him to obtain life. So they told me, and that is what they meant. Most assuredly have they caused me to think of life. When I hold the mediators in my hand I am holding life, and when I pass them on to the others, to my relatives and to my sisters, I am passing on life to all of them. In this way were we made to think of life. I will not detain you any longer. All that I wish to say is that I am thankful. Children of the night-blessed ones, I greet you."

Then he sat down and the host rose and spoke as follows:

"You who sit in the east, you who sit in the north, you who sit in the west, and you who sit at the end of the road, I greet you all. It is good. This is what I wanted but have not been able to say. You, however, told it all in my place. It is good. Of all things this is the foremost, it is said. The instruments with which to ask life you have placed before me. That alone is enough to live on and that you have done for me. It is good. Your forefathers dreamed just as the spirits did, and how they obtained life, all of that you have told me to-night. It is good. You have said enough to obtain life. It is good. I say this because I am thankful. If you do anything, do it in the right way, I was told. I understand this ceremony, but nevertheless what I have done is the best I could do. I will now place the food before you. I am an old man, but I have always performed this affair just as I have performed it to-day, and, although I know that I have not done it in the right way, yet it was my turn to do it, and I did it. I am an old man, and for that reason I am not able to procure meat anywhere. My relatives helped me and that is why I have been able to do it. Here are four kettles of hot water. I will place them in the center of the lodge for you. The one in the east and the one in the north and the one in the west and the one at the end of the road; each one may have it. Children of the night-blessed ones, all who are seated here, to all do I send greeting."

Then the leader of the east band rose and said: "Councilors, I greet you. You who sit over there in the north, you who sit in the west, and you who sit at the end of the road, I greet you all. Children of the night-blessed ones who are in this lodge, I greet you. We are all to arise soon and that is why I announce this."

Then the leader of the north band rose and said: "We also will rise, as it is our turn. We greet you all."

Then the leader of the west band rose and said: "The time has come for us to rise. I and my relatives will now rise. We greet you all."

Then the leader of the south band rose and said: "Councilors, I greet you. I greet all who have been blessed by the Night Spirits, each one in turn. We are now going to rise."

Then the leader of the east band said again: "Councilors, I greet you. We will now greet the hot water and I will use a song."

Then the leader of the north band said: "I also will start a song. I greet you."

Then the leader of the west band said: "I also will start a song. I greet you."

Then the leader of the south band said: "I also will start a song. I greet you."

Then the leader of the east band sang a song, and the other leaders sang their songs. Each band sang its own songs, not paying any attention to the songs of the others. Each band sang different songs. This they do in order to drown the voices of the others. Should one band overcome the other, it means that that particular band would be blessed with victory in war. What they were really saying is that their songs were more powerful than the others, and that their grandfathers' songs were the holiest. Then they all danced around the lodge, single file, and made their exit from the lodge. While they were dancing, the host sat still singing and beating his drum. They carry their kettles outside. Wherever they wish to eat, there they go and dance around the kettle of food first. Then they eat their meal. They dance in different bands.

The ceremony finishes with this feast. It is customary, however, for the one who has been given the seat of honor, that is, the east seat, to give a feast immediately afterwards. Then the one who has been invited first would do the same thing, so that all four would in this manner give dances in rotation. For this reason it generally took five nights before the ceremony was over. During those five nights no one could sleep. It is from this fact that the word, "Sore-eye Dance," which is the general term used for this ceremony, originated. If a person does not sleep for five nights, his eyes generally get sore, and that is why they call this ceremony the "Sore-eye Dance."

Sometimes they perform night-spirit tricks. These would be of the following nature: A kettle is put on to boil and some individual fishes out a piece of meat bare-handed without getting burned. At other times they shoot a hole into a drum covering, using a wild-cat claw as a missile. Then they immediately mend it.

When a man is very bad they shoot him with an object and kill him. They used to be very much afraid of such people. Sometimes they take a handful of live coals and embers from the fire, put them into their mouth and then spit them out without getting burned. It is for this reason that they are called holy. Sometimes they take burnt portions of a tree that had been struck by lightning, put them in the fire, and then when they are red hot take them out again and put them in their mouths without extinguishing them. They then spit them out, and it would look like lightning. Or they would shoot one another with cold charcoal. This is all that I know.

Once a medicine-dance man and a night-blessed man became jealous and the medicine-dance man said that he would play tricks on the night-blessed man. The night-blessed man said he was quite willing to have a contest. So the two came and sat opposite each other and began their contest. Whatever the medicine-dance man did the night-blessed man did too, but always a little better. The medicine-dance man was defeated, so from that time on the medicine-dance men are afraid of the former. The medicine-dance men shot the night-blessed men with claws, but they could not kill them. Therefore they were afraid of them. The night-blessed men could kill the medicine-dance men at pleasure. The medicine-dance men were inferior. That is all.

Society of Those Who Have Been Blessed By the Herok'a

Informant, member of the Bear clan: The feast of those who have been blessed by the Herok'a is given at any time of the year. Anyone may be invited. The feast is held in a long lodge and is generally given by a number of members at the same time (or by all). Each person brings a deer and his bow and arrows. The bows and arrows are painted different colors, depending upon the color (paint) with which the individual has been blessed. The bows are all stuck in the ground between the first two fireplaces and the arrows in a row just behind them.

During the ceremony and feast the members all sing the songs with which they have been blessed. The ceremony is held before the feast and is conducted by one of the members of the society. He leads, holding a bow in one hand. The others follow, holding arrows in their hands. Only men are permitted to dance. There are certain songs, to the accompaniment of which women are permitted to dance. But the women must have passed their climacteric.

They do not use gourd rattles as at the other dances. Instead a number of deer hoofs are strung together and used in place of them. (They do not eat with their hands or with the ordinary sticks) but use instead forked sticks, whittled down at one end. The leader wears a headdress to which a horn is attached, and paints his body with the same color as his arrows. Whoever leads the dance carries a flute, which he plays before and after each song. Those following him hit their mouth with the palm of their hands and whoop.

When the dance is over, each one of the feasters takes his plate and dances out.[17]

---

[17] This account of the Herok'a Society is unfortunately merely fragmentary, but from a few additional notes obtained there seems to be little doubt that it rePresents the same type of organization as the other religious fraternities.

SOCIETY OF THOSE WHO HAVE BEEN BLESSED BY THE BUFFALO SPIRITS

Informant, member of the Bear clan: "Come, it is the time for giving the Buffalo Feast," said my father, "so tell the attendants to get ready; and you, third-born, if you see anyone, tell him about the feast that we are going to give."

So I went to Fire-starter and said, "Nephew, my father is about to give a feast, and he wants his attendants to get ready. You are to go over to his lodge and get a few more attendants to help you. We also will get ready right away." Then I greeted him and he said, "All right, I will go and get some to help me." I returned to my father and told him what I had done. He told me to go and inform those who were to take part in the feast that they were to bring food. This I likewise did and returned with the information that they would all do as desired.

Now the attendants arrived and asked what was expected of them. They were told to haul the wood and cut the poles to be used in building the lodge, prepare the fireplaces, and put the kettles on the fire. After that they were to go and tell the young women to get the food ready. When the drum was fixed and the food prepared, then the feast would begin, they were told.

"Well, Green-hair, my nephew, it is about time for you to go down toward the timber and invite the people. You, my nephew, Fire-starter, may go to those who possess war bundles and invite them. Go especially to Strikes-the-earth-with-his-wings and tell him that he must come immediately. When you come back, Green-hair, get the earth mound (*maⁿwarup'urura*) ready. Construct two of them in the lodge. Then place upon them all the things that we are going to use in the dance."

The drum, the flute, the buffalo tails, the buffalo heads were all painted and placed there.

Then the feasters arrived. He-who-strikes-with-his-wings was to sit opposite Fleet-one. When all had entered and were seated Hodja'noka arose and spoke:

"War-bundle owners, all you who have been blessed by the buffalo-spirits and are seated here, you who are taking the place of the spirits and giving counsel like them, I thank you and greet you all. You are taking the place of the spirits. Just as we ask for long life from the spirits, so do we ask the same of you. Relatives, I know I am going to tire you all out, but do not take it amiss. What we long for, aid us in obtaining. Life is what I wish.

"What I am doing now I did not originate, for my ancestor Hodja'noka was the one blessed by the buffalo-spirits. When he was a child he was blessed by them and they gave him a certain plant and blessed him with long life and with victorious warpaths. He asked to be remembered by Hodja'noka in his offerings. The buffalo-spirit told him that if he would pour tobacco for him, and give feasts and make offerings of eagle feathers, the blessings he had given him would last forever.

"All these blessings were handed down to my father. These I also was taught. This life do we pray for and we have asked you all to come and help us. We thank you for it. As soon as the attendants are finished with the preparation of the food then we will eat. Our servants may perhaps burn their hands while preparing the food, but they will obtain life by so doing. Those who possess war bundles are always told to help one another and I know that you have come here for that reason. Life I am seeking and that is why I am giving this feast. Help me, all you owners of bundles who are present here. I will now sing some of the songs that Hodja'noka taught us. You who have obtained blessings, I greet you."

Then he sang the following songs:

Song 1

Naŋgura homa'ni hiwiiê. (Repeat.)
In the road walk let him do.

Song 2

Hodja'noka hamani'winê. (Repeat.)
Hodjanoka Walk by.

Song 3

Kâra Hodja'noka hamani'winê.
Say, ·Hodjanoka Walk by.

Dancing song

Hodja'noka tcawawi're. (Repeat.)
Hodjanoka go toward.
Erehu'na.. (Repeat twice.) Wiga'rê. (Repeat twice.)
It is coming   say to them.

As soon as Hodja'noka finished his songs, then all the objects (drum, gourds, etc.) were passed to He-who-strikes-the-earth-with-his-wings, and he rose and spoke:

"Brother-in-law, councilors, relatives, all who are seated here, I greet you. You who have been blessed with bundles, I greet likewise. You are taking the place of the spirits. It is good. We are trying to encourage one another and we have come to help you. We have brought you food for the feast. We also are desirous of obtaining long life and that is why we have brought our offerings, for we know the buffalo-spirits will accept them, as they are very tempting. You who are taking the place of the spirits, I greet you."

Then he sings some songs and dances and passes the drum, etc., to the next guest and so it, in turn, is passed on until the fourth invited guest is reached. Then the drum is replaced in the center of the lodge.[18]

Informant, unknown clan:[19] Buffalo feasts are given in spring, in fall, and in midwinter. No meat is offered, but only vegetables. The buffaloes said that maple sugar is their favorite food, so when this feast is given they always have some maple sugar along with the other things. The buffalo feast always takes place in a long lodge. The attendants make the lodge and boil all the food. When the kettles have been placed on the fire those giving the feast enter. The earth mound is now constructed and tobacco offered to it. All those giving the feast pour tobacco on the earth mound, asking for victory in war. When this is finished they sing buffalo songs, starting with the initial songs. When they are ready to sing the dancing songs the feast-giver rises and speaks as follows:

"The dancing songs that we are about to sing we use because we believe that our offering will thus be accepted. It is generally the custom to do this."

He now calls on some one to lead in the dance. This individual is always taken from the Buffalo clan. He comes forward, placing the buffalo head on his own head and carrying the buffalo tail attached to himself. He leads in all the dances, the others following him. A plate of maple sugar is placed at the buffalo mound. When he approaches the buffalo mound he makes a noise like a buffalo, sticks his tongue to the plate of sugar, and licks up some of it. Those following do the same. This they do without even holding the dish, just as buffaloes eat. When they finish their dancing they pass the drum on to another person, and when it has made the circuit of the lodge they eat. Each person has his own dish. Then the leader in the dance is told that the dish of wild rice standing in the center of the lodge is meant for him, and that he can invite whomsoever he likes to help him. When all in the lodge are ready they start eating all at the same time. When those in the center of the lodge get through and the dish is empty it is thrown over their heads, and they do not stop this until the dish has been turned upside down. While they are engaged in doing this they bellow like buffaloes. They are not allowed to use their hands in turning the dish over. They must do it with their heads, for it is a sacred thing and that is the way the buffaloes used to do it. When they are all through eating the feast-giver sings a dancing song and all those within the lodge rise, take their plates, and dance out of the lodge.

---

[18] In this account it is not quite clear whether the drum is merely passed to the four principal guests or to all. At the buffalo dance witnessed by the writer in the summer of 1908 it was passed only to the four principal guests. This was also corroborated by a number of informants.

[19] The origin myth of this feast is given on page 195.

Description of buffalo dance and its origin.—Informant, member of Bear clan: The buffalo dance can be given by anybody who has been blessed by the buffalo spirits. In the beginning the Winnebago had animal forms, and they could obtain all the power they wanted, but since they left that stage of life they can obtain power only by fasting. John's buffalo feast is of recent origin. It originated with his grandfather.

A long lodge is prepared and in the center there is a pile of loose dirt. John's grandfather's name was Hodjanaga, Young-man-just-maturing. In fasting he found out that he was blessed with powers to cure the sick and be victorious in battle. While fasting, the spirits told him that he would receive what he was longing for. They told him that he would know what to do, for they would come after him. Soon they came after him and took him into camp (i. e., spirit country). When he got there, he saw an old man and a child, and he was told that it was on account of the child that he had been brought there; that the child had heard his prayers while fasting and had blessed him. Then they showed him a certain herb and told him, "This is what we give you. It will give you strength in running. Use it in time of war, and use it also as medicine for life. I have blessed you and given you what you desired and do you, in turn, make me a dog feast and give me red feathers, tobacco, and food." Then they taught him the songs and gave him a buffalo tail and a flute.

No invitation sticks are used. They go around and invite those whom they want.

When the grasses are well developed, then the Buffalo clan people make a feast to their life or clan; also in midwinter, for that is the time when all the spirits awaken from their night's sleep and turn over on the other side.

SOCIETY OF THOSE WHO HAVE BEEN BLESSED BY THE GRIZZLY BEAR

Informant, member of Bear clan: The grizzly-bear dance was given by those who had been blessed during their fasting by the grizzly bear. Women were never so blessed, and for that reason they never could participate in the dance. Different people received different blessings. We were blessed with two grizzly-bear heads, grizzly-bear hides, and paws. In the lodge constructed for the dance was placed a mound of earth called ma^{n}warap'uru. The ma^{n}warap'uru is supposed to represent a bear's cave, the four points of the cross representing the entrances to the cave and the four lines running to the center, the paths along which the grizzly bear travels when he scents a man. The place in the middle is supposed to be the habitation of the bear himself. Tobacco and red feathers are placed both in the center and at the four points. Only people who had been blessed by the grizzly bear were permitted to sing and dance. The dancing itself took place both around the lodge and around the maⁿwarapʻuru. The dancers are supposed to imitate the motions and the cries of the grizzly bear. Sometimes they whirl themselves round and round, like a grizzly bear, but their principal motion consists in stretching out their hands. In this position they will take tobacco from the maⁿwarapʻuru and eat it. They believe that they are representing the bears when they do this.

The dancers are selected by the one giving the dance. Those taking part vie with each other in exhibiting the powers with which they have been blessed, because in this way those present could see who possessed the greatest powers.

The purpose of the dance was to thank the grizzly bears for the blessings they had bestowed upon the people. (However, there seemed to be many other special occasions for which the dance was performed.)

If sick people are present at the dance they are told to put some tobacco on the maⁿwarapʻuru and ask for life.

There is a description of the grizzly-bear dance in the account of Little Priest's life which it might be well to append here in view of the brevity of the above description.

"Little Priest had been wounded in so many places that he was practically dead. He was, of course, entirely unconscious when his relatives arrived. They decided to perform the grizzly-bear dance for him. He himself had been blessed by the grizzly bears when he was young.

"The dance was to be given at the lodge of an Indian named Good Soldier. They carried Little Priest to the lodge in a blanket, so that they could sing for him and permit him to show the powers he possessed. He was unable to move on account of the wounds and the bruises he had gotten. The man who sang for him at that time was South-Wind. There were all in all ten Indians, entirely naked, except for their breechclouts. Little Priest had told South-Wind that he was a grizzly bear and that he could heal himself (no matter how badly he had been wounded).

"As soon as the songs and dancing commenced Little Priest began to move his little fingers. Soon he was able to move his arm as far as his forearm, and gradually he regained the power of moving the entire arm. Finally he sat up and began to keep time on the drum. Then he tried to stand on his feet, but owing to his weakness it was only with the greatest difficulty that he could straighten out his body. Finally he stood erect. Then he started to walk around the lodge very slowly. The second circuit he made more easily, and by the time he had made the fourth circuit he was dancing just as the other dançers were with all his strength restored. Then he walked to the ma^{n}warup‘uru, took some earth, rubbed it on his wounds, and they were healed immediately. There was only one wound that he could not heal, which was situated on a part of his back that he could not reach with his hands.''

He sang many songs while dancing. These songs were the ones that the spirits had taught him when they blessed him.

GRIZZLY BEAR SONGS

1

Newine′na newine′na ha^{n}ptca^{n}nê.
I am he, I am he, the day it is I.

2

Ha′na^{n}niŋxgu^{n}ne‵k‘tce hiniŋgai′rê nink‘tca′i^{n}niŋkᴇʀa djanûŋga′grê.
That you would be listened to you were told by the children as many as there are.

3

Ma^{n}tcō′ja^{n} ho′dadjehi‵rera.
The grizzly bear was starting to roam.

4

Wa′wonatca^{n}t$^{\epsilon}$i^{n} nihe′ka.
Shouting you can hear him.
Ho′ratca^{n}t$^{\epsilon}$i^{n} nihe′ka.
His voice you can hear.

CHAPTER XIV

THE MEDICINE DANCE

(Pls. 49, 50)

ORIGIN MYTH

What it was our father sat on when he came to consciousness is uncertain. Then his tears flowed and he began to cry. Not long did he think. He saw nothing and nothing was there anywhere. He took something from the seat on which he was sitting and made a portion of our earth.

Then he sent the earth below him. From where he sat and as he looked at his own creation, it became similar to our earth. However, nothing grew upon it and it was entirely without a covering. It had not become quiet but was spinning around.

Suddenly he thought, "If I do this, it will become quiet." Then he made a covering (hair) for it. He took a weed from his seat to make grass for the earth and earthward he sent it. That he did and then looked at his own creation. It was not quiet but still kept on turning. "This way I will do again," he thought. He took a tree and toward the earth he sent it and again looked at his creation, but still it kept spinning around. Then he sent four men, brothers, and placed one in the east, one in the west, one in the south, and one in the north, and again looked at his creation. It was, however, still spinning around. "Perhaps it will become quiet in the following way," he thought. So he made four of what are called water-spirits and below the earth he placed them, and for that reason they are called island-weights. Then he scattered a female spirit over the earth, by which stones are meant. Finally he looked at his creation and he saw that the earth had become quiet.

He had sent the stones clear through the earth, throughout its extent, and only the heads remained uncovered. He looked at his creation and saw that it had become quiet. No clouds appeared anywhere, the light of day appearing motionless, and the vibrations of heat seemed to be like spider webs going past, floating.

All the birds that were to roam over the sky, all the quadrupeds that were to be on this earth and those called subterranean animals, he placed in houses that he had made for them and scattered here and there. Then he made all those insects that were destined to live on the earth. Finally, at the end of his thinking he made us,

PLATE 49

a. EXTERIOR OF MEDICINE DANCE LODGE

b. INTERIOR OF MEDICINE DANCE LODGE

PLATE 50

a. EXTERIOR OF MEDICINE DANCE LODGE

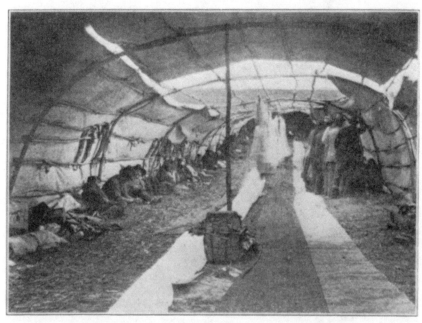

b. INTERIOR OF MEDICINE DANCE LODGE

the human beings. However, we were not even equal in strength to a fly. We were the weakest of all. Then he looked at what he had created and he liked it and sat filled with happy thoughts.

He was proud of us and gazed again on what he had created. He had, however, not made the human beings equal in strength to the others and they were on the point of being destroyed. Then he formed a human being, like ourselves, and when he had finished him, he named him the Foolish-One. "Foolish-One, to the earth you are to go. Weakly (pitiable), in every respect, I made the human beings. I made them as my last thought. Now this creation of mine, they, the evil spirits, are likely to injure, so do you, O Foolish-One, go and put things in order."

Then he sent him to the earth, but when he came on earth he did not do what he had been told. He went around the earth and accomplished nothing. (As useless) as a child crawling on all fours he was. He really amounted to nothing. Though sent by Earthmaker, he amounted to nothing. He did no good and injured the creation of Earthmaker, so Earthmaker took him back and had him sit at the right of his own seat.

Then he made another (man) and when he was finished called him the Turtle. "The two-legged walkers (human beings) whom I created as the last of my thoughts, (evil spirits) are about to exterminate Do you go and put the earth in order." Turtle went and (took along) a knife that he had been given. When he came on earth he led people on the warpath, but he did not look after the (welfare) of (Earthmaker's) creation. Earthmaker therefore took back the second man, too, and placed him on his left side.

Then he made a third (man), and when he finished him, he named him Bladder, and said, "You are to go to the earth. As my last thought, I created the two-legged walkers and they were pitiful in every way. They are now about to be exterminated and you are to rescue them. Try with all your strength."

When he came on earth he made a long lodge and created twenty men. That many younger brothers he had. Then they all started to go around this entire island and all the younger brothers were killed. Thus he failed in his mission. The work his father had sent him to do, he failed in, so (Earthmaker) took him back and placed him on his left side.

Then he made a fourth (man) and when he finished he named him He-who-wears-human-heads-as-earrings.

Then he made the last one, Hare, his body just like ours. "You are the last one I am going to create, so try with all your strength, Hare, try." He-who-wears-human-heads-as-earrings, the fourth one, failed. He therefore took him back. Hare was the last that Earthmaker, our father, wished to create. He (had created) him entirely by the force of his thoughts.

"Hare, what I am doing, you also will be able to accomplish. Try with all your power. If (the evil spirits) injure my creation, it will not be good on earth, life will not be good." Thus he encouraged him; thus he spoke to him. "Try and overcome these (evil spirits)."

So Hare was sent to the earth, and when he came on earth he said to himself, "My brothers acted in a (certain) way and failed." Hare had come up to a certain oval lodge and from this (same) house came a young woman with a little pail. She was going toward the river. "Now they (Foolish-One, etc.), were not able to do (what I am going to do)," he said. There he entered the body of the young woman in order to become a human being. There he sat in the abdomen (of the young woman), yet he heard their (human being's) cry.

He heard them crying. "My father sent me to give them advice, and here, for so very long a time, I have been sitting." Crying, shrieking, he heard them (the human beings). "So long have I been sitting here that (the evil spirits) will in the end destroy them." Seven months had he been waiting when he spoke thus. Finally, when the proper time had elapsed, he went out through an opening. Not four days after, the woman died.

He always left the house in which they lived, at night, and would roam around. Whenever he walked inside the house he would reflect much light. As soon as daylight appeared he became quiet, it is said. As soon as the sun went down, he went out. He traveled all around the earth, for its entire extent, and just before sunrise returned and became quiet. Throughout the day he sat thinking of all the work he was to do.

For the third time he again started out, at sunset, and traveled over half the extent of the earth, and all the bad spirits that were growing wild he put an end to. "Not again will they (the bad spirits) live; not for a second time will they kill any of my uncles or aunts." Just before daylight appeared, he went toward the house, and as he approached it, his heart felt good. Then he entered the house and all day he sat there wrapped in thought.

When the sun went down he went out and over to the very edge of the earth, as large as it is, he roamed, and all the bad spirits that exist he killed. Just about daylight he went up into the heavens and bang! he pursued all the bad birds that were living there and driving them together in the west, he killed them all. Very early in the morning he went to the house thinking pleasant thoughts. "The work my father sent me to do I have accomplished. The life of my uncles and aunts will now be like mine, from now on." Thus he thought as he entered the house.

"Well, Grandmother, the work my father sent me to do, I have accomplished. He sent me to look after his creation and all that I have accomplished. My uncles' and aunts' lives will hereafter be the same as my own." "But, Grandson, how can your uncles' lives be the same as yours? It is not so. The (world) is as our father created it. Not different can it be made." "The old woman must be related to them and therefore does not like it that I killed (the evil spirits)." "No, Grandson, our father has ordained thay my body (the earth) should fall in two. Lest they should cause a shortage in food (by overpopulation) he ordained that there should be death, otherwise they would crowd each other too much on earth. So, therefore, he arranged that they have a place to die."

Hare didn't like it. "Surely, Grandmother does not like it because she was related to them. She is taking their (evil spirits) part." Thus he thought. "No, Grandson, that is not so. Your heart, at present, feels sore. Your uncles and aunts will obtain enough of life; they will live to a normal old age," she told him. "Now, Grandson, get up. Your uncles and aunts will follow you. Try with all your strength (to do what I am going to tell you). You are a man, so do not look back."

Around (the earth) they started. "Not to look back," grandmother said. "I wonder why she said it." Thus he thought. So he looked back just the least bit to his left. The place he had started from caved in instantaneously. "O my! O my! A man I thought you were, a person of prominence, and I had encouraged you very much. But now, Grandson, decay, death can, in no way, be taken back." That is what she meant, it is said.

Around (the earth) they went and to the edge of the fire (that encircles the earth) they traveled, it is said. They united it (the fire) so that they (the uncles and aunts) would attain old age, so she said.

"To look back, she forbade me. But I have already made up my mind (as to the immortality of my uncles and aunts). When they become like me, then only will I be happy. Such is my thought." Then he went out and there, where the sun rises, to the east, he went and entered the house. Opposite the occupants he sat himself. What he had come for (the occupants) knew, it is said, "Well, Hare, there is nothing I can say to you. If the one ahead has anything he wishes to say to you, he will undoubtedly do so." Then he (Hare) greeted him and went out.

Toward the west he traveled. Even then not any (other) thought he had. "I can do it," he thought on the way. When he arrived at the house he entered and sat himself opposite the (occupant). "Hare, what you have come for, I know, I believe, but I will not tell you anything. The one ahead, he it is that can tell you, he it is." So he (Hare) saluted him and went out.

Toward the house of the fourth one, in the south, he went and entered, and sat himself opposite (the occupant). "Hare, what you have come for, I know, but if even those ahead could not say anything to you, how can I, the very last, say anything?"

Then he saluted him and went out in the same way that he went in. He started for his house and came there crying, it is said. "My aunts and uncles must not die!" "To all things death will come," he thought. Then he cast his thoughts upon the precipices and they began to fall, to crumble. Upon the rocks he cast his thoughts and they crumbled. Under the earth he cast his thoughts and all beings that were living under the earth stopped moving and their limbs stiffened (in death).

Up above also he cast his thoughts and the birds began to fall down (dead).

Then when he entered the house he took his blanket and wrapping himself in it, lay down crying, it is said. "Not the entire earth will suffice for us," he thought, "and in some places there will not even be enough earth."

After a while the news reached our father. "To utterly destroy us they will try" (the people were saying). That Hare was not feeling well, was the news that reached him. Then he (Earthmaker) said to the first man he had created, "Hare is not feeling well and you are to go after him." Toward the earth he came. "Hare, I have come here to fetch you." But he did not answer him and he did not even move his blanket. So the man (Foolish-One) returned. Then he (Earthmaker) said to the second one, "Hare you are to go after and bring him back here. Try very hard to (accomplish) it, for he is not feeling well." When he arrived there (he said), "Hare, I have come after you to take you back." But Hare did not even (answer). When he returned, he said, "Hare did not say anything." (Then to the third one he said), "Hare you are to go after, for he is not feeling well." When he came (to where Hare was, he said), "Hare, I have come after you, to take you home." But Hare did not even answer him. Hare was indeed not feeling well.

Then he (Earthmaker) told the fourth one, "You are to go after Hare. Be sure and bring him. Be sure and bring him. Try with all your strength." "No matter how hard it is, I will bring him" (said the fourth one). He started out and when he came to Hare (he said), "Indeed, for a very long time has your heart been sad, Hare. But let us go home now. Get up!" Then he took him back, it is said, to Earthmaker he took him. But not to Earthmaker's house did he take him, but to that opposite where the chief of the Thunderbirds lived. At his side, there they placed him. In front of the Thunderbird chief's (house) there was a mound and also a little war club painted red on one side. Thunderbird chief took the little war club and holding it lightly, shook it gently. So great was the noise (it made) that Hare got frightened and almost ran out, it is said. Then they freed him from the sad thoughts he had had on earth and restored his spirits.

Soon after that they took him to Earthmaker and (when) he had come there (Earthmaker said), "Hare, your heart must have been very sad. Indeed, for your uncles it was, that your heart felt sad. Now that their lives may be benefited, a holy teaching you are to take back to them. "Here, look at it," he said, and pointed toward the south. There a long lodge stood (revealed). At this he looked and there were old people with hair all white. "Thus your uncles and aunts will be. They will make very much noise (in this ceremony). Now look down! Some help is to be given them. Not one bad spirit will I put there." Then he (Earthmaker) pointed in that direction and said, "You are to go back there (to earth) and put this (ceremony) before them. Not alone are you to do it, but with the aid of your own friends, Foolish-One, Turtle, Bladder, and He-who-wears-heads-as-earrings." These he meant. "Your grandmother (the earth) will help you and if one of your uncles and aunts performs everything properly he will have more than one life. I will always keep the door (through which he may return to earth) open to him. When he becomes reincarnated he can live wherever he wishes. He can return (to the earth) as a human being or he can join the different bands of spirits, or finally he can become (a being) below the earth." All this he (Earthmaker) did for us.

Then Hare returned to the earth and to his grandmother. "What I have tried to obtain for my uncles and aunts, that now I have brought back with me." "Grandson, how was it possible for you to make them immortal like ourselves? As the world was created, so must it remain." "Grandmother, I say that my uncles will choose their lives for themselves, and grandmother, you are to help me." "All right, grandson, it is good," she said, thanking him. "When the time comes, my friend the Foolish-One will come," he thought. Then he struck his drum and started the songs. All of a sudden, Foolish-One came in. "That you would come, my friend, I thought, and thus you have come." "Indeed, my friend, I knew your thoughts and, for that reason, I came." Then they went out together and outside of the village they sat and discussed what they were to do. This is what they were doing. All day they discussed on the outskirts of the village. When they came to the house they entered it and sat down. "My friend Turtle will come," he (Hare) thought. Then Turtle did come. "My friend, I knew you would come, and for that reason, you have come." "Yes, indeed, your thought I knew, and for that reason I have come." Soon Bladder came. He (Hare) thought he would come and for that reason he came. Then Hare centered his thoughts on He-who-wears-heads-as-earrings, and he also came.

Their grandmother listened to them quietly, but she could not understand them. Then (after a while) Hare said, "Grandmother, what I have been trying to obtain for my uncles I have succeeded (in accomplishing). You are now going to hear of it. Come here toward the fireplace and sit down and you will hear of it. (I know) that you are anxious to help them, Grandmother." "Indeed, grandson, it is good," she said, and got up. Then she took her work and sat down near the five of them and laid her hands upon their heads. In front of her nephew, Hare, she placed her work. "If you get this for them (i. e., the medicine dance) your uncles will live well. This way they are to do forever," she said. In front of him she put her work and said, "For this thing, indeed, I thank our father." Thus she said and went back and sat down. "Grandson, what the nature of my help for you was to be, you asked? Well, look at me, grandson. For your uncles and your aunts, our father had me bring the following. I have for them that with which they will always be able to ask for life." Then she opened that part of her body where her heart was situated and very green leaves were to be seen, like an ear in shape. It was as white as a blossom. Then she opened her breast on the right side and said, "Grandson, look at me." Then unexpectedly corn was visible. "For your uncles and aunts, our father let me bring corn." A stalk became visible whose leaves were very green and whose tassels were white. These were the ears of corn that we were to eat.

Then the five of them got up and Hare said, "Our grandmother, let us greet." So they walked up and laid their hands upon her head. Then they greeted her and went around again. "It is good, grandmother, this is what I meant when I said you were to help them. You were going to help us, grandmother," I said. "You may now fix your breast."

Then he went out, proceeding toward the east, and when he got there he stopped. Then he turned toward the west. Grandmother closed her breast and entered the house. "Well, grandson, I have done it." "It is good, grandmother," said Hare. Then he went out, and when he got to the door he stopped there and thought, "This is the way it will be." And where he stood, eight yellow female snakes he threw. They became the side-poles of the lodge. Their heads he turned toward the east, and their tails he turned toward the west. The strings he used with which to tie them were rattlesnakes. The doorway was made of a black female and a male snake, the latter placed at the right. At the rear end of the house, in the west, he also made doors of blue female snakes. Then he took a reed-grass, which he had brought with him, under whose covering we were to live, and threw it over the lodge and the lodge was wrapped in it entirely. Then he took another piece of reed-grass and inside the house, at the right side, he threw it and it became white mats spread out. Then he threw a bear-skin hide in the house on the right side, and it extended along the length of the lodge. Then he made a white deer-hide extend along the entire length of the lodge, on the right side. A door he made of a real living mountain lion. This he did in order to prevent bad spirits from entering. At the door, on the west side, he placed a buffalo bull, and when this all was completed, he looked inside the lodge and then he heard these animals bellowing and roaring, it is said. Inside of the lodge, it was light.

Then he started for the lodge, first going for his friends. "Well, my friends, I am through; the house I have finished. Grandmother, stand up, for we are going to follow." He walked behind and when they came to the door, the fear-inspiring lion snapped his teeth, as he stood there. Then they went in and walked around the lodge until they came to the place where they had entered and they sat down. Then Hare sent a number of public criers, a bear and a wolf, to traverse the entire length of the earth. Along with them were sent the winged messengers, the common crow and the shrieking crow.

When the animals that had started first returned, their bodies were old and devoid of hair, and they supported themselves on staffs. When the birds who had gone returned, their wings were worn out, their eyebrows lapped over their eyes, and they looked very old indeed. They came in front of Hare's seat and said to him, "Your uncles and aunts, when they speak of you, will speak of you forever in praise. We have placed many life-giving objects within the lodge." "Well, my friends, it is good. This is what I meant. I thank you in the name of my uncles and aunts."

Then all the messengers who had been above on the earth, etc., all of them came. The four very first men he had created also came. They all stood at the door ready to enter. The oldest one started in, but he turned back, being afraid of the animals within. Three of them were afraid and therefore failed to enter. Then the youngest opened the door for them and led them in. After he entered, they, in turn, walked around the lodge, and when they got to the door, Hare placed the eldest one there and said, "My elder brother, this is your seat, the east one." Then he walked around again and at the north end he stopped and made the second one sit down. Then he walked around and, stopping in the west, made the third one sit there. Then, finally, he put the fourth one in the south seat, and went to his own seat and sat down.

Now all the other spirits began to enter the lodge. Then the first people came in and four were made to sit in the east and four were made to sit with each of the four seats. The people were of the

Bird clan, the Bear clan, the Wolf clan, and the Snake clan. The fourth one was the one they were to teach, to initiate.

Then Hare got up and spoke as follows: "My friends, I have had you come together, for my uncles and aunts had been living a most pitiable life. You are to teach them the life they are to live and which they are to hand down from generation to generation. That is what I ask of you. What I want, you have heard. I leave everything to be done and said by those in the east."

Then he, the one in the east, arose and spoke, "Our friends, the uncles and aunts of the Hare, we are to teach the meaning of life, so that they may hand it down from one generation to the other. Only today, for the first time, have we discussed this thing for them. Life (all that life consists of—wealth, honor, and happiness) they shall have from now on." The four of them said, "What the one ahead said (we say)." When they finished, they returned.

Now Hare got up again and said, "My friends, that is what I wished for my uncles and aunts. This council-lodge I made for them, and as long as they follow the precepts taught in the creation-lodge they will be invulnerable. For that reason this seat has been made for them, that whosoever desires may sit therein."

All day long the spirits taught him, and when the sun was on the treetops, when it was time to stop, the spirits dispersed, taking with them as they went half the light within the lodge. They rubbed against the door-poles as they went out. They pushed them in deeply so they would not fall.

Then Hare spoke, "Grandmother, I will be sitting ready for any one of my uncles and aunts who will perform this ceremony that we have taught them well. With tears my uncles and aunts will come to me and my heart will feel sore. I will go above and sit down and if any person performs this ceremony that we taught him well, then he will be as I am, if you will but look at me, grandmother. Look at my body, grandmother." And behold, like a very small boy he was. "If any one repeats what we have done here, this is the way he will appear."

"Look at me," Hare said for the second time; "Look at me!" There he stood a full-grown man. Then, for the third time, he said, "Grandmother, look at me." There he stood a man in middle age; his hair was interspersed half-and-half with gray. Then she looked at him for the fourth time, and his hair was covered as if by a swan (i. e., it was all white), and he leaned tremblingly on his staff, standing in the east. "Well, grandmother, if any of my uncles and aunts performs this ceremony properly this way they will live."

"It is good, grandson. However, not only your uncles but your aunts, likewise, will be that way if any of the latter performs the ceremony properly. "Look at me," she said, and when he looked at her, there stood a very young woman, her hair like a shawl. "It is good, grandmother, and I thank you in the name of my aunts. Then for the second time she said, "Look at me." He looked at her and there stood a woman in middle age, her hair almost gray. "Well, grandmother, it is good, that is what I meant." Then for the fourth time she said, "Grandson, look at me." He looked at her. Her hair was entirely dried up, in the nape of her neck there was a hollow, and like a duck looking at the sun, she appeared. Her chin, like a wooden poker, burnt short, there she stood trembling. "Well, grandmother, this is what I meant when I said that you were to help me. My uncles and aunts that is what I wished for them, and I thank you."

ORGANIZATION OF THE BANDS

The medicine dance of the Winnebago consists of five bands. A sixth band is temporarily formed whenever the ceremony is given in honor of a deceased member.

For purposes of description it will be best to divide each band into three parts—the leader, his two assistants, and the rest of the band. Leadership depends upon a thorough knowledge of the ceremony and its complete esoteric significance, which is in the possession of only a few individuals in each band. This knowledge can be obtained solely by purchase and religious qualifications. These religious qualifications, to which might be added moral as well, play little part at the present day, but there can be no doubt that they were essential in the past. The leader likewise often possessed other characteristics, such as those of warrior and shaman.

The two assistants were generally men who had purchased sufficient information and privileges to entitle them to help the leader in certain details of the ceremony. The drummers, rattle holders, dancers, etc., were always recruited from their ranks. Eventually they might become the leaders. Those who were neither leaders nor assistants possessed a knowledge varying from that of elementary information, required for admission, to that entitling them to the position of assistant.

There is a priority of position in the lodge, depending on priority of invitation. The band invited first occupies the east position; that invited second, the north; that invited third, the west; and that invited fourth, the south. The east is the position of highest honor; the south, that of the lowest. Between the bands there exists an order of invitation based on tradition, the exact nature of which is unknown. According to one informant, if one band invited another, the latter in turn would be obliged to give it the position of honor; but as there are five bands, this can apply only to special cases. Whatever may be the order, it is certain that each band has ample occasion to occupy all five positions.

There are two ways in which a man can join the medicine dance. He may simply apply for admission to any of the five leaders, or he may take the place of a deceased relative. In the former case, if his payment is satisfactory, and he has the other qualifications, he is accepted. In the other case, his relatives decide to have him take the place of a deceased relative. This latter form of candidacy is by far the more common. At the present day initiation requires the payment of about $300 or $400, in the form of goods and tobacco. Of this, a portion is given to the leader of the ancestor host's band during the four nights' preparation, and the rest to the leaders of the other four bands during the ceremony proper.

Exactly how much information an individual obtains on entering can not be determined. Much depends on the amount of the payment. The minimum knowledge would amount to an acquaintance with the bare externals of the ceremony, its general significance, and such knowledge of the legendary origin of the lodge as a single recital could give. The new member is not initiated into the symbolism of the ritualistic myths, and consequently a large portion of the same must be unintelligible to him. What he obtains is practically only the right to hold the otter-skin bag and to use it in a certain way. He may not take part in any of the forms of dancing or singing, nor may he even shoot at will. He very rarely remains in this condition long, but takes the first opportunity to purchase additional knowledge and privileges.

There are three kinds of members—mature men, women, and children. The privileges of women differ from those of the men, in that the women do not have to take the sweat bath, may never become assistants, and are allowed to dance only in a certain way. In other respects they have the same privileges as men. In practice there are certain privileges that women never have, but this is due to the fact that either they do not care for them or they are not in a position to buy them. Children belong to a quite different category. Although they possess an otter skin, they have not even the power of making it effective. There does not seem to be any evidence indicating that women were ever excluded from membership.

Prescribed duties of the bands.—The duties of the host, called the ancestor-host, are as follows:

1. To rehearse the songs and rituals with his band four nights previous to the ceremony proper. At this rehearsal the candidate is always present and is instructed in the ceremony.

2. To send out invitation sticks and tobacco to the leaders of the other four bands. The messengers are always his sisters' sons.

3. To begin the four nights' ceremony preceding the ceremony proper.

4. To receive the leaders and assistants of the other four bands before the sweat-lodge ritual, and to begin the same.

5. To begin the ceremony proper.

6. To take part in the main portion of the ceremony proper:

(a) To welcome the four bands.

(b) To lead the candidate to the secret brush and instruct him in certain precepts.

(c) To act as preceptor of the candidate before he is shot with the sacred shell.

(d) To turn the candidate over to the charge of the leaders of the east and north bands.

(e) To relate certain of the myths.

(f) To deliver specific speeches and to perform the actions that constitute the basic ritual of the ceremony proper. This will be discussed later.

The east is known as Those-who-sit-first, Where-the-day-comes-from, Where-the-sun-rises. All these terms are used frequently. The duties of the leader are:

1. To assist the ancestor host in passing upon the eligibility of a candidate.

2. To take part in the following portions of the ceremony proper:

(a) Accompanied by his two assistants, to take part in the brush ritual.

(b) To take charge of the candidate after he has been handed over to him by the ancestor host.

(c) To shoot the sacred shell into the candidate's body.

(d) To relate certain of the myths.

(e) To perform the basic ritual.

The north band is known as Where-the-cold-comes-from. The leader has the same duties as those of the east leader. The myths recited are of course different.

The west band is known as Where-the-sun-goes-down. The leader has the duty of reciting certain myths and performing the basic ritual.

The south band is known as He-who-sits-at-the-end-of-the-road or Where-the-sun-straightens. The duties of the leader are the same as those of the leader of the west band, except that the myths he recites are different.

The distribution of the gifts to the different bands is as follows: The leader of the east band receives one-half of the number of blankets, the upper half of the new suit worn by the candidate, and one-quarter of the food.

The leader of the north band receives one-half of the blankets, the lower half of the suit, the moccasins, and one-quarter of the food.

The leaders of the west and south bands receive each 3½ yards of calico and a fourth of the food.

The ancestor host receives various gifts of food and tobacco from the leaders of the other bands. He receives his payment from the candidate before the ceremony proper.

The candidate is present at the four nights' ceremony of the ancestor host's band, preliminary to the ceremony proper. At the latter ceremony he sits to the right of the ancestor host's band. He is not dressed in his new suit until after the secret ceremonies in the brush.

There are facial decorations distinctive of the different bands: The host's band and the candidate paint a blue circle on each cheek, but its significance is unknown to the writer.

The regalia used are simple and few. They consist of eagle, hawk, squirrel, beaver, and otter-skin bags (pls. 51–53), a drum, gourd rattles, and invitation sticks. The otter-skin bags are always beaded and contain the sacred shell and various medicines. A few red feathers are always inserted in the mouth of the otter-skin bag. The gourds contain buckshot at the present time and are painted with blue finger marks.

Division of the ceremony.—The medicine dance is divided into five well-marked parts. The first part (I) consists of the two nights' preparation preceding the sending out of the invitation sticks. This takes place at the home of the ancestor host in the presence of the members of his band and the candidate. The second part (II) consists of the four nights' preparation preceding the sweat-lodge ritual. Each band has its own four nights' preparation, although that of the ancestor host begins before the others. The third part (III) consists of the rites held in a sweat lodge, specially constructed for this purpose near the medicine lodge, on the morning after the four nights' preparation. The participants are the ancestor host, the leaders of the east, west, north, and south bands, each with his two assistants, and the candidate. The fourth part (IV) consists of the ceremony proper, which in turn must be divided into the night ceremony (*a*) and the day ceremony (*b*). The fifth part (V) consists of the rites held in the brush, at which the secrets of the society are imparted to the candidate. Special guards are placed on all sides of the brush to prevent the intrusion of outsiders. The participants, besides the candidate, are the ancestor host, the leaders of the east and north bands, each with his two assistants, and all other individuals who have bought the privilege of attending. These ceremonies take place at dawn preceding the day ceremony.

Two feasts and one intermission interrupt the main ceremony. The feasts always take place at the end of the ritual of the east band—i. e., generally at noon and at midnight. The intermission

PLATE 51

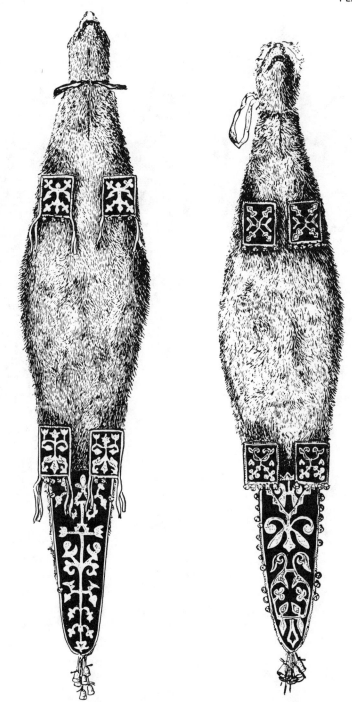

OTTER-SKIN MEDICINE POUCHES USED AT MEDICINE DANCE

PLATE 52

POUCHES OF ANIMAL SKINS USED AT MEDICINE DANCE

PLATE 53

SKIN POUCHES AND FEATHER FANS USED AT MEDICINE DANCE

generally lasts from dawn preceding the day ceremony until 7 or 8 a. m. The intermission begins as soon as the drum and gourds have been returned to the ancestor host and ends as soon as the people return from the brush ritual.

The first and second parts are concerned entirely with a recital of certain ritualistic myths and a rehearsal of the songs and the specific ritual of each band used during the remaining parts.

Types and component elements of the ceremony.—For purposes of greater clarity, the speeches, songs, and types of action will be carefully differentiated and referred to by some designation characterizing their essential traits. These speeches, songs, and types of action together form combinations which may be regarded as units, and they will therefore also be referred to by some designation characteristic of their function.

1. Types of speeches—(1) Salutations: No formal salutation is used during Parts I and II, the individuals being addressed by their relationship terms. In Parts III, IV and V the salutations are invariably the same. The ancestor host and his band are addressed as follows: "The-one-occupying-the-seat-of-a-relative (deceased) and you-who-sit-with-him, do I salute." The east is addressed, "You-who-represent-the-place-where-the-sun-rises"; the north, "You-who-represent-the-place-where-the-cold-comes-from"; the west, "You-who-represent-the-place-where-the-sun-straightens," or (preferably) "You-who-represent-the-end-of-the-road."

The appellations of the bands, as before stated, refer to the creation myth and the four guardian spirits whom Hare visited for the purpose of inquiring into the necessity and meaning of death. Hare was compelled to travel around the earth, which is conceived of as an island, and received no answer until he came to the spirit at the end of the road. In the dramatic performance of the medicine dance the lodge typifies the earth and the four bands and their leaders typify the four spirits. The ancestor host's band typifies the ancestor of the Winnebago.

(2) Speeches: Under this head will be treated (*a*) speeches of welcome; (*b*) speeches of acceptation; (*c*) speeches of presentation; (*d*) speeches explanatory of the significance of the ritual; and (*e*) speeches of admonition, addressed exclusively to the candidate. This does not exhaust all. There are many others, generally short, that can hardly be classified. In their content, as well as in the order of their succession, the speeches must follow a traditionally determined sequence. In practice this is certainly not always true, but to the mind of the Winnebago these speeches appear as old as the ceremony. It is their firm belief that any departure from the accepted type will interfere with the efficacy of the ceremony.

(a) Speeches of welcome: When the leader of the east band enters after the ancestor host has begun the ceremony (IV, b), he addresses the latter as follows: "It was good of you to condescend to invite me to this dance. I am a poor pitiable man and you believed me to be a medicine man. However, I know you will show me the true manner of living, which I thought I possessed, but which I in reality did not." In this strain he continues, weaving into his speech references to the ritual connected with his band and offering thanks for the beautiful weather (should it be a clear day). In concluding he thanks all again, and informs them that he will sing a song. With slight alterations the leaders of the other bands address the ancestor host similarly. The ancestor host's answer of welcome is as follows: "Whatever I desired you have done for me. All night have you stayed with me and by your presence helped me in the proper performance of this ceremony. I am ready with a dancing song, and when I have finished and sit down I shall pass to you tobacco and other means of blessing (the gourds and the drum). All who are present do I greet."

(b) Speeches of acceptation: After the ancestor host has been presented with food he thanks the donors as follows: "You have had pity on me. You have been good to me and have given me to the full whatever I desired. You have filled my heart with the blessing of thankfulness. In return I give you a blessing. Here is some food for you. It is not anything special, nor is it as much as it ought to be, and I know you will remain hungry. It was prepared for the spirits of the four quarters (whom you represent), but it is lacking in all those qualities which would have made it acceptable to them. Such as it is, however, may its presentation be a means of blessing to you."

(c) Speech of presentation: East presents the food to the ancestor host with the following words: "I have not very much to tell you, because I am too poor, but our ancestors told us to give you food. This little that I give is all that I can, being a person of so little importance."

(d) Explanatory speeches: These are of so specific a nature that no single one can be considered typical.

(e) Speeches of admonition: "Nephew, now I shall tell you the path you must walk, the life you must lead. This is the life Hare obtained for us. This is the only kind of life—this that our ancestors followed. Listen to me. If you will always help yourself, then you will attain to the right life. Never do anything wrong. Never steal, never tell an untruth, and never fight. If you meet a woman on the left side of the road, turn to the right. Never accost her nor speak familiarly with a person whom you are not permitted thus to address. If you do all these things, then you will be acting correctly. This is what I desire of you."

2. Types of songs: The songs may be divided into two groups—
(1) Those that are sung in connection with myths and after the
speeches of a more general nature, and (2) those that are sung to
accompany definite and specific actions. These latter can therefore
be most conveniently divided into (a) minor dance songs, (b) major
dance songs, (c) initial songs, (d) terminal songs, (e) loading songs,
and (f) shooting songs. The medicine men distinguish only between
four kinds of songs—major and minor dance, terminal, and shooting
songs. Each has a different rhythm and music. For purposes of
description, however, the above division is more convenient.

3. Types of action—(1) Blessing: Either hand is held outstretched,
palm downward, and moved horizontally through the air. It is
always used when entering and leaving the lodge and on any occasion
where an individual has to pass from one part of the lodge to another.

It is always rendered as "blessing" by the Indians, and they particularly insist upon the fact that the "blessing" was not conveyed
by any words used in connection with the action, but by the action
itself. Each person who is thus passed answers with a long-drawn-
out "ho—o—o" and with an obeisance of the head.

A modification of the above is the "blessing of the head," which
consists of a simple laying of the hand upon the head, both the giver
and the recipient keeping their eyes fixed upon the ground, the recipient slightly bending his head. A few mumbled words accompany
this action.

(2) Direction of walking in the lodge: Individuals always walk contrary to the hands of the clock. A person in the east band must
make the entire circuit of the lodge in order to pass out. In only
exceptional cases can this rule of passing be broken, and that is when
an old and especially privileged member crosses from his seat to that
directly opposite him during the shooting ceremony. I was given to
understand that this was an extremely expensive privilege.

4. Types of ritual: Parts III, IV, and V can be so analyzed that
they fall into a fairly well-defined number of units, consisting of
speeches, songs, and movements. These units are nine in number.
Artificial distinctions have been avoided in this division, as far as
possible. The units are (1) entrance ritual; (2) exit ritual; (3) fire
ritual; (4) presentation-of-food ritual; (5) shooting ritual; (6) initiation ritual; (7) sweat-lodge ritual; (8) smoking ritual; (9) basic ritual.

Of these, (3), (5), (7), (8), and (9) are found in Part III; all except
(7) and (6) in Part IV (a); and all except (7) in Part IV (b). (5)
does not actually occur in Part III, but is described in detail in the
myth related there. The order in which we will discuss these ceremonial units is not the order in which they follow one another
in the ritual. Some are interwoven with one another. Both these
factors will, however, be considered in the description of the entire
ritual, following the description of each ceremonial unit.

(1) Entrance ritual: The band enters the tent, makes one complete circuit, and stops. The leader now delivers a short speech, followed by a song. The band then continues to the west end, where another speech is delivered and another song sung. After this the band continues again, and stops at the east end, where the leader talks and sings. Now all sit down. After a short pause the leader again rises and walking over to the ancestor host, talks to him, gives him some tobacco, and returns to his seat. Each band entering repeats the same ritual. This applies, however, only to Part IV (a) and (b).

(2) Exit ritual (Part IV (a) and (b)): The east leader rises and speaks, followed by north, west, and south. Each one then speaks again and, all singing, all walk toward the entrance in such a way that the south, north, and west bands make complete circuits of the lodge, thus enabling the east band to precede them. Near the entrance all stop singing and say *"wa-hi-hi-hi"* four times and pass out. This exit ceremony differs slightly in the two divisions of IV.

(3) Fire ritual, Part III: The ancestor host rises and goes to the leaders of the four other bands individually; and after he has blessed them they respond; then all rise, make four circuits of the lodge, and sit down again. The leader of the east band now rises, holding in his hand the invitation sticks and some tobacco, delivers a speech, then goes to the fireplace and kindles the new fire.

(8) Smoking ritual: The leader of the east band pours tobacco into the fire, first at the east, and then at the north, west, and south corners. He then lights his pipe, puffs first toward the east, then toward the north, west, and south, after which he passes his pipe to the leader of the north band, who takes a few whiffs and in turn passes it around to the next member of the lodge. When the pipe has made the complete circuit it is placed in front of the fireplace. In the meantime the ancestor host has returned to his seat, and after a short pause, rises, speaks, and sings again. This smoking ceremony occurs after each entrance ceremony, IV (a) and (b), and before both feasts of IV (a) and (b).

Presentation-of-food ritual (Part IV, a and b).—The leader of the east band rises and brings meat, berries, wild potatoes, etc., to the ancestor host, delivering a minor speech at the same time. Each of the other leaders repeats the same ceremony. When all have finished, the ancestor host rises and thanks them.

(5) General shooting ritual (Part IV, a and b): The leaders of the east, north, west, and south bands, holding their otter skins in their hands, rise and, accompanied by three men, make a complete circuit of the lodge. They first speak in undertones to these three men, giving them directions. At each end the leader of the east band speaks, and then, singing, walks toward the west end, saying "yoho—

o—oya—a" three times, and ending with a long-drawn-out "*yo—ho.*" At the west end both he and the leader of the south band speak. Then chanting "*yo—ho*" again, they all walk toward the east end. Here the leader of the east band speaks twice. All now place their otter skins on the ground in front of them, and east speaks again. At the conclusion of his speech, all kneel in front of the otter skins and cough, at which the sacred shell drops from their mouths upon the otter skins. They thereupon pick it up, and holding the shell in one hand and the otter skins in the other, make a circuit of the lodge four times, increasing their speed each time, and singing. All this time the shell is held in full view of the spectators, on the outstretched palm of the right hand. As they near the east end of the lodge, at the end of the fourth circuit, standing in front of the ancestor host's band, they supposedly swallow the shell, and fall down, instantaneously, head foremost, as if dead. Finally they come to, and coughing up the shell they put it into their otter-skin bags, and then making the circuit of the tent, shoot four members of the ancestor host's band, four of the east, four of the north, two of the west, and two of the south band. Each person as he is shot falls prostrate upon the ground, but recovering after a few moments, joins those making the circuit of the tent. Each leader now takes his drum and gourds to the fireplace. Then the general shooting commences. Each person possessing the right shoots one individual, until all the members have been shot. As each person is shot he falls to the ground, feigns unconsciousness, and then slowly recovers. The slowness or speed of his recovery depends exclusively upon the privileges he possesses and the number of years he has belonged to the society. As soon as each person shot recovers he falls in line immediately after the last one shot. While all are thus walking around a half dozen people at the fireplace sing shooting songs to the accompaniment of drums and gourds. The amount of noise at this point is quite considerable.

(6) Initiation ritual (Part IV, *b*): All the members of the ancestor host's band and the candidate make one circuit of the lodge, taking their otter skins with them. As they pass around they gently touch the heads of the members with the mouth of the otter skin, saying "*Yoho—o—o*", to which the members respond with "*Ho—o—o.*" After the circuit, all return to their seats, with the exception of the candidate, who remains at the east end in front of the fireplace. After a pause the ancestor host joins the latter and delivers a speech of the admonition type. The candidate first faces the south and then the north. During the speech the ancestor host touches him on his head and on his chest and makes him face first south and then north. When the speech is over the ancestor host sings and takes the candidate to the west end of the tent.

The tent is now prepared for the initiation proper. Two lŏng strips of calico are stretched from the west to the east end of the lodge. They are about a foot and a half wide and are separated from each other by the fireplace. At the west end a much shorter strip of the same material is stretched along the width of the lodge across the two long strips. Upon this the candidate is placed. When these preparations are completed the ancestor host arises and going to each of the four leaders speaks to them in an undertone. He then returns to his seat. The leaders of the east and north bands now arise and make the complete circuit of the lodge. First the former and then the latter speaks. Then the former speaks twice. After that the leader of the north band delivers another speech and, together with his partner, walks to the west end of the lodge, where the candidate is kneeling. The two leaders here speak again. Both now take their sacred shells, swallow them, and walk to the east end (pls. 52, 53).

Here they speak again and hold their otter skins in readiness for the shooting, but first jerk them forward twice toward the four cardinal points, saying "*dje-ha-hi, dje-ha-hi*," and concluding with "*e-ho-ho-ho*." Standing upon the two calico strips in a slightly bent position and holding the otter skin tightly in their hands, they now run rapidly toward the reclining form of the candidate, making loud threatening sounds in a quavering voice, and strike his body twice with the mouth of the otter skin, emitting two short sounds as of an animal who has succeeded in capturing his prey. The candidate falls prostrate to the ground instantaneously. He is immediately covered with a blanket upon which are placed the otter skins of the two leaders. A number of people especially privileged now gather around the covered figure, dance, sing, and shout to the accompaniment of the shouts of the other members of the society, all of whom seem in a frenzy of excitement. When the noise has somewhat abated the blanket is removed and the figure of the candidate is shown, still apparently unconscious. He comes to slowly and finally succeeds in raising himself and sitting up. He then coughs violently, and the shell which has apparently been shot through his body falls out of his mouth. After this his recovery is rapid. He is then undressed and the finery and new buckskin suit, moccasins, etc., are distributed to those to whom it is customary to give them. He now returns to his seat, to the right of the ancestor host's band, where some female relative, generally his mother, dresses him in an ordinary suit.

(7) Sweat-lodge ritual (Part III): The east leader rises and with his two assistants makes the circuit of the sweat lodge, while the north, west, and south leaders each with two assistants join him. At the east end the leader makes four steps with his right foot, each

time saying, "*Wa-hi-hi.*" He then makes the circuit of the lodge four times. After the third circuit he goes directly to the heating stone, "in defiance of the rule," as he himself says, but with the hope that through this defiance he will gain additional strength. After he has made the fourth circuit he seizes the two entrance lodge poles and, shaking them gently, shouts "*e-ho-ho-ho.*" All now sit down. The ancestor host now takes four sticks and smears them with a special kind of greenish clay and hands them to the leader of the east band. The latter seizes them and holds them tightly with both hands. By this action he is supposed to obtain strength. The sticks are then passed in rotation to the leaders of the north, west, and south bands, all of whom repeat the same ceremony.

(9) Basic ritual (Part IV, *a* and *b*): This ritual is that upon which the ritual for the ceremony proper (Part IV, *a* and *b*) is built. In a certain sense it may be justifiable to consider all the above ritualistic complexes with the exception of the entrance and exit rituals as parts of this basic ritual. The important religious function of the medicine dance is the "passing" of the blessing, consisting of speeches, songs, and the blessings, going from one band to the other, for the greater benefit of both the host and his guests. These blessings are symbolized by the drum, the gourds, the songs, the speeches, and the specific actions in which each band participates. The ceremony begins when the ancestor host delivers his first speech and ends when drum and gourds are returned to him. All that takes place between the ancestor host's first speech up to the time that the drum and gourds are pláced before the members of the east band constitutes the unit that I have called the basic ritual. Into it are thrust as intrusive elements other rituals, so that it is at times extremely difficult to discern the basic ritual itself. But it is there and remains intact, for as soon as an intrusive ritual is finished it is taken up and continued to the end. Such a ritual as the general shooting or the initiation, or such myths as the origin myth, require hours; and yet as soon as they are over the basic ceremony continues from the point where it has been interrupted.

The east leader rises, speaks, then sits down, and, together with the other members of his band, sings a song (initial song). When this is finished he rises and speaks again, sits down, and commences a song called the minor dancing song. While he and a few others are singing, drumming, and using the gourd rattles, other members of his band, as well as members of the other bands who so desire, and who have bought the privilege, come to his seat and join in the dancing. When this is over he and a few others, either from his own or from some other band, go to the fireplace, where the leader delivers a speech, and begin the major dancing songs, in which the privileged members participate. After this the drum is tied to one of the privileged members, generally the one who has been drumming, and the circuit is made twice, the leader and his two assistants at the head, followed by the other members of his band. Two stops are made at the west and two at the east end, where songs, called completion songs, are sung. Then the circuit is made four times, all chanting "*Wa-hi-hi*," slowly at first, then faster, the speed of the walking corresponding to that of the chanting. Then with a final strong "*e—ho—ho*" drum and gourds are deposited in front of the next band. All now return to their seats, where before sitting down the leaders deliver a short speech.

This basic ritual is repeated by each band in the manner described. As it is so often broken up by the intrusion of other rituals it will be best to divide it into four parts. These parts are never broken up. Whenever intrusive elements occur, they either precede or follow.

The first part consists of all that takes place between the first speech of the leader and the completion of the initial song. The speech referred to is the one that follows the smoking ritual, which may, on the whole, be reckoned as belonging to the introductory ritual, such as the entrance ritual. The second part consists of all that transpires between the second speech and the conclusion of the minor dancing song. The third part consists of all that happens between the speech at the fireplace and the completion of the major dancing songs. The fourth part includes everything between the completion of the major dancing songs and the last speech the leader makes, after he has passed the drum and gourds to the next band.

The most bewildering intrusion is that which follows the second part. Before the leader and his assistants go to the fireplace the elaborate general shooting ritual takes place. After the specially designated men of each band have been shot, those privileged proceed to the fireplace. Here they sing the shooting songs until the ritual is over. The first set of drummers and gourd rattle holders are often relieved by a second set. It is only when the shooting songs have been completed that the leader and his assistants proceed to the fireplace to begin the third portion of the basic ritual.

Ceremony as a whole: As stated before, there are certain speeches and types of action that can not be fitted into the above description. This is especially true of myths; and these, with the exception of the content of the myth, will now be considered in connection with the description of the entire ritual as related to me by B. The ceremony begins with an account of the manner in which B. was induced to join the society. Upon his acceptance and payment of the required amount of material, the ceremony began.

The first two nights consisted of an informal salutation, two explanatory speeches, and four myths, the latter in no way connected with any part of the medicine dance. The last three myths dealt with the legendary account of the origin of the Winnebago medicine dance and its dissemination among the tribes.

At sunset the leader of the band to which the candidate has applied for admission gathers together the members of his band and all retire to a little lodge near his home, in order to begin the four nights' preparation. What actually takes place during these four nights is not as stereotyped as the other rituals connected with the medicine dance. There is a general rehearsal of songs, speeches, and other elements of the ceremony. The speeches are not actually rehearsals of those to be delivered during the ceremony proper, but refer to the purpose of the medicine dance much in the same way as do some of the speeches in the ceremony proper. A large number of miscellaneous myths are likewise related. The candidate who is present in the lodge of his future ancestor host is likewise instructed in as many things as an uninitiated member is allowed to know. This instruction consists in the teaching of certain myths and types of action.

On the morning after the last of the four nights the candidate is given some sacrifical tobacco and told to go in search of a stone for the sweat bath. He selects a stone that he can carry on his back easily. Before picking it up he pours tobacco on it. As soon as the stone is brought to the lodge of the host it is heated. The candidate is now dispatched for some oak branches, four pieces of oak wood about 2½ feet in length, and some grass. The grass is used for improvised seats; the oak wood for the four construction poles of the sweat lodge. They are placed in the east, north, west, and south points, respectively. It is not permitted to trim the tops of the oak wood. When all the bands have gathered near the medicine lodge and retired to their improvised lodges, the ancestor host and the candidate go to the lodge of the east leader, that is, to the lodge of the band first invited, and greet him by touching his head with their hands.

He answers with "*Ho—o—o.*" The leader of the first band rises and, accompanied by his two assistants, goes to the sweat lodge. The ancestor host then goes to the lodges of the other bands and greets the leaders in a similar manner. After the leader and assistants of the band last invited have entered the sweat lodge the ancestor host, the candidate, and his assistants enter, and the ceremony is begun.

After the ceremonial salutation and an introductory speech the ancestor host, as the leader of the band giving the medicine dance may now be called, rises, and taking his invitation stick and some tobacco, approaches the leader of each band, and blessing him, thanks him for coming, assuring him at the same time to how great a degree his presence will contribute toward the success of the performance of the ritual. He then returns to his seat. The leaders thank him in turn. Now follow the fire and smoking ritual, which in turn are followed by twelve speeches of a general and explanatory character. Then comes the "strengthening" ritual, and immediately after two exceedingly long myths, describing the initiation of the first man into the secrets of the lodge, as well as the symbolic meaning of the shooting ritual. All now undress and take a sweat bath. Female candidates are excluded. A number of short speeches follow, and the whole concludes with the exit ritual.

The drum and gourds are used to accompany the songs. The basic ritual is perhaps present to a certain extent. The writer, however, was not permitted to witness the ritual, and for this reason the procedure seemed somewhat hazy to him.

When the ritual and the sweat baths are over there is a slight pause. The candidate, the ancestor host, and his band enter the medicine lodge, and after taking their seats sing a few songs. When the last song is concluded the other bands enter in the order of their invitation. Now comes the entrance ritual, followed by the smoking ritual. Thereupon the ancestor host rises and delivers the opening speech of the basic ritual. The ancestor host does not go through the entire basic ritual at this time, because he is not permitted to begin the shooting ritual. Soon after the beginning of the basic ritual by the ancestor host, generally after the second speech, gourds and drums are passed to the leader of the east band. This one rises and begins the basic ritual, which he interrupts at the end of the second part, in order to begin the general shooting ritual. When that is finished he continues the third and fourth parts of the basic ritual. Then drum and gourds are passed to the north band. Its leader now in turn begins his basic ritual, but stops after the second part, where the presentation-of-food and the smoking rituals intervene. It is now about midnight, and the feast is given. As soon as the feast is finished and the lodge has been cleared of food and eating utensils, the leader of the north band continues up to the third and fourth parts of the basic ritual. The leaders of the west and south bands perform the basic rituals without any interruption, except, of course, that of the general shooting ritual between the second and third parts. The drum and gourds have now reached the ancestor host, who goes through the third and fourth parts of the basic ritual. There is, however, some doubt as to whether this is always done. Then follows the exit ritual and all pass out to rest for a few hours.

A short time preceding dawn the candidate and the leaders of the east and north bands and the ancestor host, each with two assistants and all other members who are privileged to do so, leave the lodge and walk to the brush where the candidate is to be initiated into the mysteries of the sacred shell and the shooting. Each band must have one or more of its members present at this ritual. When they are near the place set aside for the secret ritual the order of marching, which up to this time has been of no consequence, changes into that of single file, the leader of the east band leading. When they have arrived at the proper place, all stop. The east leader now informs those present that he is going to make a road for the candidate symbolical of the path of life, which forms the basis of the sweat bath and medicine dance. Singing, he circles the spot four times. At the end of the fourth circuit he stops and all turn around and face east. The leader of the north band has also the right to go through this ritual, but he does not always do it. Repeating the ceremony is, in all probability, connected with extra expense. All now sit down and the specific rites of the brush ritual begin.

The ancestor host rises and, taking the candidate with him, goes to the leader of the east band and speaks to him. Then he and the candidate return to their seats. The east leader now relates to the candidate a portion of the story of the journey to the land of the spirits and to the lodge of Earthmaker. When this is finished the two leaders teach the candidate how to go through the actions incidental to the shooting, the swallowing of the shell, and the recovery from its effects. When they think that he is sufficiently adept in all these actions they dress him in his new suit, put on a new pair of moccasins, decorate him with finery, and return to the medicine lodge.

The rites generally last until about 8 in the morning, so that when those who have participated in the brush ritual are returning the other members of the medicine dance are also about ready to begin the day ceremony, the principal one of the entire medicine dance. The ancestor host again precedes the other leaders in entering the lodge. Then follows the entrance ritual. During this ritual the drum is struck four times at stated intervals. The smoking ritual now follows. When it is concluded the ancestor host rises to begin the basic ritual, which is interrupted at the end of the second part. Gourds and drum are passed to the east band, whose basic ritual is also interrupted at the end of the second part. Now follows first the initiation of the candidate into the medicine dance and then the general shooting ritual. When the east leader has concluded, drum and gourds are passed to the north band, whose basic ritual is not interrupted as on the preceding day. At the conclusion of the basic ritual of the north band the food-presentation ritual follows, then the smoking ritual, and finally the feast. After the feast the leader of the west band narrates the origin myth of the medicine dance, which is continued by the leader of the south band. The presents are then distributed. After this, the basic ritual is continued by the leader of the west band, followed by that of the south band, and finally the drum and gourds go to the fireplace. The exit ritual now begins, and at about sunset the entire ceremony of the medicine dance is over.

On the whole, it must be said that the main difference between (a) and (b) of Part IV, setting aside the initiation, lies simply in the number of myths told and the greater length of the speeches.

Personal Accounts of Initiation

1. J. B.'s account: I was about 13 years and over when they told me that they would make me a member of the medicine dance. I liked it very much. Some people do not like it at all when they are asked to join the medicine dance. I, however, liked it very much. The medicine dance I am going to join, they told me. Very much did my parents desire me to do it. If I wished to live a holy life, that is what I should do, they told me.

Then, when everything was in readiness for my initiation, we moved on to the village where the ceremony was to take place. At night they were to sing at the medicine dance, and they, my relatives, were to join in the singing with them. There they also preached to me. They told me that this rite, the medicine dance, was a good thing. I did not even then think that those who were to initiate me into the medicine dance would kill me when they shot at me, as was the popular belief.

Never had there been such a life, they said, as the one I was going to live, now that I was about to join the medicine dance. Never at any time would I have thought of such a life. Those who were about to make me join the medicine dance told me that the Indians, when they hear of it, will expect me to do great things, that they will speak well of me, and like me. That is all I can now think of concerning that matter.

Now, those who are about to make me join the medicine dance are preparing to show me the shells, and for this purpose they are taking me into the brush. There they, the elders, preached to me. I was not the least bit frightened when, after this, they prepared to shoot me with the sacred shell. Indeed, I was not the least bit worried about it, nor did I think to myself, "I wonder how it is going to be?" Then those who already belonged to the medicine dance, those whom I had dreamed of all this time, shot me. When they shot me I didn't die. That thought was in my mind; but when they shot me, as a matter of fact, I didn't even lose consciousness. Almost immediately I knew how to do it (i. e., to shoot). They liked it very much. Everything they told me to do I did immediately, nor was I backward about anything. The shaman liked it. Never had anyone learned as quickly as I had, they were saying. "That augurs well for him," they say. I thought then that the medicine dance was true.

When we returned from the brush I entered the lodge. Not in any direction did I look, not once did I speak, not once did I move around, not once did I change my position. Just as they told me to sit, that way I remained sitting. As many Indians as were gathered in the lodge, all of them, I failed to notice. Not once did I, by chance, permit my glance to wander from side to side. I was doing everything exactly as I was told. The shaman liked it.

Whenever thereafter a medicine dance was given I attended it. Whenever I went in at night I remained there until it was all over, not going out once. And during the day ceremony not once did I permit my glance to wander outside. Never did I permit myself to lie down from fatigue; nor did I permit my glances to wander outside, because there was much noise there, or because some people were doing funny things. Not even within the lodge did I glance. Indeed, I never allowed my glances to wander in any direction. All the holy things I was told to do, I did. This is a holy ceremony, and I was bashful in its presence.

If at any time any of my leaders in the medicine dance wished to give the ceremony I would stay in his house together with those who had been invited. I would do all the work for him, sing the medicine dance songs, etc. All the different things he was supposed to do, all that I would do for him.

When his wife cooked, I carried the water for her, I made the fire, and helped her with the dishes. All the work she liked to have done in the house, I did for her.

All the clothes I possessed I gave to him. Money I gave to him, and the food he needed I procured for him. Whenever he gave a feast, in addition to what he cooked, I would put a special pail of food on the fire for him. When he ate it he was thankful.

"My son, what do you think I possess, that you are doing all this for me?" But I continued; and when I killed a medium-sized buck I made a feast in his honor, and all the clothing he needed, I gave him. Then I also gave him a costly repeating rifle, the one I used in hunting. All these things I offered him. Then I gave him an eagle, so that he could make a medicine pouch out of it. Money I also gave him, and gourds. Thus I acted, feasting him and offering him gifts all the time. I worked for him all the time.

One day he said to me, "My son, you have been treating me very well. Even my own brothers never treated me the way you have been doing. I thank you. All my relations hate you, but don't pay any attention to them. You are from a different family and I am teaching you various things (that belong to them), they say. They want me to stop instructing you. My father left the medicine dance for me to take care of. I am in complete control of it. Not one of these people, my kindred, has ever done anything for me in their lives. My ancestors said that you are my relative for what you have done. I can not teach my relatives the details of this ceremony, as I would have done had they acted correctly. My knowledge of this ceremony belongs to you, for you have paid for it. My remote ancestors told their descendants, as it has passed down from mouth to mouth to us, that whosoever pays careful attention to all that pertains to this ceremony, that whosoever has a good memory, he is the one to whom it should be taught. Thus they spoke.

"My son, you alone have been good to me," he said. "This ceremony you will learn. Our son, He-who-stands-on-a-cloud, and you have been kind to me. Both of you will live a long life. Never divide this ceremony in two. Never keep anything separate, but do, the two of you, counsel about everything. If one of you knows anything, tell it to the other. Two people are necessary to make the ceremony truly efficacious for either one. Never dislike one another.

"My younger brother, you are going to be a chief. No one else pays attention to this ceremony. You alone are doing it. If at any time I should leave your presence, when I am about to go I know that you, oh my son and brother, I will leave behind me, peacefully traveling along. Thus I will think as I am about to depart. Thus my ancestors told me."

Thus in trying to obtain information I made myself pitiable. I tried to be blessed. I performed all kinds of work. Even woman's work I did. Thus I kept myself in a pitiable condition, and for that reason my brother-in-law blessed me. He blessed me with the ceremony of his ancestors. He told it to no one else but to me; and if anyone else, at the present time, narrates the ceremony as told by our band, he is not telling you the truth. Up to the present time this ceremony was an Indian ceremony, and not a second time will I tell it to a member of the white race.

This ceremony molded me. I paid the most careful attention to it; I worshiped it in the best way I knew how. I was careful about everything in my life. I never drank. A holy life it was that I sought and most earnestly did I pray that I might live over again. That is what I yearned for. If I do everything that this ceremony enjoins upon me well, I will return to Earthmaker, they told me. This is what I wished. I was doing well as a medicine man and everyone loved me. This ceremony was made with love.

I knew all the songs. Indeed, the leader of the dance would make me sing the songs for him. As many medicine men as there were, they all liked me. I was not overbearing, but modestly did I comport myself right along. All the medicine men told me that I was doing very well, and they offered thanks in my behalf.

2. J. C.'s account of how he came to join the medicine dance: This is how it was. A grandmother of mine was the cause of it. She said that the Creator's son [21] was called the Hare; that he came on earth and brought life, she said. She said that whoever did this would live well, that their souls would always return to the place where the

---

[21] J. C. is a prominent member of the Peyote cult and, in common with other members of this cult, he has identified the Hare with Christ.

Creator sits. The first thing that they did to me was this: They took me to a lodge at night; there they talked and sang. Then the second night the tobacco bundles were made; then the great old medicine men were given tobacco. After this came the four nights' preparation. Then came the great medicine dance. Then they went after those that were going to join, one at a time. They, the medicine men, were repeating what the Hare had done. When the Hare came on earth he performed certain actions, and that is what they were repeating now. Hare had visited the different spirits, it is said, looking for a means of life, it is said. The old medicine men possessed the good tidings that Hare had brought to this earth. That is what the people desired of Hare, it is said.

When they entered, the first person to whom tobacco had been given, i. e., the one first invited, entered first. Then the others followed in turn. Then he talked; then the one who initiated me expressed his thanks, saying, "You medicine men, this affair the Hare has given you, you are repeating in order to bless us. For that reason you have come. We ask you to give to this person whom we are about to initiate the life you have obtained for us. We ask that the newly initiated one travel along that road."

Then the first person spoke, and after that they all ate. When he was through they heated a stone. After that they all entered in regular order and I was asked to go in with them. Thus I entered the sweat-bath lodge. When I was inside they told me that the stone which they had heated was a spirit. "The life that he brought I should ask for," they told me. After that we went out again.

At night we entered again. Then at about 2 o'clock they took me out to the brush. Not until then was I to learn what the medicine men really did. When we got to the brush they made me sit down and the man who was initiating me turned me over to the others. He said, "I turn him over to you. Whatever the elders have taught you, that we desire you to tell him." When he finished the first one began to talk, saying, "It is good that you are such a person. Earthmaker must have willed it so. In the olden times if a person wanted to join the medicine lodge he could not do it until he was quite old." Then he continued preaching to me. When Earthmaker first came into the world and what happened after that, how he created all things: that he told me. He told me that Earthmaker created four worlds, in each of which he placed men and women; that the heavens we see represent the last man he created and the earth we are living on the last woman he created. Then he told how *Herecgunina* was created. The story is as follows: Earthmaker created man, whom he wished to put at the head of the world, but he did not make one of his legs quite right. Then he threw him down to the earth because when Earthmaker made anything wrong he never did it over again. *Herecgunina* lived on earth from that time on, and it is said that he also created things. Indeed, it is said that he was almost the equal of the Earthmaker. He made the people very miserable. Then Earthmaker sent four of his sons (to save the people). Hare alone, of all the four, accomplished what he had been sent out for. All the rest failed. Hare obtained life for the people upon this earth.

Then the man told how the medicine lodge had been founded; how all the spirits upon the earth and all those under the earth and all those above the earth gathered together. They brought life with them. Then the medicine bags began to come. Fisrt came the eagle. He came from above. Next came the hawk, and then the squirrel, etc. The otter was the last one. Then the old man stopped talking to me and another person began to admonish me. He told me how I was to conduct myself. Then he spoke to me of the medicine-lodge road (i. e., of life) and what happens after life.

The first thing that I would meet on the road would be bad birds making a lot of noise. "Do not look at them," he told me. They would let fly at me bad-smelling saliva and phlegm, but I was not to turn around, he said. Then the road would become thickly covered with thorn bushes. It would seem almost impossible to untangle them. I was, however, not to pay any attention to them, he told me. On the road, fires would send their sparks toward me, but I was to pay no attention to them. After a while I would lose one of my relatives, but I was to keep right on. I was not to get angry nor to give up, and after a while the road would become thickly covered with poplars growing on each side. Then the hair on my temples would become gray. This is what would happen to me, he told me, if I paid close attention to this ceremony. After a while it would become foggy—i. e., my eyesight would grow dim. Then I would come to a hill, one of four hills. When I came to the last hill there I would see red cedar trees. This is what would happen to me if I paid close attention to this ceremony, he told me. My soul would return to Earthmaker and I would then be allowed to come back to this earth if I wanted to.

Then they gave me the object with which they shoot themselves— the shell. They shot me. After that they made me try to do it, and when I was able to shoot well, we all came back. It was now daylight. Now they put clothes on themselves and arose. Those who were initiating me then spread upon the ground the things which had been brought. Then the leader spoke. He told me that he would put me on the medicine-dance road. Then they sat me down there and shot me. Then the clothes that I had on were taken off and I was given other clothes. I was now told that I was standing on the medicine-dance road. After that they danced all day. In the evening they stopped. Now this is what I did; this is all I can say. I greet you, my friends.

CHAPTER XV

MISCELLANEOUS DANCES

The Hok'ixe're Dance

Informant, member of the Thunderbird clan: This is the way in which people used to bring scalps to one another. When a man returns from the warpath with a scalp he leaves it outside of the village and the warriors run out with their clubs and strike it and count coup (just as on the battlefield). As they count coup they call out their names Then they are told what ceremonial dress they are to wear. They then send a messenger to the person to whom the scalp is to be presented to tell him to select a pole (for the victory dance). He thanks them and says, "It is good." Then the warriors who are returning arrange themselves in a circle around this pole and dance around it. He who has obtained the first war honor leads.

The one to whom they present the scalp thanks the spirits who are in control of war powers and then raising his hand prays to the Sun. Then he sings a song and when that is finished sits down, beats the drum, and sings a dancing song, while the others dance.

Then the owner of the scalp, turning toward the spirits who are in control of war, gives the victory whoop four times. After each whoop all the other people in the lodge strike their mouths with their hands and yell. After the victory whoops have been given all dance the victory dance.

Then the man who has received the scalp lets his sisters, his aunts, and his nieces select the war presents which are always bestowed upon them. With these tied around their necks they dance. Toward evening they finish the victory dance and then all enter the (dancing) lodge. He to whom the scalp is given is the host and he sits down first. Then comes the donor and then in a row the four who have counted coup.

The ceremony begins with songs sung by the host. He first sings two war-bundle songs (*waruxa'p na*^{n}*wa*^{n}) and then two night songs (*ha*^{n}*he' na*^{n}*wa*^{n}). When these are finished the meal is eaten. Before eating, all the animal heads are placed in front of the donor of the scalp and he selects those men with whom he wishes to share them.

Then the host rises and says, "War-bundle owners who are seated here, I greet you all. Our warrior (the donor) will eat together with our grandfather, the scalp, who is standing in the center of the lodge. Place a plate for the scalp and bring it to that brave man." Then the brave warriors eat the head, and when that is finished the servants distribute meat and food to those present who have not taken part in the head eating. While they are eating the host blows on his flute and sings some songs until the eating is over. Then he rises and speaks again:

"All you who are present to give us counsel and who sit here in the place of others, I greet you. For the warriors who would counsel with us repeatedly and for the sacred speeches of our fathers do we ask. In this ceremony to-day we will select as many war-bundle owners as are present to eat together with our grandfather, who is standing in the center of our lodge (the scalp). And if they select me to eat with the scalp, poor and pitiable as I am, it would be good.

"Should sickness suddenly come upon a village all those who are sick may take part in this ceremony. For our grandfather, who stands in the middle of the lodge, is no weakling, and when they take hold of him they are obtaining supernatural powers, it is said. We are trying to trample upon the soul (*wanaŋxi'rak*) (of the scalp). If we trample upon it, all the goods of life that were still coming to him when he was killed will be transferred to us. As many as are going to take part in this dance to-night should try to make the soul of our grandfather (the scalp) more amenable to our prayers. So all you women and men see to it that you dance with all your strength. Do not take this matter lightly, for we obtain life thereby, we were told.

"Councilors of the different clans who are seated here with us, I greet you all."

Then they sang *hok'ixe're* songs and danced the *hok'ixe're* dance. All night they danced. They did not stop for a moment. Thus they tried to conquer the soul of their grandfather (scalp). They danced till early in the morning and then just as the sun appeared they carried the drum outside of the lodge to the victory post and danced the victory dance. As soon as the sun was high in the heavens they stopped. Then they went to sleep.

The second day.—Just before the sun was setting they all came and danced the victory dance again. Then the host got ready to furnish the meal again. All his female relatives who had received presents took charge of the preparation of the food, which the servants had previously obtained. As soon as the victory dance was over they entered the dancing lodge. Then the host spoke, and when he finished he sang four songs, and as soon as these were finished they all got ready to eat. Then the host said that he would give the heads of the animals to the donor and that the latter might select those warriors whom he wished to have as partners in the head eating. Then the donor selected his partners. The host then began to sing. The scalp was taken down from the post and placed in a dish near the door. The soul of the scalp still remained within it, so they tried again to make it less powerful and to conquer it, for they knew that if they succeeded in conquering it all the life that was still coming to the possessor of the scalp at his death would be obtained for themselves. Then the dancers and the feasters, indeed all who had counted coup, tried to obtain some of the dead enemy's residuary life. All tried to add some new life to their own.

When the meal was over, then the host offered tobacco to the spirits, and all those present prayed for war to the spirits to whom offerings had been made. They asked that if it be their good fortune to kill a number of people on the warpath, when they returned home they would be as thankful as they are now. All these warriors who were taking part in this dance liked it very much.

Then the host struck the drum that had been placed in front of him and sang. When he finished, he had the drum placed in front of the man who had counted first coup. Then this man sang and the drum was passed to the next man, and so on until each man had sung. After all had sung and spoken the men and women together danced around the lodge. The woman who had received the presents led the dance, carrying the scalp. The people believed that the scalp was dancing with them. All night they danced the *hok'-ixe're* dance without resting at any time, and when the sun appeared they took the drum outside to the post and danced the victory dance. Then when the sun was high in the heavens they stopped and went to sleep. In the evening when the sun was low they danced the victory dance again, and then when it was pretty dark, singing slow songs, they slowly entered the lodge again. Then they made a circuit of the lodge and placed the drum in the middle of the lodge.

The feast was now ready. All that they were to eat—deer, bear, dog—were placed in front of the feasters. Food was brought to the donor and all those who were sitting together with him, as well as all those who had counted coup and all the women who had received presents. Head eating is holy, and if one eats part of the head it is thought that it will help him greatly.

Then the host rose and spoke as follows:

"The servants who are carrying the food around here will probably not have enough to go around, but you must remember that not the men but the women are furnishing the food. Although it is little, I hope you will eat it. We will now sing four songs." Then he sang two war-bundle songs and two night songs. Before they ate the host rose and spoke, "This is a small feast and we will try to give food to our grandfather (some spirit) who is in charge of this ceremony. All who are going to partake in the head eating will sit together with the donor. A warrior will eat together with the scalp. This is all I have to say."

Then the feasters who were selected to take part in the head eating went toward the warrior and ate with him. This warrior (the donor) held a long stick in his hands with which he danced, after he had partaken of the head together with his friends. After he had finished dancing, he walked to the center of the lodge and stuck the stick in the ground and (sat there), eating alone with the scalp. Then all the feasters ate again, and when they were finished the host sang a number of songs and passed (the drum) to the donor, who sang whatever songs he desired; either war-bundle songs, night songs, buffalo songs, or sore-eye dance songs. When the songs were over, all danced. Then the drum was passed to the one who had counted coup first and he spoke as follows:

"The spirits blessed our grandfather and taught him many speeches for this occasion. These we will try to repeat to-day. Even if we do not repeat them correctly, the Night Spirits will not take such a mistake amiss, we were told. Indeed, if I only knew one thing (a song or a speech) they would bless me. We wish to trample upon the soul of our friend (the scalp) and if you, my friends, do the same and repeat the holy speeches of your grandfathers, we will surely accomplish our purpose. Life we wish to obtain, so let us start our songs. That is what I wanted to tell you. Now let us beat the drum and sing. I greet you all."

Then the drum and tobacco were taken to the one who had counted coup second. He spoke as follows:

"The songs and speeches that my grandfather used, those I, too, will use. I, too, desire to trample upon the soul of our friend (the scalp). Life I desire, and I will therefore start up some songs. I can not do what my ancestors did, but I will do the little I know. I greet you all."

Then the drum and tobacco were passed to the one who had counted coup third, and he spoke as follows:

"What our grandfather said, that I am trying to say now. I do not know any songs or speeches, however. I did not listen to what my parents told me, so now when I might have asked the spirits for many things, I can not do it. I do not know what to say and my eyes fill with tears at my discomfiture. But I have myself to blame for it. Now I will start up some songs. I greet you all."

Then they brought the drum to the one who had been fourth to count coup and placed tobacco in his hands. Then he spoke as follows:

"It is good. Those in the east have given me tobacco and I will now offer it to the spirits in their behalf. You have helped to trample upon the soul of our friend (the scalp) and you have tried to gain additional life. I also desire life. Our ancestors were equal to the spirits in their power and they asked each other to help one another in obtaining life. I will try to ask for that which you have asked. I greet you all."

Then all the war-bundle owners in the lodge greeted each other, and the drum was passed around until every one in the lodge had sung. Then they danced the *hok'ixe're* dance until early dawn and when the sun was about to appear they took the drum to the post and danced the victory dance until the sun was high in the heavens. Then they went to sleep. All day they slept, and toward evening of the fourth night, when the sun was low, they began the victory dance again. When it was dark they entered the lodge and placed the drum in the center. Then the attendants put dog meat in the kettles. When all was in readiness and all the feasters had entered the lodge the host offered tobacco to the spirits for whom food was being prepared and spoke as follows:

"After we have sung four songs the meal will be ready to be served. The attendants, it is true, have not cooked very much and it will doubtless not be enough for all, but I think that there will be a little portion for every one. When I have finished the four songs, then the donor for whom this ceremony is being given will select the people who are to eat with him. Then the attendants will distribute the portions of meat, in addition to the heads, and then we will all start to eat."

Then all ate. The donor after first eating with his friends ate alone with the scalp. Then some of the men arose and gave thanks. Finally the host rose again and said, "Whatever little it was in my power to do, I tried to do. All have tried to help me. It is really good. I am really unable to say what I wanted, but it is good. As the drum passes around, may it be of some help to every one."

Then the drum is passed to the one who had first counted coup. He sings and then it is passed to the other three who counted coup, who likewise sing. From them it is passed to all the other people in the lodge who have not sung yet. Then all dance the *hok'ixe're* dance and toward dawn the drum is taken outside to the post and the victory dance is given. If the donor had lost a child the others now wipe off his tears and tell him not to cry any more; and they make the mourner feel joyful again. When it became (full) daylight they danced the victory dance and walked four times around the pole. Then they went to the grave of the child that had died and danced the victory dance there and stuck the scalp in the ground, for the soul of the child. There it would wither and the father would feel happy. This is the end.

The Herucka Dance

The *Herucka* is a social dance and is frequently given when visitors from other tribes are present, presents being given on this occasion. Men and women take part in it and are generally dressed in their best clothes. A few customs that were noticed at a performance in 1908 might be mentioned here.

If a man drops anything during the dance he himself may not pick it up. Only a warrior who has been wounded has the right to do so. The object dropped is returned to the owner, who, however, must always give it to his sister or niece.

It is at times customary for a man to dress himself in rags and beg for food, etc. He generally represents himself as an extremely poor man and pictures his destitution in a manner best calculated to amuse everyone.

Wagers of horses are very commonly made at this dance.

The dances indulged in are mainly victory dances and the songs known as *Herucka* songs are always victory songs. Many borrowed songs are sung at this dance.

A large drum is always used, around which sometimes as many as 10 drummers sit. The drum consists of an ordinary tub over which skin has been tightly drawn. It is supported by two carved sticks, to which it is firmly attached, so that the bottom is about a foot from the ground. It is painted in the following manner: Two rather narrow lines of paint across the center of the drum, one blue and the other green. The portion of the drum next to the yellow line is painted blue, and that next to the blue line red. No meanings for the colors were obtained.

Watconaŋk'êwê Feast
(afraid-to-eat-greens feast)

Informant, member of Beaver clan: Just about roasting-ear month people would commence to fast and continue until the green corn is ripe enough to be eaten. They fast so that all the plants may strengthen the tribe.

The fast generally takes place in a special lodge, from under which all the grass has been cut, for the faster must not come in contact with anything that is green. When the fasting is over a feast is given at which all those present eat "greens" for the first time.

The Captive's Death Dance

Before putting a captive to death it is customary to tie his arms behind him in such a manner that his hands have a little freedom. Then they put a gourd in his right hand and a lance in his left hand

and permit him to dance and sing. This is called the *waŋgeniŋke-i*ⁿ dance.[22]

"So then the turtle was told to dance his death dance—i. e., *waŋgeniŋke-i*ⁿ dance. Both of his arms were tied behind above the elbows. Only thus was he permitted to walk. His wrists were tied in front, so that he could not stretch out his arms. His ankles were tied in such a way that he could not take any long steps. He carried a gourd in one hand and a sacred object in the other, and with these he danced up and down the village, performing his death dance and singing and shaking his gourd. Many people came to see him. He stopped and changed his song, singing, "O death, O death! You young women come here to see me. I am anxious for death."

. . .

(It seems that it is customary to grant any wish the captive makes while dancing this dance.)

The Farewell Dance

When a person is about to go on the warpath he goes around the village dancing and asking for volunteers to accompany him. New volunteers join him as he dances and sings. When the dancing is over these volunteers tell the people how their forefathers encouraged them to go on the warpath, etc.

At the beginning and end of each song they strike their mouths with their hands and give a whoop.

FAREWELL SONGS

I

Hi′skê weje′ji yare′naⁿ da′tcuⁿ wa′ŋkênaŋgre wajaⁿ ana′ŋgere; hi′ske
Truth he speaks I hope, war leaders, what he says, truth
  weje′ji yare′nAⁿ.
  he tells I hope.

II

Cuŋkena′ŋgere je′ske hidanaŋkik'iⁿna dotcû′ŋkera waŋga′niŋge: je′ske
Those dogs like I think of myself war leader a man I am: Thus
  hidanaŋkik'iⁿna.
  I think of myself.
  (I. e., I don't value my life any more than that of a dog.)

III

Jige′ ya′rageni\nAⁿ wajaⁿ s'iⁿp'anai′na dotcu′ŋkera; jige′ yare′nAⁿ.
Again I desire it something a long time war leader; again I desire
  (I. e., it is a long time since I have been on the warpath.)

IV

Ga ai′recke xawa′niŋktcane\nAⁿ dotcuⁿ wuŋkerarëcke xawa′niŋktcanenAⁿ
Even that they say will disappear war leader even he will disappear.
  (I. e., I don't value my life any more than the war-leader does.)

---

[22] The following description of this dance, contained in one of the versions of the myth, " Turtle on the warpath," is no doubt fairly accurate.

THE SOLDIER'S DANCE

Informant, member of the Bear or Soldier clan: [23] The object of performing the soldier dance (fig. 37) is to strengthen the members of the Bear clan. They dance with the emblem of the Bear clan, the whittled stick (*namaŋxî'nixîni*), in their hands. The dance is also given whenever a council in which tribal affairs are discussed is held. On such an occasion the men take their drums to the council lodge and dance there, followed by the women.

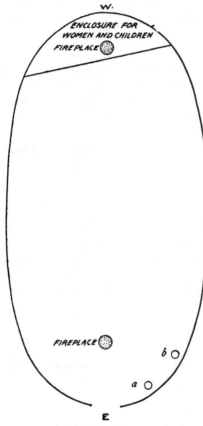

The principal leader—i. e., the chief of the Bear clan (*ma'nanp'e hû'ŋgera*)—appoints a person who is in charge of the ceremony (*ma'nanp'e hak'o'hiduk'ôno'na*).

The ceremony begins with the chief of the clan marching around the village with some followers and stopping here and there to dance and give the soldier whoop. The members of the Bear clan are supposed to be strengthened by the blessings of all the animals who have claws. Should anyone be sick in the village, this strength of theirs would be sufficient to cure them. Then they return to their lodge and are put in control of the entire village.

FIG. 37.—Plan of Soldiers' dance. *a*, Leader. *b*, Assistant.

As soon as the time for the dance is at hand the soldiers give their whoops and an old warrior is selected to tell of his war exploits. He always makes it a point to tell of some exploit that seemed at first foolhardy—how he tried to do something that generally meant death, but how he succeeded by reason of his fearlessness. It is with such a heart, he tells them, that they must dance the soldier's dance. Then they all dance and sing. When they are finished, they let the women dance.

---

[23] Throughout this work soldier is used to connote something quite different from the word warrior. The Soldier clan is the Bear clan, and the Warrior clan is the Hawk or the War-people clan.

The soldier dance is a hop up and down with both feet and in no particular order, anywhere around the singers. It is held in the open air.

I

Mananp'e'ra na^{n}ji^{n}winê.
Soldiers get up.

II

Waja^{n}nija^n tcɔxigi'ji na^{n}ji^n'a^{n}djê.
Something difficult get ready.
(I. e., whenever there is anything difficult to do you must get ready.)

III

Mananp'e'ra newine'n$_A$^{n} hu'nagiredra.
Soldiers I am he whom they spoke of.

IV

Mananp'e'ra hi'ja^n wine'n$_A$^{n}.
Soldier one I am.
(I. e., I am a soldier, and if there is anything to do I'll do it.)

Ceremony of Uangeru
(begging ceremony)

A dummy is made of grass and dressed with whatever objects the maker wants to get. If he wants a horse he puts a bridle crosswise around the body of the dummy; if he wants clothes, he dresses him up in Indian clothes. Then the man places this dummy anywhere near a gathering, or where he expects a gathering to take place. He sits near it. As soon as any warrior sees the dummy he goes over to it and either kicks or strikes the man who made it, giving him at the same time one of the objects he wanted. Any person may do the same. They may not stop kicking the man until some warrior who had at some time or another cut up an enemy in war cuts up the dummy. Then all stop, and as soon as his bruises permitted him, the man would get up and pick up the gifts brought to him.

Feast to Buffalo Tail

A grandfather of mine called Cokeboka fasted at Neceda, Wis. There he was blessed by a young buffalo bull calf belonging to a herd. The calf said, as the herd went by, "Father, keep going in the road; mother, keep going in the road." He meant a warpath instead of the road they were going in. The man was to go on a warpath, from which he would return victorious.

They used to make offerings to this tail alone, apart from the war bundle. The braided grass was to be used for smoking. The feast is given in spring after the grass grows up, and in midwinter. Ground corn is boiled in making the feast.

Kikre Waci and Tcebokona^{n}k Dances

There is a pleasure dance called *kikre waci* and a dance called *tcebokon$_A$^{n}k* (wearing buffalo headdresses). The latter is of Sioux origin.

CHAPTER XVI

THE PEYOTE CULT

GENERAL DESCRIPTION

Owing to the great importance of one of the modern cults found among the Winnebago, the so-called Mescal or Peyote, it will be discussed here in some detail. Not only is this cult of great prominence in the life of the modern Winnebago, but as its inception and progress can be followed out in considerable detail it is of great significance for the study of their religion.

The ceremony is generally held in a building called by the Peyote worshipers a church, although it frequently takes place in the open also. In the early days of its organization as many meetings as possible were held. In 1910 there was a tendency to restrict the number and to have them generally take place on Saturday night. In 1913, after the first enthusiasm of the new converts had died out, the author was informed that the meetings were rarely held more than once a week. Around Christmas and beginning with July a series of meetings was held, lasting from a week to 10 days, as a rule. The Christmas meetings were not prominent in 1910, but the July ones seem to have been held from the beginning. They represent, of course, merely a substitution for the older pagan ceremonies and games that were held about that time.

In the early days the ceremony was opened by a prayer from the founder, and this was followed by an introductory speech. Thereupon the leader sang a Peyote song, to the accompaniment of a drum. Then another speech was delivered, and when it was finished the drum and other regalia were passed to the man to the right. This man, in turn, delivered a speech and sang a song, and when he was finished, passed the regalia to the third man, who subsequently passed it to the fourth one. The fourth man, when he was finished, returned it to the leader. In this way the regalia passed from one person to another throughout the night. It not infrequently happens that one of these four gets tired and gives up his place temporarily to some other member of the cult. At intervals they stopped to eat or drink peyote. At about midnight the peyote, as a rule, begins to affect some people. These generally arise and deliver self-accusatory speeches, and make more or less formal confessions, after which they go around shaking hands with everyone and asking forgiveness.

PLATE 54

a. PEYOTE LEADERS

b. BURIAL HUTS

PLATE 55

b. JOHN RAVE

a. OLIVER LAMERE

In 1910 the cult already had a rather definite organization. There was, at every performance, one leader (pl. 54, *a*) and four principal participants. John Rave (pls. 5, *b*; 55, *b*), the Winnebago who introduced the peyote, was always the leader whenever he was present. On other occasions leadership devolved upon some older member. The four other principal participants changed from meeting to meeting, although there was a tendency to ask certain individuals whenever it was possible. The ritualistic unit, in short, is a very definite one, consisting of a number of speeches and songs and in the passing of the regalia from one to the other of the four participants.

During the early hours of the evening, before the peyote has begun to have any appreciable effect, a number of apparently intrusive features are found. These, for the most part, consist of speeches by people in the audience and the reading and explanation of parts of the Bible. After the peyote has begun to have an appreciable effect, however, the ceremony consists exclusively of a repetition of the ritualistic unit and confessions.

There is an initiation consisting of a baptism, always performed by John Rave. It is of a very simple nature. Rave dips his fingers in a peyote infusion and then passes them over the forehead of the new member, muttering at the same time the following prayer:

"God, his holiness."

This is what the Winnebago words mean, although some of the younger members who have been strongly permeated with Christian teachings translate the prayer into, "God, the Son, and the Holy Ghost."

Whenever the ceremony is performed in the open a fireplace in the shape of a horseshoe is made. At one end of this fireplace is placed a very small mound of earth, called by Rave "Mount Sinai," and in front of this a cross is traced in the earth. Upon the small earth mound are placed the two "chief" peyote, the Bible and the staff. The latter, called by Rave the shepherd's crook, is always covered with beadwork, and generally has a number of evenly cut tufts of deer hair on the end and at intervals along its length. The sacred peyote, known as *huŋka* (i. e., "chief") are exceptionally large and beautiful specimens. They are regarded by a number of people, certainly by Rave, with undisguised veneration.

In addition to the above, there is found a large eagle feather fan, a small drum, and a peculiar small type of rattle. To my knowledge, this type was unknown among the Winnebago before its introduction by the peyote eaters.

JOHN RAVE'S ACCOUNT OF THE PEYOTE CULT AND OF HIS CONVERSION

During 1893-94 I was in Oklahoma with peyote eaters.

In the middle of the night we were to eat peyote. We ate it and I also did. It was the middle of the night when I got frightened, for

a live thing seemed to have entered me. " Why did I do it?" I thought
to myself. I should not have done it, for right at the beginning I
have harmed myself. Indeed, I should not have done it. I am sure
it will injure me. The best thing will be for me to vomit it up. Well,
now, I will try it. After a few attempts I gave up. I thought to
myself, "Well, now you have done it. You have been going around
trying everything and now you have done something that has
harmed you. What is it? It seems to be alive and moving around
in my stomach. If only some of my own people were here! That
would have been better. Now no one will know what has happened
to me. I have killed myself."

Just then the object was about to come out. It seemed almost out
and I put out my hand to feel it, but then it went back again. "O, my,
I should never have done it from the beginning. Never again will I
do it. I am surely going to die."

As we continued it became day and we laughed. Before that I
had been unable to laugh.

The following night we were to eat peyote again. I thought to
myself, "Last night it almost harmed me." "Well, let us do it
again," they said. "All right, I'll do it." So there we ate seven
peyote apiece.

Suddenly I saw a big snake. I was very much frightened. Then
another one came crawling over me. "My God! where are these
coming from?" There at my back there seemed to be something.
So I looked around and I saw a snake about to swallow me entirely.
It had legs and arms and a long tail. The end of this tail was like
a spear. "O, my God! I am surely going to die now," I thought.
Then I looked again in another direction and I saw a man with horns
and long claws and with a spear in his hand. He jumped for me and I
threw myself on the ground. He missed me. Then I looked back
and this time he started back, but it seemed to me that he was directing his spear at me. Again I threw myself on the ground and he
missed me. There seemed to be no possible escape for me. Then
suddenly it occurred to me, "Perhaps it is this peyote that is doing
this thing to me?" "Help me, O medicine, help me! It is you who
are doing this and you are holy! It is not these frightful visions that
are causing this. I should have known that you were doing it.
Help me!" Then my suffering stopped. "As long as the earth
shall last, that long will I make use of you, O medicine!"

This had lasted a night and a day. For a whole night I had not
slept at all.

Then we breakfasted. Then I said, when we were through, "Let
us eat peyote again to-night." That evening I ate eight peyote.

In the middle of the night I saw God. To God living up above,
our Father, I prayed. "Have mercy upon me! Give me knowledge

that I may not say and do evil things. To you, O God, I am trying to pray. Do thou, O Son of God, help me, too. This religion, let me know. Help me, O medicine, grandfather, help me! Let me know this religion!" Thus I spoke and sat very quiet. And then I beheld the morning star and it was good to look upon. The light was good to look upon. I had been frightened during the night but now I was happy. Now as the light appeared, it seemed to me that nothing would be invisible to me. I seemed to see everything clearly. Then I thought of my home and as I looked around, there I saw the house in which I lived far away among the Winnebago, quite close to me. There at the window I saw my children playing. Then I saw a man going to my house carrying a jug of whisky. Then he gave them something to drink and the one that had brought the whisky got drunk and bothered my people. Finally he ran away. "So, that is what they are doing," I thought to myself. Then I beheld my wife come and stand outside of the door, wearing a red blanket. She was thinking of going to the flagpole and was wondering which road she should take. "If I take this road I am likely to meet some people, but if I take the other road, I am not likely to meet anyone."

Indeed, it is good. They are all well—my brother, my sister, my father, my mother. I felt very good indeed. O medicine, grandfather, most assuredly you are holy! All that is connected with you, that I would like to know and that I would like to understand. Help me! I give myself up to you entirely!

For three days and three nights I had been eating medicine, and for three days and three nights I had not slept. Throughout all the years that I had lived on earth, I now realized that I had never known anything holy. Now, for the first time, I knew it. Would that some of the Winnebagoes might also know it!

Many years ago I had been sick and it looked as if this illness were going to kill me. I tried all the Indian doctors and then I tried all of the white man's medicines, but they were of no avail. "I am doomed. I wonder whether I will be alive next year." Such were the thoughts that came to me. As soon as I ate the peyote, however, I got over my sickness. After that I was not sick again. My wife had suffered from the same disease, and I told her that if she ate this medicine it would surely cure her. But she was afraid, although she had never seen it before. She knew that I used it, but nevertheless she was afraid of it. Her sickness was getting worse and worse and one day I said to her, "You are sick. It is going to be very difficult, but try this medicine anyhow. It will ease you." Finally she ate it. I had told her to eat it and then to wash herself and comb her hair and she would get well, and now she is well. Then I painted her face and took my gourd and began singing very much. Then I stopped. "Indeed, you are right," she said, "for now I am well." From that day on to the present time she has been well. Now she is very happy.

Black Water-spirit at about that time was having a hemorrhage and I wanted him to eat the peyote. "Well, I am not going to live anyhow," he said. "Well, eat this medicine soon then and you will get cured." Consumptives never were cured before this and now for the first time one was cured. Black Water-spirit is living to-day and is very well.

There was a man named Walking-Priest and he was very fond of whisky; he chewed and he smoked and he gambled. He was very fond of women. He did everything that was bad. Then I gave him some of the peyote and he ate it and he gave up all the bad things he was doing. He had had a very dangerous disease and had even had murder in his heart. But to-day he is living a good life. That is his desire.

Whoever has any bad thoughts, if he will eat this peyote he will abandon all his bad habits. It is a cure for everything bad.

To-day the Indians say that only God is holy. One of the Winnebagoes has told me, "Really, the life that I led was a very bad one. Never again will I do it. This medicine is good and I will always use it." John Harrison and Squeaking-Wings were prominent members of the medicine dance; they thought much of themselves as did all the members of the medicine dance. They knew everything connected with this medicine dance. Both of them were gamblers and were rich because they had won very much in gambling. Their parents had acquired great possessions by giving medicines to the people. They were rich and they believed that they had a right to be selfish with their possessions. Then they ate peyote and ever since that time they have been followers of this medicine. They were really very ill and now they have been cured of it. Now if there are any men that might be taken as examples of the peyote, it is these three. Even if a man were blind and only heard about them he would realize that if any medicine were good, it is this medicine. It is a cure for all evil. Before, I had thought that I knew something but I really knew nothing. It is only now that I have real knowledge. In my former life I was like one blind and deaf. My heart ached when I thought of what I had been doing. Never again will I do it. This medicine alone is holy and has made me good and has rid me of all evil. The one whom they call God has given me this. That I know positively. Let them all come here; men and women; let them bring with them all that they desire; let them bring with them their diseases. If they come here they will get well. This is all true; it is all true. Bring whatever desires you possess along with you and then come and eat or drink this medicine. This is life, the only life. Then you will learn something about yourself, so come. Even if you are not told any-thing about yourself, nevertheless you will learn something of your-self. Come with your disease, for this medicine will cure it. What-ever you have, come and eat this medicine and you will have true knowledge once and for all. Learn of this medicine yourself through actual experience.

If you just hear about it you are not likely to try it. If you desire real knowledge about it try it yourself, for then you will learn of things that you had never known before. In no other way will you ever be happy. I know that all sorts of excuses will run through your mind for not partaking of it, but if you wish to learn of some-thing good, try this. Perhaps you will think to yourself that it will be too difficult and this will seem an excuse to you for not trying it. But why should you act thus? If you partake of it, even if you feel some uncertainty about its accomplishing all the good that has been said of it, I know that you will say to yourself, "Well, this life is good enough." After you have taken it for the first time, it will seem as if they are digging a grave for you, that you are about to die; and you will not want to take it again. "It is bad," you will think to yourself. You will believe that you are going to die and you will want to know what is going to happen to you. The coffin will be set before you and then you will see your body. If you wish to inquire further about where you are going then you will learn something you have not known. Two roads there are, one leading to a hole in the earth and the other extending up above. You will learn something that you had not known before. Of the two roads, one is dark and the other is light. You must choose one of these while you are alive and so must you decide whether you wish to continue in your evil ways or whether you will abandon them. These are the two roads. The Peyote people see them. They claim that only if you weep and repent will you be able to obtain knowledge. Do not, as I said before, listen to others talking about it, but try the medicine yourself. That is the only way to find out. No other medicine can accomplish what this has done. If, therefore, you make use of it, you will live. After they have eaten peyote people throw aside all the (evil) ceremonies that they were accustomed to perform before. Only by eating the peyote will you learn what is truly holy. That is what I am trying to learn myself.

It is now 23 years since I first ate peyote, and I am still doing it (1912). Before that my heart was filled with murderous thoughts. I wanted to kill my brother and my sister. It seemed to me that my heart would not feel good until I killed one of them. All my thoughts were fixed on the warpath. This is all I thought of. Now

I know that it was because the evil spirit possessed me that I felt that way. I was suffering from a disease. I even desired to kill myself; I did not care to live. That feeling, too, was caused by this evil spirit living within me. Then I ate this medicine and everything changed. The brother and sister I wanted to kill before I became attached to and I wanted them to live. The medicine had accomplished this.

O. L.'s Description of the Peyote Cult

(Pl. 55, a)

John Rave belongs to the Bear clan, the members of which had the functions of what might be called sergeants-at-arms. He and his ancestors used to be in charge of the *manupetci* (i. e., the sergeants-at-arms lodge), to which all malefactors would be brought for punishment.

Rave, although he belonged to this highly respected class of people, was a bad man. He roamed from place to place. He has participated in all the ceremonies of the Winnebago, the medicine dance alone excepted. He had been married many times. Up to 1901 he was a heavy drinker. In that year he went to Oklahoma and while there ate the peyote. He then returned to the Winnebago and tried to introduce it among them, but none with the exception of a few relatives would have anything to do with it. This did not in any way discourage him, however, and he continued using the peyote, now and then getting a few converts.

There was not very much religion connected with it in the beginning and the reason people drank it was on account of the peculiar effects it had upon them. Nevertheless these Peyote people preached good things and gradually lost all desire for intoxicating drinks or for participating in the old Winnebago ceremonies. Then Rave began to do away with the old Indian customs. About four or five years ago the membership in the Peyote religion began to increase, for many people now noticed that those connected with the Peyote cult were the only people in the tribe leading a Christian life.

At this time the Bible was introduced by a young man named Albert Hensley (pls. 8, *d*; 9, *d*). He, too, had been a bad person, although he had been educated at Carlisle. Like Rave, he was a heavy drinker and fond of wandering.

During the last few years our members have increased so fast that now almost half the tribe belong to our religion. We all make efforts to lead a Christian life and we are succeeding very well.

We use the New Testament, especially the Revelations.

Our meetings take place at any time. We gather together in the evening, and as soon as everything is in readiness the leader arises and offers a prayer called, "Turning themselves over to the care of the Trinity." Then all sit down and the leader makes the regular announcements. The peyote is then passed around, either in the dry condition or steeped. The leader thereupon starts the singing. These are some of the songs:

1. Ask God for life and he will give it to us.
2. God created us so pray to him.
3. To the home of Jesus we are going, so pray to him.
4. Come ye to the road of the Son of God; come ye to the road.

Then Albert Hensley calls upon 12 educated members to translate and interpret certain portions of the Bible for the nonreading members. He arranges with the leader to have the singing stop at certain places so that some of these young men can speak. When these are finished, other individuals are called upon to give testimony. Hensley always talks and so does Rave.

John Rave baptizes by dipping his hand in a diluted infusion of peyote and rubbing it across the forehead of a new member, saying, "I baptize thee in the name of God, the Son, and the Holy Ghost, which is called God's Holiness."

The peyote eaters wanted to get baptized and unite with the church in Winnebago, but the clergyman in charge would not permit them, so they went and did their own baptizing through their leader, John Rave, who, though he is not educated, is full of real intelligence and religion.

If a person who is truly repentant eats peyote for the first time, he does not suffer at all from its effects. But if an individual is bullheaded, does not believe in its virtue, he is likely to suffer a good deal. This I know from my own experience. After eating peyote I grasped the meaning of the Bible, which before had been meaningless to me.

If a person eats peyote and does not repent openly, he has a guilty conscience, which leaves him as soon as the public repentance has been made.

Old men and women who had been brought up to worship animals and all kinds of spirits have cast them all away and in many instances burned their idols, not because they were told to do so but because they felt that way.

Whenever at our meetings a person wishes to pray, he does so; when he wishes to cry, he does so. Indeed, we show no timidity about worshiping God in the right way. In the Bible one often reads of Christ casting out the devils and of the people shouting, etc. So does the peyote act on us in the beginning, although afterwards its effects abate.

If a peyote eater relapses into his old way of living, then the peyote causes him great suffering.

At first our meetings were started without any rule laid down by the Bible, but afterwards we found a very good reason for holding our meetings at night. We searched the Bible and asked many ministers for any evidence for Christ's ever having held any meetings in the daytime, but we could find nothing to that effect. We did, however, find evidence that he had been out all night in prayer. As it is our desire to follow as closely as we can in the footsteps of Christ, we hold our meetings at night. Then, too, when we pray we wish to get as far away as possible from earthly things, and the night is the best time, for then we are not likely to be bothered by anything.

We have made earnest efforts to become Christians since we began drinking and eating this peyote, but many people say sarcastically that we have drunk ourselves into Christianity, and that we are demented. I am a peyote eater, but I have never found a demented person among them. We claim that there is virtue in the peyote. To you who do not believe and desire to find out let me quote the fourth chapter of the First Epistle of St. John:

"Beloved, believe not every spirit, but try the spirits whether they are of God; because many false prophets are gone out into the world.

"Hereby know ye the spirit of God. Every spirit that confesseth that Jesus Christ is come in the flesh is of God."

We claim that you can not find out anything by standing off at a distance and only talking about it. We claim that some earthly things can have the virtue of God, for instance, the Bible, which is entirely made up of earthly material—the ink, the paper, the cover— yet it has survived the ages.

J. B.'s Account of the Leader of the Peyote [1]

(Pl. 3)

Among the Winnebago there is a man named Little-Red-Bird, and when he reached middle age he began to travel around the world and learn different Indian languages. He used to travel inland a good deal. Once he joined a circus and crossed the ocean. He felt so ill while crossing that he wanted to die. Suddenly a wind came up and he got very frightened. He did not know what to do. Then he prayed to Earthmaker. When he came to the other side of the ocean there he saw a big island and a big city (London), and in this last place they held their circus. The chief of that country (the king) he met there.

When he came back to his own people he told them that on the other side of the ocean the Thunderbirds did not thunder. All they did was to drizzle. There was no lightning either. As he crossed the ocean on his return it thundered and lightened.

When he came home he was very glad to see his relatives and he offered tobacco in thanksgiving.

---

[1] The narrator was a very lukewarm follower.

Shortly after this he traveled again and came to a band of Indians who were eating peyote. It was his custom to try everything when he went visiting. He did not realize what he was doing when he ate this medicine, but he did it anyhow. After a while he began to think of his manner of life, and he felt that he was doing wrong. All the evil he had done he remembered. Then he prayed to God. Suddenly it occurred to him, "Perhaps I am the only one doing this." Then he looked around and watched the others, and he saw them praying in the same manner.

Not long after that he came home, taking with him some of this medicine. He knew it was holy. At home he offered tobacco to it and kept on eating it. Soon it cured him of a disease he had. He tried to induce some of the others to try it, but they refused. After a while a few tried it, and the peyote movement began to spread. All the old customs that they had been accustomed to observe they abandoned. They gave up the medicine dance and the ceremonies connected with the clans. For that reason, therefore; the conservative people hated them; their own brothers and sisters hated them, for they had abandoned what were considered holy ceremonies.

ALBERT HENSLEY'S ACCOUNT OF THE PEYOTE [2]

(Pls. 8, d; 9, d)

I am 37 years old. It was 37 years ago that my mother gave birth to me in an old-fashioned reed lodge. When I was a year old she died and my grandmother took care of me. I had come into the world a healthy child, but bad luck was apparently to pursue me, for when I was 7 years old my grandmother died. Then my father took care of me. At that time he began to be a bad man; he was a drunkard and a horse thief. He would frequently get into trouble and run away, always taking me along with him, however. On one occasion we fled to Wisconsin, and there we stayed two years. We got along pretty well, and there my father married again. By his second wife he had three children.

After a while he got into trouble again, and misfortune followed misfortune. People were killing each other, and I was left alone. If at any time of my life I was in trouble it was then. I was never happy. Once I did not have anything to eat for four days. We had fled to the wilderness, and it was raining continually. The country was flooded with high water, and we sat on the top of a tree. It was impossible to sleep, for if we went to sleep we would fall off into the water, which was very deep. The shore was quite far away. As we were prominent people, we soon heard that my

---

[2] This account is of great importance, because Hensley introduced a large number of Christian elements into the ceremony, the principal one being the Bible.

father had been freed. We were very happy, and went back to our people.

At that time a young man named Young-Bear was starting for Nebraska, and he said that he would take me along. I was very happy. So in that manner I was brought to this country. Here I have had only happy days. When my father got married everyone disliked me. When I worked I was working for my father, and all the money I earned I had to give to him.

After a while I went to school, and although I liked it I ran away and then went to school at Carlisle. I wanted to lead a good life. At school I knew that they would take care of me and love me. I was very shy and lacked a strong character at that time. If a person told me to do anything I would always obey immediately. Everybody loved me. I stayed there six months. I was also taught Christianity there. When I came back to my country the Episcopalian people told me that they wanted me to be diligent in religious matters and never to forsake the religion of the Son of God. I also desired to do that. I entered the church that we had in our country and I stayed with them six years.

At that time the Winnebago with whom I associated were heavy drinkers, and after a while they induced me to drink also. I became as wicked as they. I learned how to gamble and I worked for the devil all the time. I even taught the Winnebago how to be bad.

After a while they began eating peyote, and as I was in the habit of doing everything I saw, I thought I would do it, too. I asked them whether I could join, and they permitted me. At that time I had a position at the county commissioner's office. I ate the peyote and liked it very much. Then the authorities tried to stop the Indians from eating peyote, and I was supposed to see that the law was enforced. I continued eating peyote and enjoying it. All the evil that was in me I forgot. From that time to the present my actions have been quite different from what they used to be. I am only working for what is good; not that I mean to say that I am good.

After that I married and now I have three children, and it would not have been right for me to continue in my wickedness. I resolved that thereafter I would behave as a grown-up man ought to behave. I resolved never to be idle again and to work so that I could supply my wife and children with food and necessities, that I would be ready to help them whenever they were in need. Here in my own country would I remain till I died. This (peyote) religion was good. All the evil is gone and hereafter I will choose my path carefully.

I know the story about the origin of the peyote. It is as follows:

Once in the south, an Indian belonging to the tribe called Mescallero Apache was roaming in the country called Mexico, and went hunting in the high hills and got lost. For three days he went without water and without food. He was about to die of thirst but he continued until he reached the foot of a certain hill, on top of which he could find shade under a tree that was growing there. There he desired to die. It was with the greatest difficulty that he reached the place and when he got there, he fell over on his back and lay thus, with his body stretched toward the south, his head pillowed against something. He extended his right arm to the west and his left arm to the east, and as he did this, he felt something cool touch his hands. "What is it?" he thought to himself. So he took the one that was close to his right hand and brought it to his mouth and ate it. There was water in it, although it also contained food. Then he took the one close to his left hand and brought it to his mouth and ate it. Then as he lay on the ground a holy spirit entered him and taking the spirit of the Indian carried it away to the regions above. There he saw a man who spoke to him. "I have caused you to go through all this suffering, for had I not done it, you would never have heard of the proper (religion). It was for that reason that I placed holiness in what you have eaten. My Father gave it to me and I was permitted to place it on the earth. I was also permitted to take it back again and give it to some other Indians.

"At present this religion exists in the south but now I wish to have it extended to the north. You Indians are now fighting one another, and it is for the purpose of stopping this, that you might shake hands and partake of food together, that I am giving you this peyote. Now you should love one another. Earthmaker is my father. Long ago I sent this gospel across the ocean but you did not know of it. Now I am going to teach you to understand it." Then he led him into a lodge where they were eating peyote. There he taught him the songs and all that belonged to this ceremony. Then he said to him, "Now go to your people and teach them all that I have told you. Go to your people in the north and teach them. I have placed my holiness in this that you eat. What my father gave me, that I have placed therein."

Then he told him to go home. He thought he had been dead, but it was really his spirit that had left him. After a while the man got well again.

There were many peyote near the place where he was lying and these he picked before he started. Then he went back to his lodge. He thought he had been lost, but it seemed hardly possible to him that this was the case. His being lost in the hills seemed to symbolize to him the condition of the people before they had eaten the peyote; they would be lost and then find their way again.

On his return he built a peyote lodge and for four nights he taught the people how to eat peyote. He did not, however, teach it as he was told, nor did he teach it thoroughly. These to whom he taught it used it for a purpose different from what it was intended.[3] They used it for war and for horse stealing. They, however, continued to eat the peyote, but they really ate too much of it. After a while the leader began thinking that the medicine might harm them, so he told them to hide it. The man did not know that even at that time a big war party was coming upon them. This tribe was almost destroyed.

They lost the peyote. One day, however, it was taught to a Comanche. He ate it and prayed to Earthmaker. Then it was taught to the Cheyenne and to the Arapaho and to the Caddo. The Tonkawa, the Apache, and the Mescallero Apache were the ones who had lost the medicine. When these other tribes began to eat this medicine they heard about it and they remembered that they also had long ago eaten it.

There was an old man in Oklahoma who knew the mescal country very well and he went down to old Mexico and stayed there for a year. When he returned he taught it to the Oto and the Oto taught it to us.

It is a true religion. The peyote is fulfilling the work of God and the Son of God. When the Son of God came to the earth he was poor, yet people spoke of him; he was abused. It is the same now with the peyote. The plant itself is not much of a growth, yet the people are talking about it a good deal; they are abusing it, they are trying to stop its use. When the Son of God came to earth the preachers of that time were called Pharisees and Scribes. They doubted what the Son of God said and claimed that he was an ordinary man. So it is to-day with the Christian Church; they are the Pharisees and Scribes, they are the doubters. They say that this is merely a plant, that it is the work of the devil. They are trying to stop its use and they are calling it an intoxicant, but this is a lie. If they will but come and see this ceremony they will realize this.

J. B.'s Peyote Experiences

When my father and mother asked me to come to the Missouri River (Nebraska) I knew they had eaten peyote and I did not like it. I had been told that these peyote eaters were doing wrong, and therefore I disliked them; I had heard that they were doing everything that was wicked. For these reasons we did not like them. About this time they sent me money for my ticket, and since my brothers and sisters told me to go, I went. Just as I was about to start my youngest sister, the one to whom we always listened most attentively, said to me, "Older brother, do not you indulge in this medicine eating (peyote) of which so much is said." I promised. Then I started out.

[3] This is clearly Hensley's interpretation.

As soon as I arrived (in Nebraska) I met some people who had not joined the peyote eaters and who said to me, "Your relatives are eating the peyote and they sent for you that you also might eat it. Your mother, your father, and your younger sister, they are all eating it." Thus they spoke to me. Then they told me of some of the bad things it was reported that these people had done. I felt ashamed and I wished I had not come in the first place. Then I said that I was going to eat the medicine.

After that I saw my father, mother, and sister. They were glad. Then we all went to where they were staying. My father and I walked (alone). Then he told me about the peyote eating. "It does not amount to anything, all this that they are doing, although they do stop drinking. It is also said that sick people get well. We were told about this and so we joined, and, sure enough, we are practically well, your mother as well as I. It is said that they offer prayers to Earthmaker (God)," he said. He kept on talking. "They are rather foolish. They cry when they feel very happy about anything. They throw away all of the medicines that they possess and know. They give up all the blessings they received while fasting and they give up all the spirits that blessed them in their fasts. They also stop smoking and chewing tobacco. They stop giving feasts, and they stop making offerings of tobacco. Indeed, they burn up their holy things. They burn up their war bundles. They are bad people. They give up the Medicine Dance. They burn up their medicine bags and even cut up their otter-skin bags. They say they are praying to Earthmaker (God) and they do so standing and crying. They claim that they hold nothing holy except Earthmaker (God). They claim that all the things that they are stopping are those of the bad spirit (the devil), and that the bad spirit (the devil) has deceived them; that there are no spirits who can bless; that there is no other spirit except Earthmaker (God)." Then I said, "Say, they certainly speak foolishly." I felt very angry toward them. "You will hear them, for they are going to have a meeting tonight. Their songs are very strange. They use a very small drum," said he. Then I felt a very strong desire to see them.

After a while we arrived. At night they had their ceremony. At first I sat outside and listened to them. I was rather fond of them. I stayed in that country and the young peyote eaters were exceedingly friendly to me. They would give me a little money now and then and they treated me with tender regard. They did everything that they thought would make me feel good, and in consequence I used to speak as though I liked their ceremony. However, I was only deceiving them. I only said it because they were so good to me. I thought they acted in this way because (the peyote) was deceiving them.

Soon after that my parents returned to Wisconsin, but when they left they said they would come back in a little while. So I was left there with my relatives, who were all peyote followers. For that reason they left me there. Whenever I went among the nonpeyote people I used to say all sorts of things about the peyote people, and when I returned to the peyote people I used to say all sorts of things about the others.

I had a friend who was a peyote man and he said to me, "My friend, I wish very much that you should eat the peyote." Thus he spoke and I answered him, "My friend, I will do it, but not until I get accustomed to the people of this country. Then I will do it. The only thing that worries me is the fact that they are making fun of you. And in addition, I am not quite used to them." I spoke dishonestly.

I was staying at the place where my sister lived. She had gone to Oklahoma; she was a peyote follower. After a while she returned. I was then living with a number of women. This was the second time (there) and from them I obtained some money. Once I got drunk there and was locked up for six days. After my sister returned she and the others paid more attention than ever to me. Especially was this true of my brother-in-law. They gave me horses and a vehicle. They really treated me very tenderly. I knew that they did all this because they wished me to eat the peyote. I, in my turn, was very kind to them. I thought that I was fooling them and they thought that they were converting me. I told them that I believed in the peyote because they were treating me so nicely.

After a while we moved to a certain place where they were to have a large peyote meeting. I knew they were doing this in order to get me to join. Then I said to my younger sister, "I would be quite willing to eat this peyote (ordinarily), but I don't like the woman with whom I am living just now and I think I will leave her. That is why I do not want to join now, for I understand that when married people eat medicine (peyote) they will always have to stay together. Therefore I will join when I am married to some woman permanently." Then my brother-in-law came and she told him what I had said, and he said to me, "You are right in what you say. The woman with whom you are staying is a married woman and you can not continue living with her. It is null and void (this marriage) and we know it. You had better join now. It will be the same as if you were single. We will pray for you as though you were single. After you have joined this ceremony, then you can marry any woman whom you have a right to marry (legally). So, do join tonight. It is best. For some time we have been desirous of your joining but we have not said anything to you. It is Earthmaker's (God's) blessing to you that you have been thinking of this," said he.

Therefore I sat inside the meeting place with them. One man acted as leader. We were to do whatever he ordered. The regalia were placed before him. I wanted to sit in some place on the side because I thought I might get to crying like the others. I felt ashamed of myself.

Then the leader arose and talked. He said that this was an affair of Earthmaker's (God's), and that he (the leader) could do nothing on his own initiative; that Earthmaker (God) was going to conduct the ceremony. Then he said that the medicine (peyote) was holy and that he would turn us all over to it; that he had turned himself over to it and wished now to turn all of us over to it. He said further, "I am a very pitiable (figure) in this ceremony, so when you pray to Earthmaker, pray also for me. Now let us all rise and pray to Earthmaker (God)." We all rose. Then he prayed. He prayed for the sick, and he prayed for those who did not yet know Earthmaker. He said that they were to be pitied. When he had finished we sat down. Then the peyote was passed around. They gave me five. My brother-in-law said to me, "If you speak to this medicine (peyote), it will give you whatever you ask of it. Then you must pray to Earthmaker, and then you must eat the medicine." Hovever, I ate them (the peyote) immediately, for I did not know what to ask for and I did not know what to say in a prayer to Earthmaker (God). So I ate the peyote just as they were. They were very bitter and had a taste difficult to describe. I·wondered what would happen to me. After a while I was given five more and I also ate them. They tasted rather bitter. Now I was very quiet. The peyote rather weakened me. Then I listened very attentively to the singing. I liked it very much. I felt as though I were partly asleep. I felt different from (my normal self), but when I (looked around) and examined myself, I saw nothing wrong about myself. However, I felt different.from (my normal self). Before this I used to dislike the songs. Now I liked the leader's singing very much. I liked to listen to him.

They were all sitting very quietly. They were doing nothing except singing. Each man sang four songs and then passed the regalia to the next one. (Each one) held a stick and an eagle's tail feather in one hand and a small gourd rattle, which they used to shake while singing, in the other. One of (those) present used to do the drumming. Thus objects would pass around until they came back to the leader, who would then sing four songs. When these were finished, he would place the various (things) on the ground, rise, and pray to Earthmaker (God). Then he called upon one or two to speak. They said that Earthmaker (God) was good and that the peyote was good, and that whosoever ate this medicine (peyote) would be able to free himself from the bad spirit (the devil); for they said that

Earthmaker forbids us to commit sins. When this was over they sang again.

After midnight, every once in a while (I heard) someone cry. In some cases they would go up to the leader and talk with him. He would stand up and pray with them. They told me what they were saying. They said that they were asking (people) to pray for them, as they were sorry for their sins and that they might be prevented from committing them again. That is what they were saying. They cried very loudly. I was rather frightened. (I noticed also) that when I closed my eyes and sat still, I began to see strange things. I did not get sleepy in the least. Thus the light (of morning) came upon me. In the morning, as the sun rose, they stopped. They all got up and prayed to Earthmaker (God) and then they stopped.

During the daytime I did not get sleepy in the least. My actions were a little different (from my usual ones). Then they said, "Tonight they are going to have another meeting. Let us go over. They say that is the best (thing) to do and thus you can learn it (the ceremony) right away. It is said that their spirits wander over all the earth and the heavens also. All this you will learn and see," they said. "At times they die and remain dead all night and all day. When in this condition they sometimes see Earthmaker (God), it is said." One would also be able to see where the bad spirit lived, it was said.

So we went there again. I doubted all this. I thought that what they were saying was untrue. However, I went along anyhow. When we got there, I had already eaten some peyote, for I had taken three during the day. Now near the peyote meeting an (Indian) feast was being given and I went there instead. When I reached the place, I saw a long lodge. The noise was terrific. They were beating an enormous drum. The sound almost raised me in the air, so (pleasurably) loud did it sound to me. Not so (pleasurable) had things appeared at those affairs (peyote meetings) that I had lately been attending. There I danced all night and I flirted with the women. About day I left and when I got back the peyote meeting was still going on. When I got back they told me to sit down at a certain place. They treated me very kindly. There I again ate peyote. I heard that they were going to have another meeting near by on the evening of the same day. We continued eating peyote the whole day at the place where we were staying. We were staying at the house of one of my relatives. Some of the boys there taught me a few songs. "Say, when you learn how to sing, you will be the best singer, for you are a good singer as it is. You have a good voice," they said to me. I thought so myself.

That night we went to the place where the peyote meeting was to take place. They gave me a place to sit and treated me very kindly. "Well, he has come," they even said when I got there, "make a place for him." I thought they regarded me as a great man. John Rave, the leader, was to conduct the (ceremony). I ate five peyote. Then my brother-in-law and my sister came and gave themselves up. They asked me to stand there with them. I did not like it, but I did it nevertheless. "Why should I give myself up? I am not in earnest, and I intend to stop this as soon as I get back to Wisconsin. I am only doing this because they have given me presents," I thought. "I might just as well get up, since it doesn't mean anything to me." So I stood up. The leader began to talk and I (suddenly) began to feel sick. It got worse and worse and finally I lost consciousness entirely. When I recovered, I was lying flat on my back. Those with whom I had been standing were still standing there. I had (as a matter of fact) regained consciousness as soon as I fell down. I felt like leaving the place that night, but I did not do it. I was quite tired out. "Why have I done this?" I said to myself. "I promised (my sister) that I would not do it." So I thought and then I tried to leave, but I could not. I suffered intensely. At last daylight came upon me. Now I thought that they regarded me as one who had a trance and found out something.

Then we went home and they showed me a passage in the Bible where it said that it was a shame for any man to wear long hair. That is what it said, they told me. I looked at the passage. I was not a man learned in books, but I wanted to give the impression that I knew how to read, so I told them to cut my hair, for I wore it long at that time. After my hair was cut I took out a lot of medicine that I happened to have in my pockets. These were courting medicines. There were many small bundles of them. All these, together with my hair, I gave to my brother-in-law. Then I cried and my brother-in-law also cried. Then he thanked me. He told me that I understood and that I had done well. He told me that Earthmaker (God) alone was holy; that all the things (blessings and medicines) that I possessed were false; that I had been fooled by the bad spirit (devil). He told me that I had now freed myself from much of this (bad influence). My relatives expressed their thanks fervently.

On the fourth night they had another meeting and I went to it again. There I again ate (peyote). I enjoyed it and I sang along with them. I wanted to be able to sing immediately. Some young men were singing and I enjoyed it, so I prayed to Earthmaker, asking him to let me learn to sing right away. That was all I asked for. My brother-in-law was with me all the time. At that meeting all the things I had given my brother-in-law were burned up.

The fact that he (my brother-in-law) told me that I understood pleased me, and I felt good when daylight came. (As a matter of fact) I had not received any knowledge.

After that I would attend meetings every once in a while, and I looked around for a woman whom I might marry permanently. Before long that was the only thing I thought of when I attended the meetings.

On one occasion we were to have a meeting of men and I went to the meeting with a woman, with whom I thought of going around the next day. That was (the only) reason I went with her. When we arrived, the one who was to lead asked me to sit near him. There he placed me. He urged me to eat a lot of peyote, so I did. The leaders (of the ceremony) always place the regalia in front of themselves; they also had a peyote placed there. The leader placed a very small one in front of himself this time. "Why does he have a very small one there?" I thought to myself. I did not think much about it.

It was now late at night and I had eaten a lot of peyote and felt rather tired. I suffered considerably. After a while I looked at the peyote and there stood an eagle with outspread wings. It was as beautiful a sight as one could behold. Each of the feathers seemed to have a mark. The eagle stood looking at me. I looked around thinking that perhaps there was something the matter with my sight. Then I looked again and it was really there. I then looked in a different direction and it disappeared. Only the small peyote remained. I looked around at the other people but they all had their heads bowed and were singing. I was very much surprised.

Some time after this (I saw) a lion lying in the same place (where I had seen the eagle). I watched it very closely. It was alive and looking at me. I looked at it very closely, and when I turned my eyes away just the least little bit it disappeared. "I suppose they all know this and I am just beginning to know of it," I thought. Then I saw a small person (at the same place). He wore blue clothes and a shining brimmed cap. He had on a soldier's uniform. He was sitting on the arm of the person who was drumming, and he looked at every one. He was a little man, perfect (in all proportions). Finally I lost sight of him. I was very much surprised indeed. I sat very quietly. "This is what it is," I thought, "this is what they all probably see and I am just beginning to find out."

Then I prayed to Earthmaker (God): "This, your ceremony, let me hereafter perform."

As I looked again, I saw a flag. I looked more carefully and (I saw) the house full of flags. They had the most beautiful marks on them. In the middle (of the room) there was a very large flag and it was a live one; it was moving. In the doorway there was another one not entirely visible. I had never seen anything so beautiful in all my life before.

Then again I prayed to Earthmaker (God). I bowed my head and closed my eyes and began (to speak). I said many things that I would ordinarily never have spoken about. As I prayed, I was aware of something above me and there he was; Earthmaker (God) to whom I was praying, he it was. That which is called the soul, that is it, that is what one calls Earthmaker (God). Now this is what I felt and saw. The one called Earthmaker (God) is a spirit and that is what I felt and saw. All of us sitting there, we had all together one spirit or soul; at least that is what I learned. I instantly became the spirit and I was their spirit or soul. Whatever they thought of, I (immediately) knew. I did not have to speak to them and get an answer to know what their thoughts had been. Then I thought of a certain place, far away, and immediately I was there; I was my thought.

I looked around and noticed how everything seemed about me, and when I opened my eyes I was myself in the body again. From this time on, I thought, thus I shall be. This is the way they are, and I am only beginning to be that way. "All those that heed Earthmaker (God) must be thus," I thought. "I would not need any more food," I thought, "for was I not my spirit? Nor would I have any more use of my body," I felt. "My corporeal affairs are over," I felt.

Then they stopped and left, for it was just dawning. Then someone spoke to me. I did not answer, for I thought they were just fooling, and that they were all like myself, and that (therefore) it was unnecessary for me to talk to them. So when they spoke to me I only answered with a smile. "They are just saying this to me because (they realize) that I have just found out," I thought. That was why I did not answer. I did not speak to anyone until noon. Then I had to leave the house to perform one of nature's duties and someone followed me. It was my friend. He said, "My friend, what troubles you that makes you act as you do?" "Well, there's no need of your saying anything, for you know it beforehand," I said.

Then I immediately got over my trance and again got into my (normal) condition, so that he would have to speak to me before I knew his thoughts. I became like my former self. It became necessary for me to speak to him.

Then I spoke to him and said, "My friend, let us hitch up these horses and then I will go wherever you like, for you wish to speak to me and I also want to go around and talk to you." Thus I spoke to him. "If I were to tell you all that I have learned, I would never be able to stop at all, so much have I learned," I said to him. "However, I would enjoy telling some of it." "Good," said he. He liked it (what I told him) very much. "That is what I am anxious to hear," said he. Then we went after the horses. We caught one of them but we could not get the other. He got away from us and we could not find him. We hunted everywhere for the horse but could not discover where he had run to. Long afterwards we found it among the whites.

Now since that time (of my conversion) no matter where I am, I always think of this religion. I still remember it and I think I will remember it as long as I live. It is the only holy thing I have been aware of in all my life.

After that whenever I heard of a peyote meeting, I went to it. However, my thoughts were always fixed on women. "If I were married (legally) perhaps these thoughts will leave me," I thought. Whenever I went to a meeting now I tried to eat as many peyote as possible, for I was told that it was good to eat them. For that reason I ate them. As I sat there I would always pray to Earthmaker (God). Now these were my thoughts. If I were married, I thought as I sat there, I could then put all my thoughts on this ceremony. I sat with my eyes closed and was very quiet.

Suddenly I saw something. This was tied up. The rope with which this object was tied up was long. The object itself was running around and around (in a circle). There was a pathway there in which it ought to go, but it was tied up and unable to get there. The road was an excellent one. Along its edge bluegrass grew and on each side there grew many varieties of pretty flowers. Sweet-smelling flowers sprang up all along this road. Far off in the distance appeared a bright light. There a city was visible of a beauty inde-scribable by tongue. A cross was in full sight. The object that was tied up would always fall just short of reaching the road. It seemed to lack sufficient strength to break loose (of what was holding it). (Near it) lay something which would have given it sufficient strength to break its fastenings, if it were only able to get hold of it.

I looked at what was so inextricably tied up and I saw that it was myself. I was forever thinking of women. "This it is to which I am tied," I thought. "Were I married, I would have strength enough to break my fastening and be able to travel in the good road," I thought. Then daylight came upon us and we stopped.

Then I thought of a man I used to know who was an old peyote-man. He always spoke to me very kindly. I went over to see him. I thought I would tell him what had happened to me. When I arrived there he was quite delighted. It was about noon and he fed my horses and asked me to eat with him. Then when we were through eating, I told him what had happened to me. He was very glad and told me that I was speaking of a very good thing. Then (finally) he said, "Now I shall tell you what I think is a good thing (for you to do). You know that if an old horse is balky, you cannot break him of (this habit); even if you bought him and tried to break him (of this habit) you would not succeed. If, indeed, you succeeded it would only be after very hard work. However, if you had a very young horse, you could train it in any way you wished. So it is in everything. If you marry a woman who has been in the habit of marrying frequently, it would be difficult for her to break herself of a habit she loves. You are not the one she loves. If you marry her you will lead a hard life. If you wish to get married, take your time. There are plenty of good women. Many of them are at (government) schools and have never been married. I think you would do best if you waited for some of these before marrying. They will return in the middle of the summer. So, don't think of any of these women you see around here, but wait until then and pray to Earthmaker patiently. That would be the best, I think." I liked what he told me and thanked him. I decided to accept his advice, and I did not look around for women after that. I was to wait about three months and (during that time) I paid strict attention to the peyote ceremony.

On one occasion while at a meeting, I suffered (great pain). My eyes were sore and I was thinking of many things. "Now I do nothing but pay attention to this ceremony, for it is good." Then I called the leader over to me and said to him, "My elder brother, hereafter only Earthmaker (God) shall I regard as holy. I will make no more offerings of tobacco. I will not use any more tobacco. I will not smoke and I will not chew tobacco. I have no further interest in these. Earthmaker (God) alone do I desire (to serve). I will not take part in the Medicine Dance again. I give myself up (to you). I intend to give myself up to Earthmaker's (God's) cause." Thus I spoke to him. "It is good, younger brother," he said to me. Then he had me stand up and he prayed to Earthmaker (God). He asked Earthmaker (God) to forgive me my sins.

The next morning I was taken home. My eyes were sore and I could not see. They took me back to a house and there they put a solution of the peyote into my eyes and I got well in a week.

One night, when I was asleep, I dreamed that the world had come to an end. Some people Earthmaker (God) took, while some belonged to the bad spirit (the devil). I belonged to the bad spirit (the devil). Although I had given myself up (become a peyoteman), I had not as yet been baptized. That was why Earthmaker (God) did not take me. All those who belonged to Earthmaker (God) were marked, but I was not. I felt very bad about it when I woke up, although I had only dreamed about it. I felt very bad indeed. I wanted them to hurry and have another peyote meeting soon. I could hardly wait until I reached the place where the next meeting was to take place. I immediately told the leader (what I wanted) and asked him to baptize me and he baptized me in the morning. After that morning I felt better.

Then I went to work and I worked with a railroad work-gang. I was still working when the time for the midsummer celebration approached. I always went to the peyote meeting on Saturday nights.

The old man was right in what he had told me. The girl students returned in the summer. Shortly (after they returned) a man, a friend of mine who had gone around with me, asked me if I wanted to get married. "Yes, I do," I answered. Then he said, "Listen, I have been thinking of something. What kind of a woman do you wish to marry?" I told him what I had in mind. Then he said, "Come home with me. I have a younger sister. I want her to marry a good man; I would like to have her marry you," he said. Then I went home with him. When we got there (and discussed the matter) the girl gave her consent. The parents also consented.

So there I got married and what I expected has taken place and I have lived with her ever since. On one occasion, after she was used to me, she told me this. (Before she had married she had determined that) if she ever got married, she would not care to marry a very young man. "I wanted a man who ate peyote and who paid attention to the ceremony." Such a man she desired and such a man was I, she said. She loved me, she said, and she was glad that she had married me. This is what she had asked Earthmaker (God) in prayer. "And indeed it has happened as I wished," she said. She believed it was the will of Earthmaker (God) that we had done this, she said. She was therefore glad (that she had married me). Together we gave ourselves up (to the peyote) at a peyote meeting. From that time on we have remained members of the peyote (ceremony).

Many things are said under the influence of the peyote. The members (would) get into a kind of trance and speak of many things. On one occasion they had a peyote meeting which lasted two nights. I ate a good deal of peyote. The next morning I tried to sleep. I suffered a great deal. I lay down in a very comfortable position. After a while a (nameless) fear arose in me. I could not remain in that place, so I went out into the prairie, but here again I was seized with this fear. Finally I returned to a lodge near the lodge in which the peyote meeting was being held and lay down alone. I feared that I might do something foolish to myself (if I remained there alone), and I hoped that someone would come and talk to me. Then someone did come and talk to me, but I did not feel better, so I thought I would go inside where the meeting was going on. "I am going inside," I said to him. He laughed. "Alright, do so," said he. I went in and sat down. It was very hot and I felt as though I were going to die. I was very thirsty but I feared to ask for water. I thought that I was certainly going to die. I began to totter over.

I died, and my body was moved by another life. It began to move about; to move about and make signs. It was not I and I could not see it. At last it stood up. The regalia—eagle feathers and gourds —these were holy, they said. They also had a large book there (the Bible). These my body took and what is contained in that (book) my body saw. It was a Bible. The regalia were not holy, but they were good ornaments. My body told them that; and that if any person paid attention to Earthmaker's (God's) ceremony, he would be hearkening to what the Bible said; that, likewise, my body told them. Earthmaker's son (God's son) said that he was the only way. This means that one can only get life from the Word. (My) body spoke of many things and it spoke of what was true. Indeed it spoke of many things. It spoke of all the things that were being done (by the pagan Indians) and which were evil. A long time it spoke. At last it stopped. Not I, but my body standing there, had done the talking. Earthmaker (God) had done his own talking. I would be confessing myself a fool if I were to think that I had said all this, it (my body) told me.

After a while I returned to my normal human condition. Some of those there had been frightened, thinking that I had gone crazy. Others had liked it. It was discussed a good deal. They called it the "shaking" state. It was said that the condition in which I was, was not part of Earthmaker's (God's) religion. I was told that whoever ate a lot of peyote would, through the peyote, be taught the teachings of Earthmaker (God). Earthmaker's (God's) ways and man's ways were different. Whoever, therefore, wished to help this religion must give himself up (to it). If you ate a good deal of this peyote and believed that it could teach you something, then it assuredly would do so. That, at least, is the way in which I understand the matter.

Once we had a meeting at the home of a member who was sick. The sick would always get well when a meeting was held in their home, and that is why we did it. At that meeting I got into the "shaking" condition again. My body told (us) how our religion (peyote) was an affair of Earthmaker's (God's) and even if one knew only a portion of it, one could still see (partake of) Earthmaker's (God's) religion.

Thus it went on talking. "Earthmaker (God), His Son (Christ) and His Holiness (the Holy Ghost), these are the three ways of saying it. Even if you know one (of these three), it means all. Every one of you has the means of opening (the road) to Earthmaker (God). It is given to you. With that (your belief) you can open (the door to God). You can not open it with knowledge (alone). How many letters are there to the key (the road to God)? Three. What are they?" There were many educated people (there), but none of them said anything. "The first (letter) must be a K, so if a person said K, that would be the whole of it. But let me look in the book (the Bible) and see what that means," said the body. Then it (the body) took the Bible and began to turn the leaves. The body did not know where it was itself, for it was not learned in books. Finally in Matthew, chapter 16, it stopped. There it speaks about it. "Peter did not give himself up" (it says). "For a long time he could not give up his own knowledge. There (in that passage) it says Key." That is the work of Earthmaker (God). At least so I understand it. He made use of my body and acted in this manner, in the case of the peyote.

Then I go about telling (every one) that this religion is good. Many other people at home said the same thing. Many, likewise, have joined this religion and are getting along nicely.

On one occasion, after I had eaten a good deal of peyote, I learned the following from it: that all I had done in the past, that it had all been evil. This was plainly revealed to me. What I thought was holy, and (by thus thinking) was lost, that I now know was false. (It is false), this giving of (pagan) feasts, of holding (the old) things holy, the Medicine Dance, and all the Indian customs.

J. B.'s Account of His Conversion

I was at the old agency. There they were to try me for murder. At night, as I sat in jail, certain people came to me and told me that they had a gallon jug of whisky, and that if I was free that night, I should come and drink with them. They would wait for me. That same night there was a peyote meeting at John Rave's house and my brother Sam invited me to go there. Sam stood around there waiting for me. He was very low in spirits. He knew of the other invitation I had received and he told me that he would go with me wherever I went. I wanted very badly to go to the place where they had the liquor, and should have done so if Sam had given me the least chance. However, I could not get rid of him, so I decided to go to the peyote meeting. When I arrived there, we found just enough room in the center for myself and Sam. Sam sat at the right of me and John Bear at the left. In front of me there was some peyote infusion, and some peyote ground up and dampened.

As we sat there Sam began to cry and I began to think. I knew why Sam was crying; he wanted me to take some of the peyote. After a while I began to think of my own troubles. But I thought it wasn't the proper way of taking it just because I was in trouble.

Then I thought of the other peyote eaters, how much they must be wanting me to take it. After a while I spoke to Sam and said, "I am going to eat this medicine, but . . ." Then I began to cry. After a while he tried to get me to say the balance, but I couldn't. I drank some of the solution. As the others saw that I was willing to take it they gave me a big ball of dampened peyote. However, I didn't like that and I asked for some more peyote in the dry state. I sat there asking for more and more peyote. This I kept up all night. When morning came I stopped. Just then Harry Rave got up to speak, and no sooner did he get up than I knew exactly what he was going to say. This must be the way of all peyote eaters, I thought. I looked around me; and suddenly I realized that all those within the room knew my thoughts and that I knew the thoughts of all the others. Harry Rave spoke and finished his speech; but I had known it all before he said a word. Then A. Priest, who was leading the meeting, arose and asked the rest to get up, so that they might turn themselves over to Christ. I also rose; but when I got up I was seized with a choking sensation. I couldn't breathe. I wanted to grab hold of Bear and Sam, but I didn't, thinking that I was going to stand whatever was coming to me. When I made up my mind to that, I felt relieved. Then I knew what the real meaning of turning one's self over to Christ meant.

In the morning they stopped the meeting and everyone seemed happy and glad. I, however, was very serious and wondered why they were all laughing. Every once in a while they would come and talk to me. I wondered why they did it, when they knew what was going on within me. For that reason I wouldn't answer them.

That week there were four meetings, and I went to all of them and ate very much peyote. The fourth meeting was at the usual place, John Rave's house. I sat with Sam as usual. At night I became filled with peyote. All at once I heard a voice saying, "You are the one who is to tell of the medicine dance." And I thought that Sam was speaking to me, so I turned around and looked at him, but he hadn't said a word. Soon I realized that nobody near me had said anything, and I began to think, "Why should it be I? Why not one of the others?" I rather pushed the idea from me; but no sooner had I done so than I began to have a tired and depressed sensation. This passed all over me. I knew that if I got up with the sincere purpose of giving in to the power that was wanting me to speak of the medicine dance I should be relieved. However, for some reason, I know not why, I felt like resisting.

The next morning I asked to be baptized, and said that I would thereafter have nothing more to do with offerings to the spirits;

that I would not give any more feasts; and that I would not have any more to do with the medicine dance. From that day on I quit all my old beliefs. I did not feel like saying all this, for indeed my heart was turned just the other way, but I couldn't help it, for I was filled with the peyote.

From that time on, at every meeting that I attended, I could not rid myself of the idea that I must tell of the medicine dance. At all such times a feeling of heaviness would come over me. There I would be with but one thing on my mind; should I, or should I not, tell of it? I did not want to, and thought of all sorts of excuses— that I was not a member of the Nebraska division, etc.

I was in this frame of mind while living with John Walker. There I received word that I would be wanted to tell of the medicine dance. From that moment I could not rest easy. I went to the barn and prayed and wept, asking that God might direct me. I went about but could not sit quiet. My wife stayed around me crying. As I stood there, someone drove up with a white team. Then I thought of all the unhappiness I would cause to members of the medicine lodge if I told the secrets of the medicine dance; and I asked myself if it really would not be a sin to cause so much misery. The man who was driving the white team was John Baptiste, and he told me that I was wanted to tell of the medicine dance. I got ready and entered the buggy. I was still crying and praying. Then it occurred to me that I would like to see John Rave. No sooner had I thought of this than John Rave appeared in the road. I got out and shook hands with him and told him where I was going and for what purpose, and asked him what he thought of the matter. He began to thank me for the work I was going to do and said, "This is what we should try to do, to help one another and to work for our Creator." Then he thanked me again. Perfect happiness now came over me and I went to Sioux City and got married legally. From now on I was entirely filled with the desire to tell all that I knew about the medicine dance. "This must be the work assigned to me by the Creator," I thought; and yet I have rejected the idea all the time.

On Paul's last trip, although I had not finished the translation, I didn't care to have any more to do with it, and said that somebody else should finish the work, my excuse being that I was busy. So, as soon as I heard that Paul had come, I packed up and hurried out west as quickly as possible, for I knew that he would bother the life out of me if he found me. However, no sooner had I reached the home of my friend than I was seized with an attack of rheumatism, with which I had never been afflicted before, and the next morning Paul appeared with a wagon to take me back to Winnebago. Now I know that the telling and the translation of the medicine dance is my mission in life, and I am willing to tell all to the full extent of my knowledge.

JESSE CLAY'S ACCOUNT OF THE ARAPAHO MANNER OF GIVING THE
PEYOTE. CEREMONY WHICH HE INTRODUCED AMONG THE WIN-
NEBAGO IN 1912

I went to Oklahoma once as the guest of an Arapaho Indian.
While there I witnessed the Arapaho manner of holding a peyote
meeting and was very much impressed with it. A year later this
Arapaho came to visit me in Winnebago, and while he was with us
a few of my friends urged me to hold the peyote ceremony according
to the Arapaho method. I held several meetings at which my
Arapaho friend led.

Now these are the instructions that Arapaho Bull gave me.

The person giving the ceremony must get up at sunrise so that
he can tell exactly where the sun is going to rise. He must place a
stick and make the drawing of a cross on the earth just in that
direction from which the sun is about to rise. He does this in order
to get the correct location for the tipi and the fireplace. Then he
marks a circle around the cross. Then he makes a diagonal mark
through the center of the circle, thus making the circle resemble a
star. The circle is the outline of the tipi. Then another diagonal
mark is made so that the drawing resembles, to their minds, a peyote. A fireplace which resembles a half-moon is placed right in
the center of the lodge. After that the tipi poles are raised, 12 in
number. Finally the whole is inclosed in canvas. When finished
it is supposed to represent the earth. It is then ready to be
entered. Special preparations are made for entering. The drummer with his drum and the leader and those behind him with
all their regalia march up to the door. Before these enter, however, an attendant, called the fireman, spreads sage all over the
lodge, from the seat of the leader to the door and back again. Then
he starts a fire, always placing the left fire sticks first. When they
are all thus lined up outside of the door the leader offers a prayer.

"May the Creator be with us when we enter this lodge."

The leader now enters and, proceeding along the left side of the
lodge, marches to his seat, and there he stands with his drum until
the lodge is filled. After all have entered they sit down. Then the
fireman who sits to the right rekindles the fire. The leader now
spreads out his articles—a gourd, a drumstick, a staff, and the
feathers. He then takes 12 sage leaves and lays them out in the
form of a star, first making a cross-shaped object and then filling
this into the desired form. On top he places the peyote, and, leaning
against that, he places a flute made of an eagle bone, the mouth of
the flute resting against the peyote. Then he puts an otter-skin cap
at the foot of the flute. After a while the leader takes the peyote
he is going to use in one hand and some cedar needles in the other,

and, going to his seat, where all the other objects are spread out, he sits down and prays. He prays that all the participants may be strengthened by the prospective meeting. He offers up thanks for the peyote and prays that all may be in the proper spirit that night. Then he throws the needles in the fire and holds the peyote over the smoke of the cedar. When this has been finished he returns to his seat, eats one peyote, and gives one to the drummer. After they have eaten these he passes four peyote in turn to those on his left until the peyote comes to the one sitting nearest the door. Four peyote are given to the one nearest the door that he, in turn, may pass them to those on the other side of the door and so on until the leader is reached again. Before the peyote is eaten, the leader gets up and talks. He instructs the people as to the nature of the meeting and tells them that those who wish to go out must do so after the midnight water is drunk and not until after the leader returns from outside. No one is to go out while anyone is singing, praying, or eating peyote. He then speaks of the special prayers that are to be offered up and asks them to offer general prayers for all nonmembers and even for their enemies. After that the leader again offers up a prayer and smokes all the objects he had spread before his seat. Then the songs are to start, all, however, first eating peyote.

(When the fire first starts and thereafter, throughout the night, it is supposed to represent light, just as God said, "Let there be light.")

The first song is always the same and is called the starting song. Those that follow are peyote songs. When he has finished these songs he passes the singing staff to the right of the drummer. When this one has finished the staff is returned to the leader, who passes it on to the left, and then in rotation it goes to the one sitting near the door. The drum, when it is handed on, is always passed under the staff. The fire is always replenished, but toward midnight special care is taken in this regard and the coals are placed in the shape of a crescent between the fire and the earth crescent, and the fireman sweeps first around the left and then around the right side. Then exactly at midnight the leader calls for his singing staff and his drum, no matter where they happen to be, and, taking the singing staff and sending the drum to the drummer, he blows his flute and sings. The song he sings then is called the midnight song. After that three peyote songs are sung, it making no difference which they are. As the leader starts his midnight song the fireman takes up his position at the doorway opposite the fireplace and the leader. When the second song is started the fireman turns around to the right and goes out and gets water and soon comes back with it. When he reenters he makes the figure of a cross on the ground where he stood just before he left and places water on it. Then he squats down on his knees.

When the leader stops singing he walks to the crescent by the fireplace and begins praying again. After the prayer he burns some more cedar needles. The reason for drinking water at midnight is because Christ was born at midnight and because of the good tidings that he brought to the earth, for water is one of the best things in life and Christ is the savior of mankind. After the leader has made his prayer and the cedar is burned, then the fireman reaches over toward the smoke and makes a motion with his body as if he were drawing the smoke over himself. He then takes the water and brings it over to the leader. The leader takes a bunch of feathers and, dipping it into the water, sprinkles it on the peyote, then on the fire, on the sage, and finally all over the lodge, beginning with the doorway and then going around. The water is then drunk in a regular order, first by the leader, then by the drummer, and then by all the other people. After all these things have been done the leader returns the staff to the man from whom he had taken it at midnight. As soon as this man starts the singing again the leader takes his flute and goes outside. He goes toward the east for a short distance, and there he sits down and offers up a prayer for the people. Then he blows his flute, and going to the south of the lodge repeats the same procedure. This is also repeated for the west and the north. When the singing within the lodge has stopped, he returns and takes his seat.

The purpose of going to the four directions and blowing the flute is to announce the birth of Christ to all the world.

After the leader has reentered the singing continues as before. At daybreak the fireman fixes the fire in the same way as at midnight. The staff, drum, etc., is now passed to the leader, who as soon as he has received everything takes his flute and blows on it. Before doing this, however, he puts on his otter-skin cap. The purpose of blowing the flute just at that time is to represent the trumpet of the Day of Judgment, when Christ will appear wearing His crown in all glory. The putting on of the otter-skin cap represents the crown.

The song used on this occasion is called the water song. After the first song is finished the fireman opens the door and a woman enters carrying water, which she pours over the cross which the fireman had sprinkled at midnight. The fireman then spreads something for her to sit on, between the water and the door.

When the leader has finished his four songs, he lays down his staff, etc., and, taking some cedar needles, offers up a prayer of thanks, and as he finishes he throws the cedar into the fire and sits down while the woman gathers the smoke toward her in the same way as the fireman had done on the previous night. Then the leader takes a drinking cup and sends it toward the woman. The fireman now rises and pours water on the impressions he had made when drawing the cross on the earth, and the woman drinks some water from the cup, which she then returns to the leader. The water is then returned to her and she passes it around the lodge, beginning at the left. When it reaches the leader again, he takes out the same cup which he had handed to the woman and drinks out of it. The water, however, is passed on until it reaches the door. The fireman would then take it and bring it back to where it had been placed when first brought in. The woman rises and goes around the fire-place from left to right, taking the water with her. Finally the leader takes his singing staff and sings four songs. When these songs are finished, the woman places some food just outside the door. The fireman goes outside and brings in this food, placing it in a line between the fire and the door. Four things are brought in—water, corn with sweetened water, fruit, and meat. When the food is brought in the leader puts away all the objects he had spread out before him, which the fireman takes out of the lodge. The leader then offers up a prayer of thanks and says grace. The four kinds of food are passed around the lodge, beginning with the entrance, from left to right. After they are returned they are placed in line again, only in the reverse order from that used before. The fireman then takes them outside. While the people are eating the door remains open.

(During the evening the leader represents the first created man, the woman dressed up is the New Jerusalem, the bride waiting for the bridegroom. The cup used by the leader and the woman is supposed to symbolize the fact that they are to become one; the water represents the God's gift, His Holiness. The corn represents the feast to be partaken of on the Day of Judgment and the fruit represents the fruit of the tree of life. The meat represents the message of Christ and those who accept it will be saved.) [4]

The above descriptions represent the Peyote cult as it was given between 1908 and 1913. It is quite clear that a definite organization exists consisting of a unit of five positions occupied by the leader and four helpers. No specific requirements, with the exception, of course, of that of being a peyote eater, are associated with the right to occupy these positions.

No specialized features have become associated with the positions of the four helpers. As indicated before, John Rave is always the leader when he is present, but the position of leadership can be delegated to others. This is always of a temporary nature. It may be significant to note that whenever delegated the leadership is always delegated to men who have been among the first of the converts, outside of Rave's immediate family, and who were leaders in the old

[4] J. C.'s account ends here.

pagan ceremonies. In 1910 this delegation of leadership was clearly a recent tendency, conditioned, on the one hand, by the size of the reservation and the impossibility of Rave's being everywhere, and, on the other hand, by Rave's frequent absence on proselytizing missions. In 1913 it had already become customary for a number of men to hold the position of leader even when Rave was present. A further complication was introduced when Jesse Clay began giving the peyote ceremonies in the Arapaho manner, for he then stood in the same relation to his method of giving the ceremony as Rave stood to the older form. As we shall see, there was, even in 1908, a separatist movement led by Albert Hensley, which, if it had succeeded, would have given Hensley the same leadership that Rave enjoyed before him and that Clay subsequently acquired.

DEVELOPMENT OF THE RITUALISTIC COMPLEX

From the accounts given by various members of the Peyote cult it is quite clear that Rave became interested in the peyote on one of his many trips to Oklahoma. According to the verbal account he gave, which differs in some respects from the account he subsequently dictated on the particular visit which resulted in his first eating the peyote, he was in a most distressed and unhappy condition of mind owing to the loss of his wife and children.[5] He went away from Winnebago with the intention of staying away as long as possible from the scene of his loss.

Rave's account of his conversion gives a sufficiently dramatic picture of how he first ate the peyote and its immediate effects. In response to numerous questions as to how he was first induced to eat the peyote he always said that it was because he had been so frequently asked. It is, however, far more likely that he was passing through an emotional crisis at that particular time, and the requests that he partake of it and the inducements held out to him, made it easier for him to succumb then than on his previous visits.

To judge from Rave's remarks, his first belief in the peyote had nothing of the nature of a conversion to a new religion. It seems to have been similar to the average Winnebago attitude toward a medicinal plant obtained either as a gift or through purchase. There is only one new note—stimulation by a narcotic.

Rave states that the peyote cured him of a disease with which he had been afflicted for a long time. After repeated requests his wife also consents to being treated; so he paints her face and, taking the rattle, sings peyote songs while she eats the peyote. His attitude

---

[5] In the account Rave himself gives he speaks of seeing his wife and children. As his verbal statement was corroborated by other people, we are inclined to believe that in his dictated account of his conversion he had forgotten the actual state of affairs. It may, of course, be that in his ardent desire to show the marvelous effects of the peyote he permitted his memory to play him false.

throughout, both from his own testimony and from that of others, seems to have been practically the attitude of the Winnebago shaman. He even offered tobacco to the peyote.

We have, then, at the beginning the introduction of apparently only one new element—the peyote, with possibly a few Christian teachings. Everything else seems to be typically Winnebago, and in consonance with their shamanistic practices. On the whole, the extension of the Winnebago cultural background seems to have been so instantaneous that so far as the specific cultural traits of the Winnebago are concerned there was hardly anything new at all. This view does not, of course, interfere in the least with the fact that to the Winnebago themselves the presence of the peyote represented the introduction of a new element.

The elaboration of the peyote practices at Rave's hands is the most difficult problem to trace on account of the lack of data. In the account that he gives of his conversion there is no evidence whatsoever of any antagonistic attitude toward the old Winnebago manner of living. When the author met him, however, for the first time, in 1908, this passive attitude had changed to one of violent hatred for the old Winnebago customs. Why and under what circumstances this change took place we do not know. It probably represented the interaction of many elements, the hostility of the tribe, the drawing of issues sharply around certain points, and the gradual assumption on the part of Rave of the rôle of a prophet who had solved the problem of the adjustment of the Winnebago to the surrounding white civilization. Offhand, one might be inclined to believe that Rave's insistence upon breaking with the past was due entirely to the influence of the Christian elements incorporated in his new religion. It is, however, extremely doubtful whether such an assumption is necessary. There seem to have been comparatively few Christian elements in the religion before Albert Hensley's influence had made itself felt, yet many of the old war bundles had been destroyed long before that time, and the peyote eaters were looked upon with cordial dislike by the conservative members of the tribe. The admonition that only a complete break with the past could save the Winnebagoes and enable them to compete successfully with the white intruders had been given to the Winnebagoes once before by the famous Shawnee prophet. What the latter claimed, however, was that the various sacred objects used by the Winnebago had lost their power, and that that power must now be renewed. This he thought could only be done by returning to the old manner of living which he claimed the Winnebago were no longer following. Such a claim was, after all, not revolutionary. It is not, therefore, the break with the Winnebago present-day viewpoint that characterizes Rave's attitude, but the fact that instead of returning to the older, purer life as the Shawnee prophet proposed to do, he substituted an alien religion. It was because he was introducing an alien religion, not because he was introducing a new religion, that he was so intensely hated by the conservative members of the tribe.

When this hostility was at its height a new convert, Albert Hensley, revolutionized the entire cult by introducing the reading of the Bible, postulating the dogma that the peyote opened the Bible to the understanding of the people, and also adding a number of Christian practices. He, like Rave, had been in Oklahoma. He brought back with him many peyote songs, generally in other languages, dealing with Christian ideas, upon which subsequently Winnebago songs were modeled. He also introduced either baptism itself or an interpretation of baptism, and induced Rave to attempt a union with the Christian Church. He seems to have been the only prominent man connected with the peyote who was subject to epileptic fits. He had the most glorious visions of heaven and hell while in his trance, and these he expounded afterwards in terms of Revelation and the mystical portions of the New Testament. Hensley's additions represent a second stratum of borrowed elements, all of which are in the nature of accretions as far as the peyote itself is concerned. The Bible is explained in terms of the peyote. Neither Hensley nor his followers ever interpreted the peyote in terms of the Bible, although other elements of the old Winnebago culture were so interpreted. These elements, however, represented features that even in the old Winnebago cults exhibited a great variability in interpretation.

Rave's attitude toward the innovations of Hensley seems to have been that of a benevolent acquiescence. He himself could neither read nor write. Yet he immediately accepted the Bible and added it to his other regalia. As such it always seems to have remained. To Rave, after all, the peyote was the principal element, and if Hensley chose to insist that the Bible was only intelligible to those who partook of the peyote why that naturally fell within its magical powers. From the entire omission in Rave's account of the Peyote cult of the more important things that Hensley introduced and from the fact that whenever Hensley's influence was not dominant there seems to have been little Bible reading, it seems justifiable to say that Rave's attitude toward these innovations was merely passive.

There never was any rivalry between Rave and Hensley. The latter was, however, a much younger man, quick-tempered, conceited, dogmatic, and withal having a strong mixture of Puritan Protestant ideas. A conflict developed after a while and in a very interesting manner. Rave had allowed a man with an extremely bad reputation, who had been admitted as a member of the Peyote cult, to occupy one of the four positions. Hensley violently protested, on the ground that a man of X.'s character could not properly perform the rites associated with that position. Rave, however, retorted that the efficacy of the peyote, of any position connected with its cult, was in no way connected with the character of the performer, and that it was inherent in the peyote and in the Peyote ritual. Thereupon, after much parleying to and fro, Hensley formally seceded, taking with him a number of followers. The bulk of the peyote eaters, however, remained with Rave, and within a comparatively short time a number of Hensley's followers returned to Rave, so that in 1911 Hensley had merely a handful of people. Since then he has ceased to be a force, although his innovations have been retained by a number of the younger Peyote members, especially by those who read English.

In 1911 there was no unification of the ideas of Rave and Hensley. Since then, strange to say, although Hensley's attempt to set up his own religion failed utterly, his ideas and Christian innovations seemed to have triumphed completely. This, however, has gone hand in hand with a marked dropping off of enthusiasm. It appears now as if the Peyote cult has run its course. Some of the members have recently returned to the old pagan customs, others have practically become Christians, and many have become indifferent.

Unquestionably the most interesting of recent innovations is that introduced by Jesse Clay, the account of which has been given before. This is, of course, the Arapaho manner of conducting the ceremony. At the present time it has none of the characteristics of the Winnebago ceremonial. Whether in the next few years it will develop any depends upon the interest manifested in it by the Peyote worshipers and upon the vitality of the Peyote movement in general.

It is extremely suggestive to compare what Rave introduced with the ceremony borrowed by Clay. The former introduced an isolated element, the peyote and its worship, and clothed it almost immediately in characteristic Winnebago forms. It can truly be said that although the peyote is an alien element, from the Winnebago viewpoint, everything else in the ceremony is and was from the beginning typically Winnebago. Clay's method of conducting the Peyote ceremonies, on the other hand, is entirely alien. For it ever to become popular with the large mass of Winnebago it will have to become thoroughly assimilated with the Winnebago background.

DISSEMINATION OF THE DOCTRINE

Let us now see how the ideas of Rave and Hensley were transmitted in the tribe itself, who the first and the later converts were, in what the nature of their conversion consisted, and what they, in turn, brought to the new cult.

The first and foremost virtue predicated by Rave for the peyote was its curative power. He gives a number of instances in which hopeless venereal diseases and consumption were cured by its use; and this was the first thing one heard about it as late as 1913. In the early days of the Peyote cult it appears that Rave relied principally for new converts upon the knowledge of this great curative virtue of the peyote. The main point apparently was to induce people to try it. No amount of preaching of its direct effects, such as the hyperstimulation induced, the glorious visions, and the feeling of relaxation following, would ever have induced prominent members of the old Winnebago religious societies to try it. For that reason it is highly significant that all the old members of the Peyote cult speak of the diseases of which it cured them. Along this line lay unquestionably its appeal for the most converts. Its subsequent spread was due to a large number of interacting factors. One informant claims that there was little religion connected with it at first, and that the people drank the peyote on account of its peculiar effects.

The manner in which it spread at the beginning was simple and significant—viz, along family lines. As soon as an individual had become a peyote eater he devoted all his energies to converting other members of his family. From instances that have come to our notice this lay in an insistent appeal to family ties and personal affection. A man showed unusual courtesy, showered innumerable favors upon relatives he was anxious to convert, and thereby earned the gratitude of the recipient, who at some critical moment, let us say, such as illness or mental depression, showed it by partaking of the peyote. The same methods were employed in the more general propaganda. The author knows of Peyote people who drove many miles in order to be present at the bedside of some old conservative who was ill, perhaps neglected by his relatives; bring him food, and spend the night with him in the most affectionate solicitude. They always had sufficient tact and understanding of human nature not to obtrude their purpose on the sick man too much. To the casual observer their object seemed simply that of a Samaritan. They would hardly have admitted that behind all their solicitude lay the desire to obtain a new convert. They would have claimed that their only purpose, over and above their sincere desire to comfort the sick man, was to demonstrate to their fellow Winnebago what changes the peyote had wrought in them. In this way the patient drew the inference, an inference that was likely to be drawn all the more quickly and forcibly when he contrasted the behavior of these Peyote nurses with that of his pagan relatives. The author was fortunate enough to obtain a fairly complete account of a conversion, illustrating both these features.

WHAT THE CONVERTS INTRODUCED

It is quite impossible to establish now what these converts introduced individually.   For that matter it is not necessary to assume
that they brought any specific additions to the cult.   What they did
bring were Winnebago; and with that, the emotional and cultural
setting of the old pagan background.   To one, the eating of the
peyote gave the same magical powers that were formerly associated
with membership in the medicine dance; to another, the visions were
direct blessings from God, directing him to perform certain actions;
to a third, faithfulness to the teachings of the Peyote cult became
associated with a certainty of reaching God, of being able to take the
right road in the journey to the spirit land.   Even a man so thoroughly saturated with Christian doctrines as Hensley himself felt it
necessary to introduce an origin myth; and although we know that
he borrowed it from a southern tribe, it is quite clear that in Hensley's
narrative it has already assumed all the characteristics of a Winnebago fasting experience and ritualistic myth, similar to those connected with the founders of the old Winnebago cult societies.   In its
totality the atmosphere of the Peyote cult became thus charged with
the old Winnebago background.   In 1911 it can not be said that they
had displaced the distinctive Christian elements.   Among the younger
members, especially those who had been trained in the east and could
read and write English, the influence of the Christian ideas in the
interpretation of the old pagan features is, as was pointed out before,
so strong to-day that it threatens to displace the others.

The following homily will show how the old myths were used by
the younger Peyote members to point a tale.

The old people often spoke of the Trickster, but we never knew
what they meant.   They told us how he wrapped a coon-skin blanket
around himself and went to a place where all the people were dancing.   There he danced until evening and then he stopped and turned
around.   No one was to be seen anywhere, and then he realized that
he had mistaken for people dancing the noise made by the wind blowing through the reeds.

So do we Winnebagoes act.   We dance and make a lot of noise, but
in the end, we accomplish nothing.

Once, as the Trickster was going toward a creek, he saw a man
standing on the other side, dressed in a black suit, and pointing his
finger at him.   He spoke to the man but the latter would not answer.
Then he spoke again and again, but without receiving any reply.
Finally he got angry and said, "See here! I can do that too."   He put
on the black coat and pointed his finger across the creek.   Thus both
of them stood all day.   Toward evening, when he looked around again,
he noticed that the man across the creek, pointing his finger at him,
was really just a tree stump.   "O my! what have I been doing all

this time? Why did I not look before I began? No wonder the people call me the Foolish One."

So are we Winnebagoes. We never look before we act. We do everything without thinking. We think we know all about it.

The Trickster was walking around with a pack on his back. As he walked along, someone called to him. "Say, we want you to sing." "All right," said he. "I am carrying songs in my pack, and if you wish to dance, build a large lodge for me with a small hole at the end for an entrance." When it was finished, they all went in, and the Trickster followed them. Those who had spoken to him were birds. He told them that while dancing they were not to open their eyes, for if they did their eyes would become red. Whenever a fat bird passed the Trickster he would choke it to death, and if it cried out, he would say, "That's it! That's it! Give a whoop!"

After a while one of the birds got somewhat suspicious and opened its eyes just the least little bit. He saw that the Trickster was choking all the birds. "He is killing us all," said the bird. "Let all who can run for their lives." Then he flew out through the top of the house. The Trickster took the birds he had killed and roasted them; but he did not get a chance to eat them, for they were taken away from him by somebody.

So are we Winnebagoes. We like all that is forbidden. We say that we like the medicine dance; we say that it is good and yet we keep it secret and forbid people to witness it. We tell members of the dance not to speak about it until the world shall come to an end. They are afraid to speak of it. We, the Winnebago, are the birds, and the Trickster is satan.

Once, as the Trickster was going along the road, some one spoke to him. He listened, and he heard it say, "If anyone eats me all bad things will come out of him." Then the trickster went up to the one talking, and said, "What is your name?" "My name is 'Blows-himself-away.'" The Trickster would not believe it; so he ate it. After a while, he blew himself away. He laughed. "Oh, pshaw! I suppose this is what it meant." As he went along it grew worse and worse, and it was only after the greatest hardship that he succeeded in returning home.

So are we Winnebagoes. We travel on this earth all our lives, and then when one of us tastes something that makes him unconscious we look upon this thing with suspicion when he regains consciousness.

THE ATTITUDE OF THE CONSERVATIVES

At every phase of the cult's development Rave had to contend with the hostility of the conservative members of the tribe. It would be interesting to know in what manner and degree this hostility manifested itself upon the first introduction of the peyote. As we have seen, there was in the beginning little difference between the beliefs relating to the peyote and those connected with the old Winnebago medicinal plants. Nevertheless the author was assured that hostility was exhibited to the new cult from the very start. Would the same hostility have been exhibited had this new feature represented some development from within the tribe? In other words, what it would be interesting to know, is whether the fact that the peyote was derived from without led to a hostility different in kind from that exhibited toward an innovation developing within the culture itself. No evidence could be obtained that would justify us in explaining the hostility felt by the older conservative Winnebago as due in any part to the fact that it was alien in origin. Certain elements that to-day form an integral part of the most popular of all Winnebago ceremonies were borrowed from the Sauk and Iowa, and the Winnebago realize this and mention it in the introductory myths told in connection with the preparatory rites of the medicine dance. The explanation obtained was always the same—that the hostility was due to the fact that the teachings of the Peyote people departed from those of their ancestors and that the Peyote were simply aping the habits and customs of the whites. What seems to have met with the greatest opposition from the older shamans was the denial of the doctrine of reincarnation. The Christian doctrine of the immortality of the soul does not seem to have been felt as a substitute at all. One old conservative assured the author that he had long ago prophesied the appearance of the peyote among the Winnebago. He told the author the following:

"This medicine is one of the four spirits from below, and for that reason it is a bad thing. These spirits have always longed for human beings and now they are getting hold of them. Those who use this medicine claim that when they die they will only be going on a long journey. But that is not the truth, for when they eat peyote they destroy their spirits, and death to them will mean extermination. If I spit upon the floor, the sputum will soon dry up and nothing will remain of it. So death will be for them. I might go out and preach against this doctrine, but it would be of no avail, for I certainly would not be able to draw more than one or two people away from this spirit. Many will be taken in by this medicine; they will not be able to help themselves in any way. The bad spirit will certainly seize them."

CHAPTER XVII

THE CLAN WAR-BUNDLE FEASTS

THE WAR-BUNDLE FEAST OF THE THUNDERBIRD CLAN[1]

(FIRST VERSION)

INTRODUCTORY REMARKS

The Wagigō', Winter Feast, or War-bundle Feast, as it is generally called, is one of the principal ceremonies of the Winnebago. It is to a certain extent a clan ceremonial, for the clan is the basis of its organization, but apart from that fact, it has really nothing to do with the clan and must not be confused with the specific clan feasts held once a year. A perusal of the following sketch will show clearly that we are in reality dealing with a ceremony primarily connected with success in war and that its distinctive peculiarity among the Winnebago is that it has developed into a general ceremony of thanksgiving to the spirits and developed an organization based on the clan unit. As a result of the latter fact, we find 12 war rituals all essentially the same in content and differing only in details and in the fact that the host in each of the 12 performances belongs to a different clan. The specific differences in each performance are, first, the content of the war bundle; second, the origin myths of the feast and of the songs associated with each bundle; third, the songs

---

[1] PHONETIC TABLE.—All the consonants have the same value as those in English with the following exceptions:

c is pronounced like sh in *English*.

j has the sound of z in *azure*.

tc has the sound of ch in *church*.

dj has the sound of j in *judge*.

x has the sound of ch in German *Bach*.

γ is the sonant of x.

r is a slightly trilled linguo-apical r.

ŋ has the sound of ng in *sing*.

ṇ always represents r preceded by a nasalized vowel.

t is a marked surd.

b and g are intermediate stops, except in certain positions, where they become true sonants.

ʻ is the glottal stop.

Consonants followed by ʻ represent aspirated stops.

The vowels have the following values:

ȧ has the sound of au in *aught*.

a is the short continental a.

ā is long a.

e is short open as in *pen*.

ę is short and close but not as close as the French e in *fete*.

ē is long close e.

ē̆ is broad impure, as in an accentuated pronunciation of ei in *eight*.

i is short and open as in *tin*.

į is short and close.

ī is long and close.

o is short and open.

ǫ is short and close.

ō is long and close.

ȯ is long and open.

u is short and open.

ų is short and close.

ū is long and close.

ᴀ is obscure a.

ᴇ is obscure e.

ʻ denotes nasalization.

' denotes primary stress accent.

ˋ denotes secondary stress accent.

tnemselves; and, lastly, the order in which the guests are invited (pls. 56, 57, 58).

It follows from the above remarks that in order to get a really complete account of the entire ceremony information should be obtained from each clan. The account given by any one clan will only contain the origin myth and the songs belonging to the war bundle of that clan, for although it is part of the ceremony to relate the origin myths of the various war bundles and sing the specific songs connected with them, no individual would take it upon himself to tell any but those relating to the war bundle of his own clan. Thus it will be seen that any single account is defective in some rather important particulars.

ANALYTICAL PRESENTATION OF THE CEREMONY

The ceremony falls into three well-defined parts: I, the Sweat Lodge; II, the First Division, generally known either as the Feast in honor of Earthmaker or the Feast in honor of the Thunderbirds; and III, the Second Division, known as the Feast in honor of the Night Spirits.

There is little to be said about the Sweat Lodge, for it consists exclusively of offerings of tobacco and prayers to the spirits, on the part of the one giving the ceremony, whom we will call the host.

The first division can be divided into the following component elements: (1) The preparation of the buckskins; (2) the dog sacrifice; (3) the filling of the ceremonial pipe and the smoking ritual; (4) the tobacco offering to the spirits; (5) the buckskin offerings to the spirits; (6) the feast; (7) the fast-eating contest; and (8) the basic ritual.

The second division can be divided into the following component elements: (4) The tobacco offering to the spirits; (9) the throwing out of the buckskins; (6) the feast; (10) the episode of the "Night-crazed" warrior; (11) the terminal dog ritual; and (8) the basic ritual.

(1) *The preparation of the buckskins.*—The buckskins, made as white as possible by old women, are taken into the lodge by the host and there marked in the manner prescribed for each spirit. They are then tied to a framework and rolled to the top of this frame.

(2) *The dog sacrifice.*—The dog is strangled and a pouch of tobacco is tied to each limb, and another pouch and red feathers are tied around his neck. The body is then laid in front of the war bundle, facing south, this being the direction in which Disease-giver, the spirit to whom the dog is specially sacrificed, lives.

Before strangling, a short speech is addressed to the dog in which the slayer apologizes for killing him, and assures him that in the

PLATE 56

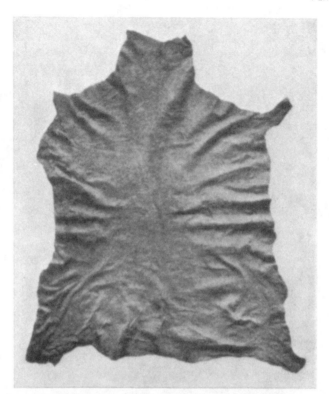

a. **THUNDERBIRD WAR BUNDLE**

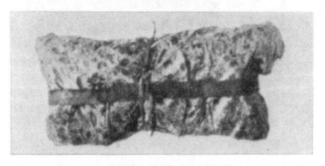

b. **HAWK WAR BUNDLE**

PLATE 57

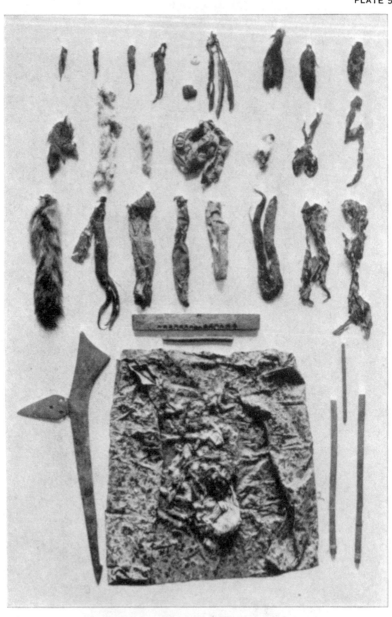

CONTENTS OF THUNDERBIRD WAR BUNDLE

PLATE 58

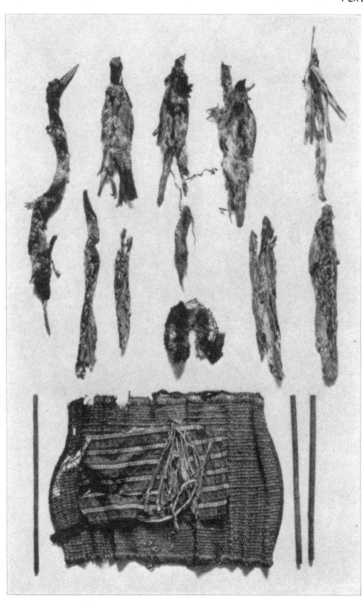

CONTENTS OF HAWK WAR BUNDLE

place to which he is going he will live far more happily than here among men.

(3) *Filling of the ceremonial pipe and the smoking ritual.*—Before the basic ritual of the first division is begun the attendants take some tobacco and, filling the ceremonial pipe, place it near the war bundle. As the first pipeful is intended for Earthmaker, the stem is directed vertically. Then as soon as the appropriate songs have been sung the attendant lights the pipe and passes it around the lodge, so that all the men may smoke. When the pipe returns to the host it is again filled.

This procedure is repeated three more times, but as in each case the offering is to a different spirit, the arrangement of the pipestem is different. At the second filling of the pipe the stem is turned to the west for the Thunderbirds; at the third, it is turned to the south for Disease-giver; and at the fourth, it is turned toward the earth for the earth and the spirits that live under the earth.

(4) *Tobacco offerings to the spirits.*—This occurs in two forms, (a) and (b).

(a) When the buckskins have been prepared and rolled up on the frameworks, then all those participating march around the lodge to the place where the war bundle is lying and pour tobacco upon it. Then they offer tobacco to all the spirits worshiped. The spirits mentioned specifically are, however, few in number, the offerings being really directed to the six cardinal points, east, north, west, south, above, and below.

(b) This is a more specific offering and all the spirits are mentioned by name and short addresses are made to them. It is repeated three times—once in the Sweat-Lodge ritual, then in the first, and lastly in the second division

In the Sweat-Lodge ritual the offering of tobacco is made to the following spirits: Earthmaker, Thunderbirds, Great Black Hawk, Night Spirits, Disease-giver, Sun, Moon, South Wind, and Eagle.

In the first division the order is different and more spirits are sacrificed to. The spirits to whom tobacco is offered are the following: Earthmaker, Thunderbirds, Night Spirits, Disease-giver, Sun, Earth, Moon, Eagle Chief, Day, South Wind, North Wind, Black Hawk, Wonaγi're Ŭaŋkcik, and Great Black Hawk.

In the second division the following spirits receive tobacco offerings: Night Spirits, Earth, Water, Pigeon Hawk, Moon, Earthmaker, Thunderbird, Great Black Hawk, Disease-giver, South Wind, and Sun.

Each spirit is addressed by name and then a handful of tobacco is poured into the fire.

(5) *The buckskin offering to the spirits.*—Short prayers are addressed to those spirits who are to receive buckskins and requests for power

are made to them. Only the following spirits receive buckskins: Thunderbird, Night Spirits, Disease-giver, South Wind, Sun, Earth-maker, Moon, Morning Star, Earth, and Water.

(6) *The feasts.*—There are two feasts, the one in the first division of the ceremony being generally known as the Thunderbird and that in the second division as the Night Spirit feast.

The guests are always divided into two divisions, the owners of war bundles and their male followers, and the women. The former, who are always warriors of repute, get the choice pieces of the deer, i. e., the heads, and the rest get the other pieces generally referred to as "the common pieces." The heads are eaten after those eating the common pieces have finished.

The host never eats at the feast he gives, but while the others are eating he plays on his reed flute.

(7) *The fast-eating contest.*—Before the heads are eaten two men belonging to the upper phratry and two belonging to the lower (i. e., generally two members of the Thunderbird clan and two members of the Bear clan) are selected to take part in the fast-eating contest. This consists of consuming an equal amount of food. The one who finishes first is considered the greater warrior. Both contestants start at a given signal and continue the contest to the accompaniment of songs sung by the other guests.

When a member of the upper phratry gives the ceremony his side always wins, and vice versa.

(8) *The basic ritual.*—After the buckskin ritual has been finished the host begins what is unquestionably the fundamental part of the ceremony, which I have called the "basic ritual." It consists of four speeches, each speech followed by a different set of songs. The first speech is followed by a set of war-bundle songs; the second by a paint set; the third by a Disease-giver set; and the last by a Night Spirit set. The last speech also contains a fasting experience of the first owner of the war bundle. When he is finished, the general feast and the fast-eating contest take place, and the basic ritual is for the time interrupted. It is continued as soon as these are finished, but not in the same manner as performed by the host. Instead of four speeches there is only one. As soon as one guest finishes speaking the other begins, and so on until all have finished.[1]

In the second division of the ceremony the basic ritual is performed in a slightly different manner. In the first place there seem to be two parts to it, the first one quite different from the basic ritual as given in the first division, and the second identical with it except that instead of seven there are only four guests called upon to speak.

In the first part of the basic ritual, as given here, the host delivers three speeches. After the first one a set of Night Spirit songs are

---

[1] Additional information on the Winter Feasts might lead me to an alteration of this last statement. In addition to the present, three more accounts of Winter Feasts were received.

sung; after the second one a dance song is sung and all the guests who so desire dance around the war bundle; after the third one the host passes the drum and other paraphernalia to the guest who is in charge of the buckskin destined for Earthmaker. This guest repeats the ritual in exactly the same manner as the host has done and then passes the drum, etc., to the second guest, and when the time comes he passes the drum, etc., to the third guest. Then the ritual of the throwing out of the buckskins intervenes, and after that the feast of the Night Spirits and the rite of those who have been crazed by the Night Spirits. Then, when these are finished, the basic ritual is continued. The continuation is, however, quite different from the first part and is identical with the basic ritual as given in the first part of the ceremony.

(9) *The throwing out of the buckskins.*—A warrior of great reputation is selected to begin the rites preparatory to the throwing out of the buckskins. One who has been blessed by the Night Spirits is preferably selected. He delivers a speech, and when he is finished the guests sing songs called "terminal Night Spirit" songs. Then the host prepares to sing a dance song, but before that he delivers a speech. Then, as the oldest men present sing, the host and the guests impersonating the spirits to whom tobacco is sacrificed take the buckskins and make the circuit of the lodge four times. An attendant precedes and another follows the procession, scattering incense consisting of branches of the arbor vitæ. Just before the fourth circuit is begun all the children smoke their hands and then touch the buckskin dedicated to Earthmaker. After the fourth circuit has been completed the buckskins are unrolled and thrown out through the top of the lodge, where the spirits are supposed to come and take them. After this, all holding tobacco in their hands walk to the fireplace and throw it in. Then, as a conclusion, all, even the women, rise in their respective seats and dance.

(10) *The episode of those who have been crazed by the Night Spirits.*— This is plainly an intrusive feature and does not take place at every performance of the ceremony. An individual who has brought himself to a state of religious frenzy strips himself entirely and behaves generally like one bereft of his senses. He sticks his hands into the boiling soup and makes a wild rush for the pot where the heads are being cooked and tries to bite them. It is believed that whoever gets the first bite will, at some future time, obtain a war honor. Then he takes the pipe placed in the center of the lodge, smokes it, and relates some war exploits. He then tells the assembled guests that in his trance he communicated with the spirits, and they told him that they had accepted all the offerings made.[2]

---

[2] There can be no doubt that we are dealing with an extremely specialized and interesting behavior, that in other tribes, and for that matter among the Winnebago themselves in other ceremonies, has an entirely different connotation.

(11) *Terminal dog ritual.*—This consists simply of a speech by the host to the assembled guests, telling them that the dog is to be sent to Disease-giver as an offering, and that he will pray to Disease-giver to preserve them from disease.

ANALYSIS OF TYPES OF ACTION AND SPEECHES

Circuit of the lodge.—This is always made in a direction contrary to that of the hands of a clock. The reason given for this method is that it is supposed to represent the journey of the Night Spirits around the earth.

Method of greeting.—This is the same as that which exists in all Winnebago ceremonies and is accurately described in my article on the Winnebago Medicine dance.[3]

Types of speeches.—This subject is of great importance because, while it is true that a certain freedom is allowed in the method of delivery and the choice of words, on the other hand, their content and to a large extent their symbolism and imagery are stereotyped. The speeches might perhaps best be divided into the following groups:

(a) *General addresses.*—These are generally delivered by the host to his guests and always contain expressions of gratitude for the kindness shown by the guests in condescending to accept his invitation.

(b) *Speeches of thankfulness.*—These are generally delivered by the guests and always contain complimentary references to the zealousness of the host in attending to his religious duties, expressions of gratitude for the invitation extended to them, and protestations, couched in the strongest terms, of their unworthiness for the honor thrust upon them and their utter inability to do aught that might insure the acceptance by the spirits of the offerings extended to them.

(c) *Speeches of admonition.*—These are plainly exhortations by the host to his band and by the leaders of the guests' bands to their bands, beseeching them to do their utmost to insure the success of the ceremony.

(d) *Speeches to the spirits.*—These are prayers varying in length and content.

THE DEVELOPMENT OF THE WAR-BUNDLE FEAST AND ITS PLACE IN THE CEREMONIAL ORGANIZATION OF THE WINNEBAGO

The ceremonial organization of the Winnebago can be divided into three types, according to the unit of organization that prevails. We find societies either based on common religious qualifications, such as being blessed by the same spirit, or those based on a fixed unit, as the five bands of the Medicine dance; organizations based on the clan, as the clan feasts; or, finally, temporary organizations based on war exploits, such as the Hŏk'ixe're dance, in which the four warriors who have counted coup on the last warpath form the units of organization. The peculiarity of the War-bundle Feast is that it belongs not merely to one of these types but to two of them.

The war bundles were originally family possessions and were, in the opinion of the writer, only secondarily associated with the clan as such. They represent a complex of blessings received from various spirits who are supposed to control the fortunes of war. They were handed down from one generation to another in the same family, but not necessarily to the eldest son, and could as a matter of default pass out of the hands of the immediate family. The individual who received the war bundle was that one who had by his interest, knowledge, character, and accomplishments demonstrated to the full satisfaction of the elder generation, more specifically to the elder generation represented by his father and close male relatives of his father's generation, that he was capable of continuing the ceremonials in a proper manner. It follows from this that he would have to be a well-known warrior. Now, it is customary among all the woodland tribes for a warrior who is about to start on a warpath to give a feast to which he invites all the other warriors, from among whom he, of course, has to draw his recruits; and at this feast he explains the nature of the contemplated warpath and his warrant—i. e., the thoroughness of the specific blessings he has received—for starting it.

In other words, we will have to picture to ourselves the war-bundle feast as originally a gathering of warriors preparatory to the starting out of a war party, in which the part of the host was always taken by the leader of the prospective war party. All of the well-known warriors were likely to have war bundles, and thus the basis for the development of what is, to all intents and purposes, a society of those who had war bundles was always present potentially. It is believed, however, that at the time the Winnebago culture was still in the formative stage this aspect of the gathering was entirely secondary, and that primarily it was a gathering of warriors for the immediate purpose of going on a warpath.

It may perhaps be interesting to go into some details of how this "society" aspect of a gathering of warriors developed. This development probably took two lines—first, a religious one, and secondly, one of definite organization. It would be quite erroneous to say that it took these lines of evolution, because it is in the nature of societies thus to develop. This originally temporary organization took these lines of development because of the presence in the war-bundle ritual of two factors—first, fasting experiences associated with the same spirits, and, second, the influence of the clan organization.

Only a small number of spirits were specifically associated with success in war, and these were Disease-giver, Thunderbirds, Sun, and

the Night Spirits.   All the warriors who possessed war bundles would
of necessity have to receive blessings from these, although in different
cases one or the other may have bestowed the more important powers.

The prominence given to the Thunderbird in the first and to the
Night Spirits in the second division give the ceremony a most marked
resemblance to societies like the Night Spirit society.   In the second
division it is even essential to have been blessed by the Night Spirits
in order to play a certain rôle.   There would thus develop the consciousness of community of interest due to the fact that as individuals
they were bound together by blessings received from the same
spirits, a feeling that was certain to be still further strengthened since,
in all likelihood, most of the possessors of war bundles belonged to
societies where this actually was the common bond.   The religious
and ceremonial aspect would thus of necessity be reinforced.   The
prayers for success on the warpath of course always existed, but
as the extraneous religious and ceremonial influences became
stronger and more insistent and as—and this should never be forgotten—the pursuit of war became less and less important, owing
to the breaking down of the culture consequent upon the advent of
the whites, these extraneous factors became, if not dominant at least
almost equal in importance to the historically older aspect; and our
original gathering of warriors, while still remaining a gathering of warriors, also became a ceremonial organization, in which offerings were
made to the entire Winnebago pantheon of spirits.   The great war
spirits were still all-important, but their position was contested by so
distinctive a peace deity as Earthmaker and such deities as Earth,
Moon, and Water.   The prayers for success in war were perhaps still
the most insistent, but prayers for life, not life merely that success in
war may be longer, but prayers for the whole content of life, were
offered up.   Disease-giver was appealed to not merely to bestow upon
man the greatest of all war honors, killing an enemy right in the midst
of his tribesmen, but also to ward off disease from the supplicants.

Still, as great as have been these extraneous influences, the character of the feast as originally one purely connected with war comes
out in numerous ways in the association, for instance, of war powers
with Earthmaker, Moon, and Earth, and significantly enough, in the
absence of the more specific religious associations such as are met with
in the Medicine dance.

Let us turn now to the development of the organization of the feast.
The development of a fixed type of organization is not absolutely
necessary.   Societies may exist only for certain occasions, such as
the return from a warpath, like the Hōk'ixe're dance or preparatory
to the starting of a war party, and be practically nonexistent afterwards.   Such are the temporary war feasts of the Ojibway, for
instance.   However, one all important circumstance prevented this

among the Winnebago, and that was the strong development of clan consciousness among them. A man was first and foremost a member of his clan, and whatever he did redounded to the credit of his clan. This clan consciousness was due to the strong individuality the more important clans possessed. They had their own traditions, functions, and customs, and each clan was quite ignorant of the customs of the other. This clan organization was extremely old and, for that reason, it is not very likely that the war bundle developed before the clan organization had matured, and from being originally the private possession of a family, became subsequently associated with the clan. It is more likely that the war bundle developed after the clan organization had fully matured, but that it remained personal property. However, owing to the fact that the possessor was always an important man, there must always have been a consciousness of a certain proprietary ownership on the part of the clan in the particular war bundle within its midst. This perhaps accounts for the fact that while the bundle can pass out of the hands of a certain family, it can not pass into the hands of another clan. Subsequently the idea developed that a family was merely the custodian of the bundle for the clan. Such seems to be the popular conception among the Winnebago to-day, and it may have represented the popular conception when the Winnebago culture was still intact. I do not believe, however, that such a view would have been accepted by the family in possession of the war bundle or by the learned class in general.

The fact that there was as a rule but one war bundle in each clan does not mean that it was developed originally through the influence of clan consciousness, although there is reason to believe that some of the war bundles arose in this way, in imitation of "clan" bundles that already existed. The reason for the small number of war bundles is to be sought in the fact that there was a very small number of individuals possessed of the necessary qualifications, and that it was probably originally associated with villages or groups of villages.[4] Whatever were the reasons for the limitation in the number of war bundles in each clan, it unquestionably strengthened the idea of clan ownership. This idea must have been powerfully reinforced again by those war bundles that actually arose out of a clan-ownership impulse. If, therefore, the actual owners resent this claim of clan proprietorship both by reason of actual possession, of inheritance and consciousness of the sacrifices and expense they and their ancestors have incurred in maintaining the ceremonies connected with these bundles it is nevertheless a fact that their viewpoint is probably wrong in so far as it is supposed to represent the entire truth, either now or in the past. The actual unit of organization found at the feast is the clan and there, at any rate, the war bundle is a clan palladium. Perhaps

---

[4] This statement is made provisionally.

this twofold interpretation really represents the war bundle in a two-fold aspect, first apart from its association with the war-bundle feast and second from its association therewith.

That the clan is the unit of organization comes out clearly from the following facts: First, there are as many buckskins offered as there are clans; secondly, the order in which the guests are invited is determined by the reciprocal relations existing between the different clans; and, thirdly, by references in the speeches. That the clan unit, on the other hand, has influenced the ceremonial aspect of the feast is apparent from the fact that offerings are made to the clan animals. For example, in the following ceremony offerings are made to the Eagle and Wona'γire Uaηkcik, who seem to be of slight importance apart from their association with the clan.

The ceremonial unit in all Winnebago societies consists of four bands, four representing the sacred number, and the ritual consists of the passing of the paraphernalia from one to the other unit until it returns to the host. The war-bundle feast corresponds to the other societies in every respect, except that instead of four there are ten bands (with the band of the host, representing the eleven existing clans of the tribe). Had not the consciousness of the relation of the war bundle to the clan been so strong the ceremonial unit would probably have been found here, as it is found in all the other ceremonies.

Summing up, then, we may say that the war-bundle feasts represent a mixed type corresponding exactly to no other Winnebago ceremony, and that beginning as a war feast it developed in addition some of the features of a secret society of the type exemplified by the Night Spirit society, with a unit of organization based on the clan; and that finally it became a general feast of thanksgiving to the entire Winnebago pantheon.[5]

CHARACTERIZATION OF THE SPIRITS MENTIONED IN THE WAR-BUNDLE FEAST

All the spirits to whom offerings are made in the war-bundle feast are guardian spirits, with the exception of Earthmaker. Some of them are conceived of as being human, while others have animal forms, and still others have an indeterminate body. The peculiar spirit, Disease-giver, has a form of his own, his body being divided into two halves, one half dispensing death and the other life. Earthmaker has no form, and in the few cases that he has been known to bless individuals he always lets his presence be known by some sign. There is generally a difference between the conception of the spirit as such and the form that he is supposed to assume

---

[5] The order in which these aspects are enumerated is not to be taken as representing a direct line of evolution.

when he appears to an individual. The Thunderbirds are conceived
of theoretically as birds, but always appear to human beings in
human shape. As it is believed by the shaman that the spirits are
a *tertium quid*, neither animal nor man, but possessing infinite
powers of transformation now into the one, now into the other, it is
rather difficult to indicate their precise nature except in this negative
way. For the ordinary individual doubtless their anthropomorphic
nature stands out most prominently.

According to shamanistic cosmology, although the greater spirits
are given control of various powers, still, in general, each spirit
is given control of some specific power. The shamanistic account
goes on to say that, upon the creation of man, Earthmaker, realizing
that he had no powers to bestow upon him, decided to give him at
least the means of obtaining those powers he had given the spirits
and presented him with tobacco, telling him that if he offered it in
the proper manner the spirits would feel constrained to accept it and
give him, in exchange, whatever powers they possessed. The popular
account of the origin of tobacco was quite different. However, it was
on the shamanistic theory that offerings were made. The arrangement
between the spirits and man was in the nature of a contract, with this
peculiarity, that the spirits did not have to accept the offerings. The
prayers are generally couched in this manner: "If you, the spirits,
accept my offerings, then grant me your blessings or a continuance
of those my ancestors received." They were, however, theoretically
always left the alternative of refusing. In practice it was not believed
that the spirits exercised their prerogative of refusal, but that in certain cases the offerings were not made in the proper fashion. The
moment the tobacco was accepted, the blessing followed of itself,
almost without the will of the spirit. This purely mechanical relation
between acceptance of the tobacco and bestowal of power comes out
excellently in one of the myths. The Winnebago are sacrificing to
the Buffalo Spirits and the smoke of their tobacco offering is ascending to the spirit-land where the Buffalo Spirits dwell. The chief of
the spirits warns the younger ones not to approach too closely to the
ascending fumes, for they are but spirits and the desire for tobacco
might get the better of their discretion and induce them to accept it.
If they do, they are lost, for they will then have to go down to the
earth and be killed. No power they possess, nor any power the chief
possesses, can save them. This "mechanical" explanation seems to
me quite significant, for it probably embodies the older point of
view and the point of view of the less enlightened Winnebago. As
such, it is to be contrasted with the later shamanistic development
with its contract and the shifting of the spirit's rôle from one of
passive acceptance to that of a spirit-deity who withholds his
approbation unless the offering is properly made.

The elements necessary to the acceptance of offerings are two-fold—the specified amount of material and the proper state of mind. The first is quite clear, but the second needs some explanation. To the Winnebago the emotional condition of a suppliant for power from the spirits is all important, and the proper emotional condition is one which they call "concentration of mind," by which they signify a complete absorption of the individual in the prayer he is making. Theoretically even the slightest interest in any other object is liable to destroy the entire efficacy of the prayer. I say theoretically, for if the prayer seems to be answered a consciousness of failure to come up to the ideal never obtrudes itself. If, however, there is reason to believe that the prayer has not been answered, then the explanation would always be that there had been either a shift of attention or a lack of emotional intensity. This is not the only explanation given for lack of success in the case of a ceremony, for there, by an extension of the principle of the "concentration of mind" to all those who participated, failure might be attributable to a large number of causes.

The popular explanation was, I believe, different. Failure was either not discussed at all and looked upon from the common-sense point of view as one of life's accidents or, if explanation was necessary, regarded as a sign that the spirits had not been tempted to accept the alluring offers.

It would, however, be erroneous to believe that much philosophizing took place over failure. Failure that entailed the death of an individual was likely to call forth not explanations as to what the failure was attributable, but desire for revenge.

With the exception of food and tobacco, which were extended to all, the offerings to the various spirits differed in nature. To the eleven great deities (i. e., including Hē'rok'a, who is not mentioned in the following account) tobacco, food (i. e., both soup and meat), and buckskins were offered. There was, however, further differentiation. To the great war deities red eagle feathers were offered in addition; to Disease-giver and Thunderbird two dogs were sacrificed; to Earth and Sun herbs and maple sugar were given; and to the Moon, bear ribs.

Having thus briefly sketched the general nature of the spirits connected with the war-bundle feast and the general theory of the offering, we will turn to a specific enumeration of the spirits.

Earthmaker.—Variously known in Winnebago as Mą'ųna, Earthmaker, Wajągų'zɛra, Creator, and Waxopī'ni Xe'tera, Great Spirit. Mą'ųna is, by far, the most usual appellation; Wajągų'zɛra is found only in rituals, and Waxop'ini Xe'tera is more or less obsolete, although not within the popular cycles relating to the Trickster, Hare, Turtle, Red-Horn, and the Twins.

Earthmaker has all the characteristics of a supreme deity. He is conceived of as formless and as never being visible to man. He is a benevolent deity, but apart from the interest he manifested in creating the world and all that exists upon it and in sending the great Transformer heroes, Trickster, Turtle, and Hare, he has taken little active interest in the affairs of humankind. It is only as a tour de force that one can receive blessings from him. An instance of the kind will be found on page 243, [6] which is to be taken not as a myth but as, at most, a true fasting experience, which has been cast into a literary form.

The conception of Earthmaker we have been discussing is found most prominently developed in the rituals and the ritualistic myths. In how far it represents an exoteric point of view it would be difficult to determine now. A study of the nonritualistic myths, however, makes it seem plausible that Earthmaker, among the people in general, was the vague Waxōp'į'nį Xe'tera, Great Spirit, typical of the woodland area; and what appears to strengthen this view is the fact that there exists, side by side with him, that other great spirit common among the woodland peoples, the Great Bad Spirit, known among the Winnebago as Herecgū'nina, of doubtful etymology. The coexistence of these two spirits and their equal rank comes out clearly in the cycle of the Twins. The ritualistic myths have attempted to interpret this old Herecgū'nina as Earthmaker's first attempt to create man, which ended in failure. He thereupon threw him away, but Herecgū'nina imitated the creations of the former and thus brought into existence the many evil spirits that infest the earth.

Only in the older traditions is this conception of the dual deities still to be found. In practical life the more systematic conception developed in the rituals has entirely displaced it, just as the older conception of the Transformers as heroes working in obedience to no one and changing the world until it assumed its present appearance out of mere whim, has given place to a well-ordered creation in which the Transformers play the rôle of deities saving the human race at the command of Earthmaker.

Thunderbirds (Wak'ą'ndja).—They are always represented as appearing to men as bald-headed individuals wearing a wreath made of the branches of the arbor vitæ. They are in control of almost all the powers that man can imagine, but they generally bless him with success on the warpath and with a long and honorable life. They are. represented as having a spirit village in the west and as intermarrying with the Night Spirits who have a village in the east. Powerful shamans and warriors not infrequently claim that they are merely reincarnated Thunderbirds. Such is the claim of the man who is

---

[6] Cf. also Jour. Amer. Folklore, vol. 26, pp. 293–318, 1913.

.reputed to have first received the war bundle of the Thunderbird clan, as we shall subsequently see.

Night Spirits.—They are known under two names, one used generally signifying literally "night" (*hąhᵉ*) and the other used only in rituals signifying "Those-who-walk-in-darkness" (Hōk'ā'was mani'ṇa). They are in control of war powers specifically and appear to men in the form of human beings. They are supposed to cause the darkness of night.

Disease-giver (Hō'cereᵉ ̨'wahį).—This is a spirit whose counterpart does not seem to exist in any other tribe. He, like the Thunderbird and Night Spirits, is a great war deity, but as his name implies, he also presides over life and death by being the source of disease. His twofold nature has been touched on before. When prayers are offered to him he is besought to turn away his "death" side and present only his "life" side.

Great Black Hawk.—Always known as K'eredjų'sep xe'tera. A powerful war deity.

The Sun.—The Sun is known generally as *wĭ'ra*, and in rituals as Hąbani'ndjera, Light-wanderer; or as Hābanihū'ra, He-who-brings-the-light-of-day. There seems little doubt but that in the earlier history of Winnebago culture he played a far greater rôle than he does to-day or did when the culture of the tribe was still intact. According to one informant he and Fire were dispatched as Transformers to rid the world of the bad spirits. As in the older conception of Earthmaker, his former rôle comes out most prominently in the nonritualistic myths, especially in the Twin cycle. In none of the many rituals of the tribe was his cult developed. He was regarded as one of the greatest war deities.

The Morning Star.—He is always known as Wīragō'cge xetera, the great star. He, like the Sun, seems to have enjoyed a greater popularity before the rise of the complex rituals. He is purely and simply a war deity.

The Moon.—Generally known as Hąhᵉ'wįra, night-sun, but in rituals as Hąhe'regi hūrā'djone, You-who-come-at-night. The Moon is a female deity in control of many powers, but apparently of no very specific ones. She is not supposed to be one of the preeminent war deities but to be more closely associated with blessings referring to long life.

The South Wind.—Known as Rek'ū'hūhį, Wind-going-with-the-stream. He is a war deity, but not on a par with the others.

The Earth.—Generally known either as maⁿna, earth, or simply as k'ū'nįk'a, grandmother, a female deity connected almost exclusively with peace. She played a far greater rôle in the earlier phases of Winnebago religious development than she did in the later and is found as an important figure in all the nonritualistic Transformer cycles, especially in that of the Hare. Her rôle in the ritualistic myths is quite important, too, but there she has been changed from a rather indifferent and at times hostile deity to a beneficent, all-loving Mother-earth.

The Water.—Generally known as nĩŋa, water, but ritualistically as huŋge', chief. There is some doubt as to whether water or the Water Spirit is meant here. This is a deity in no way connected with war. He is most commonly associated with medicines, especially the famous "paint" medicines (wāse').

These are the more important spirits and the only ones to whom buckskins are offered in the following ceremony. The following are, however, also of considerable importance:

Eagle.—Always known as Tcaxcep, eagle. A powerful war deity and a clan animal.

Pigeon Hawk.—Always known as K'ĩrịk'ĩrĩ'sgera, pigeon hawk. A powerful war deity.

Wŏnaɤi're Ŭaŋkcik.—A term difficult to translate, but meaning, in general, a terror-inspiring man. It refers, however, not to a human deity but to a bird that is supposed to be almost identical with the hawk. It is the name of one of the Winnebago clans. A powerful war deity.

North Wind.—Known as Wazī'regị hūhī'ra, Wind-that-is-in-the-pine-region. He is associated with war, but is not a very important deity.

Black Hawk.—Known as k'eredjụ sep. What difference there is between this spirit and Great Black Hawk is not clear.

Day.—Known as hạp, day or light. The term is used in rituals, especially in the medicine dance, with the meaning of life. He is very rarely sacrificed to and his mention in this particular performance of the Thunderbird war-bundle feast is merely an illustration of the fact that offerings could be made to any spirit.

In addition to the spirits mentioned above, offerings were made at different performances of the war-bundle feast to all the other spirits and even to heroes, like Trickster, Turtle, Hare, Bladder, Red-Horn, and the Twins. In the performance as given in the following account one great spirit is omitted, Hē'rok'a, meaning, literally, "Without horns." A buckskin is always offered to him, on which is painted a small bow and arrow. He is one of the important Winnebago deities, is supposed to be a Lilliputian, and controls many of the powers relating to hunting.

In order to avoid offending any spirit they always leave a portion of tobacco as an offering to those whose names they can not for the moment think of.

DESCRIPTION OF THE WAR-BUNDLE FEAST

The present war bundle has been in the family of B. for a number of generations. Our informant obtained it directly from his father.

B. was not the eldest son, but, as mentioned before, the war bundle was always given to that son who manifested the greatest interest in it. When B. and his brothers were quite young their father took them aside one day and told them the stories connected with the war bundle and told them, in addition, that the one manifesting the greatest interest would receive it. B. immediately started getting material for a feast, and this he would give to his father, who would then give a feast. This was repeated over and over again until B.'s father felt that B. knew enough about the ceremony to conduct it himself, after which he allowed him to take entire charge of it.

The war bundle contained the following objects:

The body of an eagle (tcaxce′p).

The body of a hawk (k′eredjụ′sep).

The body of an unidentified bird (waniŋk′hīwịtcak′ī′zọk′e).

The body of a pigeon hawk (k′īrịk′ī′risge).

A deer-tail headdress (tcasintc wak′e′re).

Eagle feathers (tcaxce′p mạcū′).

Medicines (wase′).

Flutes (hījū′jụk).

War club (namạ′tce).

The birds' bodies were supposed to give the possessor, in times of war, the characteristics of these animals. The flutes were associated with different spirits and used to accompany certain songs during the ceremony proper. When blown during a fight, they were supposed to paralyze the running powers of the enemy and thus make him an easy prey. The deer-tail headdress, the eagle feathers, and the war club were all war paraphernalia and were always worn when on the warpath.

When the custodian of a war bundle decides to give a feast he has his nephews go out and kill as many deer as they can, for the larger the number of deer obtained the larger will be the number of spirits to whom they can make offerings. As a rule ten to eleven deer are killed, so that all the clans, or at least all that are still in existence, can be invited.

After the deer have been killed active preparations are begun; the invitation sticks (nạnō′ɣoṇa) are sent out, and the wood for the ceremonial lodge is gathered; and, lastly, old women who have passed their climacteric are set to work on the buckskins and ordered to make them as white as possible. In the preparation of the lodge only the nephews, nieces, and wives of the participating men take part.

The night before the ceremony proper, the Sweat-Lodge ritual takes place.

When the buckskins have been thoroughly bleached they are brought into the lodge and given to the host, who proceeds to mark them in the following manner:

The buckskin to be offered to Earthmaker is marked with a cross in green. It is quite possible that the association of the cross with Earthmaker is due to Christian influence. But if this actually has been the case it is far more likely that the Christian influence led not to the actual borrowing of the Christian cross, but rather to the identification of an old Winnebago ceremonial symbol, namely, the crossed lines representing the cardinal points, with the cross, and its association with Earthmaker (pl. 48).

The buckskin to be offered to the Thunderbirds is marked with three semicircular lines, the first red, the second white, and the third blue, to represent a rainbow (pl. 48).

The buckskin to be offered to the Night Spirits is marked with four parallel lines in charcoal (pl. 48).

The buckskin to be offered to Disease-giver is marked by dipping the three middle fingers in red paint and impressing them 12 times upon the buckskin in three vertical columns, with four impressions in each column. In addition to this an eagle feather is tied to each corner of the buckskin (pl. 48).

The buckskin to be offered to the Sun is marked with an image of the sun in red (pl. 47).

The buckskin to be offered to the Moon is marked with an image of the moon in any of its phases in green (pl. 47).

The buckskin to be offered to South Wind is marked in the same way as that to Disease-giver, except that green paint is used. A red eagle feather is attached to each end of the buckskin (pl. 47).

The buckskin to be offered to the Morning Star is marked with an image of a star in black outline (pl. 47).

These are the spirits to whom buckskins are offered in the ceremony about to be described, but the other clans seem to show variations in some offerings. Thus, for example, the spirit called "Without-horns" (Hē'rok'a) receives the offering of a buckskin in some cases. The marking for him is always a bow and arrow in charcoal. In another case Fire and Turtle receive buckskin offerings. Their markings are pictures of fire and turtle.

While the host is busy thus marking the buckskins the attendants put the meat in the kettles and place the same on the various fireplaces. There are always one or two extra kettles prepared for the women and children.

The lodge extends from east to west and has only one entrance, on the east end. The host sits to the left as you enter and opposite him sits the guest of honor, who is, of course, different in each clan, but in the ceremony to be described he belongs to the Bear clan. Then, in definite order, sit the other guests, each one opposite a fireplace. The women and children sit separated from the others at the extreme western end of the lodge (see fig. 38).

After the buckskins have been marked the host arranges them on frames. The buckskin to Earthmaker is so arranged on its frame that the head points upward; that to the Thunderbirds is so arranged that its head points toward the west; that to the Night Spirits, that its head points to the east; that to the Morning Star, that its head points to the east; and those to the Earth and Water, that their heads point downward. After they have been attached to the frame they are rolled up, and the ceremony can be said to have begun. Then the guests enter, no order being observed in the manner of entering. As soon as they have all taken their places, the oldest warrior belonging to the host's band is called upon to offer tobacco to the spirits. This he does by going to the main fireplace, offering up brief prayers, and at the conclusion of each one pouring tobacco into the fire. The first prayer is always to the fire itself.[8] When he is finished, the host takes the buckskins, unrolls them, and distributes them to the various guests. The buckskin for the Thunderbirds is always given to the guest of honor, and the others are given in the following rotation: Great Black Hawk, Disease-giver, South Wind, Earthmaker, Sun, Morning Star, Night Spirits, Moon, Earth, and Water. The buckskin to Earthmaker is assigned to the middle guest, but as he is the first guest to speak, the buckskin itself is hung on the center pole that is erected in the front portion of the lodge.

After the guests have received their buckskins they stand in their respective positions, holding the buckskin in one hand and some tobacco in the other. The host concludes his remarks, and then taking his flute, blows upon it. After this he sings two songs, accompanying himself with his gourd rattles. Then the buckskins are rolled up again, but in such a way that the markings still remain visible, and hung up just west of the first fireplace, with the exception of the Earthmaker's buckskin. The host now takes the war bundle, opens it, and places it at the foot of the center pole. He then makes the circuit of the lodge, pouring some tobacco into the hands of each invited guest. When this is finished, he pours some tobacco upon the war bundle and some into the fire and proceeds to offer prayers to all the spirits, asking each in turn for life and victory on the warpath. When he is through all the guests pour tobacco on the war bundle and into the fire. Children are often allowed to pour tobacco also, the attendants bringing them from the western portion of the lodge. After the offerings of tobacco are finished the offerings of buckskin are made. Then the basic ritual is started by the host. He takes the flutes, drum, and gourds and sings in his own place. There are many different sets of songs, and every time he starts a different set he first blows upon his flute. The songs for the Thunderbird have eight starting songs and six dancing songs. When the

<hr/>

[8] This prayer, for some unknown reason, is omitted in the following account. It was obtained, however, in connection with another account of the same ceremony.

dancing songs are begun, all the men go to the war bundle and dance around it. The flute is continually blown during the dancing. Women may dance at their end of the lodge. The basic ritual is then continued.

When the last starting song is finished the host rises and, ejaculating *ho—o—o*, pours tobacco into the fireplace four times. Just when the food is about cooked four special songs are sung. Then the Thunderbird feast takes place. All the bones that have been left on the plate of the guest impersonating the Disease-giver are taken out by the host himself, carried in an eastward direction, and placed very carefully at the foot of some tree that has been especially selected. Tobacco and red feathers are poured upon these bones. The plates used by the same person are purified with arbor vitæ. The bones left on the plates of the other guests may be thrown anywhere, provided the ground on which they are scattered has been purified. When the feast is over the basic ritual is continued. When this is finished the first division of the ceremony is concluded.

During the interval between the first and second divisions the attendants sweep the lodge and purify it with branches of arbor vitæ; and new kettles with meat are placed on the fireplaces. Then the host and guests enter. The host rises and distributes the buckskins again, and while he is doing this an attendant goes around the lodge and scatters swan feathers all over it. Some are even placed on the suspended kettles. The host, because he is going to sing Night Spirit songs, takes down the buckskin intended for that spirit, blackens his face with the embers of charcoal used in marking the buckskin, and puts some swan feathers on his head. Before the host starts singing the Night Spirit songs the pipestem is turned toward the east and the origin of the songs in question is told. Then the basic ritual is begun. When the dancing songs are being sung the guests may either go to where the war bundle lies and dance there or stay in their own places and dance. When the host has finished his part of the basic ritual, drum, gourds, flute, and tobacco are passed to the first guest, and when he is finished they are passed to the second and third guests. After that the basic ritual is for the time being discontinued and the ritual connected with throwing out of the buckskins intervenes, this in turn being followed by the Night Spirit feast. However, before the feast, as the drum, gourds, and flute are returned to the host, he has a kettle placed on the fire for the spirits living beneath the surface of the earth, and when the food in it has cooked he rises and sings paint songs (*wase'*). After the feast is over the basic ritual is continued. Some time before this ritual is finished the host takes his war bundle, wraps it up, and hangs it behind the place where he is sitting. When finally all the songs with the exception of four have been sung, the host calls upon some one with a very strong voice to give the war whoop four times. This the latter does, and after the last whoop all the guests join in. Then rising, all the guests dance out of the lodge and the ceremony is over.

398   THE WINNEBAGO TRIBE

FIRST DIVISION OF THE CEREMONY—IN HONOR OF THE THUNDER-
BIRDS

Introductory remarks by informant.—Ě′gi manī′ṇegi maniḵ′ī′sak′a,
ë′gi taniwọgī′jụra. Ho′ū′ṇa higī′rëk′djonë′nʌ ge ë′sge wānasā′
tëk′djonë′nʌ.

Nọgʌ ë′sge hʌhē′gịji īniō′k′ewe ha′ụk′djo′ṇehị gịji, ë′gi wọhọ′ṇʌ
hījak′ī′xdjị tụxụruk′ī′jị jë′sge hak′djonë′nʌ. Nọ′gʌ ë′gi djā′nọgʌ
hak′ī′jụ tëk′djonẹ′ra hadjī′rẹge je īnị-ō′kewe′ụ wak′ī′jụ ha′ụk′-
djonë′nʌ gịji. Ě′gi īnị-ō′k′ewe′ū′ṇa wak′e′wik′djonā̄′winʌ hīrụ-
cdjạ′hīrẹge′.

SWEAT-LODGE RITUAL

Wak′āwinʌ hak′ịk′ū′rucârụdji-ā̄′nʌga ë′gi wak′ā′wịra hịnụk′aị′-
nawinʌ. Ě′gi tanī′ṇa tanịwī′rọgịjụ ya′ụk′djẹ′ra hā′k′āraniwakewë̄′-
nʌ jëgū′nʌ.

Host's salutation and initial speech to participants.—"Ě′gi
wak′ūrụhi′ntccʌnʌ sā′k′erenị′k′djọgre nịk′ụrụhindjwī′nʌ. Ě′gi hītt-
cō′k′ewahī′wịra ë′gi tcōk′agā′ wāna′ị′gik′ere′regị. Ě′gi hīroit′ū′ṇa
djāsge nʌdjịrọdjaị′ṇegị, ë gi hijë′sge hak′ā′ratīk′djanịhe.

Ě′gi djāsge wawë′k′djẹgị hịtcō′k′iwahī′wịra ë′gi u′ịṇëk′djanë′nʌ.
Tanī′nịk′ p′āxụ′k′djonẹ′ra ë′gi wōtā′ hịtcō′k′iwahī′wịra wā′git-
ụxū′ru-ik′djonẹ′ra. Ě′gi sā′k′erenị′k′djọŋgrʌ nịŋk′ūrụhi′ntc rehā̄′-
wịnʌ. Ě′gi tanī′ṇa hịtcō′k′ewahī′wịra, tanī′ṇa wāgịp′āxụ′-
k′djonë′nʌ nịk′ū′rụhindjwī′nʌ.

Host's offering to Earthmaker.—"Hʌ̄hʌ̄′ Ma′′ụṇa, hī-andjenī′na,
tanī′ṇa hōjū′-ịjʌ̄ nịŋgịp′āxu′ŋk′djonāre. Ě′gi tcō′k′agā Djōbenʌŋ-
gịwi′ŋxga wāna′ị′nagik′e′regị. Ě′gi hīroit′ū′ṇa djāsge nʌdjịrọrā′-
djʌŋgị; ë′gi hʌ̄′bɛnịŋk′ hīnagī′c′ụna; djọbo′hʌ̄ jedjaị′ŋxdjị hīroit′-
ū′ṇa, tcōk′agā′ djāsge′xdji nʌdjịrọrā′djʌgị, je′e rọtcʌ̄′ŋxdjị nịgị-
tā′nʌ. Ě′gi hāŋk′e wā′wẹ-ā′k′ịnị′k′djẹra."

Host's offering to the chief of the Thunderbirds.—"Ě′gi sā′nịgọhī̄′-
regị he′rẹra hịtcō′k′ewịwī′na, wak′ā′ndja hu′ŋgɛra, tanī′ṇa hōjū′-ịjʌ̄

FIRST DIVISION OF THE CEREMONY—IN HONOR OF THE THUNDER-
BIRDS

Introductory remarks by Blowsnake, informant.—In winter, in midwinter, then it was that I used to pour tobacco.[9] That was the
time I would go out and hunt for game.

Well, to-night, a vapor bath I shall take, and if I can secure food
for boiling, that kind of a feast I shall give.   As many of the leaders
as have come, that many shall be with me as I take a vapor bath in
the sweat lodge.   We are now about to enter the sweat lodge, for
everything is in readiness.[10]

SWEAT-LODGE RITUAL

We entered the sweat lodge and undressed, and after we had
entered they (the outsiders) closed the lodge covering.   I took both
the tobacco and the other things I was to use as offerings with me.[11]

Host's salutation and initial speech to participants.—"I greet you;
I greet you all, war-bundle owners.[12]   My grandparents, especially
my grandfather,[13] had concentrated their minds upon this for me.
The fireplace with which they blessed my grandfather,[15] that I am
going to ask for myself.   However weakly I may wobble about,[16] my
elders will aid me.   I am now going to pour a little tobacco and
offer, my elders, whatever feast I am able to.   War-bundle owners,
I send forth my greetings to you.   War-bundle owners, I greet you.
Ye elders, I am about to pour tobacco for them (the spirits)."

Host's offering to Earthmaker.—"Hearken, Earthmaker, our father,
I am about to offer you a handful of tobacco.[17]   My ancestor Djōbenạgiwi'ŋxga [18] concentrated his mind upon you.   The fireplaces
with which you blessed him;[19] the small amount of life you granted
to him; all, four times the blessings you bestowed upon my ancestor,
that I ask of you directly.   Also that I may have no troubles (in
life)."

Host's offering to the chief of the Thunderbirds.—"To you, who live
in the west, our grandfather, chief of the Thunderbirds, a handful of

[9] "Pouring tobacco" is the ritualistic term for giving a feast.
[10] The informant has passed to the present tense now, for he is actually giving an account of the last War-bundle Feast he gave and imagining that the writer is present.
[11] The word tobacco in Winnebago rituals is used as a generic expression for an offering. Thus the word *taniwirogi'ju* means, literally, "What we are to offer as tobacco."
[13] Literally, "Children of the bundle."
[13] He does not really mean grandparents, but elders.
[15] The word here used for fireplace is a ritualistic one. It means, literally, "That one throws within something, i. e., an offering." It also has here the secondary meaning of food.
[16] Used metaphorically.
[17] I. e., the regular offering.
[18] An ancestor of the informant.
[19] Here "fireplaces" mean blessings, for only those who had blessings could erect fireplaces, and as a fireplace was erected for each separate spirit, the greater their number the greater the number of blessings. In all rituals it is customary to speak of blessings received, as well as of personal accomplishments, with an exaggerated modesty.

niŋgip'axų'k'djonā're. Ė'gị tcōk'agā' Djobenąŋgiwi'ŋxga ë'gị wā'nąˢịgịk'e'reregị. [Hīroitˢū'na tcā k'ī'konǫk'] hīroitˢų' hōrā'-kˢụgị, jeˢe rōtcą̄'xdji nigitā'nʌ. Tanī'na hịnągī'cųrus nʌga ˢuɩ'gị ë'gị haŋk'e' wā'wę-ak'i'nik'djege."

Host's offering to the Great Black Hawk.—"Ė'gị K'e'redjų Sep Xę'tera tcōk'agā' mą̄'djǫradjǫ'gị hīroitˢū'na djāsge ną̄djịrǫrā'-djʌgi, jeˢe rōtcą̄'xdjị nigitā'nʌ. Tanī'na hōjū'-ịjǭ nigip'āxų'k'-djonā're hī'nągịhị-ā'nʌgʌ ˢų'gị. Haŋk'e' wāwę-āk'ī'nik'dje'ge, te'-jësge nigitā'nʌ."

Host's offering to the Night Spirits.—"Ė'gị sā'nigɛregi, sā'nịk' hą̄'bōgụre'gị he'ręra, Hōk'ā'was Manī'na, tanī'na hōjū'-ịjǭ nigip'-āxų'k'djonāre hịnągip'e'rez ā'nʌga ˢųgī'. Ė'gị tcōk'agā' djagū'-ixdjị ną̄djīrō'radjǫ'gị; hīroitˢū'na djasge ną̄djịrǫrā'djǫgị je nigi-tā'nʌ. Ė'gị tanī'na hị̄'nągịhị-ā'nʌga ˢųgī' haŋk'e wā'wę-ak'ini'k'-djera."

Host's offering to Disease-giver.—"Ė'gị sā'nịk' horǫtcą̄'djeregi-ŭaŋgī'jʌ cānʌk'ī'jị; haŋk'e tˢe'p'ịhịcgū'nị canʌk'ī'jị; rō sā'nịk'-p'īṇadjā'nʌga ë'gị rō sā'nịk' hōtˢę'radjegi, Hō'cereˢų'wahị hīnigaī'-ręgị. Tcō'k'agā hą̄'badjāsge'xdji wīrarōtcą̄'djexdjị gā'djʌ ną̄'djǫradjǫ'gị. Djāsge ną̄djīrǫrā'djǫgị, hīroitˢū'na, ną̄djīrǫrā'djǫgī'jị. Haŋk'-agā' rūcˢāgenị'k'djaṇe hīragē'gịjị. Jeˢe' hōraˢŭā'nʌga. Wāni-oi'tcge tcōwę'ra wairagę'jụ ānʌga hą̄ŋk'e' wāwę-ā'k'īni'k'djera. Tanī'na hōjū'-ịjǭ nigip'āxų'k'djonā're hīnągịhị-ā'nʌga ˢųgī' hą̄ŋk'e' wāwę-ak'īni'k'djege."

Host's offering to the Sun.—"Ė'gị hịtcǫk'enī'na, Hǭbani'ndjera, tanī'na hōp'ị'jʌ nigip'axų'k'djonāre. Hīṇagīp'e'rez ā'nʌga. Ė'gị tcōk'agā' hīroitˢū'na djāsge'xdjị ną̄djịrǫrā'djʌgi, jeˢe' rōtcą̄'xdjị nigitā'nʌ. Hą̄ŋk'e wāwę-ak'īni'k'djera."

Host's offering to the Moon.—"Ė'gị Hịk'ârǫk'enī'na Hą̄hē'wịra, tcōk'agā' ną̄djǫradjǫ'gị hīroitˢū'na. Djāsge'xdjị ną̄djīrōrā'djǫgị, jeˢe' rōtcą̄'xdjị nigitā'nʌ. Tanī'na hōjū'-ịjǭ niŋgip'āxų'k'-djonā're hīnągī'p'erez ā'nʌga ˢųgī'. Tcōk'agā' hīroitˢū'na djāsge ną̄djīrōrā'djǫgị, jeˢe' hūṇak'ˢų'k'dje'nʌ hą̄ŋk'e' wāwę-ā'k'inik'-djege."

Host's offering to the South Wind.—"Ė'gị rek'ū'hụhīra, tanī'na hōjū'-ịjǭ nigip'āxų'k'djonā're hīnągịhịā'nʌga ˢųgī'. Tcōk'agā' hīroitˢū'na ną̄djīrōrā'djǫgị, jeˢe' nigitā'nʌ hą̄ņk'e' wāwę-āk'ini'-k'djege."

Host's offering to Earth.—"Ė'gị K'ū'nịk'a Mā'na tānī-ǫnigī'-jųnʌ. Tcōk'agā' ną̄djōra'djonʌ hīroitˢū'na ną̄djīrōrā'djonʌ, jeˢe' nigitā'nʌ. Wāwę-ak'īni'k'djege."

tobacco I am about to offer you. My grandfather Djōnenagiwi'ηxga you strengthened. The food, the deer-couple you gave him for his fireplaces, that I ask of you directly. May it be a fact that you accept this tobacco from me and may I not meet with troubles (in life)."

Host's offering to the Great Black Hawk.—"You also blessed my grandfather, Great Black Hawk. Whatever food you blessed him with that I ask of you directly. Tobacco I am about to pour for you that you may smoke it. May troubles not come upon me; that I ask."

Host's offering to the Night Spirits.—"You on the other side, who live in the east, who walk in darkness, [20] tobacco I am about to offer you to smoke. Whatever you blessed my ancestor with, whatever fireplaces you blessed him with, those I ask of you. If you smoke this tobacco never will I be a weakling."

Host's offering to Disease-giver.—"You who live in the south; you who look like a man; who art invulnerable; who on one side of your body present death and on the other life, Disease-giver, as they call you. My ancestor in the daytime, in broad daylight, did you bless. With food you blessed him. You told him that he would never fail in anything. You told him that you would avoid his home.[21] You placed animals (i. e., food) in front of him that he should not be troubled about obtaining them. An offering of tobacco I make to you that you may smoke it and that I may not be troubled by anything (in life)."

Host's offering to the Sun.—"To you, Light-Wanderer, an offering of tobacco I make. May it be my good fortune that you accept it. Whatever fireplaces you blessed him (i. e., my ancestor) with, those I ask of you directly. May I not be troubled by anything in life."

Host's offering to the Moon.—"You also, Grandmother Moon, blessed my ancestor with food. With whatever you blessed him, that I ask of you now directly. An offering of tobacco I am about to make for you now, so that you may smoke. Whatever blessings you bestowed upon my grandfather, I pray you to give me now, so that by reason of it I may never become a weakling."

Host's offering to the South Wind.—"To you, too, South Wind, I offer a handful of tobacco, that you may smoke it. May it so happen that you accept it and that I am spared troubles (in life). With whatsoever you blessed my ancestor, that I ask of you."

Host's offering to Earth.—"For you likewise, Grandmother Earth, will I pour tobacco. With whatever blessings you blessed my grandfather, those I ask of you. May I in that way never become a weakling."

---

[20] Hōk'āwas Manina, "those who walk in darkness," is the ritualistic name of the Night Spirits.
[21] I. e., that you would not permit disease and death to enter it.

Host's offering to the Eagle.—"Tcaxce'bera tcik'o'nǫk, tcōk'agā' wāna'ịṇ₄gik'erewī'gi, hīroit'ū'ṇa nǫdjīrōrā'djawigi, je nigitā'wịn₄. Tanī'ṇa hōjū'-ịjǫ nigip'āxu'k'djonā're. Hī'ṇagip'e're̜z ā'n₄ga 'ụgī' hǫŋk'e' wāwe-ak'īnị'k'djera."

Host's general offering to the spirits.—"Hāhǫ' djā'n₄ga tcōk'agā' wāna'ị'ṇ₄gik'erewigi; hanǫ'tcị hak'ī'cdjek tanị-ō'nigijụwịn₄. Ė'gị tanị-ō'waxụjǫ tcōk'agā' Djōbenaŋgiwi'ŋxga nǫdjīrō'radjawiga. Je'e' ẽgị tcowe'regi hō'ū'ṇa higiṛǫk'ǎrohō'n₄, djā'n₄ga tcōk'agā' hiroīt'ū'ṇa ragik'e'rewigi, je'e' woīnak'ụwi-ā'nǫga. Hǫŋk'e' wāwe̜ā'k'īnịk'dje're, jẽ'sge̜ nigitā'wịn₄. Niŋk'ū'rụhindjwī'n₄ wajō'-k'ịna.

THE DOG RITUAL

Cuŋgerī'jǫ wajị'ṇụk'ū'-ịṇẽk'djonē'gị xụnụni'ŋgere'djǫ hip'ā' hīrak'ā'rara p'ị'ŋxdjị hīranǎ'n₄. P'ịŋxdjị xetehịranǎ'n₄. Hǫŋk'agā' hǫdjī'nanị xetehī'ranǎni. Niŋk'djo'ŋk' e̜wanī'ṇera wīk'īsge'xdjị hīranǎ'na. Warū'djɛra p'ị'ŋxdjị hīrak'ā'rairanǎ'n₄. Wǫgīxete'-xdjịnǎna na ni'ŋkdjoŋk e'wanī'na djāsge wāwōgixetē'n₄gɛra jẽ'sge hīcge wōgixe'teranǎ'n₄. Cuŋk'djo'ŋk' ẽ'gị wajaī'nǫk'ū'n₄ hīge'regi cuŋk'djęga nǫbịruxai'tcaṇęgị t'e̜hīre'k'djaṇęgị k'e'nị t'e̜hī'ranị t'e̜'hī k'ǎrohō'xdjịṇęgị ẽgī'djị cuŋkdjega· ǔaŋk· nǫbịruxā'djɛra hīk'ǎrohō'djęga cu'ŋk'djęga hok'ā'rakịt'anǎ'n₄.

"Hisuŋk'ā'xdjị, sā'niŋk' yǫratcǫdje'regị hōrawace'rek'djonē'n₄ Hōcere'ụ'wahīra ẽdjōrace'rek'djonē'n₄ yahī' p'īc'u'ŋk'djonē'n₄ rahī'gị. Wonā'ɣirẹra ǔaŋkci'goī'e'ṇa p'īa'e'uŋk'djā'wị, te'jẽsge ragitā'k'djęn₄."

Ė'gị cu'ŋk'djęga haŋk'e' gisawī'nịne waginai'e'ụwi-ā'n₄ga toxǫ'-rụcgǫ rūsā'gwịre e ǫŋk'e' wa'ịni'ŋk'djonën₄. Wā'ịwahī'ra rǫɣi'-ras'ā'je aī'rẹn₄. Waxǫp'ī'nị xete'j₄ nǫbịgī'rụxatc hīrek'djịṇē'gị p'ịhī'na'ị' hīres'ā'je.

Ė'gị cuŋgɛrā' t'e̜hī'regi wajịnụk'ū'-ik'ǎrǫhō'ga cuŋgoŋk'ā' higịk'-ǎrǫhō'je wa'ụje'. Tanī' warụcị'jǫ 'ụje' ẽgị mǫcū'cụtc hōgicge'-dja hīrarū'sgịtcce, ẽ'gị cuŋk nǫbīrụxā'djǫŋk'ā nǫb'ʻị gīgī'je. Ė'gị jige' tā'ni warụcị'ṇa jigịjǫ' 'ụje' djo'p'ī'wị tanị warụcị'ṇa ǔā'n₄ga hoigīcge'dja mǫcū'cụtc hīrarū'sgịtc wāt'ǫ'pce waī'za hidjō'bịk'e hịjǫ'can₄ wāwịrō'gịcge'je cuŋgoŋk'ā. Ė'gị warụɣā'bɛra rụcgaī'ran₄ga warụɣa'pǫŋk'a warụɣā'p tcōwe'dja horotcǫ'djerẹgi hap'ā'hị t'ǫbị'reje.

GENERAL PLACING OF THE TOBACCO

Tcahā'e'ǔǫŋge'dja jūra rūcdjai'nan₄ga ẽ'gị hōnawǫ'ṇa djīk'erehī' k'ǎrǫhoī'regi ẽ'gị wa'ū'-ịṇeje wagigō'nₐŋk'a tanī' hiŋk'ịrụp'o'n₄ hīrā'n₄ga warụɣā'p ẽdja t'ǫ'bịrẹje. Waxǫp'ī'nị warā'djirẹra djanₐŋgā'k'ị hanǫ'tciŋxdjị. Hīdjā' wagīt'ǫ'p wā'ū'-ịṇes'ā'je ǔaŋk

Host's offering to the Eagle.—"To you, a pair of Eagles, my ancestor prayed. The blessings you bestowed upon him, those I ask of you. I am about to pour a handful of tobacco for you. May you accept it and ward off trouble from me."

Hosts general offering to the spirits.—"Hearken, all ye spirits to whom my ancestor prayed; to all of ye, I offer tobacco. My ancestor Djō-benągiw'ŋxga gave a feast to all those who had blessed him.[22] However, as it is about time to proceed to the next part (we will ask you once again) to bestow upon us all the blessings you gave our ancestor. That we may not become weaklings, I ask of you. I greet you all."

THE DOG RITUAL

When they decide to use a dog (as a sacrifice) they take the greatest care of it from its infancy upward. With great kindness do they rear it. They never strike it when rearing it. Just like their own child do they treat it. They take great care of its food. They love it very much, just as they love their own children. Thus is the dog loved. If they are going to sacrifice it, then before they kill the dog they make the following preparation and the man who is to make the sacrifice speaks thus:

"My younger brother, you are to go to the south; to the Disease-giver you are to go. There you will live better than here. War powers and life we wish to have and that you should ask for."

The dog is not to be killed by striking, but a rope is to be used and he is to be strangled to death, so that there will not be any blood. It is forbidden to shed blood. Thus they tried to make an offering to one of the great spirits.

When the dog is to be killed, the one who is to do it prepares him. A pouch of tobacco and red feathers are tied around the neck of the dog to be offered. Then the man made another pouch of tobacco and another, till he had four, and these with (eagle) feathers he tied to the four limbs, one pouch to each limb of the dog. Then the war bundle was opened and purified with cedar leaves. Then they laid the dog in front of the war bundle, making him face south.

GENERAL PLACING OF THE TOBACCO

When they have finished arranging the buckskins and are about ready to start the singing, then the feasters mix tobacco and strew it over the war bundle. They offer this tobacco for all the spirits who exist. Even the man who originally obtained the war bundle

---

[22] "And we are repeating this now," should be added. The word for feast here means literally; "tobacco pouring."

sarūsgī'tcga djānₐga warựγā'pdjęga ë'dja hīcge horo'k' hīdjā' tanį-āhi-ā'nịhë'k'djonē'nₐ aī'regị. Je'e' djānₐga gīgǫ̃'jị-ānₐga hą̄ŋk'e' tanị wāwọgī'jụ irā'nigị je'e' je'jësgā'nₐŋk'ā ë'dja tanị' hį̄'ņek'dje wagī''u-iņes'ā'je aī'renₐ. Ė'gị hatcindjā'cANₐ wāxọp'ī'nị warā'-djịręra tani-ō'stọhị'ra hatcā'cANₐ wak'ārak'ere'nₐŋk'ị tanị' je'e ë'dja hahī'nₐŋkce aī'ręnₐ. Wak'ā'ndjā'ra tanị-ō'stọhịra niŋge' tcī'jₐ k'ere'naŋk'ī aī'reconūnₐ. Ė'gị Hą̄hē'ra jịge' hīcge tcī'jₐ Djōbenāŋgịwi'ŋxga n̥ǎdjịrōdjaī'ņeje hōtāgera' je'e hīcge Hą̄hē'ra tanị-ō'stọhīra je'e hịgịre'nₐŋkce tcōk'agā' Djōbenaŋgịwi'ŋxga ë'je aī'rera. Ė'gị ŭaŋgere'gị jịgī'jₐ tanị-ō'stọhī'ra rākce aī'ręna. Ė'gị jịge' hīcge mą̄ņe'geręra jịge' tani-ō'stọhī'ją̄ tcī'jₐ niŋgią'kce aī'ręnₐ. Ė'gị jịge' maŋk'ū'haņęgị jịge' tanị-ō'stọhī'jₐ niŋgią'kce aī'rena. Tcī se'redjịjₐ tanị' hīk'īrụp'o'nₐ tcị-ō'kịsā'gedja t'ą̄bEna'-ŋk'a je'e tanị' hą̄ŋk'e' hīk'īrụp'o'nanị rūsaŋk'ī'hị hīwace'xdjị. Hīdjā' t'ą̄bịręs'ā'je tanị' je'e rōhą̄'ŋxdjị jënₐ' hiną'ị'ņes'āje k'īgō'nₐŋk'a tcīroī'xdjị-ā'ŋk'a. Tanị' je'e rohą̄'ŋxdjị wagịrā'sgep hīreje'je wagịgō'nₐŋk'a rōgụ' wa'ụnā'ŋkcANₐ. Ė'sge k'īgō'nₐŋk'a hak'ịk'ā'razịres'ā'je waxọp'ī'nị tanị gihī'nₐ. P'ị̄'je aireconū'nₐ. "Hītadje' wa'ụwi'ŋge tanị rōhą̄' rasge'bịna'ị'wịne wōnā'γịre hịk'ụrụxū'rụkce aīrē'na. Tanị wagihī'nₐ. Ė'gị hīcge' wagịgō'-nₐŋk'a warūtctco'na wak'ā'rajī'nₐŋkce wagịxonā'winₐ tanịhū'ra k'igoī'mịnₐŋkra wāwọgī'jụra." Cgą̄'ụ'-iņe rōhą̄' rasgep wānₐgī''-ị 'u'-iņe ā'nₐga haise'retcị tanihī̓' wịrā'wajịtc hīres'ā'je.

THE TOBACCO OFFERING TO THE SPIRITS

Host's initial speech.—"Tcahā'sgara hak'e'we jejë'nọga tcō'-k'ewahī'wịra wagụdje'ra sī'jₐcA'ṇA wagịtū'cdjₐ ręhak'djonę'ra. Ė'gị wagā'xEra wawịk'āragī'ręk'djonē'nₐ. Nₐga ë'gị wawī'wāk'ārap'e'rezhị-ā'nₐga 'ụgī'jị wak'ū'ruz hīreje. Jë'sge rōā'gụ wā'uk'djonë'nₐ. Nₐga ë'gị wōho'ṇa djā'nₐga jịge' hịtcō'k'ewahī'-wịra wōho'ṇa wawīk'ārap'e'rez hīrë'je. Jë'sge rō-ā'gụ wā'ụk'dj-onë'nₐ. Nₐga ë'gị djā'nₐga sā'k'erenị'k'djoŋgEre; te tcīroī'xdjị mī'nₐgịcanₐ'gwịre. Hītọ-ịnak'ā'ragịwī'nₐ. Ėgị cindjEwat'ę' nịk'āragī'k'djonā'wi; nūnige ë'gị tọk'e'wehị nịk'āragī'k'djonawị nūnịge' hą̄ŋk'e' te'e' necewewī'nị. Hịtcō'k'ewahī'wịra ē wace'-wewịwị'ge ë'sge tcīroi'xdjị djịp hīṇagī'gịwịra. Ep'ịgā'djₐ. Sa'k'-erenị'k'djoŋgEra tcī-ō'jụ mīnₐkcā'waŋgre nịk'ū'rụhindjwī'nₐ hītcōk'ewahī'wịra. Higŭâ'na tanī'ṇa wagịp'ā'xụk'djonë'nₐ."

will be present to smoke with them, it is said. And lest (through forgetfulness) they do not think of certain spirits they have some tobacco ready for these, that they may also smoke it. Wherever it is that the spirits have their gathering places there it is that the tobacco goes. The Thunderbirds have a tobacco-gathering place, it is said. The Night Spirits have one also, it is said. The place that I spoke of as the one where Djobenāŋgiwi'ŋxga was blessed, that is the tobacco-gathering place of the Night Spirits, Grandfather Djobenāŋgiwi'ŋxga said. Up above there is also a tobacco-gathering place, it is said. And, again, on the earth there is a gathering place somewhere, it is said. Under the earth there is a gathering place somewhere also, it is said. The mixed tobacco is placed in the center of the long lodge, and though this is not pure tobacco there is plenty of it. The feasters try to consume all of it. They would smoke very much, for they desired (certain things from the spirits). Thus the feasters would encourage one another, for they, the spirits, loved holy tobacco. "Try to make them smoke as much tobacco as possible that you may obtain war powers, it is said."

He (the host) smoked for them (the spirits). He also encouraged the feasters (to smoke) and had the attendants go repeatedly to fill the pipe of the guests seated in the lodge. "Be diligent," he told them "and try to smoke as much as you can." All night he offered them tobacco to smoke, it is said.[23]

THE TOBACCO OFFERING TO THE SPIRITS

Host's initial speech.—"Six white buckskins, with enough material for as many pairs of mocassins, I am going to send to our grandparents. They will be able to recognize (the buckskins) by the marks upon them.[24] If (spirits) you recognize them, it is our desire that you take these buckskins. That is why I am doing this. I hope, also, that our grandfathers will accept our food offerings. That is why I am making them. Many are the war-bundle owners who are sitting here; the lodge tent is full of them. I am thankful for it. I am going to make you very tired; I am going to make you very hungry; but I know you never thought of that.[25] You are thinking only of our grandfathers, the spirits, and that is why you have permitted my lodge to become filled up with people. It is good. All ye war-bundle owners who are seated here within, I greet you. I am now going to pour tobacco."

---

[23] This was omitted in the account as first obtained and was told afterwards. For this reason it partakes more of a general description than of a detailed narrative.

[24] Every buckskin is marked with a symbol sacred to the particular spirit to whom it is offered.

[25] It is one of the cardinal traits of Winnebago ritualistic oratory that everything that the speaker does is to be depreciated and that any honor or consideration shown to him by his guests is to be ascribed more to a feeling of pity in their breasts than to his worth.

Host's offering to Earthmaker.—"Hǎhǎ' ᵉŭaŋgere'gi hi̜-ā'ndjɛ-
ni̜na, wajʌ'na hanǎ'tc nacᵉu̜ne're nūnige ë'gi̜ tanī'na hōjū'-ijǎ
ni̜gip'āxy̜'wīcge hīnagī'k'i̜k'djonā'wije hīrak'ī'ge ë'je aī'rɛnʌ.
Tanī'na hōjū'-ijǎ ni̜gip'āxy̜'k'djonɛhā're ë'gi̜ wagu̜dje'ra sī'jǎ
hi̜rasā ë'gi̜ wōho'nʌ wani̜-oī'tcge hi̜sgaī'jǎ wōwā'k'ona hīrasā'
warūtc xō'p'ini̜. Te jë'nọga ni̜gitū'cdjonɛhā're. Ë'gi̜ wīragī'-
p'erez ā'nọga ᵉy̜gī ë'gi̜ wotā'tc tconī'na rọhǎbōtᵉe'ki̜na, wọnā'ɣ-
i̜rɛra, ŭankci'gọᵉī'na woirọk'ī'pi̜na. Je jësge wawā'wi̜jeje. Te
jësge rōni̜gi̜ŋgy̜'wi̜ge. Wajō'k'i̜na djā'nʌga mī-ā'nọganọ'gwi̜re
mejë'nọga rōni̜gigy̜'wi̜nʌ."

Host's offering to the Thunderbirds.—"Ë'gi̜ sā'ni̜ŋgĭọhe'regi̜ hi̜tcō'-
k'eniwī'na Wak'ā'ndja hu̜'ŋgɛra, tcōk'agā' nǎdjōradjọ'ŋgi̜ji̜ tanī'-
na hōjū'i̜jǎ ni̜gip'ā'xu̜ŋgi̜. Waᵉī'nʌp hi̜nagī'gik'djonë'je. Ë'gi̜
wagu̜dje'ra sī'jǎ hi̜rasā' ni̜gitū'cdjǎ rehā'nʌ Ë'gi̜ wōho'na rōhī'-
wi̜sge hīnai̜ŋk'arabwī'ra jesgë'jǎ rọhī'ra hīk'īsgi-ā'k'i̜ǎdje'ra ni̜gitū'-
cdjǎ rehā'nʌ. Nọga ë'gi̜ warūtc xō'p'i̜ni̜ hīra'gi̜tū'tcap tejë'nọga
ni̜gitū'cdjǎ rehā'nʌ. Rā ë'gi̜ djā'nọga họk'ī̜k'ārā'djɛra hanʌ'-
gwi̜re, wō'tatc tcọnī'na rōhǎbọtᵉe'k'i̜nʌ wōnā'ɣi̜rera, enaǐ'ŋxdjinʌ
woirọk'ī'p'i̜na hi̜jǎ' haᵉy̜wije'je. Ŭaŋkcigō'ᵉi̜na mejë'nọga rọni̜-
gigy̜'wi̜na jë'nʌga ni̜gitawī'na. Họk'ī̜k'arā'djɛra ŭaŋkci'gọᵉi̜
ŭanǎdjodjai̜'sge haᵉŭǎdjā'wi̜nʌ p'i̜ ŭaŋkci'gaᵉi̜ŋk'djā'wi̜ra. Te
jësge ro-ā'gy̜wī'nʌ.

Host's offering to the Night Spirits.—"Ë'gi̜ sā'ni̜ŋk hǎbọgū'regerera
Hok'ā'was Manī'na tcōk'agā' ŭānaᵉi̜'na̜gik'e'rewigi ë'gi̜ tanīni̜gī'-
ju̜hani̜hë'k'djawi̜ra jës'ge nǎdjīrọrā'djọgi̜. Tanī'na hōjū'i̜jǎ
ni̜gip'axy̜'i̜cge waᵉī'nʌp hi̜nagik'ī'k'djera tanī'na hōjū'i̜jǎ
ni̜gip'ā'xu̜ŋk'djonā're. Ë'gi̜ wagu̜dje'ra sī'jǎ ë'gi̜ ji̜ge' wọho'na
wā'ru̜tc xō'p'i̜ni̜ hīrarū'tcap mejë'nọga reni̜gī'gi̜wina. Ë'gi̜ tcōk'-
agā' djagū' nǎdjīrōrā'djọgi̜ jeᵉe' jë'sge rọni̜gigy̜'wi̜nʌhọk'i̜k'ā'-
radjɛra djā'nʌga. Ra jë'nʌga wō'tatc tcọnī'na wonʌ'ɣi̜re woirọk'ī'-
p'i̜na hi̜jǎ' ᵉy̜k'djawī'nʌ. Nʌga ë'gi̜ ŭaŋkci'gọᵉi̜ ŭānǎdjọdjai̜'sge

Host's offering to Earthmaker.—"Hearken, Father who dwells above,[26] all things you have created. Yet if we would make an offering of tobacco you would accept it with thankfulness [27] (you said). So it has been said. I am about to offer a handful of tobacco and a buckskin for moccasins with it and a white-haired animal [28] to be cooked so that (you may have) a holy feast. These things I turn over to you. If you accept them, the first thing I wish to ask for will be (the honor of) killing (an enemy) outright, of leading warpaths, and of obtaining life honors.[29] That is what we would like to lead (i. e., a war party). That is what I would ask of you. My relatives, as many as are sitting around here, even that many ask the same things of you."

Host's offering to the Thunderbirds.—"Those in the west, our grandfather, Thunderbird Chief, you blessed grandfather, and I am now going to offer you a handful of tobacco. With thanks you will accept it (it has been said). Buckskin for moccasins, also, I am sending over to you. A feast made from one whom we regard as one of yourselves, whose body we are like.[30] I am sending along for you. Indeed a sacred feast I am offering you; that I am now sending toward you. As many of our clan members as are here, they (all) desire to make these requests: To kill an enemy outright, to lead a war party, and— O grant it to us!—a life honor. Life, that is what I pray for to you— that we ask of you. Our clan has put itself in a pitiable condition,[31] so that we may live a good life. That we ask of you."

Host's offering to the Night Spirits.—"You who live in the east, you who walk in darkness, you directed your minds toward grandfather, and for that I will pour tobacco for you, now and forever, so that you may bless me. A handful of tobacco, if we pour for you, we know it will make you thankful, and for that reason do I offer you some. A buckskin for moccasins and, together with it, a sacred feast that I am about to send toward you. With whatever you blessed grandfather, that I and all my clansmen who are here ask of you. This request, that one of us lead the war party you

---

[26] No Christian influence is to be suspected in this term of address.

[27] According to shamanistic cosmology, Earthmaker first created all the various spirits and bestowed upon each one of them certain powers. When finally he created man he noticed that he had nothing left to give him, so he decided to give him tobacco. This was to remain his exclusive possession, and not even he, Earthmaker, would be able to take it away from him. It was finally agreed that man would offer it to Earthmaker and the other spirits and receive in return therefor specific blessings.

[28] Ritualistic name for deer.

[29] "Killing an enemy outright" means killing him in the midst of his own people and without the assistance of anyone else. It was the highest war honor that a Winnebago could obtain and entitled him to wear an eagle feather in his hair. "Life honors" always refer to war honors.

[30] The whole phrase from "rohįwí'sge" to "rōhí'ra hĭk'ĭsĭkĭ-ǎ̵'djera," is the ritualistic expression for dog. The dog is referred to as "like one of ourselves" in deference to the fact that one of the clans is called wolf or dog. Thus in offering up the dog they wish to imply that they are offering up themselves.

[31] I. e., a condition which calls for pity.

hāᵋŭāhą̆'gwįre ŭaŋkci'gǫᵋį p'iąᵋ ųk'djā'wi. Te jësge rǫ'nįgigų'-wįną.

Host's offering to Disease-giver.—"Ė'gį sā'nįŋgĭorātcą̆dje'regį Hocereᵋų'wahįra, tcōk'agā' djōbenągiwi'xga īwustᵋę'k'įgį ŭānądjǫdjaĭ'sge waᵋųgī'ji. Ė'gį ną̆'djǫradjǫ'gį wǫnᴀ'ɣįre rųk'o'nᴀ xetę'ra në'cᴀną. Hīranįtce'ra wǫnᴀ'ɣįre xetehī' hįcū'rųk'onā'nǫga. Ė'gį hą̆'bEra xetehī hī'cųrųk'o'ną̆ga rōsā'nįŋk hą̆'bEra nīnë'je hīrak'ī'gegį aī'gį jīge' rosā'nįŋk hōtᵋę'ją nįnë'je. Hīrak'ī'gegį tcōk'agā' Djōbenągiwi'ŋxga ną̆djǫradjǫ'gį wīrarǫtcą̆'djegā'dją hą̆'bādjasge'xdjį harak'ī'cdjaną̆ga. Ė'gį ną̆'djǫradjǫ'gį wǫnᴀ'ɣįrera ną̆'djīrǫrā'djᴀgį, jeᵋe' nįgįtā'wįną.

Hǫk'īk'ā'radjEra djā'ną̆ga ᵋu-įnę'wira jë'ną̆ga tanī'na hǫjū'-ijᴀcᴀną̆' nįgip'āxų'k'djonā'wįre nįtā'k'atcEra. Wā'jagų'zEra wanį-oī'tcgįgįᵋū'ną̆ wanį-oī'tcge hįsgaī'ją wǫwā'k'oną̆ nįgįtū'cdją ręhā'wįną. Ė'gį wagudje'ra sī'ją. Hīrasā' wak'e'ręra hīrasā' mejë'ną̆ga nįgįtū'cdją ręhā'wįną. Tcōk'agā' Djōbenągiwi'xga djagū' nądjīrǫrā'djᴀgį jeᵋe' tanį-ǫnį'gįjųwį-ā'ną̆ga hak'ā'ratā'wigį hoici'pdjį hūnak'ų'k'djenā'wi. Tcō'k'agā Djōbenągiwi'ŋxga ë'je aī'ręną̆ wǫnā'ɣįre ŭaŋkcigoᵋī'na te jësge nįgįtā'wįną. Hagârë'ją homanī'na rakᵋųgį tcōk'agā' Djōbenągiwi'ŋxga rędjų'wanina hatci'-ndja nīhaį'regį haŋk'e' wamaci'nįnįŋk'djone hįcęje' aī'ręra tcōk'ā'.

Host's offering to the Sun.—"Ė'gį tcōk'ā' Hą̆banį'hųra hą̆bǫk'ā'hį cū'radjane tcōk'agā' Djōbeŋągiwi'ŋxga nądjǫradjǫ'gį wǫnā'-ɣįre ŭaŋkcigoᵋī'na nądjįrǫrā'djᴀgį tanī'na hōjū'iją nįgįp'ā'xų-į-ā'ną̆ga. Wājagų'zEra djagū' hīrɑk'o'nᴀ nįgigī'gįjį jeᵋe' haną̆'tcį tcōk'agā' hǫk'ī'k'aradjEra ną̆'djįrǫrā'djᴀgį djā'ną̆ga ᵋu-įnę'wįra haną̆'tcįxdjį tani-ō'nįgįjū'k'djonā'wįre. Tanī'na gā."

"Aī'ręra djagū' nįgįtā'wigį cᵋų'k'djonę'je. Hīrak'ī'k'eje tcōk'-agā' ëje aī'ręra. Wǫnᴀ'ɣįre ŭaŋkcigoᵋī'na me'jësge ronįgįgų'wįną. Tanī'na wōho'na mą̆cū'na ną̆bwe'nįgįtųxā'djwįre warak'araī'-sabā'ną̆ga ᵋųgį wǫnᴀ'ɣįrera woirųk'ī'p'įna yaᵋ ųŋk'djā'wira.

have predestined for us (we make).[32] Pitiable we are making ourselves in life, that we may live a good life (by obtaining blessings from you). That we ask of you."

Host's offering to Disease-giver.—"For you who live in the south, Disease-giver, my grandfather Djobenäŋgiwi'xga thirsted himself to death [33] and put himself in a pitiable condition. Then you who are in charge of great war powers blessed him. For you control a greater amount of war powers than any other spirit. A great amount of life you also control, for you are said (to possess two sides), one side of your body containing life and the other death. You told grandfather Djobenaŋgiwi'ŋxga that you would bless him at noon, in broad daylight,[34] and thus indeed you met him. There you blessed him with war powers; and with whatever you blessed him, that we ask of you now. Whosoever of my clan are present they all pour an offering of tobacco for you and also (give you) soup.[35] The Creator made animals for us, white-haired animals for food, and these we send to you; together with buckskins, that you may have moccasins. We also send toward you a head ornament (of eagle feathers), that also. We offer you tobacco and we ask of you to bestow upon us that with which you blessed our grandfather Djōbenaŋgiwi'ŋxga. Grandfather Djōbenaŋgiwi'ŋxga had had war powers and life, it is said; and those we ask of you. And it is said that you told grandfather that whenever you go on your warpath you will not walk upon the descendants of Djōbenaŋgiwi'ŋxga wherever they breathe.[36]

Host's offering to the Sun.—"You, grandfather Who-bring-day, who come every day, you blessed grandfather Djōbenaŋgiwi'ŋxga with war power and life and I am therefore offering you a handful of tobacco. All the (war power) the Creator controls he delegated to you and for all of that which you blessed our grandfather, as many of my clansmen as are present, we are about to pour tobacco to obtain. Tobacco, here it is."

Host then pours tobacco into the fire.

"It is said that you will do what we ask of you. You yourself told that to grandfather, it is said. War powers and life, that we ask of you. Tobacco, food, and feathers, we sacrifice to you and

---

[32] A person may be blessed with victory on the warpath directly or he may be entitled to war blessings to which near relatives were destined but which they were deprived of by an early death. The present prayer is directed toward both things, that he may enjoy the "unused" blessings of his relative and that he may not be cut off by an untimely death from the fulfillment of his own.

[33] Ritualistic expression for fasting.

[34] To be blessed in the daytime, especially at noon, was considered as particularly holy. Generally a person was blessed at night.

[35] Literally, "hot water."

[36] I. e., when Disease-giver deals out death he will avoid all the descendants of Djobenaŋgiwi'ŋxga. "Manĭ'na" is the technical word for warpath. The word for descendants really means "roots."

Ŭaŋkcigǫᶜī′ṇa racgū′nį sᶠī ŭaŋkciga⁴i′ŋk'djāwį nįgįtawī′n₄ tanį-ǫnįgī′jųwįn₄ tcōk'ā′.

Host's offering to Earth.—"Ḗ′gį jįge′ k'ū′niŋk'ā tcōk'agā′ Djōbe-nạgįwi′ŋxga nₐ̄′djǫradjǫ`gį wajạgų'zɛra djagū′ rųk'o′no niŋgįgī′gī. Tcōk'agā′ hanₐ̄′tcį nₐ̄djōradjǫ′gį djadjaī′ŋxdjį man₄'gɛre mī′naŋk'į jedjaį′xdjį p'ā danį-ǫnįgī′jų hanihë'k'djawį. Hīrage′gi djagū′ niŋgįtā′wigį hīnₐgįcᶜụ′k'dj₄nā`wį hīcë′je ë′ra. Tanī′ṇa hōjū′-įjₐ hīrani'p'ahak'djonįhā`wįn₄ djā′n₄ga wak'ī′k'aratcwira. Tanī′ṇa k'ū′niŋk'a hiŋgįrų'zwį-ₐ̄'dje. Tanī′ṇa hǫjū′-įjₐ tcį-ō′k'įsagǫ-naįī'n₄ ë′dja niŋgįp'axu′ŋk'djonā`wįre. Wǫn₄'γįrẹra ŭaŋkcigoᶠī′ṇa huŋk'ụwį-a′ndje, tejësge niŋgįtā′w′n₄. Tanī′ṇa te⁴e′ren₄.

'Nintā′k'adjɛra, woī′djᴀnᴀ narō′nį hīrasā′ reniŋgigī′wįn₄. Hīn₄-gī′p'erezwigį, ŭaŋkci'gǫᶠįṇa je⁴e′ ya⁴uŋk'djonā′wįra; jë′sge niŋgįtā′-wįn₄."

Host's offering to the Moon.—"K'ū′niŋk'a hₐ̄he′regį hųrā′djonë` n₄ ë′gį k'ū′niŋk'a tcōk'agā′ Djōbenạgįwi′ŋxga nₐ̄djǫrā′djǫŋgį tanį-ǫniŋgįjų-ā′nįhẹk'djawį djā′n₄ga hōni′ŋgera ⁴ų-įṇe′wigį. Tani-ǫwaxu′ṇa jįnadjī′wigį tanį niŋgįp'axų′wigį. Hīrak'ā′rap`erezcā`waįŋk'djonë′n₄ hīrak'ī′geje aī′rẹra. Tcok'agā′ Djōbenạgiwi′ŋ-xga djagū′ hīcųrųk'o′nǫgī′ji, jë′sge nₐ̄djōradjǫ′gį maiŋk'ī′xdjį hatā′nįhek'djawī′ra hoici'p hūnak⁴ụ′k'djonā`wį hīceje′ aī′rera.

"Tanī′ṇa te⁴e′rẹn₄."

"Tanī′ṇa ŭaŋkci'goᶠį k'aratā′ ya⁴ụ′k'djera. Wajạgų'zɛra haniŋgigī′ra nįgip'axū′ṇ₄. Wǫnᴀ′γįrẹra wak'ī′k'aradjwįra djā′nᴀga hanī′wįn₄ hagârë′j₄ naŋgū′ra hī′jₐ wawā′wigį ë′dja woirųk'ī′p'įṇa ya⁴ụk'djā′wįra nįgįtā′wįn₄. Nįntā′k'adjɛra wajạgų'zɛra wani-oī′tcgįŋgį ⁴ū′n₄ hįce′bɛra; wįwẹ′wį-ǫwįnǫ`gera nįntā′k'atc niŋgigiwī′n₄. Wā′rųtc xō′p'inį hįrā′nįŋgįtųtcₐ̄`wįn₄. Ḗ′gį wagųdje′ra sī′jₐ niŋgįtū′cdj₄ rehā′wįn₄. Wǫnᴀ′γįre ŭaŋkcigoᶠī′ṇa niŋgįtā′wįn₄ hūnak⁴ụ′gį ŭaŋkcigǫᶠī′ṇa p'ia⁴ụ′k'djā`wįn₄. Ḗ′gį jige′ k'ū′niŋk'a tcōk'agā′ Djōbenạgiwi′ŋxga nₐ̄′djǫradjǫ′gį wajạgų'zɛra wǫna′γįre ŭaŋkci'goᶠįṇa hīrųk'o′no niŋgigī′gi. Je⁴e′ tcōk'agā′

if you accept them, then we will assuredly wear war honors (some day). That we may pass through life without any troubles and that we may live long, we ask of you and offer you tobacco, grandfather."

Host's offering to Earth.—"Grandmother, you blessed Djōbenagiwi'ŋxga with whatever the Creator delegated to you. With everything that exists on the earth, for all eternity, did you tell grandfather you would bless him, and this is what we ask of you and for which we will forever offer you tobacco. You will do it, he told us you had said. A handful of tobacco we are about to send toward you, we, as many of our clansmen as are here. Tobacco do you accept from us, grandmother. A handful of tobacco there, upon him who stands in the middle of the lodge,[37] do we pour. Give us war powers and life; for these we beseech you. Here it is, the tobacco."

The host then pours some tobacco into the fire.

"Soup, vegetables, together with maple sugar we are about to send you.[38] If you accept them, life we will obtain; that we ask of you."

Host's offering to the Moon.—"Grandmother, You-Who-Come-at-Night,[39] grandmother, you blessed grandfather Djōbenagiwi'ŋxga and now all his descendants, as many as there are, are about to offer you tobacco. Now when we come to a tobacco offering we will certainly offer some to you. And you will be cognizant of it, you assured us yourself, it is said. Whatever you are in control of and with which you blessed our grandfather Djōbenagiwi'ŋxga for all eternity, that we are to ask for at all times, they told us you had said and you will assuredly give it to us. The tobacco, here it is."

He pours tobacco into the fire.

"I am using the tobacco as a means of obtaining life for myself and my relatives.[40] The Creator gave it to me and I am offering it to you. As many of our clansmen as are here we beg of you war powers; and that if we ever go on a warpath [41] there we will obtain the war honors. Soup and the animals the Creator made for me,[42] the black-furred one [43] we are offering you; soup of bear ribs. A sacred feast we are about to hold for you. A buckskin for moccasins we are about to send out to you. War powers and life we ask of you; that you give us life, so that our days may be happy. Truly, grand-mother, did you bless our grandfather Djobenagiwi'ŋxga with what-

[37] "He who stands in the middle of the lodge" is the ritualistic name for the fireplace. He is always personified and the tobacco is generally conceived of as being poured upon his head.
[38] As the offerings are made to the earth, vegetables and maple sugar are selected.
[39] Ritualistic name for the moon. The regular name is "hahe wira" (night sun).
[40] The term "uaŋkcigosi k'aratā," literally meaning "a life beseecher," is used only in rituals and is generally taken to include any offering.
[41] "Nagū," is the regular word for warpath. Literally it means simply "road."
[42] I. e., what the Creator had placed in his way and permitted him to catch and prepare for this feast. It is in this specific significance that it is meant here.
[43] "Hi'cebEra" is both the ritualistic and deferential name for the bear.

nặdjọradjǫ'gị djadjo'nạ tanị-ǫwaxụ'ṇa hiŋgire'wigị niŋgitā'wigị hūnak⁴ụharanī'cĕk'djenā'wịnạ hicĕje. Tcōk'agā' Djōbenạgiwi'ŋxga ĕ'je aī'rẹnạ. Tanī'ṇa hōjū'ịjạ p⁴ĕdje'dja hịdjeniŋgī'giwịgị. Rak⁴a- hī'k'djone hīrak⁴ī'geje tcōk⁴agā'ĕje aī'rẹra. Tanī'ṇa hoi'cipdjị hịṇagī'k'saip'djonā'wị hīceje' tcōk⁴agā' Djōbenạgiwi'ŋxga ĕ'ra. Tanī'ṇa ga heredjịgō'.''

"Tanī'ṇa hịnạgī'hịwigị wǫnạ'γịrẹra ŭaŋkcigǫ⁴ī'ṇa pīạ⁴ụ'k'djena jĕ'sge niŋgịtā'wịnạ. Nịntā'k'adjЕra woī'djonạ sī'na nạrō'nị hīrak⁴ī'sa niŋgịtū'cdjonẹhā'wịnạ; ĕ'gị wagụdje'ra sī'jạ hīrasā' wī'ṇagịp'e'rezwịgị wǫna'γịre ŭaŋkcigǫ⁴ị'ṇa ya⁴ŭaṇịhĕ'k'djawịra. Jĕ'sge nịgịtā'wịnạ k'ū'niŋk'a hā'nạga.''

Host's offering to the chief of the Eagles.—"Tcaxcep huŋgera' ⁴ŭa'ŋgЕregi hặbāmanī'ṇa. Nĕ'cАnạ xetẹra' niṇĕ'je wǫnА'γịrẹra hīrụk'o'no. Panī'je hīrak⁴ī'gegi. Ĕ'gị ŭaŋkci'gǫ⁴ị jịge' hịcū'- rụk'onặ'jenị gigịgī'jị. Tcō'k'agā Djōbenạgiwi'ŋxga nặdjọradjǫ'gị wajặgụ'zЕra djagū' rụk'o'no niŋgigi'gị. Tcōk'agā' nặdjọradjǫ'gị manạ'gere djadjaị'xdjị nịhĕ'gị jedjaị'xdjị tanị-ǫniŋgī'jụ haṇịhĕ'- k'djonā'wịgị. Jĕ'sge tcōk'agā' hīrage'gị tanị-ǫ'waxụ niŋgī'k'- erek'djā'wị hịcĕje. Tcōk'agā' ĕ'je aī'rẹra. Hīcge' tcōk'agā' wax- op'ī'nị wāna⁴ị' rụsgī'tcgi hīcgịdjạ' wāna⁴ị' yǫrak⁴ā'rak'ereje' tcōk⁴- agā' ĕje aī'rẹra. Tanī'ṇa ga aīredjịgō'.''

"Tcōk'ā' Tcaxcep huŋgЕra' tanị-ōniŋgijū'nạ. Tcōk'agā' djagū' nạdjọradjǫ'gị je⁴e' niŋgịtā'wịnạ. Ĕ'gị wawakī'k'aradjЕra taniṇiŋ- gịp'āxụ'ŋk'djonā'wịre hịṇagī'ksapwī'gị wǫnạ'γịre ŭaŋkci'gǫ⁴ī'ṇa hūnak⁴ụ'wịgị maihā'gЕregi ya⁴ụ'k'djawī'nạ. Te jĕsge niŋgịtā'- wịnạ tcōk'ā'.

Host's offering to the Day.—"Ĕ'gị jịge hặ'pdjaṇe tanī'ṇa hīdje' nịgịgī'nạ. Nịntā'k'adjЕra wanị-oi'tcge hịsgā'ra wīwē'-wị-ǫwịnǫ'- gera warūtc xō'p'inị hīraniŋgī'tụtcap rẹhā'wịnạ. Tcōk'agā' Djō- benạgiwi'ŋxga nặdjọradjǫ'gị hīcge wīwē'wị hīdjō'rak'arak'ere'jə aī'rera. Tanī'na wǫhǫ'ṇa hīṇagịp'e'rezwịgị wōnА'γịrẹra ŭaŋkcigǫ⁴ī'- ṇa yā⁴ŭaṇịhĕ'k'djawi. Niŋgịtā'wịnạ tcok'ā'.''

ever powers the Creator put in your control. That with which you blessed grandfather it is said you would give us, too, when in the course of time we would pray to you to bestow them upon us. So it is reported our grandfather Djōbenagiwi'ŋxga said. A handful of tobacco we place for you in the fire. You would smoke it, it is said that you, yourself, told grandfather. Tobacco, you told him you would always accept, it is said. Here it is, the tobacco."

He pours tobacco into the fire.

"If you smoke the tobacco for us, war powers and happiness in life we will ask of you. Soup, vegetables, rice, and maple sugar we send out to you, and buckskin for moccasins likewise. If you accept these things from us, it will be ours to use, war power and life. That we ask of you, grandmother."

Host's offering to the chief of the Eagles.—"Chief of the Eagles, you who walk on light [44] up above. You, yourself, said that only you are the greatest one in control of war powers. That you are thus, you said of yourself. Life also you are in charge of. You blessed our grandfather Djōbenagiwi'ŋxga with whatever powers the Creator put you in control. You blessed grandfather for all eternity, [45] and for those powers we are now about to offer you tobacco. It is for that purpose you told grandfather we should have a tobacco pouring. So grandfather told us, it is said. Grandfather also made a sacred bundle [46] and to this you also added your power, grandfather said, it is said. The tobacco, here it is."

He pours tobacco into the fire.

"To you, chief of the Eagles, grandfather, do we pour tobacco. With whatever you blessed grandfather, that we ask of you. All the members of the clan offer you tobacco that you may have knowledge of it (i. e., the tobacco) and bestow upon us who dwell on the earth war powers and life. That is what we ask of you, grandfather."

Host's offering to the Day.—"To the Day [47] I pour tobacco, also soup, and a rib of a white-haired animal (i. e., a deer). A sacred meal we are about to offer to you. Grandfather Djōbenagiwi'ŋxga you blessed and you also added your thoughts, [48] it is said. If you accept tobacco and the feast, war powers and life we assuredly are going to obtain. For that we ask, grandfather."

---

[44] "Habamanĭ' ṇa," is the ritualistic name for any bird. Although rarely used except in rituals, it is yet generally known among the people, a fact that does not hold for most of the other ritualistic appellations.

[45] The set phrase which from now on we will translate by "eternity," is literally "as long as the earth lasts, that long."

[46] "Waxop'ĭ' nĭ wanąᵗĭ'rųsgĭ' tcgi" means literally, "He tied up the spirit mind or manifestation," i. e., he made a bundle of the blessings he received from the various spirits. Djōbenaṇgiwi'ŋxga is the individual who is supposed to have first received the clan bundle. The word "wanąᵗĭ" is a very difficult one to render accurately in English.

[47] Although, according to the Winnebago conception, the light of day is associated with the sun, yet the sun is not regarded as causing the light any more than the absence of the sun is thought to be the cause of darkness, but both light (daylight) and darkness are associated with special deities.

[48] "Wĭwĕ'wĭ" is not to be thought of in an abstract sense but as something quite as tangible as a material object.

Host's offering to the South Wind.—"Ė'gi jige rẹk'ū'huhī'ra tcōk'agā' Djōbenagiwi'ŋxga waxop'ī'ni wā'na⁽ị djōrak'ā'rak'ereje` ë'je tcōk'agā' Djōbenagiwi'ŋxga aī'rera. Wajagu'zEra djagū' hīruk'o'no ningigī'gi tcōk'agā' Djōbenagiwi'ŋxga nädjoradjǫ' gi djadjaị'xdjị p'ā mānʌ'gere mī'nʌŋk'ī jedjaị'xdjị p'ā, tani-oningī'p'āxu hanihë'k'djawi hīrak'ī'gegi. Tanī'na ga airë'nʌ."

"Ė'gi nịtak'ā'djEra wajãgu'zEra wani-oī'tcge hiŋgi⁽ū'nʌ hūdjō'-bimanị`ja nị'tak'atc niŋgigiwī'nʌ wak'ë'jʌ. Tanī'na hịnagī'-hịwigị` nịta'k'adjEra hīnagī'p'erezwigi wǫnʌ'ɣirẹra wotā' tcōnī'na hīrak'ī'rak wawëk'djā'winʌ ŭaŋkcigǫ⁽ī'na pīą⁽ụ'k'djā`winʌ. Me'-jësge niŋgitā'winʌ."

Host's offering to the North Wind.—Ė'gi jige wazī'rẹgihuhī'ra wak'ịp'ī'na hīceje; tcōk'agā' Djōbenagiwi'ŋxga ë'je aī'rẹra. Tanī'na nịtā'k'adjEra woī'djʌne naiŋk'anʌ'gīją hā'ra waiyā'gëk'djā`wira jë'sge nãrō'ni hīrak'ī'sa niŋgi'tūcdją rehā'winʌ. Wawī'nagip'ere`zwigị wōna'ɣire ŭaŋkcigǫ⁽ị'na wōtā'ra te jë'nuga niŋgitā'winʌ. Tcōk'ā' waxą-ī'na rohãbot⁽ẹ'ki-ë'dja hī⁽ụ'p'īnanī`je hīrak'ī'geje. Tcōk'agā' Djōbenagiwi'ŋxga ë'je aī'rẹra hā'nʌga."

Host's offering to the Black Hawk.—"Ė'gi tcōk'ā' k'eredjụ' sepEra hīcge' wōwē'wị hịgi-orak'ā'rak'ere`je aī'rẹra tanī'na hōjū'-iją niŋgip'axū'na. Wōnʌ'ɣire ŭaŋkcigǫ⁽ī'na wajãgu'zEra hīruk'o'no niŋgigī'gi, je⁽e' waniŋgitā'nʌ. Tcōk'agā' Djōbenagiwi'ŋxga nãdjoradjǫ'gi manʌ'gEre djadjaị'xdjị mī'naŋk'īji jedjaị'xdjị p'ā tanī'na rahī' ranicā'k'djonë`je hīcë'je aī'rẹra. Tanī'na hīnʌgī'wik'sā`pwigi ŭaŋkcigǫ⁽ī'na ya⁽u'ŋk'djawira wōnʌ'ɣire. Niŋgitā'winʌ hā'nʌga."

Host's offering to the Wōna'ɣire Ŭa'ŋkcik.—"Tcōk'ā' Wak'ā'ndja Wōna'ɣire Ŭaŋkhīniŋgaī'rawigi, tcōk'agā' waxop'ī'ni wāna⁽ị' rusgī'-tcgi hīcge wāna⁽ị' djōrak'ā'rak'erẹ`je aī'rẹra. Tanī' niŋgip'ā'xu-wī'nʌ. Tanī'nacʌnʌ wōna'ɣire ŭaŋkcigǫ⁽ī'na tcōk'agā' Djōbenagiwi'ŋxga niŋgitā'winʌ je⁽e maịk'ī'dją ya⁽ŭanihëk'djā`winʌ.

Host's offering to the South Wind.—"South Wind, to the bundle grandfather Djōbenạgiwi'ŋxga made you added your power, so grandfather Djōbenạgiwi'ŋxga said, it is said. That which the Creator put in charge of you, and with which you blessed grandfather Djōbenạgiwi'ŋxga, as long as the earth lasts, we are about to pour tobacco for, as you yourself told us. The tobacco, here it is."

He pours tobacco into the fire.

"A four-legged animal,[49] a coon, that the Creator made for us, we are going to give you in the form of a soup. If you accept the soup and likewise smoke the tobacco, then the first request (we wish to make) is that it might be our fortune to obtain war powers and travel safely (on the path) of life. This is what we ask."

Host's offering to the North Wind.—"Wind who lives in the north, you said 'I am the equal of (the spirit of the north)'; [50] so grandfather Djōbenạgiwi'ŋxga said, it is said. Tobacco, soup, vegetables, what a tree bears, fruit, as we call it, and maple sugar, that also we send toward you. If you accept them, the request (we make) is for war power and life; that we ask of you. To kill a person outright is an excellent power to have, grandfather Porcupine,[51] you said of yourself. So grandfather Djōbenạgiwi'ŋxga said, it is said."

Host's offering to the Black Hawk.—"Black Hawk, you also added your powers for grandfather, it is said; and a handful of tobacco I am pouring for you for that reason. Whatever war powers and life the Creator put in your control, that I ask of you. You blessed grandfather Djōbenạgiwi'ŋxga for as long a period as the world would last, and you said that you would always smoke tobacco, it is said. If you are cognizant of this tobacco, let us obtain life and war power. For these we ask."

Host's offering to the Wōna'ɣịre Ŭa'ŋkcik.[52]—"Grandfather Thunder-. bird, Wōna'ɣịre Ŭa'ŋkcik, as they call you, you added your power also, it is said. Tobacco we are about to pour for you. Tobacco only (we are giving you), so that we may obtain war powers and life; that with which you blessed grandfather Djōbenạgiwi'ŋxga for all eter-

---

[49] A ritualistic manner of speaking of a quadruped, just as it is common in rituals to speak of human beings as "the two-legged-walkers."

[50] I. e., cold does not affect me. The North Wind and the spirit of cardinal point north are of course entirely distinct.

[51] No reason is known why the spirit is here addressed as porcupine.

[52] The "Wōnā'ɣịre Ŭa'ŋkcik" are birds living in the empyrean generally identified with the hawk. Here they seem to be identified with a kind of Thunderbird. Whoever is blessed by them becomes a great warrior. The term really means "a terror-inspiring man," by reason of his great war powers. One of the Winnebago clans has this name. The explanation for the identification of the Wōna'ɣịre Ŭa'ŋkcik with the Thunderbirds is probably the following: The Thunderbird is not regarded as belonging to any particular bird species, but any bird can be either a normal bird or a Thunderbird. When used in this sense, the appellation Thunderbird is generic, and the term used in the text, "Wak'ā'ndja Wōna'ɣịre Ŭaŋkcik," is then best translated by "Thunderbird—Wōnā'ɣịre Ŭaŋkcik." Thunderbird specifically is understood to be in reality not a bird but a being in human shape. Cf. Introduction. The general conception of Thunderbird given here is touched upon also by J. O. Dorsey in his "Siouan Cults."

Ṭanī'ṇa hīṇagip'erezwī'gị ŭaŋkcigọᵋī'ṇa pĭ§̄'k'dje niŋgịtā'wịnₐ wak'ik'arā'djwira djā'nₐga hanịwī'nₐ. Jë'nụga."

Host's offering to Big Black Hawk.—"Ĕ'gị k'eredjụ'sep xetẹra' saī'rụk'ononₐ' tcōk'agā' Djōbenₐgịwi'ŋxga nₐdjōradjo'ŋgị wōna'-ɣịre ŭaŋkcigọᵋị' jeᵋe hatā'nịhëk'djā'wị tcōk'agā' hīrage'gị tanị-ō'waxụ. K'erë'k'djoṇëgị tanị-ō'waxụṇa djanₐ'hị k'e'rek'djonë'-gị jënā'hₐ nₐbịruxā'djEra djanₐgā'k'djoṇẹgị jëna'hₐ. Tanī'-ṇa wōhọ'ṇA nₐbịruxā'djEra hanₐ'tcịŋxdjị hīragī'p'erez ranịcë'-k'djonëje. Hīrage'gị tcōk'agā' Djōbenₐgịwi'ŋxga. Tanī'ṇa ga heredjīgo'."

"Tanī'ṇa hōjū'-ịjₐ hīranī'p'ahawī'cge hoici'p tanī'ṇa hīṇagī'hị haranī'cëk'djonā'wịhịtëra. Tāṇị-oṇịŋgī'jụ tanī'ṇa rahị-ā'nₐga ᵋụgị wōna'ɣịre ŭaŋkcigọᵋī'ṇa wōwō'tara te jësge niŋgịtā'wịnₐ. Nịtā'-k'adjEra rōhīk'ī'sge hīnaị'k'arapwī'ra jësgë'jₐ k'īnụ'p hak'ĭₐ'-djera, niŋk'djo'ŋgeniŋgera wak'ī'tcanₐ'gera nịtā'k'atc niŋgịgịwī'nₐ. Ĕ'gị nₐbịruxā'djera wōgụdjẹ'ra sī'jₐ ë'gị rōhịwịk'ī'sge hīnaịk'arabwī'ra jësgë'jₐ rō'ra p'ị̈ᵋụ'xdjịnₐ'naga nₐphịnịŋgịruxā'djịrẹra. Ĕ'gị wak'ere hₐbitaī'ᵋụṇa hīrak'ī'ratcap nₐbịnịŋgịtụxadjwī'nₐ. Ĕ'gị wōnₐ'ɣịre hīrụk'o'no xe'tera në'jₐ nīne. Wajₐgụ'zEra nịgụ'zEra ŭaŋkcigọᵋị' hīrụk'o'no; ᵋŭaŋgere'gi wajₐgụ'zErₐ nịgụsk'ī'. Jeᵋe tcōk'agā' Djōbenₐgịwi'ŋxga nₐdjọradjo'ŋgị djā-djaị'xdjị p'ā manₐ'gere nihë'gị maịk'ī'djₐ. Tanị-ō'waxụ hak'ere-ā'nịhëk'djawị hūnā'k'ụ'wịnₐ. Tanī'ṇa hīṇagịcụruzwī'gị wōhọ'ṇa hīṇagịp'ere'zwigị nₐbịruxā'djEra wainₐ'gịcụru'zwịgị wōnₐ'ɣịrẹra woirūk'ī'p'ịṇa yaᵋụ'k'djₐnā'wi ŭaŋkcigọᵋī'ṇa yaᵋụ'k'djā'wịra. Niŋgịtā'wịnₐ tcōk'ā'wịra djā'nₐga tcōk'agā' Djōbenₐgịwi'ŋxga, waxọp'ī'nị wā'naᵋị rūsgịtcgī' djā'nₐga wānaịdjọrā'k'arak'ere-hī'gị. Hanₐ'tcịŋxdjị hₐŋk'e' wajik'ī'nA nini'ŋk'djonịhā'wịge taninₐ'cAnₐ niŋgịp'ᵋāxụ'wịcge hₐŋk'e' wajₐ' woī'cAnₐ hīwaᵋụ'-nịk'djā'wịge hīrọhịhịk'ī'sge."

"Tanī'ṇa wōgịjū'ra te jësge aī'recAnū'nₐ. E teᵋe'rẹnₐ."

THE BUCKSKIN OFFERINGS TO THE SPIRITS

(Host speaks again.) Sāk'erenị'k'djoŋgera mīnāŋkcā'waŋgre niŋk'ụruhi'ndj rehā'wịnₐ hītcō'k'ewahī'wịra hōk'ī'djₐ wagịgī' naᵋị'nịsge haŋk'ecgẹ'ra nūnige'. Waxọp'ī'nị hōk'īdjₐ' gīgī' naᵋị'-nịsge waᵋŭanₐ'gwị nūnige' hīrụdjī'sdị hawī' nūnige. Hītcō'-

nity, may we obtain from you. If you accept the tobacco may I
and my relatives live well by reason thereof; that we ask of you.
That is all."

Host's offering to Big Black Hawk.[53]—"You, Big Black Hawk, who
are in charge of war powers,[54] blessed grandfather Djōbenagiwi'ŋxga
with war powers and life, and these we are to ask of you, you told
grandfather, and pour tobacco at the same time. As many tobacco
offerings as he (grandfather) would have liked to have had and as
many (buckskin) offerings as he would have desired, that many there
will be for you. If you accept the tobacco and feast and all the
offerings, you will assuredly give (us blessings). Thus you told grandfather Djōbenagiwi'ŋxga. Tobacco, here it is."

He pours tobacco into the fire.

"If we extend toward you a handful of tobacco, you said you would
always smoke it. If, at a tobacco offering, you smoked the tobacco,
the requests we might make are these—war powers and life. A feast
of one whom you look upon in the same way as ourselves (i. e., a dog),
one whom I have been treating like a brother, with whom the children have eaten the soup of such a one, we are giving you. An
offering of buckskin for moccasins and of one like ourselves (a dog),
whose body is well prepared, do they offer you. Food they are
offering you, asking in return for life.[55] You are the only one in
control of great war powers. The Creator placed you in charge of
life; above the Creator created you. With that you blessed grandfather Djōbenagiwi'ŋxga for all eternity. We will have a tobacco
pouring, that you may give us (these things). If you take cognizance
of the feast offerings, the buckskin offerings; if you will take them,
then we will obtain the war honors and then we will obtain life. We,
as many older people as we are here, beseech you for those powers
you added to the spirit bundle of our grandfather Djōbenagiwi'ŋxga.
We will not have enough food to go around,[56] but if we offer you
tobacco, it will not be an offense (thus to act to you) (we have been
told)."

This is what they used to say at the tobacco pouring. This it is.
(Song.)

THE BUCKSKIN OFFERINGS TO THE SPIRITS

(Host speaks again.) "War-bundle owners who are seated here,
I greet you. We are endeavoring to prepare footwear for our grandfathers,[57] but we did not really accomplish it. Spirit footwear we
tried to make, that is what we were doing, but our work was lacking

---

[53] A deity apparently distinct from Black Hawk. He is the one to whom offerings are always made.
[54] Literally "in control of grass bundles."
[55] "Hąp" is the ritualistic name for life. Literally it means "light."
[56] A ritualistic expression of modesty.
[57] I. e., offer buckskins for moccasins to the spirits.

k'ewahī'wįra hąŋk'e' wajīnę'p'įhīranī'je aī'ręra. Haŋk'e' woiyā'⁴ų hīwa⁴unįk'djā'wįge hītcō'k'ewahī'wįra wagūdje' wanī'nęra⁴. Ŭaŋge'dja hīnAŋk wagigī'k'djonā'wįnA."

Offering to the Thunderbird.—"Tcōk'ā' Wak'andjā'ra waguḍję'ra sī'ją reniŋgī'giwįnA wajok'Ianiwī'nA. WōnA'γiręra ŭaŋkcigo⁴ī'ṇa wōtara' me'jësge niŋgitā'wįnA."

Offering to Night Spirits.—"Ė'gį jįge hąbogūre'gį herera' wagūdję'ra sī'ją reniŋgī'giwįnA wōtā'ra wōna'γiręra ŭaŋkcigo⁴į'ṇa. Te⁴e me'jësge niŋgitā'wįnA."

Offering to Disease-giver.—"Ė'gį jįge Hōcere⁴ų'wahį tcōk'ā' waguḍję'ra sī'ją reniŋgigī'nA. Tcōk'ā' rōhī' saṅįŋk hąbera', rohī' saṅįŋk hot⁴ę'ruk'onA ranī'je, tcōk'agā' Djōbenągiwi'ŋxga ë'ra. WōnA'γiręra ŭaŋkcigo⁴ī'ṇa wōtā'ra te⁴e' jënuŋga roniŋgigų'wįnA."

Offering to South Wind.—"Ė'gį hītcō'k'enī'na rek'ūhųhī'ra hitcō'-k'ewahī'wįra tanī'ṇa te e'redjįgō. Tcōk'agā' Djōbenągiwi'ŋxga nądjoradjo'gį wōna'γiręra ŭaŋkcigo⁴į'ṇa nądjoradjo'gį je⁴e' djadjo'na tanī'ṇa hōjū'-iją hīdje' niŋgigī'wįgį hīnagip'e'rez harā'-nįcëk'djanë'nA hīrak'ī'gegį. Waguḍję'ra sī'ją reniŋgigī'nA. Woho'ṇa te jësge niŋgitū'cdją rehā'wįnA. Tcōk'agā' djagū' nądjirorā'djogį je⁴e' hātawī'nA hā'nAga."

Offering to the Sun.—"Ė'gį hąbanį'djiręra hī'tcōk'enī'na tcōk'agā' Djōbenągiwi'ŋxga nądjoradjo'gį djagū' nądjirorā'djogį hoici'p djadjo'na tanī'na hojū'-iją niŋgip'axų'wį-ā'nAga hātawī'gį tanī'ṇa wa-ī'nAp hīnagī'hiŋk'djonā'wį hīrage'je. Ė'je aī'ręra. Waguḍję'ra sī'ją reniŋgigī'winA. Nįtā'k'atc woī'djAnA nąrō'nį hīrak'ī'sa niŋgitū'cdją rehā'wįnA. Tanī'ṇa mejë'nuga ë'dja hįranī'na⁴įwīnA. Hīnagī'gsabį-ā'nAga ⁴uŋgi wōnA'γiręra woiruk'ī'-p'įṇa yā⁴'uk'djā'wrįa. Ŭaŋkcigo⁴ī'na ya⁴ų'k'djā'wįra wōtā'ra mejë'nuga niŋgitā'wįnA."

Offering to Earthmaker.—"Ŭaŋgere'gį hī-ą'ndjeniwī'na tanī'ṇa ŭaŋkcigo⁴į' hīk'aratā' ya⁴uŋkdjā'wįra. Hīnagī'c⁴uwį-ā'nAga hanī'-nAgiwī'nA. Ė'gį nęc⁴une're nūnige' hak'djā' hōjū'-iją niŋgip'ā'ha rehā'wįcge wa⁴ī'nAp hīnagī'k'iŋk'djonā'wįje. Hīnaga'wįje. Tcōk'agā' Djōbenągiwi'ŋxga ë'je aī'ręra. Tcōk'agā' Djōbenągiwi'ŋxga nądjōrā'djoŋgi wōnA'γiręra ŭaŋkcigo⁴į'na. Niŋgitā'wįnA tanī'ṇa hak'djā' hōjū-iją niŋgip'ā'ha rehā'wįnA. Aī'gį waguḍję'ra sī'ją niŋgitū'cdją rehā'wįna wajōhok'ī'na djasge'xdjį haniwī'nA jësge'xdjį uaŋkcigo⁴į'ṇa ya⁴ų'k'djā'wį. Niŋgitā'wįnA tanī'ṇa tcahā' nąbiruxā'djera wōho'ṇA wani-oī'tcge hįsgaī'ją wani-oī'tcge ŭaŋgī'ją niŋgitū'cdją rehā'wįnA."

Offering to the Moon.—"E'gį Hąhē'wįra k'ū'nįk'a waguḍję'ra sīją ë'gį nįtā'k'atcEra tanī'ṇa me'jësge niŋgitū'cdją rehā'wįnA.

in every respect. However, our grandfathers (the spirits) would not take offense at the (inadequacy) of our work, it is said. That we may not be weakened, for that reason it is that we are preparing the moccasins for our grandfathers. Up above we are going to send them."

Offering to the Thunderbird.—"Grandfather Thunderbird, our clan is sending you moccasins. War powers and life are the requests we make in turn."

Offering to Night Spirits.—"You who live in the east, moccasins do we send you, and the request we make, is war power and life. That we ask for."

Offering to Disease-giver.—"Disease-giver, grandfather, moccasins we send you. Grandfather, life you possess on one side of your body, and death you are in control of on the other side of your body, so our grandfather Djōbenągiwi'ŋxga told us, it is said. War power and life, that is the request we make."

Offering to South Wind.—"To you, grandfather South Wind, here is the tobacco for our grandfathers. You blessed grandfather Djōbenągiwi'ŋxga with war powers and life and you said yourself that you would bless (his descendants) whenever they offered you a handful of tobacco and you accepted it. Moccasins we are sending you. Food we are about to offer you. Whatever you blessed grandfather with that we ask of you."

Offering to the Sun.—"Grandfather Light-Wanderer, you said that if at any time we poured a handful of tobacco for you and smoked tobacco as an offering (you would give us) that with which you blessed grandfather Djōbenągiwi'ŋxga whenever we ask for it. So it is said. Moccasins we are sending you. Soup, vegetables, and maple sugar also we are about to send you. Tobacco is what we think of in connection with you. If you take cognizance of it, war honors we will assuredly obtain. Life, that is what we would like to obtain."

Offering to Earthmaker.—"You who are above, our Father, we ask life of you, extending tobacco. You made this for us; you let us have it. Indeed it is you that made it and yet you will take a handful of it that we extend to you and accept it as an offering. That is what you said to us. So grandfather Djōbenągiwi'ŋxga said, it is said. You blessed grandfather Djōbenągiwi'ŋxga with war powers and life. Bless us in turn now that we are about to offer you a handful of tobacco. We, as many clansmen as there are here, are about to send to you moccasins so that we may obtain life from you. Tobacco, deerskins as offerings, food of the white-haired animal, of a male animal, we are about to offer you."

Offering to the Moon.—"Grandmother, the Moon, moccasins, soup and tobacco, these we are about to offer you. Our request is for the

Tcōk'agā' Djōbenągiwi'ŋxga djagū' nądjirōrā'djoŋgi wōtā'ra. Je jësge niŋgitā'winᴀ."

Offering to the Morning Star.—"E'gi jige ᵋŭaŋgere'gi Wīragō'cge Xeṭera' tcōk'agā' Djōbenągiwiŋxga nądjorā'djoŋgi djagū' nądjirọrā'djoŋgi wōtā'ra jësgë'ją niŋgitā'winᴀ hā'nᴀga. E'gi tanī'ṇa wōho'ṇa nąbirụxā'djᴇra waniŋgitū'cdją rehā'winᴀ ā'nᴀga."

Offering to Earth.—"E'gi tcōk'agā' waxōp'i'ni Djōbenągiwi'ŋxga wāna'i' rūsgitcgī' nīcge' wāna'i'djọrak'ā`rak'ere gīji mā'ṇa hīk,âro'- k'enina. Mą'ᵋuṇa ẹ niᵋū'nᴀ djagū' ruk'o'nᴀ niŋgigī'gi ˋtcōk'āga' nądjīrōrā'djọŋgi Djōbenągiwi'ŋxga je'e' niŋgitā'winᴀ. Tanī'ṇa nitakadjᴇra' nąbirụxā'djᴇra waniŋgitū'cdją rehā'winᴀ wōna'ɣirẹra ŭaŋkcigọᵋi'ṇa wōtā' me'jësge niŋgitā'winᴀ tcōk'ā'."

Offering to the Water-spirit.—"E'gi jige tcōk'ā' huŋge' rōni-anī'ṇẹra tanī'ṇa wọho'ṇa nąbirụxā'djera wagụdjẹ'ra sī'ją niŋgitā'winᴀ rehā'winᴀ. Wajō'kinᴀ wōna'ɣirẹra hatụtcaip'djā'winᴀ ŭaŋkcigọᵋi'ṇa niŋgitā'winᴀ."

General prayer to the spirits.—"Tcōk'ā'wira hīrụdjī'djis zīk'djë'nᴀ nūnige' hąŋk'e' wā'jiŋgirā`wini-ą`ndje tcōk'ā'wira. Sā'k'ereni'- ŋk'djoŋgera, niŋk'ūruhi'ndj rehā'winᴀ. Ŭaŋkcik tcōwā'rēdjâ`nᴀ honihā'ra djagū' adjī'regi hąŋk'e' jësgë'ją e tụxū'ruk niŋk'- djonā'wi, nūnige hīgụ' djāsge hawī'gi here'k'djonegā`djā. Hītcō'- k'ewahī'wira hąŋk'e' waji'ṇẹp'ī'hīnanī`je aīrë'jare. Hīgụ' djasge'niŋk hagī' here'k'djonegā`dją. Niŋk'uruhi'ndjwidjīgō'." (Song.)

FILLING OF THE CEREMONIAL PIPE AND SMOKING RITUAL

First filling of the pipe.—E'gi jige' tcëk warụɣa'p nāwą hī'regi nawọ'ṇa ē kârọhoī'regi tanihū'iją hōjū-irā'nᴀga warụɣa'p ëdja, "Ŭaŋgere'gi hī-ā'ndjehihī'wira tanī'hụra hoik'e'rẹra ëdja hap'ā'hi k'ere'rënᴀ ŭaŋkdji'ṇegi hū'nąbra hāp'ā'hi k'ere'rẹnᴀ. Mā'ᵋū'ṇa ŭaŋkdji'ṇegi nᴀ ŋkce ā'nᴀ ŋkce. E'sge tanihū'ra hoik'e'rẹra ë'dja hap'ā'hi k'ere'rënᴀ. Ną'wą haisu'ntc hīrẹra tanihū-ā'k'a warūtco'- na hī'ją wa'ᵋū'nᴀ rūzā'nᴀga tae' hi-ā'nᴀga hoirā'tcge hūwā'rënᴀ haną'tcix dji k'igō'nᴀ ŋk'a hī wagigirë'nᴀ. Ŭaŋgerā'cᴀnᴀ hąŋk'e' hīnụŋgera' hīwagigī'ninᴀ. Họgīgi'ŋx tanihū'ra hi'ṇẹra rasge'p' hīrẹra' jige' hōjū'.

Second filling of the pipe.—Hīnụbo'họna wọhọ'ṇa hīdjā' wak'ere'- rẹga ë'gi k'eni nawai'ṇani warụɣa'p nawai'ṇẹk'djonë`gi tanihū-iją

things with which you blessed grandfather Djōbenągiwi'ŋxga. That
we ask of you."

Offering to the Morning Star.—"You who are above, Morning Star,
our request is that you bless us with that with which you blessed
grandfather Djōbenągiwi'ŋxga. Tobacco and food and a buckskin
offering we are about to send you." [59]

Offering to Earth.—"Grandmother Earth, you also added your
power to the spirit bundle that grandfather Djōbenągiwi'ŋxga made.
The powers Earthmaker put you in control of, and with which you
blessed grandfather Djōbenągiwi'ŋxga, those we ask of you.
Tobacco, soup, and a buckskin offering we are about to send to you
and the request that we make of you, is war power and life."

Offering to the Water-spirit.—"Water-spirit, grandfather whose
body is of water,[60] tobacco, food, and a buckskin offering for moccasins, we are about to offer you. I and my relatives desire to lay
our hands on war and life."

General prayer to the spirits.—"Grandfathers, we have probably
been very remiss in what we have done, but do not hold it against
us, grandfathers. We greet you, war-bundle owners. The life
(blessings) that those who have gone before us had, the songs that
they handed down to us, not in their manner will we be able to sing,
but still, however it be, it will be (our best). It has been said that
nothing will provoke you,[61] grandfathers. Well, however, that is the
way we will do it. I greet you." (Song.)

FILLING OF THE CEREMONIAL PIPE AND SMOKING RITUAL

First filling of the pipe.—After they have sung the first war-bundle
song, then they get a pipeful of tobacco ready and place it near the
war bundle, speaking as follows: "Our father who art above, for you
the pipe is extended; up straight above it is placed." Up straight
above it is extended to Earthmaker, they say. For that reason do
they arrange the pipe in that way. Then when the songs are finished
the attendant takes the pipe, lights it, and takes it with him to the
left side, giving all the men in the lodge an opportunity to smoke.
Women are not allowed to smoke. The tobacco in the pipe is
entirely consumed as the pipe makes the circuit of the lodge and it
is then filled again.

Second filling of the pipe.—Then there at the feast for the second
time do they place (the pipe). When they are about to sing the

---

[59] That this spirit was not mentioned before is an oversight on the part of the informant.

[60] Deferential and ritualistic name for the Water-Spirit. It may mean chief. The general name which
we loosely translate "Water-spirit" is "Wak'djexī."

[61] I. e., that no inaccuracy nor ignorance on their part will anger the spirits and cause them to refrain
from bestowing their blessings. This is, of course, an expression of ritualistic modesty, but I suspect
that there is also a reference intended here to the fact that in these degenerate days not only are
individuals no longer blessed as of yore, but certain details of the ceremony have been forgotten. I see no
reason for giving too much weight to this last fact, but it may be best to have it in mind.

hōjū'-irān₄ga waruɣa'p tcōwë'dja wak'ₐdjowak'iri'rëdjₐ tanihū'd-
jęga hoik'e'rerera hap'āhī' k'ere'ran₄ga. Ė'gi nₐwₐ̄ hīranā'n₄ nₐw₄'na haisu'ndjiregī'ji tānihū'djęga wak'āndjai̯'dja wap'ā'hi k'ere'-
n₄ŋk'a wak'andjā'n₄ŋk'a wagigō'n₄ᴄŋk'a ë'dja hadjī'regi hi̯'ŋek'-
dje'gi. Ė'sge je̯ᵉe' hīdjā' k'ere'n₄ŋk'cAn₄. Wak'andjā'n₄ŋk'a
tanī'na wōho'na nₐbiruxā'djera, wak'aragī'ᵉų wagigō'n₄ŋk'a ë'dja
wak'ā'ragų hadjī'regi. Ė'sge tanihū'djęga hijai̯djā'djęgi hi̯ŋk'dję'ge
ë'sge wa'ᵉū'n₄ŋkcAn₄ tanihū'djęga.

Third filling of the pipe.—Ė'gi wagigō'n₄ŋk'a wawigi̯wā'ŋxcAn₄
wë'n₄, "Hatci'ndja hop'ā'hi-ak'erë'k'djonë'je," ë'ra wagigō'n₄ŋk'a
hī'jₐ wë'n₄, "Sā'ni̯ŋk herotcǫ'djeregi̯ hōp'ā'hi̯ k'ere'rën₄." Ė'gi
nₐwai̯'ŋën₄ Hōcere'ᵉu'wahi̯ nₐ̄'wₐ wā'ni̯ŋgi wawi'ᵉu-i̯ṇë'n₄. Ė'gi̯
haisu'ndjirera ji̯ge' tanihū'ra hōgigi'ŋx wagigī'reṇ₄.

Fourth filling of the pipe.—Ė'gi̯ ji̯ge' tani'hura p'i̯hi̯-ōju-ā'n₄ga
ëgi ji̯ge' wawigī'waŋxcAn₄.

"Hatci'ndja hōp'ā'hī-a?" "K'erë'k'djë'je mai̯'ndja t'ₐ̄bere."
Ė'sge mai̯'ndja t'ₐ̄pce. Mₐk'ū'haṇegi huŋge ë'dja tanī'huk'a
hōp'āhi̯ t'ᵉₐp ʍₐ'ᵉu'-i̯ṇen₄, mai̯'ndja t'ᵉₐ̣ibrëga. Ė'gi wase'
nₐw₄'ṇA ṇacdjai̯'ṇegi tanī'hura hōgigi'ŋx hīwagigī'je. Ė'gi̯ k'irigī'
hₐŋk'e ōjuṇī'je jë'gų mai̯ndjat'ₐ̄'pce."

BASIC RITUAL

Host's first speech.—Sā'k'ereni̯ŋk'djǫ'gᴇra mīn₄ŋk'cā'waŋgre
hītcō'k'ewahī'wira. Ėp'ī'n₄ hīṇagī'dji̯wira. Ci̯dj wat'ᵉe'eni̯ŋk'ā'-
ragik'djonā'wi̯ nūnige hₐ̄ŋk'e' wajigī'rawīni̯-ₐ̄'dje. Tǫk'e'wehi̯
t'ᵉeni̯ŋk'ā'ragik'djonā'wi̯ nūnige waxǫp'i̯'ni̯ warā'diire cewewī'wiŋge
hi̯ŋgī'dji̯wī'ra. Ėp'ī'n₄. Haŋk'e' wajₐ̄'ni̯-ijₐ p'i̯hanī'k'djonā'wi̯
nūnige hītcō'k'ewahī'wira yoire'regi̯ herera'tcōk'agā' Djōbenₐgi-
wi'ŋxga hōnihā' gīk'ere'regi wōrā'tcgₐ na'ī'n₄. Jë'sgek'djonihā'-
wiṇ₄ tcęge'dja hōnihā'ra djasge' tcōk'agā' wagīt'ᵉų'biregi yǫwehā'-
k'djawī'je nūnige' hōnihā'ra. Hīgų' hī'jₐŋk'īra hīrap'e'rez ā'n₄ga
ë'cAn₄ hawëraī'cge p'i̯k'djonë'je; tcōk'agā' ë'je aī'reṇ₄. Hīgų'
djāsge ā'n₄ga hōnihā' higų' djāsge nanā'n₄ŋk'ī ɣāk hibrā'gi hītcō'k'ewahī'wira hīniŋgī'p'erez hī'rëk'djonëna, aī'rëra. Jë'sge
p'ewī'wiŋge hōk'ā'raga na'ī'nisge. Hōnihā' tcₐ̄te' wahā'i̯-
k'djonihā'wiṇ₄; djǫbo'h₄ hak'araī'sundjwigi ë'gi hōxgų' sak'i̯'na
herëk'djonë'nA.

war-bundle songs then they fill the pipe and place it in front of the war bundle, in the path of the Thunderbirds, extending the mouth-piece in that direction (i. e., the west). Then they would sing some songs and when these were finished, the Thunderbirds would come as feasters to where the pipe lay extended and smoke. That is why they place the pipes there. The Thunderbirds do this (i. e., smoke) as a sign of acceptance of the tobacco, food, and buckskins. So that a Thunderbird might smoke, do the feasters place the pipe there.

Third filling of the pipe.—Then the host asked the others, "In what direction shall I place this pipe?" and one of the feasters said, "Toward the south, place it." Then they sang the songs of the Disease-giver. Then when they were finished they carried around the pipe.

Fourth filling of the pipe.—Then the host fills the pipe again and again asks, "In what direction shall I place the pipe?" (and some one answers), "Place it toward the earth." So he placed it toward the ground. For those under the ground, the Water-spirits, they also place the pipe by standing it on the ground. Then they sing paint songs and when they are finished they pass the pipe around so that all may smoke. When it returns (to the host) it is not filled again but placed empty on the ground.

Basic Ritual [62]

Host's first speech.—"War-bundle owners, who are sitting here, I send forth my greeting to you. It is good that you have come (in response to my invitation). It is my purpose to make you tired from sitting, but do not for that reason think any the worse of us. We will make you hungry, hungry to the point of starvation,[63] but (we know) you came for the sake of the spirits (not for our sake). It is good. We are not going to do anything in the correct manner, but our grandfathers who live in the west taught our grandfather Djōbenagiwi'ηxga some songs and these we are going to try and repeat. We will now sing the songs just as they taught it to grand-father. We may perhaps sing only one song. However, if you know only one song and take pains about it, it will suffice (to pro-pitiate the spirits); so grandfather said, it is said. Anyhow, if we try to cry, in our efforts of singing,[64] our grandfathers will take cognizance of it, it is said. That is what we are thinking of when we try to get the spirits' attention by singing.[65] We will do our best to sing the songs,[66] and we will sing four of them; and when we

[62] For explanation see Introduction.
[63] Ritualistic depreciation.
[64] I. e., if you put yourself into a state of religious fervor, a state that I have generally rendered by the word "pitiable."
[65] The word "hōk'ă'raga" means, literally, "by voice to attract attention." "Hō" is not an instru-mental particle but the word for voice, speech.
[66] Literally, "to make one's breath visible in the form of song or speech," a ritualistic circumlocution for song.

"Sā'k'erẹra tcī-ō'jụ mīnaŋkcā'waŋgre ni'ŋk'ūrụhi'ndj rehā'wị-djịgō'." (Warụγa'p Nǎwǎ.)

Ŭaŋgī'jǎ wōgigō'mịnᴀŋk' agā'k'īnọŋk t⁵ǎp djịrā'nᴀga wë'je.

First guest's address to the young people.—"Sā'k'ereniŋk'djo'ŋgera mīnaŋkcā'waŋgre nịk'ūrụhi'ndj rehā'wịnᴀ, Hōtcintci'n watcëgera' waxōp'i'nị hīk'īsgë'jǎ hōnịhā'ra nịŋgiwawī'⁵ụ-ịnẹk'djanā're hīwacī'ra djīrehīregī'jị wanᴀŋgījịiwī'nẹ wōnᴀ'γịrẹra nǎk'īxū'ruk nǎ⁵ī'wịnẹ. Ė'gị hī'nụgEra waŋgwatcā'bwịra wōnᴀ'γịre wanᴀgīxū'ruk nǎ⁵ī'-wịnẹ. Hǎŋk'e' gā'djuŋga jë'sge hīnuxū'rugenịhahǎ'kcᴀnᴀ tcëge'-dja ŭaŋkcik tcọwā'rëdjanẹ hī'jǎ warọγī' te jësge hīga djā'nᴀga ŭaŋgị-ë'rịga jë'nuŋga hịwacī' djịrehī'rẹga. Hanǎ'tcịŋxdjị hǎŋk'ī'jǎ mīnᴀ'geninaŋks⁵ā'je. Ė'gị jịge hīnụgera' hīcge ŭaŋkci'go⁵ị wagī'⁵ụ wā⁵ụ'-ịnëje. Haịseretcị'cge wacīra' hǎŋk'agā' hōrục⁵ā'gịranịs⁵ā'je aī'rẹra. Jë'sge hanịk'ā'rajīwịge wahā'djenᴀ. Wōnᴀ'γịre ŭaŋkci-gọ⁵ị'na ë'gị wōwat⁵ẹ'gịregị hōrūxū'rugEra je aī'rẹra jë'sge p'ëwī'ŋge wahë'nᴀ. Sā'k'erẹra mīnᴀŋkcā'waŋgre niŋk'ūrụhi'ndj rẹhawịdjigō'.

Host's second speech.—Sā'k'ereniŋk'djọ'gera mīnaŋkcā'waŋgere nịk'ūrụhindj rehā'wịnᴀ.

"Hītcō'k'ewahī'wịra tcīnᴀgịdjaị'jǎ wajadjǎ'gịjị wīrọk'ū'na wawịrō'k'ụŋgi. P'ī'nᴀ hīp'erezīrë'je. Hīp'e'rez na⁵ị'nẹgi nǎdjōk'ī'djǎ cī'regị. Hī'nụk warō'nị mǎk'ǎ' aī'rëje. Hit⁵ẹ'-nuŋk'ë'jǎ nǎ'tcgera tëk' hī'regị. Hīnụgī'jǎ īwust⁵ẹ'k'iŋgījị huŋge' maŋgịtcā'wǎ wāt⁵ụ'pce huŋge' xgīcgū'nị wajagụ'zEra wajịnūk'o'no gīgīgī. Hīnuŋk'djẹga nǎdjodjaị'je. Huŋge' t⁵ẹwagik'ī'k⁵ū́-ā'nᴀga hīnụ'k'djẹga ë'dja wīrōk'u' rūsgī. P'ī'nᴀ hīp'ere'zịregị. Mǎk'aị'-k'araī'tcgagi. Tcëk'djī'nᴀ wa⁵ụ'je. Mǎxī' ŭaŋgeregī' hīwīzī'gịjǎ mǎxī'k'orascọp gīwị'x nǎjị'je. HīnụgEra wā⁵ụje' mak'aị'jǎ are finished then it will be time for us to eat.[67] Warriors who are sitting within the lodge, we send forth our greetings to you." (War-bundle song.)

Then a man sitting opposite the seat of the host gets up and speaks.

First guest's address to the young people.—"War-bundle owners, young men, those who are the proxies of spirits, are about to use a song for you and start a dance in your behalf; and when they do it, get up and try to obtain war powers by dancing. Women, you should also try to obtain war powers for your brothers by dancing. Now we are not able to obtain (the number of men) that our ancestors used to obtain in the beginning. Then, if in a speech they asked for them, as many men as there were around would immediately begin to dance. Not one of them would remain in his seat. Young women, they used to act in that way in order to obtain life also. All night they would dance and not a single one would tire of it. We encourage you to do thus; that is why I am saying this. That the obtaining of life may be easy, is the reason they told us this. Because I believe it (likewise) is the reason I am telling it to you. War-bundle owners who are seated here, I greet you all."

Host's second speech.—"War-bundle owners who are sitting here, I greet you all.

"Our grandfathers knew that one of a different tribe [68] had had a vision and obtained material for use (in life). They tried to obtain it and (finally) asked him to pity them. The medicine was called hinuŋgwā'roni.[69] They made the heart of the man of this other tribe (Hit‘e'nuŋk‘e) sad.[70] (He had obtained it in the following manner): A woman fasted [71] and one of the Water-spirits whom the Creator had placed there for all eternity, a Water-spirit for keeping (the earth) quiet,[72] blessed her with the power he had been placed in charge of. The Water-spirit had himself die and the woman there

---

[67] Literally, "fast movements" in reference to the fast-eating contest that takes place during the feast.

[68] This is not a Winnebago tale.

[69] My interpreter could not translate the name of this medicine into English. He thought that it might mean "wicked woman medicine," but this is extremely doubtful.

[70] I. e., at the idea of parting with it. What tribe is meant by "Hit‘e'nuŋk‘e," it has been impossible to find out. The word, I believe, means "those whom we can speak with" in reference to the fact that their language was intelligible to the Winnebago. I was definitely assured that neither the Oto, Iowa, or Missouri were meant. I have sometimes surmised that the Winnebago may be referring to the Mandan, whose language, from the little I have seen of it, is surprisingly close to that of the former. All that the older Winnebago could tell me about the Hit‘e'nuŋk‘e was the fact that many years ago they had been in contact with a tribe speaking a language similar to their own.

[71] Literally, "to thirst oneself to death," the ritualistic expression for fasting.

[72] He is referring to one of the four beings whom Earthmaker had placed at the four ends of the world to prevent it from moving continually, as related in the origin myth of the Medicine Dance and of the Thunderbird clan.

nᾳpwirō'ra hĭk'ī'-ǫ hī-ā'nᾳga hīwīzī'k'djᵉga hīmanᾳ'k'ī t'ᵉ'xdjᵢ cī'beregᵢ; tcīrahë'rᶸ hōwä'djᵢhūhī'je hīnᶷgenᾳ'k'a tcōwehᵢ-ë'dja k'īrᵢnᾳ'kce. Mᾳk'ō'k'onᾳηk jeᵉe' ᵉᶷk'djë'gᵢ herᵉje. Ēgᵢ ŭaηk nace'rᵉge īhᾳ'pcᴀnᾳ nīhë'ra hatë'gᵢ. Ŭaηk'djᵉga wageje', "Hak'- ĭk'ū'rᶸk'ozā'dje hᾳηk'e' ë'gᵢ ōwahū' na'iyᾳ'dje." Wajᾳ' wahī'- racge wawōgī'rakce hīrak'ā'rak'arawi-ᾳ'dje. "Hᾳhᵉ' te'e wase' nᾳwᾳηk'djonë'nᾳ ŭaηk'djᵉga djᵢgī' t'ᵉek'djonë'nᾳ. Hᾳηk'e' djīniηk'djë'nᾳ hīrak'ā'rak'arawi-ā'dje." Ē'gᵢ hᾳhᵉ'regᵢ wase' nᾳwᾳ'gᵢ ŭa'ηk'djᵉga nᴀηgadjī'je. Rōgᵢγī'ra nūnige hōk'awā'nᾳga wacᵢdjā'ᵉᶷ t'ᵉeje. Ē'gᵢ wase'nǫηk'a hit'ᵉ'nuηk'e wase' hīgaī'rᵉje tcīηa gīdjᴀī'jᾳ mejë'nᶷga."

"Wase'nᾳk'a p'īηa hīp'e'rezᵢrë'gᵉ hīgᵢk'ī'cerëje nᾳdjōk'ī'djᾳ cī'regᵢ wagᵢrū'cdjᾳ hūhī'je. Ēge wase'nᴀηk'a harūtcᾳ'bᵢregᵢ haηk'e' tcī-ǫro'gᴇregᵢ wajᵢnok'u'-ᵢnanᵢ'je. Warᶷγa'p k'ū'-ᵢnᵉje. Wase'nᴀηk'a wōna'γirēdja hī'ᵉᶷ'-ᵢnᵉgᵢ p'iηgᵢ hīp'e'reztᵢnëge. Hī'- k'aracī'cik hīrëge' warᶷγā'pregᵢ hōk'ā'rak'ā'nᴀηk hīrë'nᾳ. Hōnᵢ- hā'ra tcᾳt'ᵢ' wahā'k'djonᵢhā'wᵢnᾳ wasi-ā'nᵢ hanᵢwᵢ-ā'nᴀga wahë'k'djonᵢhā'wije warᶷγā'p nāwᾳ wahë'k'djonᵢhā'wᵢnᾳ. Wasᵢā'nᵢ hanᵢwī'gᵢ hāga wajā'nᵢjᾳ ᵉū'-ᵢnᵉwīcgū'nᵢnᾳ. Haηk'e' wasᵢā'nᵢ hīranᾳ'k'īk'ᵢwᵢ ā'nᾳga wahā'niηk'djonā'wᵢnᾳ hōnᵢhā'ra haηk'e' wawatᾳ' p'īnᵢk'djonā'wᵢ nūnige hījaηk'ī'ra hīrap'e'- rezgī'cge γak' hᵢbᵢ-ᾳ'dje aī'rᵉra. Jë'sge wahëk'djonā'wᵢnᾳ. Sā'k'ereniηk'djǫ'gᴇra mīnᾳηkcā'waηgre nᵢk'ūrᶷhi'ndj rehā'- wᵢdjᵢgō." (Wase' Nᾳwᾳ.)

Host's third speech.—" Sā'k'ereniηk'djǫ'gᴇra mīnᴀηkcā'waηgre nᵢ'ηk'ūrᶷhindj rehā'wᵢnᾳ. Tǫk'e'wehᵢ t'ᵉeniηk'ā'ragᵢ-ānᾳηgwī nūnige' hōk'ā'raga nᾳ'ī'nᵢsge wāhanᾳ'gwᵢre.

Tcōk'agā' Djōbenᾳgiwi'ηxga ŭaηgī'jᾳ hot'ᵉ'rᶸk'onā'ᵢjᾳ sā'niηk' yorǫtcǫ'djeregᵢ naηk'ī'jᵢ waxōp'ᵢ'nᵢ warā'djᵢrᵉra djānᶷηgā'k'ᵢ hī'cᴀnᾳ hīraitce'raje wōna'γire rūk'o'nᴀnᾳ xetë'jᾳ herëje. Ē'gᵢ hᾳbᵢrᶸk'onaī'jᾳ hereje ë'gᵢ hōt'ᵉ' rūk'o'naᵢjᾳ herëje. Tcōk'agā' wīrarǫtcᶸ'djᵉgādjᾳ hak'idjā'je wāgeje' wōna'γire ŭaηkci'go'ᵢ nᾳdjᵢ- rǫrā'djǫgᵢ. Ē'gᵢ wageje, "Hagᾲrë'jᾳ hak'ārak'ᶸ'ᵢcge rᵉdjū'na djadjaᵢ'xdjᵢ hĭp'ā' ninë'gᵢ jedjaᵢ'xdjᵢ p'ā hatci'ndja naηk'ī'jᵢ hᾳηk'e' wamā'ninᵢηk'djonë'nᾳ hōwajairë'cge, hōni'ηk wacī'nᵢna took the material (the remains of the Water-spirit).[73] That it is good, they knew. Then she tried her medicine. The first time she did the following: Up above, almost near the sky, a hawk stood whirling around. The woman dipped her forefinger into the medicine and then she pointed it at the hawk and it fell dead; she made it fall through the top of a house; right in front of the woman it landed. She wanted to use it as a medicine bag. Then she dreamed that they had taken a man from his home that he might fast. She said to the man, "Put forth all your strength and don't try to come here." She also told his relatives to watch him. "To-night I am going to sing a paint song and if he comes he will die. Take care of him that he doesn't come." That night she sang a paint song and the man came running to her. She forbade him but he came anyhow and he died dancing. This medicine is called hit⁸e'nuŋk⁸e medicine, referring to the name of another tribe, and that is how it acted.

"They (our ancestors) knew that it was good paint and he (one of them) tried to get him (the Hit⁸e'nuŋk⁸e) to bless him with the paint (the latter had obtained from the woman). When they obtained it, they never used it in their own midst (i. e., among themselves). They made a medicine-bundle of it. The paint-medicine, it is good to use in war. That they knew very well. They were very sparing in their use of it (because it was so valuable). They placed it in their war-bundle. Paint-songs we are about to use, yet we are singing for the war-bundle. If, indeed, we had paint medicine we would amount to something. We are not going to sing as if we thought ourselves in possession of paint-medicines nor will we sing them correctly. Yet if we knew only one, if we could (in singing this one) bring ourselves to the state of crying (it would be all right), it is said. That is why we say it." [74] (Paint song.)

Host's third speech.—"War-bundle owners who are seated here, I greet you. I know that I am causing you to famish with hunger, but we are doing this in an attempt to get the attention (of the spirits). One in control of death who dwells in the south [75] and who of himself possesses greater war power than all the other spirits that exist, blessed grandfather Djōbenagiwi'ŋxga. He is in control of life and in control of death. He met grandfather in the middle of the day and blessed him with war powers and life. He said (to our grandfather when he blessed him), "If I should ever go on the warpath, your descendants, as many as they are and wherever they live, I will not tread upon, should they get sick.[76] However, your posterity never will get sick. Should they ever have a bad illness,

---

[73] The Winnebago believe that the "bones" of the mythical "Water-spirits" possess the most magical qualities when powdered and mixed up into medicines. All "paint medicines" are made of "Water-spirit bones."

[74] All these sentences are, of course, expressions of ritualistic modesty.

[75] I. e., Disease-giver.

[76] Cf. note 36, p.409, for explanation of these words.

haŋk'e' hōwajai'raniŋk'djonë'nạ. Ė'gi 'ụ'iṇẹgi ŭaŋkci'gọ'į'ṇa hīranī'nA ī'rawi̞-ā'nạga tanīō'niŋgi̞jū'i̞rawigi̞ hījū'jụgī'jạ."

"Hōcere'ụ'wahi̞ra ë'xdji̞ wā'ụje' wak'ạ'tcAŋk wagigī'je ëje. Ŭaŋkci'go'į'ṇa hōwajā' cici'k' ɛ̞ụ-i̞nā'nạga tani̞-ōniŋgī'jụ-i̞rā'wigi̞ hījū'jugEra wōho'na tanī'ṇa mặcū'ṇa cuŋksgā'ri̞jặ tejë'nụga nặbinạ'gi̞cụrụxadji̞-ā'nạga. "E'gi̞ hījū'jụk wak'ạtcạ'k niŋgī'-gi̞wi̞ra hōwe'ū'ṇa rū-ā'γi̞ra c'ụwi̞'nạ. Nābi̞rụxā'djera hīnạ hīṇagī'-gīwigi̞ hījū'jụgEra hōcewe'u'wigi̞. Ŭaŋkci'gọ'į hōwatcehī'ra hījặ tcōrā'jụ wac'ụ'gi̞. Howajā' cici'k 'ū'nạ jedjai̞'ŋxdi̞ p'ā hanạnt-cgaī'sdjonë'nạ. Hạŋk'e' hawīdje'djạ hījặ hōwajā' cici'k 'ū'.nĭk'-djonë'nạ."

Hōcere'u'wahi̞ra ewë'nạ. E howajā' cicī'k 'u'wahīra wëge jësgëk'djonë'nạ. Te'jësge tcōk'agā' DjōbenAŋgi̞wi'ŋxga nặdji̞rọd-jaī'ṇeje. Hōni̞hā'ra tcặt'i̞ djīrehā'k'djonẹhā'winạ. Sā'k'ereniŋk'-djọ'gEra mīnaŋkcā'waŋgre niŋk'ūrụhi'ndj rehā'wi̞dji̞go. (Hōcere'u'-wahi̞ Nặwạ.)

Host's fourth speech.—"Sā'k'ereniŋkdjọ'gera mi̞naŋkcā'waŋgre niŋk'ūrụhindj rehā'wi̞nạ. Hīrọ-ā'gEregi hak'araī'suntc djik'djonā'-wi̞nạ. Tcōk'agā' Djōbenạgi̞wi'ŋxga hặbọgū'regi̞ hōk'ā'was manī'-ṇa waxōp'i̞'ni̞ wāna'i̞ djok'arak'e'rëje. Tcōk'agā' Djōbenạgi̞wi'-ŋxga p'e'rez na'i̞ŋgī'ji̞ tọk'e'wehi̞ īwu's t'ẹ'k'i̞je ŭānạdjōdjai̞'sge wa'ụje. Tcëk'djī'ṇA hatī-ā'gi̞nặ'tcgi̞ djōbạ'họna gā'dja hōk'ā'was manī'ṇa hagū'i̞regi̞. Rok'o'no gū'i̞reje nīhā' gū-i̞reje hi̞gī' kīridje'-reje. 'Uaŋkcige' īwust'ẹ' rak'i̞'ge nặdjōni̞djā'wi̞nạ. Hặhẹ' wīgaī'-rẹra jë'sge wahadjā'wi̞nạ. WōnA'γi̞rẹra ŭaŋkcigọ'į'ṇa nặdji̞rọrā'-djAnạ hīgaī'reje'. Woruxū'djgadjạ djagŭânā'cge, 'Te'e hặhẹ' wāna'genạ hī'regi̞?' Wọrụxū'tcgadjạ te wā'ni̞ŋk xonū'ni̞ŋk hecë'-pge wā'nAŋkce. Gīcdjahë'regi̞. Jige hīraī'tcera nặntcgẹ'ra të'kce.' 'Tcak'o'! Jëgu tcë'k dje!' hīreje. Jë'gu hati̞ā'gi̞nặdjera ji̞ge' p'i̞hī' hīwajā'je jë'gu hạŋk'e' wā'rụdjenī'je. Hak'e'wëhạ nAŋgā'dja. Ė'gi̞ hặbọgū'regi̞ hặhẹ'ra hagū'-i̞regi̞. Rọk'o'no hagū'-i̞reje nīhā' gū-i̞reje, ë'gi̞ hīdjā' k'ĭridje'reje, 'Uaŋkcige' nặdjọni̞djā'wi̞nạ.

they have the means of obtaining life by praying for it,[77] by offering tobacco and a flute.[78]

"Disease-giver himself made these things holy. Thus they would obtain life, if they had any illness, by offering you reed flutes, food, tobacco, feathers, a white dog, and by making you at the same time an offering of buckskin hides. (Thus Disease-giver spoke to our grandfather when he blessed him:) 'A holy flute I made for you, and I forbade you to blow upon it, yet you did it. Now, hereafter, if you offer me a sufficient number of buckskins, you may blow upon it. A different life from that of others will you lead, if you do that. You will be able to cut off (stop) a bad disease caused by someone else. Nor will this one (who was ill) ever have another disease.' [79]

"Thus Disease-giver spoke. This is what the one who causes disease said. That is how they blessed our grandfather Djōbenạgiwi'ŋxga. A song I am now about to start. War-bundle owners who are seated here, I greet you." (Disease-giver song.)

Host's fourth speech.—"War-bundle owners who are seated here, I greet you. The last (song) we will now finish. You who are in the east, Night Spirits, you also added your blessing to the spirit bundle of grandfather Djōbenạgiwi'ŋxga. So that he might know (be blessed by) the spirits, grandfather Djōbenạgiwi'ŋxga starved and thirsted himself to death [80] and made himself pitiable. At first he fasted four nights and the Night Spirits came to him; with mighty sounds they came.[81] There they stood (and said), 'Human, you have thirsted yourself to death and we bless you (for that reason). We who speak are the spirits who are called Night Spirits.' They blessed him with war power and life, they said. Then he looked and (said to himself), 'I wonder whether these really are the Night Spirits that speak.' So he looked at them and they were small birds called *hecë'pge*.[82] They had fooled him. Then once again was his heart sore. 'Well! I will die,' he thought (fasting). So he fasted again and once again he rubbed on (the charcoal). For six nights he continued to fast. And again from the east the Night Spirits came. They came making a great noise and they stood near him (and said), 'Human, we bless you. You have thirsted yourself to death and you have made your heart sore. We felt sad on your account. With

---

[77] A rather curious expression used only in elevated language and meaning, literally, "to obtain with the mouth"—i. e., either by speeches, prayers, or singing. The expression would hardly be permitted in ordinary Winnebago.

[78] He does not mean by offering flutes, but by playing on them. Reed flutes are generally contained in the blessings of most spirits, but they seem to be more closely connected with the Disease-giver and the Buffalo.

[79] This, I believe, is the meaning of the last three sentences. They are somewhat obscure, and I do not guarantee the correctness of the rendering.

[80] Ritualistic expression for fasting.

[81] All powerful spirits are supposed to approach with loud noises. This is also characteristic of the Ojibway spirits.

[82] English equivalent unknown.

I'wus tᵉe'rak'i̯ŋge nᾳtcge̜'ra nīte̜'gEra. Nᾳtcge̜'ra niŋgite̜gwī'nᴀ.
Wōna'ɣi̯re̜ra ŭaŋkcigoᶜꞮ'ṇa nᾳdji̯rọrā'djᴀgi,' hiŋaī're̜nᴀ gījī'.
Wōrūxū'tcce, 'Djagŭā'hᾳhe̜' wanᴀ'ŋgenᴀ hi̯re̜gā'dja?' hīreje. Te
hᾳŋk'e' hᾳhe̜' wanī'nᴀŋkce. K'awī'cge, tcōxdjī, ci̯'k'ok'ok' jejë'-
sge wā'naŋkce gīcdjā'k'e wā'naŋkce kī'ji. Ė'tcᾳ nᾳtcgë'ra tëk'djī'-
je, 'Tcak'o! gīji̯ tcëk'dje,' hīreje' gīji̯. Hatā'ginᾳdjЕra. Jige'
p'īhꞮ' hīwā jā'je. Hatagi̯nᾳ'djenaŋk'ā haru̯wo'gahᾳ naŋgā'dja.
Ė'gi̯ jige hᾳbọgū'regi̯ hᾳhe̜'ra nᾳwᾳgū'-i̯reje. Nīhā'gū'-i̯reje
higī' k'īri̯dje' regi̯ wagaī'reje,' Hītcu̯cge', nᾳdjọni̯djᴀ'wi̯nᴀ. Hīgu̯
k'ī'ni sᵉī hīrā'ɣagwī'nᴀ. Ŭaŋkcige' hiŋk'agā' hījᴀ' nᾳdjwadjā'-
wi̯ni̯nᴀ. Wōna'ɣi̯re̜ra ŭaŋkcigoᶜꞮ'ṇa djagū' gīp'Ꞇ' cᵉu̯ŋk'djë'nᴀ,'
hīgaī'reje gīji. Wōru̯ɣī'tcce te, 'Djagŭā'nacge hᾳhe̜' wanᴀ'gЕnᴀ?'
hīregī gadjᾳ. Te hᾳŋk'e' hᾳhe̜' wani̯nᴀ'kce. P'atcō gīsge wi̯'ɣЕra
djānaga tcap'ōxgë'ra cë'pgi. Jësge wā'nᴀŋkce djā'nᴀga wāniŋk
cīci'geni̯ŋerā k'īji̯. Hī'kcakcā'-i̯re hīreje' Djōbenᾳgiwi'ŋxga.
Tcak'o! Hatagi̯nᾳ'djeregi jë'gu̯ tcë'k'dje' he̜re̜je. Hatāgi̯nᾳ'-
djera jige' p'īhꞮ' wajaje jë'djuŋga mᾳcdjᾳ' ākce.

Tanī'ṇa nᾳbā'k'ī hōjū' hᾳhꞮô'wak'īri̯rë'djᴀ hōp'ā'hi nᾳji̯-ā'nᴀga
tanī'na nᾳbō'ju̯ ëdjōp'ā'hi tanī'ṇa wagīwā'hᾳ nᾳbā'k'ī nᾳji̯-ā'nᴀga
nᾳdjọk'īdjā'xdji̯ ākce. Je'djuŋga mᾳcdjᴀ' nᾳtcge̜'ra tëkce gīji̯.
K'e'repọnᾳ'ijᴀ nᾳgā'dja. Ė'gi̯ hagŭadjī'reje. Ŭaŋkcige',
haniŋk'oā'dji̯nᴀ. Hīrọnᴀ'gi̯re̜je hᾳbōgū'regi̯ hap'ā'hi̯ hōwā'ni̯-
ak'araī'reje; hᾳhe̜' tci̯nọ'gЕra hatci'ndjanᴀŋk'ī ë'dja hanī-a̯'gi̯rë'je.
Hᾳhe̜' hu̯ŋera e hagū'hi̯ wagigī'je. Tcīnoŋk'īsā'gedja tcīseredjī'jᴀ
hᾳbōgū'ra hap'ā'hi-ā'kce. Ė'dja hani-o'-i̯k'awraī'reje. Hᾳhe̜'
djā'nᴀga xete-ā'k'ī waji̯ru̯k'o'nonoŋk'ī'ji̯ jë'nu̯ŋga tcīroixdjī-a̯'kce.
Hōk'awā'regi̯ wahi̯sọ'sgara sī kocᵉọ'gedja hīp'ā' hīnᴀ'p'ogerë'je.
Tcī-ā'k'a wōhọ'ṇa p'ëdjera' djanagā'k'ī wọhọ'ṇa gōdjōwai'reje
hadjāje. Ė'gi̯ tcahā'ra tcīsā'niŋk tcōwë'ra ᶜuni̯nᴀ'je. Ė'gi̯ wagaī'reje
ŭaŋkcige' hīgu̯k'ī'ni̯ sᵉīarawë'nᴀ; hīgu̯k'ī'ni̯ nᾳtcge̜'ra ni̯te̜'kce.

war power and life we bless you,' they said. Then he looked at them. 'I wonder whether they really are the Night Spirits?' he thought. They were not the Night Spirits who were speaking to him. The birds that spoke were the *kawī'cge*, *tcōxdji*, and *cị'k'ok'ok'*.[83] They were the ones that spoke and they were the ones that fooled him. Instead of feeling sad this time, however (he said), 'I don't care what happens; I am willing to die (in order to get the blessing),' he thought to himself. Then he began fasting again. He rubbed the (charcoal) over (his face) again. Seven nights he fasted. And once again from the east the Night Spirits came singing. They came and stood (before him) and they said, 'Nephew, we bless you. So long have you been sad and cried to us piteously (that we will bless you). No one did we ever bless before. In war and life you shall do just as you wish,' they said. Then he looked again. 'I wonder whether those speaking are really the Night Spirits?' he thought. But they were not the Night Spirits. They were the bluebird, *gị'sge*,[84] and duck, and as many of them as there were, their breasts were dark. As many birds as there were, they were bad. 'My, O my! How they abuse me!' he cried. At first Djōbenạgiwi'ŋxga had thought in his fastings that just to spite them he would fast again. Now he rubbed (charcoal on his face) again and wept bitterly.[85] Both hands contained tobacco and he stood in the direction from which the Night Spirits came and weeping, put himself in the most abject condition.

"Now, indeed, to its very depths did his heart ache. Ten nights did he fast. Finally they (the Night Spirits) came after him. 'Human, I have come after you.' He followed (the spirits) and they took him to the east; to the site of a Night Spirit village they took him. The chief of the Night Spirits had sent this one to go after him. In the village was a long lodge standing in the east. There they took him. As many Night Spirits as there were in control of powerful blessings, of that many the lodge was full. When he entered he walked in white feathers up to his knees.[86] Many kettles and much food he saw stretched right across (the lodge). On the outside, a buffalo hide stretched almost across the entire lodge. Then they said to him, 'Human, without giving up, long you have suffered; your heart has, indeed, been sad. They, as many spirits as there are

[83] English equivalents for the first two unknown. The last is probably the robin.

[84] English equivalent unknown.

[85] He wept bitterly not so much on account of his disappointment as for the purpose of bringing himself into a state of religious ecstacy. The change of attitude from one of spite to realization that not in such a way were blessings from deities like the Night Spirits to be obtained is very well brought out here. It was a cardinal tenet of the religion of the devout shamans that your success in obtaining blessings was in direct proportion to the motives and intensity of feeling you brought to your prayer. To throw away your life through mere disappointment was deemed absolutely unethical, (a thought that) is brought out quite distinctly in the systematic teachings given to the young.

[86] The lodges of the Night Spirits are supposed to be strewn with white feathers as a sign of holiness. As far as known no symbolism is attached to it.

Ha⁶e'nįnë'na djanīsgë'k'djera tcī-ō'jų-ā'gere mejë'nųga hanā̧'tcį hā̧hę' wa⁶ŭa'ŋkcaᴀna. Ė'gi ne hā̧hę' wīrųk'o'nᴀnꞏ4 ⁶ŭįṇë'nꞏ4. Wōgųzǫtcī'ra hacdjaco'nᴀŋgre, te⁶e hōnik⁶ų'-iṇëna. Wōhǫ'na djasgā'gere haŋk'agā' cūrųc⁶ā'geniŋk'djonë'nꞏ4. Tcahā' nā̧bįrųxā'-djera djanꞏ4gā'cdjare tejë'nųga taṇi-ō'waxu rak'ere'ranicek'djon-ënꞏ4. Hoici'p djasgā'gere jësgā'nįhëk'djanë'nꞏ4. Hā̧hę' tcīnǫ'-geregį wōgųzǫtcī'ra hōnįk⁶ų'-įnënꞏ4. Wōnᴀ'ɣiręra djagū' c⁶ųṇanac⁶į c⁶uŋk'djonë'nꞏ4. Ė'gį ŭaŋkcigǫ⁶ị'ṇa djadjaį'xdjį p'ā. Taṇi-ō'-waxų'ṇa ⁶unā'nįhë'gį jedjaį'xdjį p'ā hoici'p'djį, tanī'ṇa wōhǫ'na tcahā' nā̧bįrųxā'djera mācų̄' cūdjera' hoici'p'djį wōgų'zǫtcįra hācdjare. Ė'gį djī-ā̧'gik'djonë'nꞏ4 hoici'p hīniŋgį p'erez hīranihë'-k'djonë'nꞏ4.

"Tcōk'agā' Djōbenągįwi'ŋxga, te'jësge hįgaī'ręgį. E ë'je. K'aratā' wahë'k'djᴀnā'wina hōnįhā'ra tcā̧t⁶į wahā'wigį. Sā'niŋk' hā̧bǫgūre'rera tcōk'agā' Djōbenągiwi'ŋxga hōnįhā'ra djāsge'xdjį gīk'ere'regį haŋk'e' jësge'xdji hōwehā'wiṇįcge hītcō'k'ewahī'wira haŋk'e' wajiṇe'p'įhī'nanįje. Aī'rejare. Hōnįhā'ra hījąk'ī'ra hīrap'e'rezk'ī'cge ɣak hįbį-ā̧'dje airera. Jë'sge wage' wahëk'-djonā'wigadją. Sā'k'ereniŋk'djǫ'gᴇra mīnaŋkcā'waŋgre niŋk'ūru-hindj rehā'wįdjįgō'." (Hā̧hę' Nā̧wꞏ4.)

<h2>THE FEAST</h2>

Host's speech.—"Sā'k'ereniŋk'djǫ'gera mīnaŋkcā'waŋgre niŋk'-ūrųhi'tccᴀnꞏ4. Hījąk'ī'ra wāxōp'į'nįna wājągų'zᴇra gījį e waŋgā⁶ū'nꞏ4 here nūnįge' wajā̧'gere e anā̧'tc ⁶u nūnįge' djagū'rįja nįtā'k'atc hiŋgigī'wįge tanī'ṇa warūtc xō'p'ini hīrak'ī'rųtcap hagįtū'cdją rehak'djonā'wįnꞏ4. Djasgī'hīwį-ā'nꞏ4ga; djāsge haīcge hiŋgīp'e'rez hīranā'gųnį hīnęga hīwecu'nųgādja. A'nꞏ4ga, 'Ŭaŋkci'-gᴇra hījā̧ sāk'ererëra niŋgenꞏ4'k'ī ë'dja wōhǫ'djęga warā'djerā'nꞏ4. Ė'gį jįge sā'niŋk' hoire'regį herera' tanī'ṇa wagigī' na⁶ī'nīsge rǫhī'-wīk'īsgawį waŋgaik'ā'rabįrā'wira jësgë'ją. Warūtc xōp'įnį tanī'ṇa hīrarū'tcap hagįtū'cdją rehā'wira yoire'regį wak'ā'ndja huŋgera. Djāsge' haīcge hiŋgip'e'reziranā'gųnį. Hīṇęga hīwā⁶ū'cunųgā'dją ā'nꞏ4ga. Jįge sak'erë'ją hīdjā'naŋk'ī wōhǫ'ṇa e-ā'ratc."

in the lodge, that many talked of what was to happen to you. And I, I am the chief of the Night Spirits. This creation-lodge just as you see it (i. e., with all it contains) I give to you.[87] You will never be in want of food. You are to offer as many buckskins as you see here and tobacco for all time. Thus it shall be. The "creation-lodge" of the village of the Night Spirits I give to you. You can go on as many war parties as you wish and obtain as much life. As many tobacco offerings as they (i. e., you and your descendants) continue to give, all the tobacco, food, buckskin offerings, red feathers, as many as there are, they will all come to the "creation-lodge" that you see, and we will accept them.'

"Thus did they speak to grandfather Djōbenągiwi'ηxga. So he said. We will do this that we may ask (blessings) for our relatives and sing songs. Even if we do not perform everything in just the manner that the spirits in the east (told) our grandfather Djōbenągiwiηxga, we know that our grandfathers (the spirits) will not be offended. So they say. Even if you know only one song, if you bring yourself to the point of crying in your efforts (it will be all right). Thus we mean to say it. War-bundle owners, who are seated here, I greet you." (Night Spirit song.)

THE FEAST

Host's speech.—"War-bundle owners who are seated here, I greet you. Every spirit that the Creator created he made for us,[88] but whatever food he made for us all those things we were to offer up (to the spirits) together with tobacco and the sacred feast. What we are to do, what I can do to make these things known to them, that is what we should think of and talk about. (This is what the Creator said): Let (the host) call upon a warrior, a young man present at the feast. For the one who lives in the west he should make offerings of tobacco and attempt to be like (the spirits), so that one of our own members should be considered (by the spirits) as the same as themselves.[89] A sacred feast and tobacco together with it we are about to offer to the chief of the Thunderbirds in the west. What can I do that they might have knowledge of these (offerings)? Thus we should be thinking, (the Creator) said. A war-bundle owner who is present we should call upon (to take charge of) a kettle." [90]

---

[87] The lodges of the spirits are always called "creation lodges" in reference to the fact that it was by the assembled spirits in these lodges that at the beginning of the world everything was set in order. The principal "creation lodge" was that of Earthmaker, to which the soul of a dead individual wandered after death and from which he was sent to the world again if he chose to take human form once more.

[88] I. e., that they might give us blessings.

[89] I. e., impersonate the spirits. It will be remembered (cf. Introduction) that each guest is supposed to impersonate a spirit.

[90] Host's speech ends here. What follows is description.

Ė'gį jįge wōhaį'ją sairak'ā'rara K'aradjų' Sep [103] Xetera higai regi wọhaī'ją hīranā'ᵉįŋgį jįge' hīcge jeᵉe' nįŋge' waratcce.

Ė'gį jįge Hōcereᵉu'wahīra wōhaį'ją hagįk'ere'ręgį jįge jeᵉe' nįŋge' wā'ratcce.

Ė'gį jįge' hīcge Rek'ū'hūhį hįgaī'ręgį wōhaī'ją hagįk'ere'regį ë'gį jįge wāratcce'.

Ė'gį jįge hᶏbawī'ra wōhᶏ' gīk'ere'ręgį jįge jeᵉe' hīcge ŭaŋk hīdjahī' wāratcce.

Ė'gį jįge' Wīragō'cge Xetera wahā'gįk'ere`regį jįge nįŋge' wāratcce.

Ė'gį jįge tcōni'xdjį wōhᶏna'djįra nīhera jeᵉe' wōk'e'ra djanᶏ'hī hī'regį ŭaŋgera hįna rūse, jë'nųga hak'ītcᶏ'k'djęge. Ė'gį jįge hīnų'bera wōhᶏ' harā'djįręra hīcge'sge k'ūruzā'nᶏga.

Wap'e'nᶏŋkce ŭaŋgera djā'nᶏga wap'arā'djįręra.
Ė'dja jįge hīcge hanᶏ'tc wōk'e'ra djanᶏgā'gį jë'nųga hīnā' k'ūruzįrë'je.   Hanᶏ'tcįŋxdjį wasgë'ra wawōk'ā'rajų-irā`nᶏga, wamoŋk'ā'rajejërā`nᶏga.   Wōrū'djįracanᶏ hap'e'djįnᶏ`geregį.
Ė'gį jįge djānᶏga tcīroju-ā'k'a hotā' hᶏŋk'e' wap'ā' rūdje'dja waradjįrā'nįŋgi. Wōkį-ō'nįŋge wawōgijū'reje. Ė'gį djānᶏga ŭaŋgera hīnų'gera waᵉŭaŋk'ī'jį hanᶏ'tcįŋxdjį hak'ī'tcgus wasgë'ra wawọgī'jų nī'regį.
Ė'gį wap'ā' rūdje'naŋk'ā. Ŭaŋgwā'cọcera waᵉū'naŋkce. Haŋk'e' ŭaŋgwacọce'nįna wōk'lō'nįŋge wawōgī' jųhīrë`je. Hīnųgera' ŭaŋk hᶏŋk'e' wacōce'nįna wap'ā' rūdjenᶏ'k'ā. Ŭaŋgerā'canᶏ wap'ā'rūtc rūxū'rugenᶏ`kcenᶏ. Hᶏŋk'e' hīnų'gera wap'ā'rūtc wagīgī'naŋkce. Ŭaŋgwā'cọcera hōtā' wagīgō'naŋk'ā gīk'įrī'regį wagįk'ī'rįnaŋk'a hīnųgwā'tcabera hītcujọ'wahīra hītcų'-įwahī'ra, jeᵉe' wawīrō'k'arapū'nųnᶏ erë'naŋk'e. Tcī-ō'k'īsā`gedja wap'ā'-rūtc wak'aragī'nᶏ wak'įrī'djęga. Hīnųwa'tcabera hītcujọ'wahīra hīnų'k wajā'wahīra hį'nuŋk tci-ō'k'īsā`gedja wap'ā rūdjenᶏ'k'a wajᶏ woitō-į'xetexdjįją herege'. Hanᶏ'tcįŋxdjį hīrak'ī'k'arajī nᶏ'-kcanᶏ.
Ė'gį wọrū'djera hap'e' djīnagī'regį hanᶏ'tcį wagįgō'nᶏŋk'a wak'ūrųhi'ndjerhį-ā`naga wëje.
"Wasge'ri-ọwīdje`dja    herecunųgā'dją    wak'ā'ragāk'djonihā'-wįnᶏ. Sa'k'ereniŋk'djọ`gera mīnaŋkcā'waŋgre nįŋkūrųhi'ndj rehā'-wįdjigo." (Wā'rudj Nᶏwᶏ.)

[103] The "e" of keredju has become assimilated to the "a" of the preceding word.

And a war-bundle owner for the second kettle should be called upon—a kettle offered in connection with him whom we call Great Black Hawk.

Then they call for someone to take charge of the kettle placed for Disease-giver.

Then they call for someone to take charge of the kettle for the spirit whom they call South Wind.

Then they call for someone to take charge of the kettle for the Sun.

Then they also select another man to be in charge of a kettle put on for the Morning Star.[91]

Then the first one who had been called upon for a kettle takes as many pieces of food as there are individuals in his band who eat with him. The second one who had been called upon also takes enough pieces (for his band).

Those who are going to eat the head have to wait.[92]

Then all took enough pieces to suffice for their band.

Then they (the attendants) put the pieces of meat in plates and cut them up into small portions. Now all are in readiness for the meal. Only some of those in the lodge are called upon to eat the head. The plate of the others is filled with ordinary cuts (of meat). As many men and women as are present, for that many do they cut up the pieces of meat evenly and place them in the plate.

Only warriors are head eaters. Not to warriors do they give common pieces. Women and men who are not warriors can not take part in this head eating. Only men can take part in the head eating. They would not permit women to eat the head. However, those of the feasters who were warriors and had brought home war trophies would speak a good word for the trophy bearers, their sisters, their neices, and their aunts,[93] and these would be allowed to sit in the midst of the head eaters. The sisters or the aunts, whatever women were allowed to sit among the head eaters, considered it a very great honor. Thus all were encouraged to do.

Now (the preparations being finished) all are waiting for the meal and the host gets up and speaks.[94]

"I greet you all. When it (the meat) gets into the plate, then it is the time to try to get the spirit's attention by singing. War-bundle owners, who are seated here, I greet you all." (Eating song.)

---

[91] In the first division of the ritual seven kettles are prepared; in the second division, four.

[92] The eating of the deer's head is the greatest honor that one can obtain in this ceremony, and only warriors are permitted to take part in it.

[93] When a warrior returned from a successful war party with the first war honor, i. e., if he had counted coup first, he was given a wampum necklace, and this he presented to his oldest sister or to the daughters of his father's brother or mother's sister or to his mother's sister.

[94] This is the continuation of his speech that had been interrupted by the preparations for the meal

436 THE WINNEBAGO TRIBE

The Fast-Eating Contest

Tcĕk'djī'ṇa warū'djera here k'ậroḥō'gị ĕ'gị wagigō'nᴀηk'a
hījạk'ī'ra hịdjaī'ra p'īranaηk'ī'gị hōtū'djera p'ịxdjị hōtadjū'gera
aīdjā'xdjere'xdjị hīrā'nᴀga warūtctco'na hanậ'tciηxdjị rūtcop'-
djịnë'je. Hᴀηk'e' hōce'rek' hīdjā' wajậ' nīheḥī'ranịje horọcdjanā'-
cge hᴀηk'e' niηge' nīheḥī'ranīje. Hīrūcdjậ'xdjị hī'regị ĕ'gị wagigō'-
naηk'a nậji-ā'nᴀga wë'je.
"Sā'kereηiηkdjọ'gera mīnaηkcā'waηgre niηkūruhi'ndj rehā'-
wịnᴀ. Waniηgik'ī'k'aratc xetẹ'ra wak'ạdjaī'k'īk'ā'ratc hījạ'
hidjā'naηk'ī warūdj sāk'ụ' haratcec. Hījậ' tcōk'ā'rak'ere 'ụxdje
hīgeje. Ĕgị jịge' maị'djerëjạ hụndjk'ik'ā'radjī'jạ je'e warūsā'k'ụ
haratcce' wëje. Wā'niηgik'īk'ā'radjera djamᴀga'k'ī je'e' hererā'-
nᴀga ĕ'gị maṇë'girera djanᴀgā'k'į wōnᴀ'γirẹra hak'ik'ŭe'k.
Wagī'gi wa'ụk'djonë'je, waniηgik'arā'djiạ maṇe'gerëjạ hīk'ī'ụ
wagigik'ậroḥō'nᴀ wōnᴀ'γirẹra hak'ik'ŭe'k' wagigī' wa'ụηk'-
djonë'nᴀ. Ĕ'gị hīnụ'wiηk'e hījậ'cᴀnᴀ k'ūrụzịrā'nᴀga warụγa'p
tcōwë'dja warutc sak'ụ' ịk'ậrohoī'rënᴀ. Warū'djera nawā'sge
xetera' nụp'ī'wị hịk'ịk'ī'naηxdjị wōjū'-ịranᴀga ĕ'dja wak'arë'renᴀ
warụγa'p tcōwë'dja. Wasgẹ'naηk'ā wak'andjaī'k'ịk'arā'djenᴀηk'a
hījạ' tcōk'ë're wasgẹ'naηk'ā hījạ' djī-ā'mịnaηgịrë'nᴀ, ĕ'gị jịge
hịndjik'ịk'ā'radjᴇnaηk'ā hījạ' tcōk'ẹ're wasgẹ'djonë'djẹga hadjị-
ā'mịnᴀηkce. Ĕ'gị agī'xdjị k'īk'o'nọgịrëje hīdjō'bịk'e. Wagigō'-
naηk'a jujū'k' djīrehi-ā'nᴀga nậ'wạ djirehī'gi. Warūtc sak'ū'ṇa
hīk'ịdjaī'xdjị hānịmiηgịrëje. Tcōnị 'ŭaηge'dja xetẹna'ηk'a tcebị-
reḥị-ā'nᴀga īrō'k'aradjị'djịṇë'je, ĕ'gị wëje, "Ahū'-ịrasā'naηgre īra
xete'renᴀ. Haηk'e' warūdje'dja wanậ'p'ịnị wā'ụnạ'kcᴀnᴀ."
Ĕ'gị wanaina'nᴀηk'a wai'rẹje k'e'ni tcebrịā'ni nạbō'jụ rūzịrā'nᴀga
hoḥō'bịrẹra. Waī'rënᴀ. Maị'djere xetẹ'naηk'a wā'naηkce,
"Haηk'e' wōgī'zọk hīwanaī'ṇanịgā'djạ manā'geregere īra xetẹ'rẹnᴀ
'ŭa'genaηgere djasge'xdjinᴀηgre, hᴀηk'e' niηge' ragajenī'naηkcᴀnᴀ
ëje?" Hoḥī'rẹnᴀηk'ā wanā'kcᴀnᴀ. Ĕ'gị k'īgậ'ra wap'ā'warad-
jịrëje. Jenuηgā'djạ te'e'.

"Warū'dj nậwạ djīrehī'giwagigō'nᴀηk'a warū'djṇa hīk'ịdjaī'xdjị
warū'djera djīk'erehī're warū'djenaηk'ā hīk'ūhë'xdjị xāpge' tcẹbī'
nā'ī'ṇe tcōnī' tcẹbī'djegācge wajậ'nijậ herehīrana'ī'ṇe.

The Fast-Eating Contest[95]

As soon as the meal is about ready and the host thinks that (the food) in the kettle belonging to the first guest is about cooked and when it is soft and just right, then the attendants take it and cut it up. They do not leave any bones in it, nor do they leave any of the hard parts. When they have prepared it, then the host rises and speaks.

"War-bundle owners who are seated here, I greet you. One of the great ones belonging to the Bird clan,[96] a member of the Thunderbird clan, has called for a fast-eating contest. One of his followers will represent them (i. e., their clan), he has told me. Now a member of the Earth people, one of the Bear clan, must be selected[97] for the fast-eating contest, he said. As many of the Bird clan people as there are present, they all will try to take from those of the Earth people present the war honor (belonging to the fast eating). That is why they have it, so that the Bird and the Earth clans may compete for it,[98] that they might take a war honor from one another." Then both of the contestants took (the food) in front of the war bundle, and they get ready for a fast-eating contest. Two wooden bowls with exactly the same amount of food are placed in front of the war bundle. Then the Thunderbird clansman, with a follower (taking) a plate, sits down, and afterwards the Bear clansman, also with a follower, sits down. Now they hold themselves in readiness, the four of them. The feasters now start playing on their flutes and begin singing songs. The fast eaters (i. e., the contestants) start simultaneously. The upper people (phratry), the great ones, devour it first and shout, striking their mouths. "Those with wings[99] have large mouths. They can never be beaten in eating." The defeated ones took the meat in their hands and ate it up and gave the war whoop. The leaders of the Earth people said, "We have not been beaten fairly, for the upper ones have greater mouths, so how could they fail?" Thus the beaten ones said. Then they called for the heads. That is all.[100]

As soon as the host starts the eating song,[101] all the guests began to eat at a moderate pace, then they try to eat fast because they believe that it is an honor to be the first to have finished.

---

[95] This detailed account was left out in the general description and inserted afterwards. For that reason there may be a number of unnecessary repetitions. I have not tried to adjust this insert to the text proper, but have preferred to place it just where my informant desired it.

[96] This is a rather unusual appellation for the upper phratry.

[97] This is the regular name for the second of the two Winnebago phratries.

[98] This is only one of the ways in which these two phratries compete.

[99] Ritualistic name for the Bird clans.

[100] I believe it is considered correct form to permit the phratry to which the host belongs to win in this contest. Those who win get the choicest pieces of the deer head.

[101] Neither the host nor any of those who belong to his band eat during the feast.

"Ge ësge ëgi jige k'igō'naŋk'ā hījạ wa^ɛinạ̈'tcịcge hīgụ djasgẹ'gi tcẹbī'k'dje jësgë'ge. Ė'sge warūc^ɛā'gera hạŋk'e' p'ịnī'je hōk'īrā'-genaŋk'e. Ė'sge p'ëjege'regi haŋk'e' warūc^ɛā'genī na^ɛī'naŋkce. Ė'gi jige hanạ̈'tc worū'djɛra jë'gụ hī'regi hanạ̈'tc djagū'cANạ tụdjī'regi tcëbī'xdjinë'gi.

CONTINUATION OF THE BASIC RITUAL

Speech of first guest.—Ė'gi tcōnị'xdjị wohadjịranịhë'nạ wa^ɛī'nạp cANạ wë'nạ.

"Warōγī'ra hōk'ịk'ā'radjera mī'naŋkcā'waŋgre niŋk'ūrụhi'ndj rehā'wịdjịgō. DjanАga sā'k'ererẹra mīnaŋkcā'waŋgre hanạ̈tciŋxdji niŋk'ūrụhindj rehā'wịdjịgō. Warōγī'ra hōk'ī'k'arā'djera warōγī' p'anai'nạxdjị wa^ɛụ'wị-ā'nАga waxōp'ị'nị warā'djịrẹra hanạ'cgenị gī'k'aratc mīnạ'genaŋgere. Ėp'ịgā'djạ sā'k'ere hīwatcā'bwịra waxōp'ị'nị gīk'arā'djera te'jësge hīnạ'gere. E te^ɛe' ŭaŋkcik hīyahạ'gwịgā'dja. Hōtā'jị jë'sge hīrụxū'rugwịje te^ɛe' ewa^ɛụ'ịnẹge haŋk'e' waŋgajëdjā'nị-ahaŋk'ā'dja. Warọγī'ra waxọp'ị'nị warā'-djịrẹra hījạ̈k'ī'ra hīraitce'ranАŋk'ị, tanī'ṇa wọhọ'na gịgī'rẹra ë'gi tcahā' nạ̈bịrụxā'dj era. Te jë'nụga. Mạ^ɛū'na ŭaŋgere'gịnaŋk'ī wōnА'γirera ŭaŋkcigo^ɛị gītairā'nАga. Djasgehị-ā'nАga haŋk'e' wawịŋgịp'e'res hīranị'k'djẹje wawịŋgī'p'erez hīregī'jị. Ŭaŋkci-gọ^ɛị'ṇa wirā'rụxe warọγī'ra ha^ɛuŋk'djā'wị; uaŋkcigọ^ɛī'ṇa hiraṇạ'-k'īk^ɛị'ŋxdjị ^ɛŭịṇawī'ra waxōp'ị'nị tanī'ṇa gịgī'rẹra. Waxōp'ị'nị wōnaŋkcī'wịṇa djā'nАga wak'ịk'arā'djwịra ha^ɛụ'xdjịwị-ā'nАga. Wahā'dj wịreconanë'cge p'ịgā'djạ. Ė'gi ŭaŋkcigọ^ɛị'ṇa hīraṇạ' k'īk^ɛị'wịre ẹp'ī'nạ wa^ɛia'nạpge wahā'nАŋkcANạ. Ė'gi c^ɛagwahā'ra hījạ hītcō'k'eniŋk' hī'regi waxōp'ị'nịna haŋk'ī'jạ eọ'rakcigenījạ aī'rera je^ɛe' hīŋgịwewī'rẹge. Warọγī'ra wawak'ī'k'aradjera waxọp'-ị'nị honaŋkcī' hịŋgịgī'rẹra. Ep'ịgā'dja. Wawarọgiγī'rẹra mạ^ɛū'na.

"Hak'ūrụhindj rehā'nАga. Ė'gi warọγī'ra wak'ūrụhi'djanАga; ë'gi sā'kereniŋkdjọ'gera tcī-ō'jụ mīnaŋkcā'waŋgre niŋk'ūrụhi'ndj rehawịdjịgō'."

"Ė'gi hīnụ'bra wōhọ'ṇa radjịrā'nịhë'ra wa^ɛī'nАbik'arọho'nạ wë'nạ."

Speech of second guest.—Warọγī'ra wajaniwī'na mīcanaŋgā'naŋk'a niŋk'ūrụhi'ndj rehāwịdjịgō'. Ė'gi sāk'ereni'ŋk'djoŋgera higī' acā'-

Even if a feaster gets satiated, he must continue to eat until everything is finished. They tell one another that it is not good for any one to fail (and leave any food). Whatever food there is they must finish it all. All that is cooked must they eat.

CONTINUATION OF THE BASIC RITUAL

Then the one who was called upon for the first kettle thanked them and said:

Speech of first guest.—"Councilors [102] and relatives who are seated here, I greet you all. As many war-bundle owners as are seated here, I greet you all. The councilors of the clans have enjoined upon us earnestly to offer up sincere prayers to all the different spirits who are seated here (in the persons of the guests). It is good that our war-bundle owners offer up prayers in this way. It is for this reason that we are still living. Some of us can not accomplish much in that line and that is why so many of us are gone already (i. e., are dead). This ritual was made for one who is the very greatest of all the spirits, for whom they have offered tobacco and food and offerings of buckskin. Thus they have done. Earthmaker, who dwells above, they have asked for war power and life. Indeed, how would it be possible for (the spirits) not to take cognizance and accept (these offerings).[103] If we follow the preaching (of our host), life (we will obtain); life we will feel ourselves in connection with through the holy food that they (the host and the members of his band) have offered up. We have (had the honor too) of impersonating the spirits, I and my relatives. The meal likewise was excellent. It is good that they have brought us in connection with so much life and it is to thank them that I am saying this. That one of their ancestors whom they called grandfather (and whose place I am taking) was not one to speak foolishly, it is said, and still his place they thought of for me (unworthy as I am). They have given me (the part) of a councilor of their own clan and (the privilege) of impersonating a spirit. It is good. Earthmaker they have prayed to.

I greet him. To the enjoiner (host) I send my greetings; to all the war-bundle owners who are seated here, I send forth my greetings.

Then the second one who was called upon for a kettle gets ready to thank them and says:

Speech of second guest.—"Host and relatives, as many as are seated here, I send forth my greetings to you. War-bundle owners that

---

[102] The word means, literally, "enjoiners" and refers to the injunctions and instructions the elder people give to the young.

[103] I. e., the offerings are so wonderful that the spirits would have to be blind not to see them. This and the following sentences are formulaic compliments always paid to the host by the invited guests.

nₐŋk'i niŋk'ūruhi'ndj rehā'wįdjįgō'. Wawik'ī'k'aradjera warǫyī' p'onaī'nᴀ wa'ųwinā'nₐga djā'nₐga hinu'gera niŋk'djo' ŋgeniŋgera hanā̰'tciŋxdjį waŋgirǫp'o'nuhī'rawį wā'una'ŋk'adjₐ. Djagū'ijₐ wōxe'teje! Ŭaŋkci'gǫᵉ'laŋgerë᾽cᴀnₐ wōxe'teje? Warōyī'ra wawak'i'-k'aradjera waxōp'į'nį k'īsgë'jₐ hōnįhō'k'īranaŋgere waxōp'į'nį wanₐᵉį̰' rūsgī'tcgį djadjo'na tanį-ǫwaxų'na hįgįrë'regį waxǫp'į'nį tanī'na gīk'arā'naŋk'į jedjonai'xdjį hǫ'u'nįgere᾽regį. Hōwarë'ra waxōp'į'nį hīnₐcge'nį gīk'arā'tc mīna'ŋgįrā᾽naga. Wōnᴀ'yįrᴇra hadjaī'regį sᵉīrë'djₐ ŭa'ŋgᴇra tūdjįrā'nₐga hak'arā'gware. Wa'ų'-įnegį hōwarë'ra. Hōp'lǫwai'rek'djonë'gadjₐ, wōnᴀ'yįrᴇra. Hagârë'ja hak'īdjai'regį hak'įt'ₐ'p hĩk'ârǫhoī'regį ë'dja waxōp'į'nį waradjīrᴇ'ra wōnᴀ'yįre rūk'o'nonₐ tanī wawǫrā'giju-ā᾽nₐga. 'Tcōk'ā'wahī'ra gāsge niŋgįgī'wicunū᾽nₐ wįrā'gegiji.' Hōwarë'ra wōna'yįre rūk'o'nonₐ hōnī'niŋgįhanₐk'ī᾽cge haŋk'e' rak'arap'-erezenį'k'djonë᾽nₐ hōwarë'ra hak'įt'ₐ̰'bįregį. Wap'ahį-ǫk'ë'ra hōrawë'k'djenₐ hījū'gemāna māna nįjū'-įtajenī᾽sgecge hījū'g-emǫk'ë'ra hōwawë'k'djenₐ racgū'nįxdjį haragī'xebįk'djonë'nₐ.
Ë'gį jige ŭaŋgerī'jₐk'īra hak'īkŭe'gįrë'cge nī-ₐ'cinįcawaiŋk'-djonë᾽nₐ. Waxōp'į'nį nįtā'k'atc g²gī'ra p'įnₐ'gį tanī'na wōhǫ'na rōhₐ̰' tatcë'bragį waxōp'į'nį warₐ̄'djįrᴇra ë'cᴀnₐ wak'āndjā'naŋgere wōna'yįre rūk'o'nonₐ᾽nₐ xete'reje hahī' hīsge'xdjį p'įraī'cge. Djadjo'na wak'andjā'ra hagū'-įregį rājᴇra hīnip'e'rezįrek'djonë᾽nₐ hahī' wak'andjā'ra hagū'-įrëcge rajᴇra nįnā'djįranaga, "Ėdjagį tanį hiŋk'djawī'nₐ," hīniŋgaī'regį. Uaŋgena'ŋgere hījₐ̰' tcëk xete-hū'ga me'jësge hīrak'ī'k'arājī'rëk'djonë. Hotak'ī'ra te jësganaŋk'ā'-dja. Te'e ep'iŋgā'dja. Warǫyī p'onaina wa'-ūne djā'nₐga ŭaŋgera gī'jį jë'nuga hīrǫp'ū'nu wai'unaŋk'ā'dja. Wī-oire'regį hītcō'-k'ewahī᾽wįra nįtā'k'adjera wagįgī'rᴇra tanī'na tcahā'sgera k'arap'i-e'sge wagįrū'cdjₐ rehī'rᴇra. Wōnaŋkcį hiŋgįgī'rᴇra djanₐga' hōk̨'-ik'arā'djeniŋgᴇra ŭaŋkci'gǫᵉį ŭanₐ̄djōdjaį'sge ha'ŭahaŋgwī'ra jë'-nuga. Uaŋkcigǫᵉį̨'na hīranₐ'k'īk̨ᵢ'ŋxdjį̨. Wajₐgų'zᴇrₐ wōjū'-įŋgīᵉū'nₐ yak'aragustį-ā'naga ŭaŋkcigǫᵉį̨'na hīranₐ'k'īk̨'i᾽wįnₐ way-anₐbwī'na. Warǫgiyī'rᴇra sā'niŋk yoire'regį herᴇra wak'ūruhi'-ntc rehā'nₐ. A'nₐga ë'gį warǫyī'ra hōk̨'įwįk̨'ā'radjᴇra mī'naŋkcā᾽-

are here, I send forth my greetings to you. Those of the various clans (present) have counseled me repeatedly and all the women and children have pleaded in my behalf (with the spirits). What love that was! And what does life consist of but love? The clan coun- cilor is repeating the songs (that were obtained) when the sacred bundle was made, so that when the time for the tobacco offering to the spirits came, they would have the tobacco that they have kept all this time (ready). Now, sure enough, the time has arrived and they are sitting prepared to pray to all the various spirits. Long ago when they saw war they cooked the man they were to go after.[104] That is why they did it. A good (prosperous) warpath they will surely have. When they are actually in the midst of their warpath and are about to rush for one another (i. e., the Winnebago and his enemy), let him pour tobacco to the various spirits who are in con- trol of war. If you say 'Grandfather, thus we used to offer you,' although you may not know (by any word or direct sign) whether those in control of war have answered you, (you will know it) as soon as the rush upon the enemy takes place and, although you go where the bullets and arrows rain hardest, you will pass out of the reach of the bullets and will pass safely out (of all danger). If the people rush for a man to bestow the war honors upon,[105] you will be the one. If you give the sacred feast in the proper way, if you burn up much tobacco and food, then the various spirits, especially the Thunderbirds, who are in control of the greatest war power, (will bless you) for the excellent way in which you have (prayed to them). Whenever the Thunderbirds come they will remember you; and when they come they will even call you by name and say, 'Let us smoke here.' [106] When the young begin to grow up, one of the men encourages them. Only a few, however, are like this. It is good. He (the host) has preached and pleaded for as many men as are present. They (the host and his band) have made offerings of food to our grandfathers who live in the west (the Thunderbirds) and pleasing offerings of tobacco and buckskin have they sent out to them. They have permitted me to impersonate (this spirit) and have thus given life to myself and my unimportant clansmen, who have been living in so lowly a condition. With real life have we felt ourselves connected (through your actions). With life have we felt ourselves connected by means of that vessel which the Creator gave me as a

---

[104] Here the literal translation is nonsense. The real meaning is that the spirit of the enemy they are to kill on the warpath is present in the food offered up at this feast. This is a characteristic Winnebago con- ception. For another example, see a version of the origin myth of the Thunderbird clan bundle, where the hero, by drinking a certain liquid, has not only a vision of the people he is going to kill, but even hears their dying groans.

[105] This refers to the custom of running out to greet the returning warriors in order to conduct them into the village and bestow the war honors upon those who have counted coup.

[106] I. e., if a person makes it a habit to offer tobacco, the spirits will say, "Let us stop at such and such a man's place as we go along and have a smoke."

waŋk'a niŋk'ūruhi'ntc rehā'wịnʌ. Ě'gị sā'k'erẹra tcī-ō'jụ mīnaŋkcā' waŋgre hanậ'tciŋxdjị niŋk'ūruhintc rehawịdjịgō'.

Speech of third guest.—Ě'gị jịge tanī'ṇa wōho'natc hīarā'nịhẹra wak'ūruhindj rehī'nʌ. Wo'ī'nọbEra hīraī'djịge. Warọγī'ra hok'ī'- wik'aradjrera mīnaŋkcā'waŋk'a niŋk'ūruhi'ndj rehā'wịnʌ. Ě'gị sā'k'ereni'ŋk'djoŋgEra wōnaŋkcī' mī'naŋkcā'waŋgre niŋk'ūruhi'ndj rehā'wịdjịgō. Ěpịŋgā'djʌ. Jë'nụga jësge'cgụnị ārē'cge aīre te'eje wajʌ p'onaī'naŋgadjʌ. Hōk'ī'wịk'aradjEra warọγī' p'onaī'na. Ě'gị hītcō'k'ewahā`yanī'nënʌ huŋk'ū'-ịṇeje aīrera. Hagârë'jʌ īṇë'k'ī hịwatcgậ'xgi waxōp'ị'nị wa'yʌŋginạbī'k'djẹgị hịhanậ'je? Hiŋgaī'- rẹra hījaī'tcōk'ehawī'gị haŋk'e' wajā'nịjʌ herenī' nūnige ẹwewī'ṇege waxōp'ị'nị hōnaŋkcị' hiŋgigī'rẹra. Ěp'ịŋgā'djʌ. Djasgë'jʌ sā'niŋk yoire'rẹgị wōnʌ'γịre hīrụ'o'nora wak'ā'ndja huŋgra hīrak'ī'saniŋ- gEnʌŋkce saīrak'ā'rara wōnʌ'γịre hīrụk'o'nonʌ ŭaŋkcigo'ị' hīrasā' nậdjịrọdjaī'ṇẹgị waxōp'ị'nị hīk'īsgë'jʌ hōnịhō'k'īra`naŋgre djasge hiā'-nʌga haŋk'e' wawịgī'p'erez hīranị'kdjeje? Wawiŋgip'erez īrẹgī'jị hīcge wīrā'tūxe ha'uŋk'djā'wịra. Wōnʌ'ŋkcị hiŋgigi' rawịra. Ěp'ịŋgā'djʌ. Hōwarë'ra hak'īk'ụ'wịgadjʌ wajōk'ī'ŋgEra stō- ā'k'ịwị-ā'nʌga ŭaŋkcigo'ị'ṇa hīranʌ'k'īk'ịwnā'ịwịra. Ěp'ịŋgā'djʌ. Wawarō'gịγịrẹra K'eredjụ' Sep Xetẹga, hak'ūruhi'ndj rehā'nʌga. Ě'gị warọγī'ra niŋk'ūruhi'ndj rehā'wịnʌ. Waxōp'ị'nị wōnaŋkcī'ṇa sa'k'ereniŋk'djo'ŋgera tcī-ō'jụ mīnaŋkcā'waŋgre niŋk'ūruhi'ndj rehawịdjịgō'.

Ě'gị jịge hīcge ŭaŋgịdjanë'jʌ wọhọ'ṇadjịrẹra wa'ī'nʌp hīk'ârọhō'nʌ wë'nʌ.

Speech of fourth guest.—"Sā'k'ereniŋk'djo'ŋgera mī'naŋkcā'waŋgre niŋk'ūruhi'ndj rehā'wịnʌ. Warọγī'ra mīnaŋkcā'waŋk'ā wā'jạnị- wī'nʌ niŋk'ūruhi'ndj rehā'wịnʌ. Ě'gị wājʌ' p'onaī'nacgūnije hagī'jʌ jë'sge hiṇuxū'rugadjë'je ŭaŋgī'jʌ wājʌ' p'ị p'onaị'naxdjị 'uŋgā'djʌ. Ŭaŋkciginā'ŋgere hōtak'ī'racge c'aganʌgịxguṇ ẹgā`djʌ measure.[107] To those preached to, who are in the west, I send forth my greetings. To the host and those of his clan who are seated here, I send forth my greetings. To all the war-bundle owners who are seated within the lodge I send forth my greetings."

Speech of third guest.—"To all who possess tobacco and food do I send forth my greetings. The means for my feeling thankful has come to me.[108] Councilor (i. e., host) and members of his clan who are seated here, I send forth my greetings. And to you, war-bundle owners, who are impersonating (the spirits) seated here, do I send forth my greetings. In my thoughts I used to think that this is the way it was to be done, they said, but it has actually happened.[109] Thus did the clansmen, the councilors, sit acting. This (place of honor) belongs to their (the host's) grandfather (i. e., ancestor, the original impersonator), yet they gave me this position! If at any time a person (finding) me alone (had asked me) if I wanted to offer up thanks to the spirits (i. e., take part in this feast), how could such as I have said anything? They told me that they had thought of one of their ancestors in connection (with this feast), one who had been of no importance and that I was to impersonate the spirits (in his place).[110] It is good. How could the spirits who dwell in the west at the side of the chief of the Thunderbirds who is in control of war power help but recognize one who impersonates them, sings their songs, and whom, withal, they have blessed with control of a war bundle and given life? And if they recognize them, we, too, will follow them.[111] They have given us the place (of the spirits). It is good. Most assuredly have I helped myself and my relatives in gathering around here, for we have been brought in connection with life. To those they have preached to (who represent) the Big Black Hawk, do I send forth my greetings. And to the host and the war-bundle owners who are impersonating the spirits do I send forth my greetings."

Then another person whom they had called upon for a kettle gets ready to express his thankfulness and says:

Speech of fourth guest.—"War-bundle owners, councilors, relatives who are seated here, I send forth my greetings to you. This is indeed a marvelous performance and he who was able to do it is surely a marvelous man. Very few people listen to the counsel of their parents, but he was one of those who did, and (for that reason) he

---

[107] A rather curious circumlocution for stomach.
[108] I. e., now that it is my turn to speak and offer prayers, I can thank those who have invited me and the spirits.
[109] I. e., in my fondest imaginings I used to think that the ideal way to give the feast was the manner in which I see it given here. How could I have imagined that such a thing was actually possible. This is intended as a compliment to the host.
[110] This is, of course, all modesty.
[111] I. e., they will recognize us too.

te⁴e' jësgë'ją wa⁴ųnaŋk'ā'dją, wā'ją p'onaĵ'ṇaxdjį wa⁴uŋgā'dją.
Waxǫp'į'nį hōk'īk'ā'radjɛra hīnącge'ni gįk'arā'tcnaŋgre waxǫp'į'nį
k'īsgë'ją sarūsgī'tcgį wōcgǫ' hanįgī' djagū' ëgī'jį ë'xdjį hanį-
ǫgiwā'naŋgre. Ëp'iŋgā'djąwōcgǫ' eanī'nɛra k'arak⁴ų' wa⁴ųnaŋk'ā'dją.
Wōhǫ'ṇa gīksā'benądje'xdjį wōnaɣī're rūk'o'noṇa wagīk'e'rererā'-
nĄga tanī'ṇa hīwace'xdjį wagīt⁴ų'bįranĄga nąbįrųxā'djɛra hīk'-
īrā'ra wagī'jų-įrā'nĄga. Tcahā'sgara k'arap'į-e'sge higįtcą' wagįjū'-
įrā'nĄga wak'e'rɛra mącū' cūdjɛra k'arap'į-e'sge wōnĄ'ɣire rūk'o'-
noṇa. WōnĄ'ɣire hīk'aratā' hi⁴ū'naŋgre. Djasge' hī-ā'naga hąŋk'e'
wagīksā'p hīranį'k'djëje? Wawiŋgip'erezįrë'gį wōnaŋkcī'ṇa wīrā'-
rųxe hī⁴ųŋk'djā'wį, wonĄɣįrë'ra ŭaŋkcigǫ⁴į'ṇa."

"Ŭaŋgɛnū'nīgꞮą s⁴īredją'xdjī nądjįrǫdjaī'ṇęgį k'aratā'naŋgre
wōk'araik'aĵ'regį ŭaŋkcigǫ⁴į'ṇa p'į⁴ųŋk'djā'wį. P'ëdjok'e'rëją
ë'gį hī⁴ŭaha'ŋgwįre ŭaŋkcigǫ⁴ī'ṇa hį⁴ų'ŋk'djawį tā wā'naŋk'ā'dją
hąŋk'e ë'cana wak'īk⁴ų'nīnaŋk'ā'dją. Tcëge'dja ŭaŋgenū'nįŋgra
waī'rɛje, "Haŋk'e' hątā'gįnątc cūrųxū'rugenī'nĄ waxǫp'į'nį nįtā'-
k'atc gigī'ra p'į'ṇa wap'ā'hį k'ūrųk'ā'razre." Wawīk'ā'ragaī'regį.
Hōwarë'ra ŭana'ŋeręgā'dja. Në wajā'nįją ⁴ųinį-ā'nĄga waxǫp'į'nį
nįtā'k'adj gigī'regį wōnaŋkcī'ŋk'djera. Hiŋgį⁴ū'įnare waxǫp'į'nįna
warā'djįrɛra hījąŋk'ī'ra hiraī'tcerananḳa rōhąbōt⁴ę'k'į hīrūk'onaī'-
ją. Ë'gį rōhī' sānįŋk hąbįrųk'o'nadjëgį ë'gį hōt⁴ę'ruk'ō'nają hereje. Tanī'ṇa gigī'rɛra wōho'na wanį-oī'tcge hį'sgara wanioī'tcge
ŭaŋgī'ją tcahā'sgara mųcū'ṇa tanī'ṇa k'arap'į-e'sgexdjį. Hǫcere⁴-
ų'wahįra gīrųcdją' rehī'rare wōnᴀ'ɣire ŭaŋkcigō⁴į' hīk'ā'rata
hī⁴ū'įnare. Waxǫp'į'nį naŋk'e'we nadjesgë'ją nąpįrųxā'djeregį.
Wahëna'ŋgere waxǫp'į'nį hanąŋxgų'ṇe p'īnā'ŋkcį nūnįge wawįwų-
ā'gįt⁴ęk'djera. Tcōk'agā' węwįna'nĄga wōnᴀ'ŋkcį hiŋgigī'rɛra.
Waxǫp'į'nį warā'djįrɛra hąŋk'agā' rajɛra hǫ-įni'ŋge radjī'nanįs⁴ā'je
aī'rɛra. Hōnaŋkcį' gīgįrere hak'ūrųhį'ntcgį rajɛra tajerehā'-
kdjonā're hąŋk'e' woī'ya⁴ų naį'jįnįk'dje. Tanī'ṇa gigī'rɛra tcōk'ā'
Hocere⁴u'wahįra hak'ūrųhi'ndj rehā'nĄga. Ë'gį warųɣī'ra niŋk'-
ūrųhi'ndj rehā'wįnĄ. Ë'gį jige waxǫp'į'nį wō'naŋkcī'na tcī-ō'jų
mīnāŋkcā'waŋgre niŋk'ūrųhi'ndj rehā'wįdjįgō.

has done so well. The members of the clan have been sincerely worshiping the spirits. He who made the war-bundle ritual was like a spirit in power and what he told them to do they are doing in every detail. It is a good work that they are doing. Sufficient food they are offering to those who are in control of war powers that they might easily be cognizant of it. They have placed plenty of tobacco and different offerings of buckskin within their reach. A pleasing white buckskin they have strung out and offered to you; a pleasing red feather as a hair ornament (have they also offered to you). They have offered these things, so that they might ask for war from those who are in control of war. How, indeed, would it be possible (for the spirits) not to recognize these offerings? And if they recognize them, then we who are impersonating (the spirits) will also receive the benefit of the blessings of war and life (intended for the host).

"Long ago our ancestors asked (the spirits) to bless them so that, having been blessed with life, they might live happily. Here we are (sitting around) a fireplace and the life that they (host and his band) have asked for, the spirits not only are extending to them but to every one. In the early times the old men said, 'You are not able to fast and offer up proper food to the spirits so as to clear away the weapons (held) against you.'[112] Thus they spoke to them (the younger people). Just as (the older people would have liked it) so they are doing. I, who do not amount to anything, have nevertheless been permitted to take the place of a spirit to whom food is offered. This they have done for me, (given me the place) of that very spirit who is the very bravest of them all, the one who is in control of the power whereby one can kill (an enemy) outright! One side of his body controls life and the other death. Now they are about to offer him the food of a white animal, of a male animal (i. e., a dog), a white buckskin, feathers, and tobacco, all objects that please him very much. To Disease-giver they are about to extend these things, so that therewith they may ask him for war power and life. It is a fear-inspiring spirit that they have been making offerings to. I, who have listened to the spirits (through the host's kindness), surely don't have to say anything in their behalf.[113] They thought of their grandfather when they asked me to impersonate this spirit. Of all the spirits, his is the name that one can not speak of lightly, it is said. If I greet the name and speak about this spirit whom they have asked me to impersonate, may I not be weakened by uttering (his name). Those who are about to offer food to you, grandfather Disease-giver, send forth their greetings. To the host do I send forth my greetings. To the war-bundle owners who are seated here do I send forth my greetings."

---

[112] By denying that they can do it he tries to spur the young people to redoubled efforts. The weapons are the obstacles encountered in life.

[113] I. e., this feast will speak for them, more than any words I can utter.

Ė'gį ŭaŋgī'ją wōho'radjįrë'ra hīcge je'e' wo-ī'nǫbra hīradjī'ge nąjį-ā'nąga wak'ū'rųhintc rehī'ną wë'ną.

Speech of fifth guest.—"Warǫγī'ra hōk'įk'ā'radjɛra nīnaŋkcā'- waŋgera niŋk'ūrųhi'ndj rehā'wįną. Ė'gį wōnaŋkcī'na tcī-ō'jų mīna- ŋkcā'waŋgre niŋk'ū'rųhindjwī'na. Ėp'ī'ną. Ėp'ī'nį-ëgī'jį hąŋk'e'- hōsge waniŋk'djë'ra. Me'ë'caną gā'djųŋga ŭaŋkcik'į'yahaŋk'ā'dją sak'e'rẹra tejë'sge hīnaŋgre. ewa'ų'-įnẹge. Te jedjaį'ŋxdjį p'ā hįxgįxgį-āhaŋk'ā'dją hōtẹjī jë'sge hīnųxū'rukce sā'kerë'ra waxǫp'į'nį tanį-ō'gįjų warūp'īna ëwa'ū'-įnẹge. Hąŋk'e' waŋgage'- djani-ahā'ŋk'adją. Warǫγī' warųp'īną niŋk'djo'ŋgɛniŋgɛra hīnų'- ŋgera ŭaŋkci'k hūnųbi'maniṇa p'ëdjōk'e'rëją huŋgiwatcā'bwįra ë'gį k'erena'ŋgere. Huŋgiwatcā'bwįra p'ë'djerōk'ā'wak'aįrānąga. Hąŋk'e ë'caną wak'īk'ų'nįnaŋk'ā'dją. Te'jësge hī'naŋgre ẹje'e' hīnį-ąbā'haŋk'adją. Rek'ū'hųhį'ra rājera rajerehī'rare hąbįrųk'o'- noną ë'caną. Xetẹje' jë'sge hīp'ere'zįrẹge. Üaŋgenū'-iją waxǫp'- įnį hīk'īsgë'ją Djobenąŋgiwi'ŋxga hįgaī'regį rājɛra rajɛna'ŋgere. Waxǫp'į'nįna djānaga p'ī'ną hanąŋxdjįŋxdjį wōwë'wį k'īk'ere'- regį. Je'e' k'aradjįrā'naga waxǫp'į'nį kīk'arā'djɛnaŋgre. Hīsge'xdjį wā'naŋk'ā'dją ŭaŋgenū'nįŋgɛra nādjǫdjai'ṇẹgį hīgų' hąp te'e' ŭaŋkcigo'į' je'e' hī-ųnā'ŋk'adją. Wǫna'γirẹra djasage'xdjį nądjį- rǫdjai'ṇẹgį. Hąŋk'e' gīcdjaŋk'e' ranigā'dja. K'aratā'naŋgre hīsge'- xdjį wanaŋk'ā'dją wōk'araik'aī'rëcge. Hąŋk'e' hīk'arap'e'rezɛ- nįnaŋk'ā'dją te'jësge p'ewī'ną. Wa'īa'nąpcaną wōną'γirẹra ŭaŋkci'g'ǫ'īṇa hīraną'k'īk'į Rëk'ū'hųhįra. Tanį-ō'gijū-įrā'nąga tanī'na gīgįrā'nąga tcahā'sgara mącū'cụdjɛra hīrak'ī'rụtcap gīwahā'rehī'rare. Tanī'na k'arahi'ŋk'djonë'gadją gījį ŭaŋkci'- go'į'na hage'dja wīrō'naŋk hī'uŋk'djā'wira. Hōk'ī'k'aradjɛŋaŋgɛra waxǫp'į'nį hōnaŋkcį' gigī'rawįra. Hā'ụwį-ā'nąga ŭaŋkcigį'į p'į'- ŋxdjį hiŋgīgriā'wįra. Wa'įną'bwįną. Warǫγī'rẹra Rek'ū'hųhįra hak'ūrụhi'ndj rehā'nąga. Ė'gį warǫγī'ra niŋk'ūrụhi'ndj rehā'- wįdjįgǫ. Ė'gį wōnʌ'ŋkcįṇa tcī-ō'jų mīnaŋkcā'waŋgre niŋk'ūrụhi'ndj rehā'wįdjįgǫ.

Then another man who has been called upon for a kettle rises as the "means of blessing" comes to him and greeting, says to them.[114]

Speech of fifth guest.—"Clan councilors who are seated here, I greet you all. You all within this lodge who are impersonating the spirits, I greet you. It is good. If we say it is good, we mean it.[115] That we are living [116] is because they have done this for us (i. e., asked us to participate in the feast). That we have been able to move about so long (i. e., are still living) is due to the fact that the war-bundle owners knew how to offer tobacco to the spirits. It is for that reason likewise that we have not been killed. Expert in their preaching to the youths and maidens, our chiefs have also kept the fireplace for us two-legged walkers.[117] Our chiefs have piled more fuel upon the fire that it may start up.[118] And not for themselves are they doing this. What they are doing is to enable us to obtain life. The name of South Wind they have uttered; he who alone is in control of life. They knew that he was a great (spirit). An old man, one who was like a spirit (in his power), called Djōbenągiwi'ŋxga, they are speaking of. As many good spirits as there are, that many added their thoughts (power). Of this they are reminding the spirits whom they are worshiping. Sincerely are they saying it. The life they blessed the old man with, that life they are using. With war powers they blessed him. They did not fool him. Because they have made their requests sincerely is the reason that (the spirits) have given them these things in return. I feared that they might not take cognizance of them (i. e., their offerings). However, now I thank them (the host, etc.), for we have been as though connected with war power and life through South Wind. Tobacco they have poured for him, and white buckskin and red feathers have they extended to him. He will smoke the tobacco and we will follow in the path of life as a consequence. As though we were a member of their clan they have made us by (permitting us) to impersonate the spirits. What we have done will give us plenty of life to live on and for this we are indebted to them. We are thankful for it. Those who have been preached to, the South Wind I greet. Councilor (host), I send forth my greetings to you. You who are seated here and are impersonating the spirits, to you also do I send forth my greetings."

---

[114] By "the means of blessing" he means the opportunity to speak and sing.

[115] Literally, "It is not for nothing that we say this."

[116] I. e., have been blessed with life.

[117] The reference to the fireplace is twofold here. First as host it is incumbent for the owner of the Thunderbird clan bundle to take charge of the fireplaces; and, secondly, it is his duty to do so because fire is the sacred possession of the clan. "Two-legged walkers" is the ritualistic name for human beings.

[118] To be taken figuratively as meaning "blessings," since in adding fuel they are cooking the sacred food.

Hīcge ŭaŋgī'jᶏ wo̞honā'djir̞ẹra wo⁶ī'no̞bEra k'ara-ë'k'djonë'ra
wë'nᶏ.

Speech of sixth guest.—"Waro̞γī'ra hok'īk'ā'radjEra mīnaŋkcā'-
waŋgEre niŋk'ūru̞hindj rehā'wi̞djigo̞. Ë'gi̞ ji̞ge sā'k'ereni'ŋk'djoŋgera
mīnaŋkcā'waŋgre niŋk'ūru̞hindj rehā'wi̞djigo̞. Hōkī'wi̞k'aradjEra
waro̞γī' p'onaī'na wa⁶u̞'i̞na'nᶏga. Tcōk'agā' hagȃrë'jᶏ waigë'nᶏ.
Hagȃrë'jᶏ ŭaŋkci'g arēdji̞regī'ji̞. Waxo̞p'i̞'ni̞ tanī'na gīgī'regi̞.
Wōk'ë'ra djanᶏhī' mᶏtcā'naŋk'ī jenᶏ'hi̞ wak'ᶏtcā'ŋgᶏge. Nūnige
wap'aī'rasara hīdjōhaī'ne̞gi̞. Wap'ā'naŋk'a hᶏŋk'e' wadje'rasa
jë'sge rūdji̞ranī'je. Hᶏŋk'e' wap'ā'ra hinu̞'gEra wawi̞gī'ra e-ë'rani̞je
aī'rera. Wok'e' wak'ᶏtcā'ŋgEra hagȃrë'jᶏna wap'aī'rasara hījo̞haį'-
ne̞gi̞ji̞ ŭaŋkcik tcu̞cgū'ni̞ ānaga. Wōk'e' wak'ᶏtcā'ŋgera ni̞-ā'-
ni̞nᶏdji̞regī'ji̞ jedjerë'nᶏ haŋk'e' wōnᶏ'γi̞re rak'ī'p'īni̞-ā'nᶏga
hᴀŋk'e' waizā'ra hījᶏ' rak'īk'ūru̞xu̞'rugni̞-ā'nᶏga waxo̞p'i̞'ni̞ wajᶏji̞
wa⁶i̞nᴀ'ginᶏ'bge ë'ji̞ waī'zara hījᶏ' nᶏk'īk'ū'ru̞xu̞ru̞k'e' k'īji
waxo̞p'i̞'ni̞ wa⁶i̞nᶏ'ginᶏpgi waxo̞p'i̞'ni̞ warā'dji̞re̞ra nāni̞ŋxgu̞'-
nanȃna. C⁶agwahā'ra hi̞ŋgaī'ra nūni̞ge ëgi̞ji̞ ji̞ge waigaī'rënᶏ,
'Tcōk'āni̞ŋk,' wëje aī'rena. 'Waxo̞p'i̞'ni̞ wāna⁶į' rūsgītcgī'ji̞
ŭaŋgere'gerera mane̞'gir̞e̞ra. Ī'ra īrōk⁶ū'-i̞ne̞je waxo̞p'i̞'ni̞ waī're̞ge
woro'γi̞-o̞djā'djak'dje hi̞gaī'regi̞. Ī'ra hīrak'ī'ware hōk'īk⁶ŭᶏhū'-
i̞regi̞.' Ë'gi̞ hī-ā'ndjwahā'ra hīcge ī'ra hu̞ŋk⁶u̞'nege hi̞ŋgaī're̞ra.
Hawā⁶u̞' waxo̞p'i̞'ni̞ wa⁶īa'ŋgi̞naiŋk'dje̞ge hīhananȃ'na. Waxo̞p'i̞ni̞
waradji̞rë'jᶏ ni̞tā'k'atc gīgī'rare, waxo̞p'i̞'ni̞ xetë'jᶏ gi̞k'arā'-
dji̞rehī'regīji̞. Ni̞tā'k'atcrᶏ tanī'na wārūtc xō'p'i̞ni̞ tcahā'sgara
k'arap'i̞-e'sge gīrū'cdjᶏ rehī'rare. Hᶏbi̞taī'⁶u̞na hᶏbik'ā'rataī're̞ra.
Në wō'naŋkci'ŋk'djawi̞ra sak'ere̞ganaį'xdji̞-aŋge. Nūni̞ge në wajᶏ-
harë'regi̞ ŭaŋkcik⁶į'. Ŭanᶏdjo̞djaį'sge ha⁶ŭahā'ŋgwi̞ra ŭaŋkci-
go̞⁶i̞'na hīranᶏ'k'īk⁶i̞ŋk'djā'wi̞ra hōwarë'ra. Hīto-ā'k'īk⁶i̞ŋxdji̞'-
wi̞nᶏ. Wīgi̞p'erezeregī'ji̞ nīcge ŭaŋkcigo̞⁶į'na ë'dja yā⁶u̞ŋk'djā'-
wi̞ra. Hōk'ī'wik'arā'djEni̞ŋkra hak'īk⁶u̞'ŋxdji̞ ā'nᶏga. Ëp'i̞ŋ-
gā'dja. Waro̞γī're̞ra Wīragō'cge Xe'tera hak'ū'ru̞hindj rehā'nᶏga.
Ë'gi̞ waro̞γī'ra hōk'ī'wik'arā'djEra mīnaŋkcā'waŋk'a niŋk'ūru̞hi'-

THE CLAN WAR-BUNDLE FEASTS

Then another man to whom a kettle has been given gets ready to express his thankfulness and says:

Speech of sixth guest.—"Host and members of your clan who are seated here, I send forth my greetings to you. To you also, war-bundle owners who are seated here, do I send forth my greetings. The members of this clan have often preached to me. My grandfather once told me the following: 'Some day there will be a dearth of people (for a feast). There they will offer tobacco to the spirits and as many pieces of meat as they cut that many will be holy. There also they will cook heads. Heads are not to be eaten by those wearing dresses (i. e., women). Women are not permitted to scatter their food in eating, we are told.[119] Some day if they boil these holy pieces, the heads, they will be in need of people to invite to the feast. If they call upon you for one of the sacred pieces, even if at that time you had not yet obtained a war honor, if you had not counted coup,[120] still if you offer up thanks to the spirits for anything; still more so, of course, if you had been able to count coup and you thanked them for all this, they will listen to you.'[121] My grandfather told me, 'Thus they spoke to me,' he said, it is said, 'Little grandfather, the spirits up above gave (your ancestor) a war bundle to those of the Earth phratry. They gave them a mouth for speaking (in offering thanks), but they told him that it was forbidden to speak to outsiders about this matter. They gave them a mouth that they might speak to one another (i. e., members of the same clan)'.

"My father gave the information to me. For that reason, they told me, I am in a position to thank the spirits. One of the greatest of the spirits they have offered tobacco to, to one of the greatest of the spirits they have prayed. Tobacco, food, a sacred white buckskin, pleasing to their eyes, they have extended to them. With offerings of life[122] they have asked for life. We have been asked to impersonate (the spirits), even although there are plenty of war-bundle owners. But the host is a relative of ours and therefore wishes me to live. A pitiable existence we had been living (until they saw to it) that we were brought into connection with life. Proud we are of it. For if they (the spirits) accept their gifts, we also will be able to utilize the life (obtained). Clan members, we did as we pleased here. It is good. Those preached to, the Morning Star,

[119] In eating the deer head and in the fast-eating contest the meat is devoured so fast that the food is literally scattered in the process of eating. Whether there is an implied warning that a man should not be found in the same class as the women I do not know positively, but it is quite likely.

[120] Literally, "a limb." The four coup counts are likened to the four limbs of the human body. As such they are always referred to.

[121] The whole meaning of the speech up to the present is the following: Should they in the future want to give a feast and lack of the proper people cause them to call upon you, even if you had counted coup only once, the spirits would listen to you. And yet here I am and haven't even counted coup once and yet I have the effrontery to expect them to listen to me.

[122] I. e., with offerings of deer and dogs.

ndjwīna. Ė'gị wōnaŋkcī'ṇa mīnaŋk'cā'waŋgre niŋk'ūruhindj rehā'-wịdjịgō.

Ŭaŋgera hak'e'we wahoṇā'djịrẹra hīro-ā'genịxdjị hīrak'e'wera wë'nʌ.

Speech of seventh guest.—"Waroγī'ra wajō'k'ịna mīnaŋkcā'waŋk'a niŋk'ūruhindjwī'nʌ. Ė'gị wajā̧'nịjạ e tūxū'rugEnị nūnịge rōhī'ra haŋk'e' wa'ịŋk'īnobrā'jị wajị'ṇohī'ranịje aī'rera. Jë'sge wage-wahë'k'djonẹgā'dja. Ŭaŋkcigoị'' hīrak'ī'racdjạ'nʌgi haŋk'e' wajịṇohī'ranịje aī'rera. Jë'sge p'ẹ'wiŋge. Hagaī'ra wok'e' wak'ạtcā̧'ŋgera hījā̧ wō'naŋkcị hiŋgịgī'rẹra wa'īnʌbrā'jị hiŋk'-īhahā̧'xdjịconū'nʌ. Haŋk'e' wōnʌ'γịre ëwagī'gi tūxū'rugEnị'-k'djena. Nūnịge ŭaŋkcigo'ị'na hīranạ'k'īk'ị 'ŭiṇā'wịra. WōnʌA'-γịre rūk'o'nonʌ xetë'jạ wōgịhaị'ṇẹra hō'naŋkcị gīgī'rawira. Ėp'iŋgā'djạ waxọp'ị'nị wa'iŋgī'nʌbra rōk'īγī'rëjạ aira nūnịge hā̧bịrak'ī'racdjonʌ rọhī'ra ha-ë'kinʌ jë'jị haŋk'e' wajī'ṇohịrā'nị gādjạ. Yarā'nʌga waihëconaŋgā'djạ wa'iyā'nʌpdjị. Nūnịge wajā'nịjạ ë tụxū'ruk'ī'jị wīrọto' wahā'nạje. Hitcō'k'ewahī'wịra hā̧banī'hụra hābō'k'ahi hū'djaṇe wōna'γịre hīrụk'o'no xe'tera ŭaŋkcigo'ị' hīrụk'o'naịjā, tanī'ṇa wōhọ'ṇa k'arap'ị-e'sgexdjị nā̧bịruxā'djEra tcahā'sgara wak'e'rẹra mejë'nụga gīrụ̄'cdjạ rehī'-regị. Wōhọ'ṇa në waxọp'ị'nị hōnaŋkci'ŋk'djera hiŋgai'rẹra. Wa'ịya'nʌpdjī'nʌ djā'nʌga wak'īk'ā'radjEniŋgwī'nʌ stō-ā'k'īwī-ā'nʌga hā̧bitaī''ụṇa jë'nụgāniŋk waxọp'ị'nị hōnaŋkci'wịnʌ. Ep'iŋgā'djạ. Wok'e-ō'niŋgeregị haitcerarë'cge rōk'o'no iyarā'-noŋgEra te'ë'jị waxọp'ị'nịna wajīṇụk'onaī'ja wọhʌ'gịk'e'reregị në wōnaŋkci' gīgịrā'wịra Wa'īyā'nʌbwịnʌ. Waroġī'γịrẹra hak'ūrụhi'ndj rehā'nʌga. Ė'gị waroγira wakuruhindj anaga. Waxopini wonaŋkcina tci-oju mīnaŋkcā'waŋgre niŋk'ūrụhi'ndj rehā'wịnʌ.

Te'e' jëgụ'hịregị wa'ī'nạbra hanā̧'tcị aī'regị ëgị hōracdjai'jạ wagigō'nʌŋk'a hicgi-ā'ga nạjị-ā'nʌga wa'inʌ'pcanʌ.

Terminal speech of host.—"Sā'k'ereniŋk'djoŋgera mīnaŋkcā'waŋgre niŋk'ūrụhi'ndj rehā'wịnʌ. Ėp'iŋgā'dja. Djagū'xdjiniŋk rū-ā'gụ wa'ụanʌ'gwịra. Hōk'ī'wik'ā'radjEra hanā̧'tciŋxdjị hōgīgâ'ra.

I send forth my greetings. To the host and all the clansmen sitting with him, do I send forth my greetings. To those who are impersonating the spirits I also send forth my greetings."

Then the sixth one for whom a kettle has been placed, the last one, speaks.[123]

Speech of seventh guest.—"Host and your relatives who are seated here, I greet you all. I am not able to say anything (i. e., I don't amount to anything), but I can at least thank for the body.[124] It is no harm to do so, we are told.[125] That is what I mean and why I say it. To speak of life is surely no harm, we are told.[126] Thus I thought. If ever I obtained the position of one who impersonated (a spirit) and (partook) of a sacred piece of food, I felt that I would be beside myself with thankfulness and gratitude. Not of war power will such as I be able to speak. In spite of that, they have seen to it that I came in connection with life. They have permitted me to impersonate one of the spirits who is among the greatest in the control of war power. It is good to thank the spirits and at the same time to preach to one another, it is said. To speak to one another of life and of the body(?) certainly there is no harm in it. Thus I thought, and that is why I am saying this. I am very thankful. If I could only say something (that would be of any value) to the spirits I would say it. You, grandfather, who come every day, you who are in control of great war power and life, tobacco, food, an offering of a white buckskin pleasing to the spirits, and a head ornament—that is about to be sent toward you. I was to be one of those impersonating the spirits at the feast, they told me. I am deeply grateful for the honor, to all those of the various clans that are gathered together here with offerings and who are impersonating the spirits. It is good. Even had I eaten a common piece of meat I would have considered myself well repaid, but I have actually been put in charge of a spirit who controls something. We are thankful. To those to whom we preached (i. e., the Sun) I send forth my greetings. To the host I send forth my greetings. To those who are sitting in the lodge impersontaing the spirits I send forth my greetings."

When they are through greeting each other, at the end, the host rises and thanks them, saying:

Terminal speech of host.—"War-bundle owners who are seated here, I greet you all. What I long for is exactly what we have been doing. All the members of the various clans have pleaded for us in

---

[123] This is a mistake of the informant. It should be the seventh one. He seems, however, not to be counting the person who partakes of food offered to Earthmaker.

[124] I. e., the dog(?).

[125] I. e., there is no harm done if even a worthless person like myself thanks for the food of the dog, even although by doing this he is actually taking part in the feast.

[126] I. e., there is no harm in obtaining life for one another by delivering speeches and offering up prayers to the spirits.

P'iŋxdjị hiŋgigī'rawịra. Ė'p'iŋgādjạ. Djagū'xdjị ŋọ-ā'gụ waᶜŭa'-nᴀgwịra hanặ'tciŋxdjị p'ị'xdjị ụgịgaī'rawịra. Ėp'iŋgā'djạ warọgī'-gọgị djagū' rōrā'gụ wacᶜū'conọgᴇra. Sā'k'erẹra djā'nᴀgā'k'ī hānặ'-tciŋxdjị huŋgịgaī'rẹra. Ėp'iŋgā'djạ wajᴀ'ŋa xū'rug. P'ịŋxdjị wahị-bịrā'nᴀga. Ėp'ī'nᴀ p'iŋxdji. Tcëbịnagī'gịwịra haizā'xdjị tcëbwa-irā'gịgịwịra. Cᶜagwarā'wịga waxọp'ị'nị hoīt'etᶜe' nặdjwawịrodjaī' ŋẹgị hanặ'tciŋxdjị wawī'rak'aracawi-ā'nᴀga wajạ' ŋaxū'rug p'ị'xdjị wacā'wira. Ėp'ī'nᴀ wa'yā' nᴀbwịnᴀ ĵë'sge rū-ā'gụ waᶜŭā'nᴀgwī'ra.'' "Sā'kereni'ŋk'djoŋgere mīnaŋkcā'waŋgre nirk'ūrụhi'ndj rehā'-wịdjịgō'.''

SECOND DIVISION OF THE CEREMONY—IN HONOR OF THE NIGHT SPIRITS

Introductory remarks.—Ė'gị wọhọ'ŋa hīnụbọ'hoŋa hīdjọwak'ere'-regị warūtcᴀ'na wōhaịk'ịce'rẹra. Hoicibi'regị ë'gị wōhọ'ŋa waxọp'ị'nị djagū'cᴀnᴀ wagịrū'cdjaŋehịrëk'djanë'gị ĵëgụhī'regị ëgị wagịgō'nᴀk'a tanịwọgī'jụra ᶜu-ịk'ârọhō'gị taniwaxū'nᴀ. Wë'je.

THE TOBACCO OFFERING

Offering to the Night Spirits.—"Tcōk'agā' Djōbenᴀŋgịwi'ŋxga nặdjō-radjặ'gịjị hặbọgure'regerë'ra hặhẹ' huŋgera tcī'jạ wōgụ'zọtcịra ha'cinịwịŋgiji. Wak'ặtcᴀ'ŋk rak'aragị-aradjë'gị. Nặdjịrọrā'djạwī'je ë'ra. Hagârë'janᴀ tanị-ọwaxū'nᴀ hiŋgī'rẹwịgị tanī'ŋa hōjū'-ịjạ niŋgịp'axụ'wị-ānᴀga. Wōnᴀ'ɣịrẹra tcōk'agā' djagū' gịp'ị' ᶜuŋk'-dje. Nặdjịrọrā'djạwịgị je'e' hakaratā'wịnᴀ. Tcōk'a' hặhẹ' huŋgra tanī'ŋa te'e'rënᴀ.''

"Tcī-ōk'īsakọnᴀjị'ŋẹgị hīdje' niŋgigī'gị hoici'pdjị. Wōgụ'zọtcị wak'atcᴀ'ŋk hacī'nịwị-ë'dja tanī'ŋa wōhọ'ŋa wā'rūtc xōp'ịnị hīrarū'tcap wagūdjẹ'ra sī'jạ, te ĵë'nụga niŋgịtūcdjanëhā'wịnᴀ.''

Offering to Earth.—"Ė'gị Mana hīk'ârok'e'nịwịha, tcok'agā' Djōbenᴀŋgịwi'ŋxga niŋgịtā'wịnᴀ wọnᴀ'ɣịrẹra ŭaŋkcigọ-ị'ŋa niŋgịtā'-wịnᴀ. Djadjaī'ŋxdjị p'ā mīcā'naŋk'e jedjaị'ŋxdjị p'ā tanī'ŋa nịtā'k'adjᴇra wagūdjẹ'ra sī'jạ te ĵë'nụga k'ūnịk'ā niŋgịtū'cdjạ rehā'wịnᴀ.''

Tanī'ŋa te'e'rëna.

"Hītcōk'īsā'gᴇnᴀjī'ŋa ë'dja hīdje' niŋgigīgī'nᴀ wōhọ'ŋa nặbịrūxa'-djᴇra waniŋgịtū'cdjạ rehā'wịre. Hoici'pdjị hīrak'a'rap'erez ranịcā'-k'djonë'je tcōk'agā ë'je aī'rera. Wak'īk'ā'radjwịra wōnᴀ'ɣịrẹra ŭaŋkcigọ'ị'ŋa hīrak'-ī'īroī'tcᴀ wawë'k'djawịx.

song. Very good have they been to us. It is good. This is what I have longed for, what we have been doing and all the good they have said about us. It is good when you give a feast to do just what you wish. The war-bundle owners, as many as there are here, have spoken for me. It is good to obtain something when asking for it. Very well have they spoken. It is good; it is very good. You have eaten (the food) in my behalf; very carefully have you eaten it up for me. All the sacred speeches that they blessed him (our grandfather) with you have repeated so that you might obtain real life, you said. It is good and I thank you, for we have done here exactly what I have longed for. War-bundle owners who are seated here, I greet you."

SECOND DIVISION OF THE CEREMONY—IN HONOR OF THE NIGHT SPIRITS

Introductory remarks.—Then the attendants get ready to put on the kettles for the second feast. When they are finished arranging the food that is to be turned over to the spirits the host prepares his tobacco and gets ready to pour it. Then he speaks the following:

THE TOBACCO OFFERING

Offering to the Night Spirits.—"To you, grandfather Djobenąŋgiwi'ŋxga, does the council lodge of the Chief of the Night Spirits, standing in the east, belong. Holy you have kept it. You (Chief of the Night Spirits) were the one who blessed him with it, he said. When the time comes for the tobacco pouring we will offer you a handful of tobacco. War power he liked to obtain by doing this. With what you blessed him, that we ask you to give us in return. Grandfather, Chief of the Night Spirits, tobacco, here it is.

"Here in the fire I shall place tobacco for you at all times. Tobacco, holy food, and buckskin for moccasins, all those things I will send to your sacred creation lodge."

Offering to Earth.—"You who are our grandmother, Earth, you blessed grandfather Djobenąŋgiwi'ŋxga with life and war powers. As far as you extend, that far, O grandmother, do we spread out for you tobacco and food and moccasins. Here is the tobacco. Here in the fire shall I place tobacco; and food and offerings of buckskin will we send to you at all times. You will always accept them, grandfather said, it is said, so that our clansmen may travel in a straight path of war and life." [127]

---

[127] That is, may nothing intervene to prevent them from enjoying all the blessings they have received in war and life.

Offering to the Moon.—"Niŋgitā'wįnᴀ ë'gį k'ū'nįk'a. Hīcge
tcōk'agā' Djōbenᴀŋgiwi'ŋxga wāna'ı̨'ṇagįk'ere'regį waragę'je
djadjaı̨'ŋxdjį p'ā maiŋk'ī'djᴀ hōniŋgᴇra' djadjaī'ŋxdjį p'ā
ranįcë'gį jedjai'ŋxdjį p'ā tanī'ṇa hōjū'-įjᴀ hiŋgiwaxū'-įṇegį hoici'-
pdjį wa'ī'nᴀp wagįk'i-ā'nįhëk'djonën'ᴀ. Hīrak'ī'gęje aī'ręra.
Tanī'na ga airędjįgō'."

"Djānᴀga hōk'ī'wįk'aradjᴇra ŭaŋkcik'į' ŭānᾳdjọdjai'sge ha'ŭ-
ahᴀ'ŋgwįra wōnᴀ'ɣįręra hīrak'ī'roitcᴀ wawë'kdjawįra, te'jësge
niŋgitā'wįnᴀ nįtā'kadjᴇra wagụdje'ra sī'jᴀ mejë'nụga niŋgitū'cdjᴀ
rehā'wina. Tcọwe'regį gāgụ' tëk'djanįhā're wōnᴀ'ɣįręra ŭaŋkcigọ'ī'ṇa ya'uŋk'djā'wį."
Offering to the Water.—"Ě'gį jįge nī'na huŋge rōni-anī'wįṇęra tcōk'-
agā' Djōbenᴀŋgiwi'ŋxga nᾳdjọradjọ'ŋgį. Gā eredjįgō'.
"Tanī'ṇa tcī-ọk'įsā'k hōnajį'ṇęgį niŋgip'axụ'gįjį, rak'arahī'
ranįcë'k'djonë'je hīrak'ī'geje, aī'rera. Nįtā'k'adjᴇra wagụdję'ra
sījᴀ niŋgitū'cdjanįhā'wįnᴀ. Wōnᴀ'ɣįręra ŭaŋkcigọ'ı̨'ṇa te'e'-
niŋgitā'wįnᴀ hoici'p hīrak'ā'rap'erezdanë'je tcōk'agā' ëra.
Tcōk'agā' Djōbenᴀŋgiwi'ŋxga hīcge tanį-ō'waxụ niŋgī'k'erëk'djā'wį
hīrak'ī'gęje aī'rera. Ga airędjįgō'."

"Tanī'ṇa hōjū'-įjaįcge hīrak'ā'rap'eresk'e hīrak'ī'gęje aī'rera
wōhọ'ṇa tanī'ṇa hīrasā' niŋgitū'cdjᴀ rehā'wįnᴀ. Ŭaŋkcigọ'ı̨'ṇa
wōna'ɣįręra wak'ī'k'aradjwįra te'jësge rọ-ā'gọ'ı̨'ṇa."
Offering to North Wind.—"Ě'gį jįge' waxᴀhī'ṇa tcōk'agā'
waragë'je rōhᾳ'bọt'e'k'ı̨-ë'dja hī'upⁱ-ā'nįnᴀ, hīrëk'ī'gęje aī'rera.
'Wazī'rëgį hohirare cge wak ip i na!' Tcōk'agā' hīragë'je ëra.
Wagip'axụ'wįgį hiŋgirë'wįgį hīcge wagip'axụ'wįgį niŋgįk'e'rëk'-
djawį hīrakī'ge gījī. Tanī'ṇa ga airedjigo."
"Wotā'tcōnī'ṇa wōnᴀ'ɣįręra ŭaŋkcigọ'ı̨'ṇa te'jësge niŋgitā'-
wįnᴀ."
Offering to the Pigeon-Hawk.—"Ě'gį jįge K'ⁱrįk' īrįkī'sgęra tanī'ṇa
ga ëredjįgō'. Tcōk'agā' wōnᴀ'ɣįręra ŭaŋkcigọ'ı̨'ṇa nᾳdjirọrā'djoŋgī'-
gįjį hoici'pdjį niŋgitā'wįgį c'ūnanįcë'k'djane hīrak'ī'gęje tcōk'agā'
hīrak'ī'gęje ë'je aī'rera."
Offering to Earthmaker.—"Mᾳ'ụṇa taninā'cᴀnᴀ wagīp'ā'xụwįgį
taninā'cᴀnᴀrë'cge. Ěraitcë'raje hīcęje' aī'rera. Tanī'ṇa hōjū'-įjᴀ
wagip'axụ'wįgį."
Offering to the Thunderbird.—"Ě'gį wakandjā'ra taninā'cᴀnᴀ
niŋgip'axụ'-īcge. Ěraitcë'rak'djanë'je hicęje' aī'rera. Tanīṇā'-
cᴀnᴀ wagīp'ā'xụwįgį."

Offering to the Moon.—"This we ask, grandmother, of you also. You added your power to (the other blessings) of grandfather Djobenąŋgiwi'ŋxga and you said that as long as the world lasts you would willingly accept the offerings of tobacco that his posterity extended to you. Thus you yourself said, we are told. Here is the tobacco.

"As many of our clansmen as are here living in an abject condition (spiritually), may they all follow in the direct path of war. For that we are now extending to you tobacco, food, and moccasins. And may we in the future travel in the path of war and life."

Offering to the Water.—"You likewise, Chief of the Water, whose body is water, blessed grandfather Djōbenąŋgiwi'ŋxga. Here it is (the tobacco). If we poured tobacco into the fire, you said you would always smoke it, it is said. Food and buckskin for moccasins we are about to extend to you. War powers and life, that we ask from you in return, for you said that you would always accept (our offerings), we are told. When you blessed grandfather Djōbenąŋ-giwi'ŋxga you said that we should pour tobacco for you at all times, it is said. Here it is.

"You would recognize the offering of tobacco and the tobacco with the food that we sent forth to you, you said, it is said. We desire war powers and life for our kinsmen."

Offering to North Wind.—"You likewise, Porcupine,[128] told grandfather, 'For killing an enemy outright, I am useful, it is said. I am even the equal of the one who blows from the north!' Thus you told grandfather, it is said. When the proper time has arrived we should pour tobacco. Tobacco, here it is.

"Our first request is for war power and life."

Offering to the Pigeon-Hawk.—"Here is tobacco for you, too, Pigeon-Hawk. You blessed grandfather with war and life and it is said you told him that you would always give him what we asked of you."

Offering to Earthmaker.—"For Earthmaker, who is the foremost, you said we should pour tobacco, so for him we (pour) tobacco.[129] A handful of tobacco we are about to offer to you (Earthmaker)."

Offering to the Thunderbird.—"To you, also, Thunderbird, I am about to pour tobacco. It will be one of the foremost offerings, you said, it is said. Tobacco we pour to you."

---

[128] Porcupine is also associated with the North Wind in the first division of the ceremony.

[129] I. e., we even have the effrontery to offer him tobacco as if people like ourselves could ever obtain a blessing from so great a deity as Earthmaker! The order in which the offerings to the various spirits are made is rather peculiar, for that to Earthmaker should, I believe, come first. I suspect that my informant was probably in error in the arrangement given above, a fact easily explained when it is remembered that he tried to visualize a ceremony he had not given for some time.

Offering to Big Black Hawk.—"Ë'gị jịge K'eredjụ'sep xetera' tanī'ṇa hōjū'-ịjạ wịgịp'āxụwī'cịdjịgō`."

Offering to Disease-giver.—"Ë'gị jịge Hocere⁶ụ'wahịra tcōk'ā' tanī'ṇa hōjū'-ịjạ taniṇā'caṇạ reniŋgịgī'nạ."

Offering to South Wind.—"Ë'gị Rek'ū'hụhịra tcōk'ā' taniṇā'-caṇạ wīgịp'axụ'wịgị taniṇā'canarë`cge. Ë hīraitcë'ra raik'araī'p-djoṇe hīceje' aī'rera."

Offering to the Sun.—"Tanī'ṇa hīdje' niŋgịgī'nạ tcōk'ā' hạbanị-hū'ra. Tanī'ṇa hōjū'-ịjạ taniṇā'canaxdjị` hīdje' niŋgīgī'nạ."

BASIC RITUAL

Host's first speech.—"Sā'k'ereni`ŋkdjoŋgEra mīnaŋkcā'waŋgre ni-ŋk'ūrụhi'ntc rehā'wịnạ. Hōk'ā'was Manī'ṇa hōnịhā'ra · tcok'agā' djāsge gīk'ererẹ'gị Tcīwoit⁶ẹ'hịga Hōk'ā'was Manī'ṇa wawī'p'erez na⁶iŋgī'jị. Hạtā'gịnạdjā`nạga īwust⁶ẹ'k'iŋgị hītcō'k'ehịwahī`wịra mạ⁶ā'k'ī wāna⁶ị'ŋgịk'ere`regịjị. Tcōk'agā' Tcīwoit⁶ẹ'hịga wë'je, nịŋgị-ọwadjī'jạ hereje' hịk'īgë'je hạbọgụregịnā'ŋgEre hạhẹ' hīyuŋgī'wịnạ ë ⁶ūnịhë'je ëgị jịge sā'niŋk yoire'rẹgị wak'ā'ndja huŋgra hīniŋkhī'gị ë anạ'tc hī'je ë'sge mạ⁶ā'k'ī c⁶agwahī. Nūnịge' wagī'nạtcgị p'ịhī' nạdjōdjaī'ṇeje. Ë'sge hagârë'jạ t⁶ẹgījī' mạ⁶ā'k'ī họrak'djë'k'djonëje ë'je airë'nạ. Ë'sge hōnịhā' gụ'se hạhẹ' nạwạ'ṇa djagū'xdjị ëgī'jị jë'sge tūxū'rụik'djawī`je. Nū'nịge hōnịhā'ra hījạ'ŋk'īra hīrap'e'resgī`cge haŋk'e' hịtcge' warā'niŋk'djonë'nạ; hījạŋk'ī'ra hīrap'e'resgị ë'caṇạ hawërā'-īcge γak'ịnbErā'gị hīgụ' erë'nạ. Haŋk'e' tō-ị' wacā'niŋk'djonë'nạ wōna'γịre haxī'rị ŭaŋkcigọ⁶ị' haxī'rị wacëk'djonë'nạ aī'rëŋạ. Jë'sge wahëk'djoneḥā'wịgā`djạ.

Sā'k'ereni`ŋk'djoŋgEre mīnaŋkcā'waŋgre niŋk'ūrụhi'ntc rehā'-wịnạ." (Hạjẹ' Nạwạ.)

Host's second speech.—"Sā'k'ereni'ŋk'djoŋgera mīnaŋkcā'waŋgre niŋk'ūrụhi'ndj rehā'wịdjịgọ. Ë'gị hak'araī'sundjwịgị ë'gị hīnaŋgī'-djịcerëk'djā`wịra c⁶agwarā'wịga hōnịhā'ra waxọp'ị'nị hōk'īrā'ra djagū' adjī'regị waworak'ā'rak'īcarā`k'djạwịra. Jësge niŋgịtā'-wịnạ. Hīwacī'niŋera tcạt⁶ị' wahairā'nạga ë'gị tacdjạ'wịgị

Offering to Big Black Hawk.—"To the Big Black Hawk we also offer a handful of tobacco."

Offering to Disease-giver.—"To you, grandfather Disease-giver, I also send tobacco."

Offering to South Wind.—"To you, also, grandfather South Wind, I send tobacco. You would consider it foremost, you said, it is said."

Offering to the Sun.—"Here I place tobacco for you, too, grandfather Sun. A handful of tobacco here I place here for you."

BASIC RITUAL

Host's first speech.—"War-bundle owners who are sitting here, I greet you. The songs that the Night Spirits placed within the reach of grandfather Tcīwoit'e'higa,[130] those he tried to learn. He fasted and thirsted himself to death for the blessings our grandfathers (the Night Spirits) gave him (spread) over the length of the earth. Our grandfather Tcīwoit'e'higa said that he had come from somewhere in the east and that a Night Spirit chieftainess was his mother and that the son of the chief of the Thunderbirds was his father; that his parents lived beyond the confines of this earth.[131] When he fasted to be blessed by (these spirits) over again,[132] they blessed him. If at any time he should die he would be able to visit the earth again, he said, it is said.[133] The song he was taught, the Night Spirit song, that we will try to sing. Even if you know only one song, you will not bore them (the spirits) with it; for if you bring yourself to the state of weeping in your efforts, it will be (acceptable). If you do not put on any embellishments when you pray (literally, cry) for war and life (it will be acceptable), it is said. Thus we should say it.

"War-bundle owners who are seated here, I greet you." (Night Spirit song.)

Host's second speech.—"War-bundle owners who are seated here, I greet you. When we finish (our part of the ceremony), may you help us by repeating the spirit songs your ancestors gave you to be handed down (from one generation to another). That we ask of you. Now we will start a dance song and when we are finished singing, our

---

[130] Literal translation, "Kills within the lodge."

[131] What Tcīwoit'e'higa means by saying that these spirits were his parents is that he is a reincarnated spirit that has chosen to be born of human parents. Such claims were by no means rare even in late Winnebago history and there is, as a matter of fact, a powerful shaman living in Wisconsin now who claims that he is the reincarnated Hare (Wacdjinge'ga).

[132] Before coming to the earth as a human being, he had of course been told that he would receive certain blessings, but nevertheless he had to fast for them just as a human being does. However, shamans who obtained their powers in this way were always supposed to obtain them more easily than other people. For an illustration of this cf. the account of a shaman's blessing in the "Reminiscences of a Winnebago Indian" by myself in Amer. Jour. Folklore, XXVI, 1913.

[133] That is, become reincarnated.

ë′gi̧ hītcōk′i̧wahī′wi̧ra wīdjā′dja tcabi̧rë′ra manī′ṇ ̈ek′djë ̔ra.   Jë′sge
ni̧ngi̧tā′wi̧nʌ.   Sā′k′ereni ̔ŋk′djoŋgɛre mīnaŋkcā′waŋgre ni̧ŋk′ūru̧hi′-
ndj rehawi̧djigō′.''   (Nʌ̧′wʌ̧ Hīwacī′ra.)
Hak′araisu′ndji̧regi̧.

   Host's third speech.—''Ë′gi̧ sā′k′ereni ̔ŋk′dː̧oŋgɛra mīnaŋkcā′-
waŋgre ni̧ŋk′ūru̧hi′ndj rehā′wi̧nʌ.   Hōk′ā′raga nʌ̧′inī′sge wa-
ʿŭanʌ̧′ŋgwi̧ra jedjai̧′ŋxdji̧ p′ā jë′gu̧ hīdje′ hawi̧-ā′nʌga.   Ë′gi̧
hīraniķ′ī′k′ūru̧xë ̔k′djonehā ̔wi̧je. ̔ Hi̧hë′ra wīrǫrā′gɛra manī′-
ṇ ̈ek′djera jë′sge hōni̧ngī′tawi̧nʌ.   Sā′k′ereni ̔ŋk′djoŋgɛra mīnaŋkcā′-
waŋgre ni̧ŋk′ūru̧hi′ndj rehā′wi̧djigǫ.''
   ''Ë′gi̧ tcëk′djī′ṇa sā′ni̧ŋk hoiratcge′ hǫwā′rëje ṇ ̈ëγârupâ′rogɛra
warūtcā′naŋk′ā hījʌ̧′ waʿu̧je′ rūhā′k′erëje.   Sā′k′erejʌ̧ hōwahīre-
gi̧nā′ŋk′ī ë′dja hītce′gīgi̧gi̧gi̧ tcōwehī-ë′dja gīk′ereje′ p′eγ sǫ′soγra
wīrō′ragɛra m ̇īnaŋkcā′waŋk′a.   E′gi̧ tanī′ṇa nʌ̧bō′ju̧ gigī′je.''
   Speech of first guest.—''Warǫγī′ra hōk′ī′k′aradjɛra mīnaŋkcā′-
waŋgre ni̧ŋkūru̧hi′ndj rehā′wi̧djigǫ.   Ë′gi̧ hōnaŋkcī′ṇa waxǫp′i̧′ni̧
tcījū mīnaŋkcā′waŋgre ni̧ŋk′ūru̧hi′ndj rehā′wi̧djigǫ.   Ëp′i̧ŋā′djʌ̧.
Warǫγī′ra hītcō′k′ewahī′wi̧ra tani̧wǫgī′ju̧ hi̧ŋgigī′rare.   Hōk′ā′was
Manī′ṇa hʌ̧bǫgū′regi̧rȩra tcōk′agā′ hīcge wāna ̔i̧′gi̧k′erë ̔reje
hī′k′i̧gë ̔je aī′rera.   Hagârë′jʌ̧ hōni̧hā′ra tcʌ̧t ̔i̧′ wagī′gi̧k′djonā′-
wi̧gi̧ tanī′ṇa hagip′ā′xu̧wī′ge hi̧ŋk′ā′rap′erezī ̔k′djonëje, ë′je aī′rera.
Tanī′ṇa hōgū′-i̧jʌ̧ hagip′axu̧′ŋk′djonā ̔re k′arahī′je gīji̧.   Hōk′ī′-
wi̧k′aradjɛra warǫγī′ra ŭanʌ̧djǫdjai̧′sge waʿu̧naŋgre hīcge′
ŭanʌ̧djǫdjai̧′sge wahanaŋk′ā′dja wīgip′e′rezi̧rā ̔nʌga, tanī′ṇa hīcge
hi̧ŋgip′e′rezi̧rë ̔gi̧ wōk′ī′dji̧rë ̔jʌ̧ hereje aī′rera Jë′sge p′ewi̧-ā′nʌga.
Wīrǫrā′gera tcʌ̧t ̔i̧′ djīrehā′k′djonare waxǫp′i̧′ni̧ nāŋxgū′ṇe p′īnʌ̧′-
ŋkce nūni̧ge hōni̧hā′ra djagū′adjī′regi̧ jë′sge hōtā′tcgʌ̧ŋk′djonā ̔re.
Hījʌ̧′ŋxdji̧ hīsgë′ra hatūxū′rugānʌga ʿu̧ŋgī′ji̧.   Hitcō′k′ewahī ̔wi̧ra
Hōk′ā′was Manī′ṇa wōhǫ′ṇa tanī′ṇa nʌ̧bīru̧xā′djɛra naixdjī′na
wawi̧gī′p′erzi̧rëjë ̔je.   Hire wahë′k′djā ̔wi̧nʌ.   Warǫγī′ra hōk′ī′-
wi̧k′aradjɛra mīnaŋkcā′waŋgre ni̧ŋk′ūru̧hi′ndj rehā′wi̧nʌ.   Ë′gi̧
waxǫp′i̧′ni̧ hōnaŋkcī′ṇa djā′nʌga mīnaŋkcā′waŋgrë ̔cge ni̧ŋk′ūru̧-
hi′ndj rehā′wi̧djigǫ.''   (Hʌ̧hȩ′ Nʌ̧wʌ̧.)

   Second speech of first guest.—''Mʌ̧ʿu̧ṇa hōk′araī′ci̧pgi̧ hīdjā′-
gi̧kerȩ ̔ranaŋk′a wë′je.   Waroγī′ra hōk′ī′wik′aradjera mīnaŋkcā′-

grandfather, the drum, will start to walk (in your direction).[134] That we ask of you (i. e., to help us also in our dancing). War-bundle owners who are seated here, I greet you." (Dance song.)

When the dancing is finished the host speaks again.

Host's third speech.—"War-bundle owners who are seated here, I greet you. We are now trying to do our best to attract (the spirits' attention) to what we are doing and that is why we are placing (the drum) (in front of the guests). What I said about the messenger who is about to walk,[135] that I am going to speak of to you. War-bundle owners who are seated here, I greet you."

Then the attendant first moves the drum to the left side, and places both the drum and the rattle in front of the war-bundle owner who is next (in turn). He also places tobacco in his hand.

Speech of first guest.—"Host and his relatives who are seated here, I send my greetings to you. To you who are sitting here impersonating the spirits I send forth my greetings also. It is good. The host and our grandfathers pour tobacco for me. Those in the east, the Night Spirits, added their blessings also, grandfather said, it is said. If at any time we sang the songs and poured tobacco for them he would take cognizance thereof, he said, it is said. The handful of tobacco we poured they would smoke. The clansmen and councilors who are living in as pitiable a condition as I myself who am speaking will be helped, should the spirits accept their offering, just as I will be helped if they accept my tobacco. Thus I thought. The messenger that they have caused to come my way so that the spirits might hear my words,[136] I am unworthy of. What our ancestors have handed down I can merely guess at.[137] O, that it were my good fortune to say even one thing (as they desire it)! Would that the Night Spirits, our grandfathers, would accept the food and the tobacco and the offerings of buckskin! It is with that wish that we say this. Host, members of this clan who are sitting here, I send my greetings toward you. All who are sitting here impersonating the spirits, I send my greetings toward you." (Night Spirits' song.)

When the person in charge of the kettle in honor of Earthmaker[138] has finished, he says (again):

Second speech of first guest.—"Host, and your clan who are sitting here, I greet you. You who are sitting here impersonating spirits, I

---

[134] I. e., the drum will be passed from one guest to another. This constitutes the Basic Ceremony. Cf. Introduction.

[135] The drum is known variously as "*wĭdjă'dja*," the public crier, or as "*wĭrŏ'ragᴇra*," the messenger, i. e., literally, "the one through whom something is told." In this second term is included, however, not only the drum but also the gourds. The sound of the drum and the gourds translates into a language intelligible to the spirits what the Indians are pleading for.

[136] I. e., the drum.

[137] I. e., my knowledge is so imperfect that I will have to take chances at saying the right thing.

[138] This is probably a mistake on the part of the informant. It should be Night Spirit.

waŋk'a niŋk'ūruhi'ndjrehā'wįnɅ. Waxop'į'nį hō'naŋkcī'rēcge djā'-nɅga mīnaŋkcā'waŋgre niŋkūruhi'ntc rehā'wįnɅ. Waxop'į'nį wīdjā'dja tcabįrē'ra manįgīgī'rẹra te tcōni'xdjį hamanī' 'ųįnā'wįra. Wajọk'ī'ŋgEra djā'nɅga hanįwī'nɅ jë'nyga nɅtci'ŋxdjį wįrō'-ragEra watytcabwī'ra ŭaŋkcigọ'į'na hīranɅ'k'īk'ī'wįnɅ. WọnɅ'-ɣįre gīxe'we. Wa'ūįŋgā'dja wīrō'ragEra mā'nį-aŋgra jedjaį'ŋxdjį p'ā hoicɅhage'. Wahë'nɅ. Warọɣī'ra wak'ūruhi'ndjānɅga. Sā'-k'ereni'ŋk'djoŋgra mīnaŋkcā'waŋgre niŋk'ūruhi'ndj rehā'wįdjįgọ."

"Ė'gį te'ẹ'jį hōk'araī'cipānɅga. Ė'gį jįge hīcge hīnybe'dja jįge ŭaŋgī'jɅ sak'erejā'naŋk'į ë'dja hīnybọ'hona nẹɣarup'â'rogEra ë'dja gīk'ere'regį tanī'na nɅbō'jy gīgī'regį. UagEna'ŋk'a wë'je rūsgī'."

Speech of second guest.—"Waroɣī'ra wak'ī'wįk'aradjEra mīnaŋkcā'-waŋk'ā niŋk'ūruhi'ndjwī'nɅ. Ė'gį waxop'į'nį ōnaŋkcī'na mīnaŋk-cā'waŋgrēcge niŋk'ūruhi'ndjwīnɅ. Ėp'įŋgā'djɅ. Sā'k'ere-yatcā'-bwįra wā'rūtc ŭaŋgō'kuk'ū'-įnāwį-ā'nɅga. Ė'gį jįge wā'rūtc rajī'cge here nūnįge' wanap'į'ŋxdjį wani-oī'tcge k'arap'ī-e'sgexdjį rūtc waŋgagįgī'rawįra. Ė'gį je'e' cAnAnē'cge p'įŋgā'djɅ. Ė'gį waxop'į'nį wōgī'hu wa'y'nAŋgEra ŭaŋkcigọ'į'na tā wā'y'naŋgEra. HɅŋk'e ë'cAnA wak'īk'ū'nįnaŋkā'dja tcīroī'xdjį hahā'ŋgwįre te anā'tciŋxdji newaŋgā'wagį 'ū'-įnāwįge wa'y'nAŋgEra. Jë'djuŋga hoixtcɅ'ŋxdjį jįge në'xdjį tanįwọgī'jy waŋgagįgī' rawįgā'dja. Wįrō'ragEra hamanī' 'u-įnā'wįra. Wa'įya'nabwī'nɅ. Në wajā'nįjɅ 'y-įnį-ā'nɅga tegasgë'je wajɅ' yarā'naŋkce. Tcok'ā' ewewī'nẹgį wagī'unā'wįgadjɅ. Tcok'agā' hɅbọgure'gį herera' Hōk'ā'was Manī'na hōnįhā' gīgy'zįregī'jį. HɅhẹ' tcọnī'na hōxdjan'pdjį hagū'naŋk'ī'jį tanī'na hīdje' wagī'gįk'djonë'ra hōnįhā' ra hɅŋk'e' erewahā'winī'cge nɅdjọŋgįdjairā'wįgį e tanī'na hiŋgįhį'nẹk'djā'wįra hā'nɅga. Ė'gį warọɣī'ra hōk'ī'wįk'aradjEra waxop'į'nįna hīnɅ-cge'ni gįk'arā'tc mīnaŋkįrā'nɅga wawįŋgįp'erezįrë'jëje. Yā're wahëk'djonįhā'wįgadjɅ. WōnɅ'ɣįre xīrīra' ɣak'įbį-Ʌ'dje. Hagârë'jɅ nābįrūxā'djerā'nɅga waxop'į'nį wīdjā'dja tcabįrë'ra hamanįnī'nẹgį HɅŋk'e' wajɅ̂' waxdjō' ho'ū'įjɅ hereniŋk'djonë'nɅ. Djagū' rọgy' wānaŋk'e' warọɣī'ra hīcge jë'sge haxīrį-Ʌ'dje hiŋgaī'-rẹra c'agwahā'ra. Jë'sge hįhë'wahëk'djonẹgā'djɅ. Hīgŭâ'na wīrō'-ragEra tcɅt'į' djīrehā'k'djawįra Warọɣī'ra mīnaŋkcā'waŋk'a niŋk'ūruhi'ndj rehā'wįnɅ. Ė'gį sā'k'ereni'ŋk'djoŋgre niŋk'ūruhi'ndj rehā'wįdjįgo."

Hīraī'sundjEra wawī'y' rūcdjā'ŋgį ë'gį hįwacī'ra djīrehī'-k'djonë'gį wë'je.

Second speech of second guest.—"Wā'rọɣįra hōk'īk'ā'radjEra mīnaŋkcā'waŋgre niŋk'ūruhi'ndj rehā'wįnɅ. Ė'gį niŋk'ūruhi'ndj greet you. The messenger of the spirits (the drum) they have caused to walk in our path, first.[139] This drum has brought me and all my relatives who are here in touch with life. We have done this in order to obtain war power. The messenger that has walked thus far I have annoyed.[140] That is why I am saying this. Host, I greet you and yours. War-bundle owners who are seated here, I send my greetings toward you."

When he has finished, then for the second time they pass the drum to another warrior and they place tobacco in his hand. This man, taking the tobacco, speaks as follows:

Speech of second guest.—"'Host and members of your clan who are seated here, I greet you. You seated here who are impersonating the spirits, I greet you. It is good. Food you have given our warriors. There is plenty of ordinary food, but you have made us eat nice food, of animals that we like very much.[141] Even (common food) would have been good enough for us. They are boiling food for the spirits so that they might ask them for life. You are not merely doing this for them, but you are doing this for all those people who are present in this lodge. You have filled us full (of blessings and honors) and you have permitted us to pour tobacco. You have caused the messengers (the drum and the rattle) to walk over to us. We are thankful. Do I or does anything I say amount to anything ?[142] You thought of your grandfather (the spirit) and that is why you did it. Those in the east, the Night Spirits, taught him songs. The first nice evening that they start the Night (songs?), then I will offer tobacco for them. Even if we don't sing the songs correctly, they (the spirits) may still take pity on us and smoke our tobacco. The host and the members of his clan prayed earnestly to the spirits who are sitting here that they accept (these offerings). It is with this thought (before me) that I speak in this way. War powers let us cry for. 'When they give the feast, when they see to it that the sacred criers (i. e., the drums) come to you, remember that you should not take things lightly on that occasion. What the host desires do thou also pray for,' my ancestors told me. That is why I will say it. Now we are about to drum. Host who is sitting here, I greet you. War-bundle owners who are seated here, I greet you all."

When they finished the terminal song, then he got ready to start the dancing song and he said:

Second speech of second guest.—"Host and his relatives who are seated here, I send my greetings toward you. War-bundle owners

---

[139] I. e., they have given us the place of honor so that the drum will be passed to us first.

[140] I. e., I have made requests of the spirits by means of the drums and the rattles.

[141] I. e., we have been asked to eat the deer head.

[142] Question implying a negative answer.

rehā'wįnʌ̞ wō'naŋkcįnā'ᶜge mīnaŋkcā'waŋgre niŋk'ūruhi'dnj rehā'-widjigọ."

Ė'gį hįwacī'ra wawī'ᶜụ' rūcdjo'ŋgį wak'ūruhi'ndj rehī'je wë'je.

Third speech of second guest.—"Warọγī'ra mīnaŋkcā'waŋk'a niŋk'-ūruhi'ndj rehā'wįdj įgō'. Ėp'įŋgā'dja. Wįrō'ragEra watutcā'bwįra wọnʌ'γire gīxe'we waᶜụwī'ra. Ė'gį ŭaŋkcigọᶜį' gīxe'we waᶜụwįgā'-dja. Djagū' rọgụ' waᶜu'naŋgEra. Hʌ̞ŋk'e' wajā'nįją̞ naxū'ruk tūxū'rugEniŋk'djonā' nūnįge' hįgụ' djasge'hagį hë'rek'djonë'ge jëgụ'niŋk djik'e'we-ā'nʌ̞ga wīrō'ragEra jedjaį'ŋdjį p'ā hoicą̞'-hanʌ̞ga. Warọγī'ra hōk'ī'wįk'aradjEra mīco'nʌ̞ŋkcawaŋk'ā' niŋk'-ūruhi'ndj rehā'wįdjįgō'. Sā'k'ereni'ŋkdjoŋgere mīnaŋkcā'waŋgre niŋk'ūruhi'ndj rehā'wįdjįgọ."

Ė'gį jįge ᶇëγârupâ'rogEra rūhāk'ere'regį hītanī'họna tanī'na hīrasā' tanī'na harūtcā̞'pgį wë'je.

First speech of third guest.—"Warọγī'ra hōk'īk'ā'radjEra mīnaŋkcā'-waŋgre niŋk'ūruhįdjwī'nʌ̞. Ė'gį waxọp'į'nį wō'naŋkcī'na djā'nʌ̞ga tcį-ō'jụmīnā'ŋkcawaŋgre niŋk'ūruhindjwī'nʌ̞. Ėp'ī'nʌ̞ waxọp'į'nį wįdjā'djatcā'bįrëra manį-ā'ŋgra horo'k hamanī' ᶜu'-įᶇëra. Ėp'įŋgā'-dją̞. Hā̞bōgūre'girëra Hōk'ā'was Manīna wōk'ī'ra hūhī'rera hītcōk'ewahī'regį wawōk'ā'rahīra. Hūhī'rera hīcge wīrō'ragEra hamanī' ᶜu'-įᶇera hītcō'k'ewahī'wįra hōnįhā'ra djagū'ādjī'regį hīcge wawā'k'arak'ītak'djawī'na. Hītcō'k'ehawįgī'jį hā̞hẹ' wįgaī'regį hōnįhā' gik'ererë'je ë'ra. Hagârë'ją̞ hōnįhā tcā̞tᶜį wahak'djā'wįgį tanī'na hōjū'-įją̞ wagįp'āxụ'wįgį k'arahī'ᶇëk'djanë'nʌ̞ hįgaī'rëje ë'nʌ̞. Tanī'na Hōk'ā'was Manī'na hīdje' wagigī'k'djonā'wi-ā'nʌ̞ga warọγī'ra tanī'waxụ hiŋgįgī'rawī'ra tanī'na hīdje' wagįgiwī'nʌ̞. Hīcge hī'cᴀnʌ̞ wajį'djahį yare'wahëk'djā'wįje? Warọγī'ra tanī'na wōhọ'na nā̞bįrūxā'djEra wawī'gįp'erezįrëje'je. Yāre wahëk'dje. Wọnʌ̞'γire haxīrī' wahë'k'djawįgā'dją̞. Warọγī'ra hōk'īk'ā'radjEra sā'k'ereni'ŋk'djoŋgere mīnaŋkcā'waŋgre niŋk'ūruhi'ndj rehā'wįdjįgō."
(Hā̞hẹ' Nʌ̞wą̞.)

Second speech of third guest.—Ė'gį hīwacī'ra jįge wawī'ᶜụk'ârahō'gi wë'je.

"Warọγī'ra hōk'ī'k'āradjEra mīnaŋkcā'waŋk'ā niŋk'ūruhi'ndj rehā'wįdjįgọ. Ė'gį hōnaŋkcī'nācge tcī-ō'jụ mīnaŋkcā'waŋgre niŋk'-ūruhi'ndj rehā'wįdjįgọ. Hīwacī'niŋkra tcā̞tᶜį djīrehā'k'djawįra. Wają̞'nįją̞ naxū'rug p'īᶜūna'ŋkce nūnįge hʌ̞ŋk'e' hīk'ᶜī'ŋgį p'inįᶇë'dją̞ wahë'k djonegādja. Niŋk'ūruhi'ndj rehā'wįdjįgọ." (Hīwacī'ra Nʌ̞wą̞.)

Third speech of third guest.—Ė'gį hįwacī'ra haisu'ntcgį wë'je.

"Wīrō'ragEra hamanī'wįnawī'ra jedjaį'ŋxdjį p'ā hoicā̞' hawī'nʌ̞. Ė'gį djā'nʌ̞ga hōk'īk'ā'radjEra watūk'o'zwįra hīmaįcdjaŋk'djā'wįra who are seated here impersonating the spirits, I send my greetings toward you."

When the dance songs have been finished, then greeting, he says as follows:

Third speech of second guest.—"'Host who art sitting here, I send forth my greetings to you. It is good. It is to obtain war that we accept the drum. It is to gain life that we are doing this. We are doing this because he (the host) wishes it. Nothing can be gained by anything I would say, but nevertheless, howsoever small its value may be, let us start the drum. Host and members of his clan who are seated here, I greet you. War-bundle owners who are seated here, I greet you."

Then they pass the drum to the third person and he, taking the tobacco, says as follows:

First speech of third guest.—"Host and relatives who are sitting here, I greet you. You sitting within this lodge who are impersonating the spirits, I greet you. It is good that the drum of the spirits has been made to walk in our direction. It is good. They have sent us the means for imitating the Night Spirits who live in the east; for impersonating our grandfathers. The drum which they have caused to walk in our direction, the songs that they have handed down, we will also repeat them. Our grandfathers, who are called the Night Spirits, it is for them that these songs have been offered, he said. If at any time we sing these songs and offer a handful of tobacco, surely they will smoke the tobacco, our grandfathers said, it is said. Tobacco we place here for the Night Spirits. The tobacco that the host has poured for us, here we offer it. How could I have thought of anything else to say? That the spirits may recognize the offerings of the host, the tobacco, the food, and the buckskin; that is why I speak. To plead for war power piteously; that is why we speak. Host, members of his clan, war-bundle owners who are seated here, I greet you." (Night Spirits' song.)

Then when he is about to use the dance songs he says as follows:

Second speech of third guest.—"Host and members of his clan who are seated here, I greet you. You also who are seated within this lodge impersonating the spirits, I greet you. An insignificant dance song we are about to use. I know that I am unable to obtain anything by singing. However, one should not be discouraged, and that is why I am saying this. I greet you all." (Dance song.)

When the dance is finished he speaks again.

Third speech of third guest.—"We have been annoying the messenger that walked in our direction (the drum). As many clansmen as have taken hold of it, that many have been strengthened. Thus have we jejë'sge rōgụ. Wīdjā'djera watūtcạbwī'ra wa⁸iyā'nₐbwī'ra. Jed-jaị'ηxdjị p'ā hoicạ' hawī'nạ. Warọγī'ra niηk'ūrụhi'ndj rehā'wịd-jịgọ. Wō'naηkcī'ṇacge hanₐ'tcịηxdjị niηkūrụhi'ndj rehā'wịdjịgọ.

The Throwing Out of the Buckskins

Warūtco'na tanī' hok⁸ū'-ịnānₐga ë'gị warūγa'pk'ere hījaị'-naitcẹ'ra warọγi'ra warūp'ī'naηk'ī ˙te⁸e' warọγī'ra wārūp'ī'naηk'e ë'sge naịjị waxọp'ị'nị warā'djirëra hīp'e'rezịragenī'gụnị. Hīraī'rege wajₐ ṇaxū'rugenₐ hīraī'rege ŭaηgЕra hok'o'nogịrë'nₐ waxọp'ị'nị hanₐηxgū'ịṇe nₐdje'xdjịjₐ wak'ātcₐ'gī-ācge jịge' wa⁸ū'naηk'e jịge' ŭaηk'īk'ū'rụxụrugī'jₐ wa⁸ū'naηk'e waxọp'ị'nị hīk'ārap'e'-rezịrë'jₐ wa⁸ū'naηk'e hₐhẹ' hīhₐtë'jₐ wa⁸ū'naηk'ū'nị hīraī'rẹge. Ë'sge tcahā' gīci'p gīgī'rëk'djë'ge. Nëγarụpâ'rogЕra hīdjā' gīk'ererë'nₐ tanī'ṇa nₐbō'jụ gīgī're wë'nₐ.

Speech of prominent guest.—"Warọγī'ra hōk'īk'ā'radjЕra mīnaηkcā'waηgre niηk'ūrụhindjwī'nₐ. Hōnaηkcī'ṇa tcīrō'jụ mīnaηkcā'waηgre niηk'ūrụhi'ndjrehā'wịdjịgọ. Sā'k'ereni'ηk'djoηgere mīnaηkcā'waηgre niηk'ūrụhi'ndjrehā'wịdjịgọ. Ёp'ī'nₐ sā'k'ere ahīwatcā'bwịra warọγī'ra p'anaī'ṇₐxdjị wa⁸ū'ịṇā'nₐga. Ë'gị nₐdjọwā'ηgọdjaī'nawịge tcīwaηgō'jụịrā'nₐga warūdj waηgōk⁸ū'-ịṇawị-ā'nₐga. Ë'gị jịge tāṇịwōgī'jụ waηgagīgī'rawị-ā'nₐga. Ёp'iηgā'dja. Hiηk'ī-ō'sge hīwā'nịk'dje djādjīga waigë'nₐ. Hagârë'jₐ ŭaηkci'k haranī'na-īrā'naga waxọp'ị'nị wagụdje' gici'p niηgigī'regị, hₐηk'e' wahehe' wagị⁸ụ'nanịje aī'rẹnₐ. Wajā'nịjₐ nīnī-ā'nₐga waxọp'ị'nị wagụdje' gīci'bịnịηgigī'regị. Niηgīa'k' hitcō'k'ewahī'wira mₐ'āk'ī'ₐ wawīk'ī'p'erez hit⁸ẹ' ⁸ū'-ịṇeje. Hₐhẹ'ra naηgiwaī'ṇẹje ë'gị hīcge wak'andjā'ra hōk'ī'dje hₐhẹ' naηgiwaī'ṇẹje hagak'ī'tcecanₐ wawīgī'wa⁸ₐ mīnₐgịrë'je."

Hₐhẹ'ra nāwₐ'ṇa racdjā'ηgi hīcgagā' wak'andjā'ra nawₐ'ṇa hijai'ηgiwa⁸ₐ' aires⁸ā'je jë'canₐ hₐhẹ'ra wak'andjā'ra hak'īcdjek hₐhẹ' naηgiwaī'ṇẹje. Hagârë'jₐ ŭaηkci'k hīranā'nị-ịnānₐ'ga waxọp'ị'nị wagụdje' gīci'p niηgigī'regị wāna⁸ị' wagīk'ere'xdjị-ₐ'dje. Hₐηk'e' cgadjenī'cge wajā'nịjₐ ānī-ₐ'dje. Warọγī'naηk'a ŭanₐdjōdjaī'sge wōnₐ'γịre haxịrī're hicdjaηīrūxụxụnā'ηgra. Ŭaηkcigọ⁸ị' haxī'rị tanī'ṇa wōhọ'ṇa nₐbịrūxā'djЕra mₐcū'ṇa hak'arā'nị waγā'gЕnaηgra. Ŭanₐdjōdjaī'sge waxọp'ị'nị nịtā'k'adjЕra ogЕnī'ṇegị, sinị-ō'rahọtc k'īnā'nₐga wawë'k'īnā'nₐga. Naịηxdjị wajā'nịjₐ gāsge wawëje'je! Hiraī'rẹge wa⁸ū'naηgra haηk'e ë'djahī annoyed it. Host, I greet you. You who are impersonating the spirits, all of you, do I greet."

THE THROWING OUT OF THE BUCKSKINS

Then the attendants give that war-bundle owner who is regarded as the foremost, as an expert, tobacco, for it is about time now that the various spirits should accept (the offerings).[143] Therefore they select a man who is proficient, one who has very likely been blessed by the Night Spirits and one therefore to whom they are likely to listen, a holy person, a man who has attained war honors. He is likely to be the best one to make the spirits cognizant of the buckskins. So they brought the drum for him to his place, and placed tobacco in his hand. Then he spoke as follows:

Speech of prominent guest.—"Host and members of his clan who are seated here, I greet you. You seated in this lodge who are impersonating the spirits, I greet you. War-bundle owners who are seated here, I greet you. It is good that the war-bundle owners have done so much for the host. He has brought us the means of blessing and caused us to come into this lodge and has fed us. He has permitted us to offer tobacco. It is good. Not insincerely should we speak on such an occasion, our father told us. If at any time the spirits pay any attention to a human being and permit him to offer them moccasins, rest assured that they will not let a weakling do this. If you are of any importance the spirits will accept the moccasins you have offered them. Indeed, my son, our grandfathers on both ends of the earth will have knowledge of these offerings,[144] they told each other."

For the Night Spirits they sang and alternately they would start up a song for the Thunderbird as they sat there.

After finishing a Night Spirit song, then they would start up one for the Thunderbird, and then they would sing Night Spirit songs and Thunderbird songs together. "If at any time they consider you a man and accept the moccasins you have offered them, use your power. Above all, be careful that you do not say anything in a frivolous manner. The host putting himself in a pitiable condition has with copious dropping of tears besought the spirits for war power. For life he has also besought them and has prayed to them with offerings of tobacco, food, buckskins, and feathers. Putting himself in a pitiable condition he has hunted for the spirits,[145] weakened himself through exposure to cold, and caused himself untold sufferings. Oh that I could have done similarly! It is for this (these laudable rea-

---

[143] I. e., that the buckskins should be placed where the spirits can get them.

[144] I. e., the Night Spirits living in the east and the Thunderbirds living in the west.

[145] I. e., hunted the deer that are used at the feast both for eating and for the buckskin offerings.

hīxdjahī′ nawāni̥-ǎ̱′ndje warǫγī′ra tanī′na- hak′ārā′ni̥ γāgeneηk′a.
hīcge taniwǫgī′ju̥ niηgigī′regi̥. Hīcge′ hǎbi̥taī′ᵋuna hanī′ γagā′dje
warǫγī′ra djasgā′naηk′a. Hīcge′ jësgā′dje wajōk′īdji̥rë′ja herëge′-
djini ŭaηgenū′nᴀηgᴇra tcëge′dja rë′djǎ ŭǎdjī′rëna k′īdji̥re′ ᵋūi̥nā′-
nᴀga. Wajā′ni̥jǎ ᵋu-i̥në′ga hastō′ ᵋu̥-i̥në′ga ṇūxū′rugi̥resᵋā`je. Ge
jë′sge hī-adjī′rëje tcege′dja waxǫp′i̥′ni̥ k′isge ŭaηkcik′i̥′negi̥rë`cge.
Tanī′na hak′arani̥ γagi̥rë′je djadjī′ga hiηgë′rᴀ. Hōk′ā′was Manī′na
tanī′na hīdje′ wagigī′k′djonege. Niηk′ūru̥hi′ndj rehā′wi̥djigō.
(Hahe′ Nǎwǎ hīraī′suntc.)

Speech of host.—Ë′gi̥ teᵋë′ji̥ hīraī′sundjera hōk′araici̥bā′nᴀga ë′gi̥
hi̥wacī′ra wīk′u′ηk′djanë`gi̥.

"Sā′k′ereni`ηk′djoηgera   hōk′īk′ā′radjᴇra   mīnaηkcā′wangre
niηk′ūru̥hi′ndj rehā′wi̥djigǫ. Hīwacī′ra hī′u̥-i̥nëk′djonā′re ë′dja
hītcō′k′ewahī′wi̥ra wagu̥dje′niηk wagi̥tū′cdjǎ rehā′k′djoni̥hā`wi̥ra.
Ë′gi̥ ŭaηgᴇrǫwaī′re wak′ā′ragīk djani̥hawīnᴀ. Hōsge jeᵋe′ wak′ā′-
rak′ rehā′ge wahë′nᴀ. Sā′k′ereni′ηk′djoηgᴇre hōk′īk′ā′radjᴇra
mīnaηkcā′waηgre niηk′ūru̥hi′ndj rehāwi̥djigǫ."

Üaηkxete′naηk′a nǎwǎ hīwacī′ra djīrehī′gi̥. Ẇagīgâ′ra tcahā′
nǎbi̥ruxā′djᴇra wak′ūru̥cibi̥rā′nᴀga hanǎ′tci̥ hījaηk′ī′cᴀnᴀ tcahā′-
naηk′a hanī′ wacī′rëje tcīrō′gigi̥ηx djōbo′hǎ hōgīgi′ηx hīrëk′djonë′gi̥.
Warūtctco′na hījǎ tcōwë′dja wōtā′p′onᴀ hanī′wanije ëgi̥ ji̥ge
wagixo′nonᴀ hījǎ′ hage′dja wazip′â′rasge hōtā′p′ona wagigī′ manīje.
Ë′gi̥ tanī′na hōgigi′γi̥rā`nᴀga hōk′ī′ri̥rë`djǎ ji̥ge hīrǫ-ā′gᴇra
hōgigi′ηx hīdjǫbo′hona haraī′rëk′djā`ṇëgi tcahā′ nǎbi̥ruxā′djᴇra
tcōwë′xdji̥ ë′dja hanī′′ manī′naηk′ā Mǎᵋū′na tcahā′ nǎbi̥ruxā′-
djᴇra gīrūcdjǎ′ ṇëhī′rega jeᵋe′ wagaī′rëje hanᴀ′txi̥ηxdji̥
niηk′djǫηgᴇniηgrā′cge hīk′ī-ō′wi̥re nǎbᴇrotā′p′onᴀ hīwi̥-ā′nᴀga.
Hīk′ī-ō′wi̥re jë′sge hī′rëje hīro-ā′gedja hanǎ′tci̥ηxdji̥ hīgu̥′
p′ëjegerë′ra hanǎ′tci̥ηxdji̥ hīk′i-oī′rëje Mǎᵋū′na tcahā′naηk′a
k′urusgī′ ësᵋīnī-ǎ̱′bi̥rëk′djë`ge ë′sge hīk′ī-oī′rëje ë waᵋū′naηkcᴀnᴀ.

Hīdjōbo′hona hōhū′-i̥rëdja hagī′regi̥ tcahā′ra ë′dja wōwap′â′rok
hīrā′nᴀga tcīráhë′dja hōwaī′re wahī′rënᴀ. Tanī′na nǎbᵋā′k′ī
nǎbᴇrōre′xdji̥ wanī′ waᵋū′-i̥negi̥ tanī′na p′ëdje′dja wōwaxū′-i̥neje.
Ë′gi̥ hanā′tci̥ηxdji̥ wagigâ′ra tcahā′ra wak′ā′rani̥ tcīrǫwā′gi̥ηx
wak′ā′rani̥na`ηk′a ë′gi̥ k′īgâ′ra djā′nᴀga tcīrǫju̥-ā′k′a niηk′djoηgᴇ
niηgᴇrë′cge hī′nuηgᴇra ŭaηgera′ hanā′tci̥ηxdji̥ nᴀji-ā′nᴀga wacī′-
rëje homī′nᴀηgᴇra wō′naηk′ārajīnā`nᴀga wacīrë′nᴀ. Jeᵋë′ji̥ jëguā′-
nᴀga.

Ë′gi̥ ji̥ge k′eni̥ tcahā′ra uaηgerǫwaī′rewahī`rani̥ wai̥reconū′nᴀ
haηk′ī′jǎ nǎwī′ni̥ne hǎhe′ cᵋakrā′ hǎbi̥djā′nᴀga hagū′naηkcᴀnᴀ
hījǎ′ hīsagŭǎ′ni̥k′ererawī-ë`ge haηk′e′ hījǎ′ hahe′ cᵋā′k′ hīsagŭǎ′-

sons) that they (the host and his band) have done this. Do not say anything frivolously, for the host has offered in your behalf tobacco and tears. Cry that you may obtain life, even as the host and his people have done. Act thus so that you may be of help to one another even as our ancestors of old were. If people act together they will accomplish their purpose. That is what they did in the beginning and that is why they lived like spirits at that time. They cried and made offerings of tobacco, grandfather said. For the Night Spirits shall you pour tobacco here. I send forth my greetings to you." (Terminal Night Spirit song.)

After they have finished the terminal Night Spirit song then (the host) gets ready to use the dance song, but (first) speaks as follows:

Speech of host.—"War-bundle owners who are seated here, I greet you. The dance song they are about to use and then they will get ready to throw out the offerings of buckskin to the spirits. Now let us put them above. This is what I wished to tell you. War-bundle owners who are seated here, I greet you."

The host and the others now take the buckskins and dance around the lodge four times.

When he (the host) starts the oldest men sing the dance songs. Then the feasters take the buckskin offerings down and all, one by one, dance around the lodge four times. An attendant precedes them carrying cedar incense and one follows them carrying the same. After they have made the circuit of the lodge for the third time, just before they begin the fourth circuit, those carrying the buckskin that is to be thrown out for Earthmaker and who march at the head of the procession, let the children, after they have smoked their hands, touch the buckskin. After that all touch it for (they believe) that if they touch this buckskin they will obtain long life thereby.

After they have made the fourth circuit they roll up the buckskins and throw them out through the top of the lodge. They hold tobacco in both hands when they do this and this tobacco they pour into the fire. Then all the feasters, those who had buckskins and the others who were within the lodge, the children, the women, indeed, all the people, rise and standing near their seats dance. Thus they did.

Before throwing the buckskins through the top of the lodge they would tell the people not to sleep, for otherwise some of the old Night Spirits who are about at the approach of day might strike them

468 THE WINNEBAGO TRIBE

niŋk'ererawī`gī, cdjĕk'djānịhā'winʌ. Ge'djinị rọɣīna'ŋkcana. Jeʻë'jị
tcahā'ra ʻŭa'ŋgɛra họwaī're wahịrā'nagagị jë'ji ẹ'p'ā' niŋk'djo'-
ŋgɛnʌŋgɛra hịjʌ' ną̄djë'kcge ʻu'ŋk'dje aī'rẹcʌnū'nʌ."

Ě'gị jeʻë'jị nawanịhë'ra wë'nʌ.
Speech of first guest.—"Warọɣī'ra hōk'ị'k'aradjɛra mīnaŋkcā'-
waŋk'a niŋk'ū'rụhindjwī'nʌ. Watū'tcabwịra hīmaị'cdjaŋk'djā`-
wịra djā'nʌga wajō'k'īṇa watụtcabwī'ra. Ěp'iŋgā'dja. Jedjaī'-
ŋxdjị p'a hoicʌ' hawī'nʌ, wirō'ragɛra! Warọɣī'ra hōk'ịk'ā'-
radjɛra mīnaŋkcā'waŋk'a niŋkuruhindj rehawina. Waxōp'ị'nị
wōnaŋkcī'ṇa djā'nʌga tcị-ō'jụ mīnaŋkcā'waŋgre niŋk'ūrụhindj
rehā'wịdjịgọ."
Ṇẹɣârụp'o'rogera warụtcā'djega rūzā'nʌga tcịọk'īsā'gedja
k'īrịdje'hịje.
Wagịgō'naŋk'a tʻą̄pdjịrā'nʌga, wë'je.
Speech of host.—Sā'k'erenị'ŋk'djoŋgɛre mīnaŋkcā'waŋgre niŋ-
k'ūrụhi'ndj rehā'wịnʌ. Ěp'iŋgā'djʌ. Djagū' rụ-ā'gụnaŋxdjị
jësgë'ją̄ hanị'ụnʌ'gịgawịra. Haną̄'tciŋxdjị haị'seretc djagū'
ru-agu'nʌ hūnagịgā'wịra. Ěp'ī'nʌ. Cʻagwarā'wịga waxọp'ị'nị
wāna ʻị' rūsgī'djịranʌga. Ě'gị waxọp'ị'nị agịɣe'ɣebɛra djagū'ra
ịcĕk'djā'wigị hīniŋk'ā'ragairā`wigị jë'sge haị'seretc hōrak'ā'rak'ịcā`-
rawịra. Ěp'iŋgā'djʌ. Haŋk'e' hīnʌɣịcā'rawịnị. Wajʌ' raxū'-
ruk'p'ị'ŋxdjị wacahịbrā'wịra. Ěp'ī'nʌ. Wā ʻyā'ną̄pcʌnʌ ë'ge haị'-
seretc cindjwatʻẹ' niŋk'ā'ragịwī'ra here nū'nịge ë'gị tok'e'wehịniwị.
Nū'nịge ë'gị sā'niŋk hą̄bọgū'regị hererā' hōk'ā'was manī'na wōhaị'-
niŋgīją̄ hīdjā' wagịk'ere'rera hīrọ-ā'gɛniŋxdjị nawā'naŋgre ë'niŋk
p'arịdjā' gịk'ererĕk'djonēgā`djʌ. Ě'gị jịge mā'naŋgre wọhaī'-
niŋgījʌ hīdjā' gịk'erë'rera hịjʌ' haradjī'regị hīdjā' gịk'ererë'nʌ.
Ě'gị jịge wë'nʌ hą̄hẹ'wịra nịtā'k'atc gigī'rëra jịge hījʌ' hīdjā'
gịk'erë'renʌ. Ě'gị nīṇa wọhịhaī'ṇera jịgī'jʌ haratcce. Ě'gị
tcaxce'bɛra wọhʌ'gịk'erë`rera. Jịge jë'cge ŭaŋgịjʌ haradjirë'ra.
Ě'gị jịge wọxʌhī'ṇa wọhʌgịk'ererë'nʌ, jịgī'jʌ hanʌ' djịrēnʌ. Ě'gị
wë'nʌ.

Second speech of host.—"Haŋk'e' hītcōk'ewahī'wịra djā'nʌga
tcọk'agā' wāna ʻị'ŋgịk'erë'regị haną̄'tciŋxdjị, haŋk'e' wajiŋk'ī'ṇa
wahā'niŋk'djonā`wị nūnige' hīhī'hịk'isge wā'wanaŋgwịgā`dja
haŋk'e' hītcō'k'ewahī'wịra wajị'ṇe p'ịhī'ranije tcōk'agā ë'ra.
Ě'sge hīgụ' djasgë'niŋk' tūxụrugwī'ra jë'sge hawa ʻụwịgā'dja.
Jịge' haŋk'e ṇë'cʌnʌ wa ʻụnịgā'dja djā'nʌga wajọk'īṇa'ŋgera.
Jë'nụga djasgehōp'ī'niŋgɛra hatụxū'rugwịraɣ. Jë'sge hawā ʻụwịgā'-
djʌ. Ě'gị sā'k'ereniŋk'djoŋgɛra mīnaŋkcā'waŋgre niŋk'ūrụhi'ndj
rehawịdjigō."

with their canes, and if they did this such a person would surely die.[146] For that reason do they warn them not to sleep. However, as soon as the men have thrown the buckskins outside then any child who desires may sleep without danger.

After the song had been sung he (first guest) speaks as follows:

Speech of first guest.—"Host and members of his band who are seated here, I greet you. By coming in connection with the drum I and my relatives have been strengthened. It is good. To such an extent have we annoyed the drum. Host and members of his band who are seated here, I greet you. As many as there are [who are seated within the lodge] impersonating the spirits, I send forth my greetings to you."

Then the attendant takes the drum and places it in the middle of the lodge.

The host rises and speaks as follows:

Speech of host.—"War-bundle owners who are seated here, I greet you. It is good. What I have longed for, that you have completed for me. All night have you prayed for me. It is good. Blessings did the spirits give your grandfathers. What you were to say to the spirits that they (your ancestors) told you and that you have repeated here all night. It is good. You weren't selfish in your actions. You wished to obtain something for all of us. It is good. I am thankful to you, for you must have inconvenienced yourselves greatly by sitting here all night and you must in addition have suffered from hunger. Now in addition to the kettle that has been placed in honor of those who live in the east, the Night Spirits, the last band to sing will also receive a head. A kettle is also to be placed in honor of the Earth."

Then he said that food was to be placed in honor of the Moon, as well as a kettle (for soup). Then they named a person to be in charge of a kettle in honor of the Water. Then they called upon one to take charge of the kettle in honor of the Eagle. Then they placed one in charge of the kettle for Porcupine. Then he (the host) spoke again.

Second speech of host.—"I realize that our grandfathers did not bless me much and that I have hardly enough food to go around, but we will nevertheless do it, for it is said that our grandfathers will not be insulted thereby, grandfather said. That is why we give this feast, however little it be that we obtain. And I am not the only one, for all my relatives are doing the best in their power that we may obtain (blessings). That is why we give the feast. War-bundle owners who are seated here, I greet you."

---

[146] They speak of the Night Spirits appearing toward dawn as old in reference to the gray light of morning which they compare to the white hair of an old person. For the same reason these old Night Spirits have canes just as an old man has a cane.

FEAST TO THE NIGHT SPIRITS

Ĕ′gi djānaga waradjirā′nihera hiniŋk‘e′hi wōk‘e′ra djanaga wawigī′k‘arabiregi. Hanā̄′tc hīnʌ k‘ūruziregi ĕ′gi djanaga haŋk‘e′ wap‘ā′idja haŋk‘e′ horok‘u′-inanigi warutco′na hanā̄′tciŋxdji hīk‘īsge′xdji wawogijū′-ireje. Ĕ′gi hanā̄tc jĕ′gu hī′regi wagigō′-naŋk‘a jujū′k djirehī′gi warūdjɛra hīk‘idjaī′xdji. Warū′djirĕje. Ĕ′gi warū′djɛnaŋk‘a haŋk‘e rūx‘ex‘erani′ŋk‘dje. Ĕ′gi jige′ haŋk‘e′ wōk‘e′ra wōcgatc hīrani′ŋk‘dje. Ĕ′gi hūce′rĕgra haŋk‘e′ woi-e′raniŋk‘djĕ‵nʌ. P‘ī′ŋxdji stŏ wahirā′nʌga p‘īŋxdji′ nige′ wawaxu′-iṇĕk‘dje hurĕ′jak‘ira. Ĕ′gi jige k‘īgō′nʌŋk‘a haŋk‘e hai′-seretc wacgi-erā′cAnʌ airani′ŋk‘dje ŭaŋk‘ik‘ū′ruxurugɛra niŋge′-cAnʌ mīnʌ′giregi p‘ĕtc ĕ′dja. WoṇA′ɣire hok‘aragana′ŋkcAnʌ hōtotco′ṇa djasge hī′regi. Ĕ′gi wōk‘ī′zara djasge hī′regi jĕ′jesge haī′seretc horā′girĕje. Hōtcitci′ṇa hīcge wanaŋxgu′ haī′seretc hīres‘ā′je. WoṇA′ɣire wagigō′naŋk‘a tā wa‘u′nAŋk‘e hīdjā′ wōrā′nʌ nā‘i′ waires‘ā′je.

RITE OF THOSE WHO HAVE BEEN CRAZED BY THE NIGHT SPIRITS

Ĕ′gi jige hijā′ ‘u′naŋk‘u hā̄hě′ rūdjā′niŋgirega. Wak‘ātca′-ŋk‘dji wa‘uŋge′. Wainiṇā′cge hanā̄′tciŋxdji hōcârodjɛraī′res‘aje aī′renʌ. Ĕ′gi ṇaṇok‘ā′xdji haŋk‘e′ wajā′nijʌ hīk‘īk‘ā′ɣɛni tcīrō′-gigiŋx wacī′rega. Ŭaŋgɛra hanā̄′tciŋxdji hap‘ĕ′xdji mīnA′gires‘aje. Hā̄he′ wōgihai′ṇegi hatci′ndja djĕgi haŋk‘e′ nūniniṇes‘ā′je. Yahī′ tcawaī′res‘ā‵je. Ĕ′gi wōhʌ′djega xere′ haracā′cakdjĕ‵cge hā̄hě′ rudjā′nigirā‵djega wa‘usa‘je nā̄bi‘ŭa′nAga. Wohʌ′djega p‘āra hatcindjā′naŋk‘i rūɣes‘ā′je rūɣegu′gi ŭaŋgɛra hak‘ik‘uegires‘ā‵je. Hijʌ′ tcōni nige′ ratce′ na‘i′ wa‘u-iṇes‘ā′je. Hīgu′ p‘ĕje wanaci-ā′naga tcōni nige′ ratce′gi hīgu′ djasgĕ′ga ŭaŋgonaŋgires‘ā′je. Ge ĕ′sge hījʌ′ jejĕsge hīga aī′gi hak‘ik‘ŭe′gɛnaŋk‘ā rūcdjaī′ṇega ĕ′gi wagigō′naŋk‘a tanihū′ tci-ō′k‘isā‵gedja k‘ere′naŋk‘a rūzā′nʌga tani-ō′giju hīres‘ā′je tanihī′ rūcdja′ŋgi. Ĕ′gi wōrā′gɛnaje wagigō′-naŋk‘a wōhʌ′ djagū′cAnʌ girū′ziregi nā̄biruxa′djɛra djagū′cAnʌ girū′ziregi je′jĕsge hō′rakɛnʌ‵je hagaī′racge waī′res‘aje wagigō′-naŋk‘a tanī′ṇa, wōho′ṇa, nā̄biruxā′djɛra hanā̄′tciŋxdji wagirū-zirĕ′je hīgaires‘ā′je je‘e′ wajap‘ī‘u wa‘u′iṇecAnA. Haŋk‘e′ wōgigō′ hōk‘ahī′xdji wa‘u′-iṇanis‘ā‵je airecanū′nʌ. Uaŋkcik wakatcaŋk wau-inesaje. Hanʌga ĕ′gi wagigâ′ra k‘igoī′ra nīhě′ra rucdjaīṇegi hanā̄′tciŋxdji warū′djɛra jĕguhī′regi ĕ′gi ŭaŋk wap‘ā′ warā′djira nīhě′ra tcōnī′ŋxdji woha′ nā̄djirā′nihera t‘ā̄pdjirā′nʌga wĕ′je.

Feast to the Night Spirits

Those who were called on for kettles now took the pieces of meat that had been counted for them (by the attendants). The attendants divided the pieces evenly for all those who did not eat heads. As soon as the distribution was finished then the host started playing his flute and all began to eat at the same time. The feasters are careful that they spill nothing and that the utmost precautions are taken. It is not proper to scatter the bones. They are afterwards gathered up and thrown in a consecrated place. Never do they talk frivolously throughout the night. Those who had obtained war honors as they sat near the fire would now tell of their war exploits— how many warpaths they had been on and how many fights they had been in. All night do they talk in this way. All night would the boys listen, it is said. They are asking for war powers; that war might come their way—that is why they do this (recount their war exploits).

Rite of Those Who Have Been Crazed by the Night Spirits

As they do this some become crazed by the Night Spirits.[147] A religious frenzy comes over them.[148] All their clothes would be cast off, it is said. All naked, without any apparel, would the man dance around the lodge. All would sit waiting. They (these crazed ones) would not be in ignorance about the place where food was being boiled for the Night Spirits, and they would go toward it. Even if the kettle was boiling over the crazed ones would stick their hand in it. Similarly, as soon as the head was taken out from the place where it was being boiled, then these men would make a rush for it and try to get the first bite. Whoever was able to get the first bite would surely, at some later time, receive war honors. When they are finished with the rush for the head, then the feaster (i. e., the successful one) takes the pipe placed in the center of the lodge and smokes it. When he has finished he would tell of his war exploits and also tell them what offerings had been accepted by the spirits. That the one who has just come out of his trance would tell them. They (the spirits) told the feaster (i. e., the crazed one) that they had accepted all the things that had been offered—the tobacco, the food, and the buckskins; that the feasters had done well.[149] However, not at every feast would a man become crazed, it is said. A holy person he would have to be. When the feasting is over and all have finished their meal, then the first one to whom a head had been apportioned and for whom a kettle had been placed rises and speaks.

---

[147] I. e., they get into a state of religious ecstasy through worship of the Night Spirits.

[148] Literally, "holiness comes over him."

[149] Apparently the one supposed to be crazed by the Night Spirits sees them in his ecstatic vision and finds out whether they are satisfied or not with the offerings.

Speech of eighth guest.—"Warǫγī'ra wajō'nįwįna niŋk'ūrụhi'ndj rehā'wįdjigǫ. Ě'gị waxǫp'į'nị ōnaŋkcī'ṇa mīnaŋkcā'waŋgre niŋk'ūrụhi'ndj rehā'wįdjigǫ. Ěp'iŋgā'dja sa'k'erejanaįŋxdjị cā'waŋge. Nūnige' waxǫp'į'nị nįtā'k'atc gịgī'regị ṇë wona'-ŋkciŋk'djë'ra wō'naŋkcị hiŋgigī'rare ëp'iŋgā'djạ. Hạŋk'e' wajạ̄'-hage ë'sge te'jësge jiŋgigī'niŋgā'dja. Wōnʌ'γire hōtatcgạ̄' wa'ụwịgā'dja, ŭaŋkcigo'ī'ṇa hīranạ'k'īk'įwịra. Ěp'iŋgā'djạ. Djanagā' wajǫk'ī'niŋgEra jë'nụŋga hak'įwịk'u'ŋxdjiwįnʌ̣ ŭaŋkcigǫ'ī'na hīranạ'k'īk'į̇'ŋxdjịwịnʌ̣'. Hītcōk'ewahī'wịra hạbōgū'regị naŋk'ī'jị hījạ' huŋgenaŋkce eyanatcị'ŋxdjị wawịrụk'ona'naŋkce gījị wōnʌ'γire hīrụk'onai'jạ hereje' tcōk'agā' nạ̄djǫdjạ'je tcīnʌ'gịdjạ hōk'īra'djEra hanạtci'ŋxdjị nahī' gīgịje' gịgịgịjị. ŪdjEro'gedja idjaī'niŋgera γerahe' naŋk'ā'raxgūje ë'je aī'rera. Je'e' tcōk'aga' wëwī'ṇëge waxǫp'į'nị hōrtaŋkcị hiŋgigī'-raje. Tanī'ṇa wōhǫ'ṇa nạ̄bịrụxā'djEra haŋk'tgịp'e'rez p'ịnị wajạ̄' 'u-ịṇes'ā'je! Warǫγī' p'onai'ṇạxdjị wa'u'-ịṇā'nʌga wịgịp'e'-rezịregịjị hīcge djānaga wōnaŋkcī'ṇa wīrā'rụxe hī'uŋk'djā'wịra. Te'jësge ŭaŋkcik xetera' adjī'rënʌ̣, 'Waxǫp'į'nị tanī'ṇa gīgị hīrā'-nagị wagịzō'xdjị-āndje haizō'xdjị wamịŋgī'naŋgā'djǫ. Tanī'ṇa rǫhạ̄'ŋxdjị rasge'p naɫa'ndje tanī'ṇa rǫhā'ŋxdjị carasge'pgịjị je'ë'cge waxǫp'į'nị warā'djịrẹra wōnʌ'γire hīrụk'o'nʌnʌ̣ waŋgigịp'e'rezịnaŋgwī'je aī'recʌnūnʌ̣. Hịjạ' tanī'ṇa rǫhạ̄'ŋxdjị rasge'pgị hạ̄hë'ja waŋgịk'ịk'ū'rụxurugEnʌ̣'je aī'recʌnūnʌ̣. Hītadje' wa'ụ'ịṇe. Hotcintci'niŋgwī'ra të'gị wōnʌ'γire ōk'īk'ū'-rụxurugEra wōwat'e'giniŋkce ŭaŋgEnū'niŋgEra aī'recʌnūnʌ̣.

Tanī'ṇa wǫhǫ'ṇa nạ̄bịrụxā'djEra wagịksā'bịregi hage'dja wōna-ŋkcī'ṇa hīwīrā'rụxe hī'uŋk'djā'wị.

"Ŭaŋkcigǫ'ī'ṇa wōnʌ'γirẹra hīγanạk'īk'iŋk'djā'wị. Wa'īyā'nʌpce hīhë'ge wāhā'naŋkcʌnʌ̣ djagū' eresgā'nʌŋgre. Warụγa'bEra wōk'ā'ragịhonʌ̣ p'īṇā'gị tānị-ǫk'aragī'jūra p'īṇā'gị hagârë'jʌ rǫhạ̄'-bǫt'ek'ina hījō'rawëgị warụγā'bEra manịŋgī'cdjaŋk'djonë'nʌ̣. Hạŋk'e' t'ẹhịp'i raninịŋk'djonë'nʌ̣. Warǫγī'ra mīnaŋkcā'waŋgre hōk'ịk'ā'radjEra niŋk'ūrụhi'ndj rehawịdjigǫ. Waxǫp'į'nị ōnaŋkcī'ṇa mīnaŋkcā'waŋgre niŋk'ūrụhi'ndj rehā'wịdjigǫ."

CONTINUATION OF THE BASIC RITUAL

Speech of eighth guest.[150]—"Host and relatives, I send my greetings toward you. You seated here who are impersonating the spirits, I send my greetings toward you. It is good that there are so many war-bundle owners here. It is good that they have given me the opportunity of impersonating the spirits, by placing me in charge of the food that they offer to them. Though I am not related to the host, he has done this for me. That I may grope for war powers, feel myself in connection with life, that is why we do it. It is good. As many of my relatives as are here, they all worked splendidly so that we might be connected with life. He who is the leader of our grandfathers who dwell in the east (the Night Spirits), who is in control of all things, who is in control of war powers, he blessed our grandfather and he caused him to swallow as many people of other tribes as had been preordained for him. Within his stomach our grandfather heard their cries, he said, it is said. Thus thinking of my grandfather they asked me to impersonate the spirits. How could the spirits do anything but accept the offerings of tobacco, food, and buckskin! They have had a very great feast, and surely if the spirits take cognizance of it, all those who have been impersonating the spirits will also be permitted to participate (in the blessings) to follow. Our ancestors handed down to us from generation to generation the following: 'When you offer food to the spirits, sit down to your undertaking with the greatest possible attention and care. Try to smoke as much tobacco as possible, for if you smoke much tobacco then all the spirits who are in control of war powers will pay attention to you, it is said. If a man smokes very much tobacco in one night, then he will be able to obtain a war honor, it is said. Try your hardest. Young men, it is easy to obtain war powers, the old men used to say. If the spirits accept the offerings of food and tobacco and buckskins, then afterwards those who have impersonated them will participate in the blessings that follow.'

"We feel that we have been connected with life and war power. It is for that reason that I say these words of thanks. If you give the feast for the war bundle well, if you pour tobacco well, then, if at some time or another you have a chance to kill an enemy outright, the war bundle will strengthen you greatly. No one will be able to kill you.

---

[150] I. e., eighth guest to receive the buckskins, continuing the numeration from the first division of the ceremony.

474 THE WINNEBAGO TRIBE

Wa'i̯'nap tcōní'ŋxdjįn̄, ë'gį jįge hīnu̯bra wǫhᴀ' n̄djįrë'ra
wë'n̄.

Speech of ninth guest.—"Warǫγī'ra hōk'ik'ā'radjᴇra mīnaŋkcā'-
waŋgre niŋk'ūru̯hi'ndj rehā'wįdjįgǫ. Ë'gį hōnaŋkcī'n̄a mīnaŋkcā'-
waŋgre niŋk'ūru̯hi'ndj rehā'wįdjįgǫ. Ėp'ī'n̄. Warǫγī'ra ŭaŋkcik'į̯
waŋganaŋgi'į̯'wiŋge. Waxǫp'i̯'nin̄a wōnᴀγire rūk'o'nᴀn̄
ŭaŋkcigǫ'į̯' hīru̯k'o'nᴀn̄ djānu̯gᴇra p'ī'n̄a herera jë'nu̯ŋga
gīk'a'radjᴇnaŋgre. Ŭaŋkcigre hōwajā'jairēcge waru̯γap ke'renᴀgre
te'jëgu̯ hī'regį wǫgigâ'ra harak'u̯'įn̄egį; hōwajā'ja hīranįhë'ra
han̄sgā'bįranᴀga hōwajā'ra rūcdjaį'n̄es'ā'je aī'rera. Hu̯ŋgiatcā'-
bįwįra p'ëdjōk'e'rera hōk'ā'wak'a wa'u̯'įn̄ëje tejëgu̯ hī'regį
djadjįga ëcᴀnū'n̄. Te'ë'cge djadjįga waxǫp'įnį nįtā'k'atc gīgįra
p'į̄je. Hu̯ŋgįrā'gᴇra hīsge wë'ra yap'e'rez nūnįge haŋk'e' tūxū'-
rugᴇnįge haŋk'e jë'sge hanį-adjegā'dj̄. Anᴀga ë'gį, 'Hagârë'-
j̄ wōnᴀ'γire hacdjak'djo'n̄egį hak'īt'ǫ'bįk'ârǫhoī'regį, haŋk'e'
nana γicaraniŋkdje, tcōk'a wīrā gāsge niŋgī'gįwįcᴀnū'n̄ tanihū'ra
p'į niŋgī'gįwįcᴀnū'n̄ wǫgī'hǫn̄a p'į niŋgī'gįwįcᴀnū'n̄ hōk'ī'dj̄
niŋgī'gįwįcᴀnū'n̄. Gāsge wa'įn̄ëk'djë'n̄ k'īzaī'k'ârǫhoī'rare. Ë'gį
hīcegī'jį hōnī'niŋgihanᴀk'ī'cge haŋk'e' nan̄ŋxgunik'djë'n̄ wap'ai'-
niŋk'djį warak'djek'djë'n̄. Hīk'įgaī'rëje hīsgë'ra hīp'ere'zįrëge.
Ë'sge hak'ik'ā'rajįrëje. Te'e' warǫγī'ra hōk'ik'ā'radjᴇra jë'sge
hīwa'u̯'naŋk'ādj̄. Ėp'iŋgā'dj̄. Waj̄' p'į ponaī'na rūxū'-
rugįrëgā'dj̄. Mā'n̄a kâ'rok'ehī'wįra wǫgihaį'n̄era. Tanī'n̄a tcāha
nābįru̯xā'djᴇra tejë'nu̯ŋga gīrucdjǫ'n̄ehįhįrë'ra wōnᴀ'γire
hīk'āratā' hī'ŭwa'u̯'įn̄era. Ėp'ī'n̄. Kârǫk'ehįhī'wįra hōnaŋkcį
Hiŋgigī'rare hīk'ârǫk'ehįhīwįra hak'ūru̯hi'ndjanᴀga. Ë'gį warǫγī'ra
wak'ūru̯hindjā'nᴀga hage'dja djanᴀga tcį-ō'ju̯ mīnaŋkcā'waŋgre
niŋk'ūru̯hi'ndjᴇrehawįdjįgō'.

Hįtanī'n̄a wōh̄'n̄a harā'djįrëra wa'įnai'pdjonë'n̄ wë'n̄.

Speech of tenth guest.—"Warǫγī'ra hōk'īk'ā'radjᴇra mīnaŋkcā'-
waŋgre niŋk'ūru̯hi'ndj rehā'wįn̄. Ėp'ī'n̄. Warǫγī'ra waxǫp'i̯'nį
warā'djįre tanī' hīragik'arana'ŋk'į jedjonaį'xdjį hīgįrë'regį tanį-ō'-
waxū'n̄. Warǫγī'ra ponaī'na wa'u̯'įnai-anᴀga. Waxǫp'i̯'nį
hīk'īsgë'j̄ ŭaŋkcigǫ'į djōp gūcį'gįxdjįn̄ë'dj̄ ŭaŋgī'j̄ djagū'
ëgī'jį jedjaį'ŋxdjį p'ā djagū 'u̯'wacigį ë'xdjį heregigī're naŋgre.
Ėp'iŋgā'dja. Ŭaŋkci'gįj̄ ŭaŋkcigį'į'n̄egį s'īrëdj̄'ŋxdjį here
nūnįge' jedjaį'ŋxdjį p'ā h̄hę'te'e hadjanaŋgwī'gadj̄.
Han̄ŋk'āraxgu̯ŋxdjī'n̄era djagū'xdjį ëgī'jį gī'u̯'ŋxdjįn̄egā'dj̄.
Hotajį jë'sge hīnu̯xū'rugᴇnįgā'dj̄ tanį-ō'waxūn̄ᴀ. Djan̄hī' hītcō-
k'ewahī'wįra djanᴀga' tanį-ō'hįn̄ᴀ k'ere'rek'djone Djōbenaŋgį-

"Host and members of his clan who are sitting here, I greet you. You seated here who have impersonated the spirits, I send forth my greetings to you."

Then the second person for whom they had put on a kettle spoke.

Speech of ninth guest.—"Host and members of his clan who are seated here, I greet you. To you, seated here, impersonating the spirits, I send my greetings. It is good. The host has tried to make us live. All those present here have been pleading to the spirits who are in control of life and war powers. If any Indians are sick and the keepers of the war bundle give this feast then their illness will be overcome; they will recover from their disease, it is said. My father said that the people used to add more fuel to the fireplace of our chiefs when they do this. My grandfather told me that even if I (insignificant as I am) who speak were to make an offering of food to the spirits it would be good. I knew that he always spoke the truth, yet I knew that such as I could not do anything. (Thus grandfather spoke to me), 'Some day when you are in the presence of war and the rush is about to be made, you will not be frightened for you can say to the spirits, "Grandfathers, I always gave you something to smoke, boiled food for you, and gave you the material for moccasins. Now I wish to go to the fight that is to take place." If you speak to them thus, though you do not hear them answering you, (you will recognize their answer in the fact) that without any effort you will be victorious.' They told the truth to one another, for they were certain of these things. That is why they encouraged one another. This is what the host and the members of his band are doing. It is good. A laudable thing they have done. They have boiled food for our grandmother, the Earth. They have offered her tobacco and buckskins and have as a reward received war powers. It is good. Our grandmother whom they made me impersonate, I greet. Host and all those who are seated within this lodge, I send forth my greetings to you."

Then the third one whom they called on for a kettle rose to thank them and said:

Speech of tenth guest.—"Host and members of his clan who are seated here, I send my greetings toward you. It is good. The host has given the tobacco offerings to the various spirits at the proper time. They (host and clan members) have accomplished very much. Once long ago, four generations back, a man like a spirit in power had told them what to do and since then they have been repeating it. It is good. Their ancestors long, long ago first gave (this feast) and yet even to-day we have seen it. They (host and his relatives) listened attentively to what they said and they have repeated it exactly. We, ourselves, could not accomplish anything if we gave a feast. When in former times they had feasts in honor of our grandfathers, wi'ηxga hīgaī'regį hīrahī'rega waxǫp'į'nį tanįhį'gįgįra waxǫp'ī'nįna hīnącge'nį gīk'arā'djεnaηgre. Jë'sge djadjaį'ηndjį p'ā hī-adjī'rera hī-ā'wįp'erezwī'gadją. Djadjaį'ηxdjį p'ā hoici'pdjį wǫrū'γįra ka'rak'ų'įnera jësgehī'ra wająp'ī'ją herera' hīp'e'reztįwįgā'dją. Nūnįge hąηk'e' hōtajī jë'sge hįnūxurugεnįgā'dją te'ë'jį wahā'-nAgre hąηk'e jë'sge tūxū'rugεnįgā'dją k'īk'ū'rųc'ak ŭaηkcigǫ'įgā'-dją. Haηk'agā' waxǫp'į'nį tanī'na hījąηk'ī'xdjį wagįtūxū'rug tūxū'rugεnįgā'dją. Hōtā' waxǫp'į'nį tanį-ō'gįjųra p'įhī'nAηgre ë wa'ų'įnëge ŭaηkcigǫ'ī'na p'ī'nįηk hi'ŭadją'wįcgųnį. Yarëcanū'nĄ. Waxǫp'į'nį tanī'na gįgī'regį hōnaηkcī'gįgįrë'ra ëp'įηgā'dją. Hąhę'-wįra tanį-ō'gįjūrëgį wǫhĄ' gīk'e'reregį nąpgįrųxā'djeregį. Je'e ë'dja hap'ā'hį wīrū-ā'gįt'e'gį hīraī'rege waigį'u-įna'nęgųnį te'ë'jį. Hąηk'e' wają'nįją ë tųxū'rug 'ų-įnį-ā'nĄga rōhī'ra. Wa'įk'ī'-nĄbra. P'ĳe aī'rera. Jë'sge wāge' wahā'naηk'adją. Warųgįγī'-rera hąhę'regį hū'djane hak'ū'rųhintc rehā'nĄga. Ė'gį warǫγī'ra nįηk'ūrųhi'ndj rehawįdjįgō. Ė'gį waxǫp'į'nį wōnaηkcī'na mīnaηk-cā'waηgre nįηk'ūrųhi'ndj rehawįdjįgō."

Speech of eleventh guest.—"Warǫγī'ra mīnaηkcā'waηgre nįηk'ūrųhi'-ndj rehā'wįdjįgǫ. Ė'gį waxǫp'įnį wō'naηkcī'na tcį-ō'jų mīnaηkcawa-ηgre nįηk'ūrųhi'ndj rehawįdjįgǫ. Warǫγī'ra wōnA'γįre haxī'rį mīnĄ'-ηgįranĄga. Ė'gį jīge tanī'na ŭaηkcigǫ'į' k'aratā' hī'ųnëk'djë'ra tanī'na hak'ā'ranįnā'nĄga ŭaηkcigǫ'į' ta mīnaηgįrā'nAga. Ė'gį wōnA'γįrera p'ī'nĄ hīp'e'rezįrege tairā'nAga hīcdjā'nįrūxųxų'-nAηgre. Ŭaηkcige'dja t'e'ra p'ī'je waī'zara hīją' nąk'īk'ūrųxū'-ruk'į hįją' ŭaηgwā'cǫcegį ŭaηk djanĄgā'gere haną'tcįηxdjį wąją' p'į 'ų'wa'ų'djera. Hīp'e'rezwinânĄ. Ė'gį hąηk'e' wanaį'cgųnį naηk'ų' ŭaηgwā'cǫcenaηk'a jë'sge djīnA'ηgεnį wa'ų'naηkcanĄ. Hawë'xdjį k'ī-ā'nAga jë'sge k'īrūxų'rug wa'ų'naηk'adją ŭaηgwā'-cǫcenaηk'a. Warǫγį'ra hawë'xdjį k'īnā'nAga; tanį' waxų' hįrā'-nAga. Waxǫp'į'nį wǫgī'hanĄgre waxǫp'į'nį nąbįruxā'djεnaηgre me jëgų'įhīgį cAnAwonaγįre-ā'gεre hįηk'ī'rūxųrugī'k'dje. Wajągu'-zεra jë'sge hī'nĄ. Hąηk'ī'ją hatā'gįnąntc hīp'e'rezεnįηge hąηk'e' wǫnA'γįre-ā'gere hīcdjagā' ruxū'rug p'įnī'je. Ŭaηkxetenī'nįηgre ādjī'rënĄ hąηk'ī'ją hątā'gįnątc rųxū'rugεnī'cge waxǫp'į'nį tanį-ō'gįjūra waxop'į'nį nįtā'k'atc gīgįrā' waxǫp'įnį nąbįrųxā'djεra p'įhī'ra wǫnA'γįre hīrųxū'rukce. Hōrā'gεnaηkcAnĄ hīp'e'rezįrā'-nAga wā'naηkce. Te jësge warǫγī'ra hōk'īk'ā'radjεra mīnA'-ηgεnAηgre nāηxgū'įnege wa'ų'nAηgεra. Djāsge' hī-ā'nAga hąηk'e' wǫnA'γįre rųxū'ruk p'ī'nį wa'ų'naηkce! WǫnA'γįre nųxū'rugįregį nīcge hage'dja wīrā'rųxe hī'uηk'djā'wįra. Ŭaηkcigǫ'į'nA hīrana'-ηk'ik'į waxǫp'įnį wōnaηkcī'wįra waxǫp'įnį warā'djįre xetë'ją tanī'na him whom they call Djōbenaŋgiwi'ŋxga gave them tobacco to smoke and he worshiped the spirits sincerely whenever they came to him. Thus these people have done for a long time and that is why we are recognized by the spirits. As often as they gave this feast they gave it for the honor of the spirits. They have done well and we are very well acquainted with the spirits as a consequence. Yet I myself who am now speaking can not do anything; I can hardly be said to have lived (i. e., lived the life of a respectable man). I am unable even to put on one kettle in honor of the spirits. Those who have given this feast to the spirits have done well and perhaps, as a consequence, we may be able to obtain just a little of the blessings of life. So I thought. It is good (I tell you), who have made offerings to the spirits, who are impersonating the spirits. He who has been given the kettle in honor of the Moon expresses his thanks. They gave this to me so that we might plead for them (with the spirits). Not anything of consequence can we say. We are thankful. It is good, it is said. That is what I wish to say. Those counseled, I greet, the spirit who comes at night. Host, I send forth my greetings to you. You impersonating the spirits, I send my greetings toward you."

Speech of eleventh guest.—"Host and his clansmen who are seated here, I send my greetings toward you. Those impersonating the spirits, I send my greetings toward you. The host and his people sit here crying for war powers. Tobacco they offer, asking for life; the tobacco that they possess they sit here offering that they may obtain life. They know that it is good to have war powers and that is why they ask for it with tears in their eyes. It is good to die in war. If you can kill one enemy, then you will be a brave man and all the men will say that you have done a good deed. We would all know it. However, not without effort can men become braves. They must suffer to obtain this honor. The host has made himself suffer; they have poured tobacco. If we do as they did and make feasts for the spirits and offer them buckskins, then we will be able to obtain war powers for ourselves, and only then. That is what the Creator would do. Not without fasting, not white faced,[152] are war powers obtainable. Yet the old men long ago said that if one could not fast, still if he poured tobacco for the spirits and offered them food and if he made excellent offerings of buckskin to the spirits, war powers might be obtained. Thus the elders spoke and they knew of what they were speaking. The host and the clansmen sitting with him listened (to the elders) and that is why they performed (this ceremony so well). How could we ever obtain war powers as they have done? All we hope is that we may obtain some of the war powers that will follow (as a result of the feast here

---

[152] I. e., not without blackening one's face as is done in fasting.

nįtā'k'atc gigī'rɛra nąbịruxā'djɛra wagịrū'cdjAnẹhī'rɛra hoici'p
wīk'ā'rap'erez hīranịhë'k'dje aīregị. Jë'sge ya'wa'ų hąŋk'e hoī'-
niŋge gīxā'wanịnaniŋkdjịnẹge hōwarë'ra hąŋk'ō'niŋge wawë'k'ịrani'-
ŋk'dje. Wājągụ'zɛrȧ ë jë'sge hīge jesgë'nȦ. Warọgịγī'rɛra
hak'ūrụhi'ndj rehā'nAga. Ė'gị warọγī'ra niŋk'ūrụhi'ndj rehā'-
wịdjịgọ. Ė'gị jịge waxọp'ị'nị hōnaŋkcī'na djānAga mīnaŋkcā'waŋgre
niŋk'ūrụhi'ndj rehā'wịdjịgọ."

Host's terminal speech.—Wagịgâ'ra wë'nȦ, nąji-ā'naga wa'ịną'-
pcAnȦ wajōk'ī'ra.
"Sā'k'erenị'ŋk'djoŋgre mīnaŋkcā'waŋgre niŋk'ūrụhi'ndj rehā'-
wịdjịgọ. Ėp'ī'nȦ. Wā'jo ŭanądjōdjaị'sge ha'ụ'wịnȦ hīnagī'-
zōxdjị-ā'nAga. Haị'seretcị mīnaŋgịcā'naŋgịrā'nAga. Ėp'ī'nȦ.
Haizō'xdjịniŋk tcẹbịnagī'gịwịra. Ėp'ī'nȦ. Ė'gị wë'nȦ wagịgō'
hīrūk'o'nAdjẹga wọnA'γịre rūk'o'nAnA djānaga wōgụzɛra'naŋk'ị
jesgë'xdjị wawọgī'ragịrëje aī'rẹra. Ŭaŋgī'ją wọnA'γịre hīrūk'o'-
nAnȦ djanAŋgā'k'ị ŭaŋgɛregị Wajągụ'zɛra hōmịnọ'gɛnoŋk'ị ëp'ā'
ëgị maịhā'gɛregị ë'gị maŋk'ūhą'nẹgị ë'gị je'e' aną'tciŋxdjị
wawọgī'rak rehī'k'djera, ŭaŋgī'ją ŭąharatcce. NawȦ'na djōp'ī'wị
ya'uŋk'djonā're hīją' hīp'ā' waŋgā' họjedjai'ndja, 'ŭącōnuŋk'dje
djọbo'hą hōtcąt'ị' hīk'dje' hīgẹ'gị djọbo'hą wak'dje 'ŭąnAŋgere
jë'sge ë'je ë'gị jë'jị jëgụ hīrā'nAga."

TERMINAL ADDRESS TO THE DOG

Ė'gị cuŋk nąbịruxā'djɛra. Hōcere'ụ'wahịra gīrụcdją' rehī'rẹra.
Wọgī'gọ ŭaŋk'djị-ë'dja hīrụ-ā'k'djịnȦ wōcgọ' je'e' ë rụ-ā'gɛra
herë'nȦ wagịgō'nAŋk'a nąji-ā'nAga wak'ūrụhi'ntccAnȦ.
Host's speech to Disease-giver.—"Sā'kereniŋk'djoŋgere mīnaŋkcā'-
waŋgre niŋk'ūrụhi'ndj rehā'wịdjịgọ. Tcëge'djârëdją ŭaŋgɛnū'-
nịŋgra hītcōk'ehā'wịra wë'je ŭaŋgī'ją wị-orotcọ'djereginaŋk'a
wọnA'γịre hīrūk'onaị'ją hereje'. Rọsā'niŋk hąp 'ụje ë'gị hōt'ẹ'
rūk'onaị'ją hereje' hīk'ịge'je. Tcōk'agā' nądjọdjo'ŋgi rëdjụ'
wanī'na hatci'ndja hīrā'nịhẹgị hoici'pdjị wawịp'e'rez nịhëk'djonë'je
ë'je, ë'nȦ. Djadjo'na tanị-ō'waxụ hā'k'erewịgị hīgụ' p'ejë'ga
haną'tciŋxdjị tanịwōgījū'regị hąŋk'e' hōcere'raniŋk'dje ë'je aī'rẹra.
Jë'sge wa'ụ' tanịwọgī'jụ hīrẹs'ā'je. Rōhiŋk'isgā'wịje hagịtū'cdją
rehā'wịra hịją'niŋk tanị cawaŋxu'ŋk'djawịgị c'uŋkdjā'wịge họnịŋgī'-
tawīnȦ. Niŋk'ūrụhi'ndjwịdjịgọ."
Horucdjo'nȦ he'regị hīrọ-ā'gera haną'tciŋxdjị tanịwọgī'jụ
wagịgī'nȦ ŭaŋgɛra hī'nụgɛra niŋk'djo'ŋgɛra haną'tciŋxdjị.
Haŋk'ī'ją jeginịhā'nịje k'īgâ'ra haną'tc tanịwọgị'jụ hīreje ë'gị
hanātcị'ŋxdji họ-erë'ra herë'nȦ.

given). We feel ourselves connected with life, for surely one of the great spirits will take cognizance of the tobacco, food, and buckskins that we who are impersonating the spirits have offered. Surely they (the spirits) will not care to see (these offerings) lost nor let us cause ourselves to suffer in vain. Thus the Creator said. As counseled ones do, I greet you.[153] Host, I send my greetings toward you. You seated here impersonating the spirits, I send my greetings toward you."

Then the host arose and thanked his guests.

Host's terminal speech.—"War-bundle owners who are seated here, I greet you. It is good. We were living in an abject condition, so you performed this ceremony most carefully for us. All night have you been sitting here. It is good. With the greatest care have you eaten. It is good. That is what those who are in charge of feasts, who are in charge of war powers, counseled us, it is said. I shall now call on a man who can make himself heard by all the spirits who are in control of war power, including those who live above where the Creator lives, to those who live on the earth, and those who live under the earth. I will now sing four songs and when I begin them that will be the end (of the ceremony). Then the man is to give the war whoop four times."

This he said to them. Then the victory whoop was given four times.

Terminal Address to the Dog

Then the dog is sent forth as an offering to Disease-giver. There at the place where the last guest has been(?) the host rises and greets all.

Host's speech to Disease-giver.—"War-bundle owners who are seated here, I greet you. In the beginning one of my grandfathers told me that the man in the south is the greatest one in control of war powers. One side controls death and the other life, he said. He blessed our grandfather and his descendants wherever they might be and he said that he would at all times remember them. Whenever we pour tobacco, then those who offer tobacco will not take sick, he said, it is said. That is the reason they pour tobacco, they said. We are extending to you one like ourselves (the dog), and we have told all, that all who wish to pour tobacco may do so. I greet you all."

When the time has come, then all pour tobacco, the men, the women, and the children. Not one was there left of those who had poured tobacco. They had all scattered.

---

[153] Apparently the name of the spirit he is impersonating has been omitted here. It is the Water.

480 THE WINNEBAGO TRIBE

ADDENDA

Warūtc sakᵉụ'ṇa hīgụ' rūcdjai'ṇaga ë'gị wap'ā' waradjᴇra rūcdjaī'ṇanᴬga ë'gị wap'ā' warā'djịręga k'enị ŭaŋgᴇra' hīṇak'ū'-rụxịraṇị ë'gị wagịgō'naŋk'a wak'ūrụhi'ndjịrehī'je. *Speech of host.*—Sā'k'ereni`ŋk'djoŋgᴇre mīnaŋkcā'waŋgre niŋk'ūrụhi'ndj ɾehā'wịdjịgọ. Hītcō'k'e wahā'wịgị wa'ụ'iṇ̱ẹs'ā`je hoici'-pdjị hījạ' wanᴬyī'rak hōk'ā'ratcgạs'ā`je p'ị hīp'e'rezịręge. Hītcō'k'e wahā'wịgị hījạ' Wanịhë'ga hīgaī'regị hoici'pdjị ë wanᴬyī'rak hōratcgạs'ā'je. Wanayī'rak hōratcgā̧'djęga Wanịhë'ga hīgaī'regị wanayī'rak hōratcgā̧'djęga ŭaŋgịk'ị'je ë'sge p'ī'nᴧ hīp'e'rezịręje Wanịhë'ga hīgaī'regị ŭaŋgwā'cọce xeteje' hạŋk'e' Hịk'ī'sge p'inᴧ wa'ụje'. Tōgịjạ'djaṇe tōtco'ṇa hīk'ā'wakcᴀnᴧ rọyī'res'aje haŋk'e' hōp'ịnị hōwaī'res'ā`je. Ė'sge rọyī'res'aje. Nūnịge Wanịhë'ga tōgī'jạ tōtco'ṇa djōbọ'hạ hīk'awā'kcaje aīrecanū'nᴧ. Ė'sge wanayī'rak hōk'aratcā̧'djęga ë waŋgịk'ịk'ū'rụxụrukce. Hahī' wak'ạtca'ŋkce hahī' sak'ị jë'cge. Ė'sge hoici'p'djị hījạ' wanayī'rak hok'aratcgạs'ā'je. Hịjā̧ jë'sge hak'djonā'wịnᴧ wọhᴧ' tcōni'xdjị djā'wine. Ė ë'dja horok nā̧djona'gịdjạwịgị hīdjo'rogᴇniŋk 'uŋk'djë'ge. Jë'jësge niŋgịtā'wịnᴧ. Sā'k'ereniŋk'-djoŋgᴇre mīnaŋkcā'waŋgre niŋk'ūrụhi'ndj ɾehā'wịdjịgō`.

After they have finished the fast-eating contest and eaten the heads and before the men are picked out [154] then the host greets all.

Speech of host.—"War-bundle owners who are seated here, I send forth my greetings to you. Our grandfathers used to say that if one would take a chance at becoming a ghost [155] then the spirits would consider it especially good. There was one man among our grandfathers who was called He-who-shouts-in-the-distance and he put himself in the position of one who desires death. This warrior, He-who-shouts-in-the-distance, was a great man, an unequaled person. Now in summer it is forbidden to go on a warpath, for no good could come of it. That is why they forbade it. Yet He-who-shouts-in-the-distance went on the warpath four times during the summer, they said. Thus he became one who risked his life. In this way he proved that he was a great man. Finally he became holy and was permitted to carry the war bundle.[156] Thus does one do to be a person who takes risks with his soul.[157] Thus we will do at the very first feast we give. May (the spirits) also have pity upon us [as recompense for] the kettle of which they will partake. That is what we ask. War-bundle owners who are seated here, I greet you."

[154] I. e., before the men to whom kettles had been assigned were called upon to speak.
[155] I. e., risk one's life in a brave way.
[156] It is one of the greatest privileges a warrior can obtain to carry the war bundle when on the warpath.
[157] I have purposely translated this phrase, "wanaɣⁱ' rak hŏratcgǎ' dją" in three different ways to give all the different shades of meaning it possesses.

The War-bundle Feast of the Thunderbird Clan

(SECOND VERSION)

Informant, member of Thunderbird clan:[1] There were originally four warriors. The youngest one was the bravest and the most powerful. He claimed that his father was a Thunderbird and his mother a Night Spirit. He is the one who made the bundle about which we are going to speak.

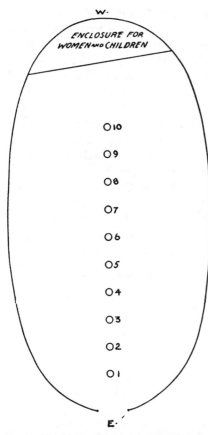

The lodge (fig. 38) is prepared by the nephews and the women relatives of the host, generally his nieces and wives. The invited guests arrive toward evening, while the women are still preparing the buckskins. These buckskins are to be made as perfectly white as possible. Only those women who have passed their climacteric are permitted to do this. As soon as the buckskins are prepared the kettles are put on the fire. The buckskins are taken by the host and marked with the specific symbols associated with the different spirits. (For the markings, see pls. 47, 48.) These buckskins are then tied to a stick. That for Earthmaker is attached to the stick with the head pointing upward; that for the Thunderbird has the stick and the head of the buckskin facing the west; that for the Night has the stick and head of the buckskin facing east; that for the Star also faces east, as do all the others not mentioned. When the sticks have been prepared and the buckskins attached to them, the latter are rolled up upon the sticks. Whosoever of the guests is the oldest feast-giver then arises and pours tobacco, first for the fire and then for all the other spirits. When they start the fire for the first time they use the old ceremonial fire sticks. With that the ceremony begins. When the old man is

Fig. 38.—Plan of Thunderbird clan war-bundle feast. 1, Buckskin for earthmaker. 2, Buckskin for disease-giver. 3, Buckskin for thunderbirds. 4, Buckskin for night-spirits. 5, Buckskin for morning star. 6, Buckskin for sun. 7, Buckskin for moon. 8, Buckskin for water-spirit. 9, Buckskin for earth. 10, Buckskin for heroka.

---

[1] This is a generalized account.

through, the buckskin is taken down, unrolled, and the thunder-buck-skin given to the band sitting opposite the host. The other buckskins are then distributed in rotation, except that the buckskin to Earth-maker is given to the guest who occupies the middle position in the lodge. All the guests remain standing with their unrolled buckskins, holding them by the sticks and keeping tobacco in their other hand, while the old man speaks to them and blows first upon a flute. Then, to the accompaniment of a gourd, he sings two songs. After that the buckskins are rolled up again in such a way that the markings remain visible, and hung up again on sticks that are placed near the individual invited guests, just west of the first fireplace. There they have a pole for Earthmaker, at whose foot the war bundle is placed and opened. Tobacco is then poured into the hands of each of the invited guests by the host. He offers tobacco especially for those individuals for whom he has prepared buckskins and kettles, asking each of them in turn for life and for victory on the warpath. When he finishes he pours some tobacco into the fire and some upon the war bundle. All the persons invited then, in turn, do the same. If the host has any chil-dren present in the lodge, he has them do the same. Children are always escorted by the attendant. The host now takes the gourds, drum, etc., and, remaining in his own place, sings different sets of songs. As often as he starts a new set, he blows upon his flute. The songs of the Thunderbird consist of eight starting songs, sung slowly, six dancing songs, etc. As soon as the dancing songs are begun, all the men in the lodge come around the war bundle and dance, blowing the flute, etc. Women may dance likewise, but they must remain in that part of the tent especially assigned to them.

Before the contents of the kettle are cooked the host sings four sets of songs. As soon as the first set has been started the attendants get as many pipes as possible and bring them to the war bundle. They also place there a large pipe with stem directed toward the west and a large pile of tobacco. These pipes are then passed back to the various guests in order to be smoked.

After the first set of songs is over the large pipe is taken and lit by one of the attendants and passed around the lodge, in ceremonial manner, each member taking a puff and passing it to the next one. When the songs to the Disease-giver are sung, the pipe is placed against the center pole with stem directed south. Before the Disease-giver songs are sung the story of their origin is told. At the end of the last of the initial songs the old man with tobacco in each hand says *Ho—o—o—o-!* He then pours tobacco into the fireplace. He is really presenting it to the Disease-giver. Then dancing songs are used as before. Usually dog meat is put in the kettle designed for the Disease-giver.

When the songs of the Night Spirit are sung the stem of the pipe is pointed eastward.

Four songs are sung before the cooking is finished, in honor of the Thunderbird. The feast is then spread, and all those in the lodge smoke and dance. The attendants take the kettles down and take the food out. While the kettles are still on, however, branches of cedar are carried around the lodge to purify it. Before distributing the food, while the singing is still going on, the attendants count the number of people in the lodge and cut the meat into a corresponding number of pieces. As each kettle is supposed to suffice for any one band, a number of small sticks about the size of a toothpick, corresponding to the number of people present in each band, is placed in each kettle. After the last four songs are used the host arises and calls for the kettle that is to be given to the person opposite him. The attendant brings it and tells him how many pieces of meat there are in the kettle. The host then speaks about his intentions in offering the kettle to the spirits; that he is seeking life and victory in war, and that he begs all those present to intercede for him. He then calls for the other kettles. There are generally one or two kettles for the women and children. When the feast is spread out and they all have their food, the host tells them that they may now eat whenever they think proper. He himself does not eat anything, but merely sings, shaking the gourds that he holds in his hand.

The Disease-giver is considered the most sacred of all the spirits, and for that reason all the bones and the plates that have been used in connection with his particular kettle are purified with cedar branches. The host carries these bones out of the lodge himself and buries them under the foot of some tree. He also takes tobacco and red feathers along with him on this occasion. As the other spirits are not considered to be as sacred as the Disease-giver, the bones from the kettles offered to them can be buried anywhere, provided the ground has been purified.

After the first invited guest has finished his meal he rises and thanks the host. He then tells the story of how he, or his ancestor, obtained the war bundle, and assures the host that he feels confident that so great a feast as this in which he is taking part will most certainly be recognized by the spirits. He also adds that inasmuch as he and the other invited guests have partaken of this feast they also hope to receive life and strength in proportion to the blessings bestowed upon the host. The other invited guests, in turn, speak in the same way.

While this is going on the attendants are preparing the kettles for another lot of meat. The whole tent is swept again and purified and the kettles are once more placed upon the fireplaces. The host now rises and, holding tobacco in his hand, informs each spirit of the par-

ticular kettle assigned to him.   Then he pours out tobacco.   Now one
of the attendants goes around the lodge and scatters small swan
feathers in every direction, even putting some near the kettles.

The host then prepares to sing night songs, but before doing so he
takes down the buckskin assigned to the Nights, blackens his face
with the ember used for marking that buckskin, and puts swan
feathers upon his head.   It is said that those who during their
fasting time visited the land of the Night Spirits saw swan feathers
scattered all over the land, and that is why they use them now.   The
host now has the pipe turned toward the east and before singing the
night songs tells the origin of these songs.   He asks all the other
invited guests present to help him with his songs and apologizes for
asking so much of them.   He now uses two sets of songs.   When
the dancing songs are sung all the men who so desire may come
around the war bundle and dance, and some may even dance near
the places where they sit.   When he has finished his songs he passes
the drum, gourds, flute, and tobacco to the invited guest opposite
him.   This one now arises, pours out tobacco, and tells the origin of
his particular war bundle and sings the night song connected with it
for the benefit of the host.   He then repeats the same actions that the
host has done.   The drum, etc., are now passed to the next man, and
so on until daylight.   Some one especially selected is given the honor
of singing those songs that are connected with the taking down of
the buckskins, and when this one starts his song all the invited
guests in whose honor kettles have been put on the fireplace take
down their buckskins and, holding them in their hands, walk around
the lodge four times.   An attendant precedes them, walking backward and purifying the path.   The buckskin with the cross marked
on it is generally carried first.   The fourth time they make the
circuit all those in the lodge first hold their hands over the cedar
incense and then touch the buckskin, because Earthmaker is going to
use it for moccasins, so that, by touching it, they might become
strengthened.   After they had made the circuit for the fourth time
they rolled up the buckskins and threw them through the openings in
the roof of the lodge, so that the spirits for whom they were intended
might receive them.

After the buckskins have been thrown out tobacco is poured into
the fireplace and all the people take their places and dance.   When
the drum has made the entire circuit of the lodge—that is, when it has
again returned to the host—the latter rises and sings the so-called
paint songs.   A short time before that a number of kettles had been
put on the fireplace for the so-called lower spirits.   The host then
declares that the feast is ready and that whenever they wish to
the guests may begin to eat.   The rites of the preceding feast are
now repeated.   Toward the end of the feast the host takes his bundle,

wraps it up, and hangs it behind him in the lodge, but he keeps the flute unpacked.   When all but the last four songs have been finished he calls upon some one who has a rather strong voice to give the war whoop, which he does, at the end of the song.   This war whoop is given so that all the spirits might hear it.   When he is through all the other guests give war whoops four times, and the feast is over.

The War-bundle Feast of the Thunderbird Clan

(third version)

Informant, member of the Thunderbird clan: When the feast is ready, the buckskin prepared, and the kettles of meat put on to boil, then the host rises and says as follows:

"Warriors and sons of warriors who are present here, I greet you all.   You have put aside all the wrongs I have done you and accepted my invitation.   I am glad of it.   You have filled my lodge. It is good.   Our four great ancestral fathers were all warriors.   The oldest one was called Whirling-Four, the second one Sitting-Chief, the third one Wabanansaka, and the fourth one Kills-Within-Lodge. When in battle, Kills-Within-Lodge was bullet-proof.   He used to wear a belt which when full of shot he would loosen and his blanket-belt would be full of bullets.   He is the one that made this bundle. With it one can obtain victory and blessings.

"The blessing we ask of you is war; for ourselves and for all who are present.   We have offered kettles to all the spirits and we will also pour tobacco for them.   This is why I am speaking to you, warriors, and you taking the place of the spirits.   All in this lodge I greet.   I greet you all."

He takes tobacco and gives some to each of those who have been especially invited.   Then he goes to the fireplace and throws some tobacco into the fire, saying: "Here it is.   Here it is.   To you who stand in the center of the lodge, to you I offer tobacco.   You encouraged us to believe that when we call upon some of your fellow-spirits, it would be only necessary to put tobacco upon your head, and that you would deliver the message.

"This is the first blessing we ask—namely, that our weapons and not those of our enemies be made sharp.   And if in a vision we be directed to go on the warpath, may we receive the complete blessing, even though we be in the midst of the battle.   Therefore do we lay all these birdskins that are used in war here in the center of our lodge.   We pray that if we use one of them we will be able to avoid danger and that we be granted long life.   For that reason, grandfather, Fire, do I pour tobacco to you.   Here it is.   Here it is.

"And thou, grandfather, Earthmaker, I offer tobacco to you. I offer tobacco to you. It was you who made the tobacco, yet we were told that even you cannot take it from us unless we offer it to you willingly, because you ordained it thus. I offer tobacco to you, that I may become a warrior and have long life. This I ask of you. A white-furred animal, a deer, with its hide, the buckskin, and its meat as food, do I offer to you together with tobacco. The hide you may use for moccasins. Here it is.

"And you, Big Black Hawk, you who are in charge of war weapons, I offer tobacco to you, that my prowess as a warrior, if I be blessed with any, may be great and audacious. Even if it is only a single enemy (that I encounter), may I be the victor. May we go through battle without injury. A kettle containing half of a deer, with its hide for moccasins, we offer to you. Here it is. Tobacco we offer to you. Here it is.

"You who live in the place of the setting of the sun, Thunder-chief, tobacco I offer to you. When my grandfather made his war bundle you added your power; and whatever knowledge of warcraft you possessed you taught him. For that we now ask you. One of our members[2] whom we feed like a baby, we offer to you together with tobacco. Here it is.

"You who live in the east, who walk in darkness, tobacco we offer to you. When our grandfather, Kills-Within-Lodge, made the spirit bundle you added your war power. We ask that when we take this bundle up we may be able to gain victory without any effort on our part. This we ask of you. As our children become big enough to go on the warpath may you see to it, in your mysterious manner, that we have war. We offer you tobacco and also a kettle containing a female deer with hide for moccasins. These we offer you. Here it is.

"You who live in the south, you who give us sickness, to that part of your body which contains life, we offer tobacco. In the bundle that our grandfather made you added your war power. That power we now ask of you. In the middle of the day you blessed our grandfather. That blessing we ask of you again. One of our members who wears a headdress,[3] do we offer to you, and likewise a deerskin for moccasins. All these together with tobacco we offer you. Here it is.

"To you, grandfather, the Sun, I offer tobacco. You blessed my grandfather, Kills-Within-Lodge, with your power when he made his war bundle. The blessing that you gave him, that do I ask of you. Let that be your first gift. May we have victory in war: and in the presence of the weapons of our enemies, make us safe. If there be any men (enemies) to whom death has been ordained, may we be

---

[2] He is referring to the dogs eaten at this feast.
[3] I. e., a deer.

the ones who will be the victors. It is said of you that even if a prayer be offered to you in silence, along with the tobacco, you will hear it. Here we offer you tobacco, deer for food, and buckskin for moccasins. This, grandfather, is our prayer and our offering.

"To you, grandmother, the Moon, do we offer tobacco. We desire to have victory in battle. The blessings you bestowed upon our grandfather, Kills-Within-Lodge, when you blessed him with the powers of a warrior, those give to us now. The blessings that were not fulfilled by him (that is, all those blessings that death prevented him from using) we ask that they may be fulfilled by us. Tobacco and deer for food and buckskin, all these we offer to you. Here it is. Here it is.

"To you, Morning Star, do we offer tobacco. When my grandfather was blessed with your power, while he was making his war bundle, he was to give you tobacco for smoking and food at midnight. That is what we are trying to do, although we are lacking in all the essentials necessary for success. However, we wish to be prepared in times of trouble and that is why we ask, grandfather, that we be blessed with life. A kettle with tobacco, enough buckskin for moccasins, and tobacco we offer to you.

"To you, grandmother, the Earth, do we offer tobacco also. We pray for victory in war and for all the medicines that are necessary to obtain it, so that we may bind ourselves with medicine; that we may use the flowers of the earth for paint—all that is red and all that is blue—this we ask of you. Should there be anything better, we ask that you arrange it so that we obtain it. Tobacco and corn for food do we offer to you, and should you need more tobacco we will send it along. Here it is.

"To you, Eagle Chief, you who blessed our grandfather with power to conquer in war while he was making his bundle of spirit-power, do we offer tobacco. For all that he told us to retain and which he said was powerful in the bundle, I am making this feast. I am trying to-night to make a feast in honor of the spirits. To you and to the hawk I offer this kettle."

All the kettles which are to be used at this feast have by this time been put on. The nephews act as attendants and place the kettles on the fireplaces. Those spirits for whom no kettles are placed on the fire receive tobacco as an offering. After the host has offered tobacco to these latter spirits, he returns to his place and sits down. Then the war-bundle owners to whom tobacco had been given get up in turn and with one hand pour tobacco into the fire and with the other upon the war bundle. The host then rises and speaks as follows:

"Sons of war, and you who stand in the footsteps of the spirits, all you who are in this lodge, I greet you. We are boiling hot water for the spirits. We will try also to use some of the songs that were taught to the owner of the bundle when he was blessed. We will perhaps make you smoke poor tobacco and tire you out by making you sit too long, and we will probably keep you hungry too long, but we know that you have served at these feasts and that this ceremony is good and that you know how to carry it on. It is good that you act thus. They say that if we sit up all night at a feast we will be able to obtain victory in war and long life. For this purpose you have come here and intend to sit with us. We are very glad. We will be at your service and as soon as the attendants have the food ready you shall receive some. To those sitting in the place of the setting of the sun, the Thunderers, we will sing the songs they taught our grandfather. We will attempt to sing them for you. If we can remember them, we will use about four."

After he has concluded, the members of his band sing the Thunderbird songs and when they are finished they sing the dancing songs.

When these are over the host speaks again.

"Sons of wars, I greet you. We are delivering our speeches as fast as possible. When our grandfather was blessed he fasted, denying himself water. He suffered much. It was then that the spirits had compassion upon him. One of the spirits met him in broad daylight, one day, at noon. He blessed him with victory in war and with the life, or good half, of his body,[4] and with the right to hand on this blessing for generations. As long as the people offer red feathers and tobacco and make feasts in his honor, so long will he not trouble them with disease. He said that these were the things he liked—dog, red feathers, and tobacco. These are the things that we accordingly offer him. We will now use his songs, which are in another language. I suppose we will make a great many mistakes, but it is said that even if a person knows only one song he should try and use it, for through it victory in war and long life can be obtained. With this thought before us we will try. We were also told that we must leave nothing undone.

"Sons of wars, and you who represent the spirits, I greet you."

Now the slow songs are sung, and after they are finished, the dance songs. Then the host rises and speaks again.

"Sons of war, I greet you. After we have used four lots of songs we will have the feast. The attendants will have the food ready about that time. The songs that we will attempt to sing will be Thunderbird songs and the songs of the different spirits that accompany this bundle, the Sun, the Moon, the Morning Star, the Earth, the Water, the Daylight, and the Eagle. The songs of all of these spirits we will try to use and sing.

---

[4] Evidently it was the Disease-giver who blessed him.

"Sons of war, I greet you."

After these songs are sung the host speaks again.

"Sons of wars, I greet you. We will sing the dancing songs. If anyone cares to dance he may do so. They say that through dancing, also, we may obtain victory in war. Therefore you women may dance and help your brothers. Dancing also is a means of obtaining life. We will now sing about four songs if we can remember them."

When the songs are over the leader says:

"Warriors, I greet you. We will sing another lot of songs and then we will have our feast. This lot of songs was sung by our grandfather, who obtained victory with them, so he added them to his bundle. So we are told. These songs can also be sung by watchmen in the camp, or on the warpath, or before the rush for the enemy, as well as while crossing rivers and in scouting. We will now try to sing them. Warriors all, who are seated here, I greet you."

The host then sings the slow songs and then the dancing songs. Then he continues:

"Warriors, I greet you. The next four songs we sing will be for all the spirits for whom we have placed these kettles of tobacco and buckskin for moccasins. The first kettle over the first fireplace is a big deer head, which our chief will partake of. This kettle is in honor of Earthmaker. The kettle will be placed for our chief. We know that he has been attentive to the spirits and that he has the right to forbid us to do wrong.

"The next kettle will be put on in honor of the war spirits who live in the place of the setting of the sun. It will be placed before the Thunderbird clan people. It is our desire that the spirits remember us for these our offerings. For that reason we will turn over to them a kettle with tobacco and enough buckskin for moccasins.

"The kettle on the second fireplace we intend to offer to the war spirit, the Big Black Hawk. Together with the kettle, we are offering tobacco and buckskin. It will be placed before Strikes-the-Tree. He understands this affair better than we do. He understands what our intentions toward the spirits are and he can therefore best make them understand us. Another kettle on the same fireplace we intend for the sun. We have already made known our intentions to him by offerings of tobacco and buckskin. That kettle will be placed for our grandfather, who understands and can perform these things better than we can.

"On the third fireplace there is a kettle for our grandmother who comes up after the dark—the Moon. That will be placed before my nephew. He knows how to take care of a war bundle. That we wish should be made known to the moon he will make it known, as he knows how to do it.

"The next kettle is in honor of the Morning Star. We offer tobacco, buckskin, and food to him. This kettle is to be placed before my uncle, as he knows how to make offerings to spirits better than we do. All that we wish is that the spirits should know that we have done this; and he understands how to make this known to the spirits. Warriors, I greet you. The kettles have now all been put on by the attendants and we offer to you all that they can hold. It will be lacking in every way, but, warriors, you understand how to divide it. Knowing this, we know that you will all get some. Whenever you get ready you can start eating. In the meantime we will sing."

After singing four songs those present partake of the feast. When the feast is over, the guest who received the first kettle rises and speaks:

"Elders and you who are mere participants, who have partaken of our feast, and you warriors, I greet. It is truly good. Who would not say it is good? Relatives, a lesson this has been to me, the fact that I have been invited. It is indeed a real pleasure for me to be here, but I have been accorded an even greater honor in that I have been given a kettle, and especially that it should be just that kettle that we offer to the greatest spirit, Earthmaker. For him have I eaten and for him have I smoked the tobacco that was offered. We will be strengthened by the blessing that it brings us. All our relatives that had anything to do with this offering will be strengthened. How can the spirits help recognizing such an offering? It is said that if we wish anything of the spirits and we offer tobacco to them they would accept and recognize it. Surely such an offering as this (in which we have participated) will be received by the spirits, and assuredly they will bless our host with victory, just as he has wished it. I am thankful that I had something to do with it. I consider that my life has been renewed. I therefore greet him, Earthmaker, and I greet the host and the warriors who are representing the spirits. I greet them all."

Then the guest who had received the second kettle rises and speaks:

"Hosts and relatives who are sitting around me, I greet you all. It is good. Who would nòt say that it is good? I do not intend this as mere imitation of the preceding speaker, but my grandfather taught me to be thankful at all times for such an affair as this. I did not gain honor in war, and (for my presence here) I am consequently all the more thankful. It is good. He has honored me together with the spirits when he offered to them tobacco, buckskin, and food and when he asked them for victory and life. How could such a one go unblessed? Do not the spirits even know our thoughts? I thank all the relatives that have partaken of this spirit food, through which they will be strengthened. Again I say, it is good. In my thoughts I greet you, feasters. Spirits of war, elders, warriors, I greet you."

Then the third speaker rises and speaks:

"Elders and relatives, I greet you. Warriors within this lodge, I greet you also. It is good. Who would not say it is good? Many times have they done this to us in the past. They understand and know how to make examples for us to follow. They have made offerings of tobacco, of food, and buckskin for moccasins to all the spirits. They have gathered us together and given us places of honor that we may obtain life thereby. They have given us spirit-food to eat in the presence of our relatives. The blessings they receive will also strengthen us in life. With these thoughts we have partaken of the feast. While boiling the water, the attendants have burned their hands, and surely they will for this reason take part in war, with honor. It is good that it is thus. What spirit could overlook such an offering? It must surely be known to them. Again I say it is good. You feasters, host, and warriors, I greet you all."

Then the fourth speaker rises and speaks:

"Elders and relatives, I greet you. Host and feasters, I greet you. It is good, the previous speakers have told me. Most certainly it is good. The chiefs have up to now asked blessings for the Winnebago fireplaces. Our host has also made offerings to all the spirits and asked victory and life for our women and children. I hope we minor ones will also receive blessings. A spirit named Kills-Within-Lodge came upon earth in the flesh and caused this (feast) to be made, and to this day it is so. It is good. With war he was blessed, we all have heard it told. It is good that we have partaken of this food, for we have been told that all meat partaken in feasts strengthens us with spirit blessings. I want to thank all of the relatives and feasters who are here, and for that reason I am speaking. Feasters, I greet you all; I greet you all."

Then he speaks again:

"It is good, my relatives, that the spirits have been given offerings of food, tobacco to light their pipes, and buckskin to use for moccasins. Now it is the midnight of the spirits, and we have all heard that at this time they turn over in their beds in spirit land, and whoever offers tobacco to them now can be assured that they will smoke it. For this reason the people have added food and moccasins. They will surely bless them with the victory and life for which they have asked. We believe that those who have partaken of the feast will be blessed, for it is said that the spirits even know our thoughts. This is what I think. I am sure I have been strengthened by it. Feasters, I greet you all. You likewise, Grandmother Moon, I greet."

The kettles are now put on again.

Now the host speaks again:

"Warriors, I greet you. It is good that you have told one another my wishes and spoken about the things that are usually discussed at this ceremony. I say again that it is good to hear such words from you. We are making you suffer, but the attendants are putting on the kettles again. I will therefore give all the spirits for whom kettles have been prepared smoking material again. I greet you all."

Then he begins to pour out tobacco for the spirits. As often as he calls upon a spirit so often does he pour tobacco into the fire, saying as follows in each case:

"Here it is, the tobacco, grandfather, who are in the middle of the lodge. We have been told that you said you were the mediator between (the spirits and human beings). It is said that if we place on your head tobacco for the spirits you would see to it that our offering had not been made in vain. So I pour tobacco for you. Here it is.

"To you, in the South, the Disease-giver, grandfather, I offer tobacco. A four-legged animal,[5] one of our own members, we have put in the kettle for you. Tobacco, food, feathers, and buckskin we offer you. You blessed our grandfather and met him in the middle of the day. With the blessing with which you blessed him do you now bless us. This we ask of you—that fever (disease) may not come upon us, and that we may have victory and life. This we ask of you because you claim that you are in charge of these things. Grandfather, in return for all the things that we ask you, we offer tobacco for your pipe. The same we offer to your grandfathers, those under the light, those who walk in darkness.[6] My grandfather you blessed. The things that you taught him we ask for. Our offerings are poorly given, and not of the best kind, but it is said that your feelings can not be hurt since you permitted our grandfather to enter your spirit-home. We pour tobacco for you, Nights, that victory may come our way, and that you might walk faster so that day may come to us sooner. Men's tobacco, food, and buckskin we offer you. Here it is.

"Morning Star, tobacco we offer you, with buckskin and food. When our grandfather made a bundle of spirit-powers, you added your blessing of warrior prowess. That is what I ask of you—that we may have victory whenever we meet the enemy. It is said that if we wait till then we might not receive your blessing. That is why we ask it now. We pour tobacco for you.

"To you, the chief of the Eagles, I offer tobacco. In our grandfather's fasting you blessed him with victory in war. That which he

---

[5] Cf. note 2.
[6] I. e., the Night Spirits.

would have used were he alive do I ask of you. And if we take the feathers that are in this war bundle on the warpath, may it so happen that even if we see only one enemy we may be the ones to have the war honor. This is what we ask of you and for this we offer tobacco to you.

"To you, Hare, do we offer tobacco. Here it is. The blessing you bestowed on our grandfather, that we ask of you, the so-called nephew. Victory in war and life we ask, should we ever go on the warpath; that we may conquer without effort and that we may be safe in the midst of the weapons of our enemies.

"To you, the Turtle, we offer tobacco. Here it is. Men's tobacco we offer you that you may fill your pipe. Our offerings are lacking in every respect, for we have no kettle for you. But we can not offend you, it is said. You have, in truth, power in war and that is why we ask you for victory in war. Grandfather, we offer you tobacco.

"To you, grandmother, the Earth, do we offer tobacco. We offer you men's tobacco. We ask victory in war from you. When our grandfather made a bundle of spirit-power, you added your power. For that reason we have been keeping tobacco for you. Here it is. Grandmother, we offer tobacco to you.

"To all those who have blessed our grandfather with spirit-power— for we do not know you all—we offer tobacco to those on earth and to those above. It is our desire that you bless us with the blessings you conferred upon our grandfather. Grandfathers, warriors, I greet you all. I am sorry that I have been boring you with my talk, and that I have perhaps made you smoke too much. But we wish to obtain victory and life, and it is said that patience gains both of these. Knowing this, you have faithfully sat through this whole ceremony. I thank you, and yet I must ask more of you. I must ask that the drum and songs be sent around the lodge as soon as I get through singing. As the Nights go around the earth at night so will the drum go around this lodge. I will now use the songs of the Nights, that is what I mean. Warriors, I greet you."

After singing slow songs he sings dancing songs, and then he speaks again:

"Warriors, I greet you. As I said before, you may sing the songs of the Nights. Your songs are certainly more spirit-like, and they have the power of obtaining life. I now send the drum to you."

Then the attendants take the drum, together with some tobacco, and carry it across the lodge, to a place opposite the host, and place it in front of one of the guests belonging to another clan. He also puts some tobacco in the hands of this person. Then the one about to sing rises and speaks as follows:

"Feast-givers and relatives, as well as you guests who are present, I greet you all. It is good that I have been honored by being placed in the path of the drum. It is said that so great is the sacredness attached to this affair that one must not refuse to accept the drum as it passes around the lodge. I also feel honored at the offering of tobacco. Indeed I feel saved, and I pray that whosoever comes in contact with these things may be strengthened thereby. As soon as I have offered the tobacco I will use the songs of our fathers. We do not know them as well as we ought to, but we will try nevertheless. It is said that if you only know one song, you must try to use it even to the point of tears; just as it is said, that if you cry after a victory you must put aside all sense of shame. Thinking of these things I will now try to sing. Tobacco I offer you."

He throws it into the fire, saying at the same time, "Grandfathers, Night Spirits, I offer you tobacco. I know that we will spoil your songs, but it is said that you are merciful and that you will sing them again to yourselves correctly. If we make any mistakes have pity on us, grandfathers, and we ask you to walk faster so that daylight may come soon. Here is the tobacco. We offer it to you."

Then he sings slow songs, and then dancing songs. One of the attendants now comes forward with tobacco in his hand, and takes the drum and moves it to another of the invited guests. He also gives this person some tobacco. This one then rises and thanks all the other people in general and says approximately the same as the man before him, praising them for all the things he could think of, accepting the tobacco, and then offering it to the spirits and to the fire. He particularly asks the Nights to walk faster so that morning might come to them sooner. After he sings his songs, which like the others are Night songs, the drum is taken and moved to another of the invited guests. Thus it passes from one to another until it has made the entire circuit of the lodge. Generally at about dawn it reaches the place of the host, from where it had started on the previous day. He sings certain songs which are called the old night songs, because the old nights are not supposed to come until approaching daylight and because their hair is white from age. When they come they bring light. All those who may perhaps have fallen asleep at this time either wake up or are awakened, for the Nights who now come are old and carry canes which, when directed toward a sleeping person, causes him to die. After the host has finished the old night songs he sings the dancing songs.

The buckskins are then taken down and carried around the lodge. All those present now arise and dance in their special places, as the buckskin passes them. The host and his invited guests now take their buckskins in one hand, holding tobacco at the same time, and pass around the lodge in single file. Thus they go around the lodge four times. The fourth time they make the circuit they stop at the first fireplace and throw the buckskins through the holes of the lodge. It is supposed that the old Night Spirits seize them at this moment and carry them up to the sky with them. The singing now ceases, and all the people take their seats again. The drum is now taken and placed in front of the host's place. He thereupon rises and speaks as follows:

"Ye warriors, as many as you are who are sitting here, I greet. It is good that you have complied with my wishes and that the spirits have already taken their buckskins and their food, and that they have left our presence. But nevertheless we will sing our last song, even if it appears that they are being sung into empty space. I know that you have already had compassion upon me, even although I am making you suffer with hunger, but let us, nevertheless, sing one more song, and then we can rest. My grandfather used these songs in time of war, and never did he miss a war honor when using them. These we will now use. You, warriors, and those of you who possess holy paints, it must seem shameful to you for me to speak this way. For we have no holy paint. However, we will not sing them with the intention of making people believe that we have holy paints, but simply because we have used them in war and found them good. That is why I am about to use them now, and that is why they belong to this bundle. Warriors, you may hear. Know you that I will use these songs in seeking victory and life. Nor will the dancing be limited merely to those who possess paint, but to anyone of the warriors here present. This will be the last dancing song. I greet you all."

Then he sings some songs, both the slow and the dancing songs. After that he rises and says the following:

"Warriors who are seated here, I greet you. I suppose it is enough that I have made you suffer with hunger all night. As soon as the attendants can get around to it the food will be placed before you again. I know that it will be lacking in every respect, but let me appeal to your good natures. On this first fireplace there is going to be a kettle for the Disease-giver. A four-legged animal, one of his own members, we will offer to him, together with tobacco and deerskins. We are also going to send to him a little four-legged animal, one with whom our children have been fond of playing. He is now in front of us. Whoever wishes to offer tobacco to the Disease-giver can do so now, and as soon as the feast is over and the bones are gathered, we will take them and, strewing tobacco upon them, place them outside. Let me tell you again that anyone who wishes may offer tobacco and ask of the Disease-giver that he keep illness away from him. Women are not permitted to partake of this kettle, so see to it that only men eat of it. As I said before,

O warriors, the food will be lacking in every respect, but try, nevertheless, to have it pass around.

"We also have a kettle on the fireplace for the Nights, which the attendants will put on in honor of the father of my wife and my own father. We offer, likewise, tobacco and deerskin along with this kettle, to the Night Spirits, so that we may obtain victory and life. That is what we wish. As I said before, I will not have any too much food for you. But they say the spirits are merciful.

"To the Morning Star we will also offer a kettle. We will have it put on for Ku′nu, as he understands these affairs better than we do and knows better than we how to ask the spirits for blessings. We offer, in addition to the kettle, tobacco and buckskin, asking victory and life from the spirits in return. As I said before, warriors, our grandfather never failed when he had this bundle. That is why we have kettles put on the fire in honor of it.

"To our fourth brother we will offer another kettle, in honor of the chief of the Eagles, praying for life and victory. Warriors who are seated here, I greet you all. Whenever you get ready to eat you may do so, and we will, during that time, sing some of our songs."

Then they sing Earthmaker songs. These songs were songs that a certain person called Wegi′ceka obtained in his blessings from all the spirits, but they were taught to him by Earthmaker.

After Wegi′ceka had been blessed by all the spirits there was just one lacking, and that was Earthmaker. So he fasted more and more, almost to the point of death, crying and longing for a blessing from Earthmaker. Finally he was told that he was to be blessed by him. At the appointed place and time a being wearing dark clothes and carrying a cane that looked fear-inspiring stood before him, like the blue of the sky. "Wegi′ceka," he said, "I bless you. You have inflicted suffering upon yourself and have hungered and thirsted on my account. With everything that I possess do I bless you; with victory and with the power to heal the sick, with riches and with good fortune as a hunter, and even with the power of having women become enamored of you—with all these things I bless you." Then he turned and walked away and Wegi′ceka saw that it was a bluejay. He felt very much humbled and so he fasted again. Four times was he treated thus. Finally he even sacrificed one of his own children, and then he was told that at a certain time and place, about the hour of noon, he would meet Earthmaker. When he came there some one said, "Wegi′ceka, I bless you. You have humbled yourself and cried unto me. I bless you. Heretofore I have blessed nobody. You are the first one." Thus he spoke, and he gave him the cane and four songs. Those are the songs which we use at the end of our feast.

After these songs are finished and the invited guests and the others present have finished eating, the feast is practically over, with the exception of a few remarks. The host rises and speaks as follows:

"Warriors and guests, I greet you all. It is good that we have this life-power to use in our travels through life. The spirits caused us to make offering and have also given us a chance to sing the songs of our forefathers. This they made us do. It is good. Our guests have shown us a great example in that they have offered enough buckskin for all the spirits and enough food and tobacco. What spirit could let such an offering pass unnoticed, without bestowing a blessing? It is said that even if you wish something and do not express it in words, still if you pour tobacco into the fire you will obtain what you wish. If that is the case, how much greater must the efficacy of the offerings be that were made here! You Feast-givers and relatives, I consider it a blessing that I was permitted to be present here. But that blessing was even increased when I was called upon to partake from a kettle offered to one of the greatest spirits. I feel that now I will surely be able to live. They say that the one called Disease-giver has victory and life in one half of his body. Therefore I greet the Disease-giver. Feast-givers, warriors, all you who are present, I greet you."

The second singer now speaks.

"Elders and ye other guests who are present, I greet you all. It is good. It is good. Who could say otherwise? Relatives, a great example has been set us. We have seen buckskins for moccasins, tobacco, and food offered to the spirits, and we ourselves have been permitted to represent these spirits by proxy, that we also might live and be strengthened; that if we should ever chance upon the enemy we might remain safe and unharmed. Such, in substance, were the tearful prayers of our leaders to-night. They prayed for victory and life, and made their offerings to the Nights, of deerskin, tobacco, and food. Most assuredly have the Nights accepted these offerings, for they have walked fast as we asked, and the night has been very short. They certainly have answered our prayers. It is good. We likewise feel that the fact that we have been here with our relatives and partaken of everything will strengthen us in life. Feast-givers and guests, I greet you all. Warriors and singers, I greet you."

Then the third one rises and speaks. He says about the same thing as the former. The fourth one does the same. When they are finished, the host rises and thanks them because they have said and done the things that he had most at heart. He speaks as follows:

"Warriors, as it is the custom, so we will now sing four more dancing songs and then we will call upon someone to make his voice known to the war-spirits. If any of you wish to offer tobacco,

you can do so, and the women likewise can join, because we have
rolled up our bundle. To the dog that we have here, an offering of
tobacco can be made." Thus speaking, he sings. After he has
finished the song, someone specially called upon gives the war
whoop, in which the rest join. In this manner they sing four times,
and the ceremony ends. They have a dog around whose neck they
tie a red rag, together with a bundle of tobacco, and to each of
whose limbs they also tie a bundle of tobacco. This dead dog is to
be placed wherever the bones that remain of the feast are buried,
generally under some tree. It is supposed that the dog will go
directly to the Disease-giver together with the tobacco and there
be taken over by him.

Notes on the Thunderbird clan war-bundle feast.—Informant, member of the clan: Place of honor at the feast is given to the bravest
man present. Scalps, etc., are always brought to those keeping
the war bundle.

Contents of bundle: Black hawk (main thing), two wolf tails,
buffalo tail, snake, weasel, three flutes—one red, one black, and one
blue.

Black hawk used in time of war. If I were leading the war party
I would carry it and it would be able to fly. It had a small bundle
of medicine tied around the neck, on each wing and each leg. A red
flute always went with it.

The two wolf tails could be taken on any warpath. It gives an
individual the power of running. The medicine tied to it is to be
smeared over the body in order to prevent fatigue. It is also used
in hunting.

Buffalo tail gives fleetness and indicates that the man received
strength from the buffalo spirit.

Weasel and snake could be put around the neck and worn over
the shoulders in times of war. Gives the power of these respective
animals in wiggling.

Flutes, blue in connection with the buffalo, red in connection
with the black hawk, and black in connection with the night spirits

THE WAR-BUNDLE FEAST OF THE BEAR CLAN

Informant, member of the Bear clan: The people were about to go
on a hunt, it is said. They returned. Four deer had been killed.
And again they went, and this time three deer were killed. But it was
not sufficient, so they went out again, and when they returned it was
found that they had killed only three deer. "Well," they said, "this
will be all right. We have ten deer. Perhaps they will last as food
until dawn."

They told the attendants to get ready the lodge and to build the
fireplaces. They told them also to have the wood and the buck-

skins ready. Then they told them to make some invitation sticks. Only four invitation sticks were to be made, and they were to tie tobacco to each of them. The lodge was now ready (fig. 36). They had fixed the vertical poles and had tied them with prickly cedar sinews. The vertical poles they painted blue.

Then he who was to be the host told the attendants to take the invitation sticks to certain people. "Bring the first one to my friend, Mąnuba'ga. See that you give it to him. I am sure that he will be here soon after. The second stick you may give to Ką-o'saga. The third one you may give to Mązihimain'iga. Be sure that you bring them to all those who possess war bundles."

The attendant did as he was told and returned and told the host that it was done. "I have seen all of them and told them to make ready. They will soon come and sit down."

All were now in the lodge and were seated. The old man, Kaɣi'ga, was the host. All his posterity were there. He had placed meat in the kettles over the fireplaces. The first kettle was for Earthmaker and the second for Turtle. "Put them on," he said to the attendants. "Put the third one on for the Thunderbird, and the fourth one for the Fire, the fifth one for the Earth, the sixth one for the Morning Star, the seventh one for Without Horn, and the eighth one for the Nights. Then put on a small kettle for Disease-giver and a full kettle for the Ruce'we.

"Hao, we will pour tobacco for them my friend, Mąnuba'ga. Whenever we can obtain a 'counciling' we always do this, for in that way we help one another. You who are sitting here for me, bundle owners, as many of you as there are within this lodge who are taking the place of the spirits, all of you I greet. War-bundle owners, all of us are thus. When you obtain a council feast for yourselves, then you will help one another. We are putting ourselves in a very pitiable condition, so you must have thought of us, and that is why you came at our bidding. It is good. And we are going to make you fearfully tired. But I beg of you, nevertheless, to continue until the end. We are now going to sing."

They get up and the guests hold tobacco in their hands. Then they sing and weep. The one who was fasting at that time stood at the war bundle crying. Then they sang the following songs:

> Human, four chunks of meat I give you.
> Human, four chunks of meat you will eat.
> I made it for you, for you who carry the war bundle.

Thus they spoke standing and weeping, pouring tobacco upon the war bundle. This they did. Then Turtle songs were used. That is what they call them. After that they used Thunderbird songs, and then what are called friends' songs. Finally they used the songs they obtained when Disease-giver blessed them. Four songs they had given them. Then songs that were associated with the drum that they use in the Night-Spirit dance were sung. The feast was now ready.

"Make ready the kettle in front of the fireplace; take the most prominent parts of the animal out of it; make the second kettle you put on also ready. Hurry up, for we are about to have a fast-eating contest. The lower clans and the upper clans will contest. They will try to partake of war. Make ready. You, Mąnuba'ga choose a person, and do you, Kaɣo'saga, do the same."

Now they were ready to have the fast-eating contest. They all sat down.

"Now listen," said the host, "as soon as the flute is blown they will begin the contest. Then will be the time for all the feast givers to sing."

Now, this is one of the songs they sang:

Where they eat, there you went, it is said.

Now they finished. Mąnuba'ga was defeated and Kaɣo'saga won. The guests filled their dishes, and the kettle that had been put on for Earthmaker was taken down and placed before Mąnuba'ga, so that he might select the best parts. Then the second kettle that had been placed on the fire for Earthmaker was put in front of Kaɣo'saga. The third kettle that had been offered to the Thunder-spirits was placed in front of Nązihima'nįga. The host then, in turn, mentioned by name all the invited guests and told the attendants what kettles were to be brought to them. As soon as the dishes had been distributed each one began to eat. They never waited for one another to start. While they were eating the members of the host's band sang. When the meal was over Mąnuba'ga rose and spoke as follows:

"Councilors, relatives, uncles, I salute you all. As many spirits as are in charge of life you have mentioned during the ceremony. Tobacco and food you have sent to them as offerings. I am sure that for that reason they will give you all that you have asked, and I also feel that I, myself, will be able to obtain something on which I can live, and that should I encounter on the warpath an enemy whose death has been ordained, it will be my fate to kill him. Thus I have been thinking, and that is why I have been sitting here. War-bundle owners, as many of you as are sitting in this lodge—war-bundle carriers, as many of you as are here—you have, indeed, had tobacco poured out for you to-day; and tobacco has also been offered to the powers that you have tied up in your bundles. I feel grateful for the fact and that I have been invited to attend, and that is why I am saying this. Councilors, war-bundle owners, all who are seated in this lodge, I salute you."

The leaders of all the other bands say practically the same.

After the speeches were all over the offerings were taken down and thrown outside through the opening in the roof of the lodge and then night songs were sung. Before throwing the offerings out they marched around the lodge carrying them in their hands. At the approach of dawn the drum, gourds, etc., have about made the entire circuit of the lodge, and as soon as they reach the host he begins to sing the night songs. After these he sings turtle songs, and then the songs are over. The host now calls upon some one to give the war whoop, so that the spirits in the west may hear their voices. Nanhį'tcoga gave the war whoop. All joined in, and the feast was over.

Descriptive notes on the Bear clan war-bundle feast.—Informant, member of clan: About the middle of winter, in the month called deer-breeding month, the Winnebago used to go out hunting, and they gave a feast to all the spirits who had blessed them.

They are very careful not to have the kettles boil over, because they believe that a man's soul (*naγi'rak'*) might be wandering about and is likely to come down along the chain of the kettle. If it doesn't boil over, the man is likely to conquer the possessions of this spirit (of an enemy) in the next battle.

The invitation sticks are sent out only to men who own a war bundle, and the clans are invited in the following fashion: First the Wolf, then the Hawk, and then any order.

The contents of the war bundle represent the following: The crow means strength in running. The turtle and the spear, the blessings which enable one to get out of difficulties, the former referring especially to difficulties in crossing water; they also enable their possessor to foretell when enemies are approaching and to tell an individual how many enemies he is going to conquer. The flute represents the voices of musical birds. When an enemy hears them it paralyzes him and he can not run.

INDEX

Page

ADOPTION—
customs of... 91
name used after... 80
AGRICULTURE 67–69
ALLIANCES OF THE WINNEBAGO 10–11
ALPHABET, SYLLABIC, used by Winnebago.... xi
ALTPETER MOUNDS—
form of 52
location of 51
number of 52
AMERICAN MUSEUM OF NATURAL HISTORY,
acknowledgment to xvi
ANIMALS—
method of slaughtering 65
mythological classification of 138
power of transformation of 149
ARAPAHO BULL, instructions given by 367
ARAPAHO PEYOTE ceremony 367–369
ARBOR VITAE, use of, in purifying rites.... 397
ARCHEOLOGY OF THE WINNEBAGO 28–55
ARROWHEADS—
authorship of 38–39
distribution of 31
types of 40
ARROWS, five types of 62
ATKINSON'S CAMP, location of 51
ATTENDANTS AT FEASTS, duties of 281
AXES, COPPER, types of 40
AZTALAN, description of 40–42
BANDOLIERS, described 61
BAPTISM, as practiced by Peyote cult 341–347
BEAR CLAN—
customs of 179–180, 100–105
dance for benefit of 338
feast of 273
functions of 152, 178
importance of 178
insignia of 178
known as Soldier clan 170
lodge of 178, 181
origin myths of 177
personal names 188–189
relations of, with Wolf clan 179
songs of 187
symbol of 155
war-bundle feast of 499–502
BEAR FEAST, origin myth of 153–154
BEAR HUNT, description of 63–64
BEGGING CEREMONY 339
BIBLE, use of, in Peyote religion 346
BIG FOX'S VILLAGE, location of.................... 3
BIG HAWK'S VILLAGE, location of 3
BINGHAM MOUNDS. See Rufus Bingham
mounds; Ira Bingham mounds.
BIRD CLANS, feast of 270–273
BIRDS, use of, in making medicines 214

Page

BIRTHS, customs concerning 78
BLACK EARTH MEDICINE FEAST, mention of 270
BLACK HAWK—
characterization of 393
offering to 381, 415
BLACK HAWK'S CAMP, location of 51
BLACK HAWK'S ISLAND, camp site 51
BLACK WATER-SPIRIT, cured of consumption 344
BLACK WOLF'S VILLAGE, location of 3
BLADDER, the hero, offerings to 393
BLESSING—
act of, in medicine dance 313
passing of 318
special, for warfare 109, 112, 120
BLINDNESS, belief concerning 215
BLOWSNAKE, JASPER—
acknowledgment to xvi
remarks by 399
BOAZ, FRANZ—
acknowledgment to xvi
BONE, ARTIFACTS OF, from mounds 54
Bow, of simple type 62
BRACELETS 61
BROWN, C. E.—
acknowledgment to xvi
quoted on copper implements 39–40
quoted on garden beds 55
quoted on intaglio mounds 33
BUCKSKINS—
ceremony of throwing out, to
spirits 383, 465, 496
marking of 395
offering of, to spirits 381–382, 417
preparation of, for War-bundle
feast 380, 394, 482
BUFFALO CLAN—
functions of 152, 195
funeral customs 106–107
origin myth of 195–197
personal names 198
songs 197
BUFFALO CLAN FEAST, participation in 158
BUFFALO HUNT, description of 64
BUFFALO SOCIETIES, number of 269–270
BUFFALO SPIRITS—
myth of 389
society of those blessed by 296–299
BUFFALO TAIL, feast to 334
BURIAL MOUNDS—
in group at Rice Lake 44
in upper Baraboo Valley 43
See Conical mounds.
BURIALS—
customs connected with 92–107
earth, clans employing 139
Goldthorpe 51

	Page
in conical mounds	36
in stone chambers	55
of the Thunderbird clan	163
scaffold, clans employing	139
two methods of	92
BUZZARD DECORAH'S VILLAGE, location of	
CALENDAR OF THE WINNEBAGO	76–77
CANFIELD, W. H.—	
intaglio mounds discovered by	42
plat by, of Man mound	54
CANNIBALISM—	
envoys eaten	6
indications of	170–171
CANOES	75
CAPTIVES, dance at death of	336
CARCAJOU MOUNDS, location of	51
CARDINAL POINTS, offerings to	381
CARLEY, SAM, acknowledgment to	xvi
CEREMONIAL ORGANIZATION, influence of clan on	156
CEREMONIES—	
Arapaho Peyote	367–371
Begging	339
four types of	269
of Medicine dance	314–326
of Night feast	281–295
of return of war party	110
of Soldier's dance	338
of stepping over grave	103
of throwing out buckskins	383, 465, 496
of wake	93–96
CHIEF—	
a peacemaker	161, 162
duties of	271, 272
functions of	161–162
lodge of, a refuge	161
relation of, to his people	271
selected from Thunderbird clan	272
CHIEF FEAST—	
food served at	271
object of	271
property of four Bird clans	270, 271
symbolism of	273
time of	270, 273
CHILDREN—	
decapitation of, in war	113
instruction of	132
treatment of	130
CHISELS, COPPER, types of	40
CHOUKEKA'S VILLAGE, location of	3
CIRCULAR MOUNDS, map showing distribution of	29
See Conical mounds.	
CLAN ANIMALS—	
as guardian spirits	147–148
as property mark	155
attitude toward	147–148
relationship to	148–150
CLAN CONSCIOUSNESS	387
CLAN FEASTS	270–273
nature of	269
CLAN SONGS—	
of Warrior clan	171, 172
use of	156

	Page
CLANS—	
conception of tie between members of	150
immaterial possessions of	155
influence of, on ceremonial organization	156
list of	142–143
marks of identification	155
names of, discussed	134
organization of	142–144
political functions of	151–153
preceded by village groups	137
property marks of	31, 155
reciprocal relationships of	153
seating of, in council lodge	115
songs of	156
specific possessions of	154–155
unit of organization in War-bundle feast.	388
See Bear clan, Bird clans, Buffalo clan, Deer clan, Eagle clan, Elk clan, Fish clan, Hawk clan, Pigeon clan, Snake clan, Soldier clan, Thunderbird clan, Warrior clan, Water-spirit clan, Wolf clan.	
CLAY, JESSE—	
a Peyote leader	371
account by, of Peyote ceremony	367–371
innovations of	373
CLOTHING, MEN'S, described	58
COKEBOKA, blessed during fast	339
COMPOSITE MOUNDS, interpretation of	36
CONCH SHELL CACHE, location of	51
CONICAL MOUNDS—	
as burial places	36
distribution of	30, 43
joined to linear	44
made by Sioux	28
number of	35
of Lake Koshkonong	52
See Burial mounds.	
CONTEST, FAST-EATING	437
COPPER, use of, by Winnebago	37–38
See Implements, copper.	
CORN—	
feast of	336
varieties of	69
CORPSE, preparation of, for burial	98, 101
See Burials.	
COSMOLOGICAL IDEAS, types of	115
COUNCIL LODGE—	
order of entering	115
seating arrangements in	116–117
COUNCILS, held for all important undertakings	115
COURTING, medicine used in	215
CREATION LODGE, meaning of	433
CROOKS, in possession of Bear clan	153, 154
CUP-AND-BALL GAME	74
CUSTOMS—	
adoption	80, 91
berry time	68
birth	78
burial	92–107
"counting coup"	110
general social	78–91
marriage	90–91

	Page
of Bear clan	179–180, 100–103
of Buffalo clan	6–7
of Wolf clan	190
puberty	87–90
war	110–113

See Facial decoration, Fasting, Feasts.

DANCES—
Buffalo, origin of	299
Captive's death	336–337
Farewell	337
for benefit of Bear clan	338
Grizzly Bear	299–301
hok'ixe're, after war party	270, 331–335
kikre waci	339
Medicine	311–326
of the Buffalo feast	298
of the Herok'a society	295
of the Night Spirit society	156, 290
Soldier's	130, 238–239
Tcebokonaᵃk	239
Victory	331–335

DAY—
characterization of	393
offering to, in War-bundle feast	381, 413

DAYTON VILLAGE, location of ... 3
DEATH, concept of ... 265–266
DECORA, position of wife of ... 145
DECORA FAMILY, origin of ... 17, 19–21

DEER—
division of, at War-bundle feast	382
killed for War-bundle feast	394

DEER CLAN—
customs of	198
dog names of	198
origin myth of	199–201
personal names of	201
song of	201

DEITIES—
attitude toward	231
list of	237
offerings to	263

See Spirits.

DESCENT—
conception of, from animals	149
reckoning of	137, 144, 145

DHEGIHA, twofold organization of ... 133
DICE GAME, women's ... 74

DISEASE—
concept of	265
cured by Peyote	371

See Sickness.

DISEASE-GIVER—
associated with success in war	385
characterization of	388, 492
conception of	120, 239
defied by man	261–262
most sacred of spirits	484
offering to, in War-bundle feast	381, 382, 401, 409, 419, 457
refusal of blessing from	254

DIVISIONS OF WINNEBAGO ... 133, 137
functions of ... 135, 139
DIXON, ROLAND B., quoted on Ohio mounds 28
DOG NAMES IN THE CLAN ... 153, 163, 181

DOG RITUAL, terminal ... 384

DOGS—
eaten at feast	281
sacrifice of	380, 390, 403, 479

DORSEY, J. O.—
list of clans by	143
list of names by	173
monograph by	133

DOTY ISLAND, Winnebago village on ... 3, 32, 39
DRAVES MOUNDS, location of ... 51
DRUM, description of ... 336
DUGOUTS ... 75
DUMB-BELL MOUNDS ... 45, 52

EAGLE—
characterization of	393
offering to, in War-bundle feast	381, 388, 403

EAGLE CHIEF, offering to, in War-bundle feast. ... 381, 413, 488
EAGLE CLAN, of little importance ... 172
EARRINGS, modern ... 61

EARTH—
characterization of	392
conception of, as a deity	237
offering to, at War-bundle feast	382, 401, 411, 421, 453, 488

EARTHMAKER—
a peace deity	386
attempt to secure blessing of	243
characterization of	390–391
conception of	237
myth concerning	120
offering to, in War-bundle feast	381, 382, 399, 407, 419, 455, 487
world ruled by	268

EARTH MOUNDS ... 28–55
EARTHWORKS AT AZTALAN ... 40–42
EATING CONTEST, at War-bundle feast ... 382

EFFIGY MOUNDS—
as property marks	31, 155
at Fond du Lac	50
at Lake Koshkonong	53
at Pishtaka	46
bear type	42, 43, 51
bird type	47, 51, 53
distribution of	30–31
explanations of	31
goose, where found	51
made by Winnebago	28
mammal	48, 53
number of	35
panther or water-spirit type	42, 51
possible purpose of	50
representations of clan animals	31, 32, 50
significance of distribution	1
turtle and allied forms	48, 53
types found	45, 50
unknown animal	48
water-spirit type, where found	51
Wingra group	46

ELK CLAN—
customs of	201
functions of	153, 201
origin, myth of	202
personal names of	202

	Page
EVIL, concept of	263–264
FACIAL DECORATION—	
as clan mark	156
of Bear clan	180
of Elk clan	201
of Medicine dance	314
of the dead	96, 98
of Thunderbird clan	163
of Warrior clan	171
FAREWELL DANCE	337
FAREWELL SONGS	337
FAST-EATING CONTEST	437
FASTING—	
a test of religious attitude	229
blessings obtained by	118–119
experience in	227
for war powers	109–112
instruction for	121, 123
personal accounts of	245, 261
FEASTS—	
afraid-to-eat-greens	336
at adoption	91
at wake	93, 94, 97
in honor of chief	271–272
invitations to	281
naming	80
of Bear clan	273
of Buffalo society	296–299
of Medicine dance	314
of Night-blessed children	281–295
of those blessed by Herok'a	295
of Thunderbird clan	379–399
of War-bundle ceremony	382, 433–435
to buffalo tail	339
to Earthmaker	78
FEATHERS, used as war insignia	113–114
FIRE—	
a possession of the Thunderbird clan	162
regarded as a spirit	118
FIREPLACES, ARRANGEMENT OF, when on the warpath	141
FIRE RITUAL of the Medicine dance	318
FISH CLAN, personal names of	202
FISHING	66
FLETCHER AND LA FLESCHE, reference to monograph by	133
FLUTE, played by host at feast	382
FOND DU LAC, effigy mounds at	50
FOOD—	
at Bear feast	273
kinds of, served at feast	271
offering of, to spirits	271
preparation of	68–70
preservation of	70
FOOTBALL GAME	73
FORT ATKINSON, intaglio mound at	43
FOSTER, DR., list of names by	274
FOUR, the sacred number	388
FOX INDIANS—	
expedition against	6
relations of, with Winnebago	10–11
FRENCH, first contact of, with Winnebago	17, 19–29
"FRIENDSHIP" RELATION of clans	139, 153
FULTON MOUNDS, location of	51
FUN HUNTER'S POINT MOUND	51
GAMBLING—	
wagers of horses	336
See Dice game, Moccasin game.	
GAMES	72–75
cup-and-ball	74
dice, women's	74
football	73
kicking	73
lacrosse	73–73, 142
moccasin	73–74
played at wake	97, 105
tree	75
GARDEN BEDS OF WISCONSIN, described	55
GENERAL ATKINSON MOUNDS—	
form of	52
location of	51
number of	52
GENTES, discussion of names of	134
See Clans.	
GHOSTS, SOCIETY OF THOSE BLESSED BY	269
GIFTS, at wake	97, 105
GODS. See Deities, Spirits.	
GOLDTHORPE BURIALS, location of	51
GRAVE POSTS, markings on	96, 107, 114
GREAT BAD SPIRIT, a creation of Earthmaker.	391
GREAT BLACK HAWK—	
characterization of	392
offerings to	381, 401, 417, 457, 487
GREAT SPIRIT, identified as Earthmaker	390
GREEN BAY—	
home of Winnebago	29
settlement on	32
GREETING, ceremonial	384
GRIZZLY-BEAR DANCE, a religious society	156
GRIZZLY-BEAR SOCIETY	269, 299
GUARDIAN SPIRIT—	
conception of	242
offerings to	382
HABITAT OF WINNEBAGO	4, 28–30
HABITATIONS OF WINNEBAGO	56–58
HAIGHT'S CREEK MOUNDS, location of	51
HAIRDRESSING	61
HANGA—	
a division of the Omaha	133
a division of the Osage	133
HARE, THE HERO—	
identification of, with Christ	328
offerings to	393, 494
world ruled by	268
HARRISON, JOHN, conversion of	344
HAWK CLAN—	
functions of	152
identical with Warrior clan	144, 170
HEADDRESS—	
buffalo, society of those wearing	270
described	61
HENSLEY, ALBERT, a Peyote leader	371
account by, of Peyote	349–352
conversion of	346
innovations of	373
HEROK'A—	
characterization of	393
feast of those blessed by	295

Page
HERUCKA, a social dance — 336
Heruka songs, always victory songs — 336
HOARD MOUNDS—
location of — 51
number of — 52
HODJANAGA, fasting experience of — 299
HOK'IXE'RE DANCE described — 331–335
HOSPITALITY, instruction in — 122
HUNTING — 61–66
HUNTING CUSTOMS — 65–66
ICTACUNDA, a division of the Omaha — 133
ICTUNGA, a division of the Kansa — 133
IDEALS, SOCIAL, connected with religion — 229–230
ILLINOIS INDIANS, defeat of Winnebago by — 6–7
IMMORTALITY, belief in — 121
IMPLEMENTS—
copper — 31, 37, 39, 40, 54
stone — 39, 54
wooden — 70–71
INITIATION, into Medicine dance — 319, 326–330
INSIGNIA OF WAR — 113–114
INSTRUCTION, SYSTEM OF—
to children — 132
to daughter — 129–132
to son — 118–132
INTAGLIO MOUNDS—
discovered by Lapham — 42
located near earthworks — 42
possible meaning of — 33
where found — 31
INVITATION STICKS—
making of — 281
order of sending — 502
presentation of — 281
IOWA TRIBE, legendary origin of — 2
IRA BINGHAM MOUNDS and village site — 51
IRON WALKER'S VILLAGE, location of — 3
JENKS, A. E., quoted on rice gathering — 68, 69
JOHN SON MOUNDS, location of — 51
JOKING RELATIONSHIP — 126
JONES, W., quoted on the Fox Indians — 233–234
KANSA, divisions of — 133
KARRAYMAUNEE'S VILLAGE, location of — 3
KETTLES—
offerings of, to the spirits — 434–435, 484
soul descending chain of — 502
KEWASKUM'S CAMP, location of — 51
KICKAPOO, territory occupied by — 29
KICKING GAME — 73
KNIVES, COPPER, types of — 40
KOSHKONONG CREEK MOUNDS AND VILLAGE SITE — 51
KUMLIEN MOUNDS—
location of — 51
number of — 52
LACROSSE—
ceremonial — 142
game of — 72–73
LAKE KOSHKONONG—
archeologic map of — 51
mounds of — 49, 50, 52–54
LAKE MENDOTA, effigy mounds at — 50
LAKE WAUBESA, effigy mounds at — 50
LAKE WINGRA, effigy mounds at — 50
LAMERE, OLIVER, acknowledgment to — xvi
LAMERE and RADIN, paper by, on Winnebago funeral — 100
LAPHAM, I. A.—
Man mound described by — 54
work of, on mounds — 28
LA VALLE MAN MOUND—
outline of — 49
plat of, by Canfield — 54
LEGENDS, MIGRATION, of the Winnebago — 2–4
LEGGINGS, pattern of — 58
LE SELLIER MOUNDS—
location of — 51
number of — 52
LINEAR MOUNDS—
as defensive works — 34–35
as lodge bases — 35, 36
as snake effigies — 35, 36
at Madison — 45
at Pishtaka — 46
classes of — 33–34
explanation of — 31
in Wingra group — 46
interpretation of — 34
made by Sioux — 28
number of — 35
of Iowa County — 45
of Lake Koshkonong — 53
purpose of — 44–50
where found — 31
LITTLE DECORAH'S VILLAGE, location of — 3
LITTLE PRIEST, grizzly bear dance given for benefit of — 300
LITTLE PRIEST'S VILLAGE, location of — 3
LITTLE-RED-BIRD, account of life of — 348–349
LODGES—
arrangement of, for War-bundle feast — 482
bark — 56
ceremonial — 57
ceremonial circuit of — 384
constructed by women — 58
council — 115
creation — 433
gable — 56, 57
menstrual — 88
of Bear clan, diagram of — 181
of Bear clan, position of — 181
of chief, a refuge — 272
orientation of — 395
purification of — 397, 484
reed matting — 56
sweat, form of — 57
LOGE BAY MOUNDS AND GARDEN BEDS — 51
LOOKOUT MOUNDS, location of — 51
MAN EATER'S VILLAGE, location of — 51
MAN MOUNDS—
described — 54–55
interpretation of — 33
outlines of — 47, 49
MAGIC, SYMPATHETIC — 206
MANITO, discussed by W. Jones — 234
MANITOWOC COUNTY, effigy mounds in — 50
MARRIAGE—
customs connected with — 90–91

Page

instruction of women for 129–130
regulated by twofold division 135
MASCOUTIN, territory occupied by 29
MEDICINE DANCE—
a religious society 156
admission to 312
duties of bands of 312–314
five bands of 311
paper on, by Radin 270
MEDICINES—
classification of 206
formulas for 217–219
stench-earth, uses of 211
use of 123–124, 215
MENOMINEE, territory occupied by 29
MESCAL. See Peyote.
MESSMER GARDEN BEDS, location of 51
MIAMI, territory occupied by 29
MIDJSTEGA, stories told of 206, 207–210
MIGRATIONS—
Siouan 1–2
Winnebago 1–4
MILWAUKEE PUBLIC MUSEUM, acknowledg-
ment to xvi
MISSOURI TRIBE, legendary origin of 2
MOCCASIN GAME 173–174
MOCCASINS, patterns of 59, 60
MOIETIES 137–142
MOON—
characterization of 392
female deity 238
offering to, in War-bundle feast 381,
382, 401, 410, 419, 455, 587
MORGAN, LEWIS H., list of clans given by.... 143
MORNING STAR—
characterization of 392
offering to, at War-bundle feast 382,
421, 588
spirit associated with war 238–239
MOUND PRAIRIE, West Group 43
MOUNDS—
age of 31, 36–37
builders of 28
distribution of 29, 30
types of 31
works on subject of 28
See Altpeter mounds, Bingham mounds,
Burial mounds, Circular mounds,
Composite mounds, Conical mounds,
Dumbbell mounds, Effigy mounds,
Intaglio mounds, Kumlien mounds,
Le Sellier mounds, Linear mounds,
Man mounds, Noe Springs mounds,
Oral mounds, Tadpole type, Turtle
mounds.
MOURNING, period of 98, 102, 105
MUSICAL INSTRUMENTS 175
MUTILATION, sign of mourning 98
MYTHS—
of Buffalo spirits 389
used by Peyote members 376–377
See Origin myths.
NAMES—
of animals 67

Page

of gentes, discussion of 134
of months 76–77
of newborn child 79
of trees 67
of tribes and peoples 27
of vegetables and fruits 67
used after adoption 80
See Names, personal.
NAMES, PERSONAL—
discussion of 145–147
of Bear clan 188–189
of Bird clan 173–177
of Elk clan 102
of first four children 203–205
of Fish clan 202
of Snake clan 202
of Water-spirit clan 194–195
of Wolf clan 192–193
NAMING FEAST 80
NECKLACES 61
NEVILLE, A. C., on habitat of the Winnebago 32
NIGHT-BLESSED CHILDREN, SOCIETY OF 281–295
NIGHT SONGS, singing of 485
NIGHT-SPIRIT DANCE, a religious society 156
NIGHT SPIRITS—
associated with success in war 485–486
ceremony in honor of 453
characterization of 392
episode connected with 383
feast to 471
offering to 381, 382, 401, 407, 453
rite of those crazed by 471
society of those blessed by 269
NOE SPRINGS MOUNDS—
described 52–53
location of 51
number of 52
NORTH MOUNDS, location of 51
NORTH WIND—
characterization of 393
offerings to 381, 415, 455
OFFERINGS TO DEITIES 263
OGDEN MOUNDS, location of 51
OJIBWAY WAR FEASTS, nature of 386
OLD GRAY-HEADED DECORAH'S VILLAGE,
location of 3
OLD LINCOLN, stories concerning 206, 207–211
OMAHA, names of divisions of 133
ONE-EYED DECORAH'S VILLAGE, location of.... 3
ORENDA, discussed by Mr. J. N. B. Hewitt 234
ORGANIZATION, TWOFOLD, discussion of 133–142
ORIGIN MYTHS—
of Bear clan 177, 181, 187
of Bear feast 253–254
of Buffalo clan 195–197
of Medicine dance 302–311
of Thunderbird clan 164–170
of Warrior clan 171–172
of Water-spirit clan 194
OSAGE TRIBE—
divisions of 133
OTO TRIBE, legendary origin of 3

Page

OVAL MOUNDS, distribution of 30
PAINT MEDICINE—
   made of Water-spirit bones 425
   use of 427
PAINTING, FACIAL. *See* Facial decoration.
PEABODY MUSEUM, acknowledgment to xvi
PEET, STEPHEN D., theory of, regarding
   linear mounds 35
PESHEU'S VILLAGE, location of 3
PEYOTE—
   curative power of 375
   effect of 341–344
   experiences with 352–366
   See Peyote cult.
PEYOTE CULT—
   Arapaho ceremony 367–371
   connected with teachings of Shawnee
     prophet 21, 25, 26
   development of 371–374
   dissemination of 374–375
   essential change made by 247
   general description of 340–341
   reference to belief of 328
PIGEON CLAN, of little importance 172
PIGEON HAWK—
   characterization of 393
   offering to 381, 455
PIGEON HUNT, described 65
PIPE—
   ceremonial, ritual of 421–423
   ceremonial use of ...94, 97, 100, 101, 110, 381
   See Pipes of peace.
PIPES OF PEACE, custodianship of 135–136
PONCA, divisions of 133
POPULATION 5, 6, 136
PORCUPINE, associated with North Wind.... 455
POTAWATOMI, territory occupied by 29
POTTERY—
   for cooking 71
   from mounds 54
PRAYER—
   for success in war 108, 109
   general, to spirits 421
   object of 263
   to avert illness 272
PROPHETS—
   a development of contact with whites.... 21
   notes concerning 26
   See Shawnee Prophet.
PUBERTY CUSTOMS 87–90
PUBLIC CRIER, duties of 162
QUAPAWS, legendary origin of 2
QUARRIES, in Winnebago territory 38
RADIN, MAX, acknowledgment to xvi
RATTLES—
   of deer hoofs 295
   of gourds 292, 295
RAVE, JOHN—
   a Peyote leader 341, 370
   account by, of Peyote cult 341–346
   acknowledgment · to xvi
   conflict of, with Hensley 373–374
   conversion of 346
RED-HORN, offerings to 393

Page

REINCARNATION, belief in 266–268, 378
RELATIONSHIP—
   joking 85–86
   terms of 80–83
RELIGION, of the Winnebago 229–268
RELIGIOUS EXPERIENCES 243–261
RICE, gathering of 68
RITUALS—
   basic, of War-bundle feast 382,
               423–453, 457–481
   of the Medicine dance 317–322
   Shooting 322, 324
   See Ceremonies, Smoking, Ritual.
ROCK RIVER MOUNDS AND VILLAGE SITE 51
RUFUS BINGHAM MOUNDS—
   location of 51
   number of 52
RUSH LAKE VILLAGE, location of 3
SARCEL'S VILLAGE, location of 3
SARROCHAU'S VILLAGE, location of 3
SAUK AND FOX, territory occupied by 29
SAUK COUNTY, effigy mounds in 50
SCALPS, used in Victory dance 110, 331–335
SECRET SOCIETIES, qualification for member-
   ship in 269
SHAMAN, patients cured by 222–227
   See Shamanism.
SHAMANISM, practices of 206–228
SHAWNEE PROPHET—
   admonitions of 372, 373
   Peyote cult connected with teachings
     of 21, 25, 26
   teachings of 21–25
SHELL, SACRED, rites of 324–325
SHIRT, BUCKSKIN, pattern of 58
SHOOTING RITUAL, of the medicine dance.322, 324
SICKNESS—
   averted by feast 271–272
   belief concerning 123
   See Disease.
SIOUAN TRIBES, migrations of 1–2
SIOUX, mounds made by 28
SKARLEM MOUNDS, location of 51
SKINNER, ALANSON—
   quoted on Menominee 38
   quoted on men's clothing 58
   quoted on tanning 71
SMOKER'S VILLAGE, location of 3
SMOKING RITUAL—
   of Medicine dance 318
   of War-bundle feast 421
   See Pipes, Tobacco.
SNAKE CLAN, personal names of 202
SNAKES, use of, in medicine 214
SNOWSHOES 75
SOCIETIES—
   basis of 384
   Buffalo, feast of 296–299
   Herok'a, feast of 295
   See Secret societies.
SOLDIER CLAN—
   different from Warrior clan 338
   See Bear clan.

SOLDIER DANCE, of Bear clan 180, 338–339
SONGS—
   associated with clans 192
   Farewell 337
   Herucka 336
   night 485
   of Bear clan 273, 500, 501
   of Buffalo clan 197
   of Buffalo feast 297
   of Grizzly Bear dance 298
   of Medicine dance 317, 322
   of Soldier dance 338
   of Thunderbird clan 163
   of War-bundle feast 396–397
   of Warrior clan 171–172
   of Wolf clan 192
SOUL—
   concept of 268
   descending kettle chain 502
SOUTH WIND—
   characterization of 492
   offering to 381, 382, 401, 415, 419, 457
SPEAR HEADS, types of 40
SPEECHES—
   at funeral 101–103
   at wake 93–96
   at War-bundle feast 423–433, 439–453
   by member of Thunderbird clan 272–273
   of acceptance 316
   of admonition 316
   of Medicine dance 315
   of presentation 316
   of welcome 316
   to deceased at funeral 99–100
   to dog, before sacrifice 380
   types of, at War-bundle feast 384
SPINDEN, H. J. See Will and Spinden.
SPIRITS—
   brought into relation with man 262–263
   characterization of 388–390
   concept and nature of 99, 235–240
   corporeality of 236
   indefinite number of 236
   of the cardinal points 120
   offerings to 271, 381, 390
   power and localization of 240–241
   prayer to 421
   relation of, to man 241
SPOTTED ARM'S VILLAGE, location of 3
SQUEAKING-WINGS, conversion of 344
STOUT, A. B.—
   quoted on Lake Koshkonong mounds .. 52
   quoted on linear mounds 33–34
   theory of, regarding linear mounds 36
   work of, on Wisconsin archeology 28
SUN—
   associated with success in war 385
   characterization of 392
   conception of, as a deity 238
   offering to, in War-bundle feast 381,
      382, 401, 409, 419, 457, 487
SUPERNATURAL POWER, concept of 233–234
SWEAT BATH, in initiation ceremony 323
SWEAT LODGE, form of 57

SWEAT LODGE RITUAL—
   of Medicine dance 320
   of War-bundle feast 380, 381, 399
TABOO, mother-in-law and father-in-law 87
TADPOLE TYPE OF MOUNDS 52
TANNING, description of 71–72
TAY-E-HE-DAH MOUNDS AND VILLAGE SITE 51
TAYLOR HOUSE MOUNDS, location of 51
TCIJU—
   a division of the Osage 133
   a division of the Ponca 133
   and Ictacunda, identical terms 133
TCIWERE, twofold organization of 133
THIEBEAU POINT VILLAGE SITE 51
THOMAS, CYRUS, work of, on mounds 28
THUNDERBIRD—
   associated with success in war 385
   ceremony in honor of 399
   characterization of 391
   conception of 239
   offering to, in War-bundle feast 381,
      382, 399, 407, 419, 455
THUNDERBIRD CLAN 159–163
   chief selected from 161
   feast of 270–273
   functions of 152
   funeral ceremonies of 98–100
   importance of 159
   known as Chief clan 170
   origin myths of 159–160
   symbol of 155
TIME, DIVISIONS OF 76–77
TIPI—
   of simple construction 57
   used on the hunt 58
TOADS, use of, for poison medicine 215
TOBACCO—
   account of origin of 18, 389
   ceremonial use of 93, 97, 103, 282, 300, 381
   offering of, to spirits 122, 272, 405, 453–457
   placing of, in War-bundle feast 403
TOTEM—
   descent from 149–150
   See Clan animal, Totemism.
TOTEMISM 137–139
TRADITIONS OF THE WINNEBAGO 7–10, 11–21
TRANSFORMATION, power of, of animals 149
TRANSFORMER HEROES 391
TRANSPORTATION 75
TRAPS FOR GAME 62
TRAVEL AND TRANSPORTATION 75
TRAVELER, the ruler of the world 268
TREE GAME 75
TRICKSTER—
   offerings to 393
   stories of 376–377
   world ruled by 268
TURTLE, THE HERO—
   offerings to 376, 494
   world ruled by 268
TURTLE CREEK, effigy mounds on 50
TURTLE MOUNDS 33
   not connected with Winnebago clans ... 50
TWINS, THE HEROES, offerings to 376
TWOFOLD GROUPING, discussion of 137–139

Page

UANGERU, ceremony of 339
UTENSILS, cooking and eating 70–71
VESSELS, WOODEN 70–71
VICTORY DANCE 331–335
VILLAGE GROUPS—
  as social unit 136–137
  present names of 137
VILLAGES—
  divisions of 140
  location of 3, 29
  organization of 140
  plans of 140, 141
WAGIGO'. See War-bundle feast.
WAJAJE, a division of the Ponca 133
WAKE—
  description of 92–98
  origin, myth of 106–107
WALKING-PRIEST, conversion of 344
WAR BUNDLES—
  contents of 394, 499
  meaning of contents of 502
  ownership of 162, 385
  possession of 154
  transmission of 145
WAR-BUNDLE FEAST—
  a ceremony of thanksgiving 379
  clan basis of 157
  description of 393, 397
  development of 384–388
  divisions of 380
  nature of 269
  of Thunderbird clan 379–499
  origin of 385
WAR CLUBS—
  of Thunderbird clan 162
  possession of 154
  symbol of Thunderbird clan 155
WARFARE—
  blessings for 109, 112, 120
  customs of 110–113
  exploits of 471
  honors in 119
  reasons for 109
  responsibility in 108, 109, 120, 161
WAR FEASTS OF THE OJIBWAY, nature of .. 386
WAR PARTIES—
  influenced by religion 130
  manner of conducting 110–113
  return of 110
WARRIOR CLAN—
  effigies representing 166
  functions of 152, 171
  identical with Hawk clan 144

Page

lodge of 170–171
not Soldier clan 338
origin myth of 171–172, 271
privilege of 110
rights of 231
songs of 171, 172
WASHINGTON DECORAH'S VILLAGE, location
  of 3
WATER—
  characterization of 393
  offering to, in War-bundle feast..181, 182, 455
WATER-SPIRIT—
  conception of 239–240
  offering to 421
WATER-SPIRIT CLAN—
  customs of 194
  functions of 153, 193
  origin myth of 194
  personal names of 194–195
WATERTOWN VILLAGE, location of 3
WEST, G. A., description by, of Aztalan 40–42
WHIRLING THUNDER'S VILLAGE, location of.. 3
WHITE CROW'S VILLAGE, location of 3, 51
WHITE OX'S VILLAGE, location of 3, 51
WILL, G. F., and SPINDEN, H. J., quoted
  on Siouan migrations 1–2
WINGRA MOUNDS, effigies 51
WINNEBAGO—
  attack on, by Illinois 6–7
  first meeting of, with whites 5
  name for themselves 5
  separation of, from Siouan kindred 2, 4
  territory occupied by 4, 28–30, 32
  tribes once composing 4
WINNEBAGO COUNTY, effigy mounds in 50
WINTER FEAST. See War-bundle feast.
WOLF CLAN—
  customs of 190
  functions of 153, 190
  origin myth of 190–192
  personal names of 192
  position of 143
  songs of 192
WOMEN, instruction concerning treatment
  of 122, 127
WONAɣI'RE UANKCIK—
  characterization of 393
  offering to 381, 388, 415
  identified with thunderbirds 415
YATA, a division of the Kansa 133
YELLOW THUNDER'S "FORTY," location of .. 3
YELLOW THUNDER'S VILLAGE, location of 3

8016